1993

Learning Disabilities

Fourth Edition

Learning Disabilities

Theories, Diagnosis, and Teaching Strategies

Janet W. Lerner
Northeastern Illinois University

Houghton Mifflin Company   Boston
Dallas   Geneva, Ill.   Lawrenceville, N.J.
Palo Alto

Cover photograph by James Scherer. Frontispiece photograph by Bobby Carey/The Picture Cube.

Part and chapter opening photographs: Sybil Schackman/Monkmeyer (Part I); Alan Carey/The Image Works (Part II); Jean-Claude Lejeune/EKM-Nepenthe (Part III); Suzanne Arms/Jeroboam (Part IV); Peter Vandermark/Stock, Boston (Chapter 1); Frank Siteman/EKM-Nepenthe (Chapter 2); Costa Manos/Magnum (Chapter 3); Elizabeth Crews (Chapter 4); Sybil Shelton/Peter Arnold (Chapter 5); Jerry Howard/Positive Images (Chapter 6); Mimi Forsyth/Monkmeyer (Chapter 7); Alan Carey/The Image Works (Chapter 8); Kent Reno/Jeroboam (Chapter 9); Alan Carey/The Image Works (Chapter 10); Phyllis Graber Jensen/Stock, Boston (Chapter 11); Lionel J-M Delevingne/Stock, Boston (Chapter 12); © Susan Lapides (Chapter 13); Teri Leigh Stratford (Chapter 14); Jerry Howard/Positive Images (Chapter 15).

To Eugene

Contents

Preface

The field of learning disabilities continues to be a dynamic discipline, responsive to advances in education and changes in society. The fourth edition of *Learning Disabilities: Theories, Diagnosis, and Teaching Strategies* reflects these advances and changes.

Children and youth who are destined to become educational discards unless their learning disabilities are recognized and treated are likely to be found in any classroom. The condition of learning disabilities is perplexing: although such students are not blind, many do not see as normal students do; although they are not deaf, many do not listen or hear normally; although they are not retarded in mental development, they do not learn. Many of these students exhibit other behavior characteristics that make them disruptive in the classroom and at home. Such individuals are the concern of this book.

Audience and Purpose

Learning Disabilities: Theories, Diagnosis, and Teaching Strategies is an introductory text, written for both undergraduate and graduate students who are taking a first course in learning disabilities. It is designed to provide a broad view of the field of learning disabilities for present and future special teachers, school psychologists, administrators, language pathologists, counselors, and other professionals preparing to work with the learning-disabled individual. This book is also intended for both preservice and inservice regular classroom teachers who are often responsible for teaching learning-disabled students mainstreamed in their classrooms. In addition, the text can serve parents seeking necessary background information to better understand the problems their children face.

The approach of the book is eclectic so that readers may gain a comprehensive overview of this complex subject. Teachers need to understand the diverse theoretical approaches to the field; have knowledge of assessment procedures; possess skill in the art of clinical teaching; and develop familiarity with teaching techniques and materials. This book deals with each of these essential areas.

Revisions in This Edition

Up-to-date information and coverage of new issues and topics is contained in this thoroughly revised text. Many chapters including those on early childhood, adolescents and adults, reading, math, and social disabilities have been completely rewritten to make them current and to reflect the latest research. In addition, treatment of preschool, adolescent, and adult populations is now positioned centrally in the text and referred to, when appropriate, throughout the entire book.

The revision also includes sections on microcomputer uses in learning disabilities and new ideas and approaches being used with learning-disabled students, such as metacognitive learning strategies and Feuerstein's Instrumental Enrichment. Many short "Case Examples" are provided to illustrate major points, and two longer extended "Case Studies" are presented to offer practical applications of the theories and procedures. The text strives to provide a fair and clear explanation of new and controversial issues in the field, such as eligibility criteria, increasing prevalence rates, ecological systems, and diverse theories of assessment and intervention. Finally, a greatly expanded art program offers thirty new photographs that serve to illustrate aspects of learning disabilities instruction.

Coverage and Features

This book is organized into four major sections. Part One is an overview of learning disabilities and includes important features of PL 94-142. Chapter 1 presents learning disabilities as a field in transition. Chapter 2 looks at the field's historical perspectives and emerging directions.

Part Two deals with the assessment-teaching process. Assessment and clinical teaching are viewed as interrelated parts of a continuous process of trying to understand students and to help them learn. Assessment is discussed in Chapter 3, with special emphasis on the development of the individualized education program (IEP). Chapter 4 examines clinical teaching and elements that make teaching successful. In Chapter 5, the various systems for delivering education services are discussed.

Part Three deals with theoretical issues and expanding directions. Chapter 6 examines basic theories of learning disabilities. Chapter 7 discusses medical aspects of research, assessment, and treatment. In Chapter 8, the specific problems of the high-risk preschooler are examined. In the last chapter in this Part, Chapter 9, the focus is on the learning-disabled adolescent and adult.

Part Four bridges the gap from theories to teaching strategies, dealing with the heart of the problem—teaching learning-disabled children and youth. The chapters are organized by academic areas. Each chapter has two sections: the first section explains the theoretical framework for teaching that particular content area; the second section offers teachers practical suggestions and methods. Chapter 10 discusses problems in motor and perceptual development. Chapter 11 looks at oral language, specifically listening and speaking. Chapter 12 analyzes the area of reading—both reading skills and reading comprehension. Chapter 13 reviews written language, including handwriting, spelling, and written expression. Chapter 14 analyzes disorders in mathematics—concepts, skills, and problem solving. Chapter 15 discusses social and emotional implications of learning disabilities.

In order to make this text easy to study and more appealing to use, the following features have been included:

Chapter Outlines for each chapter present the major headings and provide a handy checklist or organizational aid for students to use in learning chapter material.

Introductions to each chapter offer an overview of the chapter's contents and give students a framework into which they can fit new ideas.

Summaries conclude each chapter and highlight, in a clear point-by-point format, the major ideas presented in the chapter.

Key Terms, which follow each chapter, list the most important terminology and provide an opportunity for students to review their knowledge of key chapter concepts.

Case Examples, short illustrative vignettes and discussions, are interspersed throughout all chapters to demonstrate real-life situations.

Case Studies are included to provide longer more comprehensive cases and are designed to show practical applications.

Appendixes contain useful information for teachers. Appendix A is an extended Case Study. Appendix B consists of a phonics quiz and a brief review of important phonics generalizations. Appendix C is a listing and brief description of commonly used tests. Appendix D contains a listing of publishers' addresses. Appendix E is a glossary of important terms.

Study Guide with Cases

The _Study Guide with Cases_ that accompanies this text is a supplementary manual designed to help students learn the content and concepts presented in this textbook. It provides practice in using the field's important specialized vocabulary and in understanding key concepts and systems. It also provides applications of ideas, brief quizzes for review, and illustrative case studies.

Each chapter is divided into seven parts: (1) _Objectives_, major goals of the chapter; (2) _Terms You Should Know_, a series of key vocabulary terms and definitions for students to match; (3) _Key Points_, questions about the key ideas of the chapter; (4) _Seeing the System_, questions related to tables and drawings presented in the text; (5) _Application and Synthesis_, open ended activities, discussions, and debate questions; (6) _Rapid Review Questions_, a multiple choice quiz on the chapter; and (7) a _Case Study_, a brief case that illustrates a topic in the chapter, with accompanying questions.

The final section of the _Study Guide with Cases_ contains answers to the questions of each chapter.

Acknowledgments

Learning Disabilities: Theories, Diagnosis, and Teaching Strategies grew out of my experiences working in public schools with students who had reading and learning disabilities and in teaching learning disabilities courses in colleges and universities. The work was considerably influenced by feedback from students enrolled in the courses I have taught. Also, students and colleagues alerted me to new concepts, programs, assessment instruments, and intervention strategies. In particular, I would like to acknowledge the critical suggestions and helpful feedback of a number of faculty members at Northeastern Illinois University: Dr. Rosemary Egan, Dr. Kenneth James, Dr. Jeffrey Messerer, Mrs. Gertrude Meyers, and Dr. Margaret Richek. I am also indebted to many authors of books and articles, to speakers at conferences, and to educators in school districts and universities with whom I have worked. In addition, I have been fortunate in having had the opportunity to keep abreast of the current scene by listening to and meeting with professionals and parents at conferences held in various communities throughout the country. I am grateful to Northeastern Illinois University for having provided the conditions needed to complete this work.

I wish to thank the following reviewers, who read the manuscript at various stages and provided helpful suggestions and criticisms: Dr. Jerome Ammer, C. W. Post College (New York); Dr. Judith A. Bondurant, State University College at Buffalo; Dr. Roger Carlsen, University of Dayton; Dr. Charles A. Chrystal, State University College at Buffalo; Dr. Robert J. Evans, Troy State University (Alabama); Dr. Robert N. Freeman, Georgia Southern College; Dr. Michael Hannum, University of Tennessee—Knoxville; Dr. Kathleen Harris, California State University—Los Angeles; Dr. Jeffrey Hummel, SUNY at Buffalo; Dr. Virginia Laycock, College of William and Mary; Dr. Bob MacMillan, University of the Pacific; Dr. John A. Merica, University of South Florida; Dr. Peggyann Reed, San Jose State University; Dr. Steven C. Russell, Bowling Green State University; Ms. Nancy Saltzman, University of Colorado; Dr. Marilyn Smith, Kansas State University; Dr. Ruth Steinberg, University of Wisconsin; Dr. Saroj Sutaria, Kent State University; Dr. Carol Thornton, Illinois State University; Ms. Nancy Warnock, Eugene Public Schools; Dr. J. Barbara Wilkinson, Oklahoma State University.

The editorial staff at Houghton Mifflin offered persistent and creative guidance. Dr. Samuel A. Kirk played a continuing role in the making of this book: as my first college instructor in special education, and as a stimulating and provocative scholar and writer. I wish to acknowledge my family—Susan, Laura, Dean, James, and Aaron. Finally, thanks to my husband, Eugene, who continues to provide the encouragement and support every author needs.

Janet W. Lerner

Learning Disabilities

Overview of Learning Disabilities

PART *1*

Learning Disabilities: A Field in Transition

Chapter **1**

Introduction

*T*his is a book about learning disabilities, a problem which impedes learning for many children, adolescents, and adults, affecting their schooling and adjustment to society. In Part 1, which is an overview of the field of learning disabilities, there are two chapters. Chapter 1 introduces basic concepts, and Chapter 2 offers an historical perspective.

This introductory chapter gives the reader an idea of the scope of the field. The discussions involve definitional issues, characteristics and subtypes; the problems at different ages and stages of life; the prevalence of learning disabilities in our schools; and the interdisciplinary nature of the field.

The Enigma of Learning Disabilities

There is a growing concern for children and youth with learning disabilities. The enigma of the youngster who encounters extreme difficulty in learning, however, is not new. Children from all walks of life have experienced such difficulties throughout the years. In fact, some of the world's most distinguished people had unusual difficulty in certain aspects of learning.

Some Eminent People with Learning Disabilities

Nelson Rockefeller, who served as vice president of the United States and governor of the state of New York, suffered from severe dyslexia, extreme difficulty in learning to read. His poor reading ability kept him from achieving good grades in school, and the affliction forced him to memorize his speeches during his political career (*Time*, September 2, 1974). In describing his feelings about growing up with a learning disability, Rockefeller (1976) recalled:

> I was dyslexic . . . and I still have a hard time reading today. I remember vividly the pain and mortification I felt as a boy of eight when I was assigned to read a short passage of scripture at a community vesper service and did a thoroughly miserable job of it. I know what a dyslexic child goes through . . . the frustration of not being able to do what other children do easily, the humiliation of being thought not too bright when such is not the case at all. But after coping with this problem for more than 60 years, I have a message of hope and encouragement for children with learning disabilities—and their parents. (pp. 12–14)

Thomas Edison, the ingenious American inventor, was called abnormal, addled, and mentally defective. Writing in his diary that he was never able to get along at school, he recalled that he was always at the foot of his class. His father thought of him as stupid and Edison described himself as a dunce. Auguste Rodin, the great French sculptor, was called the worst pupil in his school. Because his teachers diagnosed Rodin as uneducable, they advised his parents to put him out to work, though they doubted that he could ever make a living. Woodrow Wilson, the scholarly twenty-eighth president of the United States, did not learn his letters until he was nine years old and did not learn to read until age eleven. Relatives expressed sorrow for his parents because Woodrow was so dull and backward (Thompson, 1971).

Albert Einstein, the mathematical genius, did not speak until age three. His search for words was described as laborious, and, until he was seven, he formulated each sentence, no matter how commonplace, silently with his lips before speaking it aloud. School work did not go well for young Albert. He had little facility with arithmetic, no special ability in any other academic subject, and great difficulty with foreign languages. One teacher predicted that "nothing good" would come of him. Einstein's language disabilities persisted throughout his adult life. When he read, he heard words; writing was difficult for him; and he communicated badly through writing. In describing his thinking process, he explained that he rarely thought in words; it was only after a thought came that he tried to express it in words at a later time (Patten, 1973).

These persons of eminence fortunately were able somehow to find appropriate ways of learning, and they successfully overcame their initial failures. Many youngsters with learning disabilities are not so fortunate.

CASE EXAMPLE

Tony—The Puzzle of Learning Disabilities

The case of Tony illustrates the enigma of learning disabilities and the difficulty parents encounter. Tony's parents have long been aware that their son has severe problems in learning. As an infant, Tony was colicky and had difficulty in learning to suck. His early speech was so garbled that no one could understand him, and frequently his inability to communicate led to sudden temper tantrums. The kindergarten teacher reported that Tony was "immature"; his first-grade teacher said he "did not pay attention"; and succeeding teachers labeled him "lazy" and then "emotionally disturbed." Tony's distraught parents attempted to find the source of his learning problems to alleviate his misery and theirs. They desperately followed suggestions from many sources that led to a succession of specialists and clinics dedicated to treating such difficulties.

One clinic detected a visual problem, and as a result Tony received visual training exercises for several years. Another clinic diagnosed Tony's problem as a lack of neurological organization and instituted a lengthy series of motor exercises. An opinion of emotional disturbance at another agency led to years of psychotherapy for both Tony and his parents. A reading tutor analyzed the problem as a lack of instruction in phonics, and Tony received intensive phonics instruction for a period of time. The family pediatrician said that the boy was merely going through a stage and would grow out of it. Yet despite this wealth of diagnosis and treatment, Tony still cannot learn. He is unhappily failing in school, and, understandably, he has lost faith in himself.

The problems encountered by Tony and his parents are typical. Each specialty viewed Tony's problem from its own perspective and therefore saw only part of the picture. What is needed, instead, is a unified interdisciplinary approach to the problem of Tony's learning disabilities—a coordinated effort, with each special field contributing its expertise to the analysis and treatment of the child. A unified procedure is required to mobilize the team and coordinate the efforts of the various participating professions.

Definitions of Learning Disabilities

The term learning disabilities was first introduced in 1963. A small group of concerned parents and educators had met in Chicago to consider linking the isolated parent groups active in a few communities into a single organization. Each of these parent groups had identified the children of concern under a different name—including perceptually handicapped, brain-injured, and neurologically impaired. If the groups were to join, they needed to agree on a single term to identify the children. When the term *learning disabilities* was suggested at this meeting, it met with immediate approval (Kirk, 1963). The organization today known as the Association for Children and Adults with Learning Disabilities (ACLD) was born at this historic meeting.

Although the term *learning disabilities* had immediate appeal and acceptance, the task of developing a definition of learning disabilities proved to be a challenge. Indeed, defining this population is considered such a formidable task that some have likened learning disabilities to pornography: each is "impossible to define but you always know it when you see it."

Thus, defining learning disabilities in a way acceptable to all has continued as a debatable issue since the inception of the field. Although a number of definitions have been generated and used over the years, each has been judged by some to have certain shortcomings.

The Federal Definition

Probably the most widely used definition is the one incorporated in Public Law (PL) 94–142, the Education for All Handicapped Children Act (U.S. Office of Education, August 23, 1977). This definition is the basis for federal and state law, as well as for many school programs.

There are actually two parts to the federal definition. The first part appears in the major body of the rules and regulations of PL 94–142 and was adopted from a 1968 report to Congress of the National Advisory Committee on Handicapped Children. This definition reads:

> "Specific learning disability" means a disorder in one or more of the basic psychological processes involved in understanding or in using language spoken or written, which may manifest itself in an imperfect ability to listen, think, speak, read, write, spell, or to do mathematical calculations. The term includes such conditions as perceptual handicaps, brain injury, minimal brain dysfunction, dyslexia, and developmental aphasia. The term does not include children who have learning problems which are primarily the result of visual, hearing, or motor handicaps, of mental retardation, of emotional disturbance, or of environmental, cultural, or economic disadvantage.

The second part of the federal definition is considered operational and appears in a separate set of regulations applying to PL 94–142 concerned with learning disabilities (U.S. Office of Education, December 29, 1977). It states that a student has a specific learning disability if (1) the student does not achieve at the proper age and ability levels in one or more of several specific areas when provided with appropriate learning experiences, and (2) the student has a severe discrepancy between achievement and intellectual ability in one or more of the following areas: (a) oral expression, (b) listening comprehension, (c) written expression, (d) basic reading skill, (e) reading comprehension, (f) mathematics calculation, and (g) mathematics reasoning.

In brief, the federal definition of learning disabilities in PL 94–142 contains the following major concepts:

1. The individual has a *disorder in one or more of the basic psychological processes.* (These processes refer to intrinsic prerequisite abilities such as memory, auditory perception, visual perception, and oral language.)
2. The individual has *difficulty in learning,* specifically, in the areas of speaking, listening, writing, reading (word recognition skills and comprehension), and mathematics (calculation and reasoning).
3. The problem is *not primarily due to other causes,* such as visual or hearing impairments, motor handicaps, mental retardation, emotional disturbance, or economic, environmental, or cultural disadvantage.
4. A *severe discrepancy exists between the student's apparent potential for learning and the student's low level of achievement.*

Other Definitions

Another definition that is proving to be influential was proposed by the National Joint Committee on Learning Disabilities (NJCLD) in 1981 (Hammill, Leigh, McNutt, and Larsen, 1981). (This group consists of representatives from several organizations concerned with learning disabilities: The American Speech-Language-Hearing Association, The Association for Children and Adults with Learning Disabilities, The Council for Learning Disabilities, The

Division of Children with Communication Disorders, The Division for Learning Disabilities, The International Reading Association, and The Orton Dyslexia Society.) The NJCLD definition states that

> Learning disabilities is a generic term that refers to a heterogeneous group of disorders manifested by significant difficulties in the acquisition and use of listening, speaking, reading, writing, reasoning, or mathematical abilities. These disorders are intrinsic to the individual and presumed to be due to central nervous system dysfunction. Even though a learning disability may occur concomitantly with other handicapping conditions (e.g., sensory impairment, mental retardation, social and emotional disturbance) or environmental influences (e.g., cultural differences, or inappropriate instruction, psycholinguistic factors), it is not the direct result of those conditions or influences.

Important concepts in the NJCLD definition include the following:

1. *Learning disabilities are a heterogeneous group of disorders.* (Individuals with learning disabilities exhibit many different kinds of problems.)
2. *The problem is intrinsic to the individual.* (Learning disabilities are due to factors within the person rather than to external factors, such as the environment or the educational system.)
3. *The problem is thought to be related to a central nervous system dysfunction.* (There is recognition of the biological basis of the problem.)
4. *Learning disabilities may occur along with other handicapping conditions.* (There is recognition that individuals can have several problems at the same time, such as learning disabilities and emotional disorders.)

Other definitions of learning disabilities have been proposed. For example, a widely used resource for physicians and psychologists, the *Diagnostic and Statistical Manual of Mental Disorders (American Psychiatric Association*, 1980), defines and describes attention deficit disorders (ADD). *Attention deficit disorders* refers to poor attending ability, which often serves as a diagnostic symptom of learning disabilities for physicians. (See Chapter 7 for a discussion of attention deficit disorders.)

As the field has gained recognition, many countries throughout the world have developed their own definitions of learning disabilities. For example, most of the provinces in Canada have programs for learning disabilities, and Ontario's special education Bill 82 contains a definition of learning disabilities. In England, the Warnock Report identifies and defines children with "specific learning difficulties." Many other nations are developing learning disabilities programs and are engaged in research.

Need for Several Definitions

What conclusions can be drawn from this review of definitions of learning disabilities?

1. Learning disabilities has become an established discipline. The problem is widely accepted and recognized, and learning-disabled individuals are being identified by many disciplines, professions, organizations, and in many nations of the world.
2. The goal of finding a single definition of learning disabilities acceptable to all may be unfeasible. The nature of the problems of learning disabilities is highly individual, and solutions applied to those problems must be adaptive and flexible. Some scholars are suggesting that there are several types of learning disabilities and a different definition is needed for each.
3. There appears to be a need for several definitions of learning disabilities. Different definitions are required by various professions, populations, age levels, and degrees of severity.

Common Elements in the Definitions

The various definitions of learning disabilities have several common elements: (1) neurological dysfunction, (2) uneven growth pattern, (3) difficulty in academic and learning tasks, (4) discrepancy between achievement and potential, and (5) exclusion of other causes. The nature of each of these elements and problems that surround each are examined in the following section.

Neurological Dysfunction

Although not always stated directly, implied in many of the definitions is the idea that learning disabilities are related to atypical brain function. Since all learning originates within the brain, the presumption is that a disorder in learning can be caused by central nervous system dysfunction. Educational and environmental events can, of course, modify the process of learning and influence brain function, making it worse or better.

In many cases the neurological condition is difficult, if not impossible, to ascertain by medical examination or external medical tests. Often, therefore, the central nervous system dysfunction is presumed and determined through observation of behavior. As noted in Chapters 7 and 12, there is growing evidence derived from sophisticated brain research to support the presumption of neurological dysfunction. Teachers are chiefly concerned with behavioral and educational aspects, but the medical contributions remain important. The medical profession played a key role in the historical development of the field (see Chapter 2) and currently takes an active part in research, diagnosis, and treatment (see Chapter 7).

Uneven Growth Pattern

This element of the definition refers to an irregular or uneven development of the various components of mental ability. Mental ability, or the intellect, is not a single capacity; rather, it is composed of many underlying mental abilities. For the individual with learning disabilities, these component abilities or subabilities do not develop in an even or normal fashion. That is, while some of the components are maturing in an anticipated sequence or rate, others are lagging in their development, thereby appearing as symptoms of the learning problem. This uneven growth pattern is also called *developmental imbalances* (Gallagher, 1966), *intra-individual differences* (Kirk & Kirk, 1971), or *modality strengths and weaknesses* (Chapters 6 and 10). The key phrase within the federal definition referring to this component is "Specific learning disability means a *disorder in one or more of the basic psychological processes.*"

The concept of an uneven growth pattern has become the basis of much of the diagnosis and remediation in learning disabilities. It is this element of the definition that has caused a lively debate within the field about the utility of information about processing deficits for teaching a student. A discussion of this "processing debate" appears in Chapters 6 and 10.

Difficulty in Academic and Learning Tasks

The specific problem that the student encounters in learning may occur in the acquisition of speech and oral language, in reading, in arithmetic, in handwriting, in motor skills, in written expression, in thinking, or in psychosocial skills. (See Part 4 for discussions of each specific area of learning.) The federal definition lists seven specific academic areas in which learning disabilities can be detected. The learning tasks affected are wide-ranging. This part of the definition has created some conflicts with other professions. If the focus is on the student's reading problem, the reading specialist in the school is also concerned; if the presenting problem is a language disorder, the speech and language teachers share the responsibility.

Discrepancy Between Achievement and Potential

Another element common to many definitions of learning disabilities is the identification of a gap between what the student is potentially capable of learning and what the student in fact has learned or achieved. This imbalance between achievement and potential is highlighted in the operational portion of the definition: "The child has a severe discrepancy between achievement and intellectual ability in one or more of seven areas."

This element of the definition stresses the criterion of underachievement. Emphasis on underachievement minimizes other aspects of the definition—especially the concept of disorders in basic psychological processes. Since there are many reasons besides learning disabilities for an individual to be underachieving, such as poor teaching, lack of motivation or

A specific learning disability may occur in one of many areas—for example, in reading, math, motor skills, thinking, or psycho-social behavior.

(Michael Kagan/Monkmeyer)

interest, or psychological or emotional factors, the criterion of underachievement alone is insufficient.

To determine if a discrepancy exists between potential and achievement, one must ask three essential questions, each of which raises critical problems. The questions concern the determination of (1) potential, (2) achievement, and (3) severe discrepancy.

1. *What is the individual's potential for learning?* To make a judgment about a person's potential, ability level, or capacity, professionals generally use an intelligence, or IQ, test. Currently, IQ tests are under severe criticism from many segments of our society. Critics have charged that they are inaccurate measures of intelligence, that they are racially and culturally biased, and that they are of questionable use because scores may vary depending on the test being used. Thus, the question of whether we can effectively measure potential remains a highly debatable issue.

2. *What is the individual's achievement level?* Tests used to measure the individual's performance level are also suspect. Many reading tests, for

example, have been questioned in terms of their validity, reliability, standardization, and measurement of error (Farr, 1969). The applicability of the scores in other achievement tests widely used in the measurement of learning disabilities has also been questioned (Salvia & Ysseldyke, 1981). Another problem is the lack of standardized tests for several of the areas of learning disabilities identified in the federal law, for example, written expression.

3. *What degree of discrepancy between potential and achievement is considered "severe"?* The important word here is *severe*. A one-year discrepancy at second-grade level is more severe than a one-year discrepancy for an eleventh-grade student. Thus, one must ask, "Should a severe discrepancy be determined by a fixed amount of time (one year, three years), or should a ratio or some statistical measure or formula be used?"

Each state, school district, or evaluation team must establish its own method of determining a "severe discrepancy." Some schools and some of the state education agencies have developed quantitative measures to determine severe discrepancy. A discussion of various ways to establish "eligibility criteria" appears in Chapter 3. A key question is how a quantitative technique to measure the discrepancy can be coupled with the human factors, such as clinical observations made by an astute teacher. There is a growing acceptance (as noted in the discussion of the NJCLD definition) of the idea that other impairments may occur concomitantly with learning disabilities.

Exclusion of Other Causes

Many of the definitions state that the learning problem is not primarily the result of other causes. That is, the students are not mentally retarded, emotionally disturbed, visually handicapped, hearing impaired, or culturally, socially, or economically disadvantaged. Such a limitation is often difficult to implement in practice. Teachers who work with other kinds of exceptional students frequently observe that their students appear to have two handicaps—their primary impairment, plus learning disabilities. Moreover, it is not easy, when evaluating an individual, to ferret out which problem is primary and which is secondary.

The incorporation of an exclusion clause into the definition has its origin in the need to establish learning disabilities as a separate and discrete category. This was important at the time the field was first established in order to obtain sufficient funds and appropriate legislation for the learning disabled apart from the other categories of handicapped individuals (Kirk, 1974).

Diverse Characteristics of Learning Disabilities

When considering the learning and behavior characteristics of learning disabilities, we must keep certain cautions in mind. The term *learning disabil-*

ities encompasses a cluster of disorders, and no one individual will display all of them. For example, some learning-disabled individuals have a mathematics difficulty whereas others excel in mathematics. Hyperactivity and perceptual disorders are symptomatic problems for many students but not for all. Further, certain kinds of characteristics are more likely to be exhibited at certain age levels. Young children are more likely to be hyperactive than adolescents. In addition, deficits are manifested in different ways at different age levels. For example, an underlying language disorder may appear as a delayed speech problem in the preschooler, as a reading disorder in the elementary-age student, and as a writing disorder in the secondary student. The implications of each of these learning and behavior characteristics are complex, and they are discussed in detail throughout this book. With these cautions in mind, the common characteristics of learning disabilities can be listed as follows.

Disorders of attention: hyperactivity, distractability, attention deficit disorders (Chapter 7)

Failure to develop and mobilize cognitive strategies for learning: organization, active learning set, metacognitive functions (Chapters 6 and 8, and Chapters 11 through 14, especially Chapter 12)

Poor motor abilities: fine and gross motor coordination, general awkwardness and clumsiness, spatial problems (Chapter 10)

Perceptual problems: discrimination of auditory and visual stimuli, auditory and visual closure and sequencing (Chapter 10)

Oral language difficulties: listening, speaking, vocabulary, linguistic competencies (Chapter 11)

Reading difficulties: decoding, basic reading skills, reading comprehension (Chapter 12)

Written language difficulties: spelling, handwriting, written composition (Chapter 13)

Mathematics difficulties: quantitative thinking, arithmetic, time, space, calculation facts (Chapter 14)

Inappropriate social behavior: social perception, emotional behavior, establishing social relationships (Chapter 15)

Thus, there is a cluster of general learning and behavior patterns that characterize learning disabilities. Each individual student, however, will exhibit only some of these characteristics. During the evaluation process, the assessment team determines which characteristics the individual student exhibits and how they impede that student's learning.

Subtypes of Learning Disabilities

As noted earlier, learning disabilities comprise a heterogeneous group of symptoms and characteristics. There is much research interest in classifying subtypes of learning disabilities. Research in this area may help to clarify the definition and lead to more effective assessment and remediation. There is evidence that learning disabilities are not a "single syndrome" and that the learning disabilities population falls within a number of subtypes.

Kirk and Chalfant (1984) suggest two types: *developmental learning disabilities* and *academic learning disabilities.* Developmental learning disabilities include the prerequisite skills that a student needs in order to achieve in academic subjects (attention, memory, perceptual skills, thinking skills, and oral language skills). Academic learning disabilities refer to school-acquired learning (reading, arithmetic, handwriting, spelling, and written expression). Other classifications of learning disabilities subtypes were reviewed by McKinney (1984), who reported on eight subtype research studies.

In a study using a cluster analysis technique, McKinney (1984) identified four subtypes of learning disabilities. The following characteristics were found in the four subtypes: *Subtype I* (33 percent), average verbal skills, deficits in sequential and spatial skills, poor in independence and task orientation, conceptual strengths on the intelligence test, Weschler Intelligence Scale for Children-Revised (WISC-R), mild learning disability in reading and math, 60 percent male; *Subtype II* (10 percent), poor in general information, arithmetic and picture arrangement on WISC-R, severely impaired in academic areas, rated low by teachers on behavioral scales, judged less considerate and more hostile by teachers, very poor in task orientation; *Subtype III* (47 percent), 93 percent male, above average conceptual skills on WISC-R, mildly impaired in academics, poor task orientation, socially extroverted: *Subtype IV* (10 percent), moderately impaired in academic areas, no evidence of behavioral deficiencies, average verbal skills, deficits in sequential and spatial skills.

This research in subtypes of learning disabilities is promising and may help to clarify the definition, find more homogeneous diagnostic groups, and promote better ways to make decisions on teaching and placement.

Widening Age Span of the Learning Disabilities Population

When the small group of parents and professionals first sought to obtain help for their children and promote the field of learning disabilities, their efforts focused on the pressing needs of the elementary-level child. Since that time, however, we have come to realize that learning disabilities become evident at many stages of life and that the problem appears in a different form at each stage. Each age group (preschoolers, elementary children, adolescents, and adults) needs different kinds of skills. Therefore, certain characteristics of learning disabilities assume greater prominence at certain age levels.

Learning Disabilities at the Preschool Level

Educators are generally reluctant to label preschoolers as learning disabled. Since growth rates are so unpredictable at young ages, it is very difficult to make a diagnosis for the preschooler. Instead, very young children who appear to have problems are simply viewed as "high-risk" children. Experience and research show that intervention for the young high-risk child is very effective and educational efforts have a high payoff.

Among the characteristics seen in learning-disabled preschool children are inadequate motor development, language delays, speech disorders, and poor cognitive and concept development. Common examples of problems at the preschool level are the three-year-old who cannot catch a ball, hop, jump, or play with manipulative toys (poor motor development); the four-year-old who does not use language to communicate, has a limited vocabulary, and cannot be understood (language and speech disorders); and the five-year-old who cannot count to ten, name colors, or work puzzles (poor cognitive development). In addition, preschoolers often exhibit behaviors of hyperactivity and poor attention. The problems and treatment of the preschool child are so unique that a special chapter is devoted to this age group (Chapter 8).

PRESCHOOL USUALLY NOT A LABEL

Learning Disabilities at the Elementary Level

In many children, learning disabilities first become apparent when they enter school and fail to acquire academic skills. Often the failure occurs in reading, but it also happens in mathematics, writing, or other school subjects. Among the behaviors frequently seen in the early elementary years are inability to attend and concentrate, poor motor skills as evidenced in the awkward handling of a pencil and in poor writing, and difficulty in learning to read.

In the later elementary years, as the curriculum becomes more difficult, problems may emerge in other areas, such as social studies or science. Emotional problems also become more of an impediment after several years of repeated failure, and students become more conscious of their poor achievement in comparison with peers. For some students, social problems and the ability to make and keep friends increase in importance at this age level.

Learning Disabilities at the Secondary Level

There is a radical change in schooling at the secondary level, and adolescents find that learning disabilities begin to take a greater toll at this level. The tougher demands of the junior and senior high school curriculum and teachers, the turmoil of adolescence, the continued academic failure all sometimes combine to intensify the learning disability. Adolescents are also concerned about life after completing school. They may need counseling and guidance for college and career and vocational decisions. To worsen the situation, a few adolescents find themselves drawn into acts of juvenile delinquency.

Since adolescents tend to be overly sensitive, emotional, social, and self-concept problems often accompany a learning disability at this age. Most secondary schools now have programs for learning-disabled adolescents.

Though this age group is considered throughout the book, some of its unique features, as well as special programs designed for it, are discussed in Chapter 9.

Learning Disabilities in the Adult

By the time they finish schooling, many students either overcome their learning disabilities or succeed in reducing them so that they no longer have a severe problem as adults in society. For others, however, the problem continues, and vestiges of their disorder hamper them as they grow older. Difficulty in reading, as well as social problems, may limit their career development and also hinder them in making and keeping friends. We are finding that many adults are voluntarily seeking help in later life to cope with their learning disabilities. Problems of adults are discussed further in Chapter 9.

Prevalence of Learning Disabilities

Estimates of the prevalence of learning disabilities vary—ranging from 1 percent to 30 percent of the school population—depending on the criteria used to determine eligibility. The number of children and youth identified as learning disabled depends largely on the definition and identification procedures selected. The more stringent the identification criteria, the lower will be the prevalence rate. Conversely, the more lenient the criteria, the higher will be the prevalence rate. If only severe cases of learning disabilities are admitted to the program, a low percentage of children will be identified. If mild, as well as severe, learning disabilities are admitted for service, the prevalence rate will rise.

Several studies have attempted to measure prevalence of learning disabilities. In one early study of 2,800 third- and fourth-grade pupils, the researchers found that 7 to 8 percent had learning disabilities (Myklebust & Boshes, 1969). In another study of 3,000 second-grade children, Meier (1971) found that 15 percent had learning disabilities. The National Advisory Committee on Handicapped Children (1968) recommended to Congress that a conservative estimate of 1 to 3 percent be considered as a prevalence estimate until research provides more objective evidence.

Since the implementation of Public Law 94–142, the Education for All Handicapped Children Act, in 1977, we have an actual count of how many children and youth receive special education services each school year. This information is made available through the student's *Individualized Education Program* (IEP). Census data from the IEPs are collected by each school district and reported to each state education agency, and state totals are reported to the Department of Education. Consequently, we now have valuable information about the number of learning-disabled students being served and other demographic information.

TABLE 1.1   **Students Receiving Special Education Services, Ages 3–21: School Year 1983–1984**

Handicapping Condition	Percentage of Total School Enrollment*
Learning disabled	4.63
Speech impaired	2.89
Mentally retarded	1.92
Emotionally disturbed	.93
Deaf and hard of hearing	.19
Multihandicapped	.15
Orthopedically handicapped	.14
Other health impaired	.14
Visually handicapped	.08
Deaf-blind	less than .01
Total	11.09

Source: U.S. Department of Education, *To assure the free, appropriate public education of all handicapped children*, Sixth Annual Report to Congress on the Implementation of PL 94–142, The Education for All Handicapped Children Act, 1984. Personal communication with the Office of Special Education and Rehabilitation, U.S. Department of Education.
*The percentages are based on handicapped children ages 3–21 as a percent of total school enrollment for preschool through twelfth grade.

More than four million students in the nation have been identified in all categories of handicap, which is about 11 percent of the total school population. As shown in Table 1.1, learning disabilities is the largest category of exceptionality, comprising over 4 percent of the total school population. Some 40 percent of all handicapped students receiving special education services are learning disabled.

In addition to the number of students served, other information is available through the child count data. For example, there is information on sex differences. Although it has been estimated over the years that there are more boys than girls with learning disabilities, the child count data now support this estimate. About 72 percent are boys and 28 percent are girls, or about two and a half times more boys than girls (U.S. General Accounting Office, 1981).

An analysis of the number of students classified as learning disabled since PL 94–142 was first implemented reveals an interesting trend. Table 1.2 indicates that there has been an increase in the number of students classified as learning disabled over the years. Figure 1.1 shows an increase in learning disabilities as a percentage of the total school population, from 1.89 percent in 1977–1978 to 4.40 percent in 1982–1983.

The National Association of State Directors of Special Education

TABLE 1.2   **Number of Learning-disabled Children and Youth, Ages 3–21**

Year	Number of Identified Learning-disabled Students
1976–77	797,212
1977–78	969,423
1978–79	1,135,559
1979–80	1,281,379
1980–81	1,468,014
1981–82	1,627,344
1982–83	1,745,871
1983–84	1,811,451

Source: U.S. Department of Education, *To assure the free, appropriate public education of all handicapped children*, Annual Report to Congress on the Implementation of Public Law 94–142, The Education for All Handicapped Children Act, 1979–1984. Personal communication with the Office of Special Education and Rehabilitation, U.S. Department of Education.

(NASDE) (1983) offers the following reasons for the increase in the number of children and youth classified under learning disabilities.

1. *Improvement in procedures for identifying and assessing learning disabilities.* Factors such as more awareness of learning disabilities, public pressure to adequately serve these children, and improved assessment techniques have led to the identification of many children who may previously have gone undetected.
2. *Liberal eligibility criteria for learning disabilities.* Some states have more lenient eligibility criteria than others. Some local school districts permit students with a wide range of learning problems to be classified as learning disabled.
3. *Social acceptance/preference for the learning disabled classification.* Some students who once would have been classified as mentally retarded or behavior-disordered are increasingly classified as learning disabled so that they can receive special services. Many parents and administrators prefer the learning disabilities classification because it does not carry the stigma of other handicap classifications. Over this period, there has been a decrease in the percentage of children identified as mentally retarded.
4. *Cutbacks in other programs and lack of general education alternatives for children who experience problems in the regular class.* Over this period, there has been a decrease in the funding of other special programs (such as Chapter I programs, which are federally funded remedial programs in regular education) and a lack of adequate remedial programs for students experiencing difficulty in the regular classroom.

FIGURE 1.1
**Learning-disabled Children and Youth, Ages 3–21 Served Under PL 94–142
and PL 89–313 as a Percentage of Total School Enrollment***

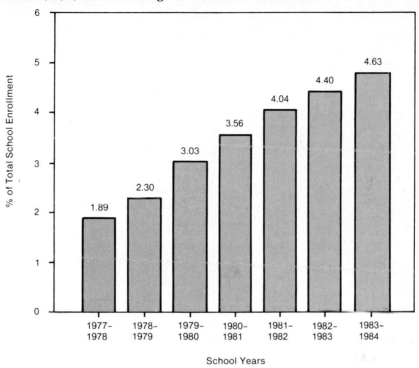

School Years

*Note: Number of LD Children ages 3–21 served as a percentage of estimated Fall enrollment (ages 5–17)

Sources: U.S. Department of Education. *To assure the free, appropriate public education of all handicapped children,* First through Sixth Annual Report to Congress on the Implementation of Public Law 94–142, The Education for All Handicapped Children Act, 1979–1984.

U.S. Department of Education, *National enrollment statistics,* 1979–1984, National Center for Education Statistics.

Personal communication with the Office of Special Education, U.S. Department of Education.

5. *Court order.* There have been a number of judicial decisions to re-evaluate minority children because the classification of mental retardation was judged discriminatory. Many of these children are being reclassified as learning disabled.

Disciplines Contributing to the Study of Learning Disabilities

Four disciplines make major contributions to the study of learning disabilities: education, psychology, language, and medicine. In addition, other professions in the helping and research fields participate in and advance the

FIGURE 1.2
Learning Disabilities: An Interdisciplinary Field

work done for the learning disabled. Such a mingling of professions has resulted in a multidisciplinary breadth to the body of thought concerning learning disabilities. (See Figure 1.2.)

Education

The contributions of the field of education have a practical framework, for educators must deal with the reality of teaching the child. Kirk and Gallagher (1983) note that education often begins where medicine stops. Classroom teachers, reading specialists, special educators, and physical educators focus on the learning behavior of the student. The educators' expertise includes knowledge about subject area sequences, understanding of the relationships among curricular areas, acquaintance with a variety of school organizational patterns, and knowledge of materials and methods. The very term *learning*

Learning disabilities affect people differently in various stages of life; each age group requires different intervention and teaching strategies.

(Sally Stone Halvorson/Monkmeyer)

disabilities, with its emphasis on the learning situation instead of the causes of the disorder, demonstrates the impact of educators on the field.

Psychology

Psychologists, particularly specialists in child development, learning theory, and school psychology, have had significant influence in shaping the field. The psychological perspective has also led to a keener awareness of the psychodynamic consequences of learning disabilities.

School psychologists have had an especially direct influence since they observe, test, evaluate, and characterize the outward behavior of children. The work of child development specialists, focusing on the developmental processes of the normal child, has become the basis for many concepts of the atypical child. Learning theorists have enriched the field with their analysis of school-subject content areas in behavioral terms, identifying tasks to be taught and behaviors to be expected. Reinforcement theory, operant conditioning, and behavior modification are among the contributions of learning theorists to learning disabilities research and training.

Language Disciplines

Professionals in the fields of speech and language pathology, language development, linguistics, and psycholinguistics recognize that many of their concerns overlap with the concepts of those in the field of learning disabilities. Speech and language pathologists have produced research on ways to assess language disorders and teach those who have them. The work being done in linguistics (the study of the nature and structure of human language) and in psycholinguistics (the study of the relationship of language development to the thinking and learning processes) has also added to the learning disabilities knowledge base. A renewed interest in the puzzle of language acquisition, kindled by recent work in psycholinguistics, increases our understanding of the child with learning disabilities. Knowledge of how the normal child learns language is invaluable in developing the ability to diagnose and treat language difficulties in children. Conversely, study of the language disorders of exceptional children can clarify the understanding of the normal child's language acquisition.

Medicine

The medical specialties (represented by both practitioners and researchers) contributing to the field include pediatrics, neurology, ophthalmology, otology, psychiatry, pharmacology, endocrinology, electroencephalography, nursing, and school nursing.

Medical specialists are, by education and practice, cause-oriented— always searching for the etiology, or source, of a health problem. They view learning disabilities as pathological conditions and therefore their major contributions have been in identifying the causes of learning disorders. Physicians are the key specialists for the medical diagnosis.

Other Professions

Many other professionals play important roles in the research and literature on learning disabilities. Optometrists have made key advancements concerning the visual function. Audiologists have contributed important concepts relating to hearing and auditory perception and training. Social workers, occupational therapists, and guidance counselors have also been instrumental in the growth of the field. In addition, research findings from fields such as genetics and biochemistry also provide important information.

One must also consider parents as vital contributing members of the interdisciplinary team. They have known their child for the longest period of time and have the most at stake. The parents' input and help can be both extremely supportive of and enriching to the understanding of the learning-disabled student.

The Learning Disabilities Teacher as a Coordinating Agent

The learning disabilities specialist can serve as the agent responsible for coordinating the efforts of the contributing disciplines. One crucial role of the learning disabilities specialist is to build a cooperative interdisciplinary team that works together, rather than to permit team members to pursue splintered and isolated approaches that sometimes work at cross-purposes with one another. Although the learning disabilities specialist cannot be an expert in all of these contributing fields, she or he can receive intensive interdisciplinary training that includes the basic concepts of the other specialists and what they do. The learning disabilities specialist should be equipped to serve as a highly skilled coworker and coordinator.

Without a coordinated effort, each professional may see the student with learning disabilities in terms of her or his own perspective, much as the fabled blind men of India are said to have "seen" the elephant. In the proverbial tale, one blind man felt the elephant's trunk and concluded an elephant was like a snake; another, feeling the leg, said it resembled a tree trunk; the third, feeling the tail, believed the elephant was like a rope; the fourth touched the ear and thought the elephant was a fan; the fifth felt the tusk and likened the elephant to a spear; while the last man, feeling the side, said the elephant was like a wall. Similarly, since each professional sees but one part of the learning disabled student, there is a risk that each may blindly misinterpret who the student actually is. An important task of the learning disabilities specialist is to integrate the various professional services in order to effect an understanding of the whole person.

Summary

• This chapter introduced the field of learning disabilities by presenting accounts of the lives of accomplished people who experienced severe learning problems as children; discussing and evaluating several definitions of learning disabilities; analyzing five elements common to most definitions of learning disabilities; looking at the expanding age range of the learning disabilities population; discussing the prevalence of learning disabilities; and describing the contributions of the various disciplines involved in the learning disabilities field.

• Learning disabilities have affected the lives of many eminent people as children, including Nelson Rockefeller, Thomas Edison, Auguste Rodin, and Albert Einstein.

• Defining learning disabilities has proved to be a formidable task. The federal definition that appears in PL 94–142 has become the basis for state and local district definitions and many learning disabilities programs. The operational part of the federal definition states that a student can be identified as learning disabled if the evaluation team finds a severe discrepancy between his or her achievement and intellectual ability in one or more of several areas: oral expression, listening comprehension, written expression, basic reading skill, reading comprehension, mathematics calculation, and mathematics reasoning. In addition to the federal definition, others have been proposed, including one by the National Joint Committee on Learning Disabilities (NJCLD).

• There are five elements common to most definitions of learning disabilities: neurological dysfunction, uneven growth pattern, difficulty in academic and learning tasks, discrepancy between achievement and potential, and exclusion of other causes. Each adds to our understanding of learning disabilities, but each element also raises certain issues in the field.

• Learning-disabled students display many different and diverse characteristics. No one individual will exhibit all characteristics. In addition, certain difficulties are more prevalent than others at particular ages. The possible characteristics include problems in: attention; cognitive strategies for learning; motor abilities; perception; oral language; reading; written language; mathematics; and social behaviors.

• There is recognition that learning disabilities affect people differently in various stages of life. Preschoolers, elementary-age students, adolescents, and adults manifest different problems and characteristics. Each age group requires different intervention and teaching strategies.

• It is difficult to determine the prevalence of learning disabilities because the number of students classified as learning disabled depends on the method and criteria used for identification. The more stringent the criteria, the fewer the number of students who will be identified. The percentage of students classified as learning disabled is increasing for several reasons, including improved procedures for identifying learning disabilities; social acceptance and preference for the learning disabilities classification; and a decrease in other types of remedial services. The identified learning disabilities group is now over 4 percent of the total school population.

• There are several disciplines that participate in the study of learning disabilities, making it a multidisciplinary field. These disciplines are education, psychology, language, medicine, and other helping and research professions. Each specialization has important contributions to make to the field, and the learning disabilities teacher often acts as the coordinator of these diverse contributions.

Key Terms

potential for learning	attention deficit disorders	handicapped children
present levels of achievement	central nervous system dysfunction	heterogenous intrinsic
severe discrepancy	prevalence	Public Law 94–142

147,227

Historical
Perspectives

Chapter 2

Introduction

*T*his chapter traces the roots of the field of learning disabilities by reviewing the work of individuals who generated concepts that have advanced the thinking of the field. Each contribution was built upon earlier theories and, in turn, inspired further research and investigation. Wiederholt (1974) divides the history of learning disabilities into three distinct periods: (a) the *foundation phase* (about 1800–1930), marked by basic scientific investigations of brain function and dysfunction; (2) the *transition phase* (about 1930–1960), when research findings about brain dysfunction were applied to the clinical study of children who were not learning and professionals began to develop assessment and treatment methods for those children; and (3) the *integration phase* (about 1960–1980), characterized by the rapid growth of school programs for the learning disabled, the eclectic use of a variety of theories, assessment techniques, and teaching strategies, and the enactment of legislation designed to protect the rights of handicapped children and youth. To update this history, we have added a fourth period, the *contemporary phase* (1980 to the present): a time of emerging directions, expanding the scope of the field. During this period, the concept of the age levels of people affected by learning disabilities was broadened. Learning disabilities services were integrated into both special education and regular education systems. New ideas and research findings were incorporated, and computer technology began to be used to help learning-disabled students. These four periods are illustrated in the time line in Figure 2.1.

The Foundation Phase: Brain Research

The foundation phase, 1800–1930, consisted of basic scientific research on the brain and its disorders. Many of the early brain researchers were physicians involved in the study of their adult patients whose brains had been damaged by stroke, accident, or disease. These scientists gathered information by first studying the behavior of the patients who had lost some function, such as the ability to speak or read. Then if the patient died, they examined the patient's brain through autopsy in an attempt to correlate the loss of function with specific damaged areas of the brain. We shall briefly review here the highlights of this foundation period.

A widely held belief in the nineteenth century was the notion of *phrenology:* that abnormal behavior and brain function could be predicted by examining the shape of a person's skull. Bumps on the head were thought to reveal information about the brain. Paul Broca (1878) rejected the phrenology notion with his discovery during autopsies that certain areas of the brain (in the

FIGURE 2.1
Time Line: Historical Phases of the Field of Learning Disabilities

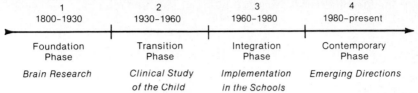

left frontal lobe) were damaged in adult patients who had lost the ability to speak and subsequently died. The importance of his discovery is widely recognized, and the loss of the ability to speak is often called *Broca's aphasia.* Carl Wernicke (1908) followed up on Broca's work, describing another portion of the brain (the temporal lobe), to which he attributed the understanding of speech, or listening comprehension. Both Broca and Wernicke hypothesized that specific localized areas of the brain governed particular activities.

John Hughlings Jackson (1874) was critical of this localization theory, contending that the human brain was more than a collection of independent centers. He believed that parts of the brain were intimately linked and that damage to one part would reduce overall general functioning. Sir Henry Head (1926) produced a work on aphasia that was the culmination of a lifetime of collecting scientific data. He conducted many clinical observations, developed a system for data collection, and created a test for aphasia. Head believed that aphasics did not suffer from generalized impairment of intellectual ability even though they had sustained brain damage evidenced by language difficulties.

James Hinshelwood (1917), a physician, studied the condition *word blindness,* which he defined as the inability to interpret written or printed language despite normal vision. Reporting on the case of an intelligent boy who was unable to learn to read, Hinshelwood speculated that the problem was due to a defect in the angular gyrus, a specific area of the brain.

Kurt Goldstein (1939), a physician who treated brain-injured soldiers during World War I, hypothesized that brain damage affects an individual's behavior. Among the characteristics he noted in the brain-injured soldiers were perceptual impairment, characterized by foreground-background difficulties; distractibility to external stimuli, and perseveration (the behavior of being locked into continually repeating an action). Heinz Werner and Alfred Strauss continued the work of Goldstein, expanding the study from brain-injured soldiers to brain-injured children.

Brain research did not end in the 1930s, although the field of learning disabilities proceeded from the *foundation* phase of brain study to the *transition* phase—the clinical study of learning problems in children. In fact, with today's advancements in scientific technology providing more sophisticated ways to study the brain, interest in brain research has grown. Some of the more recent research findings about the brain that have implications for learning disabilities are discussed in Chapters 7 and 12.

The Transition Phase: Clinical Study of Children

During the transition phase (about 1930–1960), scientific studies of the brain were applied to the clinical study of children and translated into ways of teaching. Psychologists and educators developed instruments for assessment and remediation, and they studied specific types of learning disorders found in children.

A number of professionals played important roles in evolving the field. Foremost among them was Samuel T. Orton (1937), a neurologist, whose theory of the lack of cerebral dominance as a cause of children's language disorders (see Chapter 7) led to the development of a teaching method known as the Orton-Gillingham method (see Chapter 12). The Orton Dyslexia Society, created to honor Orton and continue his work, is an active force in the field of learning disabilities today. Grace Fernald (1943), an educator, also contributed to this period of growth. Establishing a remedial clinic at the University of California in Los Angeles, she develped a remedial approach to teaching reading and spelling (see Chapters 12 and 13). Mildred McGinnis (1963), a speech pathologist, was another early investigator and teacher of children with language disorders and aphasia.

The scholars who helped develop the field during this period and are considered pioneers in the study of learning disabilities include William Cruickshank, Ray Barsch, Marianne Frostig, Newell Kephart, Samuel Kirk, and Helmer Myklebust, Since their contributions are described in detail elsewhere in this book, they are therefore not included in this chapter of historical highlights. Rather than trace the development of the transitional phase through accounts of individual achievements, we will examine the progress reflected in the changes in terminology during this period. The progression of terms—brain injured, Strauss syndrome, minimal brain dysfunction, and finally learning disabilities—occurred because each of these terms filled a need at the time but each had inherent shortcomings. Some of the terms identified the biological *causes* of the problem; others described the behavioral *consequences*.

The Brain-injured Child

Pioneering work conducted by Alfred Strauss and Laura Lehtinen (1947) was reported in their book, *Psychopathology and Education of the Brain-Injured Child.* They identified in it a new category of exceptional youngsters, calling them *brain-injured children.* Strauss observed that these children had previously been classified as mentally retarded, emotionally disturbed, autistic, aphasic, or behaviorally maladjusted. Most of the subjects of Strauss's studies exhibited such severe behavior disturbances that they were excluded from the public schools. Further, the medical histories of these children indicated that they had suffered a brain injury at some time during their lives (before, during, or after birth).

Seeking a medical explanation for the behavioral characteristics he observed, Strauss concluded that the behavior and learning patterns of these children were manifestations of brain injury. Strauss's hypothesis was unique at the time because the behavioral abnormalities of many such children had been explained by others as having emotional origins. Strauss further speculated that other children who exhibited characteristics similar to the subjects in his studies had also suffered an injury to the brain that produced the abnormal behavior and learning characteristics.

Strauss hypothesized that the brain could have been injured in any of three periods in the child's life: *before* birth, the prenatal stage; *during* the birth process; or at some point *after* birth. An infection such as German measles (rubella) contracted by the mother early in pregnancy and affecting the fetus exemplifies a cause of brain injury before birth. Brain injury during birth could result from any condition that would seriously reduce the infant's supply of oxygen during the birth process (anoxia). After birth, the brain could be injured by a fall on the head or an excessively high fever in infancy or early childhood. In some cases, such events produce other handicapping conditions, such as mental retardation or physical impairments; but Strauss contended that these events could also precipitate behavior and learning problems.

Strauss identified the following behavioral and biological characteristics of brain-injured children:

Behavioral Characteristics

Perceptual disorders. When looking at a picture, the child with perceptual disorders sees parts instead of wholes, or sees figure-ground distortions that may confuse the background with the foreground. An example of the need to see an object as a whole rather than as unrelated parts is the identification of a letter. When asked to identify the capital letter "A," the child with perceptual disorders may perceive three unrelated lines rather than a meaningful whole.

Figure-ground distortion refers to an inability to focus on an object without having its setting interfere with the perception. The ambiguity in perception that the normal observer senses in the following illustrations can help one understand the unstable world of the child with a perceptual disorder. In Figure 2.2, one is to determine if the picture is of two faces or a vase. In Figure 2.3, one is asked to look at the drawing and then to sketch it from memory. Even copying Figure 2.3 may prove to be difficult. The illustrations contain a reversible figure-ground pattern that produces a confusion or a shifting of background and foreground, much like what a perceptually impaired child constantly experiences. One teacher noted that whenever she wore a particular dress with polka dots,

FIGURE 2.2

Do you see two faces or a vase?

children with perceptual disorders seemed compelled to touch in order to verify what they thought they perceived.

Perseveration. A child with perseverative behavior continues an activity once it has started and has difficulty in changing to another. For example, a child may not be able to stop after writing the letter *a* the three times required in a writing lesson, but, instead, continues this activity until the entire page is filled with a's. One such child continued the activity onto the desk and up the wall.

Conceptual disorders. A child with conceptual disorders is unable to organize materials and thoughts in a normal manner. This is a disturbance in the cognitive abilities, and it affects comprehension skills in reading and listening. One ten-year-old girl was unable to differentiate the concepts of *sugar* and *salt* and usually confused the words symbolizing the concepts.

Behavioral disorders. Children with behavioral disorders may be hyperactive, explosive, erratic, or othewise uninhibited in behavior. The child who is continually in motion, blows up easily, and is readily distracted from the task at hand is exhibiting behavioral disorders.

Biological Characteristics

Soft neurological signs. This term refers to subtle, rather than obvious or severe, evidence of neurological abnormalities. An awkwardness in gait, for example, is considered a slight neurological sign. The inability to perform fine motor skills efficiently is also included in this category.

FIGURE 2.3
Examine this drawing and then try to sketch it from memory.

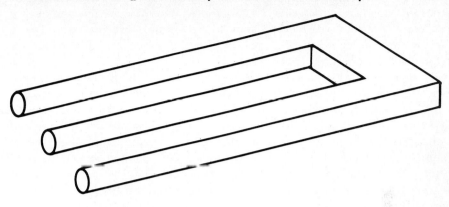

A history of neurological impairment. This refers to evidence in the medical history of brain injury that occurred before, during, or after birth.

No history of mental retardation in the family. Strauss felt that it was important to rule out familial or inherited types of mental retardation. Since his interest was in the effect of brain damage on a child with a potentially normal brain, he therefore excluded from his investigation those children who had mental retardation due to inherited factors. (Strauss's research subjects included youngsters with known brain injury who fell within the normal and above-normal intelligence ranges, as well as some whose scores fell within the mentally retarded ranges.)

In Strauss's thinking, children could be diagnosed as brain injured without hard evidence of any of the three biological signs. Since his research subjects were known to have suffered a brain injury and also exhibited the identified behavioral characteristics, Strauss hypothesized that other children who showed similar behavior characteristics could be presumed to have suffered a brain injury at some time in their lives.

Strauss's initial work alerted physicians to events that might be related to brain injury. An alarmingly large number of possibilities have been suggested as potential causes of such injury. In the prenatal stage, injury could result from such conditions in the mother as the RH factor or from diseases during pregnancy such as rubella. It could also be caused by the mother's smoking or using alcohol, or by medication she had taken during pregnancy. During the birth process, insufficient oxygen, prematurity, a long, hard labor, difficult delivery, or a purposely delayed birth could injure the baby's brain. Childhood diseases such as encephalitis, and meningitis, dehydration or extremely high fevers accompanying illnesses, and head injuries sustained in accidents have also been linked to brain injury.

It must be remembered, however, that these events are merely potential causes of brain injury. Many children with case histories of such events apparently escape harm whereas other children who evidence clear symptoms of brain injury have no such events in their case histories. Even in cerebral palsy clinics, which deal with gross brain damage, the causes of about one-third of the cases are obscure.

Besides developing a theory of the brain-injured child, Strauss and Lehtinen (1947) presented a plan for teaching. Their suggested methods, materials, and settings differed dramatically from those of a regular classroom. For example, they designed a learning environment that reduced distraction and hyperactivity: all stimulating visual materials such as bulletin boards or pictures were removed, and the window panes were painted to conceal overstimulating outside views. Further, they recommended that the teacher avoid jewelry and dress in a manner that would reduce distractions. The students' desks were placed against a wall, behind a screen, or in a partitioned cubicle. Special materials were constructed to aid students in the perception of visual forms and in the organization of space and form. The authors advised that many of the commercially prepared teaching materials designed for normal students were unsuitable for those with brain injuries.

Strauss's work filled a great void. It offered an alternate diagnosis for children who previously had been given many other labels: badly behaved, emotionally disturbed, lazy, careless, or stupid. To parents who had been blamed for causing psychological situations that created learning disorders in their children or who had been told that their children did not fit into a public school setting or who had been vainly seeking a diagnosis, this framework was most welcome. It provided a meaningful, logical, and hopeful analytic view of their problem children.

Thus, Strauss and his coworkers laid the foundation for the field of learning disabilities by (1) perceiving a homogeneity in a diverse group of children who had been misdiagnosed by specialists, misunderstood by parents, and often discarded by society; (2) planning and implementing educational settings and procedures to teach such children successfully; and (3) alerting many professions to the existence of a new category of exceptional children.

Strauss Syndrome

Questions about the assumptions and implications of Strauss's theories and methods arose soon after the publication of his book. The term *brain-injured children* proved to be confusing. Not all children with brain injuries have learning disorders. For instance, some persons afflicted with cerebral palsy, a condition caused by brain injury, do not have learning problems and have earned Ph.D. and M.D. degrees whereas others have severe mental defects. Many professionals questioned the value of the term *brain injured* as a means of describing, categorizing, diagnosing, and teaching children. They found it difficult to use in communicating with parents, there was frequently no hard medical evidence of brain injury, and it appeared excessively condemning on the child's school records. Parents understandably reacted in a negative, traumatic, or guilt-ridden manner when told their child had a brain injury.

Stevens and Birch (1957) recommended that the term *Strauss syndrome* be used instead of *brain injured* to describe the child who could not learn and did not easily fit into other classification schemes. This term focused on an expanded set of behavioral characteristics and also paid tribute to an early pioneer in the field.

Thus the term *Strauss syndrome* was introduced to describe the child who exhibited several of the following behavior characteristics (Stevens & Birch, 1957, p. 348):

1. Erratic and inappropriate behavior on mild provocation
2. Increased motor activity disproportionate to the stimulus
3. Poor organization of behavior
4. Distractibility of more than ordinary degree under ordinary conditions
5. Persistent faulty perceptions
6. Persistent hyperactivity
7. Awkwardness and consistently poor motor performance

Development of Other Terminology

Others suggested alternative terminology to overcome the shortcomings of the term *brain injured.* Doll (1951) suggested *neurophrenia,* and Lewis, Strauss, and Lehtinen (1960) used *the other child.* Others described this child as *perceptually handicapped,* which was actually one of the behavioral characteristics identified by Strauss.

Some researchers and clinicians noted that children exhibiting the Strauss syndrome were only a portion of the children with learning disorders. For example, some children who could not learn readily were not hyperactive but hypoactive: quiet, without excessive movement, and even withdrawn. Further, while in some children perceptual disturbances accompanied learning problems, in many others they did not.

So many new terms were being suggested that Clements (1966) tried to sort them out. He identified thirty-eight different terms that were being used to refer to the brain-injured child and divided them into two categories: those that identified "organic aspects" (cause-related terms) and those that identified "consequences" (behavior-related terms). An example of an organic label is *neurological dysfunction;* an example of a consequence label is *hyperkinesis.*

Minimal Brain Dysfunction (MBD)

Clements (1966) and others recommended the term *minimal brain dysfunction.* Clements classified children with various brain impairments along a

TABLE 2.1   **Classification Guide of Brain Dysfunction Syndromes**

Minimal (Minor, Mild)	Major (Severe)
1. Impairment of fine movement or coordination	1. Cerebral palsies
2. Electroencephalographic abnormalities without actual seizures, or possibly subclinical seizures, which may be associated with fluctuations in behavior or intellectual function	2. Epilepsies
3. Deviations in attention, activity level, impulse control, and affect	3. Autism and other gross disorders of mentation and behavior
4. Specific and circumscribed perceptual, intellectual, and memory deficits	4. Mental subnormalities
5. Nonperipheral impairments of vision, hearing, haptics, and speech	5. Blindness, deafness, and severe aphasia

Source: Minimal Brain Dysfunction in Children (p. 10) by Sam Clements, 1966, Washington, DC: Department of Public Health Services (Publication No. 1415).

scale that ranges from mild to severe. At the severe end of the scale are children with obvious brain damage, such as cerebral palsy or epilepsy. At the opposite end of such a scale are children with minimal impairments that affect behavior and learning in more subtle ways. Clements concluded that the term *minimal brain dysfunction syndrome* was the best way to describe the child with near-average intelligence and with certain learning or behavioral disabilities associated with deviations or dysfunctions of the central nervous system. This term differentiated the minimally involved child from the child with major brain disorders. Table 2.1 illustrates this continuum.

Critics of the term *minimal brain dysfunction* note that the so-called major brain injuries on the scale of the conceptualized brain dysfunction may or may not be accompanied by difficulties in learning. While some individuals with obvious brain injury, such as cerebral palsy, have no learning difficulties, others show mental subnormalities, infantile autism, and childhood schizophrenia. Some educators have found that minimal brain dysfunction does not properly describe the behavior or learning characteristics of the child. The question then arises of how much is *minimal.*

Chalfant and Scheffelin (1969) suggested a variation, *central processing dysfunctions.* They defined this condition as a disorder in the analysis, storage, synthesis, and symbolic use of information.

Learning Disabilities

In most cases, the dysfunction of the brain was inferred through observation of behavior, analysis of the individual's reaction to learning situations, or the sampling of behavior through psychological tests. Since it is impossible to look at the physical brain injury inside the child's skull or to know for certain that specific cerebral tissue has been damaged, one has to conjecture about the brain injury on the basis of behavioral symptoms.

Therefore, we needed a term that accurately and meaningfully described the behavioral symptoms. In 1963 Samuel Kirk first proposed the term *learning disabilities* at an initial ACLD organizational meeting of concerned parents and professionals. Accepted immediately, *learning disabilities* appears to be a satisfactory term for the present. It is an umbrella concept, encompassing many diverse types of learning disabilities without specifying the area of the student's learning deficiencies. Its advantages are that it avoids the medical complications, focuses on the educational problem, and seems to be acceptable to parents, teachers, and students. Since *learning disabilities* has now been written into law in the United States and other countries throughout the world, the term will probably continue to serve as a recognized way to refer to individuals with the problems that are the concern of this book.

The Integration Phase: Rapid Expansion of School Programs

During this period (about 1960–1900), learning disabilities became an established discipline within the schools throughout the country. The field grew with extreme rapidity: learning disabilities programs were organized, teachers were trained, and classes were started. (A few events that occurred in a later phase are discussed in this section because they are a logical extension of and closely related to a major event of the integration period.)

Rapid Growth of Public School Learning Disabilities Programs

One of the first attempts to establish a public school program was accomplished by Cruickshank, Bentzen, Ratzburg, and Tannhauser (1961). This demonstration–pilot project adapted and refined the educational methods proposed by Strauss and Lehtinen (1947) for brain-injured students. The Cruickshank study provided a detailed description of the program, as well as a report of its effectiveness. The general plan for teaching these students called for the following conditions in the teaching environment:

1. Reducing unessential visual and auditory environmental stimuli
2. Reducing to a minimum the space in which the student works
3. Providing a highly structured daily school schedule
4. Increasing the stimulus value of the teaching materials

By the 1960s and in the 1970s, public school programs were rapidly being established throughout the nation. The forces at work included parental pressures for school programs, an increase in professional information, the availability of teacher-training programs, and the beginnings of state laws requiring services for learning-disabled students. The early programs were mostly for students at the elementary level, and they followed the traditional delivery system in special education at that time, self-contained classes. Later in this period, resource room programs were introduced and the schools began to serve older students. Also, many new tests and teaching materials were developed to serve the growing learning-disabilities populations in the schools.

Development of Learning Disabilities Organizations

During this period, parents and professionals organized to further the cause of learning disabilities and strengthen efforts to help students. A critically important event was the establishment, in 1963, of an organization for parents and professionals that today is called the *Association for Children and Adults with Learning Disabilities* (ACLD). Over the years ACLD has been extremely effective in furthering the cause of learning disabilities by bringing the problem to the attention of legislative bodies, teachers, and other school personnel, and by helping parents when they discover that their child has learning disabilities.

In 1968 the Council for Exceptional Children (CEC) established a separate division for special educators interested in learning disabilities. This division was reconstituted in 1982 under the name Division for Learning Disabilities (DLD).

Another independent organization for professionals in learning disabilities—an outgrowth of an earlier CEC division—was established in 1982 as the Council for Learning Disabilities (CLD). In addition, many professional organizations in fields such as reading, speech and language, and pediatrics have subgroups or special-interest committees concerned with learning disabilities.

Thus, during the integration phase, parent and professional organizations were effective in bringing professionalism to the field and helping to develop school programs.

Increased Legislative Support

Learning disabilities advocates achieved a major feat when, in 1969, Congress passed the Children with Specific Learning Disabilities Act. For the first time, learning disabilities was acknowledged in federal law and funding provided for teacher training.

Child Service Demonstration Centers

In the 1970s federal funding supported the development of learning disabilities model programs throughout the country. Called Child Service Demonstration Centers (CSDS), these projects provided the opportunity for innovation and experimentation. Mann et al. (1984) evaluated the overall effect of these demonstration projects and found them beneficial: many of the services they developed were replicated in other sites, a remarkable number of materials were developed and disseminated, and they succeeded in serving as vehicles to stimulate and spread learning disabilities practices throughout the nation. The demonstration projects led to the training of many teachers, provided help for many students, and promoted the development of new teaching materials and methods for the learning disabled.

Learning Disabilities Research Institutes

In 1978 the Office of Education sponsored five Learning Disabilities Research Institutes to conduct research on basic issues related to the field of learning disabilities. A different area of learning disabilities was targeted for investigation at each of these institutes, and the research generated has increased our understanding of learning disabilities.

The research findings of these institutes are reported in relevant areas in this book. In addition, the summaries of the research findings of the five institutes can be found in *Exceptional Education Quarterly* (1983). The areas of research and locations of the Learning Disabilities Research Institutes are listed below (The *DLD Times,* 1983):

> LD Adolescents/Learning Strategies Curriculum. University of Kansas, Lawrence, KS 66044. D. Deshler, Director.
> Social Competence/Communication. University of Illinois at Chicago, Chicago, IL 60634. Tanis Bryan, Director.
> Cognitive Theory/Controlling Attention. University of Virginia, Charlottesville, VA 11903. D. Hallahan, Director.
> Improving Basic Skills. Columbia University. New York, NY 10027. F. Conner, Director.
> Assessment and Evaluation. University of Minnesota, Minneapolis, MN 55455. J. Ysseldyke, Director.

Public Law 94–142

The legislation that has had the greatest influence on the establishment of learning disabilities services in our public schools has been the federal law known as Public Law 94–142, the Education for All Handicapped Children Act. Passed by Congress in 1975, the law became effective in 1977. Under this landmark legislation, all handicapped children and youth aged three through twenty-one have the right to a free, appropriate public education. Further, each state must have a plan that complies with the federal law. As a result, this law has affected schools in every part of the nation (U.S. Office of Education, 1977).

Under PL 94–142, handicapped children are defined as those who, because of their impairments, need special education or related services. In addition to learning disabilities, the federal categories of handicapping conditions are as follows: mentally retarded, hard of hearing, deaf, speech impaired, visually handicapped, seriously emotionally disturbed, orthopedically impaired, other health impaired, deaf-blind, and multihandicapped.

Public Law 94–142 is considered civil rights legislation that guarantees education to the handicapped. It has profoundly altered educational practices, which had earlier led to neglect and substandard treatment of handicapped children. This remarkable law is the outcome of what has been called the "quiet revolution,"—one hundred years of a slowly growing awareness and support of handicapped people.

Several critical features of PL 94–142 have implications for identifying assessing, and serving the learning-disabled students. They are discussed in the relevant sections of this book. Among these important features are the *Individualized Education Program,* or IEP (discussed in Chapter 3), *procedural safeguards* (also discussed in Chapter 3), *the least restrictive environment* and the *continuum of alternative placements* (discussed in Chapter 5), and *parental involvement* (discussed in Chapters 3 and 5).

In 1980 Congress established the Department of Education, under which the Office of Special Education was established in 1983. It is heartening to note that the Department of Education saw fit to maintain Public Law 94–142 as a separate categorical program and to continue to appropriate special funds to support it. This victory was due, in part to the hard work and persistent efforts of parents and professionals in educating Congress to the special needs of handicapped children and youth.

A law passed by Congress in 1983, PL 98–199, underscores the federal role in special education by extending and affirming many of the features of PL 94–142. PL 98–199 contains these major features (Council for Exceptional Children, 1984):

Restoration of the National Advisory Committee on the Education of Handicapped Children and Youth

Permission to use federal funds under the preschool incentive grant program to serve handicapped children below age three

Establishment of grants to states for developing and implementing comprehensive plans to provide early childhood education to all handicapped children from birth

Expansion of model demonstration postsecondary education programs, including vocation, technical, continuing and adult education

Establishment of a new program to stimulate and improve secondary special education and transition to postsecondary education, as well as vocational, rehabilitation, continuing education, employment, independent living, and other adult services

Refocusing of personnel preparation resources on the preparation of special education personnel, and requiring colleges and universities receiving grants to meet state and professionally recognized standards

Establishment of grants for parent training and information

Establishment of a new clearing-house for disseminating information on federal laws, career and job opportunities in special education, and available services and programs in postsecondary education for the handicapped

Emphasis of federal research on the improvement of teaching methodology and curriculum and the application of new technologies to improve instruction

The Contemporary Phase: Emerging Directions

The 1980s reflect emerging directions in learning disabilities. In a relatively new field, one expects many changes in direction and the development of new concepts and ideas. Some occur as a natural extension of ongoing programs; others result from shortcomings experienced in earlier programs; and still others come about because of outside pressures. In this section, we shall look at the major trends of this phase: the widening age span of the learning-disabled population, mild and severe learning disabilities, the cross-categorical concept, regular education and mainstreaming, and some implications of computer technology.

Expanding Age Span of the Learning-disabled Population

One obvious direction in the field of learning disabilities is the concern for an extended age group of individuals with learning disabilities. When programs first began in the early 1960s, they were developed for children of elementary school age; now there is interest in individuals who are younger or older than that initial age group.

Learning disabilities specialists are very concerned about the high-risk preschool child—aged three to five, or even younger than three. If we can identify youngsters in the early childhood years before they fail and if we can provide successful intervention for these preschoolers, then the learning failure may be prevented or mitigated. Chapter 8 discusses the problems of the high-risk preschool child who is likely to encounter school failure without an intervention program.

At the other end of the school continuum are the adolescents with learning disabilities who are in secondary schools. This is an emerging age group with special needs, and secondary schools have developed many services for it. The learning-disabled adults are yet another subgroup in the field receiving recognition. The problems of learning-disabled adolescents and older individuals are discussed in detail in Chapter 9.

Mild and Severe Learning Disabilities

Just as the widened age span of the learning disabilities population has become apparent, so has the possible extent of the disability. The severity of the learning disability must be determined to properly place and teach the student. Students with mild learning disabilities and those with severe problems have quite different needs. Some schools find it useful to differentiate three levels of severity in learning disabilities: mild, moderate, and severe.

Students with severe learning disabilities require special attention and may need the environment of a self-contained classroom for most of the day.
(Alan Carey/The Image Works)

Many students with learning disabilities have mild handicaps: although they need supportive help and special teaching, they can probably get along, at least for part of the day, in the regular classroom, that is, they can be mainstreamed. For these students, the regular teacher can often make changes in instruction within the regular classroom that will benefit them. They may also receive special services in the resource room setting. Students with mild learning disabilities usually have a disability in just one or two areas of learning.

Severe learning disabilities pose a very different problem. These students are likely to lag significantly in many areas of learning and to have concomitant social, emotional, or behavioral problems as well. The educational services needed for severe learning disabilities are quite different than those required for mild learning disabilities. These students probably need the environment of a self-contained classroom, contact mainly with one teacher, and special services for most of the day. Because of the intensity of their problems, the special class should be much smaller than the regular classroom. However, students with severe learning disabilities can gradually be mainstreamed for special subjects or activities as they are ready or be placed in the resource room as their progress permits. Thus more adjustments and adaptations in the school environment and in the educational treatment are required for students with severe learning disabilities.

Moderate learning disabilities fall somewhere between. These students will probably need services in the resource room, and perhaps some will need more frequent and intensive instruction in a special class. One large-scale study analyzed data on the severity of the handicap of students receiving special services (Pyecha, 1981). This study found that about 44 percent of students with learning disabilities were rated as mild, 51 percent as moderate, and 5 percent as severe.

Cross-categorical Concept

The cross-categorical concept provides a new view of special education in which the field of learning disabilities plays a pivotal role. According to this concept, rather than perceiving each category of special education as distinct, we should emphasize the common characteristics among the categories and instruct students from this perspective.

The categorical system in special education evolved, historically, as the field of special education developed The field of special education encompasses several kinds of atypical children. Each category of handicap (visually impaired, hearing impaired, mentally retarded, physically handicapped, speech impaired, emotionally disturbed, learning disabled, etc.) became established individually over the years when there was sufficient interest in that particular area of exceptionality. Now some special educators have asked whether the traditional categorical approach offers the best way to think about handicapped students (Dunn, 1968; Hobbs, 1975; Reynolds, 1982; Blackhurst, 1982; Lilly, 1982; Brady, Conroy & Langford, 1984) suggesting a cross-categorical system as an alternative for several reasons.

1. *The categories of exceptionality are not discrete and separate entities but have much in common with each other.* Thus, students in the areas of learning disabilities, emotional disturbance, and mental retardation often are not easy to differentiate. Moreover, assessment procedures and treatment methods often overlap.
2. *A cluster of court decisions supports claims of discrimination through the categorical placement of children in special education programs.* In response to class action lawsuits, the courts have judged that special education classes (particularly mental retardation) can be discriminatory, often causing social or psychological harm (Gilhool, 1982). The term *six-hour retarded child* is used to describe students who have been labeled as mentally retarded by school personnel but are "retarded" only during the time they are in school.
3. *The question of whether categorical placement is beneficial academically.* Some research suggests that mentally retarded children placed in

categorical settings did not achieve significantly better than similar children who were instructed in the regular classroom (Meyers, Macmillan, & Yoshida, 1980).

4. *Categorical labels may stigmatize the student.* However, one report indicates that the process of labeling can be beneficial as well as detrimental (Hobbs, 1975). It can stigmatize the students and adversely influence expectations and attitudes of teachers, but it may also provide a means for professionals to communicate with one another, for labels help highlight a problem. Moreover, labels seem to be necessary; when one set of labels is removed, a new set tends to evolve in its place.

Functional Categories of Learning

An alternative to the classification system that will cut across the commonalities of the categories has been suggested: a functional system that will focus on teaching and on the learning disorders common to several categories. Functional categories could be divided by areas of learning problems rather than by types of exceptionality.

Figure 2.4 shows a matrix relating the historical categories of special education to the functional categories of learning. Decisions regarding budgeting, curriculum planning, and placement could be based on functional activities rather than on historical categories (Lerner, 1973).

The field of learning disabilities has a unique position in the cross-categorical movement, for it deals with the various areas of learning that are important for success in school. It has the potential to act as a core for special education. Since most categories of special education involve students who face learning problems, knowledge of learning disabilities should help all teachers who deal with handicapped students.

Generic Teacher Certification

Many states are moving toward the "generic" certification of special education teachers: certification for teaching children in several categories of exceptionality, including learning disabilities. To obtain such certification, a teacher would have to train in several areas of exceptionality. A recent survey indicated that fifteen states gave only generic certification; thirteen states gave only categorical certification (certification in only one area); and twenty-one states gave both generic and categorical certification (Beech, Blaski, Crump, & Smith, 1983). These varied certification practices create difficulties when teachers are trained in one state and seek employment in another.

Cross-categorical Grouping

Some special educators are proposing a cross-categorical grouping and placement of students for instruction. They suggest that three categories—learning disabilities, emotional disturbance, and educable mental retardation—be clustered when the handicap is considered mild (Hallahan & Kauffman, 1982).

FIGURE 2.4
Matrix of Historical Categories and Functional Categories

HISTORICAL CATEGORIES	Pre-academic	Oral Language	Reading	Written Language	Vocational Education	Arithmetic	Social Development	Cognitive Strategies	Other
Mentally Retarded									
Visually Impaired									
Hearing Impaired									
Orthopedically Impaired									
Speech Impaired									
Emotionally Disturbed									
Learning Disabled									
Others									

(Column heading: FUNCTIONAL CATEGORIES)

Not all special educators advocate this kind of cross-categorical grouping for instruction. Many schools and parents see virtue in maintaining separate placement for instruction for students with learning disabilities. Parents of learning-disabled students are especially concerned that their children can be lost in the shuffle of cross-categorical placement. They point out that such classes can become a "dumping ground" for students with a variety of unrelated problems. The resulting diversity of learning and behavior problems would impede teachers in helping the learning-disabled student. Many parents and teachers warn, therefore, that learning-disabled students should not be grouped arbitrarily with students with a variety of educational and behavioral needs.

Learning Disabilities and Regular Education

The rapid growth of special education in the past has been in the direction of removing atypical children from the mainstream of regular education and placing them into special education programs. Regular education supported this movement, which had the effect of transferring and the responsibilities of educating children with a variety of learning problems to the domain of special education. Now the trend is reversed, and learning-disabled children are being brought back into regular classrooms. Many special educators are suggesting that regular education take on more of the responsibility of educating handicapped children (Lilly, 1982; Reynolds, 1982).

Changes occurring in regular education make it more adaptable to the problems of the atypical student. Schools today are more concerned with individual differences and they have more flexible organizational patterns and curriculum. Classroom teachers have more training in special education, and they have a greater variety of materials and media at their disposal.

When the learning-disabled student is placed in a regular classroom, it is essential that additional guidance be available to help both the student and the classroom teacher. Learning disabilities teachers should be prepared to serve in this capacity.

Among the benefits learning-disabled students gain from placement in a regular classroom is the opportunity to be with nonhandicapped students. Providing services to learning-disabled students in the regular classroom is known as mainstreaming, and it requires that regular teachers and learning disabilities teachers work cooperatively. (Mainstreaming as an educational delivery system is discussed in greater detail in Chapter 5.)

The Implications of the Microcomputer

The microcomputer has literally exploded onto the educational scene, bringing its promise of new solutions to old educational problems and challenging the way we think about learning. To meet this promise and challenge, the learning disabilities teacher must be aware of the computer's power and potential, as well as its limitations. The microcomputer appears to be much more than a mere technological addition to our teaching tools. It is revolutionizing many aspects of our business and personal lives to such an extent that some predict that the computer will soon be as handy and useful as a pencil. Thus, microcomputers have the potential of changing many of the traditional ways we have been teaching (*Computers, Reading, and the Language Arts,* 1983.)

Since the ways for using the microcomputer affect many areas of learning disabilities, specific applications of this technology appear throughout this text. For example, its use in administering and scoring tests and other assessment instruments and in writing an *Individualized Education Program* (IEP) appears in the chapter on assessment (Chapter 3), and a discussion of its use in teaching writing skills through word processing is included in the chapter on written language (Chapter 13). Chapter 12 deals with applications to teaching reading and Chapter 14 discusses applications in mathematics.

The full impact of "high tech" on learning disabilities is still speculative. However, a national survey of microcomputers in the schools shows that a majority of the schools (53 percent) now have microcomputers (Center for the Social Organization of Schools, 1983). At the high school level, the survey found that 85 percent have microcomputers. So many new models of microcomputers are appearing on the market and such a proliferation of software packages is being created that it becomes difficult to sort them all out. The professional journals are beginning to carry computer review sections

The microcomputer allows the learning-disabled student to work at a self-established pace and to review material repeatedly.   *(Martine Franck/Magnum)*

(for example, the monthly computer courseware review in the *Journal of Learning Disabilities*). New journals dedicated to microcomputer use in special and remedial education are being developed (for example, *Computers, Reading in the Language Arts*). In addition, many conferences are dedicated to this subject (for example, the Council for Exceptional Children has had several special conferences on microcomputers). Some schools now have a computer specialist on the staff, and workshops on computer literacy are popular in-service courses. There are also computer literacy self-instructional programs (such as the *Computer Connection for Teachers*).

Some of the microcomputer software packages appear to have much promise for helping learning-disabled students. Because of the computer, the teaching of writing may change drastically in the near future. The *Bank Street Writer* has been one of the most successful software packages for teaching writing through word processing (see Chapter 13). A programming language called LOGO is simple enough to be used in a functional way by very young children or to develop organizational and cognitive skills in learning-disabled students of all ages. Older students can learn BASIC, a very useful and powerful programming language. Another popular logical thinking program is

Gertrude's Secrets (for ages four to ten) and *Gertrude's Puzzles* (for ages eight to thirteen).

One of the most common uses of the microcomputer is for individual tutoring and for drill, practice, and review. Software packages written for teaching mathematics, phonics, grammar, and content area subjects are spilling out onto the market. Students can work at their own pace, reviewing the material over and over until it has been learned. The microcomputer has more patience than any human teacher in repeatedly teaching a skill. (*Wiz Works* and *Alligator Alley* are popular drill and practice type of programs.)

The microcomputer also aids in assessing and developing teaching plans. The computer can be used to actually test or to rapidly score and analyze tests given through another medium. For example, there are programs available for analyzing performance on the *WISC-R* (Wechsler Intelligence Scale for Children-Revised). The computer is also useful in generating specific educational plans from the assessment data and in locating and finding appropriate techniques and materials. For example, there are programs that can help in writing individual education programs (IEPs). One outcome of these programs is that they can serve as a teacher's aide, freeing up more time for teaching (Walker, 1983).

Microcomputers also allow teachers to write their own "author systems" to remediate the specific disabilities of an individual student or a small group. Though not easy, such an activity would certainly be within the spirit of "clinical teaching."

In addition, the computer can help reduce the administrative chores of teaching. Administrative chores such as the keeping of records, filling out repetitive forms, preparing district status reports, and special education information management can be eased by harnessing the technology of the microcomputer (Bennett, 1984).

Among the fast-placed changes in the microcomputer field are the development of "peripherals" (machines that are attached to the basic microcomputer, such as the printer). Peripherals that may prove to be especially valuable educational tools for learning-disabled students are the Koala Pad that will permit the student to draw on the computer screen instead of using the keyboard to write instructions, and the Speech Synthesizer that will produce the sounds of words that are programmed.

However, there are several limitations in using microcomputers to solve the problems of learning disabilities. Microcomputers are still expensive and so are the software packages. Even in the schools that do have microcomputers, student-computer ratio is low, and each student is allotted very little time to use the computer. Also, many of the exisiting programs do not meet the needs of learning-disabled students, and many students have not acquired the typing skills needed to use the computer efficiently. How to find the school time for adding computers to the curriculum is another problem that has not been solved. The task of increasing computer literacy among learning disabilities teachers also poses some difficulty since many teachers are still skeptical about the place of the microcomputer as an educational tool in the classroom.

Despite these limitations, it appears that microcomputers are here to stay. They will have a tremendous impact on the field of learning disabilities and play a growing role in the assessment and remediation of learning-disabled students. Specific applications are presented in the relevent chapters in this book.

The world of the microcomputer brings with it a strange new set of technical terms. The following may provide some help in getting through the maze of the new jargon.

A Brief Glossary of Microcomputer Terminology

Back-up   A reserve copy of the program.

Boot   The process of starting up the computer.

Bug   An error.

CTRL   Stands for "control."

Cursor   A blinking square showing the current position on the screen.

Disk, diskette or floppy disk   A flexible plastic record that contains programs.

DOS   Disk Operating System. A program that enables the computer to read and write information on a disk.

Menu   The selection of programs available on a disk.

Peripheral   An accessory that can be attached to the computer, such as a printer.

RAM   Random Access Memory. The main memory of the computer, which stores current programs. This memory is lost when a computer is turned off. The content of RAM changes with each program. A "64K" computer has 64,000 characters of RAM available.

ROM   Read Only Memory. This memory is built into the computer. It is unalterable and permanent. It does not disappear when the computer is turned off. It holds important programs that must be available to the computer.

Software   Another name for computer programs. It controls the computer hardware and performs tasks.

User-friendly   Makes it easy for the user to get answers or help.

Learning Disabilities Organizations

There are several active organizations today devoted or related to children and youth with learning disabilities. Brief descriptions and addresses of these organizations appear below:

ACLD: An Association for Children and Adults with Learning Disabilities. This is a parent organization with active professional participation as well. There are state and local chapters of this national organization. ACLD, 4156 Library Road, Pittsburgh, PA 15234.

CLD: Council for Learning Disabilities. An organization for professionals.

Council for Learning Disabilities. Department of Special Education. University of Louisville, Louisville, KY 40292.

DLD: Division for Learning Disabilities. This organization for professionals is a unit within the Council for Exceptional Children (CEC). Council for Exceptional Children, 1920 Association Drive, Reston, VA 22091.

Orton Dyslexia Society, Inc. This organization honors Samuel T. Orton, a physician who studied children with language disorders. The organization succeeds in combining the interests of both medical and educational professionals interested in dyslexia and language-learning disorders. It has state and local units as well as the international organization. Orton Society, Inc., 8415 Bellona Lane, Towson, MD 21204.

American Speech and Hearing Association. A professional association for speech and hearing pathologists. American Speech and Hearing Association, 9030 Old Georgetown Road, Washington, DC 20014.

International Reading Association. An organization for persons interested in all aspects of reading. International Reading Association, 800 Barksdale Road, P.O. Box 8139, Newark, DE 19711.

Journals and Periodicals

Some journals and periodicals containing articles, research, program descriptions, tests, materials, and organizational activities are listed below:

Academic Therapy. 20 Commercial Blvd., Novato, CA 94947.

Asha. American Speech and Hearing Association, 9030 Old Georgetown Road, Washington, DC 20014.

Bulletin of the Orton Society. Orton Society, Inc., 8415 Bellona Lane, Suite 115, Towson, MD 21204.

Elementary English. National Council of Teachers of English, 111 Kenyon Road, Urbana, IL 61801.

Exceptional Children. Council for Exceptional Children, 1920 Association Drive, Reston, VA 22091.

Exceptional Education Quarterly. 531 Industrial Oaks Blvd., Austin, TX 78735.

Exceptional Parent. P.O. Box 102, Boston, MA 02117.

Focus on Exceptional Children. 6635 E. Villanova Place, Denver, CO 80222.

Journal of Applied Behavior Analysis. Department of Human Development, University of Kansas, Lawrence, KS 66045.

Journal of Learning Disabilities. 101 E. Ontario, Chicago, IL 60611.

Journal of Reading. International Reading Association, 800 Barksdale Road, Newark, DE 19711.

Journal of Special Education. 1115 Fifth Avenue, New York, NY 10003.

Learning Disabilities Quarterly. Council for Learning Disabilities. Department of Special Education, University of Louisville, Louisville, KY 40292.

Reading Research Quarterly. International Reading Association, 800 Barksdale Road, Newark, DE 19711.

The Reading Teacher. International Reading Association, 800 Barksdale Road, Newark, DE 19711.

Remedial and Special Education. PRO-ED. 5341 Industrial Oaks Blvd. Austin, TX 78735.

Teaching Exceptional Children. Council for Exceptional Children, 1920 Association Drive, Reston, VA 22091.

Summary

- The history of the field of learning disabilities can be divided into four phases: (1) the foundation phase, (2) the transition phase, (3) the integration phase, and (4) the contemporary phase.

- The foundation phase covers the period from 1800 to 1930. It was an era of basic scientific research on the brain and its disorders.

- The transition phase covers the period from 1930 to 1960. During this time researchers conducted clinical studies of children who were having difficulty learning, and psychologists and educators developed instruments for assesment and remediation. The progress of the field was marked by a series of terms that were used to describe the child who was not learning. The term *brain-injured child* was introduced by Alfred Strauss. Other suggested names included Strauss syndrome and minimal brain dysfunction (MBD). The term *learning disabilities* was first proposed in 1963.

- The integration phase occurred between 1960 and 1980. During this period there was widespread and rapid implementation of learning disabilities programs in the schools across the nation.

- The contemporary phase began after 1980. This period represents emerging directions, such as the widening age span of the learning disabilities population; the increasing recognition of the range of learning disabilities from mild to severe; the cross-categorical concept; learning disabilities and regular education; and implications of computer technology.

Key Terms

impulsivity	cross-categorical grouping	minimal brain dysfunc
perseveration	aphasia	tion
mild learning disabilities	perceptual disorders	PL 94–142
distractability	soft neurological signs	brain-injured child
mainstreaming		

The Assessment– Teaching Process

PART 2

Chapter Outline

Assessment

Introduction

The three chapters of Part 2 highlight the integral elements of the assessment–teaching process: assessment (Chapter 3), clinical teaching (Chapter 4), and placement for instruction (Chapter 5).

Assessment and teaching should be interrelated in the continuous process of trying to understand a troubled student and to help that student learn. Attention to only one of these components splinters the effort. For example, the merely routine teaching of skills or the use of methods and materials without considering the unique problem of a student would not only waste time but might also harm the student. Similarly, if assessment results only in selecting a label (such as dyslexia) or a presumed cause of the learning problems (such as a lesion in the angular gyrus or perhaps an overindulgent mother), it cannot provide sufficient guidelines for devising strategies to help the student learn.

This chapter investigates several aspects of assessment: its purposes, the effects of the law (particularly Public Law 94–142) on the assessment-teaching process, the decisions that must be made, the kinds of assessment information obtained, special topics related to assessment in learning disabilities (eligibility criteria and using computers for IEPs); and it starts a case study.

Purposes of Assessment

Assessment is the process of evaluation that takes place in forming judgments about students. The major reason for assessment is to gather pertinent information about a specific student for making the crucial decisions about placement and teaching. The data about the way a student performs certain tasks are synthesized, analyzed, and interpreted.

The process of assessment serves several broader purposes as well. Salvia and Ysseldyke (1981) specify five purposes of assessment that are pertinent for learning disabilities.

1. *Screening:* to detect pupils who may be eligible for learning disabilities services
2. *Placement:* to aid in decisions about the most appropriate environment for teaching identified students
3. *Program planning:* to assist in the design of education programs for individuals or groups
4. *Program evaluation:* to measure the effectiveness of a program
5. *Review of student progress:* to monitor a student's achievement and progress

The Influence of the Law on the Assessment Process

The rules and regulations of education laws have greatly influenced our assessment and teaching practices. The most substantial influences have been brought about by the federal legislation known as Public Law 94–142, the Education for All Handicapped Children Act, and the law's counterpart in each state. Because of the law's effect on the assessment and teaching of exceptional students, it is important that teachers know its requirements. Two segments of PL 94–142 that directly shape assessment procedures are discussed in this section: the provisions related to the *individualized education program* (IEP) and procedural safeguards.

The Individualized Education Program (IEP) as an Assessment–Teaching Process

One of the major provisions of PL 94–142 is the requirement that an *individualized education program* (IEP) be formulated for each student identified as handicapped. The IEP serves two purposes:

1. *As a written plan for a particular student.* The IEP is a written statement developed by the IEP, or case conference, team, which prescribes specific educational objectives and placement for an individual student.
2. *As a management tool for the entire assessment-teaching process.* The IEP also serves a much broader purpose than the written document itself. As the core of the entire assessment-teaching process, it involves all the assessment evaluation as well as teaching procedures. It becomes the critical link between the learning-disabled student and the special teaching that the student requires.

Thus, the IEP is intended as a management tool for insuring that the education designed for the handicapped student is appropriate for that student's special learning needs and that the special educational services are actually delivered and monitored (Turnbull, Strickland, & Brantley, 1982; Lerner, Dawson, & Horvath, 1980). The stages of the IEP as the assessment-teaching process are illustrated in Figure 3.1.

Procedural Safeguards

Several other regulations in PL 94–142 affecting assessment procedures are known as *procedural safeguards.* They are designed to protect the rights of handicapped students. The most important of these safeguards are summarized below.

1. Parents must *consent in writing* to having their child evaluated and to the plans and placement set forth in the written IEP.

FIGURE 3.1
Stages of the IEP as an Assessment-Teaching Process

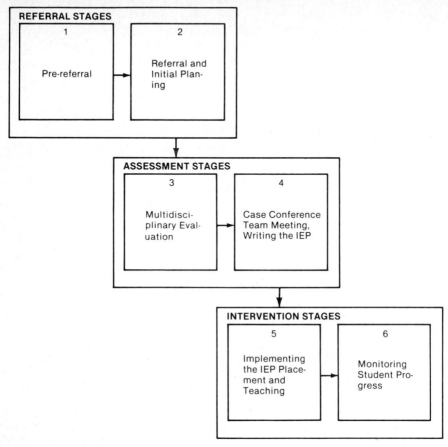

Source: Adapted from J. Lerner, D. Dawson, and L. Horvath, *Cases in learning and behavior problems: A guide to individualized education programs* (Boston: Houghton Mifflin, 1980), p. 3.

2. The assessment must be conducted in the *student's native language* and the findings reported to the parents in the parents' native language.
3. Tests and procedures used for the evaluation and placement must be *free of racial or cultural bias.*
4. The parents have the *right to see all information* collected and used in the decision making.
5. Parents and students have the right to an *impartial due process hearing* if they disagree with the IEP decisions.
6. The *confidentiality* of all reports and records of the students is protected under the law.

Stages of the Assessment-Teaching Process

The assessment-teaching process follows a sequence of stages. There are three broad stages: referral, assessment, and intervention. The case study described at the end of this chapter and continued in Chapters 4 and 5 illustrates the assessment-teaching process.

The *referral stages* begin the process and involve prereferral and referral actions. The *assessment stages* are the core of the process and involve the tasks of developing and writing the IEP. The *intervention stages* occur after the written document has been completed and involve the teaching and the monitoring of student progress. Each of these broad stages is subdivided so that there are six stages in all. These six stages meet the legislative mandates of the IEP.

Referral Stages
1. Prereferral activities
2. Referral and initial planning

Assessment Stages
3. Multidisciplinary evaluation
4. The case conference team meeting and writing of the IEP

Intervention Stages
5. Implementation of the teaching plan
6. Review and monitoring of student progress

1. ***Prereferral activities***   This refers to action by teachers prior to referring a student for a special education case study. In this stage the classroom teacher attempts to use selected methods in the classroom to help the student overcome the problem. Research has found that the most important decision that gets made is the decision by a teacher or parent to refer a student for a psychoeducational evaluation. Once students are referred, the probability is very high that they will be declared eligible for services (Ysseldyke, 1983). The prereferral procedures, therefore, are a preventative measure that often serves to make referral unnecessary.

   Many learning disabilities programs now require evidence of the prereferral activities before the referral is initiated (Lieberman, 1982; Geraldi & Coolidge, 1983). Prereferral activities include the establishment of a building assistance team within the school to which classroom teachers can go for help, teacher consultation with the building team about a student's academic and behavior problems, and the implementation of suggested interventions in the classroom.

   One example of a prereferral procedure is called the *teacher assistance team* (Chalfant & Pysh, 1983; Chalfant, Pysh, & Moultrie, 1979). In this particular example, a team of three regular education teachers in the school, plus the referral teacher, meet to brainstorm and to help the referring teacher develop a plan to enhance the student's performance in the classroom. This prereferral procedure has succeeded in substantially reducing the number of learning disabilities referrals. Another benefit is that fellow teachers work together in solving classroom problems.

2. ***Referral and initial planning.*** The initial referral of a student for evaluation can come through several sources: the teacher, the parent, or other professional persons who have contact with the student, or a self-referral by the student. Once the referral is made, school personnel must follow up the referral. Parents must be notified of the school's concern and must give written permission for an evaluation. In addition, decisions must be made about the general kinds of assessment data needed and who will be responsible for gathering this information.

3. ***The multidisciplinary evaluation.*** At this stage, specialists representing various disciplines obtain the necessary information by assessing academic performance and behavior in areas related to the suspected disability. The multidisciplinary evaluation is conducted by personnel who represent several psychoeducational specialties (for example, school psychologists, social workers, school nurses, speech-language pathologists, learning-disabilities specialists, reading specialists, and others).

Several features of the law regulate the multidisciplinary evaluation. Testing must be administered by trained personnel. The tests must be appropriate, validated for the purpose used, and be free of cultural or racial bias. Evaluation materials must be administered in the student's native language. The evaluation team must represent several disciplines and include at least one teacher or other specialist in the area of the suspected handicap. That means that if a learning disability is suspected, at least one person knowledgeable about learning disabilities would be involved in the evaluation. In some cases, the multidisciplinary specialists responsible for collecting the assessment data meet as a team (Pfeiffer & Naglieri, 1983). This multidisciplinary team should not be confused with the case conference, or IEP, team. In the multidisciplinary team, specialists administer tests, obtain other evaluation data, and determine the student's eligibility for learning disabilities programs. In the case conference, or IEP, team, participants meet to make decisions and write the IEP.

Special regulations in the law require that in evaluating learning disabilities the multidisciplinary team prepare a written report of the evaluation that includes the following information:

a. Whether the child has a specific learning disability
b. The basis for making the determination
c. The relevant behavior noted during the observation of the child
d. The relationship of that behavior to the child's academic functioning

As part of the IEP process, the student's parents, teachers, and other professionals meet for discussion of evaluation findings.   *(Jonathan Goell/The Picture Cube)*

     e. The educationally relevant medical findings, if any
     f. Whether there is a severe discrepancy between achievement and ability that is not correctable without special education and related services
    g. The determination of the team concerning the effects of environmental, cultural, or economic disadvantage

Each team member must certify in writing whether the report reflects his or her conclusions. If any team members disagree with the evaluation, they must submit separate statements presenting their conclusions.

4. ***The case conference, or IEP, meeting—Writing the IEP.*** After the multidisciplinary information is gathered, the parents are contacted to arrange the case conference meeting. It is at this meeting that the IEP is written. The participants at the IEP meeting must include the following:

    a. A representative of the public educational agency
    b. The student's teacher
    c. One or both parents
    d. The student when appropriate
    e. Other individuals, at the discretion of the parents or school. Other individuals could include a variety of people: professionals who par-

ticipated in the evaluation (school psychologist, speech teacher, reading teacher, medical specialist, learning disabilities teacher); legal experts such as attorneys or parent advocates; a private psychologist or psychoeducational specialist. However, the meeting should be kept as small as possible to facilitate decision making and communication; care should be taken not to overwhelm the parents with "experts."

The content of the IEP must include these following components:

a. A statement of the student's present levels of educational performance
b. A statement of annual goals, including short-term objectives
c. A statement of the specific special education and related services to be provided to the child, and the extent to which the child will be able to participate in regular educational programs
d. The projected dates for initiation of services and the anticipated duration of the services
e. Appropriate objective criteria and evaluation procedures and schedules for determining on at least an annual basis whether the short-term instructional objectives are being met.

Before a student is placed into a special education program and services begin, the parents must agree to the IEP plan in writing.

5. *Implementation of the teaching plan.*   This is the teaching portion of the assessment-teaching process. In this stage the student is placed in the agreed-upon setting and receives instruction designed to help him or her reach the goals and objectives set forth in the IEP. This stage occurs after the IEP document has been written and involves implementation of the plan through clinical teaching (see Chapters 4 and 5).

6. *Monitoring of student progress.*   This stage calls for review (at least annually) and re-evaluation of the plan in terms of student progress. Plans must be included in the IEP to show how this evaluation will be accomplished, who will conduct it, and what assessment instruments and criteria will be used.

Some schools are turning to computers as an aid in writing IEPs. The use of microcomputers for IEPs is discussed later in this chapter.

Assessment Decisions

The purpose of the assessment is to collect and analyze information that will help in planning an educational program to improve a student's learning. The questions that must be considered in this process take into account the entire assessment procedure, including the writing of the multidisciplinary evaluation report.

1. *What are the student's present levels of educational performance?* The procedure through which the present level of performance is identified differs from one school to another. However, to determine levels of performance, any procedure must include the following steps: (a) review the information gathered by the multidisciplinary team, (b) determine subject and skill areas for which an IEP should be developed, (c) determine if sufficient evaluation data are available, (d) gather and review more evaluation data if necessary, and (e) state performance levels related to subject and skill areas to be developed (Turnbull et al., 1982). The performance level can be stated in terms of criterion-referenced skill statements, norm-referenced measurements such as grade level or age level, or a curriculum sequence level. It should be stated in observable and measurable language so that all members of the committee have the same understanding. There are several ways to obtain this information: observations, informal tests, daily monitoring, and formal tests.

2. *What additional information about the student can be gathered from reviewing the data collected by the multidisciplinary team?* The information collected by the multidisciplinary team can provide important diagnostic data about the student. The required classroom observation can indicate the student's behavior in school and how that behavior relates to the academic problem. For example, what does the student do during the independent reading activity period? The case history information gives indications about past health, absences from school, family moves, changes in schools, teachers' comments, grades over time—all of which can be valuable in understanding the student's problem. The multidisciplinary information can also indicate whether the student has the prerequisites or readiness skills for academic learning and also what the student's learning patterns are. In addition, the multidisciplinary approach can provide insight into the interrelatedness of the student's difficulties. For example, we might find that a student with a severe handwriting problem also has a severe motor problem, or we may discover that a student with a reading problem has an underlying oral language problem. It is useful to look for clusters of factors and characteristics. For example, a student who does poorly in oral expression may have a history of delayed speech and reduced motor functioning of the speech apparatus (tongue, lips, etc.) and may also do poorly in memory and listening tests. Because of the many ways in which a student's difficulties may manifest themselves, it is important that there be several objective measures, as well as clinical observations, to support the position that the student is encountering difficulty in some area of learning.

3. *Is there a discrepancy between achievement and intellectual ability?* The achievement level means the present performance level discussed in question 1. Ability level refers to the student's potential for learning and must also be measured in some way. Typically, evaluators will use an

intelligence, or IQ test. The criteria for determining a specific learning disability defined in PL 94–142 includes the existence of a discrepancy between what a student is actually learning (achievement) and what the student ought to be learning (potential).

In determining if a student has a severe discrepancy between achievement and potential, three difficult questions must be answered: (a) What has the student actually learned and how should the present achievement level be measured? (b) What is the student potentially capable of learning and how can this potential be measured? (c) What amount of discrepancy between achievement and potential should be considered significant? There are several suggested methods for measuring this discrepancy, and the issues of how to quantify the "discrepancy score" and the role of this information in determining eligibility have become subjects of intense debate. These issues are discussed in greater detail later in this chapter, in the section on eligibility criteria.

4. *Does the student have a learning disability?* Schools and states vary in the criteria and guidelines that they have established and use to determine whether a student has a learning disability. Specialists in the field likewise differ in their tactics for identifying learning disabilities (Ysseldyke, 1983). Many districts and states are placing more emphasis on quantitative data, such as "discrepancy scores" that measure the gap between performance and potential. In addition, to determine eligibility, teams should take into account other evaluation information that is less quantitative, such as observational reports, information provided by teachers and parents, and other information revealed through test performance. For example, how did the student's performance in language tasks compare to the performance in nonverbal manual-type tasks? Did attentional problems interfere with test performance? Both discrepancy scores and other kinds of data should be used to make decisions about learning disabilities eligibility. The Ohio guidelines for learning disabilities emphasize this point: "Sole use of the discrepancy score criteria to identify specific learning disabilities violates federal regulations" (*Ohio Guidelines,* 1983, p. 21).

Under the rules of PL 94–142, students with learning disabilities must be identified by category for "child count" and funding purposes.

5. *What annual goals, including short-term instructional objectives, should be set for the student?* Annual goals are general estimates of what the student will achieve in one year. Annual goals should represent the most essential needs of the student, and priorities should be set for each subject area. For example, an annual goal in mathematics could be that the student learns to multiply and divide.

Short-term instructional objectives are designed to move the student from the present performance level to the annual goal. Usually there are several short-term objectives, which are sequential, specific in terms of behavior and criteria, and manageable for both student and teacher. For the annual goal stated above, the short-term objectives could be as follows: (a) the student will add numbers involving two renamings; (b) the student will subtract numbers involving two renamings; (c) the student will multiply and divide through products of 81; (d) the student will multiply two-digit numbers by one-digit numbers; (e) the student will divide numbers by two-digit divisors.

6. *What specific special education and related services are to be provided? To what extent will the student be in regular education?* These decisions are related to where the student will be placed for the delivery of services. The various options for placement are discussed in Chapter 5. In addition, decisions must be made on the extent to which placement with nonhandicapped students is appropriate.

7. *How will the student's progress be monitored and measured?* Another decision concerns how to determine if the annual goals and short-term instructional objectives are being met. What measurement device will be used? Who will be responsible? A sample format for evaluating annual goals and short-term objectives appears in Table 3.1.

8. *What teaching plan is appropriate for this student?* It is necessary to develop a plan for teaching beyond that which is required in the IEP. The plan must take into account all the information about the student: strengths and weaknesses, developmental levels, skills learned as well as those not yet assimilated, age, interests, and attitudes. Planning strategies require that teachers have a broad knowledge of methods, materials, approaches, curriculum areas, child development, and, most importantly, the students themselves.

Finally, the assessment process involves continuous reappraisal; it must be revised and modified as more knowledge of the students is acquired through teaching and as the students themselves change as they learn.

Obtaining Assessment Information

In order to answer many of the questions listed above, data must be collected. This information can be obtained in five major ways: (1) case history or interview, (2) observation, (3) informal testing, (4) formal standardized testing, and (5) criterion-referenced testing. In practice, these five methods are not separated but are often accomplished simultaneously. One procedure may suggest the others. As a result of astute observation, specific formal tests may be selected. For example, speech misarticulation, along with frequent misunderstanding of the examiner's conversation, could suggest an auditory difficulty and lead to a decision to administer formal tests of auditory acuity and discrimination. For purposes of discussion, however, it is useful to separate these five areas of data gathering.

TABLE 3.1 Sample Format for IEP Annual Goal in Mathematics

Instructional Area: Mathematics
Annual Goal: Student will learn multiplication and division computation skills

| | Evaluation of Short-term Objectives | | | | Results of Evaluation Skills | | | |
Short-term Objectives	Tests, Materials, Evaluation Procedures to be Used	Criteria of Successful Performance	Evaluation Schedule	Date Objective Mastered	Not Existing	Emerging	Acquired
1. Student will add numbers involving two renamings	Will compute 20 addition problems requiring two renamings	85% accuracy	End of first grading period	10/10/79			X
2. Student will subtract numbers involving two renamings	Will compute 20 subtraction problems requiring two renamings	85% accuracy	End of second grading period	11/14/79			X
3. Student will multiply and divide products through 81	Will complete a fact sheet containing 20 multiplication and division facts and products through 81 within a specified time	65% accuracy	End of third grading period	1/15/80		X	
4. Student will multiply two-digit numbers by one-digit numbers	Appropriate mastery test included in mathematics text	75% accuracy	End of fourth grading period			X	
5. Student will divide numbers by two-digit divisors	Appropriate mastery test included in mathematics text	75% accuracy	End of fifth grading period				

Source: Illinois primer on individualized education programs (Springfield, IL: State Board of Education, Illinois Office of Education, 1979), p. 36.

Case History

The case history provides information, insights, and clues about the student's background and development. The following kinds of information are obtained, usually from the parents: learning problems of other members of the family (indicating possible genetic traits); the child's prenatal history, birth conditions, and neonatal development; the child's age when developmental milestones such as sitting, walking, toilet training, and talking were attained; and the child's health history, including illnesses (particularly those with high fevers) and accidents. Additional information, such as the school history, can be obtained from parents, from files, and from school personnel, including teachers, nurses, and guidance counselors.

It requires a skillful interviewer to obtain a maximum amount of useful data. The interviewer must try to establish a feeling of mutual trust with the persons being interviewed, taking care not to ask questions that might alarm parents or make them defensive by indicating disapproval of their actions. The interviewer's attitude should convey a spirit of cooperation, acceptance, and empathy while maintaining a degree of professional objectivity to guard against excessive emotional involvement and consequent ineffectiveness.

If the history taking is to be useful in making a diagnosis, it must go beyond routine questions and gather more information and impressions than the questions themselves ask. The skillful interviewer is able to gather information in a smooth, conversational manner while fulfilling all the other requirements of case-study technique. The data and impressions thus gained are integrated with information obtained through clinical observation and formal testing procedures.

Many school systems have designed screening interviews or questionnaires that are used with the parents of all incoming kindergarten children. Questions are designed to detect those children who are likely to have learning difficulty. The hope is that early detection of high-risk cases will permit plans to be made to help prevent the development of learning disabilities. Below are some questions that might be used in such a screening interview:

Questions Concerning General Background and Health:

How old is the child in years and months?
Was there anything unusual in the birth history?
How is the child's general health?
Has the child had any periods of illness or hospitalization?
Have you ever suspected that the child has poor eyesight?
What were the results of any visual examination?
Have you ever suspected that the child has poor hearing?
If an examination was given, what were the results?

FIGURE 3.2
Case History Information

IDENTIFYING INFORMATION
Child: name, address, telephone, date of birth, school, grade
Parents: father's name and occupation, mother's name and occupation
Family: siblings' names and ages, others in the home
Clinic: date of interview, referral agency, name of examiner

BIRTH HISTORY
Pregnancy: length, condition of mother, unusual factors
Birth conditions: mature or premature, duration of labor, weight, unusual circumstances
Conditions following birth

PHYSICAL AND DEVELOPMENTAL DATA
Health history: accidents, high fevers, other illnesses
Present health: habits of eating and sleeping, energy and activity level
Developmental history: age of sitting, walking, first words, first sentences, language
   difficulties, motor difficulties

SOCIAL AND PERSONAL FACTORS
Friends
Sibling relationships
Hobbies, interests, recreational activities
Home and parent attitudes
Acceptance of responsibilities
Attitude toward learning problem

EDUCATIONAL FACTORS
School experiences: skipped or repeated grades, moving, change of teachers
Preschool education: kindergarten, nursery school
Special help previously received
Teachers' reports
Child's attitude toward school

Questions Concerning Development:

At what age did the child sit up, crawl, walk?
At what age was the first word spoken?
At what age did the child begin to use sentences?

Questions Concerning Present Activities:

Can the child use pencils, crayons, scissors?
Can the child ride a bicycle?
Can the child write his or her name?
Does the child have any nervous tendencies such as bed-wetting, unusual
fears, extreme moods of depression, anxiety, temper tantrums?
Is the child overly active or restless?
Can the child use language for intelligent expression?
Does the child like to listen to stories?

What responsibilities or independent activities does the child accept and perform with some regularity?

How does the child spend time at home?

A variety of forms designed to obtain information about the case history by means of an interview have been developed. Some are quite lengthy and complete, procuring information in many categories. Working somewhat like a detective, the diagnostician must gather enough information to analyze the child's learning failure and to design an appropriate treatment procedure. Not all cases require all the information found on some forms. Case history forms generally contain questions in the categories shown in Figure 3.2.

No one case history form will be entirely suitable without revision and modification from one clinical setting to another. Each diagnostic center must develop a form that meets its own needs and provides the information it desires.

Observation

An observation of the student is required as part of the assessment of learning disabilities. Many attributes of the student are inadequately identified through either standardized test instruments or through interview. The skillful diagnostician, however, is able to detect many of these characteristics through astute observation of the student's behavior and through the proficient use of informal tests. Further, informal tests and observation of behavior provide an opportunity to corroborate findings of the other two areas of assessment. For example, the skillful observer can determine whether the behavior of a child who appears to be deaf is characteristic of children with actual deafness or of children with other types of problems such as aphasia, emotional disturbance, or mental retardation.

Norman, who was being evaluated because of poor reading, was overheard by the diagnostician warning another child that for his bad behavior he would no doubt get "H-A-L-L." The diagnostician perceptively inferred that Norman's incorrect spelling might be related to a deficit in auditory processing. A formal test of auditory discrimination was subsequently given, and Norman's poor performance substantiated that hypothesis.

An assessment of the student's general *personal adjustment* can be made through observation techniques. For example, in the testing situation the examiner observed that when the work became difficult, Ricky gave up completely and simply filled in the blank spaces with any answer; Pat tensed up and refused to continue the work, and Jane, refusing to guess and afraid to make a mistake, struggled with a single item for as long as she was permitted. Through such observations, questions such as the following should be probed: How does the student react to new situations and people? What is the student's attitude toward the learning problem. Has the school problem interfered with other aspects of the student's life? Has it drained the student's energy? Is the student's attitude one of interest or of indifference?

Motor coordination and development can be at least partially assessed by observing the student's movements and gait. How does the student attack a writing task? Does he or she contort the entire body while writing? What is the general appearance of the student's handwriting? How does the student hold a pencil? Does the student move continuously during the session or constantly touch things in the room?

One can also informally assess the student's *use of language*. Is there evidence of infantile speech articulation? Does the student have difficulty finding words? Does the student have an adequate vocabulary? Does the student speak easily or haltingly or perhaps excessively? Does the student use complete sentences or single words and short partial phrases? Is the sequence of sounds correct in words? Does the student commit major errors of grammar and syntax?

Games, toys, and information activities are useful to the diagnostician both as a means of building rapport with the student and as an aid in making informal clinical observations. For example, the student's ability to zip a zipper, tie a shoelace, button clothing, or lock a padlock gives clues to *fine motor coordination and eye-hand relationships*. Games such as phonic rummy or phonic bingo give clues to the student's *auditory skills*.

Many of the clues that can be used in planning the instructional programs are best detected by observing the pupil's everyday classroom behavior. For example, while the student is reading, the teacher can observe how he or she responds to an unknown word. Does the reader look at the initial consonant and then take a wild guess, attempt to break the word into syllables, or try to infer the word from context? Such information, gathered through observation in the classroom, can prove to be valuable data in the diagnosis.

Rating Scales of Student Characteristics

Teachers' observations of students can also be recorded in a behavior-rating scale. These scales record the teacher's judgment or impression of the student in a measurable fashion. For example, the teacher is asked to judge the student's ability to follow directions on a five-point scale. A rating at level 1 indicates that the teacher judges the student as being unable to follow directions while a rating at level 5 indicates that the student is skillful at following directions.

Teachers involved in one study were asked to judge twenty-four behavioral characteristics of children by rating them on a five-point scale (Myklebust & Boshes, 1969). A score of one represented the lowest rating of function, a score of five represented the highest, and a score of three was considered average. The behavioral categories rated are shown in Figure 3.3. Since 5 was the highest possible rating on any one factor, the highest total

FIGURE 3.3
Rating Scale of Student Behavior

	POOR 1	2	3	4	GOOD 5	
AUDITORY COMPREHENSION						
1. Ability to follow oral directions						1
2. Comprehension of class discussion						2
3. Ability to retain auditory information						3
4. Comprehension of word meaning						4
SPOKEN LANGUAGE						
5. Complete and accurate expression						5
6. Vocabulary ability						6
7. Ability to recall words						7
8. Ability to relate experience						8
9. Ability to formulate ideas						9
ORIENTATION						
10. Promptness						10
11. Spatial orientation						11
12. Judgment of relationships						12
13. Learning directions						13
BEHAVIOR						
14. Cooperation						14
15. Attention						15
16. Ability to organize						16
17. Ability to cope with new situations						17
18. Social acceptance						18
19. Acceptance of responsibility						19
20. Completion of assignments						20
21. Tactfulness						21
MOTOR						
22. General coordination						22
23. Balance						23
24. Ability to manipulate						24

possible score was 120. The mean score of children identified as normal was 81, while the mean score of the learning disabilities group was 61.

Teacher judgment of students' behavioral characteristics has proved to be a reliable technique for identifying the learning disabled, and rating scales have proved to be useful instruments (Bryan & McGrady, 1972). Two scales, the *Pupil Rating Scale* and the *Devereux Behavior Scales*, are listed in Appendix C.

Applied Behavior Analysis

Within the behavioral approach to teaching children with learning problems, the concept of observation takes on a very specific meaning since quantified observational data are required. Direct and structured observational techniques are used in this approach to provide data for measuring the student's behavior over a period of time, to determine a base line of initial behavior, and to determine and measure the events that appear to modify behavior. The data obtained through these detailed quantitative observations provide the basis for planning ways to teach and meet explicit behavioral goals in reading, speaking, and computation (Lovitt, 1975, 1977; Jenkins, Deno, & Mirkin, 1979; Deno & Mirkin, 1977).

In applied behavior analysis, assessment data are obtained directly through daily observation and measurement, rather than indirectly through tests. Lovitt (1975) characterizes *applied behavior analysis* as having five components.

Direct measurement.   The behavior of concern is measured directly rather than through tests. For example, if you want to assess Sam's reading, have him read the words in his reader. If you want to assess Alice's ability to multiply by two, have her do arithmetic examples of that type.

Daily measurement.   The behavior of concern is measured daily if possible. If Sam is given the opportunity to perform his reading task for several days in a row, then a baseline of his average performance over several days can be computed.

Replicable teaching procedures.   The instructional interventions must be clear so that they can be replicated.

Individual analysis.   The data represent the behavior of a single individual. If there are five children in an instructional group, then there would have to be five charts to show the behavior and performance of each child.

Experimental control.   This is a method to measure the effectiveness of a treatment. Data are recorded by period to show behavior at baseline, after the institution of treatment, and after the removal of treatment. Chapter 15 shows an example of applied behavior analysis measurement.

Jenkins, Deno, and Mirkin (1979) suggest that direct, daily measurement of performance can be useful in tracking a student's progress in reaching both annual goals and short-term objectives on an IEP. They believe that as an assessment method it is relevant to what is being taught, sensitive and flexible (if changes are to be made), and easy to repeat.

We discuss methods of monitoring behavior further in Chapter 15.

Informal Methods

Informal measures to assess student performance can be very useful. A practical approach is to test the student on the ordinary materials and procedures that he or she is currently working with in the classroom. For example, a teacher can select items from the student's texts. Informal measures have not been tested on large populations, nor are data available to permit comparison of a student's performance with that of a normed sample population. However, informal tests do have many advantages (Zigmond Vallecorsa, & Silverman, 1983). They permit freedom in administration and interpretation; for example, a teacher can encourage the student or give the student more time to complete the test. Such adjustments put students at ease and help assure that they give their best effort. Moreover, informal tests can be given more frequently than formal measures, can be administered over a period of time rather than in a single session, and can be assessed using a wide variety of techniques. In addition, they can be given during regular instruction periods and are less expensive than formal tests.

Informal tests can be designed either commercially or by the teacher. Moran (1978) proposes using classroom materials for informal tests because one can then examine behaviors that are as close as possible to the desired behavior. Moran gives five guidelines for informal testing: (1) test only those skills that appear to be deficient; (2) start testing at the terminal behavior and then move down to easier material, if necessary; (3) test under typical classroom conditions during regular school hours, if possible; (4) combine systematic observation of behavior with informal testing; and (5) separate skills deficits from environmental or behavior conditions.

Examples of tests are presented below for specific subject areas. Other informal tests, such as the informal reading inventory, are treated in the pertinent academic chapters in Part 4.

Informal Graded Word-Recognition Test

This sort of test can be used as a quick method to determine the student's approximate reading level. Such a test is also useful in detecting the student's errors in word analysis. An informal graded word-recognition test can be constructed by selecting words at random from graded basal reader glossaries. Table 3.2 illustrates the informal graded word-recognition test. Words from the preprimer through third-grade levels were selected from several basal reader series, and from grades four through six were taken from the Durrell-Sullivan reading vocabularies for those grades (Durrell, 1956).

The informal graded word list can be given as follows: (1) type the list of words selected for each grade on separate cards; (2) duplicate the entire test on a single sheet; (3) have the pupil read the words from the cards while the examiner marks the errors on the sheet, noting the pupil's method of analyzing and pronouncing difficult words; and (4) have the pupil read from increasingly difficult lists until three words are missed. The level at which there are two missed words suggests the instructional level at which the pupil is able to read with help. The level at which one word is missed suggests the pupil's independent reading level—that at which the pupil can read alone. The level at which three words are missed suggests a frustration level, and the material is probably too difficult.

Informal Arithmetic Test

An informal arithmetic test can be easily devised to point out weaknesses in the basic computational skills (Underhill, Uprichard, & Heddens, 1980). Otto, McMenemy, and Smith (1973) suggest that the informal survey test illustrated

TABLE 3.2   **Informal Graded Word Reading List**

Preprimer	Primer	Grade 1	Grade 2
see	day	about	hungry
run	from	sang	loud
me	all	guess	stones
dog	under	catch	trick
at	little	across	chair
come	house	live	hopped
down	ready	boats	himself
you	came	hard	color
said	your	longer	straight
boy	blue	hold	leading

Grade 3	Grade 4	Grade 5	Grade 6
arrow	brilliant	career	buoyant
wrist	credit	cultivate	determination
bottom	examine	essential	gauntlet
castle	grammar	grieve	incubator
learned	jingle	jostle	ludicrous
washed	ruby	obscure	offensive
safety	terrify	procession	prophesy
yesterday	wrench	sociable	sanctuary
delight	mayor	triangular	tapestry
happiness	agent	volcano	vague

in Figure 3.4 be used for sixth grade. The difficulty level of the test could be increased or decreased, depending on the grade level being tested.

The informal arithmetic test should include several items of each kind so that a simple error will not be mistaken for a more fundamental difficulty. Otto, McMenemy, and Smith suggest that errors can be charted:

Addition

combinations
counting
carrying
faulty procedures

Subtraction

combinations
counting
regrouping
faulty procedures

Multiplication

combinations
counting
remainder difficulties
faulty procedures

Division

combinations
counting
carrying
faulty procedures

FIGURE 3.4
Informal Survey Test: Sixth-Grade Level

ADDITION	300	37			
	60	24		234	123
	407	6	271	574	324
	2	19	389	261	451
SUBTRACTION	765	751	7054	8004	90327
	-342	-608	-3595	-5637	-42827
MULTIPLICATION	36	44	721	483	802
	$\times 10$	$\times 83$	$\times 346$	$\times 208$	$\times 357$
DIVISION	$2\overline{)36}$	$12\overline{)36}$	$6\overline{)966}$	$16\overline{)1081}$	$13\overline{)8726}$

Source: W. Otto, R. McMenemy, and R. Smith, *Corrective and remedial teaching* (Boston: Houghton Mifflin, 1973), p. 284.

Diagnostic Teaching

Diagnostic teaching is an extension of the assessment process. The perceptive teacher continues to collect assessment information while teaching the student. Typically, after giving tests, the teacher still has much to learn about the student and can do so by developing lessons that teach and test simultaneously and by noting the student's reactions to these lessons. Diagnostic teaching is also referred to as "trial lessons" or "teaching probes."

Assessment information about the student's learning styles can be obtained through short teaching lessons. For example, the following procedure can indicate if the student learns well through a sight-word method. First, teach some words visually by putting a few words on cards. Say the word while the student is looking at the word. A short time later, test the student on the word to see if the student remembers it. Students who have fairly good visual memories will have little difficulty remembering the word after a few repetitions. A similar procedure can be used in a diagnostic teaching session to assess a student's auditory and phonics learning abilities.

Several commercial tests use a similar technique to probe the student's learning style: for instance, *The Learning Method Tests* by Mills (1956) and the *Learning Styles Inventory* (Dunn, Dunn, & Price, 1982).

Roswell and Natchez (1983) describe an approach that consists of visual, phonics, visual-motor, and kinesthetic trial lessons for students at reading levels 1 to 3.

In the *visual* method, the teacher selects about five words not known by the student, such as *pencil, lady, sock*, and prints each of them on a separate card. (The examiner first administers tests to make sure the student does not already know the words.) The examiner then writes each word on another card, along with the picture of the object denoted. The examiner points to the word on the picture card, pronounces it, and then asks the student to look at the word and say it several times. After a lapse of time, the student is tested on the nonillustrated cards.

The *phonics* trial lesson consists of several parts. First, the teacher asks the student to make new words by substituting beginning consonants: change *run* to *sun, fun, bun*, and so on. Then the teacher pronounces single phonemes in one-syllable words slowly and distinctly and asks the student to combine the sounds to make a word: *k-a-t* blends to *cat*. The teacher next asks the student to substitute final consonants in short-vowel words using sounds taught in the first part: *fat* to *fan, cat* to *can, run* to *rub*. Finally, the teacher asks the student to read in mixed order the words learned through the phonic approach: *run, cat, rub, man*.

In the *visual-motor* trial lesson, the teacher chooses three unknown words five to seven letters in length (for example, *fight, missile, horse*) and presents each word separately on a card, asking the pupil to look carefully, to shut his eyes and try to visualize the word, to open his eyes and check his visual image by looking at the word again, and finally to say the word. Then the card is removed and the student writes the word from memory.

The *kinesthetic* trial lesson is attempted if all the other methods have failed. The teacher writes or prints an unfamiliar word on unlined paper, making each letter approximately two inches high. The student is told that she will learn a new way to read through her fingers. She looks at the word and traces it with her index finger while simultaneously pronouncing it very slowly. This trace-and-say process is repeated several times, and the student is then asked to write the word without reference to the model.

Other trial lesson techniques are suggested by Roswell and Natchez for older students reading at higher grade levels. Again, at the conclusion of the trial lesson session, both teacher and student have a better idea of how to begin and where to go.

Formal Standardized Tests

Formal tests are commercially prepared instruments that have been used with and standardized on large groups of students. When formal tests are given, strict procedures in administration, scoring, and interpretation are required. These tests are called *norm-referenced* because they have scores derived from their administration to a large group of children. Formal tests may have the following characteristics:

1. The test is usually available in more than one form so that a student can be examined more than once without obtaining a high score due to practice.
2. The test is accompanied by a manual giving directions for administration, scoring, and interpretation.
3. The manual contains grade norms, age norms, and possibly percentile ranks or some form of scaled scores.

4. The manual includes figures on validity (the degree to which the tests measure what they are supposed to measure). The manual also shows reliability (consistency or similarity of performance). A score of .90 indicates that if the test were given to the student again it is 90 percent likely that the student would obtain a score in the same range.

The examiner should have a sound foundation in the techniques of using and interpreting tests in general and should be thoroughly familiar with the specific test being used. Frequently, the value of a test may not be so much in the final test score as in the measurement of a particular subtest performance, the profile of all the subtests scores, or the clinical observations of the student during the test. The diagnostician who has had extensive experience with a test may find that some parts used alone yield the necessary information.

The Adequacy of Formal Tests Used in Learning Disabilities

Caution must be exercised in the interpretation of test scores. The score indicates only a small sample of behavior at one moment in time. All tests, by their very nature, give only a limited measure of a person's abilities.

Researchers have been extremely critical of the adequacy of many of the tests that are widely used to assist in decision making in the field of learning disabilities (Ysseldyke, 1983; Salvia & Ysseldyke, 1981; Ysseldyke & Algozzine, 1979; Thurlow & Ysseldyke, 1979). They have criticized the technical adequacy of the tests on three counts: (1) *standardization*, asking, "On what group was the test standardized?" (2) *reliability*, questioning "Are the test results consistent?" and (3) *validity*, asking "Does the test measure what it claims to measure?" The researchers have found many of the tests used by learning disabilities teachers to be ineffectual when judged by these criteria.

In a survey of forty-four Child Service Demonstration Centers that serve learning-disabled students, 100 percent reported that they use norm-referenced tests. Four tests used by more than half of the centers were the *Keymath Diagnostic Arithmetic Test* (Keymath); the *Peabody Individual Achievement Test* (PIAT); the *Wechsler Intelligence Scale for Children-Revised* (WISC-R); and the *Wide Range Achievement Test* (WRAT). Of the thirty tests used by three or more centers, only five were found to have technically adequate norms, only ten had adequate reliability, and only nine had technically adequate validity, according to Thurlow and Ysseldyke (1979).

There appears to be a difference of opinion between researchers who question the adequacy of tests and practitioners who find that tests offer helpful information (Salvia & Ysseldyke, 1981). Moreover, some researchers of psychological tests believe that their use in clinical settings is justified. Anastasi (1976) notes that multiple sources of data should be used in an intensive diagnosis and that if such instruments serve primarily to suggest leads for the skilled clinician to follow up, their retention can be justified. Moreover, Anastasi points out that even highly reliable tests with well-established validity do not yield sufficiently precise results for individual

Caution must be exercised in the interpretation of test scores: they indicate only a small sample of behavior at one moment.   *(Judith D. Sedwick/The Picture Cube)*

diagnosis. Clinicians should avoid overgeneralization from isolated test scores, but such data can provide a rich harvest of leads.

The student with a learning disability, however, cannot wait until we have flawless diagnostic tools. Moreover, data from informal tests and observations are similarly fallible. In spite of the doubts raised by such critical reports, formal tests can be useful in obtaining information that helps formulate an evaluation when the tests are widely used. It is important for the diagnostician to know the limitations of the test and to use the information in proper perspective. Any single score, of course, gives only a small part of the information and it should always be interpreted with extreme caution.

Formal tests can be viewed as a means of providing two levels of information about the student: (1) *general tests* sample general, or global, areas of functioning and determine whether a student is performing at, above, or below age level in a given area; and (2) *diagnostic tests* give a microscopic view of the components of some area of performance, enabling the teacher to analyze the student's functioning in specific subskills and supplying direction for remediation. Some commonly used formal tests of both types are discussed below. A listing of these tests and their publishers is presented in Appendix C; many are discussed in greater detail in this chapter.

Tests of Mental Abilities and Mental Processes

The purpose of the general intelligence tests is to assess the global aspects of intelligence, usually for classification or categorization. The most commonly used individual general intelligence tests are the revised *Wechsler Intelligence Scale for Children* (WISC-R), and the *Stanford-Binet Intelligence Scale*. While the *Stanford-Binet* yields a single score of general intelligence, the WISC-R provides a verbal IQ and a performance IQ in addition to the full-scale score. The *Slosson Intelligence Test for Children and Adults,* the *McCarthy Scales of Children's Abilities,* and the *System of Multicultural Pluralistic Assessment* (SOMPA) are also frequently used as tests of intelligence.

Such tests provide initial data for classifying a student as high, average, or low in general mental abilities. However, the general nature of such tests may limit their usefulness in analyzing the pupil's learning problem.

A second stage in the evaluation, then, is the use of tests that provide information for analyzing component mental abilities, and specific intellectual, perceptual, and/or cognitive factors. The *Woodcock-Johnson Psycho-Educational Battery—Tests of Cognitive Ability* contains subtests of mental ability. The *Kaufman Assessment Battery for Children* (K-ABC) *Mental Processing Composite* (including several subtests of sequential processing and simultaneous processing) also provides discrete mental processing subtest information. The *Illinois Test of Psycholinguistic Abilities* (ITPA) was one of the first tests of mental processes designed expressly to analyze subskills of mental function. Another diagnostic test battery that assesses several subareas of mental abilities is the *Detroit Tests of Learning Aptitude.* There are also a number of other diagnostic tests that sample only one or a few of the subareas of mental processing. Tests of visual-motor perception include the *Bender Visual-Motor Gestalt Test for Children*, the *Developmental Test of Visual-Motor Integration*, the *Marianne Frostig Developmental Test of Visual Perception*, and the *Monroe Reading Aptitude Tests*. A test that estimates visual perception development and intelligence is the *Goodenough-Harris Drawing Test*. Auditory perception tests include the *Wepman Test of Auditory Discrimination* and the *Roswell-Chall Auditory Blending Test*.

Two tests of mental abilities are described in some detail below: the *Wechsler Intelligence Scale for Children-Revised* (WISC-R) and the *Kaufman Assessment Battery for Children* (K-ABC). The WISC-R is one of the widely used intelligence tests in assessing learning disabilities, and it is likely to be part of a student's IEP assessment. The K-ABC is a relatively new test that has generated much interest.

Wechsler Intelligence Scale for Children-Revised (WISC-R)   The WISC-R is one of the most widely used tests for assessing the potential of learning-disabled students between the ages of 6 through 16. The complete test consists of five verbal and five performance subtests, plus two optional tests. A general idea of the kinds of abilities sampled in each of the subtests is given below:

Verbal Tests   These tests use oral language for administration and student responses.
>   "Information"—tests how much general knowledge the student has acquired through living in the surrounding environment.
>   "Comprehension"—assesses a student's ability to make judgments about social situations.
>   "Arithmetic"—tests the ability to do arithmetic reasoning problems within a time limit.
>   "Similarities"—tests a student's skill at detecting analogies, or similar elements in different objects.
>   "Vocabulary"—tests a student's ability to describe selected spoken words.
>   "Digit span"—(an optional test) measures the student's ability to remember and repeat a series of digits after the examiner says them.

Performance Tests   These tests are presented in a visual manner and the subject responds by performing some task.
>   "Picture completion"—requires the student to detect missing elements in pictures.
>   "Picture arrangement"—asks the student to rearrange a set of pictures so that they relate a sequential story.
>   "Block design"—asks the student to arrange small colored blocks to copy a geometric design.
>   "Object assembly"—requires the student to assemble the parts of a puzzle that represent an object.
>   "Coding"—tests the student's ability to remember associations between numbers and geometric symbols and quickly record these associations.
>   "Mazes"—(an optional paper and pencil test) measures the student's ability to find the way out of a maze.

The WISC-R is designed so that a scaled, or standard, score of ten indicates average ability for age in the particular subtest. The test yields a full-scale IQ, a verbal IQ, and a performance IQ. Information about a student's strengths and weaknesses in language and performance areas can be interpreted by comparing the verbal IQ to the performance IQ. Although the WISC-R was designed as a measure of global intelligence, examiners frequently garner additional clinical information by going beyond the global scores and analyzing the student's performance on specific subtests (Salvia & Ysseldyke, 1981).

Another type of clinical interpretation of the WISC-R is accomplished by grouping the subtests. Bannatyne (1974) suggested grouping WISC-R subtests into four categories: *spatial ability* (picture completion, block design, object assembly); *verbal conceptualization ability* (comprehension, similarities, vocabulary); *sequencing ability* (digit span, arithmetic, coding); and *acquired*

CHARLIE

12-1

"... I can't go bowling tonight, Freddie, I'm cramming for an IQ test tomorrow..."

Reprinted by permission: Tribune Media Services, Inc.

knowledge (information, arithmetic, vocabulary). The average scaled score for each category totals thirty points.

Kaufman Assessment Battery for Children (K-ABC) The K-ABC is an individually administered measure of intelligence and achievement for children aged two and a half to twelve and a half. Based on a definition of intelligence that has its roots in cognitive psychology and neuropsychology, it is described by its authors as a clinical instrument.

There are two scales of intelligence: (1) the *Sequential Processing Scale*, or tasks that involve mentally arranging stimuli in serial order (for example, the digit span), and (2) the *Simultaneous Processing Scale*, or tasks that demand primarily spatial integration of stimuli (for instance, block design).

The *Composite Processing Scale* combines the sequential and simultaneous scores. In addition there is an *Achievement Scale* and a supplemental

Nonverbal Scale (selected tests for language-disordered, hearing-impaired, or non–English speaking students).

The K-ABC contains sixteen subtests, but because of the age range of certain tests no student completes more than thirteen. Some of the subtests were adapted from neuropsychological procedures.

Sequential Processing Scale

"Hand movement"—The student must perform a series of hand movements in the same sequence as performed by the examiner.

"Number recall"—The examiner presents a series of digits, and the student is required to repeat the digits in the same sequence.

"Word order"—The student is required to touch a series of silhouettes of common objects in the same sequence as the objects were presented orally.

Simultaneous Processing Scale

"Magic windows"—The student identifies a picture which the examiner exposes by slowly moving it behind a narrow slotted window so that the picture is only partially visible at any one time.

"Face recognition"—The student selects from a group photograph the one or two faces that are briefly exposed.

"Gestalt closure"—The student names an object or scene pictured in a partially completed inkblot drawing.

"Triangles"—The student assembles several identical triangles into an abstract pattern that matches a model.

"Matrix analogies"—The subject selects the meaningful picture or abstract design that best completes a visual analogy.

"Spatial memory"—The student recalls the placement of pictures on a page that is exposed briefly.

"Photo series"—the student places photographs of an event in chronological order.

Reading Tests

There are many global or general survey-type tests of reading. Among them are the *Gates-MacGinitie Reading Tests*; the *Stanford Achievement Test: Reading; California Reading Test; Metropolitan Achievement Tests: Reading;* and *SRA Achievement Series: Reading.* These tests yield a general score of silent reading, and they give an indication of the level at which a child reads.

A diagnostic reading test differs from a general reading test in that it analyzes the processes by which the child attempts to read—it gives information on *how* the child reads rather than only indicating reading level. Analysis of specific errors, for example, might indicate poor word-attack skills, a lack of familiarity with certain phonic elements (vowels, consonant blends, diphthongs), inadequate sight vocabulary, or a slow reading rate. Some of the useful diagnostic reading tests include *Gates-McKillop-Horowitz Reading*

Diagnostic Tests, the *Durrell Analysis of Reading Difficulty, Roswell-Chall Diagnostic Reading Test of Word-Analysis Skills, Gray Oral Reading Tests, Spache Diagnostic Reading Scales, Woodcock Reading Mastery Scales*, and the *Test of Reading Comprehension* (TORC).

Tests of Other Academic Skills

Some of the general tests that measure performance in academic subjects such as reading, arithmetic, spelling, and grammar are *Iowa Every-Pupil Tests of Basic Skills*, the *California Achievement Test*, the *Metropolitan Achievement Tests, SRA Achievement Test*, the *Stanford Achievement Test,* and the *Wide-Range Achievement Test* (WRAT).

Fewer tests of a diagnostic nature are available for academic areas other than reading. Some of them are *Diagnostic Tests and Self-Helps in Arithmetic,* the *Gates-Russell Spelling Diagnostic Tests,* the *Stanford Diagnostic Arithmetic Test*, the *Peabody Individual Achievement Test* (PIAT) and the *Key Math Diagnostic Arithmetic Test.*

Motor Tests

A general assessment of motor skill can be made with the *Health Railwalking Test*. Examples of diagnostic tests that examine the component parts of motor performance are the *Lincoln-Oseretsky Motor Development Scale, Purdue Perceptual Motor Survey*, and the *Southern California Perceptual-Motor Tests*.

Language Tests

In the area of language tests, it is important to differentiate between speech assessment and language assessment. A speech test evaluates the student's skills in articulation and voice quality. A language test evaluates linguistic abilities. Many of the tests previously mentioned in this section (such as the ITPA) have subtests of language ability.

Speech screening tests of articulation are the *Templin-Darley Screening and Diagnostic Tests of Articulation* and the *Goldman-Fristoe Test of Articulation*. Two tests of the ability to understand words are the *Peabody Picture Vocabulary Test* and the *Ammons Full-Range Picture Vocabulary Test*. The *Northwestern Syntax Screening Test* and the *Test of Auditory Comprehension of Language* (Carrow) measure syntax development. Other language measures are the *Houston Test for Language Development*, the *Mecham Verbal Language Development Scale*, the *Test of Language Development* (TOLD), and the *Clinical Evaluation of Language Function*. Tests of written language are the *Picture Story Language Test*, in which the pupil writes a story, and the *Test of Written Language* (TOWL).

Social Maturity Assessment

The *Vineland Adaptive Behavior Scales* use the technique of interviewing an informant (usually the mother) to assess several areas of the pupil's maturity. Six categories of maturity are measured on this scale: (1) self-help, (2) locomotion, (3) occupation, (4) communication, (5) self-direction, and (6) socialization. The scale yields a "social age score" and a social quotient, with an average social quotient score of 100.

Screening Tests for Visual and Auditory Acuity

Since defects in vision or hearing may adversely affect the learning process, it is important for children with learning disabilities to be checked for such sensory deficits. Vision- and hearing-screening tests may be given by the learning disabilities specialist who has been trained in the administration of these tests, or sensory screening may be conducted by the school nurse or some other member of the interdisciplinary team. Those students who fail the screening tests are referred to an eye or ear specialist for a thorough and intensive professional examination.

Several vision-screening instruments help to detect students who require further testing. Among them are the *Keystone Vision Screening for Schools* and the *Ortho-Rater*. These instruments use stereoscopic slides to screen for near-vision and far-vision acuity, eye-muscle balance, and fusion.

The *audiometer*, an auditory screening instrument, aids in detecting students who should be referred for a more thorough and intensive examination. Two attributes of the student's ability to hear sound are measured: *frequency* and *intensity*. The frequency of a sound is measured by the number of vibrations that occur per second; as the frequency of sound increases, the pitch of the sound becomes higher. The intensity of a sound wave refers to the strength (or loudness) measured in decibels. The student who, in a threshold audiometric examination, exhibits hearing levels of twenty decibels or greater at any two frequencies in either ear should be referred for an otological examination. Considerable training is required before a diagnostician is able to use an audiometer and interpret the findings of an audiometric test.

Individually Administered Comprehensive Batteries

Some batteries of academic tests that can be individually administered include the *Peabody Individual Achievement Test* (PIAT), the *Woodcock-Johnson Psycho-Educational Battery*, the *Inventory of Basic Skills (Brigance)*, and the *Wide Range Achievement Test* (WRAT).

Criterion-referenced Tests

Criterion-referenced tests are suggested as an alternative to formal norm-referenced tests for several reasons: (1) the shortcomings of standardized norm-referenced tests, (2) the increasing demand for accountability, and (3) the growth of behavioral psychology concepts that advocate using criterion-referenced tests because they are closely related to treatment. The basic purpose of criterion-referenced measurements is to determine the extent to which the pupil has met specific instructional objectives. For example, does the pupil recognize -*ing* endings? Can the student use the initial digraph *sh*? Does the pupil know the meaning of the prefix *dis-*? Criterion-referenced tests are a way of measuring mastery levels rather than grade levels; they describe rather than compare performance. The thinking underlying this approach is similar to that of applied behavior analysis discussed earlier. Some criterion-referenced measurement and teaching programs and their publishers are the *Croft In-Service Reading Program* (Croft Educational Service), *Fountain Valley Teacher Support System* (Richard L. Zweig), *Individual Pupil Monitoring System* (Houghton Mifflin), *Prescriptive Reading Laboratory* (McGraw-Hill), *Read On* (Random House), *Skills Monitoring System* (Harcourt Brace Jovanovich), *Wisconsin Design for Reading Skills Development* (National Computer Systems), *Sequential Testing and Educational Programming for Secondary Students* (Academic Therapy Publications), and the *Criterion Test of Basic Skills* (Academic Therapy Publications).

Special Issues in Assessment of Learning Disabilities

This section presents two topics that go beyond the fundamentals of assessing learning disabilities discussed thus far in this chapter and require a more extended discussion. The topics of *eligibility criteria* and *using computers to write IEPs* are current issues of high interest.

Eligibility Criteria

Earlier in this chapter, the discussion focused on the decisions to be made during the assessment/teaching process. One of the most critical decisions facing the multidisciplinary team is whether the student under consideration has a learning disability. In other words, is the student eligible for learning disabilities services? If the student is deemed eligible, then the IEP, or case conference group meets to decide on placement and teaching and to write the IEP. But if the multidisciplinary team decides against eligibility, then the IEP, or case conference, meeting would not take place and the student would not receive learning disabilities services. Thus, the number of students identified as eligible for learning disabilities services is directly related to the criteria used by the multidisciplinary team in making eligibility decisions.

Responsibilities of the Multidisciplinary Team in Making Eligibility Decisions

Let us review the responsibilities of the learning disabilities multidisciplinary team. The team decides a student's eligibility for learning disabilities services by taking many factors into account. These factors are both qualitative and quantitative in nature and include exclusionary criteria, social, emotional and cultural factors, medical data, observational and developmental information, the adequacy of tests used, and whether there is a severe discrepancy between achievement and potential. All this information is consolidated in determining if the student is eligible for learning disabilities services.

As noted in Chapter 1, a problem perceived by many schools is that the number of students deemed eligible for learning disabilities services has been rising. Factors that account for this increase include (1) a greater awareness of learning disabilities on the part of parents and teachers, (2) the tendency to view learning disabilities as a preferred exceptionality, (3) the growth of learning disabilities programs at the secondary and preschool levels, and (4) a reduction in other kinds of remedial services and special education identification. The increase in the number of students identified as learning disabled has become a matter of concern for school districts, state education agencies, and the Department of Education. Consequently, pressure is mounting to seek ways to establish "eligibility criteria" that would reduce the number of students identified as learning disabled.

Thus, the "discrepancy score" has received great attention as a way to quantify the discrepancy between achievement and potential and to produce data that are specific and objective. The controversial questions are: Which of the several discrepancy-score methods will be used? How much weight will be put on the discrepancy score in relation to more qualitative factors in reaching the eligibility decision?

Methods for Determining the Discrepancy Score

The "discrepancy score," or the discrepancy between a student's potential and achievement, is measured through quantitative techniques. Currently, these four methods for determining a discrepancy score are used in schools or are being suggested by measurement specialists (Cone & Wilson, 1981; Forness, Sinclair, & Guthrie, 1983): (1) *deviation from grade level*, (2) *potential-achievement discrepancy based on grade scores or age scores*, (3) *the potential-achievement discrepancy based on standard-score comparisons*, and (4) *potential-achievement discrepancy based on regressions analysis measures*. Each of these discrepancy score methods has certain advantages as well as certain limitations. Since teachers are likely to participate on teams that develop and consider the discrepancy score, it is important that they be familiar with these concepts. The four discrepancy score methods are reviewed below.

1. ***Deviation from grade level.***   This approach to learning disabilities eligibility identifies students whose achievement scores are significantly below their current grade placement. The deviation can be the same across grades (for example, one year below current grade level) or it can

"I'm not an underachiever. You're an overexpecter."

From *Phi Delta Kappan*, September 1981. Reprinted by permission of Randy Hall.

vary, with greater deviation required for eligibility at the higher grades. Guidelines are set by the school to determine the amount of deviation from grade level needed for learning disabilities eligibility. The guidelines below illustrate the deviation from grade-level method (Richek, List, and Lerner, 1983):

Deviation from Grade-Level Eligibility Criteria

Primary grades—more than 1.0 years below current grade level
Intermediate grades—more than 1.5 years below current grade level
Junior high school—more than 2.0 years below current grade level
Senior high school—more than 2.5 years below current grade level

The deviation-from-grade-level method is often combined with an IQ cutoff level. For example, the school can determine that to be eligible for services, the learning disabilities student's IQ must be in the normal range, and the deviation from grade level must meet the school guidelines. Several schools and states determine learning disabilities eligibility in this way.

The Cone and Wilson (1981) analysis suggests that the deviation from grade level method is easy to administer, but it has many statistical shortcomings. The method discriminates against students with higher IQs who should be performing above grade level, but since they are at grade level, they would not receive services (Cone & Wilson, 1981). The method tends to identify low achievers rather than students with learning disabilities.

2. *Potential-achievement discrepancy based on age-level or grade-level scores.*   These methods of obtaining the discrepancy score are based on the discrepancy between potential and achievement when both are converted to either grade-level scores or age-level scores. These methods are the most frequently used by schools to determine learning disabilities eligibility (Cone & Wilson, 1981). The methods described here include (a) the mental grade method, (b) the years-in-school method, and (c) the learning quotient method.

Mental Grade Method (Harris, 1961).   This is the simplest method. It uses the student's mental age to assess reading expectancy. To determine reading expectancy grade, the examiner subtracts five years from the student's mental age.

$$\text{RE (reading expectancy grade)} = \text{MA (mental age)} - 5$$

Thus a child with a mental age of thirteen is expected to read as well as the average thirteen-year-old or average eighth-grade student. An MA of seven suggests a reading expectancy of the average seven-year-old, or second-grade student.

The expected reading level and the student's present reading level are compared to determine whether a discrepancy exists. For example, Tony is 10 years 0 months old and has an IQ of 120. Using the mental grade method, his reading expectancy grade is 7.0. If he reads at 4.0 grade level, he has a 3-year discrepancy in reading.

$$7.0 \text{ (RE)} = 12 \text{ (MA)} - 5$$

Years-in-School Method. The Bond and Tinker (Bond, Tinker, Wasson, and Wasson, 1984) formula suggests that the mental grade method does not take into account the years of teaching exposure and therefore gives an inaccurate expectancy in some cases, especially when the IQ is particularly high or particularly low. In the first case, it overestimates expectancy and in the second it underestimates it. These authors calculate expectancy grade with the formula

$$\text{RE (reading expectancy grade)} = \frac{\text{years in school} \times \text{IQ}}{100} + 1.0$$

Ten-year-old Tony is in the middle of the fifth grade and therefore has been in school for 4.5 years. Using this formula with his IQ of 120, his reading expectancy is grade 6.4.

$$\text{RE} = \frac{4.5 \times 120}{100} + 1.0 = 6.4$$

If he reads at 4.0 grade level, the discrepancy between his expectancy and achievement levels is 2.4 years.

Learning Quotient Method. Another method that has been suggested to quantify a learning disability first takes three factors into consideration: mental age (MA), chronological age (CA), and grade age (GA) (Myklebust, 1968). Since each factor contains certain errors, an average of the three—called expectancy age (EA)—tends to minimize error. In this method the MA is considered separately as a verbal MA and as a performance MA, as measured by the *Wechsler Intelligence Scale for Children—Revised* (WISC-R).

$$\text{EA (expectancy age)} = \frac{\text{MA} + \text{CA} + \text{GA}}{3}$$

The learning quotient is then the ratio between present achievement level (achievement age, or AA) and the expectancy age (EA).

$$\text{LQ (learning quotient)} = \frac{\text{AA (achievement age)}}{\text{EA (expectancy age)}}$$

A learning quotient (LQ) of 89 or below is one basis for classifying a child as having a learning disability.

An estimate of verbal mental age (MA) is obtained by multiplying verbal IQ by chronological age and dividing by 100.

$$\frac{\text{Verbal IQ} \times \text{CA}}{100}$$

A similar formula yields the performance MA.

$$\frac{\text{Peformance IQ} \times \text{CA}}{100}$$

An estimate of grade age (GA) is made by adding 5.2 to present grade placement (Grade + 5.2).

We can look at Tony using this method. He is 10.0 years old, is in grade 5.5, and has a WISC-R IQ of 120. His verbal IQ is 110 and his performance IQ is 130. His reading achievement score was 4.0, which gives him a reading achievement age of approximately 9.2.

$$\textit{Verbal MA} \quad \frac{11\ (\text{MA}) + 10\ (\text{CA}) + 10.7\ (\text{GA})}{3} = 10.6\ (\text{EA})$$

$$\frac{9.2\ (\text{AA})}{10.6\ (\text{EA})} = .87\ (\text{LQ})$$

$$\textit{Performance MA} \quad \frac{13\ (\text{MA}) + 10\ (\text{CA}) + 10.7\ (\text{GA})}{3} = 11.2\ (\text{EA})$$

$$\frac{9.2\ (\text{AA})}{11.2\ (\text{EA})} = .82\ (\text{LQ})$$

Thus the learning quotient method indicates that Tony has a learning disability because on the basis of his verbal mental age he has a learning quotient of 87 and in his performance mental age he has a learning quotient of 82. These quotients suggest that he has learned 87 percent of what he is capable of in one case and 82 percent of what he is capable of in the other. Both are below the cutoff point of 89.

An alternate technique of estimating expectancy age is suggested by Harris (1961, 1970). This method, which stresses intelligence but also weighs experience, involves giving mental age twice the weight of chronological age. Thus

$$\text{EA (expectancy age)} = \frac{2\ \text{MA} + \text{CA}}{3}$$

This calculation can be substituted for step 1 of the learning quotient method.

Although the potential-achievement discrepancy score based on age and grade levels is the most frequently used to determine eligibility, Cone and Wilson (1981) point out a number of statistical shortcomings. The scores do not take into account the tests' error of measurement, nor do they have a comparability of norms across tests. That is, the grade-level or age-level scores on one test are not comparable to the age- or grade-level scores on another test. For example, the mental-age-level score from an intelligence test is not comparable to the age-level score from an achievement test.

3. *Potential-achievement discrepancy based on standard-score comparisons.*   The use of standard scores is suggested to avoid some of the problems inherent in comparing age and grade scores. In this method, all scores are converted to standard scores that are based upon the same mean and standard deviation. Thus, the standard score on a mental ability (IQ) test can then be readily compared with the standard score on an achievement test. In judging discrepancy, if the difference between the obtained standard scores is greater than one or two standard errors of difference, then the student is viewed as eligible for learning disabilities services. Variations of this method include z-score discrepancy (Erickson, 1975; Elliott, 1981), the T-score discrepancy (Hanna, Dyck, & Holen, 1979), and normal curve equivalent (NCE) discrepancy.

Some school districts are using *normal curve equivalent* (NCE) scores to measure the potential-achievement discrepancy. The raw scores on potential and achievement tests are converted to NCE scores. NCE scores, which resemble standard scores, have a range from 1 to 99 with a mean of 50. Like standard scores, NCE scores have been transformed into equal units and can be compared across tests. They are reported in many test manuals and can also be converted from grade-based percentile scores or from the raw scores. In one school district using NCE scores to determine discrepancy, if the NCE achievement score is one or more standard deviations below the potential score, the student is considered eligible for learning disabilities services (LD Criteria Committee, 1983).

The Cone and Wilson (1981) analysis indicates that the standard score comparison method meets many of the statistical criteria. However, it does not usually take into account certain statistical properties (specifically, the statistical property known as regression toward the mean). The use of the standard score or the NCE score comparisons can be simplified through the use of tables showing the standard scores or NCE scores of tests that are commonly used in the school district.

4. *Potential-achievement discrepancy based on regression analysis.* Another method to determine the discrepancy score is through the technique known as *regression analysis.* Measurement experts tend to favor this procedure because it includes a correction for many of the statistical flaws of the other discrepancy score methods. Regression analysis adjusts for the phenomenon of regression toward the mean. There is a statistical tendency for scores that are especially high or low to move toward the mean when measured a second time. These high or low scores are unreliable because of the many sources of errors of measurement (Hargrove & Poteet, 1984). Regression analysis methods make statistical adjustments for this tendency. Several different models of regression analysis have been proposed (see Cone & Wilson, 1981, and Thorndike, 1965).

Shepard (1980), however, argues that regression analysis has inherent weaknesses as a way to measure the discrepancy score and should not be used because it depends on tests that have low reliability. For example, many of the tests currently used in learning disabilities assessment either fail to meet acceptable psychometric standards or the necessary correlations between the measures have not been adequately investigated (Salvia & Ysseldyke, 1981). In effect, regression analysis is a precise, sophisticated technique being used on tests that are rather gross measures of behavior. Another problem is that parents and many teachers find it difficult to understand the concept of regression analysis.

Combining Qualitative and Quantitative Data

The qualities of each of these four discrepancy score methods are different. It is acknowledged that eligibility for services should not be decided solely on the basis of the discrepancy score but that other information should be considered as well. Many parents and teachers are concerned about the relationship of qualitative and quantitative factors in the decision process and contend that there is no substitute for clinical judgment and experience (McLeod, 1979). Certainly, there are many human and clinical factors that cannot be put into any formula. Observation, informal measurements, and the experiences of teachers and parents are an important component of the eligibility decisions. Additionally, discrepancy scores focus exclusively on potential and achievement measures while ignoring other learning character-istics unique to learning-disabled individuals. Keogh, Major-Kingsley, Omori-Gordon, and Reed (1982) suggest that a common set of marker variables, or reference points, be used in describing and identifying learning-disabled subjects and that these variables may offer a promising approach to the problem of eligibility criteria.

Using the Computer for IEPs

The microcomputer is proving to be a remarkable tool for IEP management, for its facility with data management makes it possible to store, analyze, manipulate, and retrieve the information required.

While the concept of the individualized education program mandated in PL 94–142 is generally hailed as a major step forward in special education, the mechanics of developing, writing, and monitoring the IEP has presented teachers with a multitude of problems. The legal requirements surrounding the IEP have greatly increased the tasks of developing reports, record keep-ing, and monitoring student progress. Teachers often justifiably complain about the increased burden of writing and managing responsibilities and the additional paperwork.

Microcomputer programs can ease some of this burden, making the formulation and writing of IEPs more efficient during the assessment stage and the monitoring of student progress easier during the intervention stage (Hayden, Pommer, & Mark, 1983). What kinds of chores can be accomplished productively with the microcomputer?

1. *Microcomputer programs can assist teachers in creating new IEPs.* Pro-grams can be written to contain the kinds of data the particular school desires to include on the IEP—for example, demographic information, goals and objectives, the names of the participants of the multidiscipli-nary and IEP teams, dates of events, scores on tests and other assessment information, decisions and recommendations, and so forth. The com-puter requests each type of information until all data have been entered. The particular format that the school desires can also be built into the computer program.
2. *Updating records.* The student's IEP and records are stored on disk or tape and can be easily "pulled up" for modification. New information can be added to the IEP as changes occur—for example, when objectives are met, placement is changed, promotions occur, new test scores are ob-tained, observations take place, or objectives are reviewed or monitored.
3. *Printing of records.* With the microcomputer, all participants at an IEP meeting can have a copy of the IEP at the end of the meeting rather than after weeks of waiting for the material to be handwritten, and then trans-

cribed and typed. If there are errors or omissions, they can be conveniently and quickly corrected.

4. *Generation of long-term goals and short-term objectives.* The microcomputer cannot and, of course, should not replace assessment decisions made by good clinicians, but it can make preparing and writing IEP goals and objectives less tedious. A bank of educational objectives becomes an efficient aid for IEP preparation. The bank of objectives can be formulated by teachers in the school and stored in computer memory for later selection. A number of commercial IEP programs also contain a bank of objectives for various curriculum areas. The good program should include options to create new objectives and goals for a particular student.

5. *Monitoring procedural safeguards.* The microcomputer also helps ensure that the school attends to procedural safeguards mandated by federal and state agencies (Hayden, Vance, & Irvin, 1982a, 1982b). Each procedural safeguard is built into the program, and the school personnel enter the date each was attended to (for example, the date parents gave permission for an evaluation).

6. *Analyzing and interpreting test results.* Programs that score and/or analyze performance on specific tests can be purchased or written—for example, WISC-R subscore analysis and recommended intervention strategies (Vance & Hayden, 1982), the Woodcock-Johnson Psychoeducational Battery, K-ABC, and DIAL-R.

7. *Monitoring academic-skills learning.* A curriculum skills checklist can be programmed to monitor student progress. In one large school district, at first only reading and arithmetic skills were written into the computer program. Successful experience with it prompted teachers to request the addition of skills for language arts, prevocational courses, and social behavior (Minick & School, 1982).

8. *Providing parents with more detailed and comprehensive information.* In one school district, parents expressed satisfaction with computer-generated reports, saying they received more information about their child's progress than before.

9. *Creating a resource information bank.* The computer can generate suggestions for resource materials and for the locations of these materials within the school district to meet student needs. This type of inventory control has the advantages of quickly locating material and of helping teachers recognize that all materials belong to the entire school and are to be shared.

Because so many commercial programs are becoming available for IEP management, the problem of selection is no easy task. The program should meet the needs of the teacher and the school and have room for adding features that have not been preprogrammed. Many schools have found it feasible to develop their own IEP management systems tailored to the school's needs (Hayden et al., 1983; Minick & School, 1982; Vance & Hayden, 1982; Hayden et al., 1982, 1982a). The benefits of using the microcomputer for the IEP include a saving of school personnel time (of about 60 to 80 percent), an increase in the content of IEPs, greater parent satisfaction, less delay in report writing, a reduction of secretarial time needed for preparing reports, and the inclusion of statistical packages to analyze data.

Introduction to the Case Study

The first part of an extended case study is presented at the end of this chapter. Before discussing the case, however, it is important to realize that the direction of every case is influenced by the theoretical orientation of the case investigators. The theoretical orientation affects many factors: (1) how the student's learning problems are analyzed; (2) the kinds of assessment questions asked; (3) the selection of evaluation techniques and tests; (4) the interpretation of case data; (5) the recommended delivery system; and (6) the proposed instructional strategies. Because solving the puzzle of a learning disabilities case is an art, as well as a science, professionals may differ about many aspects of a case. (In addition to the case presented here, another extended case study is presented in Appendix A.)

The following case study, that of Rita G., illustrates the stages of the assessment-teaching process (shown in Figure 3.1). Information presented in this case study is based on an actual case. Identifying information has been altered to maintain confidentiality. This case study is broken into three segments, which are presented in the three chapters of Part Two. The placement of the case study is as follows:

PART I of Case Study	Stage 1. Prereferral	in Chapter Three
	Stage 2. Referral and initial planning	
PART II of Case Study	Stage 3. Multidisciplinary evaluation	in Chapter Four
PART III of Case Study	Stage 4. Case conference/ Writing the IEP	in Chapter Five
	Stage 5. Implementing the IEP	
	Stage 6. Reviewing student progress	

CASE STUDY　　　　　　　　　PART I

*RESENT
REMEDIATION*

Rita G.

Identifying Information

Name of Student: Rita G.

Age: 9.0 (Nine years - 0 months)

Current placement: Grade 3.6. Regular third-grade class.

Stage 1: Prereferral Information and Activities

Rita's third-grade teacher, Mr. Martinez, requested a prereferral staffing for Rita G. In his request, Mr. Martinez reported that Rita cannot work independently; she seems unable to organize and plan when faced with a problem task, such as thinking through an arithmetic word problem or solving problems in other curriculum areas. When doing a class assignment, she answers one or two items and then becomes distracted by other activities going on in the classroom and does not complete her work. While she recognizes words in reading, her reading comprehension is inconsistent and her work is usually not completed. On the day Mr. Martinez made the prereferral request, Rita's total morning's work consisted of writing four spelling words five times each. Mr. Martinez also reported that Rita never engaged in conversations with him, rarely asked questions either in class or of him personally. He did note that in her cumulative records her first-grade teacher described her as inquisitive, but she showed no evidence of that quality in his class.

The prereferral team meeting was held soon afterward. The team consisted of Mr. Martinez, the building principal, and the fourth-grade teacher. After discussing Rita's performance in class, the team concluded that the assigned work in the class may be too difficult for Rita. The team suggested trying to have Rita use texts and workbooks at the second-grade level and giving her individual assignments in this material instead of the regular third-grade books.

Mr. Martinez tried this approach for several weeks. Rita objected to being given different assignments from those of her classmates. She also resented being given "baby" work. She began to hide her papers at home and lost her assignment notebook; her mother reported that she purposely broke pencils when doing homework. Rita's academic functioning at school grew worse. She was failing in several subjects. Mr. Martinez decided to call in Rita's mother to discuss recommending an educational evaluation.

Stage 2: Referral and Initial Planning

Mr. Martinez met with Rita's mother to discuss her daughter's learning difficulties. Mrs. G. said that she was worried because the problem was becoming critical. Rita kept saying she was dumb and hated school, and it was becoming increasingly difficult to get her to go to school. She frequently complained of stomachaches in the morning. Mr. Martinez and Mrs. G. agreed to refer Rita for an educational evaluation in the hope that it would provide information to help plan an appropriate educational program for her. Mrs. G. signed the informed consent form so that the evaluation could proceed.

*SELF-
CONCEPT*

Mr. Martinez submitted a referral and discussed Rita's problem with the special education coordinator in the school. The initial planning for Rita's evaluation included the following kinds of assessment information: classroom observation; auditory and visual acuity; a relevant developmental and educational history; measures of intellectual aptitude; measures of present levels of academic functioning; a measure of adaptive behavior, learning strengths and weaknesses; and an interest inventory.

Note: The information gained from this evaluation is presented in the continuation of the case of Rita G. in Chapter 4.

Summary

• This chapter examines the first of the two parts of the assessment/ teaching process: the assessment of learning disabilities. Assessment is the process of gathering pertinent information about the student to make the critical decisions about teaching. The purposes of assessment include screening, placement, program planning, program evaluation, and assessment of student progress.

• Federal and state laws have greatly influenced the assessment process. Federal legislation known as Public Law 94–142 and state versions of this law have had the greatest impact.

• The IEP (individualized education program) has two functions. It is a written plan for a particular student and it also regulates the entire assessment/teaching process.

• Several procedural safeguards must be considered during the assessment process. They include obtaining parental consent, giving tests in the student's native language, using tests that are free of racial and cultural bias, assuring confidentiality, and the right to a due process hearing.

• The assessment-teaching process has six stages: (1) prereferral, (2) referral, (3) multidisciplinary evaluation, (4) case study IEP meeting, (5) implementation of the teaching plan, and (6) review and monitoring of student progress.

• Prereferral activities are activities that the teacher tries in the classroom before making the referral.

• Referral is the formal procedure of initiating the special education study for the student.

• Multidisciplinary evaluation is the process of obtaining assessment information through testing and other means. This information is obtained by various specialists in the school.

• The case conference meeting is the meeting with the parents and other school personnel at which the IEP is written.

• Implementation of the teaching plan refers to both placement and teaching to reach the prescribed goals and objectives.

• The student's progress must be reviewed and the IEP re-evaluated, at least annually.

• Several decisions must be made during the assessment process. Many of these decisions are required in the law concerning the IEP.

• Assessment information can be obtained in five major ways: case history or interview, observation, informal testing, formal standardized testing, and criterion-referenced testing.

• Eligibility criteria help to determine if the student has learning disabilities and is eligible for learning disabilities services. The multidisciplinary team takes into account both qualitative and quantitative information and may consider discrepancy scores, which measure the discrepancy between the student's achievement and potential. The four discrepancy measures are deviation from grade level, discrepancy based on grade- and age-level scores, discrepancy based on standard-score comparisons, and discrepancy based on regression analysis measures.

• The microcomputer's facility in data management makes it a useful tool for the IEP writing and management process.

Key Terms

short-term instructional objectives
annual goals
formal standardized tests
case history
present levels of educational performance

rating scales
informal assessment methods
observation
multidisciplinary evaluation
criterion-referenced tests

individualized education program (IEP)
prereferral activities
referral
eligibility criteria
procedural safeguards
diagnostic teaching

Chapter Outline

Clinical
Teaching

Chapter **4**

Introduction

*T*his chapter reviews the teaching portions of the assessment-teaching process. Assessment provides only a starting point; the process continues with teaching—a special kind of teaching required to help students handicapped by learning problems. To differentiate it from regular classroom teaching, it is called *clinical teaching.*

The goal of clinical teaching is to tailor learning experiences to the unique needs of a particular student. Using all the information gained in the assessment and through the analysis of the student's specific learning problems, the clinical teacher designs a special teaching program. Assessment does not stop when the specific treatment procedures begin. In fact, the essence of clinical teaching is that assessment and instruction are continuous and interlinked. The clinical teacher modifies the teaching as new needs become apparent. Many different intervention strategies can be used in clinical teaching.

A clinical teacher is a "child watcher." Instead of concentrating solely on what the student *cannot* do, the clinical teacher observes in detail what the student *does* do. Observing the kinds of errors the student makes is as important as observing the student's successes. Errors provide clues to many factors, such as the student's current level of development, way of thinking, underlying language system, and style of learning.

For example, a clinical teacher might make use of oral reading errors. Kenneth Goodman's (1969) studies of the analysis of errors (which he calls miscues) in oral reading show that such errors provide excellent clues to the student's mental processes underlying reading (Goodman & Gollasch, 1980–1981). According to Yetta Goodman (1976), oral reading miscues should not be viewed as mistakes that must be eradicated but as overt behavior that may reveal aspects of intellectual processing.

Clinical teaching can also be viewed as an alternating teach-test-teach-test process, with the teacher alternating roles as tester and teacher. First the student is tested; a unit of work based on the resulting information is then taught. After teaching, the student is again tested to determine what has been learned. If the student performs well on the test, the clinical teacher knows the teaching has been successful and plans for the next step of learning. If the student performs poorly on the test, then the clinical teacher must reassess the teaching plan, analyze the errors trying to determine the cause of the failure to learn, and develop a new course of action for teaching.

CASE EXAMPLES

The Clinical Teaching Approach

• Ann, a third grader, read "I saw a large white house" as "I saw a large white horse." A teacher might respond by concluding that Ann is wrong and her error must be corrected. The clinical teacher, however, would respond by thinking, "That's an interesting error. I wonder what caused that behavior. What is involved in Ann's approach to learning or her processing of information that caused her to do that?" The teaching that followed would depend on the analysis of this error—whether it is related to a deficiency in visual perception, an inadequate sight vocabulary, poor visual memory, lack of word attack skills, or too difficult a text. Subsequent teaching and testing would evaluate the analysis.

• John read "Now he had been caught" as "Now he had been catched." Again, teaching will depend on whether the clinical teacher analyzes this error as lack of phonics skills, not paying attention to word endings, or as an underlying linguistic difference between the reader and the text.

• In another area of academic performance, Debby failed the arithmetic story problem in the testing situation. Observation revealed that though she could read the words of the story and perform the arithmetic calculations required, she could not visualize the story's setting. She could not picture in her mind's eye the items to be calculated in the arithmetic story problem. The clinical teacher speculated that Debby's arithmetic failures were related to her identified difficulty in spatial orientation and visualization. This hypothesis was supported by the observation that Debby could not remember how to get to school, to the store, or to a friend's house from her home and that she constantly lost her way in the outside hall. The teaching in this case was directed toward strengthening Debby's visualization skills and the ability to visualize the situation in arithmetic story problems.

• Saul, a high school student, was failing in most of his subjects. He seemed to be uninterested and uninvolved in his school courses. Although his reading word-recognition skills were good, his reading comprehension was very poor. When questioned in class, Saul usually quickly blurted out the first answer he thought of, which was often wrong. His impulsive behavior was the same in written work. After carefully observing his behavior and responses, his teacher surmised that Saul did not have a system for learning. He did not know how to become actively involved in the learning task. He responded impulsively because he had not learned how to stop, think, and monitor his responses before answering questions. In short, he lacked learning strategies. The instruction that ensued focused on teaching Saul to become a more efficient learner.

Clinical teaching, then, implies a concept and an attitude about teaching. It requires flexibility and continuous probing by the teacher, but it does not require any one particular instructional system, educational setting, or style of teaching. The concept of clinical teaching can be applied to teaching an individual student in many settings: a regular classroom, a resource room, a self-contained classroom, or a one-to-one setting. Again, many different intervention strategies or remedial techniques can be used.

FIGURE 4.1
Diagram of the Clinical Teaching Cycle

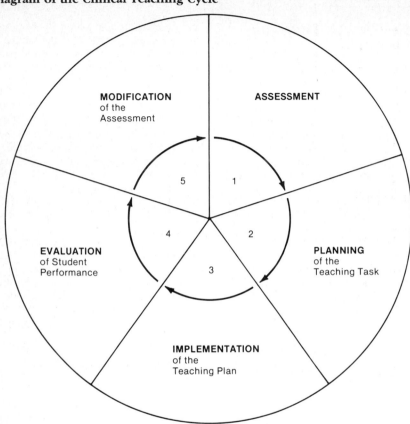

Clinical Teaching Cycle

Clinical teaching requires continual decision making on the part of the teacher. The complete clinical teaching process can be viewed as a cycle, with each stage of the process as a point along a circle, as diagrammed in Figure 4.1. The phases of the clinical teaching process are (1) diagnosis, (2) planning, (3) implementation, and (4) evaluation, leading to (5) a modification of the diagnosis, and then to new planning, new forms of implementation, and a continuing cycle of clinical teaching.

Clinical teaching differs from regular teaching in several ways. First, although in clinical teaching continual decision making is required, in the regular classroom the routine often appears to be designed to minimize decision-making points. For example, in the regular classroom, curriculum procedures are often determined not by the teacher but by the materials being used. The search for the "perfect package" to teach academic skills and "foolproof" programmed materials can be viewed as an attempt to minimize

In the clinical teaching process, continual reassessments and decisions are made about the appropriateness of teaching plans and strategies.

(Alan Carey/The Image Works)

the teacher's need to make decisions. One example of classroom methods that tend to reduce decision making is the widespread use of a highly planned basal reader, the predominant instrumental tool in reading in 90 to 95 percent of the classrooms across the country. Once a basal reader has been adopted, the teaching decisions can be largely found in the basal reader itself. The initial decision of selection can stand for five years or more. Of course, individual teachers use the basal reader in different ways; some follow the instructional manual very closely while other teachers make many adaptations and changes. The point is that this particular material has many instructional decisions built in with step-by-step and day-by-day directions in the textbook, teacher's manual, and workbooks. Thus, a basal reader can become the decision maker instead of the teacher, as Durkin (1974) has found it often to be the case.

Another difference between clinical teaching and regular teaching is that while clinical teaching is designed for a unique student, lessons and materials in the regular class are designed for the "average" student of a given grade level or classroom. Educational research that seeks to find the *best* method to teach a subject area is often designed to measure the average, or mean, achievement level that results from the use of various methods or materials rather than to study appropriate methods for teaching a unique student with a highly individualized learning style (Lerner & Egan, 1979).

To summarize, clinical teaching differs from regular teaching because it is planned for an individual rather than for an entire class, for an atypical learner rather than for the mythical "average" learner. The student may be taught within a group setting, but even so clinical teaching implies that the teacher is fully aware of the individual student's learning style, interests, shortcomings and strengths, levels of development and tolerance in many areas, feelings, and adjustment to the world. With such knowledge, a clinical teaching plan that meets the needs of a particular student can be designed and implemented. An important aspect of clinical teaching is the skill of interpreting feedback information and the need for continuous decision making.

Ecological Considerations

In clinical teaching, it is important to consider ecological factors affecting the student's learning. The phrase *ecological systems* refers to the interactions between an individual and the various environments within which that person lives and grows. A student's ecological systems include the environments of the home, the school, the social group, and the cultural milieu, all of which influence the desire and ability to learn. A complex interrelationship exists between the student and each of these environments (Richek, List, & Lerner, 1983). For example, students often react very differently in a clinical setting or a one-to-one situation than they do in a classroom. In fact, the description of a student's behavior in an individual testing setting is often so different from that of the classroom that one wonders if the same student is being described. Also, each of the environments (home, school, social, and cultural) interacts with the others to influence the student's learning and add to the student's complex ecological system.

Home Environment

The home environment is the child's first in the ecological system. The child's home experiences during the first five or six years influence the development of cognitive growth and become the foundation for later school ability.

In the home environment, parents provide both intellectual stimulation and emotional well-being. The critical relationship that develops between the infant and the mother (or primary parent figure) known as "bonding" lays the foundation for later emotional health (Bowlby, 1969). The development of ego, self-concept, and self-esteem also depends on the support and encouragement of parents within the home. Parents become role models for their child. When their child experiences school difficulties, a supportive family relationship becomes especially important.

In today's fluid society, many events that occur in the home environment profoundly affect youngsters. Moves to a new location, a divorce or the separation of the parents, death of close relatives, or the departure of older siblings from the home are often traumatic events for the youngster and affect learning. Teachers and parents can work reciprocally to help students cope with these wrenching situations.

School Environment

Students spend a substantial portion of their day in school, and the school experiences can dramatically affect their lives. Relationships with peers and with school personnel (including teachers, aides, administrators, office personnel, and maintenance staff) are an integral part of the school ecological system.

Norms and expectations for behavior in the classroom are different from those in other settings that the student is familiar with—primarily the home (Hamilton, 1983; Mehan, 1979). What teachers and students do cannot be understood solely in terms of teaching and learning academic subject matter. In addition to the formal curriculum of academic knowledge, there is a "hidden curriculum" of values and behavior taught implicitly by the complex ecological system of the school and classroom. Research conducted in schools during a lesson shows that students must learn complex rules for participation in a classroom. Not only must they learn the context of the lesson, but they also have to learn implicitly such behaviors as how to be recognized and how to state what they know (Hamilton, 1983). Learning-disabled students often have difficulty learning these hidden rules of school behavior.

Research shows that learning-disabled students often encounter unsatisfactory relationships in the school environment. They receive less praise and acknowledgement for their efforts and are more likely to be criticized, shown disapproval, and even ignored (Bryan, 1983; Gouldner, 1978). Such negative factors serve to discourage learning. The clinical teacher must be aware of how the ecological system of the school affects the student's learning and take measures to counteract these effects (see Chapter 15).

Social Environment

The ecological system of a student's social environment is another important consideration. Everyone needs satisfactory relationships with friends. For young people, these relationships create the basis for social growth and opportunities to gain confidence in social experiences. Unfortunately, for many learning-disabled students, the social sphere is another area of dismal failure, and they exhibit poor social perception abilities (Bryan, 1983; Bryan, Pearl, Donahue, Bryan, & Pflaum, 1983; Kronick, 1978; Bruinniks, 1978; Osman, 1979, 1982). When children develop normally in the social sphere, they learn social skills in a casual and informal manner, assimilating appropriate ways of acting with people through incidental experiences. Learning-disabled students, however, are often not socially perceptive or adept at discerning the nuances of everyday living. They are unaware of how their actions affect others and how their behavior is interpreted by their would-be friends. Their unsatisfying social environment, in turn, may adversely affect school learning.

The same characteristics that create the academic learning disability may also create the disability in the social sphere. Osman (1979) describes Betsy, a first grader who encountered difficulty in the social environment. Betsy had trouble both understanding verbal communication and talking to her classmates. She hugged and touched every prospective friend until the classmate backed away. She made connections with people by feeling and touching—a behavior characteristic of much younger children. When she liked someone, she wanted to show it and did so by hugging, kissing, and grabbing. The other first graders were able to play together and convey thoughts to each other by talking. They did not need to touch in order to feel liked, and they thought Betsy was strange. When Betsy sensed the other children's rejection, she became even more possessive. The more she was rebuffed, the more she tried to make a friend—the wrong way. By age seven, Betsy expected to be rebuffed by her classmates and unconsciously provoked them. She would ask "Do you like me?" at inappropriate times, inviting a negative response. Because of her complaints of mistreatment at the school bus stop, her mother had to drive her to school. This provoked taunts from the other children, which she hated. Eventually, her claim that "nobody likes me" was based more on reality than on Betsy's imagination.

Social problems and ways teachers can help learning-disabled students cope with these problems are further discussed in Chapter 15.

Cultural Environment

Finally, the clinical teacher should consider the ecological system of the student's cultural environment. Our nation's school population consists of students who come from many different ethnic and cultural groups. One of our nation's greatest challenges is the education of students from all cultures, regardless of geographic origin, socioeconomic status, or native language of the student.

In our pluralistic society, sometimes students reject the traditional values of the school, abiding instead by the perceived values of a subculture. If the student thinks that the values of the culture are different from those of the school, there is a conflict. The bilingual and bicultural school programs attempt to meet the values of both groups. The learning-disabled student from these groups has concomitant problems—those derived from learning disabilities and those related to the cultural ecological system.

Implications for Learning

Ecological research suggests that learning competencies depend on positive interactions with the various environments—home, school, social, and cultural systems—in addition to the student's knowledge of the subject matter. The flow of a classroom day is quite complex; it is regulated by subtle forms of communications and a host of teacher skills and sensitivities beyond academic knowledge and instructional techniques. The clinical teacher tries to be sensitive to the impact of the ecological system on the student's learning, attitudes, and progress.

Controlling the Instructional Variables

The teacher and the school can do relatively little about many factors related to learning disabilities. The home environment or the genetic or biological makeup of the student may be key elements producing the learning problem, but frequently such variables cannot be modified by the teacher. Some variables, however, can be changed or manipulated by the school, and these should be carefully analyzed for optimum effect.

Barsch (1965) has suggested six factors in learning that can be readjusted by the clinical teacher: space, time, multiplicity, difficulty level, language, and interpersonal relationships.

1. *Space* refers to the physical setting, which should be conducive to learning. Among the ways to modify space are the use of partitions, cubicles, screens, special rooms, and quiet corners and the removal of distracting stimuli. Other areas to be considered in space are the actual work area, the size of the paper, and the desk surface. Strauss and Lehtinen (1947) and Cruickshank, Bentzen, Ratzeburg, & Tannhauser (1961) have advised that a nondistracting school environment be provided.

   The goal of space control is to increase slowly the amount of space with which the student must contend. Gradually, students must internalize their own controls so that they can get along in an unmodified space environment.

2. There are a number of ways to control *time* in the clinical teaching setting. For the student with a very short attention span, lessons can be designed to be completed in a shorter time. For example, one row of mathematics problems can be assigned instead of an entire page. The work page can be cut into squares or strips to shorten the time required

to complete one section. In timed exercises, the time can be increased. Time can be broken into shorter units by varying the types of activity so that quiet activities are followed by livelier ones. Planned interruptions of long lessons, such as having the student come to the teacher's desk or walk to a shelf to get supplies, can be useful.

3. The *multiplicity* variable refers to the number of factors the student must deal with in a task. The teacher can control the factors the student must contend with and avoid overloading the student by limiting (a) the number of pieces of work to be dealt with, (b) the environment, or extraneous stimuli, and (c) the modality channels of various teaching methods.

The number of pieces of work can be reduced by giving the pupil fewer pages to complete or fewer spelling words to learn. The teacher can limit the number of pictures on walls and bulletin boards, control the lighting and the color of the room or furnishings, and reduce his or her own verbalization. Cruickshank et. al. (1961) urged that the elimination of unnecessary visual and auditory environmental stimuli is essential when creating a good teaching environment for brain-injured and hyperactive pupils.

For some students the modalities stimulated during learning should be limited. The multisensory approach may, in fact, actually disturb their learning. That is, stimulation of the auditory, visual, tactile, and kinesthetic sensory modalities all at the same time may prevent rather than enhance learning.

4. The *difficulty level* of material used can be modified to meet the present performance and tolerance level of the student. The concept of readiness applies here. Many students are failing tasks simply because the tasks are too difficult and the level of performance required is far beyond their present ability. Expecting a student to perform a task far beyond tolerance level can result in a complete breakdown in learning. Strauss and Lehtinen (1947) recognized such a reaction, calling it a "catastrophic response."

Another factor to be considered is the developmental hierarchy of the subject area. Certain tasks normally precede others. The student who has not learned to handle the oral language will probably do poorly in written-language tasks of reading and writing. The student with poor word-recognition skills cannot be expected to succeed in reading-comprehension exercises.

Some skills or responses must be overlearned so that they become automatic. If skills are to be utilized or transferred to new situations, they must be internalized. This internalization permits a shift from the representational level (the conscious, cognitive level) to the automatic response level (the subconscious, habitual level). For example, in reading, the student may initially use phonic skills in a conscious, deliberate way to decode words, but later the process should become automatic (at a subconscious level) for effective reading. The conscious sounding out of words may actually interfere with reading. Syntax and grammar must become automatic if the student is to understand and use language effectively.

5. *Language* can also be modified to enhance student's learning. To assure that language clarifies rather than disturbs, clinical teachers should examine the wording of directions. They should plan communication so that the language used does not exceed the student's level of understanding. For some students, particularly those with auditory language disorders, language quantity must be reduced to the simplest statements. The following techniques simplify language: reduce directions to "telegraphic speech," using only essential words; maintain visual contact with the learner; avoid ambiguous words and emphasize meaning with gesture; speak in a slow tempo; touch the student before talking; and avoid complex sentence structure, particularly negative constructions. In summary, do not overload the student's capacity to handle language.

6. The *interpersonal relationship factor,* the rapport between the pupil and teacher, is of paramount importance. Without it, learning is not likely to take place, and with it, learning frequently occurs in spite of inappropriate techniques and materials or other shortcomings. Both the pupil's self-concept and concept of the teacher must be considered. The importance of the pupil-teacher relationship is discussed in greater detail in this chapter in the section on establishing a therapeutic relationship.

A Classification System of Intervention Methods

A wide array of teaching methods is used by the clinical teacher. These special kinds of teaching are variously referred to as intervention methods, remediation instruction, instructional strategies, educational therapy, or simply good teaching. The terms will be used interchangeably in this discussion. In sorting out the many intervention methods used in clinical teaching, an organized system or classification model can provide an overall perspective. The model shown in Figure 4.2 classifies the many teaching methods into three kinds of analysis: analysis of the *student,* of the *content* to be learned (curriculum), and of the *environmental conditions* under which the learning occurs. Each analytic approach is further subdivided into three specific categories of intervention, making a total of nine. Each of the nine categories of intervention has merit, but each also has certain limitations and shortcomings. All these categories and some of the criticism directed against them are briefly examined in this section.

This classification model offers *one* working system to organize the confusion of teaching methods. Several of the categories are also discussed in greater depth later in this chapter.

FIGURE 4.2
A Classification of Intervention Methods

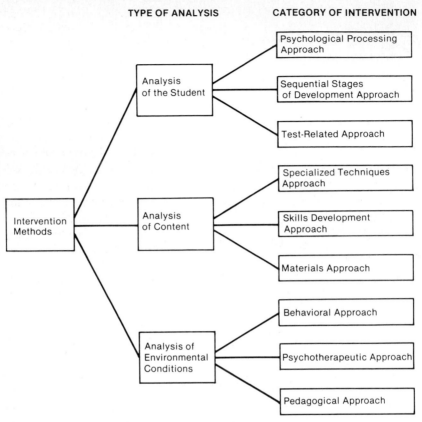

Analysis of the Student

The first three categories of intervention concentrate on an analysis of the student and how he or she functions as a learner.

Psychological Processing Approach

The approach to remediation often associated with learning disabilities is that of *psychological processing*. Psychological processing refers to the student's abilities in processing information. By assessing a student's processing abilities (visual, auditory, memory, haptic abilities, and so forth) and comparing and contrasting the areas of processing strengths and weaknesses, the teacher gathers information to plan teaching. Various authorities have suggested several approaches: one is to remediate the processing deficits; another is to teach through the student's processing modalities that are strong and intact; and a third is to do both simultaneously.

The value of the psychological processing approach has been questioned by a number of investigators (Hammill, Goodman, & Wiederholt, 1974; Hammill & Larsen, 1974a, 1974b; Salvia & Ysseldyke, 1981). They challenge the premise that instruction in psychological processing in isolation leads to improvement in academic learning (see Chapter 6).

Nonetheless, the concept of psychological processing remains a cornerstone of the field of learning disabilities. It provides a way of thinking about how a student learns and offers a framework for teaching.

Sequential Stages of Development Approach

In the *sequential stages of development* approach to remediation, the teacher analyzes the student in terms of a specific hierarchy of stages of normal development. Examples of such hierarchies are sequential stages of motor development (Chapter 10) and Piaget's developmental stages (Chapter 6). In this approach, the teaching begins at the lowest unaccomplished stage in the hierarchy, proceeding to the next stage when the student is ready. For example, according to one hierarchy model, if the youngster has inadequate gross motor skills, remediation would be geared to helping the youngster attain proficiency at that level. Once skills at this stage are learned, remediation moves on to the next sequential stage, for example, fine motor development.

Specific models and programs of the sequential approaches to remediation have been critiqued by Goodman and Hammill (1973), and others. They question the need to develop proficiency at each stage of the hierarchy as well as the transferability of skills learned in the hierarchy to areas of academic learning.

A number of remedial programs are based on the sequential stages of development theory, a framework that rests on a child development perspective. Many of the motor development programs, for example, are based on such a model.

Test-related Approaches

The *test-related* approaches to remediation analyze the student through a particular diagnostic instrument that provides a system for pinpointing areas needing remediation. The model underlying the test is accepted as the model of learning disabilities. For example, if the teacher administers the *Illinois Test of Psycholinguistic Abilities* (ITPA), this model provides the framework for remediation. Certain materials have been specifically designed for test-related approaches. Bush and Giles (1977), the *MWM Program* (Minskoff, Wiseman, & Minskoff, 1973), and the *Goal Program Language Development Game* (Karnes, 1972) provide exercises and materials designed for remediating deficit areas as indicated by the ITPA test. The authors of the *Kaufman Assessment Battery for Children* suggest that their test can be used in this manner.

The test-related approach to remediation has also been questioned by several writers (Newcomer, Hare, Hammill, & McGettigan, 1974; Hammill & Wiederholt, 1972; Hammill & Larsen, 1974a; Newcomer & Hammill, 1975; Salvia & Ysseldyke, 1981). Although the pupil may improve in the specific skill areas being tested and taught, the carry-over to broader kinds of learning is uncertain. Moreover, critics ask test makers why the areas chosen for assessment are more important than others that might have been chosen. They also question the construct validity of the tests.

Remediation in test-related approaches depends on the test being used and the quality of the theory underlying the test. The pupil's performance in the test directs the remedial procedure.

Analysis of the Curriculum

The next three approaches to remedial instruction emphasize the content to be learned rather than analysis of the student who is to learn it.

Specialized Techniques Approach

Unlike the usual developmental methods used in the regular classroom, *specialized techniques* are assumed to be highly differentiated ways of attacking specific learning problems. A specific method is sometimes named after the originator or the popularizer of the approach, for example, the Gillingham method or the Fernald method. These approaches often require the teacher to follow certain steps in a prescribed order and fashion and for a specified period of time. The same method is used for all students, regardless of each student's specific abilities.

Since most research compares methods as they affect large groups, it is difficult to know if any one particular method has been *the* best for an individual student. Few research studies have been conducted to measure the superiority of one specialized technique. In fact, on close inspection, the highly specialized techniques often turn out to be similar to remedial and developmental approaches that have been used over the years.

Skills-Development Approach

Another category of remediation that analyzes the content to be learned is the *skills-development* approach. A hierarchy of skills in a subject area (reading, arithmetic, spelling, and so forth) is postulated. The remedial specialist attempts to determine how far the student has gone along the skills hierarchy in a specific subject area, what the student does not know within the skills hierarchy, and where in the hierarchy teaching should begin. The ability to read, for example, is presumed to be composed of many skills and subskills; by mastering the component subskills, the student should master the skill of reading. The remedial specialist must have a thorough understanding of normal developmental skills in each subject area. *Criterion-referenced* systems of teaching (discussed in Chapter 3) embody the skills-development approach to remediation.

Critics have questioned the premise that a specific empirically derived hierarchy of skills exists. In the field of reading, for example, scholars note the lack of evidence to support this contention. Some students may be better able to learn by using a different set or ordering of skills (Pearson & Johnson, 1978; Downing, 1982).

The skills-development approach focuses on the analysis of the task to be learned rather than on the student who is to learn it. Because growth is assumed to proceed through a sequence of skills, each phase of developmental growth is likened to climbing the rungs on a ladder. The premise of this approach is that each rung must be touched in climbing to the top; the learner who misses some rungs may fall off.

Materials Approach

Publishers' materials become the basis of yet another category of remediation, guiding and directing the procedure of remediation. The basic decision within this approach is the choice of materials. Once this decision is made, the materials themselves, rather than the teacher, become the decision makers, guiding the skills sequence, providing practice activities, suggesting questions to be used, and giving step-by-step instructional procedures. The use of *Distar* is an example of this category of remediation.

Reliance on materials lessens the teacher's role. This is a disadvantage of the method since, as noted earlier in this chapter, clinical teaching should require constant and active decision making. Durkin (1974), after observing teachers of reading who followed the materials approach, noted that some of them had become educational clerks, allowing materials to dictate what was to be taught and how.

Nevertheless, publishers' materials can prove to be a valuable tool in remediation if they are not misused. Certainly, the clinical teacher should be familiar with a wide variety of materials.

Analysis of the Environmental Conditions Surrounding Learning

Behavioral Approaches

Another form of intervention is the *behavioral* approach. Unlike the categories discussed earlier—which analyze the student, the content to be learned, or the materials to be used—this approach concentrates on the environmental conditions surrounding learning. Based on principles of operant conditioning, the behavioral approach is used to remediate in two ways: by eliminating undesired behaviors and by establishing specific desired behaviors. Applications of the behavioral approach in learning disabilities include behavior modification techniques and applied behavior analysis.

Behavior modification is the application to human beings of the knowledge about animal behavior obtained through experimental psychology. As presented in Chapter 15, the theory states that if a response is rewarded (reinforced) when it occurs, it will tend to be repeated. Advocates of behavior modification are not concerned about the cause of a student's learning problem or how the student processes information or with a hierarchy of stages; rather, they focus on how the environment can be manipulated to bring about desired behavior. They do not search for presumptive underlying causes or explanations, but for ways of changing specific behavior.

Cases in which behavior-modification approaches to teaching were used indicate that manipulation of events that follow an act (reinforcements) improved the student's performance. Evidence of the success of the behavioral method is demonstrated by a series of graphs (Figure 4.3 in this chapter and Figure 15.2 in Chapter 15) showing the change in learning behavior.

Applied behavior analysis focuses on changing the environment of learning through directed teaching and monitoring the student's behavior on a continuous basis. This strategy can be effective both as an assessment technique (as described in Chapter 3) and as a teaching technique (as discussed later in this chapter). The success of the intervention that is the core of applied behavior analysis can be measured through the inspection of charts or graphs (Figure 4.3).

Some educators contend that behavior concepts of teaching are too narrow in scope (Hamilton, 1983), too confining for the student (K. Goodman, 1974), and do not offer a holistic style of learning (Smith, 1977). Smith believes that in the field of reading, for example, the skills that can be taught in this manner are splintered and trivial, and perhaps may not be necessary for successful reading per se. In addition to criticizing the theoretical foundations of behavioral approaches, teachers also find fault with their practical applications: they frequently complain that time does not permit the careful recording and monitoring required with the method.

Nonetheless, the field of learning disabilities benefits from behavioral approaches to teaching, and behavioral methods play a growing role in the field. Certainly, skill in both behavior modification and applied behavior analysis techniques should be among the competencies of all learning disabilities specialists (Lovitt, 1984).

Psychotherapeutic Approach

This category of remediation concentrates on the student's feelings and relationship with the teacher. The psychodynamics of remediation is too often lost in the labyrinth of materials, techniques, methods, modalities, and baseline data. These failing students are unhappy in the learning situation. Their frustrations, poor ego development, and feelings of inadequacy all lead to continued failure in learning. What is needed, this approach suggests, is to reverse this cycle by building feelings of success and establishing a healthy psychodynamic relationship between teacher and student.

Even if a child is well adjusted when entering school, continued failure in school learning is likely to have unfavorable effects. As the pupil gets older, these feelings of failure, frustration, and oversensitivity tend to increase. Consequently, in the learning-disabled adolescent, emotional problems are almost always in evidence. Many students with learning problems are, in fact, referred for psychological or psychiatric therapy.

Remediation thus involves the task of rebuilding the ego, fostering confidence and assurance, and letting students know that the teacher understands the problem and has confidence in their ability to learn and succeed. There are many reported cases of dramatic improvement in academic learning after a student had worked with a tutor who was untrained in the sophisticated skills and knowledge of the learning disabilities profession, yet able to establish a point of meaningful contact between teacher and student. Specific techniques are presented later in this chapter (in the section "Establishing a Therapeutic Relationship") and in Chapter 15.

The psychotherapeutic approach to remediation also has its critics. Despite the need for considering psychodynamic factors, many authorities question the overdependence on this approach alone. They point out that exclusive use of a psychotherapeutic approach may result in the creation of "happy failures," students who have learned to be content with their disabilities.

The emphasis in this approach to remediation, then, is on providing appropriate environmental conditions to improve the student's self-confidence and establish a healthy relationship with the teacher.

Pedagogical Approach

The last category of remediation has the old-fashioned title *pedagogy*. According to Cohen (1971), the major cause of reading failure is *dyspedagogia,* a term coined to indicate a lack of good teaching. It follows, therefore, that good teaching is itself a method of remediation. A number of research studies have concluded that the teacher is the most important variable in a pupil's learning (Bond & Dykstra, 1967). These studies have shown that students in certain classes in school did better than students in other classes, regardless of the methods or materials used, even when the data was controlled for intelligence and socioeconomic level. The most important component in these situations was not the materials or the methods but the teacher. Bateman (1974) suggests that the term *learning disabilities* be replaced by the term *teaching disabilities* to emphasize the shift in focus from something deviant or pathological within the student to inadequacies in the teacher and the teaching environment. Elkind (1983) refers to the "curriculum-disabled" student.

Despite this frequent observation that the teacher is the key ingredient for successful remediation, the research has not yet revealed precisely what qualities the successful teacher possesses. Is it empathy, kindness, ability to structure the class, enthusiasm, creativity, punctuality, ability to individualize instruction, consistency, knowledge of the field, love of children, diagnostic skills, familiarity with materials, competency in specific skills, clinical intuition, or possibly a judicious combination of all these qualities?

Ysseldyke and Algozzine (1982) state that we have not been able to define very well the behavior of good teachers. After a critical review of many studies of the competencies of effective special education teachers, they conclude that we still have little knowledge regarding the characteristics that make effective teachers. Without a clear answer to what qualities make the good teacher, the plea for "good teaching," although obviously important, is vague.

Implications of the Classification System

The classification system just presented, consisting of three kinds of analysis and nine categories, is not a rigid one. In practice these categories are not mutually exclusive, and teachers may use several concurrently. Each of the categories has strong arguments to support it; yet each is also vulnerable to criticism. Learning disabilities specialists must have a certain degree of knowledge, skill, and expertise in each of the categories but must also recognize the shortcomings and limitations of each. Each category of intervention has a contribution to make to the total system of clinical teaching.

Overdependence on one approach to remediation should be avoided. Such an error is exemplified in this fable (*A Fable for Teachers,* 1974):

A Fable for Teachers

Once upon a time the animals decided they must do something educational to help their young meet the problems of the world. A school was organized where they adopted a curriculum consisting of running, climbing, and swimming. To make it easier to administer, all of the animals took all the subjects. Of course, the duck was excellent in swimming—in fact he was better than the instructor; running, however, was a weak area for him. Therefore, he had to stay after school and drop swimming in order to practice running. Now, this was kept up until his webbed feet were badly worn and soon he became only average in swimming. However, average was an acceptable criterion in this school so no one was concerned about it—except, of course, the duck. While the rabbit was good in running, he was not up to par in swimming and suffered a nervous breakdown because of the makeup work required to improve his swimming. By the end of the year, an abnormal eel that could swim exceedingly well and also run and climb had the overall highest average and was consequently named valedictorian of the class.

The point of the fable presented on this page is that each student is different and that no one method can be relied on as *the* way for teaching in every case. After a five-year follow-up study of children with learning dis-abilities who were enrolled in special education classes, Koppitz (1972–73) concluded that "learning disabilities cannot be corrected or 'cured' by a specific teaching method or training technique. It is imperative that teachers have a wide range of instructional materials and techniques at their disposal and that they are imaginative and flexible enough to adapt these to the specific needs of their pupils" (p. 137).

Learning disabilities specialists should have knowledge and skill in each of the categories of intervention, but they should also be aware of the limita-tions of each.

Several of the intervention approaches of this classification model are discussed in greater depth in the rest of this chapter. Two approaches, one of them student-centered (psychological processing) and the other curriculum-centered (skills development), are discussed in the next section. An aspect of the behavioral approach is considered in the section on applied behavior analysis, and the psychotherapeutic approach is dealt with in the section on establishing a therapeutic relationship.

Task Analysis

Task analysis, an important concept for teaching learning-disabled students, is an analysis conducted by the teacher to obtain further information in order to understand the problem and teach the student properly. Two ways of carry-ing out this analysis are often suggested: (1) the *psychological-processing approach* to evaluate and analyze the student's processing abilities that are needed for the task; and (2) the *skills-development approach* to analyze and evaluate what is to be learned, that is, the task itself. The first analyzes the learner whereas the second analyzes the content to be learned. Each ap-proach reflects a different basic theoretical perspective of learning disabilities (see Chapter 6).

Psychological-processing Approach to Task Analysis

The psychological-processing approach to task analysis attempts to identify and analyze the processing abilities and disabilities of the learner as revealed through the learner's performance of the task. The key questions to be asked are "How does the student process information?" or "What are the student's processing dysfunctions?" The aim is to identify the psychological processes that are thought to be interfering with learning. Johnson (1967) suggests that two aspects of the task that the student is expected to accomplish be analyzed: the manner of *presentation* of the task and the expected mode of *response*. Is the student's failure caused by a lack of understanding of the task or by an inability to perform the task?

From this perspective, the task can be analyzed in a number of ways: (1) which perceptual modalities are needed for understanding and performing the task? These modalities could be auditory, visual, kinesthetic, or tactile. (2) Does the task require a single perceptual modality or several and must the student shift from one modality to another (for instance, from auditory to visual, or from visual to motor)? (3) Is the task primarily *verbal* or *nonverbal?* (4) Does it require *social* or *nonsocial* judgments? (5) What *skills and levels of involvement* (perception, memory, symbolization, conceptualization) are needed?

If a student fails a task, then the teacher analyzes whether failure is due to the manner of presentation or to the mode of response expected, and the teacher probes for the other factors that account for the failure.

For example, two spelling tasks might differ significantly in presentation and mode of response: one spelling test might require the pupil to underline the correct spelling from among four choices, and another might require the pupil to spell orally a spoken word. The visual-memory, language, and motor requirements of these two spelling tasks are quite different.

As another example, two pictures in a workbook exercise represent a *ball* and a *rake.* The teacher orally asks the child to circle the one that rhymes with *bake.* If the student fails, one can analyze the task to discover why. The manner of presentation was verbal and auditory (from the teacher) and visual (from the page). The child had to understand language, including the meaning of *rhyme* and *circle,* follow directions, and have good visual perception of the two-dimensional graphic representation of objects on the page. The mode of response was motor. Prerequisites for performing the task included previous knowledge of and experience with the items represented by the pictures, and adequate auditory memory of the sounds of the words represented by the pictures and the words spoken by the teacher, the skill to compare words and identify rhymes, and the motor ability to draw a circle. Failure to complete the task could have been due to a lack of any of these requirements.

In another task, the student is required to match a printed geometrical form with one of three choices by circling the matching form. This task, a common one in readiness tests and exercises, can be analyzed as being on the perceptual level, nonverbal and nonsocial. The presentation is visual, and the response is motor.

The use of such task analysis in examining workbooks and test materials often reveals that the name of the exercise has little to do with the abilities needed to understand and perform the task. Clinical teaching requires the ability to understand the processing demands of the task and to compare these with the abilities of the student.

Skills-Development Approach to Task Analysis

The second approach to task analysis is oriented toward analyzing the task itself so that learning experiences can be designed to direct a student to reach specific objectives. Salvia and Ysseldyke (1981) maintain that the skills approach advocates assessment of academic skills development and differential instruction tailored to move the student to the desired level of skill achievement. The emphasis is on competent skills and their integration into complex terminal behaviors. The skill of buttoning, for example, entails a sequence of component sequential subskills: grasping the button, aligning the button with the buttonhole, and so forth.

This approach places relatively little emphasis on discovering the student's abilities or disabilities but stresses the specific educational tasks to be taught. The important questions behind curriculum planning using this approach are (1) What specific educational tasks are important for the student to learn? (2) What are the sequential steps in learning this task? and (3) What specific behaviors does the student need to perform this task?

In other words, an educational objective is operationally determined. For example, reading may be the objective that is operationally defined as pronouncing certain words. The desired educational task is broken up into small component parts or sequential steps, that is, learning certain initial consonants and short vowels and blending certain sounds into words. Finally, specific desired behaviors of the student are determined for each step.

There are four steps in the skills approach to task analysis.

Step 1: Clearly state the learning task (behavioral objective).

Step 2: List all the components or subskills necessary to meet these objectives and to place these subskills in a logical teaching sequence.

Step 3: Test informally to determine what subskills the student can already perform.

Step 4: Begin teaching in sequential order the next skill in the task-analysis hierarchy.

For instance, if the objective is to have the student saw a piece of wood, this could be the instructional sequence: start with soft wood and move to hard wood; start with pregrooving the wood for the student and move to having the student make his or her own groove; start from holding the end of the wood for the student to giving him or her complete independence in sawing (Siegel & Siegel, 1977).

Integrating the Two Approaches to Task Analysis

The two approaches to task analysis—psychological processing and skills development—are often debated and contrasted in an effort to determine the better method (Salvia & Ysseldyke, 1981). As noted in Chapter 6, this debate reflects basic underlying differences in theoretical perspectives about learning disabilities. Teachers, however, need not be pressured into choosing one or the other. In fact, clinical teachers should be proficient in both types of task analysis. They must know the sequence of skills development in academic subjects and be able to analyze the tasks from this perspective. At the same time, they must also be able to shift the orientation from the subject matter to the learner and analyze the student's way of processing information. The two approaches can be combined. Siegel and Gold (1982) suggest that the clinical teacher should (1) select a relevant and appropriate task, (2) know or create a specific sequence of steps based on the hierarchy of competencies needed to perform the task, and (3) make the necessary modifications based on the individual student's profile of strengths and weaknesses. The clinical teacher must be able to identify the demands that a task will make on a student in order to prepare the student to meet each demand.

Competencies in both approaches to task analysis, then, should be part of the professional repertory of the clinical teacher:

1. *Task analysis of the learner* involves specifying how a particular student functions—the things the student can and cannot do, psychological-processing areas of strengths and weaknesses, and attitudes and emotions as they affect learning.
2. *Task analysis of the curriculum* involves knowing the content of developmental skills and the hierarchy of components needed to perform such skills.
3. *Relating the curriculum task to the learner* involves the ability to coordinate data gathered from the analysis of the learner with the analysis of curriculum skills to be learned.
4. *Making appropriate clinical decisions* involves the ability to decide on ways of using this information to bring about improvement in the student.

Practicing teachers typically report that they see no conflict between the two methods and are able to readily incorporate both in their teaching. For example, they will teach observable reading skills, such as word-recognition skills, but also use the information they have about a student's difficulty in hearing phoneme sounds and making auditory discriminations between two similar sounds. Such information about the student makes the teacher more sensitive to the problems the student is encountering in learning word-recognition skills. The student may still have to learn phonics because that is a stage individuals must go through in acquiring the skill of reading. But understanding the student's problem in acquiring this skill and taking that problem into account while teaching is what makes the difference between teaching and clinical teaching.

Applied Behavior Analysis

Chapter 3 introduced the technique of *applied behavior analysis* as it is used in assessment. The process requires direct, daily observations and monitoring of the student's behavior, thus, promoting the interrelationship of testing and teaching. The progress observed in the continuous monitoring directs the course of teaching. The technique has been used to teach reading, arithmetic, spelling, writing, and social abilities. Lovitt (1975) describes the steps involved in using applied behavior analysis in the teaching of students with learning disabilities.

1. *Identify the precise behavior* that should be taught to the student. For example, a goal might be that the student recognize sight words or write spelling words correctly.
2. *Establish the appropriate level* to which that behavior should be taught. For example, the level might be set at the recognition of fifty sight words or at the attainment of 90 percent correct answers on a twenty-word spelling test.
3. *Arrange the situation* in which the identified behavior will occur. Arrange the time, prepare the materials, and decide on a monitoring procedure.
4. *Gather base-line data* over a few days. Observe and record daily the behavior under question to see how the student performs before introducing an instructional intervention technique.
5. *Study base-line data* in terms of correct and incorrect responses, error patterns, and so on.
6. *Analyze the student's performance* in terms of (a) whether the student cannot or will not perform the task, and (b) whether the student is at the acquisition stage (just beginning to learn the task) or the proficiency stage (learning to do the task with quickness and ease).
7. *Decide if the behavior should be changed* and instruction is necessary.
8. *Select an intervention teaching technique* that is as natural and simple as possible. There are two general types of intervention teaching techniques: contingent and noncontingent. A *contingent event* happens only if a student does something; for example, a reward is given if the student says a word correctly. A *noncontingent event* occurs if it happens regardless of the quality of the student's behavior; for example, the teacher demonstrates the correct way of doing an arithmetic problem regardless of whether the answer was right or wrong.
9. *Use the intervention teaching technique* for a few days and observe and monitor the student's behavior. Make decisions about continuing the technique.
10. *Remove the teaching technique* when performance level reaches the criterion mark. Observe what happens to behavior after removal of the technique.
11. *Help the student to generalize* newly acquired behaviors.

Figure 4.3 shows an example of applied behavior analysis. In this example, the objective was to increase the rate of verbal interaction and physical

FIGURE 4.3

Example of the Applied Behavior Analysis Approach to Monitoring Task Analysis: Percent of Observations in Which Verbal Interaction and Physical Contact Occurred

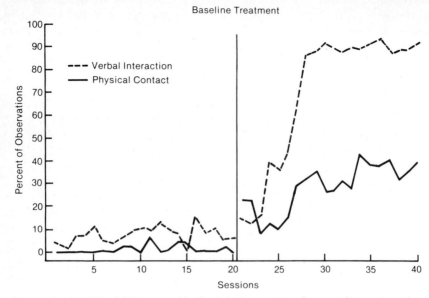

Source: A. Ford and J. Ford, "Using a cognitive discrimination exercise to foster social interaction with a withdrawn preschooler," *Directive Teacher* (Summer 1979), 24–25. Reprinted from the *Directive Teacher,* NCEMMH, The Ohio State University.

contact in a boy of five years six months who exhibited low behaviors in these areas. Students in the class were given twenty plastic cards with various complex geometric designs. When the teacher showed a sample card, the students were to sort through their cards and find a card that matched the sample shown by the teacher. In the base-line period of twenty sessions, the students were given contingent reinforcers of praise and food upon individual performance of the matching exercise. During the treatment period of twenty sessions, the rewards were given for group performance; that is, all students received praise and food when every student in the group had correctly matched the cards. Figure 4.3 shows that the pupil under study learned to increase verbal interaction and physical contact with the group during the treatment phase.

Establishing a Therapeutic Relationship

Clinical teaching does not imply a mechanistic or unsympathetic view of the student. It does demand objectivity to analyze the way a student learns and the skills to be taught and to implement specific teaching plans, but it also requires a subjective understanding of the pupil as an individual—as a whole individual with feelings, emotions, and attitudes. Abrams (1970) refers to this emotional dimension of learning disabilities as "ego status," or self-concept.

Within such a framework, Roswell and Natchez (1971) present a sensitive and empathetic description of the feelings of the student with learning disabilities. They point out that this student is a lost and frightened person who has often suffered years of despair, discouragement, and frustration. Feelings of rejection, failure, and hopelessness about the future are always present, affecting every subject in school and every aspect of the student's life.

> For twelve long years of school and after, he contends with a situation for which he can find no satisfactory solution. When schoolwork becomes insurmountable, the child has few alternative resources. An adult dissatisfied with his job may seek a position elsewhere or find solace outside of his work; he may even endure these difficulties because of a high salary or other compensations. For a child who fails, however, there is no escape. He is subjected to anything from degradation to long-suffering tolerance. Optimum conditions may lessen the child's misery, but proof of his inadequacies appears daily in the classroom. In the end, he is held in low esteem, not only by his classmates, but also by his family. (p. 2)

The clinical teacher should realize that a learning disability may influence every aspect of the student's world. Deploring such statements as "There's no point in trying to teach until the emotion problems are cured," Roswell and Natchez note that clinical teaching can provide therapeutic results. Experience has shown that success in learning has a beneficial effect on personality, enhances feelings of self-worth, and rekindles an interest in learning. In fact, these authors refer to teaching that results in such changes as "psychotherapeutic." In addition to knowledge and skill in the use of clinical teaching techniques, the clinical teacher must understand the emotional impact of failure on the student.

> Not only are his parents and teachers displeased with him, but their anxiety often becomes uncontrollable. The parents wonder whether their child is retarded or just plain lazy. If they are assured that his intelligence is normal, even the most loving parents can become so alarmed at their child's inability to learn that they tend to punish, scold and threaten, or even reward with the hope of producing desired results. Teachers also feel frustrated by their inability to reach the child.
>
> It is under such adverse conditions that the child tries his best to function. When he continues to fail, he can become overwhelmed and devastated. These feelings linger with him after school and on weekends. The notion that he does not measure up hangs over him relentlessly. (p. 68)

An important goal of clinical teaching, therefore, is to motivate students who have been failing to build their self-concept and to interest them in

It is very important for the clinical teacher to develop a strong relationship based on acceptance and respect with the learning-disabled student.   *(Elizabeth Wilcox)*

learning. To accomplish such ends, Roswell and Natchez suggest consideration of the following "psychotherapeutic principles" of teaching:

Rapport   A good relationship between the teacher and student is an essential first step in educational therapy. In fact, it has been said that much of the success in clinical teaching depends on the establishment of rapport. There must be total acceptance of the pupil as a human being worthy of respect in spite of failure to learn. A good relationship implies compassion without overinvolvement, understanding without indulgence, and a genuine concern for the student's development. Since the student lives in a continuing atmosphere of rejection and failure, the relationship with the clinical teacher should provide a new atmosphere of confidence and acceptance. It is extremely difficult for a parent to retain an accepting yet objective attitude, and the student becomes very sensitive to the parents' disappointment. Parents are often unaware of their child's reaction to their efforts. For example, one well-intentioned father, who was observed in a public library helping his son pick out a book and listening to him read, was overheard to say, "I'll tell you that word one more time, and then I don't want you to forget it for the rest of your life." This hardly reflects an attitude conducive to learning.

Collaboration   Involvement of both the pupil and the teacher in their joint task provides another step toward psychotherapeutic treatment. Pupils should be involved in both analysis of their problems and evaluation of their performance. In the same collaborative spirit, the student should take an active role in designing lessons and choosing materials.

Structure   Both structure and limits are important elements in teaching the learning disabled because they introduce order into their chaotic lives. Many of these students need such order and welcome it. Structure can be provided in many aspects of clinical teaching—in the physical environment, in the routine sequence of activities, and in the manner in which lessons are taught.

Sincerity   Children are skillful in detecting insincerity. Honest appraisal is necessary. Children soon detect dishonesty if told that they are doing well when they know they are not. Instead, the teacher might try to minimize anxiety about errors by saying that many students have similar difficulties and by conveying a confidence that together they will find ways to overcome them.

Success   Achieving goals in learning and acquiring a feeling of success are of prime importance to the learning disabled. This means that the materials selected must be at a difficulty level that will permit success.

Learning-disabled students are reluctant to read books at the appropriate difficulty level for them if the books are obviously labeled for a grade level lower than their own. Rather than identifying difficulty level by grade, the publishers of some new materials have identified difficulty levels by color-cuing the reading selections. Fourth graders who would refuse to read a second-grade book can now meet success because they do not heistate to read material at the purple level.

In addition to carefully selecting the level of difficulty of teaching materials, the teacher can also make students conscious of success and progress by praising good work, by using extrinsic rewards as reinforcement, and by developing visual records of progress through charts and graphs.

Interest   The chance of successful achievement is greatly increased when the teacher provides materials based on the student's special interests. Such interests can be determined through conversations with the pupil or by administering interest inventories. If reading material can be found in the student's area of interest, this may prove to be a strong motivation for learning. However, it is frequently difficult to find material in the student's area of interest that is also written at the appropriate difficulty level, particularly if knowledge of the subject is quite advanced. In that situation, books written on the student's difficulty level are too simple in content and therefore not interesting.

Middle-grade boys with an interest in Greek and Roman mythology have been observed to improve their reading skills greatly by devouring all the myths. The first real interest in reading shown by some high school students is stimulated by the necessity of passing a written test in order to get a driver's license. Utilizing this interest, some teachers have successfully used the driver's manual to teach reading. Series books have been the impetus for other youngsters to become readers. An interest in a series such as the Freddy books, Landmark books, or Nancy Drew mysteries or an interest in an author, television series, or movie based on a book can spark reading if the clinical teacher can capture this interest. Once a real interest is tapped, great progress can be made. One eighth-grade boy found the first book he ever read from cover to cover, *The Incredible Journey,* so fascinating that he was completely oblivious to class changes, ringing bells, and classroom incidents from the time he started the book until it was completed.

One teacher reported as follows about a boy with a reading disability who became interested in the simplified Dolch version of *Robinson Crusoe:*

> He became so immersed in the story that he would grab the book as soon as he entered the room for our daily session. At first he couldn't allow me to read any part of the story, even trying phonetically to read new words. But as the story became more exciting, he'd ask me to tell him the words because he did not want to lose the thread of the plot while seeking the correct word.

Once in a while dramatic changes occur in a student's attitude and outlook because of clinical teaching. When such changes occur because of a book the child has read, it is sometimes called *bibliotherapy.* Learning about the experiences of others fosters release and insight, as well as hope and encouragement. Fairy tales, for example, have great appeal for many children, and primary teachers are aware of the sheer delight and excitement of children when they read a simple version of the classic themes in their reading books. Students with personal problems (for example, children who are short, fat, unpopular, or physically or academically handicapped) identify with characters in books suffering similar problems and are helped by the characters' resolution of them.

One boy in a learning disabilities group in seventh grade who was without goals, direction, or adult identification, was able to identify with Houdini, the great escape artist. He read all the books he could find on Houdini in the school library and in the public library. At the same time, personality and attitude changes as well as tremendous improvement in reading were observed by his teachers. The boy who found an interest in *Robinson Crusoe* identified with the chief character and his predicaments. His teacher reported:

> Many times he would tell what he thought he would do if he were in a particular situation that Crusoe was in, and then he would be so delighted that the main character had done similarly. If Crusoe had taken another course of action, we would have to decide whose plan was better.

The right book can be a powerful tool to build interest, provide motivation, and improve reading.

CASE STUDY   PART II

Rita G.

Stage 3: The Multidisciplinary Evaluation

The multidisciplinary team consisted of the school psychologist, the school nurse, social worker, and the learning disabilities teacher. Each member of the team was responsible for administering certain tests and gathering specified evaluation information. A summary of the multidisciplinary evaluation appears below.

Classroom Observation The learning disabilities teacher and the social worker observed Rita in the third-grade class. The learning disabilities teacher's observation took place during an arithmetic lesson. Mr. Martinez was giving the class practice in solving word problems in two-digit addition and subtraction, using place value. He would read the problem to the class; students were expected to visualize the situation and then perform the calculations on paper to find the answer. The lesson was followed with practice on similar written word story problems in a workbook, and students were assigned to complete five problems. Rita did not volunteer the answer to any of the oral problems, and she did not write the calculations to find the answer to the problems during the lesson. In the seatwork portion of the lesson, Rita attempted the first problem but had difficulty staying on task. She did

not even attempt the other four problems. Inspection of her work showed she could not line up the numbers in the addition problem and consequently made mistakes in addition. She had many erasures and crossouts.

The social worker observed Rita during a fifteen-minute "free" period. During this time none of her classmates interacted with her, and she just stared out of the window for the entire period.

Auditory and Visual Acuity The school nurse tested Rita for hearing and visual impairments.

Hearing On the *Beltone Audiometer*, Rita's hearing tested within the normal range.

Vision On the *Keystone Telebinocular Vision Screening Test*, Rita's vision was tested on three occasions. Each time she had some difficulty in fusion in both far-point vision and near-point section vision. The school nurse recommended that Rita be referred to an eye specialist for further testing.

Developmental and Educational History The social worker interviewed Mrs. G. to obtain the case history information. Rita is the older of two daughters in an English-speaking household. Her father is a salesman; her mother a homemaker. Rita's birth and prenatal history were reported as normal. Her birthweight was seven pounds, ten ounces.

Rita had a high fever at six months of age and was hospitalized for two days. She had chicken pox at age five. Otherwise her medical history appears to be normal.

Mrs. G. said that motor development seemed to be normal; she crawled at six months and walked at one year, but she seemed to fall and bump into things frequently. She had much difficulty learning to feed herself and learning to dress herself. She still has trouble with certain items, such as tying shoelaces. She did not like to play with "educational" types of toys that had to be put together. Mrs. G. described her as "clutzy." Language development seemed to be normal; she babbled at six months, said her first word at about one year, and used two-word sentences at eighteen months.

She attended a nursery school at age four, but, according to Mrs. G., was not enthusiastic about going to preschool. Rita began to experience problems in kindergarten. The kindergarten teacher told Mrs. G. that Rita showed difficulty in fine motor coordination and seemed "immature" for a five-year old. The first-grade teacher said she did not always pay attention and did not complete her work. The second-grade teacher said she did not try hard enough and her work was very "sloppy." Rita does not have any close friends and usually plays with younger children.

Mrs. G. felt the major problem now was that she was failing third grade and that she did not want to go to school.

Measures of Intellectual Aptitude The school psychologist administered the *Wechsler Intelligence Scale for Children-Revised (WISC-R)*. Rita's overall performance was within the average range with a Full Scale IQ of 109. Her Verbal IQ was 128 and her Performance IQ was 87. These WISC-R scores suggest a discrepancy between the verbal and performance abilities. Her aptitude strengths were in areas that use language; her weaknesses were in tests in which she had to visualize objects in space or plan and manipulate objects,

and in arithmetic. (The mean for the IQ scores on the WISC-R is 100; the mean for the subtest scores on the WISC-R is 10.) The school psychologist noted that she seemed to give up as soon as items became difficult and did not seem to have any system for attacking challenging problems. When items became hard for her, she seemed helpless and simply said, "I can't do that. It's too hard for me." Her WISC-R scores were as follows: WISC-R Full Scale IQ 109; Verbal IQ 128; Performance IQ 87.

Verbal subtest scaled scores

Information	13
Comprehension	11
Arithmetic	8
Vocabulary	14
Similarities	14
Digit Span	13

Performance subtest scaled scores

Picture arrangement	7
Picture completion	8
Block design	8
Object assembly	7
Coding	6
Mazes	5

Present Levels of Academic Functioning The following academic tests were given by the learning disabilities teacher: *Peabody Individual Achievement Test* (PIAT), *Key Math Diagnostic Arithmetic Test, Brigance Inventory of Basic Skills, Woodcock Reading Mastery Tests,* and the *Boder Test for Reading-Spelling Patterns.* In addition, her classroom work was observed and analyzed. Her performance in mathematics, reading, handwriting, and spelling is summarized below.

Mathematics Mathematics testing included the mathematics tests of the *PIAT, Key Math Diagnostic Arithmetic Test,* and *Brigance Inventory of Basic Skills.* Rita scored substantially below grade level in all these mathematics tests. Her grade placement at the time of the test was 3.8, and her mathematics scores ranged between grade 1.8 and 2.5, making her between one and one-half year to two years below her present grade in mathematics. Her greatest mathematics problems were in the areas of numerical reasoning, word problems. She also did poorly in addition, subtraction and multiplication. Her scores were low in fractions and division, but she has not had instruction in these areas in the classroom.

Reading   Rita was given the reading tests of the *Brigance Inventory of Basic Skills,* the *PIAT,* the *Woodcock Reading Mastery Tests,* and the *Standard Reading Inventory* to test reading achievement. In general, Rita scored satisfactorily in tests of word recognition, but her performance dropped considerably when reading comprehension was required. When she was observed during the reading, she seemed to lose her place and had difficulty concentrating on the material. Her word identification and phonics skills and her reading vocabulary are adequate. Difficulties in reading appear when she is required to use higher conceptual skills in reading comprehension. Her reading comprehension is at the independent reading level of second grade. Her word recognition skills are at the fourth-grade level.

Handwriting   Rita's handwriting skills were assessed with the *Brigance Inventory of Basic Skills* and through observation. Handwriting poses a major problem for her. The third-grade handwriting curriculum calls for shifting from manuscript to cursive writing. However, Rita has resisted making the change and asked Mr. Martinez if she can continue using manuscript writing. She is left-handed and has always had much difficulty performing this visual-motor task. Her written papers are a painstaking task for her to complete and require much effort and time. Even then, the final product is usually illegible and has a very sloppy appearance. She begins many letters from the bottom to the top of a line. Tall letters are the same size as small letters. Her pencil grasp is unusual, and she keeps her nonwriting right hand in a folded tense position. Written expression could not be tested because of her extremely poor handwriting skills.

Spelling   Rita's spelling was tested with the spelling tests of the *PIAT,* the *Brigance Inventory of Basic Skills,* and the *Boder Test of Reading-Spelling Patterns.* She scored at the second-grade level. Analysis of her spelling errors showed that she usually spelled words according to phonic rules, for example, *frend* for *friend, laf* for *laugh,* and *tok* for *talk.* She showed poor visual memory for irregularly spelled words.

Adaptive Behavior   Rita was given the *AAMD Adaptive Behavior Scale—Public School Version* by the social worker. Her lowest scores were in the areas of independent functioning, vocational activity, responsibility and socialization. The results supported her mother's comments that Rita relies on other people to tell her what to do, and that she has made no friends and plays only with her young sister. It also supports the observation of Mr. Martinez that Rita lacks the motivation to organize herself to complete school work and will often "just sit there."

Learning Strengths and Weaknesses
Rita was given the *Beery Test of Motor Integration* by the learning disabilities teacher. Her score was equivalent to that of a six-year-old, or three full years below her chronological age. Although she could copy simple designs such as the circle and plus sign, she had difficulty with the triangle, diamond, and other more complicated shapes. She appears to have a weakness in visual perception abilities.

Her auditory discrimination was tested with the *Goldman Fristoe-Woodcock Test of Auditory Discrimination.* Her scores were adequate on this test, suggesting a strength in auditory discrimination.

Other learning strengths included good phonics skills, an adequate sight vocabulary, and good verbal skills.

All the specialists on the multidisciplinary team noted weaknesses in attention and concentration. Also, they noted that Rita lacked cognitive strategies to approach learning situations. She had become a passive learner and did not actively seek out ways to enhance her learning.

Interest Inventory   The learning disabilities teacher gave Rita an informal interest inventory. Rita indicated that she likes to watch television and eat. Her playmates include her younger sister and her sister's friend. Rita does not receive an allowance but earns money by taking out the garbage. She spends the money she earns on candy. In response to the question "Do you like school?" she said, "Sometimes and sometimes not." After some prompting, she admitted that a good school day meant the teacher had not yelled at her. Her favorite subject is music. She dislikes gym and arithmetic.

Note: The case study of Rita G. is continued in Chapter 5.

Summary

- This chapter reviewed the clinical teaching portion of the assessment/teaching process.

- The concept of tailoring learning experiences to the unique needs of a particular student is the essence of clinical teaching.

- The clinical teaching process can be viewed as a five-stage cycle of decision making that consists of assessment, planning, implementation, evaluation, and modification of the assessment.

- The clinical teacher considers the student's ecological environments: the home environment, the school environment, the social environment, and the cultural environment. Each has an impact on the student's learning.

- One of the critical roles available to the clinical teacher is that of changing certain variables in the school setting: space, time, multiplicity of factors, difficulty level, language, and interpersonal relationships. By modifying these elements the teacher controls certain variables that affect learning.

- A classification system of intervention classifies approaches according to the type of analysis performed: analysis of the student, analysis of content, and analysis of the environment.

- Task analysis is another strategy for clinical teaching. There are two perspectives to task analysis: the psychological-processing approach, which examines the student and how he or she processes information, and the skills-development approach, which analyzes the content of the task to be learned. Although professionals have debated the merits of each approach, many teachers find it useful to combine elements from both in their actual practice.

• Applied behavior analysis provides one approach to clinical teaching. An eleven-step process is suggested that is based on daily observation and monitoring in order to (1) identify behavior, (2) establish appropriate goals, (3) arrange the learning situation, (4) gather base-line data, (5) study base-line data, (6) analyze performance, (7) decide on necessary behavior changes, (8) select an intervention technique, (9) use the intervention technique, (10) remove the technique, and (11) help the student to generalize the new behavior.

• Clinical teaching requires not only a sound foundation in methods and practices, but also the ability to establish an understanding and empathetic relationship with the pupil. Six therapeutic principles—rapport, collaboration, structure, sincerity, success, and interest—can help in creating such a relationship.

Key Terms

remediation	psychotherapeutic relationship	behavioral approach
clinical teaching		rapport
task analysis	ecological system	psychological processing
applied behavior analysis	base-line data	skills sequence

Systems for Delivering Educational Services

Chapter **5**

*T*his chapter examines topics related to school placements, the school settings for delivering educational services to learning-disabled students. Specifically, the topics include (1) certain concepts important to special education services, (2) various placement options in the schools for learning-disabled students, (3) the role of the learning disabilities teacher, and (4) the parent-school relationship, including ways in which parents can effectively help in their child's education. This chapter also concludes the case of Rita G.

Important Concepts for Delivering Special Education Services

A critical component in the assessment-teaching process is the decision about the placement or setting in which the student will receive educational services. The case conference team specifies the recommended educational placement as part of the IEP. Thus, the special education law, PL 94–142, and its counterpart in each state heavily influence the types of delivery systems that a school provides. Three concepts stemming from this law that particularly affect the delivery of special education services for learning-disabled students are the continuum of alternative placements, the least restrictive environment, and mainstreaming.

Continuum of Alternative Placements

PL 94–142 requires that schools provide a *continuum of alternative placements* for handicapped students. This means that schools must establish an array of educational placements to meet the varied needs of exceptional students. Among the delivery options for providing instruction to learning-disabled students are regular classes, resource room classes, self-contained special classes, special schools, and other types of placements that may be needed.

Table 5.1 contains a brief list, with explanations, of alternative placements, ordered from the least restrictive to the most restrictive. The term *restrictive* as used in this context has to do with placement with nonhandicapped students. Being with nonhandicapped students is considered less restrictive; being with only handicapped students is considered more restrictive. Factors taken into account in placement decisions include the student's academic achievement levels and chronological age, the individualization and intensity of intervention needed by the student, the student's level of schooling (primary, intermediate, or secondary), and the severity of the learning disability.

TABLE 5.1 **Continuum of Alternative Placements**

Regular Class: A general type of class in which most students receive instruction, including most classes other than those that are composed of handicapped children.

Indirect Services Within Regular Class: Support services to the regular class teacher to enable the handicapped child to perform in a regular classroom setting.

Direct Services and Instruction Within the Regular Class: Activities concerned with the teaching-learning process that are provided to the handicapped student by special education personnel within the regular class.

Resource Room Services: Those activities provided in an instructional setting designed or adapted as a place where handicapped children receive a part of their schooling.

Self-contained Special Class: A class having the same special education teacher for all or most of the daily session and composed of handicapped children, for whom a program of special education is provided.

Private Day School: A school that is controlled by an individual or by an agency other than the local, state, or federal government, and usually is supported by other than public funds. The operation of the school's program rests with other than publicly elected or appointed officials. Students attend private day schools during a part of the day, as distinguished from a residential school where students are boarded and lodged as well as taught.

Special Public Day School: A nonresidential school attended by handicapped children where a program of special education is provided. This type of school is operated by publicly elected or appointed school officials who have control over the school's programs and activities and is supported primarily by public funds.

Public Residential School Facility: An educational institution in which students are boarded and lodged as well as taught. It is supported by public funds and operated by publicly elected or appointed school officials who control the school's programs and activities.

Private Residential School Facility: An educational institution in which students are boarded and lodged as well as taught. It is controlled by an individual or an agency other than local, state, or federal government, and usually is supported by other than public funds. The operation of the school's program rests with other than publicly elected or appointed officials.

Hospital Program: Formal instructional activities provided in a hospital.

Homebound Instruction: Individual instruction by a teacher usually at the home of a student who is unable to attend classes.

Note: This list of educational placements or environments is adapted from a reporting form used by the Bureau of Education for the Handicapped, U.S. Office of Education, for PL 94–142. The placements are ranked from least restrictive to most restrictive environment.

Source: J. Lerner, D. Dawson, and L. Horvath. *Cases in learning and behavior problems: A guide to individualized education programs* (Boston: Houghton Mifflin, 1980), p. 343. Copyright © 1980 by Houghton Mifflin Company. Used by permission.

FIGURE 5.1
A Model of the Continuum of Educational Program Alternatives in Relation to Restrictiveness and Severity

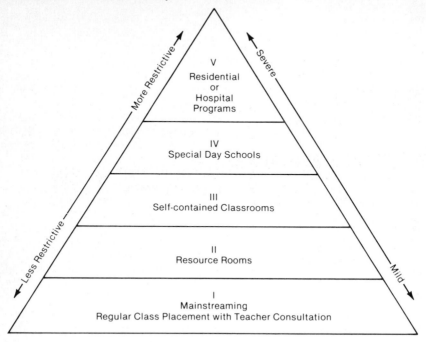

Least Restrictive Environment

The writers of PL 94–142 recognized that successful handicapped adults have learned to function comfortably in the larger society of the nonhandicapped world. The intent of the law, therefore, is to help prepare handicapped students for that integration through experiences in school with nonhandicapped peers. The feature of PL 94–142 designed to assure this integrated experience is referred to as the *least restrictive environment*. As stated in PL 94–142, "to the extent appropriate, handicapped students are to be educated with nonhandicapped students." This means that placement decisions must reflect consideration of the least restrictive environment for each student. As noted earlier, the more the placement includes nonhandicapped students, the less restrictive that environment is considered to be.

The diagram in Figure 5.1 illustrates several of the most common placement options in relation to the restrictiveness of the environment and to the severity of the learning disability. This is a version of the cascade model of the continuum of alternative placements first suggested by Deno (1970). Each level of the model, beginning with Level I and progressing through Level V, represents an increasingly restrictive placement in terms of diminishing contact with nonhandicapped students. In terms of severity, students with mild learning disabilities would be likely to receive services in Levels I or II (the

As mainstreaming flourishes, regular classroom teachers must become sensitized to the needs of the many special students they will meet in their classes.

(Jean-Claude Lejeune/Stock, Boston)

regular class or resource rooms); students with severe learning disabilities would probably receive services in Level III (the self-contained classroom). In many cases, the team recommends services from several of these placement options concurrently; for example, the self-contained class and the resource room. As a particular student progresses in learning, changes in the educational setting may be necessary so that placements suit new educational needs.

Some special educators have been critical of this interpretation of "least restrictive environment." They point out that for many learning-disabled students who cannot function in an environment with regular students, the *least* restrictive placement under the law may actually be the *most* restrictive for that student in terms of an environment for learning (Heron & Skinner, 1981).

Mainstreaming

The practice known as *mainstreaming* stems from the concept of the least restrictive environment. It is the social and instructional integration of handicapped students into a regular education class for at least a portion of the school day (Schulz & Turnbull, 1983; Schwartz, 1984). However, the term *mainstreaming* is not mentioned in PL 94–142 and is not synonymous with the least restrictive environment. The intent of the law is to provide educational experiences for handicapped students in a setting with nonhandicapped society wherever possible; it is not the intent of the law to place all handicapped students into regular classes.

In practice, mainstreaming takes several forms. In some situations, no direct special education services are provided by special educators, and the student receives all instruction in the regular classroom from the regular classroom teacher. In other situations, the special education teacher provides various kinds of assistance both to the regular teacher and to the special student within the regular class. In still other cases, the student is in the regular classroom for most of the time but also receives instruction in a special education resource room. There is a nationwide trend toward reducing the number of self-contained learning disabilities classes and increasing mainstreaming programs. It has been pointed out, however, that by excluding the self-contained program as a possible alternative form, a school no longer offers the most appropriate placement for many students. For some students, particularly those with severe learning disabilities, placement in a mainstreaming setting may become a complex failure-producing situation. A self-contained classroom may be the delivery system that best meets such students' needs.

Reasons for Mainstreaming

A number of reasons underlie the development of mainstreaming and its rapid implementation in the schools (Houck & Sherman, 1979).

1. *Reducing isolation.* Today, all handicapped individuals have the right and opportunity to take part in the mainstream of society. Students who spend their school day in an isolated special education environment are deprived of the opportunity to learn how to live and interact with normal peers, skills they will need when their schooling is over and they are out in the world.
2. *Detrimental effects of labeling.* Labeling and classification can serve many useful purposes. Indeed, federal regulations require classification according to category before funding is provided. But the labeling process creates many difficulties. Labels attached to students placed in a categorically isolated class may have detrimental effects on the student's feelings. Reger (1979, p. 532) asks: "Why is it necessary for a child to be labeled— in effect called a derogatory name—before help can be offered?" Labeling has been called stigmatizing. Worse, if it serves to impose limits on teacher expectancies and reinforces the learning problem, it can become a self-fulfilling prophecy (Rosenthal & Jacobson, 1968).

3. *Legislation and litigation.* As noted earlier, PL 94–142 requires that students be placed in the least restrictive environment, that is, with nonhandicapped students, to the extent appropriate. Thus, the law supports the concept of mainstreaming. In addition, parents have brought class action suits against schools, charging that special education placement was unjustifiable and discriminatory. In many cases this charge was substantiated, and such lawsuits have encouraged the mainstreaming movement.

4. *Trend toward integration of regular and special education.* Mainstreaming provides a way of bridging the gap between special and regular education. Changes in the philosophy of regular education make it more adaptable to the problems of the atypical student and more concerned with individual differences. Today's schools have more flexible organizational patterns, better trained teachers, more ancillary school personnel, and a greater variety of teaching materials and media. Special and regular educators have the opportunity to work to gether, and mainstreaming is a vehicle for enhancing this cooperative effort.

5. *Cost-effectiveness programming.* Administrative efforts are geared toward giving special education services to the greatest number of students for the least cost. Administrators have been accused in some instances of viewing mainstreaming as a way to cut costs rather than as a way to improve the education of the learning disabled. Mainstreaming can be effective only if it is carefully planned and has the needed support services and materials. It should not be viewed solely as a way to save money.

Problems to Be Solved in Mainstreaming

Although most educators praise the concept of mainstreaming, certain problems have emerged in its implementation. Some mainstreaming programs are instituted without sufficient preparation, planning, follow-up, and support. Because of the lack of preparation and training, many regular classroom teachers view mainstreaming with misgivings. Teachers should not be expected to have all the skills and time to successfully mainstream students representing the full range of handicapping conditions without various kinds of support and assistance (Schulz & Turnbull, 1983). In addition, not enough attention has been paid to the attitudes and sensitivity of the other students in the regular class. Nonhandicapped students must be taught to understand and accept the handicapped as fellow schoolmates. They must realize that although they cannot change the way handicapped people start out in life or prevent the occurrence of a handicapping condition, they can play a part in improving the quality of life and help make the problems and challenges less overwhelming for their handicapped classmates.

Experience and research with mainstreaming delivery systems for the learning disabled thus far lead to the following conclusions (Haight, 1984; Wang & Birch, 1984; Salend, 1984; Schwartz, 1984):

1. Regular classroom teachers are generally hesitant and sometimes fearful about providing for the needs of special students in their classrooms. If it is to succeed, mainstreaming must be viewed as a systematic process. It requires a team approach and should be a shared responsibility of all of the educators in the school.

2. When learning-disabled students are mainstreamed into regular classrooms, they often need some supportive services. A resource room can aid them in maintaining academic gains they had made in the special placement. Ryan (1984) places the responsibility for providing supportive services on the special education teacher.

3. Many learning-disabled students are not well accepted socially by peers in the regular classroom. Mainstreaming often does not lead to greater social interaction with nonhandicapped students or to more social acceptance. It has also been observed that many learning disabled students do not learn to model their social behavior after that of their classmates in the mainstreaming setting. (Bryan, et al., 1983).

4. Acceptable classroom behaviors are even more important for success in the mainstream than academic competencies. In response to a questionnaire about the qualities learning-disabled students need to succeed in the mainstream, both regular classroom teachers and special education teachers indicated that the most essential skills involved (a) interacting positively with other students, (b) obeying class rules, and (c) displaying proper work habits (Salend & Lutz, 1984). The special teacher should prepare students for the mainstream by teaching these essential skills for classroom behavior. For example, if in the regular classroom the student may have to work independently on an assignment for thirty minutes, then the special education teacher should strive to prepare the student for that situation by making the same work demands in the special education setting.

Alternative Placements

The various options of the continuum of alternative placements are described in this section. In selecting the placement for delivering educational services for a particular student, the case conference IEP team should consider factors such as severity of the handicap, need for related services, the student's ability to fit into the routine of the selected setting, and the student's social and academic skills. Often the team recommends a delivery system that combines elements of several types of placements. In the following two cases, different delivery systems are recommended.

CASE EXAMPLES

Selecting a Delivery System

• José, aged twelve, was judged to have mild learning disabilities. He has been receiving resource help for the past year. His word recognition reading skills are now at grade level, but reading comprehension and arithmetic, though very much improved, still require special education instruction. José has improved in his attention skills; he now knows how to study and can attend to an assignment for a period of thirty minutes. José still has a speech articulation disorder that requires the services of the speech and language teacher. José's IEP recommendation for placement is that he be mainstreamed in the regular classroom for most of the day but that he also receive services in the learning disabilities resource room. In addition, José will be scheduled for related services in speech therapy.

• Lucinda, also aged twelve, was judged to have severe learning disabilities. Last year she was enrolled in a special school. Now she is returning to the regular school. Her reading skills are at the primary level, and she has extremely poor skills in arithmetic, spelling, and language. In addition, she has a severe social disability and does not easily relate to adults or peers. Lucinda is returning to the regular school with great fear and reluctance. She needs a very supportive placement, one offering a predictable routine and surroundings, as well as an opportunity to develop strong social relationships with a few people. Since Lucinda has displayed a remarkable talent in creative art and enjoys working with a variety of art media, the IEP recommendation for her placement is that she receive services in a self-contained learning disabilities class, but that she also be placed in the regular art class

---

The various placement options are described below. Most learning-disabled students will be served through one of the first three placements discussed in this section: the regular class, the resource room, or the self-contained classroom.

Regular Classroom

Regular class placement is the least restrictive, and it is the delivery system usually referred to as mainstreaming. The special educator may serve as a consultant to the regular teacher, provide materials for the student, or actually teach the student within the regular education setting. As noted in the discussion on mainstreaming, if intervention for learning-disabled students in the regular classroom is to succeed, it requires careful planning, teacher preparation, team effort, and a complete support system. Mere physical placement in a regular classroom is not enough to ensure academic achievement or social acceptance. Learning-disabled students still have specific needs that require accommodation and attention. Also, even in the regular class setting, special educators must retain major responsibility for educating the learning-disabled. In-service and continuing education of regular teachers is critically important, and so is the coordinated effort of all school personnel—regular teachers, special teachers, related personnel, and administrators (Salend, 1984; Schwartz, 1984; Schulz & Turnbull, 1983).

Resource Room

A *resource room* is an educational setting that provides assessment services and remedial instruction to handicapped students on a regularly scheduled basis for a portion of the school day (Wiederholt, Hammill, & Brown, 1983). The resource room placement is the most prevalent type of placement for learning-disabled students. It is a flexible program in terms of the curriculum offered, the time the student spends in the program, the number of students served, and the teacher's time. Many educators see the resource room as a supporting element or extension of mainstreaming (Hawisher & Calhoun, 1978; Schulz & Turnbull, 1983; Wells, Schmid, Algozzine, & Maher, 1983).

Advantages of the Resource Room

The resource room offers these advantages:

1. The resource room teacher is located in the same building as the regular teachers, the administrators, and the students and may be readily accepted by them. Because resource room teachers are not tied to a single class, they can share responsibilities for students with all the teachers in the building who have students in the program. The resource room teacher's time is flexible, enabling him or her to accept many varied responsibilities.
2. Students with learning disabilities can benefit from specific resource room training while remaining integrated with their friends and age-mates in school.
3. Students have the advantages of a *total remedial program,* which is prepared by the resource teacher but may be implemented in cooperation with the regular class teacher.
4. Young children with mild but developing problems can be accommodated, thereby preventing later severe disorders from developing.
5. Resource programs are flexible enough to fit the level of the schooling. Primary school resource programs can be very different from those serving secondary school students.
6. Resource rooms can serve children without attaching a stigmatizing label. Some resource rooms are *cross-categorical* (serving various handicaps); others are *categorical* (serving only the learning disabled).

The Resource Room Teacher

A highly competent and personable individual is needed to meet the responsibilities of the resource room teacher. This teacher should be able to (1) work closely and harmoniously with other teachers and the ancillary staff, (2) make educational and behavioral assessments, and (3) design and implement individualized instruction for students referred to the resource room. The first requirement reflects a human relations skill whereas the other two are professional teacher competencies.

Since the student is in the regular classroom for a large part of the day, both diagnosis and remediation must be related to needs in the regular classroom. In planning the schedule of the resource room teacher, time should be allotted for assessment, teaching, and consultation. Teacher aides, including paraprofessionals, parent volunteers, or older pupils, are useful in enhancing the services afforded by the resource room. Many kinds of equipment and materials are needed to ensure flexibility and variety. The resource room teacher might take the initiative in developing a resource team. Such an approach would give school personnel the opportunity to interact and to develop a communication flow. Finally, it is of paramount importance that the room be well-organized and an attractive place for students.

In summary, a resource room is an administrative arrangement. Its success depends upon many factors, including the competence of the resource teacher, the support and cooperation of all levels of administration, and the availability of adequate space and materials.

Self-contained Special Classes

The self-contained special classroom within the school was one of the first approaches of the public school system to the education of students with learning disabilities. The research efforts of Cruickshank et al. (1961) resulted in demonstration classes for teaching brain-injured and hyperactive children. These classes became a prototype for many special classes for learning disabilities that followed. The classes researched by Cruickshank, Bentzen, Ratzeburgh, & Tannhauser (1961) had specially equipped rooms designed to reduce environmental distractions, and the teaching techniques were highly structured and exacting.

While some features of these early special classes have changed, many of the elements are important today. Special classes are typically small, containing about six to ten students. A wide variety of materials is available to the teacher. Often the classes are started with one or two students and additional pupils are enrolled one at a time to permit the establishment of a classroom routine before each new student is added to the class. The special class provides the opportunity for highly individualized, closely supervised, intensive instruction.

Some special classes are *categorical* (consisting of only students classified as learning disabled); other special classes are *cross-categorical* (consisting of students who have been classified as having one of several handicaps—learning disabilities, behavior disorders, or mental retardation).

Initially, most special education services were delivered through self-contained special classes. Once the student was classified as handicapped, the student was placed in the special class; no other educational option was available in the school. Regular educators readily shifted the responsibility of teaching handicapped students to special educators. In 1968, a now-famous article was published by Dunn, entitled "Special Education for the Mildly Retarded: Is Much of It Justifiable?" This article pointed out many of the detrimental aspects of special classes and reported on research that questioned the academic value of special class placement. Many other articles critical of special classes soon followed. These writings and other factors led to a marked decrease of special classrooms in favor of other types of delivery systems (resource rooms, itinerent programs, mainstreaming).

Now, many learning disabilities specialists are taking a renewed look at the value of self-contained special classes for certain students, particularly those with severe learning disabilities. The self-contained classroom seems to benefit some learning-disabled students (Smith, 1983; Carlberg & Kavale, 1980; Yauman, 1980; Boersma, Chapman, & Battle, 1979; Ribner, 1978). They appear to have a better self-concept than similar students in the mainstream. Regular class competition can set achievement criteria that the learning-disabled student cannot meet, thereby diminishing self-concept. As Smith (1983) notes, some studies indicate that certain learning-disabled students make greater strides in special classes in both academic and social areas. With its lower teacher-pupil ratio, this setting offers more intensive individualized instruction in which students spend more time "on-task" in learning. For the student with the most serious and severe learning disabilities problems, the special classroom may provide the most appropriate setting for the kind of intensive and comprehensive intervention needed.

One goal of the special class delivery system is to help students organize themselves for increased independent learning so that eventually they will be able to take part in a less restrictive environment. Usually, students begin the transition by participating in a limited way in a regular class for a selected subject. Then their participation is gradually increased until they are attending regular classes full-time. If the transition is to be effective, a good working relationship must be maintained between the teacher of the special class and the teacher of the regular class. Sometimes the transition begins by having the student receive some instruction in the resource room.

Special Day Schools

Special day schools are separate school facilities established specifically for students with a special handicap—in this case, learning disabilities. These schools are usually private and, historically, have been established when the public was either unaware of or unwilling to recognize the learning problem. Some students attend the special school full-time; others attend for half a day and may attend the public school for the balance of the school day.

The disadvantages of such programs include the high expense to parents, the traveling distance, and the lack of opportunity to be with nonhandicapped students for some portion of the school day. These schools have served well, however, as pilot programs for later classes in public schools.

Residential Schools

Residential schools provide full-time placement for students away from their homes. Relatively few have handicaps severe enough to warrant such placement. However, if the community lacks adequate alternative facilities, if the behavioral manifestations are extremely severe, and if the emotional reaction among other members of the family is debilitating, residential placement on a twenty-four-hour basis may be the only solution for both the student and the family.

Although residential schools are the oldest provision for dealing with exceptional children and youth, they have many disadvantages. Removal of the youngster from home and neighborhood, emphasis on the handicap, rigidity of institutional life, and lack of opportunity for normal social experiences are among the shortcomings of the residential school. As the public and private schools and other community agencies develop more services, the need decreases for residential placement for most learning-disabled students. Nonetheless, for certain youngsters, residential placement remains the most appropriate and has proved to be successful in helping a student learn and make an adjustment to the world.

Other Placement Considerations

Often a combination placement is a viable alternative. For example, a student could be in a self-contained classroom for a portion of the day or week and in a regular classroom for the remainder.

Itinerant Programs

Some schools, particularly those with a small enrollment, provide itinerant programs. The learning disabilities teacher travels to several schools, serving students in many classrooms by providing educational services. Students are scheduled to leave their regular classroom at a specified time for work with the itinerant teacher. They may come individually or in small groups of two to six. Sessions may be held daily or several times a week, generally lasting from thirty minutes to an hour. Care must be taken in scheduling. For example, if the pupil enjoys physical education, the teacher should avoid preempting this period for the teaching session. In addition, the classroom teacher should be consulted about the optimum time for the student to leave the classroom. If the learning disabilities teacher intends to work on reading, the regular classroom reading time may be convenient for scheduling the special therapy session. Some schools use a revolving time schedule so that a different subject is missed for each session with the itinerant teacher.

The rooms used by the itinerant teacher should be pleasant and have an abundant supply of materials. Since the student often has a short attention span, it is wise to provide a change of pace by planning a number of different activities for the teaching session.

Preschool Programs

Educational services for exceptional preschool children aged three to five have very specific requirements. These services are discussed in detail in Chapter 8. In general, preschool programs involve screening, intensive diagnosis, and a noncategorical, child development type of class. (Lerner, Mardell-Czudnowski, & Goldenberg, 1981). Early childhood programs include work in the home with parents as teachers.

Secondary School Programs

The needs of secondary students require different kinds of educational services than those at the elementary level. These alternatives are presented in Chapter 9. Problems increase at the high school level. High school staff members are likely to be primarily interested in their own specialty areas. Their concern and perspective tend to be oriented toward content rather than toward the student. Consequently, it becomes more difficult to convince the high school staff that accommodations are needed and flexibility is required to help the learning-disabled students. Scheduling, too, becomes difficult since students cannot easily miss scheduled classes. Free periods, a second English period, and release from music or art classes have provided the needed time in some secondary programs.

Further difficulties at the secondary school level stem from the increased frustration and emotional problems that accompany the learning disabilities of a student who has reached the high school level. High school students generally need direct help in finding ways to attack their content subjects.

In some high school programs, students attend their regular classes, which may be modified, but they also report to a resource room for several periods a week. Assessment and planning of programs are made by a multidisciplinary team consisting of high school personnel, such as the school psychologist, social worker, guidance counselor, and learning disabilities teacher. However, implementation and teaching are the responsibility of the learning disabilities specialist. Many students participating in the high school program may have been previously classified as having other kinds of exceptionality or other causes of school failure.

The Roles of the Learning Disabilities Teacher

The teacher of students with learning disabilities plays many roles. The jobs such a teacher performs, either as an individual or as a team member, include

(1) setting up programs for identifying, assessing, and instructing students with learning disabilities; (2) participating in the screening, assessment, and evaluation of students with learning disabilities; (3) consulting with professionals from contributing disciplines and interpreting their reports; (4) testing students both formally and informally; (5) participating in the formulation of individualized education programs; (6) implementing the educational plan through direct intervention and teaching and creating or locating appropriate materials and methods; (7) interviewing parents and holding conferences with them; (8) consulting with the regular classroom teachers to help them understand the student and to help the teacher provide effective instruction; and (9) perhaps most important, helping the student develop self-understanding and gain the hope and confidence necessary to cope with and overcome the learning disabilities.

The role of the learning disabilities teacher is difficult to define because the functions of the position are changing. It is important to be alert to emerging concepts and problems and to be able to adapt to change. Two dimensions of the job should be considered: (1) the professional teacher-competencies dimension and (2) the human relations dimension.

Professional Teacher Competencies

Learning disabilities teachers should, of course, be highly competent in all the technical aspects of their profession. The complex technical role and professional competencies of the learning disabilities teacher have been described in detail by Newcomer (1978, 1982), Fox-Reid (1982), and Freeman and Becker (1979). These technical competencies include knowledge of the theories in the field of learning disabilities, familiarity with tests, skill in assessment and evaluation, knowledge of curriculum and teaching materials, and skills in methods of teaching oral language, reading, written language, mathematics, behavior management, social-emotional skills, and prevocational and vocational skills. Most of the chapters in this book deal with these technical and professional dimensions of the role of the learning disabilities teacher.

The Human Relations Role

The second and growing dimension of the role of the learning disabilities teacher is in the realm of human relations. When the self-contained special class was the predominant method for delivering educational services, the job was relatively isolated and there was relatively little need for the learning disabilities teacher to interact with other school personnel and little interdependence of functions. As the educational services for learning-disabled students extended to resource rooms, mainstreaming, and teaming and consulting models, the need for interdependence increased. The objectives of a learning disabilities program can only be met if all the persons within the system function in an integrated fashion. Interaction, communication, and the development of common goals are needed strategies for integrating the various components of the system. The learning disabilities teacher must possess the human relations skills to bring about this integration so that everyone concerned with a student is part of a coordinated working system.

Most of the training in learning disabilities programs is geared to developing the technical professional competencies in learning disabilities teachers. Yet surveys of practicing learning disabilities teachers in the schools indicate that learning disabilities teachers rate *consulting* and *counseling* skills (a human relations function) as among the most important competencies of the job (Fox-Reid, 1982; Newcomer, 1982; Freeman & Becker, 1979).

Moreover, the consulting role is growing in importance. Increased mainstreaming makes greater demands on the learning disabilities teacher as a consultant to the regular classroom teacher. But Aloia (1983) found that learning disabilities teachers had much less confidence in their role as consultants than in their ability to perform their professional tasks well. In the consultant role, the learning disabilities teacher must establish relationships with many persons within the school.

Working with Classroom Teachers

The importance of the regular classroom teacher in helping the learning-disabled student is becoming increasingly evident. Under a resource room delivery system, the classroom teacher must coordinate efforts with the learning that occurs in the resource room. Under a mainstreaming model, the teacher must learn to work as a member of a team. At times, the learning disabilities specialist may work with the student in the regular classroom; at times, an aide or paraprofessional will work with the student in the classroom; at other times, the regular teacher will be responsible for the instructional program of the student.

Mainstreaming has created a number of unanticipated problems. Classroom teachers are often untrained in special education and unprepared to handle problems of the atypical student. They may be fearful of the responsibility and in some cases reluctant to accept this additional task. Successful integration of the learning-disabled student into the regular classroom needs careful thought, planning, and supervision. Consulting efforts have to be geared to gaining the classroom teacher's acceptance of the goals of the program and willingness to coordinate efforts to help the student. The learning disabilities teachers arrange in-service learning experiences and works with classroom teachers to modify classroom instruction. In addition, they demonstrate assessment and instructional techniques and behavior management methods, as well as introduce curricular materials and independent learning activities. All these tasks require both technical competencies and interpersonal relationship skills.

Working with Other Specialists

As the scope of the responsibilities of the learning disabilities teacher expands, the common boundaries of interest with other specialists increase. Work with various specialists in closely related disciplines, such as psychology, reading, speech, counseling, school nursing, and so forth, derives from areas of common interests.

These overlapping areas of interest, or areas of interface, may also lead to territorial conflicts. Questions of primary responsibility for a specific area may arise. Who, for example, should work with the student who has a severe reading problem? Several specialists lay claim to this child—the learning disabilities specialist, the reading specialist, and the speech and language pathologist—and all of them may perceive their expertise as encompassing the entire realm of language problems, including reading. The student with a language disorder could be served by the speech clinician or by the learning disabilities specialist. Diagnostic functions could be within the jurisdiction of the school psychologist or the learning disabilities specialist.

Such interface relationships may be the most delicate and demanding aspects of the job. The role responsibilities as perceived by the learning disabilities specialist may not mesh with the perceptions of other specialists on the staff. Coping with such differences in role perception requires both sensitivity and astute political savvy.

Working with Paraprofessionals

Many of the delivery systems make extensive use of paraprofessionals or aides—paid and volunteer nonprofessionals who undertake the task of assisting teachers (Lindsey, 1983). These individuals should be given very structured, limited, and specific assignments in working with students. Their duties must be carefully planned and supervised by either the learning disabilities specialist or by the classroom teacher. Instruction should be clear, and material should be easy to use. The precise educational responsibilities of the paraprofessional must be clear to everyone involved. At the same time, it is essential that paraprofessionals perceive themselves as working parts of the system and view their work as significant and worthwhile.

Working with Administrators

It is clear from research reported in organizational theory that if changes are to be made in the system there must be support from administrators. Without the understanding and support of the principal of the school and the superintendent of the system, it is virtually impossible to implement a successful learning disabilities program and reach established goals. Change in an organization comes from the top, and the start must be made with the top management.

The following example illustrates a difference in role perception by administrators and learning disabilities personnel. Ms. Bailey, a newly graduated learning disabilities teacher, accepted her first teaching position in Parkside School District. Her rather naïve view of the educational world, gained in part from her university training, was that learning disabilities is the center, with many other disciplines contributing to the field. When she expectantly asked the superintendent for the administrative staff and line chart, she discovered to her dismay that learning disabilities was not the focal point of the chart; in fact, it was not even on the chart. The superintendent kindly suggested that one box in the bottom left-hand corner of the chart might be considered a related learning disabilities component. The perception of the role of learning disabilities on the part of the new graduate was vastly different from the perception shown on the administrative chart. Such a discrepancy, sometimes called *cognitive dissonance* (Festinger, 1964), requires a certain amount of adjustment. Part of the consulting function is to develop common perceptions among all persons involved; certainly the administrator must be part of the communication and planning system.

Principles of Consulting

Perhaps the most difficult task of the learning disabilities specialist is that of consulting. Although consulting with the classroom teacher is of paramount importance, this function should be envisioned in terms of working with the entire school system. Unless all elements within the system operate in a coordinated fashion, the objectives and goals of the learning disabiliites program will not be satisfactorily met. This implies that the learning disabilities teacher must consult with regular teachers, related personnel, administrators, parents, and others. Ryan (1984) believes that the learning disabilities teachers should consider themselves as the specialists who are primarily responsible for developing proper attitudes and policies pertaining to the learning-disabled students within the school building.

A new set of skills is needed for the role of the consultant. For this function, learning disabilities teachers require specific knowledge, skills in analysis, synthesis, and problem-solving strategies, and an aptitude for human relations and communication. Consulting skills can be learned and taught, but that requires advanced training and preparation (Haight, 1984; Lilly & Givens-Olge, 1981).

Several principles should be kept in mind when consulting in the school system:

1. *Common goals.* It is essential that there be a common perception of the goals and objectives of the learning disabilities program among the various persons involved. All must know the purpose of the program. If individuals are working toward different purposes, there is likely to be conflict and dissatisfaction. Common goals must be perceived by classroom teachers, administrators, paraprofessionals, other specialists, and other individuals who may be involved.

Parents of a learning-disabled student may find it helpful to speak with a counselor in an attempt to gain greater empathy for their child's problems.

(Judith D. Sedwick/The Picture Cube)

child in the achievement of increasingly complex accomplishments. (Kephart, 1972, p. vi)

There has been an awakening of concern for the problem of parents of exceptional students. This has come about because (1) parent groups have been the major impetus for much of the special education legislation and the establishment of many programs; (2) recent legislation has given parents a variety of rights in regard to their handicapped child, such as the right to obtain their child's complete psychoeducational data and the right to have the final say on educational placement recommended by the school; (3) educators are realizing the important role that parents can play in helping their child; and (4) educators are recognizing the pervasive effect a child's handicap has on the parents.

Parent Reactions to Handicapped Children

The attitude of parents who have a child with a learning disorder is very different from that of parents of a youngster who does not present such a problem (Kinsbourne & Caplan, 1979). Parents of learning-disabled children may exhibit attitudes of overindulgence or overprotection. Researchers note three frequent attitudes on the part of mothers toward their handicapped children. The first attitude is reflected by mothers who reject their child or are unable to accept the child as a handicapped person. Complex love-hate and acceptance-rejection relationships are found within this group. Rejected children not only have problems in adjusting to themselves and their disabilities, but they also have to contend with disturbed family relationships and emotional insecurity. Unfortunately, such children receive even less encouragement than the normal child and have to absorb more criticism of their behavior.

A second relationship involves mothers who overcompensate in their reactions to their child and the disorder. They tend to be unrealistic, rigid, and overprotective. Often, such parents try to compensate by being overzealous and giving continuous instruction and training in the hope of establishing superior ability.

The third group consists of mothers who accept their children along with their disorders. These mothers have gained the ability to provide for the special needs of their handicapped children while continuing to live a normal life and tending to family and home, as well as civic and social obligations. The child's chances are best with parents who have accepted both their child and the defects.

Psychiatric or psychological help is often needed by the parents of children with learning disabilities. Psychiatrists are increasingly aware that the presence of a handicapping problem must be faced by both child and other members of the family. In addition to an honest acceptance of the problem, there must be recognition that improvement is often a slow process. The reaction of parents is often one of denial, followed by anger, then by a search for other diagnoses. Sometimes parents also need help of a psychotherapeutic nature in accepting the problem, in developing empathy for their child, and in providing a beneficial home environment. Guidance counselors and social workers play important roles in providing such help (Klein, Altman, Dreizen, Friedman, & Powers, 1981).

Parent Education Groups and Counseling

Establishing healthy parental attitudes and ensuring parent-teacher cooperation are, of course, desirable goals. Two procedures, parent education groups and parent counseling, can help in meeting these goals.

Parent education groups—parents meeting regularly in small groups to discuss common problems—can be organized by the school, family service organizations, professional counselors, or by parent organizations (such as ACLD). The opportunity to meet with other parents whose children are encountering similar problems tends to reduce the parents' sense of isolation. Further, such parent groups have been useful in alerting the community, school personnel, other professionals, and legislative bodies to the plight of their children.

Often the first step in parent counseling is helping the parents get over their initial feelings about their handicapped child. The initial period of reaction may be one of mourning, misunderstanding, guilt, deprecation of self, and even a sense of shame. Parents may react to these feelings by turning away in confusion, or they may overreact, become aggressive, and try to break down doors to get things done. These aggressive parents are much needed in our profession for they are the ones who keep the educators moving. Educators should empathize with parents to help them get over the initial period of reaction (Buscaglia, 1975; Kinsbourne & Caplan, 1979; Klein et al., 1981).

Some counselors view the learning disabilities problem as a family affair and involve the extended family—grandparents, siblings, and others who have close contact with the child or adolescent. Parent education sessions offer the following benefits (Silver, 1983; Klein, et al. 1981; Smith, 1980):

1. Parent groups help parents to understand and accept their child's problem. Participation in such groups is ego-strengthening, supportive, and practically helpful.
2. Parents experience many anxieties stemming from apprehension about the psychological and educational development of their children. Through parent groups they discover that they are not alone; other parents have similar problems and have found solutions.
3. Parents should realize that they are an integral part of their child's learning, development, and behavior. They can learn to perceive their children differently and learn to deal with their problems more effectively.
4. Topics that are popular at parent education sessions include discipline, communication skills, behavioral management, parent advocacy, special education legislation, social skills development, helping their child make friends, home management, and college and vocational opportunities.
5. The parents' needs are different at different stages. Parents who have recently learned of their child's problems have different needs and interests than parents who have been involved with the problem for several years. Parents of young children have different education needs than parents of adolescents.

Parent–Teacher Conferences

Parent-teacher conferences can become a bridge between the home and school. Both parents and teachers tend to shy away from conferences, parents fearing what they will hear and teachers fearing that parents will react negatively. Yet the conferences should be viewed as an opportunity to help the student. By coordinating efforts, the student's life in school and at home can work together to enhance progress. If they are compartmentalized, they may be working at cross purposes, making the student's life even more difficult.

In setting up a conference, teachers should try to reassure parents that they are going to communicate with another human being—not a cog in an impersonal system. The teacher should communicate a sincere interest in the student and respect for the parents, as well as convey a sense of confidence without being arrogant. The problem should be discussed in a calm manner, avoiding technical jargon. Parents want to understand the nature of the problem and therefore diagnostic data and current teaching approaches should be interpreted and explained. The parents must also be helped to become sensitive to the nature of the student's learning difficulties and to those tasks that are difficult.

In addition, parents usually want to know what they can do at home. Most specialists believe that at home, parents should involve the children in domestic responsibilities and not try to help them with schoolwork. Since academic learning is the area of most difficulty, students being taught academic skills by their parents might be failing consistently in front of the most important adults in their lives. Moreover, parents find that helping their children in academic areas can be formidable and frustrating. Even well-trained learning disabilities specialists who perform outstandingly well professionally often fail miserably when trying to deal with learning disabilities in their own children. Too often parents' attempts to help their children in academic areas result in harm to the child, to the parents, and to their relationship. The pressures and demands of the academic learning situation interfere with the role of the parents in developing a good self-image. Instead, suggestions for parent involvement should be related to home life (Smith, 1980). When a parent undertakes the task of tutoring, the child too often loses the parent while gaining a mediocre teacher (Brutten, Richardson, & Mangel, 1973).

Student-teacher conferences are also important to help students understand their problems. Learning-disabled students are often worried, frightened, and confused; they need to have their evaluation and teaching plan explained in words they can understand. Such a conference can help in clearing up confusion and alleviating concern. A delightful short book designed to explain learning disabilities to a student is *The Tuned-In, Turned-On Book About Learning Problems* (Hayes, 1974).

Suggestions for Parents

A book designed to give parents of learning-disabled children an overview of the field, *Something's Wrong with My Child* (Brutten et al., 1973), offers a number of suggestions to help parents make life at home easier.

1. Don't lose outside interests. Try to relinquish your child's care to a competent baby-sitter periodically. Parents need time off for independence and morale boosting.
2. Don't push your child into activities for which the child is not ready. The child may react by trying halfheartedly to please you, rebel either actively

or passively, or just quit or withdraw into a world of daydreams. If the child is forced to meet arbitrary and inappropriate standards imposed by the adult world, learning becomes painful rather than pleasurable.

3. Be alert to any hint that your child is good at *something*. By discovering an unimpaired area or native talent, give your child a new chance for success. The tasks may be small, such as folding napkins or helping with specific kitchen chores.

4. Match tasks to the child's level of functioning. For example, have easy-to-wipe surfaces and breakproof containers to reduce spills when the child uses these materials. Think about the child's problem and figure out a way to help. As an illustration, Brutten et al. suggest drawing an outline of the child's shoes on the closet floor to indicate left and right.

5. Be direct and positive in talking to your child. Try not to criticize but to be supportive and to provide guidance. For example, if the child has trouble following directions, ask him or her to look at you while you speak and then to repeat what you have said.

6. Keep the child's room simple and in a quiet part of the house—a place to relax and retreat.

7. Simplify family routine. For example, mealtime for some children can be an extremely complex and stimulating situation. Your child may be unable to cope with the many sounds, sights, smells, and so on. It may be necessary to have the child eat earlier at first and gradually join the family meal—perhaps starting with dessert.

8. Help the child learn that she or he must live with other children in a world that doesn't revolve around her or him. Because some learning-disabled children do not play well with other children, parents have to go out of their way to plan and guide such social experiences. This may mean inviting a single child to play for a short period of time, arranging with parents of other learning-disabled children for joint social activities, or volunteering to be a den mother or a Brownie leader.

9. Above all, Brutten et al. advise that all children need to learn that they are significant. They must be treated with respect and allowed to do their own work. They should learn that being a responsible and contributing member of the family is important—probably more important than learning the academic skills demanded by the school.

Teachers may wish to recommend reading materials to parents to help them become better acquainted with the problem of learning disabilities and ways of helping their children. A selection of appropriate books for parents is given below.

Becker, W. C. (1971). *Parents Are Teachers.* Champaign, IL: Research Press.

Brutten, Milton, Richardson, Sylvia O., and Mangel, Charles. (1973). *Something's Wrong with My Child: A Parents' Book About Children with Learning Disabilities.* New York: Harcourt Brace Jovanovich.

Hart, Jane, and Jones, Beverly. (1968). *Where's Hannah? A Handbook for Parents and Teachers of Learning Disorders.* New York: Hart.

Kronick, Doreen (Ed.). (1969). *They Too Can Succeed: A Practical Guide for Parents of Learning Disabled Children.* San Rafael, CA: Academic Therapy Publications.

Levy, Harold B. (1973). *Square Pegs, Round Holes.* Boston: Little, Brown.

Osman, B. (1979). *Learning Disabilities: A Family Affair.* New York: Random House.

Smith, S. (1980). *No Easy Answers: The Learning Disabled Child at Home and at School.* New York: Bantam.

CASE STUDY   PART III

Rita G.

Stage 4. The Case Conference

The case conference team that met to discuss Rita included the school psychologist, the learning disabilities teacher, Mr. Martinez (her third-grade teacher), and Rita's parents, Mr. and Mrs. G.

The case conference team agreed that Rita has a number of strengths. They include facility with oral language; intelligence within the overall normal range, with high abilities in verbal areas; an understanding and supportive family and a playful relationship with her sister; good word recognition skills in reading a grasp of phonics skills; and an above average listening-speaking vocabulary.

Her weaknesses include the following: poor arithmetic computation and mathematics word problem-solving skills; slow, laborious, and illegible handwriting, related to general visual-motor and spatial problems; and difficulty in reading comprehension. These other weaknesses were also noted: Rita has developed a passive attitude toward learning; she cannot attend to a task without becoming distracted; and she lacks organizational skills and does not use efficient learning strategies. Finally, Rita has no friends and lacks social skills.

The case conference team concluded that Rita has learning disabilities. She has a severe discrepancy between her potential (especially using the Verbal IQ score) and her achievement in mathematics calculation, mathematics reasoning, reading comprehension, and written expression. Her learning problems are not primarily the result of emotional disturbance, mental retardation, visual or hearing impairments, or environmental, economic or cultural disadvantage. Rita displays many of the symptoms of learning disabilities: visual-motor perception problems, social disabilities, poor attention, and inefficient learning strategies.

The annual goals developed for Rita focused on the following: (1) improving skills for written communication, (2) improving mathematics skills—calculation and arithmetic word story problems, (3) improving reading comprehension, (4) developing cognitive learning strategies, and (5) developing better social skills. Short-term objectives were written for each of these goals. The learning disabilities teacher and Mr. Martinez would develop more specific plans to reach each of these objectives.

The case conference team recommended that Rita be placed in the learning disabilities resource room for two hours each day and remain in the regular third-grade class with Mr. Martinez for the balance of the day. Rita's father said that he thought this would be a good arrangement because Rita would receive the special teaching she needed and still be part of the third-grade class.

The case conference team also recommended that Rita make an appointment with an eye-care specialist for further vision testing. Rita's mother said she would call for an appointment next week.

The information and decisions were written into Rita's individualized education program. The IEP was signed by all the case conference team members, including Mr. and Mrs. G.

The annual goals concerning improvement in the skills of writing for cursive and typewriting are shown below. A few selected short-term objectives for these goals are presented.

Annual Goal: Writes legibly, using cursive writing, one paragraph consisting of ten sentences.

Short-term Objectives: cursive writing

a. traces two cursive letters using a stencil.
b. copies ten letters using cursive writing in upper and lower case on a chalkboard.
c. writes legibly all letters using cursive writing in upper and lower case on paper.
d. writes name in cursive writing.
e. writes legibly five short words in cursive writing from a model.
f. writes legibly a sentence from a model.
g. writes legibly a paragraph with five sentences.
h. writes legibly a paragraph with ten sentences.

Annual Goal: Typewrites a paragraph consisting of ten sentences.

Short-term Objectives: typewriting

a. following a student instruction manual for a typewriter (or a microcomputer), learns home position for hands.

b. completes the lesson for *fff* and *jjj*.
c. completes the lessons for all the letters on the keyboard.
d. typewrites one sentence of four words with fewer than three errors.
e. typewrites one paragraph of ten sentences.

Stage 5: Implementing the Teaching Plan

The learning disabilities teacher and Mr. Martinez developed more specific plans to meet the objectives stated on the individualized education plan. A summary of these plans are discussed briefly in this section, but many more specific objectives, lesson plans, and re-evaluation procedures would have to be made.

Individual lesson plans were made to coordinate the work of the resource room and the third-grade curriculum. Rita's deficits in visual-motor skills were taken into account in planning a skills approach to arithmetic. The learning disabilities teacher and Mr. Martinez decided to use concrete materials to establish basic number concepts for addition, subtraction, and multiplication. Opportunity for drill and practice was planned by using a number of different manipulative materials and some microcomputer mathematics drill and practice software.

The microcomputer would also be used to teach Rita typing skills. After she learned how to type, the plan was to teach her word processing and then move into lessons in written expression. It was felt that it would be worthwhile to try to teach Rita cursive writing. Even though she would learn to type, there are many occasions in daily life when handwriting is a necessity. Many students find cursive writing easier than manuscript because of the unity and flow of the letters. Many students in the third-grade are reluctant to learn cursive writing. However, since her writing problem is so severe, her writing progress should be monitored very carefully and progress re-evaluated continually.

Another specific plan was to help Rita develop more efficient learning strategies. She would be taught how to self-monitor attention to keep herself on task and use self-rehearsal strategies to improve her approach to learning. The plan also included the provision of more opportunities for social interaction in the classroom through assignment to committees and peer work. These are but a few of the implementation activities.

Stage 6: Monitoring Progress and Review

Rita's progress would be reviewed informally on a monthly basis by the learning disabilities teacher and Mr. Martinez. An annual review is planned for the middle of the following year, when Rita will be in fourth-grade. She will be tested in mathematics computation, mathematics reasoning, written expression, and reading comprehension.

Summary

• Three important concepts should be considered in planning the delivery of special education services to learning-disabled students: the continuum of alternative placements, the least restrictive environment, and mainstreaming.

• The continuum of alternative placements refers to the array of education placements in the schools to meet the varied needs of exceptional students.

• PL 94–142 requires students to be placed in the "least restrictive environment." This means that they should be with nonhandicapped students to the greatest extent appropriate.

• Mainstreaming is the placement of exceptional students into the regular classroom as the recommended delivery system. For many learning-disabled students, mainstreaming is not the best placement.

• Alternative placements available to meet the needs of learning-disabled students range from the regular classroom, the resource room, and the self-contained special class to special day schools, and residential schools. Each of the placements is successively more restrictive in terms of the disabled student's opportunity to interact with nonhandicapped students.

• The role of the learning disabilities teacher is multifaceted. The technical role demands competencies in assessment and teaching. The human relations role requires sensitivity and skill in dealing with people. As learning disabilities teachers interact more and more with other school staff, the human relations aspect of the job grows in importance.

• Since learning disabilities teachers often act as consultants, they should be knowledgeable about certain principles of consulting and activities for involving school personnel.

• Parents are a vital component in the student's education. Parent education groups are effective in helping parents understand their child and his or her problem and find ways to help their child within the home.

• Parent-teacher conferences are important ways of working with parents and involving them in the educational process.

Key Terms

least restrictive environ- ment	paraprofessionals	delivery system
mainstreaming	parent teacher confer- ence	itinerant teacher
regular class	parent education groups	consulting role
resource room	continuum of alternative	residential school
self-contained special class	placements	child-teacher conference

Theoretical Perspectives and Expanding Directions

PART *3*

Theoretical Perspectives: Concepts and Implications

Chapter 6

Introduction

Part 3 examines underlying theories (Chapter 6) and emerging directions in medicine (Chapter 7), early childhood (Chapter 8), and adolescence (Chapter 9). In this chapter we will examine several theories that provide a framework for evaluating and teaching learning-disabled students and the implications of these theories. The theories cover the perspectives of the maturational view, psychological processing, academic skills mastery, and cognitive approaches.

"If you don't know where you are going, any road will take you there." This counsel is as applicable to learning disabilities as other facets of life. Theory is needed to understand the learning problem encountered by the student and to provide a basis for the methodology that will be used. Teaching without theory may follow the road that leads nowhere.

In a visit to a hypothetical classroom, we might see all the children in a room, or in a school district, or even in an entire city using the latest in educational technology—"Mother Hubbard's Cure-all," enticingly packaged material composed of colorful boxes, machines, and supplementary items. This program, which the publisher assures the user is based on extensive research and the most recent scientific evidence, is purported to cure students with learning disabilities and to improve students without learning disabilities. The program contains all teaching media: films, tapes, ditto sheets, workbooks, computers, muscle exercises, and even books. It also has a teacher's manual that describes the foolproof step-by-step directions on *how* to use the equipment. Everything is carefully described, except *why* a particular activity is to be used. The theoretical basis for the method has been eclipsed by the latest educational technology. The answer to the question of *why* a particular activity is being performed may be that the teacher's manual specified that this activity is to be completed two times a day for a period of three weeks before Book Three can be used with the audio-visual-motor-computer machine.

The point of this somewhat cynical view of pupils engulfed in orderly technology without a theoretical basis is that such activity may be wasteful. In their enthusiasm to "do something," education students often question the need to study theory. What is needed, they imply, are "practical" methods and techniques to help children. Knowledge of methods and techniques is indispensable, but one must inquire *what* techniques do and *why*. In many classrooms and clinics across the country, teachers are busily engaged in neat, orderly techniques, completing page after page or step after step in sequential fashion without knowing why. As a result, much of the work is probably wasteful of all resources—time, effort, money—and, most important, children. There has been too great an emphasis in some classes on practical arts and practical academics, with a neglect of the theory underlying the methodology.

The Role of Theory

An understanding of the theories that form the foundation of the field of learning disabilities is a basic requirement for understanding and participating fully in the field. Theory provides perspectives for examining and interpreting the various branches of the field. It is also helpful in sorting and evaluating the bewildering deluge of new materials, techniques, machines and gadgets, methods and mediums confronting the educator.

Theories in this context are meant to be working statements. As John Dewey (1946) expressed it, "They are not meant to be ideas frozen into absolute standards masquerading as eternal truth or programs rigidly adhered to; rather, theory is to serve as a guide in systematizing knowledge and as a working concept to be modified in the light of new knowledge." This process of theory building can be useful in separating what we know from what we believe or infer. Dewey contended that theory is the most practical of all things.

The purpose of theory is to bring form, coherence, and meaning to what we observe in the real world. Theory is practical in that it provides a guide for action, creates a catalyst for further research and theory building, and clarifies and structures the processes of thought. Without a theoretical basis for evaluation and treatment, decisions are based on faith in what the experts say, intuitive homilies and principles, or the bandwagon approach to decisions in education—the use of materials or techniques that appear to be popular at the moment.

Every profession is dependent upon the concepts and ideas contributed by earlier theorists. We build upon the underlying support of past theories, even though we modify and change them. Learning disabilities, if it is to continue as a dynamic and growing field of study, needs the development of conceptual models on which to base treatment.

The role of theory, then, is to provide the creative framework for meeting the challenge of learning disabilities. The theories generated in this field to understand and help atypical learners have significant applications in the fields of special education and regular education as well.

Maturational Theories of Learning Disabilities

The maturation view of learning disabilities is built on the concepts of developmental psychology, the analysis of children's thinking through the study of the sequential maturation of cognitive abilities in children. The maturational view suggests that a progression of abilities normally occurs under appropriate conditions. Knowledge of maturation and the normal cognitive development of children serves as a basis of comparison for understanding children with learning problems since the child's maturational status affects the ability to learn.

Further, the maturational perspective implies that attempts to speed up or by-pass the developmental process may actually create problems. Piaget, the famous developmental psychologist, is said to have remarked, "Every time I describe a maturational sequence in the United States, an American asks: 'How can you speed it up?'"

Maturational Lag

The concept of *maturational lag* posits a slowness in certain specialized aspects of neurological development. According to this point of view, each individual has a preset rate of development of the various factors of human growth, including cognitive function (Bender, 1957). Children who show discrepancies among the various subabilities do not necessarily suffer from central nervous system dysfunction or brain damage; rather the discrepancies show that various abilities are maturing at different rates. Proponents of the maturational lag viewpoint hypothesize that children with learning disorders are not so different from children without them. It is more a matter of *timing*, and the developmental lag in the maturation of certain skills is viewed as temporary.

The concept of maturational lag leads to a view that many learning disabilities are created when children are pushed by society into attempting academic performances before they are ready. Thus, the demands of schooling compound the distortion by introducing experiences beyond the student's readiness or capacity at a given stage of development.

Koppitz (1972–73), in a five-year follow-up study of 177 special-class pupils with learning disabilities, found that "slow maturation" described most of these children. She concluded that children with learning disabilities are more immature and more poorly integrated than most and that they need more time to learn and grow up. Many children with learning disabilities need extra time in order to compensate for slowness in neurological development—usually requiring one or two more years than other pupils to complete their schooling. Moreover, the Koppitz study indicated that when given this extra time and some help these children often do well academically.

The maturational-lag point of view also receives support from the findings of a study conducted by Silver and Hagin (1966). This study was of children who had been diagnosed and treated for reading disabilities at Bellevue Hospital Mental Hygiene Clinic. A number of years later, when the subjects were young adults aged sixteen to twenty-four, they were called back for a follow-up evaluation. At that time, they did not show difficulty in spatial orientation of symbols, auditory discrimination, or left-right discrimination,-

although they had manifested such problems as children. Through the process of maturation, many of these problems had apparently disappeared.

In an extensive study aimed at finding factors that best predicted reading failure in kindergarten children, deHirsch, Jansky, and Langford (1966) found that tests that were most sensitive to differences in maturation were the ones that best predicted reading and spelling achievement in second grade. Of the tests grouped under the category "Maturation-Sensitive Tests," 76 percent were significantly correlated with grade achievement, compared to only 17 percent of the "Nonmaturation-Sensitive Tests." DeHirsch contended that the data generated by the study supported the theory that maturational status is the crucial factor in forecasting subsequent reading achievement.

Another view of the impact of maturation on the student with learning disabilities was proposed by Kirk (1967), who suggested that during the growing stages the student normally tends to perform in functions that are comfortable while avoiding activities and functions that are uncomfortable. Since certain processes have lagged in maturation and are not functioning adequately for students with learning disabilities, they avoid and withdraw from activities requiring those processes. As a result, the neglected functions fail to develop; and consequently, the disability is intensified and exaggerated.

The maturational concept suggests that a major cause of school difficulty is immaturity. An implication of this train of thought is that younger and less mature children in a grade would experience more learning problems than older students in that grade. In fact, several research studies found this to be the case. Younger children in the early grades do have more learning problems. When the month of birth was compared with the percentage of children referred for learning disabilities services, the researchers found that the younger children (those born near the cutoff date for school entrance) were much more likely to be referred for learning disabilities services. The researchers called this phenomenon "the birthdate effect" (Diamond, 1983; Di Pasquale, Moule, & Flewelling, 1980).

Piaget's Maturational Stages of Development

Piaget, the famous Swiss psychologist, spent his life studying the intellectual development of children. His concepts of maturational stages of logical thinking suggest that cognitive growth occurs in a series of invariant and interdependent stages. At each stage, the child is capable of learning only certain cognitive tasks (Piaget, 1970). The child's ability to think and learn changes with age, that is, with passage through a series of maturational or developmental stages. The quantity, quality, depth, and breadth of the learning that occurs are a function of the stages during which the learning takes place. Piaget provided a schematic description of the normal child's stages of development.

1. The first two years of life are called the *sensorimotor* period. During this time children learn through senses and movements and by interacting

Exploring his environment by touching and examining is one important means for this toddler to learn.   *(Hays/Monkmeyer)*

with the physical environment. By moving, touching, hitting, biting, and so on, and by physically manipulating objects, children learn about the properties of space, time, location, permanence, and causality. Sensorimotor learning will be discussed in Chapter 10.

2. Piaget called the next five years of life, ages two to seven, the *preoperational* stage. During this stage children make intuitive judgments about relationships and also begin to think with symbols. Language now becomes increasingly important, and children learn to use symbols to represent the concrete world. They begin to learn about the properties and attributes of the world about them. Their thinking is dominated largely by the world of perception. The subject of perception is one of the concerns of Chapter 10.

3. The period occurring between ages seven and eleven is called the *concrete operations* stage. Children are now able to think through relationships, to perceive consequences of acts, and to group entities in a logical fashion. They are better able to systematize and organize their thoughts. Their thoughts, however, are shaped in large measure by previous experiences and depend on concrete objects that they have manipulated or understood through the senses.

4. The fourth stage, that of *formal operations*, commences at about age eleven and reflects a major transition in the thinking process. At this stage, instead of observations directing thought, thought now directs observations. Children now have the capacity to work with abstractions, theories, and logical relationships without having to refer to the concrete. The formal operations period provides a generalized orientation toward problem-solving activity.

The transition from one level to the next involves maturation. According to Piaget, the stages are sequential and hierarchical, and it is essential that a child be given opportunities to stabilize behavior and thought at each stage of development.

Yet the school curriculum frequently requires the child to develop abstract and logical conceptualizations in a given area without providing sufficient opportunity to go through preliminary levels of understanding. Attempts to teach abstract, logical concepts divorced from any real experiential understanding on the part of the child may lead to inadequate and insecure learning. The teacher may think the child is learning true concept development, but it may be only surface verbal responses.

CASE EXAMPLE

Maturational Theory

Illustrations of young children who have surface verbal skills without an in-depth understanding of concepts are frequently amusing. One kindergarten child explained with seemingly verbal proficiency the scientific technicalities of a spaceship being shot into orbit. His apparently precocious explanation ended with: "and now for the blast-off . . . 10—3—8—5—6—1!"

The maturation of the cognitive ability to categorize objects was apparent when each of three children, aged seven, nine, and eleven, was asked to pack clothes for a trip in two suitcases. Sue, the eleven-year-old, was adultlike in her thinking, packing day clothes in one case and night clothes in another. Dean, the seven-year-old, had no organizational arrangement and proceeded to randomly stuff one suitcase with as much as it would hold and then to stuff the second with the remainder. Laura, the nine-year-old, made an organizational plan that called for clothes above the waist to go in one suitcase and clothes below the waist to go in the second. The top parts of pajamas and a two-piece bathing suit were placed in one suitcase and the bottoms in the other. Each child had categorized in a manner appropriate to the individual's maturational stage.

Schools sometimes neglect the need for prelogical experiences and learning in their attempts to meet the current trend to teach abstract concepts and logical thinking in the primary grades. In instituting a modern mathematics program in one district's kindergarten, the teachers were advised that an understanding of the one-to-one correspondence was a higher and more important cognitive level than other kinds of number learning. Special learnings of numbers taught through games like "Ten Little Indians" and other counting experiences were unfortunately dropped from the kindergarten curriculum because these activities did not develop "logical thinking."

Piaget used the following experiments to illustrate that children's notions of *conservation* develop according to their maturational stage of thinking. In one of his conservation experiments, two balls of clay of equal size were placed on a scale to demonstrate to the child that they were equal. One ball of clay was then flattened. Piaget found that eight-year-olds were likely to predict that they were still the same weight whereas four-year-olds said that the flattened ball of clay weighed more. In another experiment, an equal amount of liquid was poured in two identical glasses. When the liquid from one glass was emptied into a tall thin container, five-year-olds were convinced that the tall thin glass contained more liquid, but seven-year-olds knew there was no difference in volume. From experiments such as these, Piaget concluded that the child's ability to understand the principles of conservation develops naturally through the maturational process.

Piaget's ideas about the development of cognitive structures through assimilation and accommodation and the implications for learning disabilities are discussed later in this chapter.

In summary, the maturational point of view expresses the belief that all individuals have a natural development and time for the maturation of various skills. What is sometimes thought to be a learning problem in a child may be merely a lag in the maturation of certain processes. It is important for those who have the responsibility of providing the educational environment for the child to be aware of the child's stage of maturation and of any lags in maturation that may be present. It has been noted, ironically, that with all our attempts to be "scientific" about decisions made in education, one of the most important decisions—when to teach a child to read—is based on the science of *astrology*. The star under which the child is born, the birth date, is the key determining factor of this crucial decision because it determines when the child enters school and begins formal school learning.

Implications of Maturational Theories for Learning Disabilities

Theories of maturational development have significant implications for understanding and teaching learning disabled children and youth. The theory suggests that the cognitive abilities of the child are qualitatively different from those of the adult. Cognitive abilities develop in a sequential fashion that cannot be altered. Further, as children mature, their way of thinking continually changes.

An implication, then, is that the school must design learning experiences to enhance the establishment of natural developmental growth. Instead, the educational environment may be hindering rather than assisting the student's development, learning, and cognitive growth. If the school makes intellectual demands of students that require cognitive abilities they have not yet developed, learning problems may be created. In interpreting Piaget for teachers, Furth (1970) asks for schooling that allows for the development of maturational experiences rather than demands that students perform skills for which they are not ready.

The first job of our schools, according to Furth, should be to strengthen the thinking foundation on which further learning is grounded. Without the foundation in thinking and teaching that promotes the development of the child's cognitive structure, learning is merely surface and illusory learning. In jest, some avid proponents of the maturational point of view suggest that the forcing of young children to perform academic tasks for which they are not ready (such as requiring immature preschoolers to read) should be considered a form of child abuse.

Educators frequently use the term *readiness* to refer to a state of maturational development that is needed before some desired skill can be learned. For example, readiness for walking requires a certain level of development of the neurological system, adequate muscle strength, and the development of certain prerequisite motor functions. Until an infant has these abilities, attempts to teach the skill of walking are futile. To illustrate readiness in a very different area of learning, a student must have acquired certain mathematics skills and knowledge to profit from a course in calculus.

While readiness skills are picked up in an incidental fashion by normal learners, students with learning disabilities require special attention to help them gain and strengthen the prerequisite or readiness abilities needed for the next step of learning. Although we should not force students into learning content or subject matter for which they are not ready, sensitive evaluation and clinical teaching can help students acquire the needed prerequisite abilities.

Psychological Processing and Academic Skills Mastery

Two theories in learning disabilities, a *psychological processing* perspective, and an *academic skills mastery* perspective, are often presented as alternative approaches to evaluation and remediation (Ysseldyke & Salvia, 1974). The first theory focuses on the student's abilities and disabilities; the second concentrates on the analysis of the task to be learned. While these two perspectives provide a forum for lively debate, in practice, few teachers exclusively follow either one or the other. The two methods need not be viewed as diametrically opposed procedures nor as mutually exclusive alternatives. Nonetheless, it is useful to understand each theory, along with the implications of each for understanding and teaching the learning-disabled student.

The Concept of Psychological Processing

As noted in Chapter 1, students with learning disabilities are often defined, in part, as those having "disorders in one or more of the basic *psychological processes* needed for school learning." A number of terms are used to refer to these psychological processes, including *perceptual modalities, perceptual processing, learning style, and psycholinguistic abilities*. They all describe the ways in which human beings organize and interpret data or stimuli in the world. Disorders in these basic psychological processes are referred to as *central processing dysfunctions* or *psycholinguistic disabilities*. "Processes are constituted of specific covert behaviors, which transform and manipulate information between the time it enters as a stimulus and the time a response to it is selected" (Torgesen, 1979b, p. 516).

Researchers have proposed several models of psychological processing as means of interpreting learning disabilities (Johnson & Myklebust, 1967; Kirk & Chalfant, 1984; Kirk & Kirk, 1971; Wepman, 1968). Although these models differ in certain respects, all of them specify underlying processing abilities, such as auditory processing, visual processing, kinesthetic and tactile processing, memory abilities, language abilities, and so forth. Moreover, each of these processing abilities is further subdivided. For example, visual processing comprises visual perception, visual discrimination, visual memory, and visual closure.

The concepts fundamental to the psychological processing theory are that students differ in their underlying mental abilities to process and use information and that these differences affect a student's learning. Further, students with processing dysfunctions are unable to learn from regular classroom instruction, and they need special teaching methods. In other words, the basic premise is that certain students fail to learn efficiently in school because of deficits in their psychological processing functions. The theory suggests that students with auditory processing dysfunctions, for example, will encounter difficulty with instructional approaches that are primarily auditory, such as phonics. Similarly, students with visual processing dysfunctions are likely to experience obstacles in learning to read by methods that are primarily visual, such as the so-called sight method.

According to the theory, once teachers discern or diagnose these processing abilities and disabilities, they can prescribe appropriate teaching methods. One generally assesses a student's weaknesses and strengths in processing functions through tests or observations. The information or observation should then lead the teacher to develop an appropriate teaching plan. Proponents of the theory have designed three different teaching plans, all based on knowledge of the student's processing abilities and disabilities.

Teaching Strategy 1: Training-the-Deficit Process   The purpose of this method is to help the student develop and build those processing functions that are weak. The underlying deficit abilities are strengthened and improved through practice and training. The teaching plan concentrates on the deficit process, in order to eliminate the disability and prepare the student for further learning.

Teaching Strategy 2: Teaching Through the Preferred Process
This approach uses the student's modality of strength as the basis of teaching. The contention is that instruction should be based on teaching methods and treatment procedures that take advantage of the student's strengths and circumvent his or her processing weaknesses. One method to investigate the effectiveness of teaching to a student's preferred processing modality is called *aptitude-treatment-interaction.* It seeks to identify those abilities of a student that respond successfully to treatment.

Teaching Strategy 3: The Combined Approach   The third teaching approach based on the processing concept combines aspects of the two previous methods. It advocates that the teacher not only instruct the student by a method that emphasizes the processing strengths but concurrently use teaching strategies to strengthen the processing weaknesses.

Commentary

The theory of psychological processing dysfunctions as a way of understanding a student's inability to learn became central to the field of learning disabilities during its early years of transition and integration. Many teachers and other professionals found the concept to be both a refreshing and hopeful new way to view students who could not learn and to plan teaching for them. In recent years, however, professionals are asking certain critical questions about the theory:

1. Do psychological processing factors cause learning failure?
2. Can psychological processes be measured through existing tests?
3. Does teaching based on psychological processing information help students learn?

Each of these questions is examined in turn.

1. *Do psychological processing factors cause learning failure?* The critics charge that the theory *assumes* that psychological processing disabilities are the cause of learning disabilities. Since the evidence that has supported the relationship so far is correlational, and correlation does not imply causation, the assumption cannot at present be proven. The critics argue further that since we can only hypothesize the existence of the underlying psychological processes because they are not observable phenomena, they may not, in fact, exist. They believe that hypothetical constructs should not be used in diagnosing and planning for a student

with learning disabilities; instead, they propose that teachers use the academic skills mastery approach (Mann, 1979; Salvia & Ysseldyke, 1981).

2. *Can psychological processes be measured through existing tests?* Another question concerns the tests that teachers typically use to measure psychological processes. After reviewing the research literature on such tests, Ysseldyke (1977, 1978) and Salvia and Ysseldyke (1981) conclude that current measures of ability lack the necessary reliability and validity to be used to identify students' strengths and weaknesses and make consequent decisions. In addition, Torgesen (1979b) feels that poor performance on one kind of test may not demonstrate a deficiency in a given psychological process.

It should be pointed out that many widely used achievement tests are also subject to the same criticisms of inadequate construction, validity, or reliability (Ysseldyke, 1977, 1978). In fact, Ralph Nader has charged that college entrance examinations, such as the SAT, are subject to these criticisms to such a degree that he and his investigating committee consider them to be fraudulent (Fields & Jacabson, 1980).

Another point that is frequently made concerning psychological processes relates to the age of the subject. The processing tests and teaching procedures appear to be a more important consideration in planning for a young child than for an adolescent.

3. *Does teaching based on psychological processing information help students learn?* Each of the three teaching approaches based on psychological processing information about a student has been criticized separately.

a. *Training-the-deficit process* has been the target of most of the critical research of processing. A number of critics have questioned its efficacy (Hammill and Larsen, 1974a; Hammill and Larsen, 1974b; Newcomer and Hammill, 1976; Larsen and Hammill, 1975; Vellutino, 1977; Vellutino, Steger, Moyer, Harding, & Niles, 1977). One often-cited research study was conducted by Hammill and Larsen (1974a), in which the authors reviewed thirty-eight earlier studies of process training and concluded that such training had not been conclusively demonstrated to be an effective method of teaching. The Hammill and Larsen (1974a) study itself was criticized by Minskoff (1975) on methodological grounds and by Lund, Foster, and McCall-Perez (1978) on the grounds that a reanalysis of the original data indicated that the method was effective in many cases.

Kavale (1982) analyzed the data in 161 studies through a statistical method known as meta-analysis and found that visual perception is an important correlate in the complex of variables related to reading achievement.

In general, although the research is still unclear, it does suggest that training psychological processes *in isolation* will not improve academic skills. The deficit abilities are only a prerequisite for learning; it is still necessary to teach reading skills and arithmetic skills. Research indicates that the age of the student and the severity of the problem also have an impact on the success of the method.

b. *Teaching through the preferred process* has not received as much research attention as deficit training. However, several studies have been conducted in which students were given tests to determine their modality preference and then given differential instruction (generally in reading) by a method that supposedly utilized the processing strength—either in the visual or in the auditory process (Jones, 1972; Robinson, 1972; Sabatino & Dorfman, 1974; Newcomer and Goodman, 1975). Tarver and Dawson (1978) conducted a review of fifteen modality preference studies. The results of these studies, in general, showed that there were no significantly successful learning experiences based on tailoring the method of reading instruction to the student's processing strength.

Explanations have been given for the lack of research support: the tests may not be accurate measures of modality preference, and there are methodological flaws in the research. The most obvious answer appears to be that one does not use only one modality in reading. Thus, even though a phonics method were to be used to teach auditory learners, they would still have to employ visual processes in learning phonics. Similarly, in learning sight words, students also have to use auditory abilities. In order to read, a person must use several psychological processes—not just one.

c. *The combined approach* to teaching based on the psychological processing framework advocates both teaching through the preferred process and training the deficits. This may be viewed as an eclectic method since it combines aspects of the other approaches; consequently, it is difficult to isolate effects and conduct research. At this point, therefore, little research has been reported on the combined approach.

The Concept of Academic Skills Mastery

The *academic skills mastery* approach to evaluating and teaching learning-disabled students is proposed as an alternative to the psychological processing approach. Several terms refer to this theory of instruction, including *task analysis, specific skills training, directed teaching, sequential skills teaching,* and *mastery learning*. Rejecting the notion that prerequisite disabilities and deficits cause academic failure, proponents of this school of thought recommend that educators concentrate on the academic skills that students need to learn rather than on the disabilities that impede their learning (Ysseldyke, 1978, 1983; Treiber and Lahey, 1983; Salvia and Ysseldyke, 1981; Vellutino, 1977; Bloom, 1976).

The essence of the academic skills mastery approach is the analysis of the academic task in terms of the underlying skills needed to accomplish that task. These skills are then placed in an ordered and logical sequence and students are tested to determine which of these skills they possess and which they do not. Teaching involves helping students acquire the subskills that are not yet mastered.

Ysseldyke (1978) describes the approach as the analysis of a complex terminal behavior into its component parts (called *enabling behaviors*); then teaching those enabling behaviors that a pupil does not yet demonstrate; and finally, integrating those behaviors into the terminal objectives. The theory holds that assessment be restricted to the strengths and weaknesses of specific skills and instruction be restricted to the teaching of those skills. The academic skills mastery approach does not acknowledge any special learning problems or ability deficits within the pupil other than a lack of experience and practice with the task. The underlying assumption is that academic success or failure is due to the connections between the subskills that are characteristic of a particular academic task. The theory focuses on an analysis of the task rather than on an analysis of the student. Here is a summary of the steps of the academic skills mastery approach:

1. State objectives to be achieved and skills to be learned in terms of student performance.
2. Analyze the skill to be learned in terms of specific tasks.
3. List the tasks to be learned in a sequential order.
4. Determine which of these tasks the student knows and does not know.
5. Teach through direct instruction. Do not make assumptions about the learner's ability to acquire the skill.
6. Teach one task at a time. When that has been learned, teach the next task.
7. Evaluate the effectiveness of the instruction in terms of whether the student has learned the skill.

The steps involved in teaching a student to swim illustrate the academic skills mastery approach. First, one observes the student's failure to swim when he or she sinks to the bottom of the pool or refuses to enter the water. Then, one analyzes the steps needed for swimming—for example, floating, treading water, breathing under water, kicking, and so forth. Then, one teaches the student each skill in sequence, helps the student to combine the skills, and finally observes the student swimming across the pool. Although this example is not of an academic task, the same procedure can be applied to teaching an academic area, be it reading, mathematics, or writing.

The theoretical underpinnings of the academic skills mastery approach can be found in the research from applied behavior analysis (Bijou, 1970; Gagné, 1985), as well as in the work of other educational theorists (Bloom, 1976, 1978). According to Bloom (1978), "What any person in the world can learn, almost all persons can learn if provided with appropriate prior and current conditions of learning" (p. 564). Bloom theorizes that under favorable learning conditions (such as those provided by academic skills mastery), the level of learning of students tends to rise over a series of learning tasks. Bloom, however, limits the successful application of academic skills mastery theory to the middle 95 percent of the school population. The student with learning disabilities may fall within the 5 percent that Bloom excludes. So, academic skills mastery theory may be more useful in mild cases of learning disabilities than in severe ones.

Commentary

There are several questions that have been raised concerning the academic skills mastery theory when it becomes the sole basis for thinking about children and youth with learning disabilities.

1. *Is learning composed of a set of separate and distinct skills?* Many kinds of learning cannot be viewed as a set of separate skills. For example, many authorities do not think a task as complex as reading can be sub-divided into specific measurable and observable skills. There is disagreement about what the skills are, how many there are, and what the order for learning them should be. The cognitive processes involved in the acts of reading and learning to read remain a mystery despite vast research into this area. The whole (reading) is greater than the sum of its parts (specific skills). Pearson and Spiro (1980) note that although mastering all of these skills has something to do with reading, they question whether mastery of those skills transfers to what is understood to be "reading."

2. *Can skills be ordered in a hierarchy?* The sequence of specific skills is perhaps logical and ordered from an adult point of view. The problem is that children do not learn in a logical and ordered fashion; they learn in their own unique fashion. This is particularly true of the learning disabled. Developmental psychologists (Piaget, 1970) have taught us that the thinking of children is different from that of adults. Many reading authorities believe that the whole notion of a sequence or hierarchy of skills in the field of reading is at best a pedagogical convenience. They charge that although the idea may appeal to our sense of logic, there is little evidence to support the existence of separate skills, let alone separate skills that can be placed in a hierarchy (Pearson and Spiro, 1980).

3. *Is the establishment of a set of skills a method of teaching?* Stating that a specific skill should be taught is not a method of instruction. It still begs that question of *how* that skill should be taught. In deciding how to teach, we must look at how the student learns.

4. *Are children and youth with learning disabilities different from other kinds of underachievers?* It is difficult to justify the concept of learning disabilities based only on an academic skills mastery perspective (Ysseldyke, 1982). Academic skills mastery is a recommended teaching approach for all students and for all underachievers; the theory does not

FIGURE 6.1
Building an Integrated Process-Skills Theory in Learning Disabilities

Theory of
Integrated
Process-Skills

Theory of   Theory of
Psychological   Academic Skills
Processing   Mastery

discriminate the learning disabled as a unique group (Torgesen, 1979b). Cruickshank (1977) points out that it is misleading to ignore concepts of psychological processing disorders when thinking about learning disabilities because we are dealing with complex developmental problems—not just a problem of sequential teaching.

Implications for Teaching: Combining the Two Approaches

The building of new theories depends on the foundation and experience of earlier theories. A new theory is often the effect of a synergistic combination of elements of the contributing earlier theories. Synergy occurs when the new entity created is something none of the contributing parts could achieve alone. We are suggesting that a more comprehensive theory can integrate the two perspectives—psychological processing and task analysis. As illustrated in Figure 6.1, we stand on the shoulders of the giants who have come before us.

The problems in this "processing versus skills" debate are indeed complex; we need much more information about the nature of human learning to resolve the issues. It appears, however, that elements of both views have a role to play in the solution. Concepts of psychological processing must be broadened to include other cognitive areas; views of academic skills must also be broadened to include the interaction between instructional variables and student-centered variables. As Torgesen (1979b) puts it,

> . . . we should keep the concept of psychological processes alive. The notion of deficiencies in the processing activities required for learning is essential to the

maintenance of concern with learning-disabled children as a special subgroup within the general population of underachievers. . . . Although the basic concept of processing deficiencies is important and viable, adjustments are needed in the manner in which these processes are conceptualized and measured (p. 520).

The suggested combination of the two approaches provides an excellent example of theory building, as discussed at the beginning of this chapter. Each theory has been found through experience to have certain limitations. What is needed is a broader, more comprehensive theory that can integrate both psychological processing and academic skills mastery.

Cognitive Abilities and Learning Strategies

The process of learning obviously involves thinking and knowing, or cognition. Therefore, the analysis of the nature of cognitive abilities and thinking processes is critical to an understanding of learning disabilities.

The term *cognitive abilities* refers to a collection of mental skills that are essential human functions. They enable one to know, to be aware, to think, to conceptualize, to use abstractions, to reason, to criticize, and to be creative. Cognition is the manner in which humans acquire, interpret, organize, store, retrieve, and employ information. Neisser (1967) defined cognition as the process by which sensory input is transferred, reduced, elaborated, stored, recovered, and used. Cognitive abilities develop at all stages of life and involve various kinds of behavior. For example, when a young child plays at putting pots and pans inside each other, he or she is acquiring certain cognitive skills. It is difficult to examine cognition apart from other kinds of learning since its development is intertwined with the growth of the individual, a process that includes motor, perceptual, memory, language, and social learning. A disturbance in the thinking process no doubt is an important factor for many children and youth with learning disabilities. Further, a disturbance or inadequate development in other areas of learning is likely to affect adversely the development of the higher cognitive abilities.

Piaget's Development of Cognitive Structures

Piaget (1970) recognized the importance of structuring thinking in order to learn. He observed that each person approaches the learning task with an existing cognitive structure (or, as Piaget called it, *schemata*). The learner adapts to the environment and structures new knowledge in two complementary ways, which Piaget called *assimilation* and *accommodation*.

In *assimilation*, learners incorporate new experiences into their already existing schemata, or cognitive structure. That is, the new experiences provide practice and strengthen their existing cognitive structures. In *accommodation*, learners focus on the new features of a learning task, thereby changing their cognitive structures. For example, in picking up a ball, a two-year-old girl will assimilate the grasping technique she has already acquired; but the girl will also accommodate to the new features of the ball by changing her cognitive structure (or schemata). Thus, according to Piaget, learning and cognitive development consist of a succession of changes in one's cognitive structures through both assimilation and accommodation.

The implication of Piaget's theoretical framework for learning disabilities is that what students learn depends on their existing cognitive structure, the experiences and knowledge that they bring to the learning situation. Therefore, one of the most important factors in learning is what the students already know. They must learn to use the experience, the knowledge, and the skills they already possess.

Memory Abilities and Learning

The fact that some pupils who are unsuccessful learners have poor memories, of course, was observed long before learning disabilities was recognized as a field of study. There is now a renewed interest in the role of memory in learning, in the kinds of memory operating within a learning task, and in ways to improve memory. The fields of psychology, biochemistry and neurology have directed increased attention to the mechanism of human memory.

Sensation and perception take place when the stimulus is present; they are ongoing activities. Memory pertains to sensations and data *already* received and perceived. The ability to store and retrieve previously experienced sensations and perceptions when the stimulus that originally evoked them is no longer present is called memory, imagery, recall, or sometimes "the mind's eye."

Examples of sensations and perceptions that occur only in the mind are the musician "listening" to music played at an earlier time; the cook "tasting" the sourness of a lemon to be used; the carpenter "feeling" the roughness of sandpaper used yesterday in a job; the gardener "smelling" the sweetness of lilacs while looking at the buds on the tree. McCarthy (1968) describes how she helped her three-year-old understand the qualities of memory. She explained the word "mind" by asking the youngster to close her eyes and think about a peanut butter and jelly sandwich. Yes, the child could "see" the jelly dripping down the sides of the bread; she could "smell" the peanut butter; and she could even "taste" the first bite. Where was this sandwich that had become so vivid? It was, so went the explanation, in the same place her mind was.

Memory Mechanisms

There are at least three stages of memory in which the child with learning disabilities could have difficulty: *reception, storage, or retrieval* (Howe, 1970). First, the child must *receive* the information, that is, be able to clearly understand what is to be remembered. A child may not remember something if it was not initially perceived clearly. Poor reception may also be related to

Students can be helped to develop efficient learning strategies that will enhance their ability to remember in academic tasks.   *(Lionel J-M Delevingne/Stock, Boston)*

inability to attend. Secondly, the information must be *stored* within the brain. There seem to be several stages and ways for the brain to store information. Thirdly, to remember something it must be *retrieved* from storage. Some students have difficulty getting the information back from storage. Most of us have had the experience of having a name or a word on the tip of our tongue but being unable to retrieve it.

Writers in the field of human memory refer to three types of memory storage systems: (1) a sensory storage or register, (2) a short-term store, and (3) a long-term store. Information is first contained in the *storage register;* then it is identified and retained in the *short-term store;* finally, selected information is assimilated into what already is stored in the *long-term store.* Information that is not coded successfully for long-term storage fades away and is largely forgotten. Rehearsal is needed to maintain the information in short-term store.

Effect of Memory on Other Mental Abilities

Memory is separable in concept from other facets of the intellect; it is not synonymous with intelligence. The individual may have a poor visual memory, yet excel in abstract reasoning. Conversely, a person with poor comprehension may possess an above average memory. Einstein's childhood, as noted in Chapter 1, suggests that he exhibited certain deficits in auditory memory while possessing qualities of a genius in quantitative thinking.

A fascinating account of a man who possessed an unusual ability to remember while he manifested poor abstract reasoning ability is reported by the Russian psychologist Luria (1968). The memory of this man, whom Luria referred to as "S," was so remarkable that he became a professional mnemonist, that is, a man who earns his living by demonstrating his remarkable capacity to remember. Luria had S memorize a table containing fifty numbers arranged in four columns and thirteen rows. After three minutes of study, S could reproduce the items perfectly in any pattern—column by column, diagonally, or in the form of one fifty-digit number. Moreover, he was able to reproduce the table perfectly several months later. Even after fifteen or sixteen years, S was able to repeat a series of numbers Luria had given him, and he had complete recall of the setting fifteen years earlier—Luria's clothing, the appearance of the room, and so on.

Yet this remarkable mental subskill was not accompanied by superiority in other intellectual abilities, and this isolated ability brought its own frustrations. S's problem was that although he remembered almost everything he had experienced, he lacked an ability that most of us recognize only as a limitation—the ability to forget. Because S found it very difficult to eliminate images no longer useful, his vivid imagery blocked his understanding of the meaning of written descriptions and made abstract reasoning extremely difficult for him.

The saga of Luria's subject illustrates the concept that memory is an ability that is separable from other elements of the intellect.

Kinds of Memory

Students with learning disabilities frequently have difficulty recalling what things looked like or sounded like. Memory of past experiences must be retained and compared in order to organize and interpret experience. Otherwise each experience is unique, with no connection to previous experience and learning. Memory refers to the recall of nonverbal as well as verbal experiences— for example, the inability to recall the meanings of sounds made by dogs, horns, bells, and certain voice qualities, or to recall the meanings conveyed by facial expressions. The inability to remember words, directions, and explanations exemplifies disabilities of remembering language. Memory problems can also be related to a specific perceptual process, for example, visual memory or auditory memory. There are other categories of memory that can be differentiated, such as rote memory, immediate or short-term memory, sequential or serial memory, and long-term memory.

Rote memory connotes repetition carried out mechanically without understanding. Thus, one child who through rote memory learned to repeat the alphabet without realizing the meaning of the letters asked what an "elemenopee" is.

Short-term or *immediate memory* is required in tasks in which the subject is expected to hold information in the mind for a relatively short period of time before retrieval. Tasks such as repeating digits, repeating a string of words, following a short series of instructions, remembering and reproducing designs, or spelling a word for a test are examples of tasks requiring short-term memory. Carroll (1967) found that people who had a poor aptitude for learning foreign language were also poor at the task of repeating nonsense syllables after a short delay, while people with high language aptitude had no trouble with this task.

Serial or *sequential memory* is another type of automatic response requiring a specified order to the items being recalled. For example, in saying the days of the week or in the act of counting, the order of the elements is of paramount importance. The order of the words in a sentence is crucial, particularly in the English language. The child who formulates a sentence in the order of object-verb-subject, "milk want baby," may be exhibiting a disturbance in sequential memory.

In *long-term memory,* knowledge must be retained and stored for a long period of time before retrieval of the information is required. Long-term and short-term memories are located within different structures of the brain. The phenomenon of memorizing material shortly before an examination and forgetting the bulk of it shortly afterward is well known to most students. Long-term memory requires the ability to assimilate, store, and retrieve information when it is needed. It is dependent on the learner's skill in seeing the relevancy of the material and relating it to past knowledge.

Retrieval of odd bits of long-term memory traces sometimes are triggered by strange events. For example, at a recent national education conference, a professor noted a vaguely familiar woman in the lobby. He observed her for several minutes, walked up to her, and blurted out, "Hilltop 5–4260." Indeed, that had been her telephone number some twenty-five years earlier; however, the professor could not remember the woman's name.

Helping Students Remember

Many learning-disabled students do poorly on tests of memory and in academic skills that require memory (recognizing words, numbers, facts).

Torgesen (1979a) suggests that the problem is not one of limited memory capacity but rather a difficulty in the management of intact memory capacities. In a study of children with reading disabilities, he found that these youngsters manifested a general lack of reflective knowledge about memory and memory processes, as well as a generally disorganized approach to cognitive tasks. Significant differences were found between good and poor readers in their knowledge about memory strategies, such as rehearsal, ability to generate a variety of different solutions to a memory problem, and planning for real-world memory problems. This suggests that teaching can make a difference by helping students develop memory strategies.

For efficient learning, an individual's memory in many areas of performance must become an automatic, habitual response to a stimulus. Examples of such automatic responses include remembering words when speaking, inserting the proper syntactic word form in a sentence, and remembering a word by sight when reading. Many factors have an effect on memory: the student's intensity of attention, meaningfulness of the material, interest in the subject, and the amount of drill and overlearning. Research indicates that appropriate environmental factors and teaching can help children improve in what they can remember (Torgesen, 1980, 1982; Valett, 1983).

Thus, while teaching cannot change a student's brain biologically, it can help students develop efficient learning strategies that will enhance ability to remember in academic tasks. Some of the learning strategies used by efficient learners are presented later in this chapter and in the Teaching Strategies sections of Part 4 of this text.

Cognitive Styles of Learning

There has been much recent interest in how one's cognitive approach to an academic situation influences the effectiveness of learning. Cognitive style refers to the student's general behavior and attitude when presented with a learning task. Analysis of the student's cognitive style of learning provides insight into the learning difficulties.

Reflective and Impulsive Cognitive Styles

One way of analyzing styles of learning is to determine whether the student's learning behavior is reflective or impulsive. In the *reflective* style, the student proceeds with careful deliberation, considerating alternatives before choosing a response to a problem. In the *impulsive* style, the student responds very quickly, without considering possible alternative responses.

Learning-disabled students often respond in an impulsive style, a behavior that research suggests is detrimental to school performance (Keogh, 1977; Epstein, Hallahan, & Kauffman, 1975). Teachers of learning-disabled students are very familiar with impulsive behavior. These students speak without first considering their thoughts and race through written assignments without monitoring right and wrong answers. In a matching figures task, they draw lines from one object to another without first inspecting the page. Impulsive students seem to come to decisions too quickly, without sufficient time between the stimulus and the response.

Torgesen (1980, 1982) suggests that the impulsive behavior of learning-disabled students is basically due to a lack of alternative cognitive strategies. These students respond impulsively because they do not have other ways readily at hand for coping with the learning task. The obvious solution is to help them acquire an array of useful cognitive learning strategies.

Active and Passive Cognitive Styles

Another way to view cognitive styles is to consider whether they are *active* or *passive*. Efficient learning requires an *active* and dynamic involvement in the learning process. Active learners efficiently use many cognitive strategies. They work at structuring the information (organization), asking themselves questions about the material (self-questioning), comparing the new information to what they already know (assimilation and accommodation). They are intensely involved and have a desire to learn, or motivation (Brown, 1978; Flavell, 1977).

Learning-disabled students, on the other hand, have learned to approach the learning task in a *passive* manner. They lack interest in learning probably because past learning experiences were often dismal exercises in failure and frustration. Not believing that they can learn, learning-disabled students do not know how to go about the task of learning. As a consequence, they become passive and dependent learners, a style that has been referred to as "learned helplessness" (Torgesen, 1982).

Metacognition

An important characteristic of efficient learners is that they know how to approach a learning situation; they know how to use and direct their own cognitive and thinking processes to be successful learners. Learning disabled students lack these efficient learning strategies. However, once they do learn the cognitive strategies used by efficient learners, they can apply them in many learning situations.

Metacognition refers to the awareness of one's systematic thinking strategies that are needed for learning. When people do something to help themselves learn and remember, they exhibit metacognitive behavior. Some common examples of metacognitive behavior are suggested by Loper (1980): preparing shopping lists to remember what one intends to buy, outlining difficult technical chapters to help understand and remember the material, and rehearsing and repeating what has just been learned to help stabilize and strengthen the learning. These behaviors indicate an awareness of one's own limitations and the ability to plan for one's own learning and for solving problems.

There is a parable that has meaning in this context. If you give a starving man a fish, you feed him for a day. However, if you teach the starving man to fish, you feed him for a lifetime. Similarly, if you teach a learning-disabled boy a fact, you help him for the moment; however, if you teach the boy how to think about learning, you help him for a lifetime.

Teaching Efficient Learning Strategies

What cognitive strategies are used by people who learn in an efficient and well-functioning manner? Efficient learners seem to be able to control and direct their thinking processes in order to facilitate learning and to deal with abstract concepts needed for academic learning. Efficient learners ask themselves questions; they organize their thoughts; they connect and integrate the new materials they are trying to learn with prior experience and knowledge they already possess; they try to predict what is to come; and they monitor the relevance of new information. Efficient learners exhibit an active interest in learning and solving problems. In other words, efficient learners have learned how to go about the business of learning and have at their disposal a repertoire of cognitive strategies that work for them (Deshler, Schumaker, & Lenz, 1984; Deshler, Schumaker, Lenz, & Ellis, 1984; Wiens, 1983; Brown, 1978; Meichenbaum, 1977; Torgesen, 1979a, 1980).

A characteristic of learning-disabled students is that they lack these functional cognitive learning strategies. They do not know how to control and direct their thinking to learn, how to gain more knowledge, or how to remember what they learn. Thus, what learning-disabled students need is specific instruction in how to learn. They must become aware of and acquire efficient cognitive strategies to facilitate learning and remembering. Once learned, cognitive strategies can be used in many contexts. Fortunately, research shows that learning-disabled students do improve after instruction in specific strategies for learning (Bos and Filip, 1984; Olsen, Wong, & Marx, 1983; Wiens, 1983; Gerber, 1983; Wong and Jones, 1982; Torgesen, 1982; Meichenbaum, 1977).

Instructional Techniques

Some examples of cognitive learning strategies that teachers can help students learn are presented below.

1. *Self-questioning.* The students quietly ask themselves questions about the material. This process is also referred to as verbal mediation. The internal language, or covert speech, helps organize material and behavior. Camp and Bash (1981) suggest the following types of questions:

   What is the problem? or What am I supposed to do?
   What is my plan? or How can I do it?
   Am I using my plan?
   How did I do?

2. *Rehearsal and review.* The students practice and review what they have learned. This self-rehearsal helps students remember. People forget when the brain trace, which is a physical record of memory, fades away. Recitation and review of material to be learned helps the student remember.

3. *Cognitive behavior modification.* This is an approach of the behaviorist school to teach students self-instruction, self-monitoring, and self-evaluation techniques (Meichenbaum, 1977). There are several steps: (a) the teacher models a behavior while giving an explanation; (b) the student performs the task while the teacher describes it; (c) the student talks

the task through out loud; (d) the student whispers it to himself or herself; and (e) the student performs the task with nonverbal self-cues.

4. *Use of organization.* To aid in recall, the student figures out the main idea of the lesson and supporting facts. The organization of material has a great deal to do with how fast we can learn it and how well we can remember it. Already existing memory units are called chunks, and through *chunking,* new material is reorganized into already existing memory units. The more students can relate what they are learning to what they already know, the better they will remember the material.

5. *Memory strategies.* If new material is anchored to old knowledge, students are more likely to remember it. For example, one student remembered the word "look" because it had two eyes in the middle. Some pupils can only alphabetize if they sing the "ABC" song. Some adults can remember people's names by using a mnemonic device that associates the name with a particular attribute of that individual, for example, "tall Tony."

6. *Predicting and monitoring.* The students guess about what they will learn in the lesson and then check on whether their guesses were correct.

7. *Modeling.* The teacher provides an example of appropriate cognitive behavior and problem-solving strategies. The teacher can talk through the cognitive processes being used.

Ways to use these and other cognitive strategies in specific academic areas are woven throughout various other chapters, especially in the Teaching Strategies section of this book. For example, see the Reading Comprehension section in Chapter 12. See also Chapter 9 for a discussion of learning strategies implemented with learning-disabled adolescents.

Feuerstein's Instrumental Enrichment*

An innovative and promising method of assessing intellectual potential and remediating cognitive deficits has been formulated and implemented by an Israeli psychologist, Reuven Feuerstein. This important work is receiving increasing attention from all segments of the educational and psychological community as a promising approach for meeting the needs of students with cognitive deficits. Feuerstein's work demonstrates that the human organism can be modified at all ages and stages of cognitive development. Further, with this method, the cognitive functioning of adolescents can be greatly increased. Several research reports indicate that teaching learning-disabled students cognitive processes through Feuerstein's method of instrumental enrichment is effective in improving problem-solving behavior (Messerer,

*J. Messerer, E. Hunt, G. Meyers, J. Lerner, "Feuerstein's Instrumental Enrichment: A New Approach for Activating Intellectual Potential in Learning Disabled Youth," *Journal of Learning Disabilities* Vol. 17, No. 6, June/July 1984, pp. 322–325. Reprinted by special permission of The Professional Press, Inc. Copyright © 1984 The Professional Press, Inc.

Hunt, Meyers, & Lerner, 1984; Harth, 1982; Arbitman-Smith & Haywood, 1980; Reid, Knight-Arest, & Hresko, 1981; Chance, 1981).

There are two basic components to the Feuerstein work: assessment and instruction. The assessment instrument is known as the *Learning Potential Assessment Device* (LPAD) (Feuerstein, 1979). The teaching method is called *Instrumental Enrichment* (IE) (Feuerstein, 1980).

Instrumental Enrichment is the fruit of many years of careful observation and research on the part of Feuerstein and his associates. Their studies focused on Israeli adolescents who were identified as mentally retarded, slow learners, and disadvantaged. One of the most significant results of their observations was the recognition that these students demonstrated specific "cognitive deficiencies" while engaged in problem-solving tasks. The cognitive deficiencies occurred during one or more of several phases of the problem-solving process: (1) at the *input* phase (that is, while gathering the relevant information critical to the solution of the problem); (2) during the *elaboration* phase (that is, while "operating on," or converting the input through mental manipulation to produce the desired result), or (3) during the *output* phase (that is, reporting the desired result) (Chance, 1981; Messerer et al., 1984).

The following example illustrates the three phases of the problem-solving process. Suppose six-year-old David is asked, "How many apples would you have if one person gave you two apples and another person gave you three apples?" In order for David to solve this problem, he must utilize the three phases of the problem-solving process. First, in the *input* phase, David must gather the correct data (that is, two apples, three apples, and the specified arithmetic operation of addition). Then in phase two, *elaboration,* David must elaborate on what is given to arrive at the appropriate solution (that is, apply the mathematical operation of addition to reach to solution of five apples). Finally, in phase three, *output,* David must express the derived answer (that is, the response of "five" must be expressed in oral or written form) (Messerer et al., 1984).

Feuerstein explains that cognitive difficulties may arise at any of the three levels of information processing (input, elaboration, or output), which could affect the accuracy of the student's response. Feuerstein suggests that cognitive processing difficulties result from deficit cognitive functions, and he recommends remediation through the Instrumental Enrichment method.

The Instrumental Enrichment curriculum itself consists of fifteen instruments (groups of lessons) that require from three to five one-hour sessions over the course of two to three years to complete (Feuerstein, 1980). In addition to the carefully structured materials, the most critical element of the program is the specially trained teacher, who provides "mediated learning experiences." The teacher first selects what is to be taught—specific events, concepts, ideas, principles, or other stimuli. The teacher highlights the attributes of these stimuli by interrelating them with the personal experiences of the pupils and with the problems presented on worksheets. Pupils come to

FIGURE 6.2
Instructional Enrichment: *Organization of Dots*

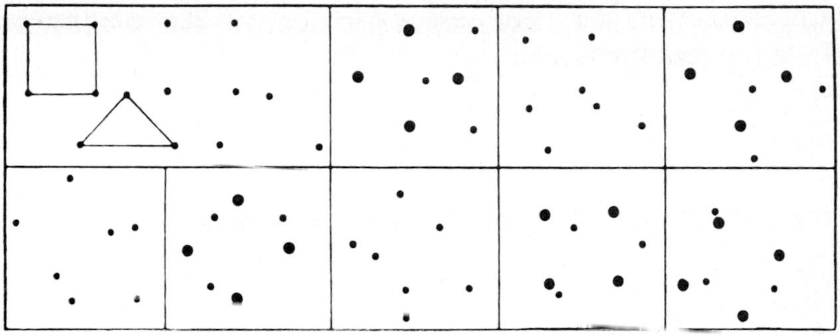

Source: Reuven Feuerstein, *Instrumental Enrichment—An Intervention Program for Cognitive Modifiability* from the program entitled Instrumental Enrichment; Organization of Dots (University Park Press, 1980). Reprinted by permission of the author.

understand that what is being discussed has a purpose that is both useful and meaningful, now and in the future. The pupils also learn that they will be able to use effectively what they are being taught.

The success of Instrumental Enrichment greatly depends on the specially trained teacher, or mediator. The program instruments themselves provide only opportunities through which mediated learning experiences can occur. It is the teacher-mediator who shapes these opportunities and brings them to the attention of the learner. Without the teacher's mediation, the pupil might fail to perceive the significant meaning of the learning experiences and thereby fail to apply them to everyday situations.

To illustrate the kinds of lessons used in Instrumental Enrichment, the *organization of dots* task is shown in Figure 6.2. The organization of dots task requires the learner to identify geometric figures embedded in an amorphous cloud of dots. For example, early lessons require the student to locate a square and a triangle in a cloud of seven dots. The teacher-mediator first orients the pupils to the presented task by asking a series of key questions designed to elicit both a definition of the problem and potential strategies for solving it. Next, the students attempt to solve the problem. Then the teacher-mediator leads a discussion in which students report the strategies that worked best. Then the teacher-mediator helps the students formulate a general metacognitive principle based on their learning experience and bridges that principle to other experiences in their own lives. In effect, the students, with the help of the teacher-mediator, develop metacognitive principles useful for future learning.

In summary, Feuerstein's work in metacognitive functioning offers new ways for understanding and remediating learning disabilities. The theory appears able to explain the difficulties experienced by learning-disabled students and provide techniques for assessment and remediation of learning disabilities.

Implications of Cognitive Approaches for Learning Disabilities

The cognitive learning strategies approach focuses on *how* students learn rather than on *what* they learn. Efficient learners use a number of cognitive strategies to help them learn and remember. However, learning-disabled students do not have a repertoire of learning strategies; they do not know how to go about learning. The teacher's role in this framework is a very critical one. The teacher helps students develop efficient learning strategies. In effect, the teacher helps students learn how to learn. Teachers can help students become aware of their own thought processes and develop accessible cognitive strategies to enhance learning.

Summary

• Theories and their relationship to teaching are a necessary framework for understanding learning disabilities. Theory building implies development of conceptual frameworks that take into account the shortcomings of earlier theories.

• Maturational theories of learning disabilities stress the natural progression of child growth and the sequential development of cognitive abilities. A state of readiness is needed for the child to acquire certain abilities. Forcing a child into trying to learn before that state of readiness has been reached can lead to academic failure or learning disabilities.

• Psychological processing refers to the way human beings organize and interpret data in the world. The student can have a psychological processing disorder in areas such as auditory processing, visual processing, or kinesthetic or tactile processing.

• Academic skills mastery is an approach to learning disabilities that emphasizes the analysis of the academic task in terms of the subskills that lead to the achievement of that task.

• Both psychological processing and academic skills mastery approaches when taught in isolation have been criticized. It is suggested that these two approaches are best taught jointly within a process-task perspective.

• Cognitive strategies refer to an individual's awareness of the thinking and learning plans needed for learning and the student's repertoire of learning approaches. Pertinent to the discussion of cognitive strategies are metacognition and cognitive styles.

• Feuerstein's theory of Instrumental Enrichment focuses on the development of learning and cognitive strategies. The role of the teacher as a mediator is critical to this approach.

Key Terms

psychological processing
  disabilities
assimilation
academic skills mastery
preoperational stage
maturational lag

cognitive abilities
instrumental enrichment
sensory-motor period
accommodation
metacognition
learned helplessness

cognitive learning
  strategies
deficit processes
passive learning style

Chapter Outline

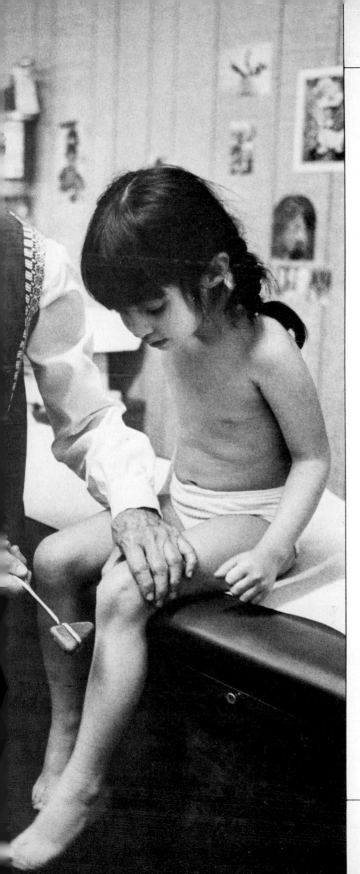

Medical
Aspects of
Learning
Disabilities

Chapter 7

Introduction

*T*he medical profession has been a vitally important participant in the field of learning disabilities. As noted in Chapter 2, physicians conducting brain research were central to the early development of the field. Very often the physician is the first professional to examine a child with learning disabilities and continues to monitor the youngster over a long period of time. In addition, when the school evaluation suggests pathological problems, many learning-disabled children and adolescents are referred to pediatricians, neurologists, psychiatrists, ophthalmologists, audiologists, and other specialists for further diagnosis or treatment. In some cases, medical personnel become key members of a student's multidisciplinary evaluation team and contribute to the IEP. Finally, medical research continues to provide new aid in prevention, diagnosis, and treatment.

This chapter discusses the value of medical information for teachers and deals with the physiology of the brain, the neurological examination, attention deficit disorders, various medical treatments, and the involvement and contributions of several medical specialties.

The Value of Medical Information for Educators

No one discipline can remain productive while in isolation, and the field of learning disabilities draws on many others, such as education, medicine, psychology, and language. Recognizing the multidimensions of learning disabilities, pediatrics, for instance, is training its doctors to become familiar with relevant educational concepts and procedures (Levine, Brooks, & Shonkoff, 1980; Feagans, 1983). It seems just as essential for teachers to learn about relevant medical aspects of the field. Medical information is useful for teachers for a number of reasons.

1. *Educators are coming to realize that we cannot artificially separate behavior and learning from what happens in our bodies.* Learning is a neurological process that occurs within the brain; no learning can take place without involving the central nervous system. Therefore a dysfunction in the central nervous system can seriously impair the ability to learn. It is important that teachers have basic information about the central nervous system and its relationship to learning and learning disabilities, and the education profession is beginning to recognize that importance. A volume in a series published by the National Society for the Study of Education bears the title *Education and the Brain* (Chall & Mirsky, 1978).

2. *Medical specialists often contribute to both the assessment and the treatment of learning-disabled students.* To understand these medical contributions, teachers need a working knowledge of certain medical and neurological topics related to learning disabilities and some knowledge of the vocabulary and perspectives of the various medical specialists.

3. *Learning disabilities teachers are often required to interpret medical reports about their students and to discuss the findings with physicians and parents.* In addition, knowledge about medication that may be prescribed for their students and the ability to provide intelligent feedback to parents and physicans about the drug's effectiveness are important teacher competencies.

4. *Scientific investigations that attempt to unravel the mysteries of the human brain and learning are fascinating in themselves.* An added lure is that these studies hold the promise of furthering our understanding of the enigma of learning disabilities, even though they may not always have an immediate application for teaching. Duane (1983) points out that collaboration between specialists in basic neuroscience and educators is needed to improve the quality of research in brain-behavior relationships. As informed professionals in the field of learning disabilities, teachers should have up-to-date information on relevant topics related to medicine.

The Functions of the Brain

All human behavior is mediated by the central nervous system and the brain. The behavior of learning is one of the most important activities of the brain. From the medical perspective, learning disabilities represents a subtle malfunction in the most complex element of the human body, the central nervous system.

The Neurosciences

The *neurosciences* are those disciplines that investigate the organism of the brain and conduct research to expand our knowledge of brain function. Much of our basic information about how the human brain deals with the learning and language processes has been derived from studies of the adult brain, usually an adult brain that has incurred some tissue damage from disease or injury. Research on the brain and behavior has been slow in coming, partly because the necessary technology was not available (Silver, 1983).

Now exciting new techniques for brain research, diagnosis, and treatment permit scientists to obtain visual images of the brain while it is functioning. Current technology offers the CAT scan (computerized axial tomography); the PET scan (position emission tomography); NMR (nuclear magnetic resonance evoked response techniques); and BEAM (brain electrical activity mapping) (Moser, 1983). Thus, it is now possible to conduct research on brain function during the act of reading or learning (Silver, 1983; Duane, 1983).

Neuroanatomic studies of the brain structure of dyslexics promise to provide additional information on the causes of learning disabilities (Galaburda, 1983). This research consists of autopsy examinations of the brain structure of young people who suffered from severe reading problems and met a sudden death. (The findings of these studies are discussed in Chapter 12, in the section on dyslexia.)

Neuropsychology

One of the neurosciences, is a discipline that combines neurology and psychology, investigating the relationship between brain function and human behavior. Most of the research in neuropsychology has been applied to the study of behavior in adults with brain injury. However, recent work in this specialized field has been directed toward research and applications in learning disabilities (Gaddes, 1980, 1983; Obrzut & Hynd, 1983; Levine, Brooks, & Shonkoff, 1980). Neuropsychologists are interested in the perceptual, cognitive, and motor deficits in learning-disabled individuals and in the relationship of these deficits to brain structure and function.

Two neuropsychological test batteries designed to assess brain functions in children are used for learning disabilities: the *Luria-Nebraska Neuropsychological Battery for Children* and the *Reitan-Indiana Neuropsychological Test Battery for Children* (Gaddes, 1980, 1983; Hartlage, 1982). These tests require intensive advanced training in neuropsychology and in the specific techniques of administering them.

The Cerebral Hemispheres

The human brain is composed of two halves, the right hemisphere and the left hemisphere, which appear to be almost identical in construction and metabolism. Each hemisphere contains a frontal lobe, a temporal lobe, an occipital lobe, a parietal lobe, and a motor strip area (see Figure 7.1). The motor area of each hemisphere controls the muscular activities of the opposite side of the body. Thus, the right-hand and foot movements originate in the motor strip of the left hemisphere. Both of the eyes and ears are represented in both hemispheres (Geshwind, 1979).

Language function is thought to be located in one hemisphere of the brain. Research indicates that in more than 90 percent of adults language function originates in the left hemisphere, regardless of whether the individual is left-handed, right-handed, or mixed. The speech area is located in the left hemisphere in the majority of right-handed people; for left-handed people, the location for speech appears to occur with nearly equal frequency in

FIGURE 7.1
The Brain

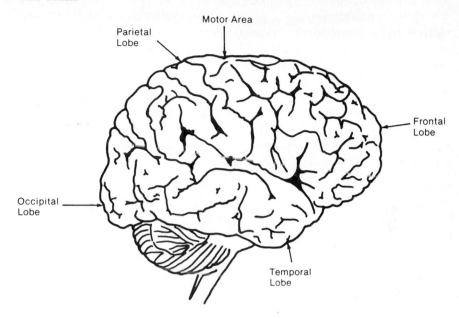

each hemisphere. Similarly, about 98 percent of right-handed and 71 percent of left-handed people have speech dominance in the left-hemisphere.

Although the two halves of the brain appear to be almost identical in structure, they differ in function. Current research suggests that although the left hemisphere appears to react to and utilize language-related activities, the right hemisphere deals with nonverbal stimuli, including spatial perception, directional orientation, time sequences, and body awareness. Thus, even though visual and auditory nerve impulses are carried to both cerebral hemispheres simultaneously, it is the left hemisphere that reacts to linguistic stimuli, such as words, symbols, and thought. Consequently, adult stroke patients with brain injury in the left hemisphere often suffer language loss along with an impairment in the motor function of the right half of the body.

However, the two hemispheres of the brain do not work altogether independently; there are many interrelating elements and functions. The learning process depends upon both hemispheres and their interrelating functions (Geshwind, 1979; Duane, 1983).

Cerebral Dominance

Orton (1937), one of the early investigators of reading and language difficulties, theorized that reversal of letters and words (which he called *strephosymbolia*, or twisted symbols) was symptomatic of a failure to establish cerebral dominance in the left hemisphere, the location of the speech area. According to Orton's theory, the interference of the right hemisphere during language activities caused language confusion. Orton's early ideas of cerebral dominance have been superseded by recent neuroscientific evidence and thinking (Hiscock & Kinsbourne, 1980). Current findings suggest that, although the left hemisphere usually specializes in the language function and the right hemisphere controls nonverbal functions, both hemispheres make specific contributions to the learning process. Faulty efficiency in either hemisphere reduces the total effectiveness of individuals and their acquisition and use of language (Kinsbourne, 1983; Duane, 1983; Geshwind, 1979).

Lateral Preference

The issue of *laterality* is a related controversial subject. The theory proposed is that a tendency to use either the right or left side of the body or a preference for one hand, foot, eye, or ear has a relationship to learning disorders. The term *established laterality* refers to the tendency to perform all functions with one side of the body, while *mixed laterality* refers to the tendency to mix the right and left preference in the use of hands, feet, eyes, and ears. A student's laterality is tested through simple behaviors such as throwing a ball, kicking a stick, sight with a tube, and listening to a watch (Harris, 1958) or through more sophisticated means used in neuroscience or neuropsychology methods (Hiscock, 1983). The research on lateral preference has not found a difference in reading ability between groups of students with established laterality and groups with mixed laterality. Hiscock and Kinsbourne (1980) conducted a thorough review of the research and concluded that the diagnostic significance of mixed laterality is doubtful. These findings suggest that at present there is dubious practical value in the determination of laterality as part of the learning disabilities assessment (Hiscock, 1983).

Right Brain, Left Brain: Hemispheric Differences

The right hemisphere and the left hemisphere appear to function differently. This duality of the brain has led to speculation that some people tend to approach the environment in a "left-brained" fashion whereas others use a "right-brained" approach. These differences in brain function warrant further discussion because the concept may provide some insight into differences in learning styles.

Differences in function between the left and right hemispheres were vividly illustrated with the so-called split-brain research (Sperry, 1968). This research was conducted on patients suffering from severe epileptic seizures that could be fatal but could not be treated with medication. Surgery was performed, severing the corpus callosum, the bundle of nerve fibers connecting the two hemispheres, thereby freeing the patients from the seizures. By splitting the two hemispheres of the brain, however, the surgery created, in effect, two brains operating within a single body, each half acting independently of the other and each seeming to have its own sensations, perceptions, and memories, as well as cognitive and emotional experiences. The ensuing research on these patients showed major differences in functions between the two brains. For example, when a picture was shown to the right brain (left eye), the subject had no recollection of seeing it when it was shown to the left brain (right eye). Visual images projected to the left brain could be described in speech and writing, but visual images to the right brain could not be described through language. Similar results occurred when the patients were asked to identify objects put into either their right hand or their left hand. When the image went to the left brain (right hand), they could identify and name the object; but when it was sent to the right brain (left hand), they were unable to identify the object.

Neuropsychologists are particularly interested in hemispheric differences, that is differences in functions between the left and right hemispheres of the brain (Hartlage & Telzrow, 1983; Gordon, 1983). A neuropsychological theory has it that sequential and linguistic tasks are related to the left-brain function while simultaneous and visuospatial tasks are related to right-brain function. Thus, activities such as reading, arithmetic, spelling, would be left-brain tasks whereas art activities, intuitive thinking, and spatial thinking would be right-brain tasks. In relation to learning disabilities, the hemispheric difference theory suggests that the sequential and linguistic tasks of the left brain are more school-oriented. Further, some learning-disabled students, who have much school difficulty, have better ability in right-brained tasks, the simultaneous and visuospatial activities (Gordon, 1983). One psychological assessment instrument that attempts to differentiate between sequential-linguistic and simultaneous-visuospatial styles of learning is the *Kaufman Assessment Battery for Children (K-ABC)* (Kaufman & Kaufman, 1983; Gunnison, Kaufman, & Kaufman, 1982). Hemispheric research, however, is still in the investigative stages and neuroscientists caution that not enough information is available as yet for applications to teaching (Kinsbourne, 1983).

The Neurological Examination

The neurological examination can be conducted by several medical specialists—the family-practice physician, the pediatrician, the neurologist, or the psychiatrist. The neurological examination of the child or adolescent suspected of having learning disabilities has two distinct components: the standard neurological assessment and the examination for minimal neurological signs.

Levine et al. (1980) point out that parents and schools may have unrealistic expectations about the results of the neurological examination. It cannot

Medical specialists, particularly those like neurologists who deal with the brain, often contribute to the assessment and treatment of learning-disabled students.

(© Joel Gordon 1978)

answer all questions, and it has potential for abuse. Despite these shortcomings, a carefully performed and judiciously interpreted neurological examination can contribute to the understanding of the functional status of a learning-disabled student. The conventional neurological examination would not reveal many of the subtle deviations called soft signs that learning-disabled children exhibit. Medical specialists carrying on research in the field of learning disabilities have noted that the conventional neurological examination often fails to find any abnormalities in patients whose primary complaint is the inability to learn (Levine et al., 1980; Levy, 1983). A number of difficulties in interpreting neurological findings should be noted.

1. A wide range of soft signs of minimal neurological dysfunction occurs among students who *are* learning satisfactorily.
2. Because the student's neurological system is not yet mature and is continually changing, it is often very difficult to differentiate between a lag in maturation and a dysfunction of the central nervous system.
3. Many of the tests for soft signs are psychological or behavioral rather than neurological tests.

For these reasons the value of the soft signs is questioned by some neurologists. Yet the supreme test of healthy neurological function is efficient learning. The key difference between human beings and lower animals is our unique ability to learn, which is attributable to the highly complex organization of our brain and nervous system. The well-functioning nervous system will facilitate learning.

The neurological examination is described by Levine et al. (1980). In the conventional neurological examination, the neurologist first obtains a careful, detailed *medical history* to provide specific information and to obtain clues to the causes of the problem. The information collected includes a family history (for clues of a genetic nature), the details of the mother's pregnancy, the birth process, and the neonatal development. The neurologist records information about all illnesses, injuries, and infections that the student has had. The developmental history of the child's motor behavior (the age at which the child crawled, stood, walked) and language skills is also important. The neurologist collects further the data on the student's hearing, vision, feeding, sleeping, toilet-training, and social and school experiences.

An *examination of the cranial nerves* gives information relating to vision, hearing, taste, facial expression, chewing, swallowing, vestibular function (equilibrium), and the ability to speak. Evaluation of the function of the various cranial nerves is derived by noting responses to certain stimuli, the condition of various organs, and the ability of the student to perform certain tasks.

The conventional neurological examination also *assesses all the components that control motor function.* A number of reflexes are tested, and the sensory nerves are assessed through tests of perception or tactile stimulation.

Electroencephalography, commonly called EEG, is a technical process of measuring the electrical activity of the brain. In this examination, electrodes are attached with a special paste to several locations on the head of the person being examined. The brain activity emanating from the various locations of the electrodes is represented on a chart by a graph-type pattern. The electroencephalographer reads the pattern that has been produced to determine if abnormalities in brain activity exist. Although abnormal or borderline EEG patterns are found in many children with learning disabilities, many investigators believe that at present a diagnosis with this instrument is rather unreliable.

Other special medical procedures that might be requested by the neurologist include x rays of the skull and the blood vessels of the brain, biochemical studies, endocrinological studies, genetic examinations, the CAT scan, and the PET scan.

Soft neurological signs can be detected in a neurological examination that is more complete than the conventional one. As previously noted, the neurological abnormalities most often seen in the patient with learning disabilities are not the gross deviations but, rather, the fine, subtle, and minor symptoms. Many of the tests used to detect these symptoms have been borrowed or adapted from psychological assessment procedures. The soft signs include mild coordination difficulties, minimal tremors, motor awkwardness, visual-motor disturbances, deficiencies or abnormal delay in language development, and difficulties in reading and arithmetic skills.

Levine et al. (1980) and Vuckovich (1968) discuss a number of tests used by neurologists to detect soft signs of central nervous system dysfunction. These tests could also be used by the teacher as an informal motor test.

Visual-Motor Tests

A number of visual-motor tests are used to evaluate a patient's ability to copy various geometric forms. Children can copy geometric forms in Figure 7.2 at the following ages:

Figure	Age
Circle	3
Cross	4
Square	5
Triangle	6–7
Diamond	7

Another visual-motor test is the *Bender Visual-Motor Gestalt Test*, in which the patient is asked to copy nine geometric forms. Another test, the *Goodenough Harris Draw-a-Man Test*, requires the patient to draw a picture of a human figure. The scoring depends on the body detail represented.

Gross-Motor Tests

These tasks indicate postural skills, movement, and balance. The normal age at which the task can be performed is:

Task	Age
Hopping on either foot	5
Standing on one foot	6
Tandem walking (heel-to-toe)	9

The child's walking gait is also observed.

Two tests of crossing the midline in execution of movements are also given:

Touching nose and left ear and then nose and right ear. Observers note the rapidity with which the automatic level of takeover of motor movements is introduced.

Finger-nose test. The patient is asked to touch a finger to his or her nose and to the examiner's finger repeatedly. Facility in alternating movement is observed.

FIGURE 7.2
Geometric Forms

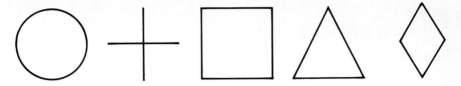

Fine Sensory-Motor Tests

Finger-agnosia test. This test assesses the patient's ability to recognize through a tactile sensation, often with eyes closed, which finger is being touched by the examiner. The tasks and the normal age at which each task can be performed are listed below.

Task	Age
Recognition of thumb	4
Recognition of index finger	5–6

Other tests of tactile perception are recognition of objects by touch, recognition of two simultaneous contacts as the examiner touches two parts of the child's body (such as face and hand), recognition of letters or numbers by touch, recognition of letters or numbers drawn in the palm of the hand, and facility in moving the tongue (vertically and horizontally).

The *finger dexterity test* requires the child to touch each finger in turn to the thumb. Each hand is tested separately.

Hyperactivity

During the neurological examination, the physician observes the patient for symptoms of hyperactivity. Hyperkinetic youngsters can only sit for a few minutes at a time and even then often fidget and wiggle excessively. They have an extremely short attention span, are likely to talk too much in class, and constantly fight with friends, siblings, and classmates. Their actions have been described as impulsive or driven. Hyperkinetic youngsters are easily distracted, racing from one idea and interest to another and unable to focus attention. The existence of hyperkinesis is interpreted as a soft sign of neurological dysfunction.

Measuring the level of hyperactivity is a difficult task, although Poggio and Salkind (1979) present a review of available measures. A frequently used instrument to measure hyperactivity in studies of drug therapy is the *Conners Rating Scales* (Conners, 1969). There are two forms of the Conners Scale— one for parents and one for teachers—in which ten questions about the student are answered on a four-point scale. These scales are distributed to physicians by Abbot Laboratories, North Chicago, IL 60064.

(The *Conners Rating Scales* appear in the *Study Guide with Case Studies* that accompanies this text.)

Attention Deficit Disorders

A recommendation stemming from the medical field is to use the term *attention deficit disorder* (ADD), instead of the earlier medical term *minimal brain dysfunction* (MBD) (American Psychiatric Association, 1980). The change in terminology was suggested because it is currently not feasible to verify the condition of minimal brain dysfunction through external, or outside, tests (such as a laboratory test). Therefore, the syndrome of *attention deficit disorder* is proposed as an alternative because this condition does not require an external text.

Attention deficit disorders are divided into two types: those with and those without hyperactivity. *Attention deficit disorder with hyperactivity* is defined as

> developmentally inappropriate inattention, impulsivity, and hyperactivity. In the classroom, attentional difficulties and impulsivity are evidenced by the child's not staying with tasks and having difficulty organizing and completing work. The children often give the impression that they are not listening or that they have not heard what they have been told. Their work is sloppy and is performed in an impulsive fashion. On individually administered tests, careless, impulsive errors are often present. Peformance may be characterized by oversights, such as omissions or insertions, or misinterpretations of easy items even when the child is well motivated, not just in situations that hold little intrinsic interest. Group situations are particularly difficult for the child, and attentional difficulties are exaggerated when the child is in the classroom where sustained attention is expected.
>
> At home, attentional problems are shown by a failure to follow through on parental requests and instructions and by the inability to stick to activities, including play for periods of time appropriate for the child's age.
>
> Hyperactivity in young children is manifested by gross motor activity, such as excessive running or climbing. The child is often described as being on the go, "running like a motor," and having difficulty sitting still. Older children and adolescents may be extremely restless and fidgety. Often, it is the quality of the motor behavior that distinguishes this disorder from ordinary overactivity in that hyperactivity tends to be haphazard, poorly organized, and not goal directed.*

The diagnostic criteria for attention deficit disorder with hyperactivity are as follows:

A. *Inattention*. At least three of the following:
   1. Often fails to finish things he or she starts
   2. Often doesn't seem to listen

---

*From the *Diagnostic and Statistical Manual of Mental Disorders* (3rd ed., p. 41) by the American Psychiatric Association, 1980, Washington, DC: Author. Reprinted by permission.

      3. Easily distracted
      4. Has difficulty concentrating on schoolwork or other tasks requiring sustained attention
      5. Has difficulty sticking to a play activity
  B. *Impulsivity.* At least three of the following:
      1. Often acts before thinking
      2. Shifts excessively from one activity to another
      3. Has difficulty organizing work (this not being due to cognitive impairment)
      4. Needs a lot of supervision
      5. Frequently calls out in class
      6. Has difficulty awaiting turn in games or group situations
  C. *Hyperactivity.* At least two of the following:
      1. Runs about or climbs on things excessively
      2. Has difficulty sitting still or fidgets excessively
      3. Has difficulty staying seated
      4. Moves about excessively during sleep
      5. Is always "on the go" or acts as if "driven by a motor"
  D. Onset before the age of seven
  E. Duration of at least six months
  F. Not due to schizophrenia, affective disorder, or severe or profound mental retardation.*

Attention deficit disorder without hyperactivity has the same features as attention deficit disorder with hyperactivity except for the absence of hyperactivity; in addition, the associated features and impairments are generally milder.

The terminology connected with attention deficit disorders is in tune with current educational, as well as medical, thinking. Many researchers see attention deficits as the most critical defect of the learning-disabled student (Hallahan & Sapona, 1983; Dykman, Ackerman, Holcomb, & Boudreau, 1983; Hallahan & Reeve, 1980; Keogh & Margolis, 1976; Ross, 1976). The focus on attentional problems appears to be of common interest to both the medical and educational fields, and, hence, an area of possible coordination between them.

The ability to concentrate and attend to a task for a prolonged period of time is essential for the student to receive necessary information and complete certain academic activities. Often we find that learning-disabled students are attending but they are attending to the wrong stimuli. The problem is *selective attention*; that is, the ability to attend to relevant (central) information in the face of irrelevant (incidental) information.

There are several separate but interrelated phases of attention. To help a student, the teacher must know with which phase the student has difficulty (Keogh & Margolis, 1976).

*From the *Diagnostic and Statistical Manual of Mental Disorders* (3rd ed., pp. 43–44) by the American Psychiatric Association, 1980, Washington, DC: Author. Reprinted by permission.

1. *Coming to attention.* This includes getting alert, getting set to attend, being motivated to attend.
2. *Focusing attention.* This includes gathering the vigilance and energy needed to carefully examine the problem and developing an interest in the problem to be solved. Impulsive children may be fast decision makers, but they make many errors, blurt out answers, jump to conclusions and guess wildly. They have to learn to focus attention, slow down, become more reflective, and monitor their answers.
3. *Sustained attention.* In this phase of attention, the student must concentrate for an extended period of time, become an active learner, and get into the problem more deeply. The teacher can provide help and guidance to increase concentration. Students need help in picking up the right cues rather than irrelevant information. Verbal mediation is also helpful in improving concentration; students learn to talk out the problem to themselves. Some learning-disabled students cannot concentrate because they cannot organize what they are to do and are therefore distracted by irrelevant stimuli. For example, when a student is told to study for half an hour, he or she may not know what to do during the study time. Specific guidelines are needed. The teacher can provide guides with such reminders as "Look carefully at the directions," "Remember, find three reasons," "Check your answers," "Did you answer each question?" or "Restate the three ways given by the author."

   The concentration time should be gradually increased and extended. Students should be aware of this objective and of progress as it is made. For example, attention and concentration can increase from doing one problem, to doing five problems to doing one page of problems. Or they can be extended from working for two minutes to working for ten minutes and then half an hour. The topic of attention and concentration is also discussed in Chapters 6, 9, and 15.

Medical Treatments

The different kinds of treatments prescribed for learning-disabled students include drug therapy, diet control, allergy therapy, and megavitamins. Treatments with a medical basis are among the most hotly debated issues in the field of learning disabilities. Some of these treatments lack sufficient empirical research and need additional scientific evidence before they can be widely accepted (Silver, 1975).

Drug Treatment

Many learning-disabled students are given medication to control hyperactive behavior and reduce attention deficits in order to enhance their opportunity to learn. Although drug therapy is a medical therapy, the teacher plays an important role in improving its effectiveness. To accomplish this, the teacher should be aware of the specific drug program a student is under in order to provide feedback to the doctors and parents concerning the effect of the drug on the student in school. With such feedback, the physician can gauge the effectiveness of the drug and make appropriate modifications.

Students with volatile behavior symptoms are most likely to receive drugs to aid in the management of behavior both at home and at school. The drug may decrease the hyperactivity and increase the length of attention span so that learning can take place.

Students with learning disabilities often have an unpredictable reaction to a particular drug or combination of drugs. Certain stimulants, used by adults as energizers, seem to have the effect of calming the behavior of children who are hyperactive, impulsive, and distractible. (Cantwell, 1980). On the other hand, sedatives such as Phenobarbital have been reported to increase activity in the lethargic and hypoactive child. There are many exceptions to these generalizations, and no specific treatment is available for pediatric patients who have been diagnosed as learning disabled because the causes and manifestations are so diverse.

Since these youngsters often have an abnormal reaction to certain drugs, some physicians have suggested that trial of a drug can be a useful diagnostic tool to indicate the presence of a neurological abnormality. An atypical reaction to a drug such as Dexedrine or Ritalin could serve as part of the data in making a diagnosis. Normal use of such drugs is as an energizer, so a calming-down reaction to the drug could be a diagnostic indication of dysfunction in the central nervous system (Kinsbourne & Caplan, 1979).

The ideal drug should control hyperactivity, increase attention span, reduce impulsive and aggressive behavior without inducing insomnia, anorexia (loss of appetite), drowsiness, or other serious toxic effects (Millichap, 1973). Because hyperactive behavior is substantially reduced at the onset of puberty, medication is typically stopped at age twelve. The following groups of drugs are prescribed: *central nervous system* drugs (Ritalin, Dexedrine, Cylert); *tranquilizers* (Librium, Mellaril, Thorazine, Serpasil); *antidepressant* and *anticonvulsant* drugs (Dilantin, Phenobarbital).

Stimulant Medications (Central Nervous System Drugs)

The three stimulant medications most frequently prescribed for attention deficit disorders are *Ritalin, Dexedrine,* and *Cylert* (Levine et al., 1980). As indicated in Table 7.1 Ritalin and Dexedrine become effective in less than half an hour; however, Cylert takes up to four weeks. The duration of action for Ritalin and Dexedrine is three to five hours. That means that unless a second dose is taken during the school day, the effects of a morning dose of the medication will wear off in the course of the day. Cylert is taken in one daily dosage and its effects are long lasting. Teachers often report that when students are taking Ritalin or Dexedrine their attention lags and hyperactivity increases as the effects of the medication wear off during the school day. It

TABLE 7.1   **Stimulant Medications Used for Treatment of Attention Deficits**

Brand Name	Generic Name	Onset of Action	Duration of Action
Ritalin	Methylphenidate	30 minutes	3–5 hours
Dexedrine	Dextroamphetamine	30 minutes	3–5 hours
Cylert	Pemoline	2–4 weeks	long-lasting

may be necessary to plan teaching activities requiring concentrated attention early in the day while the medication is most effective.

The side effects of stimulant medications include insomnia and loss of appetite. However, these side effects are usually transient and diminish as tolerance develops (Levine, et al., 1980). One study of side effects reported growth suppression in children on stimulant medications (Safer & Allen, 1973). However, a follow-up study of these children showed a rebound phenomenon, with an accelerated catch-up growth over the summer when the medication was stopped (Safer, Allen, & Barre, 1975). In another study of the effects of stimulant medication on growth reported by Gross (1976), no reduction in growth was found.

In studies of the long-term effects of stimulant medications, there have been no documented adverse consequences. Drug abuse has not been a problem for children who received stimulant medication for hyperactivity. In general, many physicians conclude that the long-term risks of medication appear to be negligible (Levine et al., 1980; Levy, 1983).

Research results on the effectiveness of stimulant medication differ in various studies. Many of the experimental studies on the effectiveness of drugs have been criticized because of poor design or inadequate controls (Egan, 1978; Aman 1980). In general, however, the short-term effect of stimulant medication has been to dramatically reduce hyperactivity. Kavale (1982) analyzed 135 studies of the effects of stimulant drug treatment on hyperactivity through the statistical procedure known as meta-analysis. His findings indicate that stimulant drug intervention controls hyperactivity. The case is not so clear for social, academic, and psychological adjustment. There is obviously a need for a comprehensive management approach that goes beyond the administration of drugs. Academic remediation and behavior therapy are important elements in such a plan.

Years of research on the effectiveness of drug treatment with the learning-disabled led researchers to the following conclusions (Conners, 1973; Levine, et al., 1980):

1. There is no simple available diagnostic category backed up by clear-cut procedures of assessment using validated methods that unequivocally leads to a prescription for drug treatment.
2. The effect of stimulant drugs, such as amphetamines, is more complex

than a simple reduction of activity level. The drugs alter the quality of the student's activity and goal directedness. They can also have a significant effect on mood, personality, concentration, perception, and motor coordination. Since the effects are least apparent to the physician treating the student in an office, close liaison of the medical personnel with the school and the family is needed.

3. Drug treatment by itself is seldom a sufficient remedy for the total set of symptoms of maladaptive behavior. Educational and psychological treatment is also needed.

4. Careful follow-up of the course of treatment is essential to regulate dosage and to evaluate the side effects and behavioral consequences of treatment. The drugs by themselves do not teach anything. The student still needs continued attention to educational instruction.

5. Despite these cautions, drugs have been shown to produce substantial academic and behavioral improvement. When indicated, they should be used. There is no support for the fear that drugs produce a susceptibility to addiction or drug abuse in later life.

All in all, drugs appear to be of considerable value in certain instances but are of little or dubious help in other cases. In a majority of cases (60 to 75 percent), a favorable response can be observed shortly after treatment is initiated. However, in a significant minority of cases (25 to 40 percent), an adverse response occurs from the outset (Kinsbourne & Caplan, 1979; Aman 1980).

School Responsibility in Medication

One problem related to the use of prescribed medication for learning-disabled children is the question of the responsibilities of the school and the teacher. Who on the school staff should be responsible for the storage and administration of prescribed medication? What are the legal implications for the teacher and the school? Most schools have not formulated written policies to regulate storage and administration of prescribed medication in the schools. To guard against potential hazard to the pupil's health, as well as to protect the school from possible liability for improper handling or dispensation of prescribed medicine, schools should develop policies regarding this matter (Nimmer & Kinnison, 1980).

Nutrition

One area under investigation is the connection between *nutrient deficiency* and learning impairment. Simopoulos (1983) and Martin (1980) summarized the research on this topic. It is known that protein and calorie deficiency in early life can result in permanent anatomical and biochemical changes in the brain. Intelligence in undernourished humans is diminished, and there is increasing evidence that minimal brain dysfunction results from undernutrition. Early malnutrition impairs growth, both of the body in general and the central nervous system in particular. The severity of the deficit is related to the age at which malnutrition occurs, the degree, and the duration. The first six months of life are a critical nutrient period because it is at this time that maximal postnatal brain cell division occurs in the human infant. Damage incurred during this period is probably permanent.

Diet

There are several diet-related theories concerning the cause or treatment of hyperactivity and learning disorders.

Food Additives

One of the most controversial and widely discussed treatment theories is that of Feingold (1975), who proposes that food additives in the child's diet induce hyperactivity. Feingold notes that artificial flavors, artificial preservatives, and artificial colors have been on the increase in the American diet and that youngsters today consume a large variety of food additives. Therapy consists of the control of the child's diet and the removal of food additives.

Numerous studies have been conducted on the Feingold diet. Most have found that the method is not effective in controlling hyperactivity (Mattes, 1983; Kavale & Forness, 1983). However, the Feingold diet continues to enjoy popularity and has many supporters (Rimland, 1983). Parents and others who are followers of the Feingold approach to hyperactivity have banded together to form local Feingold Association groups. It is estimated that 20,000 individuals are members of Feingold groups and that the diet has been tried on more than 200,000 children (Mattes, 1983).

Hypoglycemia

Another diet-related theory of the cause of learning disorders suggests that many learning-disabled children have *hypoglycemia*, a condition due to a deficiency in the level of blood sugar (Dunn, 1973; Runion, 1980). Therapy consists of the control of the child's eating pattern so that the condition can be improved. Without diet control, according to the theory, there is a decrease in the blood-sugar level about an hour after eating, and the child's energy for learning is drained.

Megavitamins

The use of *megavitamins* as a treatment procedure has also stirred interest. Brenner (1982), Alden (1979), and Cott (1972) discuss the results achieved with children who were treated by orally administered pills, capsules, or liquids containing massive doses of vitamins. Although the three authors report that this treatment is effective for children with learning disabilities, many physicians believe that further research evidence is needed before such treatment can be generally prescribed.

Allergies

According to some researchers, many children develop both diet- and environment-related *allergies* that adversely affect learning. The treatment in this approach is removal of the element causing the allergy. Crook (1977) and Rapp (1979) report success with this treatment. Among the food ingredients thought to impair learning and induce hyperactivity are sugar, milk, corn, eggs, wheat, chocolate, and citrus (Crook, 1983). In a double-blind study, O'Shea and Porter (1981) reported a significant improvement in hyperactive patients given treatment for allergies.

Medical Specialties Involved with Learning Disabilities

Pediatrics and Family-Practice Medicine

The pediatrician and the family-practice physician are the medical specialists who are usually responsible for the care of children and adolescents. The role of the child-care physician has changed and extends beyond the care of physical ailments; responsibilities today include understanding the problems of learning and behavior. Pediatricians are expected to diagnose handicapping conditions, developmental delays, atypical language, and motor and behavior growth; to know about special education services offered by the schools; and to be familiar with the rights of handicapped children under state and federal law (McDonald, Carlson, Palmer, & Slay, 1983; Levine et al., 1980; Lerner & Cohn, 1981).

The parent who becomes concerned about a child's behavior at home or poor performance in school often turns to the pediatrician for help. The parent might report that the child overreacts to everything, is constantly in motion, is silly at inappropriate times, does not see the consequences of actions, cannot control behavior, is overly affectionate, indiscriminate, and gullible. The child may have poor relations with peers, a low tolerance of frustration, and frequent temper tantrums. In school he or she may have a short attention span, be easily distracted, be disorganized in working, vary in mood from day to day, or even hour to hour. The child may have problems in reading and may not seem to understand numbers and arithmetic concepts.

Although some pediatricians have not been trained to detect the medical symptoms that indicate the likelihood of learning disabilities, many pediatricians see their role as central in the total management of the child in terms of both physical and mental health. They consider themselves to be concerned with the child's language development, school adjustment, and academic learning. Many pediatricians have commented on the change in the types of problems faced by the profession. For example, while fewer children suffer

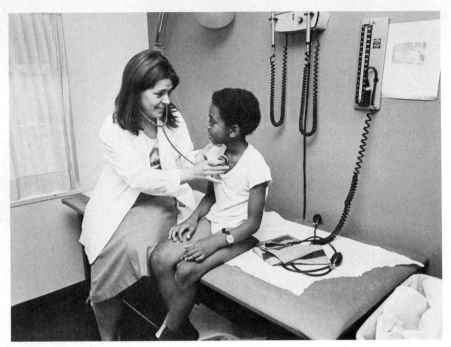

Pediatricians are expected to diagnose various handicapping conditions and to be aware of the special education services available. *(Bohdan Hrynewych/Stock, Boston)*

serious infectious diseases, biochemical abnormalities have drawn attention and gained emphasis. At present, pediatricians are increasingly being alerted to learning disabilities. They are frequently panel members at educational conferences dealing with such problems as dyslexia; they are often part of diagnostic teams in various clinical settings in which learning disabilities are encountered; and they are beginning to make referrals when a cluster of symptoms suggestive of learning disabilities is noted.

An emerging subspecialty within pediatrics is *developmental pediatrics*. The American Academy of Pediatrics has suggested that such pediatricians acquire advanced training for this specialty, which would combine expertise in child development with medical knowledge, especially in genetics, neurology, and psychiatry. The specialty would also include familiarity with the contributions of nonmedical professionals who deal with children and training in working on interdisciplinary teams.

What, in fact, is the status of the pediatrician's knowledge about handicapped children, in general, and children with learning disabilities, in particular? Shonkoff, Dworkin, Leviton, and Levine (1979) conducted one survey of ninety-seven pediatricians in New England; the American Academy of Pediatrics (1980) carried out another survey of sixty randomly selected pediatricians throughout the United States. Both studies indicated a need for a more sophisticated understanding of the dynamics of child development as well as for more expertise in the assessment and management of atypical children. The study by the Academy of Pediatrics presented revealing data on physician contact with, experience, and knowledge of handicapped children: 100 percent reported seeing learning-disabled children among their patients with exceptionalities; 58 percent of the respondents used the Denver Developmental Screening Test as a screening instrument; about 70 percent reported regular contact with special education departments in local schools; only 38 percent had participated on educational planning teams; about 73 percent reported familiarity with PL 94–142; only 27 percent felt that they had been adequately trained in medical school or residency to work with handicapped children and their families; and about 73 percent recognized the need for more training in issues involving handicapped children (Lerner & Cohn, 1981).

Neurology

If neurological impairment is suspected in a child or adolescent with learning disabilities, the individual may be referred to the neurologist, a physician specializing in the development and functioning of the central nervous system. Overt disturbances of motor function (such as cerebral palsy, epilepsies, and cortical blindness or deafness) and overt neurological abnormalities (such as the absence of certain reflexes or asymmetry of reflex responses) can be readily detected by the neurologist. However, the learning-disabled rarely have such obvious impairments. They are more likely to manifest minimal, subtle, refined deviations called *soft signs*.

The subspecialty within the field of neurology that deals with learning disabilities is pediatric neurology. Specialists in this field have the experience, training, and professional perspective to diagnose and treat children and youth with learning disabilities. As with other medical specialists, it is essential that the pediatric neurologist establish good communication with the schools to provide a comprehensive treatment program for their patients.

Ophthalmology

Whereas the pediatrician is usually the first to be consulted by the parent when the child has problems at home, the eye specialist is often consulted when the child has difficulty in school, particularly when the problem is poor reading. In fact, one of the first published papers on reading problems (Morgan, 1896) was written by an ophthalmologist. It seems axiomatic that ocular comfort and visual efficiency are desirable attributes for reading success. Because reading is so obviously related to vision, it is not surprising that the eye specialist is involved when the child fails to learn to read.

The *ophthalmologist* is the specialist in the medical field who is responsible for the health of the eye, and the *optometrist* is the nonmedical specialist concerned with vision and its measurement and correction. The ophthalmologist considers the physiology of the eye, its organic aspects, diseases, and structure. The optometrist is more likely to stress the uses of the eye. There are differences in diagnosis and treatment procedures among eye specialists. Although some treat deviations they consider significant by patching, lenses, and surgery, other specialists emphasize functional vision and the fact that visual skills are learned. Others treat weak or impaired visual skills by direct training procedures, as well as by lenses and other methods.

Visual Findings as Factors in Reading Problems

Since visual deficiency may be a factor in certain cases of reading disability, students with reading problems should have an eye examination as part of their diagnosis. Teachers should be alert to such symptoms as facial contortions, head thrust forward or tilted, tension during close work or when looking at a distant object, poor sitting posture, frequent rubbing of eyes, excessive head movements, avoidance of close work, and frequent losing of place during reading.

In the eye examination, the eye specialist checks for visual acuity, refractive errors and binocular difficulties. *Visual acuity* refers to the ability to see forms or letters clearly from a certain distance. The Snellen chart, a visual screening test used in many schools, tests visual acuity at twenty feet from the chart, that is, *far-point visual acuity*. A score of 20/20 means that the subject sees at twenty feet what the normal eye sees at twenty feet. A score of 20/40 indicates that the subject sees at twenty feet what the normal eye sees at forty feet. Other instruments are needed to assess *near-point visual acuity* at sixteen inches, the distance used in reading. Persons who pass a far-point visual acuity test may fail the near-point test.

Refractive errors are due to a defect of the lens and are of three types: (1) *myopia* (nearsightedness), (2) *hyperopia* (farsightedness), and (3) *astigmatism* (the blurring of vision due to an uneven curvature of the front of the eye). Research studies have revealed that myopia has little or no correlation with poor reading and, in fact, is found as often or more often in good readers than in poor readers (Richek, List, & Lerner, 1983). The visual screening devices that detect only the condition of myopia may not detect visual defects that appear to be significantly related to reading difficulties. Reading requires visual acuity at "near point," a distance of fourteen to sixteen inches, rather than at twenty feet. Astigmatism does not appear to be closely related to reading disability either. In some cases it is associated with better-than-average reading. Poor readers, however, do seem to have a slightly higher occurrence of hyperopia.

Binocular difficulties occur because the two eyes are not functioning together. Three binocular conditions are (1) *strabismus* (lack of binocular coordination), (2) *inadequate fusion* (poor accommodation of focus of the eye lens to fuse the two images), and (3) *aniseikonia* (ocular images of an object fixated are unequal in size or shape in the two eyes). Some research studies have indicated that problems of binocular vision have more implications for reading than refractive errors do.

Probably of greater importance to learning and reading than visual acuity or refractive errors is the process of visual discrimination and visual perception—the interpretation of visual sensory stimulation. Disturbances in visual perception, however, are not due to organic ocular abnormalities but rather to psychological or central processing dysfunctions.

Visual discrimination is the process of detecting differences in objects, forms, letters, or words. *Visual perception* is the cognition and interpretation of a visual sensation and the mental association of the present visual stimuli with memories of past experiences. The mechanisms of visual discrimination and visual perception are not strictly within the realm of the medical aspects of vision. They are, therefore, discussed more fully in a later chapter (Chapter 10) dealing with perceptual skills.

Differences in Opinion Concerning Vision and Learning

Professional differences of opinion concerning the eye and learning disabilities are reflected by the two professional specialties that deal with eye care, ophthalmology and optometry. Many optometrists are interested in developmental vision, visual perception, and visual training, as well as refractive errors. Most ophthalmologists are concerned with the organic health of the eye, as well as refractive errors. Consequently, while the optometrist may see a need for eye training for a particular child, the ophthalmologist may find nothing wrong with the child's eyes.

The American Association of Ophthalmology, in conjunction with other medical associations, issued a position paper entitled "Learning Disabilities, Dyslexia, and Vision" (Committee on Children with Disabilities, 1984), which presented the profession's opposition to visual training approaches to reading problems. Optometrists have attacked such position statements, charging that gross distortions and inaccuracies were used in reaching these conclusions (Flax, 1973). One educator who reviewed the visual training research (Keogh, 1974) concluded that while the research does indicate a relationship between visual perception and reading ability, there is insufficient evidence to support a direct causal interpretation. One problem is that the developmental training programs reported in the research use a variety of techniques, including an emphasis on language, so that it is difficult to consider visual perception independently of other program effects. It appears that additional study is needed to find definitive answers to this controversial question.

Haddad, Isaacs, Onghena, and Mazor (1984) analyzed the results of ophthalmological evaluations of seventy-three children with reading difficulties. They found that eighteen had overt refraction errors (astigmatism, myopia, and hyperopia), which were treated successfully with corrective glasses; eighteen had dyslexia but no ocular anomalies, and thirty-seven had impaired fusional amplitudes and were given orthoptic exercises. They concluded that the orthoptic exercises improved the fusional amplitudes and also helped improve the reading ability of these students.

Otology

The ability to hear the sounds and language in the environment is a crucial factor in learning. Language, for example, is learned largely through the sense of hearing. The medical specialist responsible for the diagnosis and treatment of auditory disorders is the *otologist*, and the branch of medicine dealing with the ear is called otology. A slightly broader area of medical specialization, otolaryngology, deals with the ear, nose, and throat.

The nonmedical specialist who is concerned with normal and abnormal aspects of hearing is called an *audiologist*. Audiology spans a number of functions, including the testing and measurement of hearing, the diagnosis and rehabilitation of the deaf and hard-of-hearing, the scientific study of the physical process of hearing, and the broadening of knowledge and understanding of the hearing process.

Hearing is most frequently measured with an electronic device called a pure-tone audiometer. Pure tones are produced near the outer ear, and the subject states whether or not a sound is heard. A second method of assessing hearing is through a bone conduction test. This method measures hearing in certain types of hearing loss by conducting sound waves directly to the inner ear by way of the bones of the ear. In testing for auditory disorders, two dimensions of hearing are considered—intensity and frequency.

Intensity refers to the relative loudness of the sound and is measured in decibels (db). The louder the sound, the higher the decibel measure. Ordinary conversation measures at fifty-six to sixty decibels. Davis & Silverman (1970) estimate a hearing threshold of 30 decibels as the minimum level at which children begin to encounter problems in school. *Frequency* refers to the pitch, or vibrations, of a given sound wave and is measured in cycles per second (cps). A person may have a hearing loss at one frequency but be able to hear well at another. In speech, consonant sounds such as *s, sh, z*, are high-frequency sounds; vowels, such as *o* and *u*, are low-frequency sounds.

Hearing level is the intensity level in decibels at which a person begins to detect sounds in various frequency levels. When screening children for hearing loss, the audiometer may be set at an intensity of fifteen to twenty decibels. In a comprehensive sweep check test, the child is tested at frequencies of 250, 500, 1,000, 2,000, and 8,000 cycles per second.

The prevalence rate for students handicapped with a hearing loss including both deaf and hard of hearing is .19 percent. In addition, many children suffer temporary hearing loss due to infected adenoids or tonsils, wax in the ears, or other abnormalities that can be corrected. When such a temporary impairment occurs during certain developmental stages in early childhood, it may have a detrimental effect on learning, particularly language learning.

There is increasing evidence that the common ear condition in children known as *otitis media* has a detrimental effect on learning and can result in learning disabilities. Otitis media is a condition of inflammation of the middle ear accompanied by fluid medial to the ear drum. The cause may be an infection, allergies, inflamed adenoids, or tonsils. It may cause a mild and fluctuating hearing loss that interferes with language development and acquisition of good auditory perception and can lead to learning disabilities. The case histories of learning-disabled students show a markedly higher occurrence of otitis media than is found in the non-learning-disabled population (Reichman & Healey, 1983).

A sensory hearing impairment, then, is an important consideration in diagnosing and treating a student with learning disabilities. Occurring with greater frequency than impairments in auditory acuity, however, are deficits in auditory perception and auditory discrimination. A disability in auditory perception is not related to organic abnormalities of the ear. The subject of auditory perception is discussed in greater detail in Chapter 10.

Psychiatry

Many children with learning disabilities are referred to child psychiatrists, who can play an important role in the field of learning disabilities. Many referrals to psychiatric facilities are made because of academic difficulties. As we have come to recognize the emotional factors in learning disabilities, these medical specialists began to assume important roles as members of diagnostic treatment teams. A psychiatric approach to learning disabilities should take into account the complex relationship between organic factors and psychodynamic elements. Psychiatrists often work with parents and other family members, as well as with the student. In addition, they must communicate and coordinate their efforts with the school or clinic and with the educational efforts that are being made. The child psychiatrist certainly is a very visible medical professional at conferences, in the literature, in research, and as an important member of the learning disabilities team (Silver, 1983).

Other Medical Specialties

The discussion in this chapter does not exhaust the medical specialties concerned with or contributing to the field of learning disabilities. Practitioners and researchers in the fields of endocrinology, biochemistry, and genetics are very much involved with the problems of the student who cannot learn in a normal fashion. They are treating such youngsters, are members of diagnostic teams, and are contributing important findings to the literature. The future may hold important breakthroughs from these disciplines.

Summary

• Medical information about learning disabilities has value for the teacher. Learning occurs within the brain, and what happens in the body and the central nervous system affects a student's learning. Physicians are often part of the diagnosis and treatment for a learning-disabled student. Teachers should understand the medical vocabulary and concepts of the various subspecialties in medicine. Teachers often become an important part of the medication treatment process.

• The neurosciences consist of various specialties that study the brain. One of these specialties is the field of neuropsychology, which combines neurology and psychology, and studies the relationship between brain function and behavior. Neuropsychologists are beginning to apply their research to the field of learning disabilities.

• The brain has two hemispheres—the right and the left. Each hemisphere controls different kinds of learning. Theories about cerebral dominance, lateral preference, and hemispheric differences are applied to learning disabilities, but most of these theories are still considerd speculative.

• The neurological examination for learning disabilities is conducted by the family-practice physician, the pediatrician, the neurologist, or the psychiatrist. It consists of two parts: the standard neurological assessment and the examination for minimal neurological signs.

• Attention deficit disorder (ADD) is the designation recommended by the medical profession for learning disabilities. The definition of attention deficit disorders separates two types of disorders: with hyperactivity and without hyperactivity. Teachers must determine which phase of hyperactivity is troublesome for the student: coming to attention, focusing attention, or sustained attention.

• A number of medical treatments are used for the learning disabled. Some of them lack sufficient empirical research and need additional scientific evidence before they can be widely accepted. Treatments include drug therapy, diet control, allergy therapy, and megavitamins.

• The most commonly given medications are stimulant medications: Ritalin, Dexedrine, and Cylert. Studies show that they help reduce hyperactivity and improve attention. However, students on such medications must be carefully monitored, and teachers can play an important role in this monitoring.

• The Feingold diet has been a popular treatment approach. It eliminates food additives such as artificial flavors, preservatives, and colors. Most of the research on this method has not shown it to be effective.

• Other treatments include therapy for hypoglycemia, use of megavitamins, and treatments for allergies. Most physicians feel that more research is needed for these treatments before they can be generally prescribed.

• The medical professional usually responsible for a learning-disabled child or adolescent is the family-practice physician or the pediatrician. The role of the pediatrician is shifting to include emotional and school problems, as well as physical problems.

• The pediatric neurologist specializes in diagnosing and treating conditions related to central nervous system dysfunctions in children, including those with learning disabilities.

• Often learning-disabled students with reading difficulties will be examined by the eye-care specialist. The medical specialist is the ophthalmologist; the nonmedical eye-care specialist is the optometrist. There is some difference of opinion between these two disciplines concerning the relationship of vision and reading and the role of eye exercises in treatment.

• Hearing problems would be referred to the otologist, the medical specialist concerned with hearing. The audiologist is the nonmedical specialist in hearing. Hearing loss, permanent or temporary, can seriously affect language learning and auditory perception.

• Learning-disabled individuals with accompanying emotional problems are often referred to the psychiatrist. The psychiatrist is particularly concerned with the complex relationship between organic factors and psychotherapeutic elements.

Key Terms

attention deficit disorders	megavitamins	neurology
drug therapy	electroencephalogram	lateral preference
selective attention	Feingold diet	neurosciences
neuropsychology	minimal brain	ophthalmology
cerebral dominance	dysfunction	optometry
soft neurological signs	hyperactivity	audiology
cerebral hemisphere	developmental pediatrics	food additives

Chapter Outline

High-Risk
Preschool
Children

Chapter **8**

Introduction

*T*he early identification of preschool children who are likely to encounter difficulty in academic learning and the immediate provision of an early intervention program are proving to be the most dramatic success story in education today. If such preschoolers are identified before they encounter difficulty, potential learning failure can be prevented. The benefits include a substantial financial saving for society and a significant improvement in the quality of life for these children.

We use the term "high risk" for the early childhood years because it is difficult to identify learning disabilities at the preschool level. These children have not yet failed in school learning, but we can predict that they are likely candidates for school failure. This chapter discusses information about several populations of preschool children who exhibit preacademic deficits and are considered "high risk." Among these vulnerable preschoolers are young children who have limited opportunity due to economic deprivation, children with various medical problems, children with language disorders and delays, and children who test poorly in cognitive skills, as well as children who have shown actual learning disabilities. Early childhood special programs and research usually do not differentiate among these various high-risk populations. Moreover, findings from one group of high-risk young children have crucial implications for others.

The Importance of the Preschool Years

The critical importance of the early childhood years to cognitive growth and later success is becoming increasingly evident. The work of developmental psychologists such as Piaget (1952), Bloom (1964), and Kagan (1976) shows that by the time the child fails in school much is already lost. Bloom, for example, found that 50 percent of the child's cognitive growth is completed by age four. Therefore, early detection of high-risk and handicapped children makes it possible to provide appropriate intervention during these important learning years. With early identification and treatment, many conditions can be alleviated, other problems can be overcome to a large extent, and some problems can be managed so that the children can live a better life. The benefit to society is that the number of children needing later special education services can be greatly reduced.

CASE EXAMPLE

A High-Risk Preschool Child

Lorinda was identified during the local school district's preschool screening program as a high-risk child who needed further assessment and intervention. She performed poorly on tests requiring expressive language skills and on social measures. Lorinda was three years nine months old at the time.

During an interview with Lorinda's mother, the school obtained additional information about her. Lorinda was the youngest of four children. Born six weeks prematurely, she weighed a little over four pounds at birth and had trouble breathing. She frequently suffered from colds during her first two years, and between the ages of two and three she had at least eight serious ear infections. Motor development seemed to be normal; she sat up, walked, and crawled at the same ages as her siblings. Her language development, however, was slower than theirs. Although she seemed to understand language when spoken to, she could not use it to make her wants known. She did not use any words until the age of two and even now only uses very short sentences, such as "Me want pizza" or "Him break cup." She often uses the wrong word or simply points to what she means. She still has temper tantrums, which seem to be triggered by her inability to communicate what she wants.

Her mother described her as an "overactive" child compared to the other children. She would "tear the house apart," break the crib, and take all her toys apart. They could not take her along when they would visit anyone, nor could they take her to restaurants or other places because of her volatile behavior. She never sat down, except to watch television, and that usually lasted for only a few minutes. When she turned three, her mother tried to enroll her in a small play school, but after a few days the director said she could not stay because of her extreme hyperactivity. She would grab toys from other children and hit or scratch her classmates without provocation. Also, on several occasions she had opened closed cabinets and taken out the contents.

Her mother said she suspected that Lorinda was different from the others, but everyone had told her not to worry, that she would outgrow her disruptive behavior. Lorinda's mother said she was relieved to have her daughter in the special preschool program. At last someone else recognized Lorinda's problem and would be working to help her. The hours Lordinda would be in school would offer the first break for her mother since Lorinda was born, and she was looking forward to receiving help from the school on home behavior management.

The underlying philosophy of early childhood special education is that educational experiences do make a difference in terms of child growth and development. In the controversial issue of whether the rate of cognitive growth is due to heredity or environment, the viewpoint of early childhood special educators is that environmental and educational intervention has a tremendous payoff. The "heredity or environment" controversy, which has been the subject of professional research and debate since intelligence tests were first developed at the turn of the century, can succinctly be stated as

follows: is intelligence and cognitive ability a stable and unchangeable characteristic, or can it be significantly modified through environmental conditions?
In support of the heredity position, Jensen (1969, 1978) presented data that,
he contended, demonstrates that heredity establishes the limits of a person's
intelligence. He maintained that early intervention programs that attempted
to improve intelligence were futile and doomed to failure.

In support of the environmental contribution to intelligence, an impressive collection of early childhood research studies shows that environment
does indeed make a remarkable difference. Early intervention can effectively
increase cognitive ability, improve the child's performance in school, and add
to the quality of life in later years (Reynolds, Egan, & Lerner, 1983; DeWeerd,
1981; Lerner, Mardell-Czudnowski, & Goldenberg, 1981). After analyzing
both the virtues and the pitfalls of the "heritability index" of IQ scores,
Anastasi (1976) concludes the IQ is not fixed in an individual but it is amen-
able to modification by environmental intervention. The work of Feuerstein
(1980) also supports the idea that cognitive ability can be changed (see
Chapter 6).

Obviously, both heredity and environment contribute significantly to an
individual's cognitive functioning. Even if heredity accounts for 80 percent of
the variance in intelligence, it still appears possible to raise or lower the IQ
by approximately 20 points through environmental intervention (Kirk,
Kliebhan, and Lerner, 1978). Evidence accumulated from a wide variety of
sources supports the hypothesis that environmental enrichment and stimulation have a major impact on the cognitive, language, and social development
of young children.

The Effectiveness of Early Intervention

Studies designed to measure the efficacy of early intervention are focused on
several populations of high-risk preschoolers: youngsters who are considered to have "limited learning opportunity" because of economic deprivation, children with identified medical problems, children with language disorders and delays, children whose early test scores show poor cognitive
ability, and learning-disabled youngsters. Since a differential diagnosis that
can determine the exact reason for the problem is so difficult at this age level,
children are often grouped together for intervention programs. This provides
additional time for observation and diagnostic teaching. A child who tests as
mentally retarded at two years of age may not actually be mentally retarded
when provided with effective intervention. Research reports on efficacy do
not always differentiate the various high-risk populations. Moreover, the
findings for one group undoubtedly have major implications for others. Early
childhood efficacy studies are significant because children with learning disabilities are likely to be found in all these groups and the intervention
methods can be useful for many learning-disabled preschoolers. Four phases

There is much evidence to support the idea that intervention in early childhood can effectively increase cognitive ability and improve a child's performance in school.

(B. Griffith/The Picture Cube)

of intervention studies are reviewed in this section: (1) early efficacy studies, (2) studies linked to the Handicapped Children's Early Education Program (HCEEP), (3) recent longitudinal studies, and (4) infant programs.

Early Efficacy Studies

Until the mid-1960s, there were few programs serving young handicapped and high-risk children. All that parents could find were a few private agencies or clinics and some state institutions. Virtually no public school programs were available for parents or their preschool children. During this era, however, several experiments set the stage for later work by demonstrating that young children can improve dramatically under stimulating environmental conditions.

An early landmark study reported by Skeels and Dye (1939) showed that infants classified as retarded who were taken out of the unstimulating atmosphere of an orphanage prior to the age of three years and placed into a more favorable environment increased 27.5 IQ points after a two-year period. A comparison group that remained in the unstimulating environment of the orphanage decreased in IQ by 26.2 points. Three years later the experimental children had retained their IQ increases while the IQ score of the comparison group continued to decline (Skeels, 1942). In a follow-up study twenty-five years later (Skeels, 1966), the experimental group was self-supporting; not one of its members was in an institution. In contrast, of the twelve children in the comparison group, one had died and four were institutionalized. Also, there was a marked difference in educational achievement. The experimental group had completed a median of twelfth grade, and four had received a college education. In contrast, the comparison group had completed a median of only third grade.

Other early studies were conducted by Kirk (1958, 1965) who tested the effects of preschool education on the mental and social development of young, mentally retarded children. He found that children who received two years of preschool education increased in both mental and social development and retained the increase to age eight. Children in the control group, who did not receive the preschool intervention, dropped in both IQ and SQ (social quotient).

A program designed to increase academic skills in young children from low socioeconomic status (SES) homes was conducted by Bereiter and Englemann (1966). They taught fifteen four-year-old children with a series of deliberately planned lessons involving demonstrations, drill, exercise, and problems. At the beginning of the instruction, these children were a year or more retarded in language and cognitive abilities, but within nine months, they progressed to normal levels as assessed in language and IQ tests. Moreover, after instruction, the children scored at the second-grade level in arithmetic and at the first-grade level in reading.

The HCEEP Studies

The great majority of programs for preschool handicapped children today are the result of the implementation of a federal law passed in 1968, the Children's Early Assistance Act. This act spawned the collection of model, or demonstration, projects known as HCEEP (Handicapped Children's Early Education Programs), sometimes referred to as the First Chance Network. The supporting legislation required these HCEEP programs to (a) include parents, (b) provide in-service training, (c) evaluate the child's progress, (d) evaluate the program's effectiveness, (e) coordinate activities within the public schools, and (f) disseminate information about the project to both professionals and the public (Cook & Armbruster, 1983; Swan, 1980). By 1980, there were 177 early childhood special education programs in operation under funding provided by this legislation. The early HCEEP programs first concentrated on establishing model programs; later the focus included dissemination and replication; a growing concern at present is measuring the efficacy of the programs (Swan, 1981). Thus, HCEEP legislation provided seed money to establish demonstration programs, which now are being successfully expanded, continued and adopted by public schools.

The HCEEP programs vary widely in purpose, curriculum, handicaps served, age groups, and activities. To illustrate the diversity, three successful and widely disseminated HCEEP programs are briefly described below.

The Portage Project (Shearer & Shearer, 1972) was a home-based program. The project staff traveled to the child's home to help parents learn how to work with their children in the home setting. Located in a rural area of Wisconsin, this project has been successfully disseminated in many other sites.

The Milwaukee Project (Heber & Garber, 1975) provided an all-day program to preschool children from economically disadvantaged families. The mothers of these preschoolers were tested and attained IQ scores of less than 70. The children received an intensive intervention preschool program from the age of three months to six years. Among the findings of the study were that the children who participated attained IQ scores that were 30 points higher than the scores of children in a control group.

The PEECH (Precise Early Education for Children with Handicaps) project was a cognitive/psycholinguistic model program for multihandicapped children aged three to five. Nonhandicapped children were also enrolled to provide an opportunity for the handicapped youngsters to interact with nonhandicapped peers. The children attended preschool classes for half-day (two and a half hour) sessions daily. The teachers spent the remainder of the day on other activities, such as work with parents, curriculum planning, case conferences, and IEP writing. The results of the project showed that social and academic progress persisted into the elementary grades and that there was significant language growth, the children were successfully mainstreamed, and there was increased parent involvement. In addition, the program was successfully replicated in twenty sites in a cost-effective manner, multiplying the impact of the project (Karnes, Kokotovic, & Schwedel, 1982).

Overall, HCEEP has been successful in stimulating the development of early childhood special education programs in the public schools. It has demonstrated the implementation of programs based on a variety of philosophical approaches and in diverse settings (urban, suburban, and rural).

Recent Longitudinal Studies

Several longitudinal studies show impressive long-term effects of early intervention for high-risk children (Ramey & Bryant, 1982). Two follow-up studies, in particular, have received wide publicity: the Head Start longitudinal study (Lazar & Darlington, 1979) and the Perry Preschool Program study (Schweinhart & Weikart, 1980; Clements, Schweinhart, Barnett, Epstein, and Weikert, 1984).

Perhaps the greatest opportunity to investigate the impact of early intervention on cognitive growth and later adjustment came with the Head Start programs. Funded by the Office of Economic Opportunity, Head Start began in 1964 as part of the War on Poverty. It was intended to provide compensatory educational experiences for children who might otherwise come to school unprepared and unmotivated to learn. In a follow-up study some fifteen years later, 820 children who had taken part in Head Start or similar programs in the early or middle 1960s were evaluated. The data collected in this follow-up study revealed some impressive and very encouraging information, demonstrating that the Head Start experience was very successful. The following questions were asked to measure the effectiveness of the Head Start experience, after a long period:

1. Was the student placed in a special education class during schooling or in a regular class?
2. Was the student left back a grade or more?
3. Did the student finish school by the age of eighteen?

The follow-up data revealed that the Head Start participants did significantly better on all these measures than did the control children. Moreover, the study showed that Head Start programs were "cost-effective"; that is, society saved money by providing preschool education since the investment reduced costs for special education and grade retention later (Lazar, 1979).

Another important longitudinal study, the Perry Preschool Program, was carried out by the High/Scope Educational Research Foundation of Ypsilanti, Michigan (Schweinhart and Weikart, 1980, 1981). The preschool children selected for this project had test scores showing low cognitive ability and came from the bottom 20 percent in terms of economic income. The Perry Preschool Program had a cognitive emphasis curriculum. When the participants were tested in studies at ages fifteen and nineteen, the positive effects were impressive. These students were more committed to schooling and doing better in school than peers who did not have the preschool experiences. They also scored higher on reading, arithmetic, and language achievement tests at all grade levels. Moreover, they had a 50-percent reduction in the need for special education services. They also had less deviant and delinquent behavior, and parents reported that they received greater satisfaction from their children (Clements et al., 1984).

In summary, the longitudinal evidence demonstrates that early intervention for handicapped and high-risk preschoolers is highly successful. It results in significant improvement in the children's cognitive skills, behavior, attitude toward school, and academic achievement. In terms of cost/benefit analysis, the schools get their money back with interest because there is less need for special education services and there is a decrease in the retention rate, thereby reducing the time that children spend in public school. Further, upon completion of schooling, the students are more likely to be gainfully employed—to be taxpayers rather than tax receivers—and to be citizens who contribute to society.

Infant Programs: Birth to Three

The recognition of the need for intervention during infancy (birth to age three) has been even slower than that for the three- to five-year-old population. Yet the needs of handicapped infants and their distraught, confused, and often guilt-ridden parents are probably greater than that of any other age group. One problem encountered in serving this age group is that no one agency has the responsibility for it. PL 94–142 does not cover it (beginning at best at age three), although a few states have passed laws to begin services at birth. Another law, the Developmental Disability Act (described in the next section) does include babies from birth to age two. Gallagher (1979) has suggested that the responsibility for the young handicapped child must be divided between public health and education. The Department of Human Resources should assume responsibility for the under-three age group and the state departments of public instruction should assume responsibility for children aged three years and above.

A review of the sparse literature and research on handicapped infant programs was conducted by Karnes, Linnemeyer, and Shwedel (1981). They described some infant studies, as well as seven model programs for ages 0–3, which were developed under the federal funds for HCEEP. The following conclusions can be drawn from this review:

1. *Intervention in infancy is sound practice.* The earlier the intervention, the better are the chances of reducing the adverse effects of the handicapping condition. In some cases the handicap can even be eliminated.
2. *"Bonding" is more difficult to accomplish with a handicapped infant.* Bonding is the necessary process of infant development in which a strong affective relationship is established between the baby and the

caregiver (usually the mother). With a handicapped infant, it is particularly difficult to establish this essential relationship and parents often
need direct assistance.

3. *A multidisciplinary team that also represents several agencies is important.* One profession or agency cannot provide all the knowledge, skill,
and expertise needed.

4. *Parents become the baby's first teacher.* Parents of handicapped infants
require parent training to help them in this difficult task. As key members of any team concerning their child, they must be involved in all
aspects of the program.

Legislation for Young Handicapped Children

In this section, we will review some of the important federal laws that have
supported the development of early childhood special education programs.

Public Law 94–142

Although PL 94–142 is called the Education for *All* Handicapped Children
Act, it does not actually apply to all children. Even though the legislation does
state that it applies to all aged three through twenty-one, the individual states
do not have to comply with the federal law for youngsters within the three-to-
five age group. If an individual state does not require special education for
handicapped three- to five-year-olds in the state law, then the federal law
cannot supersede the state legislation. A recent survey indicated that less than
one-third of the states (sixteen states) have mandated legislation for three- to
five-year-olds. Twenty-two states mandate services for ages four and five, and
twelve states do not require services until the children reach age six (Comptroller General of the United States, 1981).

PL 94–142 contains an incentive grant program that enables states to apply for a grant to provide preschool programs for handicapped three- to five-
year-olds. These special funds are designed to encourage the states to
develop early childhood special education programs.

PL 94–142 does not specify any requirements or recommendations for
children from birth to three years of age.

Public Law 98–199

Public Law 98–199 (see Chapter 2), passed by Congress in 1983, affirms and
extends the federal role in special education. This new act provides an expansion of early childhood education programs for the handicapped: (1) it encourages the development of programs for children below the age of three
by granting permission to use federal funds under the preschool incentive
grant program to serve handicapped children under that age; and (2) it
establishes grants to states for developing and implementing comprehensive
plans to provide early childhood education to all handicapped from birth.

Some authorities are concerned that by identifying and labeling a child at too early an age, they may actually be creating problems. *(J. R. Holland/Stock, Boston)*

Head Start

As noted earlier, Head Start programs were launched in 1964 through the Office of Economic Opportunity to provide preschool education to the nation's disadvantaged children. Project Head Start is perhaps one of the most influential and massive federal social experiments in our history. In 1972, Head Start legislation was amended to include handicapped children. Ten percent of the total enrollment in Head Start is to be reserved for handicapped children. The inclusion of handicapped children in Head Start programs called attention to the need for screening, diagnosis, and special planning.

Children's Early Assistance Act

The HCEEP programs (discussed earlier in this chapter) were funded by legislation known as the Children's Early Assistance Act, passed by Congress in 1968. This legislation, which led to the development, validation, and replication of model early education programs, has had a major impact on the well-being of many thousands of young handicapped children (Assael & Harrison, 1981).

Developmental Disabilities Act

Handicapped children from birth through two years of age are covered by the Developmental Disabilities Act. *Developmental disability* is defined as a severe, chronic disability that

1. is attributable to a mental or physical impairment or a combination of mental and physical impairments;
2. is manifested before the individual attains the age of twenty-two;
3. is likely to continue indefinitely;
4. results in substantial functional limitations in three or more of the following areas of major life activities:

   a. self-care
   b. receptive and expressive language
   c. learning
   d. mobility
   e. self-direction
   f. capacity for independent living
   g. economic self-sufficiency;

5. reflects the individual's needs for a combination and sequence of special, interdisciplinary, or generic care, treatment, or other services that are individually planned and coordinated.

The population covered by this act includes persons with severe learning disabilities originating in early childhood.

Early Identification and Assessment

Typically, identification and assessment programs for young children with special needs provide for the following phases: (1) *screening* to identify special needs children; (2) *intensive diagnosis* of selected children to determine the nature of the problem and make further referrals if necessary; (3) placement of some children in an early childhood class for *further observation and teaching*; and (4) making decisions for further educational *placement,* which might be a regular kindergarten, a transitional kindergarten, or a special class. These four stages are shown in Figure 8.1.

To avoid stigmatization, school districts often encourage *all* three- to five-year-olds to be brought in for initial screening. The steps encountered in this approach include finding the preschool children in the surrounding geographical area, notifying *all* parents that such services are available, encouraging them to bring in *all* children for initial screening, and, finally, informing parents of the results of the screening procedures.

FIGURE 8.1
The Stages of Early Childhood Special Education Programs

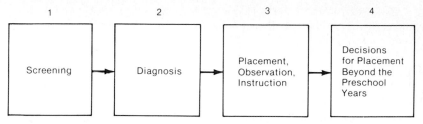

1   2   3   4

Screening → Diagnosis → Placement, Observation, Instruction → Decisions for Placement Beyond the Preschool Years

Problems Related to Early Identification

A number of important issues are inherent in providing screening, diagnostic, and treatment services for preschoolers. Some authorities are concerned with the potential dangers of early identification. By identifying and labeling a child at three or four years of age, educators actually may be creating certain problems. Since children do not mature at the same rate, readiness for school is often a matter of timing. Some children have developmental lags that may disappear by the time they are ready for formal schooling. The term *self-fulfilling prophecy* has been used by Rosenthal and Jacobson (1968) to describe effects of teacher expectancy on pupil performance. It is possible that early identification might serve to impose limits on teacher expectancies and to develop an atmosphere that reinforces the child's learning problems.

Another issue that arises is the paradox that at the time the child is identified, the learning disability has not yet occurred. If not treated, the child may or may not develop a problem. Even if a treated child is successful in a later learning situation, one can never be certain if that success was due to the early identification and treatment. Predictive validity is therefore low (Keogh & Becker, 1973). Another problem in early identification is the difficulty of determining a three-year-old's category of exeptionality. Diagnostic instruments are imprecise, and an inappropriate label may stigmatize the child. Since the nature of the handicapping condition is not easily discernible at this age, early childhood programs generally include children with a variety of handicaps: learning disabilities, mental retardation, emotional disturbances, and language disorders. Most program developers feel that it is not as important to make a differential diagnosis to determine the precise category of the preschooler's problem as it is to find and help the child. Most preschool programs are therefore cross-categorical, seeking terms that will include all of these handicaps. Cross-categorical terms, such as *developmental disabilities* or simply *early childhood services,* are often used.

Keogh and Becker (1973) summarize concerns about early detection by asking three serious questions: (1) How valid are the identifying or predictive measures? (2) What are the implications of diagnostic data for remediation or early intervention? (3) Do benefits of early identification outweigh possible damaging or negative effects of such recognition? In spite of the concerns raised by these questions, most special educators believe that effective early identification is critical and that it may accomplish much in preventing or reducing learning disorders.

Child Find

"Child Find" is a component of PL 94–142 that requires the states to actively seek out those handicapped children who are currently unserved, under-served, or inappropriately served. Much of the effort in Child Find is put into locating preschoolers with special needs. The first step in assessment is locat-ing special needs preschoolers. It is estimated that 62 percent of the pre-school special education population is currently unserved (Comptroller General of the United States, 1981).

Screening Methods and Tests

Among the ways to locate high-risk children are the use of referrals from parents, physicians, and health agencies, and the use of screening tests. There are many widely used tests for screening preschool children, including DIAL-R; SEARCH & TEACH; Meeting Street School Screening Test; Boehm Test of Basic Concepts; and the Denver Developmental Screening Test. In general, these tests are short evaluations for screening preschoolers in the areas of language, motor skills, and concepts. To provide an idea of the kinds of abiliites observed in preschool screening tests, two tests are briefly de-scribed.

DIAL-R

DIAL-R, Developmental Indicators for the Assessment of Learning-Revised (Mardell-Czudnowski & Goldenberg, 1983), is a twenty-four item instrument for screening children aged two to six. It takes twenty to thirty minutes to administer to a child. In this test, when children enter the testing area, they are greeted by a coordinator, and certain basic information is obtained from the parent. The child's picture is taken with an instant camera, and the child then progresses to various testing stations. Children are screened in the following areas:

Sensory Acuity   Children are screened for visual and auditory acuity. If visual and auditory defects are suspected, the child is referred for a profes-sional visual or hearing examination.

Motor Development   Children are screened for both gross motor and fine motor development. Motor tests include catching, jumping, hopping, skipping, building a four-block design, touching fingers (copying the tester's demonstration by consecutively touching each finger on one hand to the thumb of the same hand, and then repeating the task on the other hand);

cutting various patterns with scissors, matching and copying six shapes and six letter formations, and writing their name.

Concept Development   Items include identifying nine colors; identifying eighteen parts of the body; rote counting to eleven; showing one-to-one correspondence of 1, 3, 5, 7, and 9; demonstrating five prepositions (*on, under, corner, between,* and *middle*); identifying fourteen given concepts; naming eight letters; and sorting chips by color, size, and shape.

Language Skills   Children are screened for skills in receiving and expressing oral language. Articulation is checked by having them say fifteen words. They are asked to copy a series of clapping patterns, repeat numbers and sentences said by the tester, describe nine pictures, answer four problem-solving questions, and tell their first and last name, sex, age, address, and phone number.

Social and Affective Competencies   The child's social and affective interactions are recorded through observational notes made by the tester.

SEARCH & TEACH

(Silver, Hagin, & Kreeger, 1976) is a test described as a scanning and intervention program for kindergarten and first grade. SEARCH is a test to locate vulnerable five- and six-year-olds. TEACH is a resource book of instructional tasks designed to mesh with SEARCH.

SEARCH takes about twenty minutes to administer and score. It is composed of ten subtests: three visual perception tests, two auditory perception tests, two intermodal tests, and three body image tests. The test yields a total score to indicate vulnerability and a profile of component abilities.

TEACH is the follow-up intervention program, designed to prevent learning failure by teaching skills to vulnerable children identified by SEARCH. It follows the same components as SEARCH.

Curriculum in Early Childhood Special Education

A wide variety of curricula are used in the early childhood programs for children with special needs. The programs tend to follow the curriculum of early childhood programs, but modifications are made as needed. The basic curriculum models are (1) enrichment curriculum, (2) direct skills instruction curriculum, and (3) cognitive development curriculum. Each of these approaches is based on a different theory of child development, and a different interpretation of the interaction of the child, the teacher, and the school environment.

Enrichment Curriculum

This curriculum is based on a maturational view of child development. The enrichment perspective is often considered the "traditional" program of the nursery school. It is a "whole child" approach, promoting the child's physical, social, emotional, and intellectual growth. It assumes a natural growth sequence for the young child's abilities. The school provides opportunities for the child to enhance these natural growth processes with a learning environment that is enriching, encouraging, and nurturing. The teacher capitalizes on occasions for incidental and informal learning. Many Head Start programs follow this curriculum.

Direct Skills Instruction Curriculum

This curriculum is based on the belief that direct intervention is the best method to bring about the desired learning in young children. The role of the educator is to carefully plan and structure learning experiences to build specific academic skills. The educator determines the kinds of behaviors that are needed to perform such academic tasks as reading and arithmetic and then teaches these behaviors directly to the child as early as possible. The DISTAR program (Berieter and Englemann, 1966) follows such a curriculum.

Cognitive Development Curriculum

Many of the concepts and curriculum programs of this approach stem directly from the ideas of Jean Piaget (1952). The major concern is the way that children develop cognitive abilities—memory, discrimination learning, problem-solving ability, concept formation, verbal learning, and comprehension. Unlike the skills instruction curriculum, the cognitive approach does not train specific academic skills such as reading or arithmetic. Instead, the activities are designed to encourage the development of thinking skills in children. The Perry Preschool Program provides an example of this curriculum (Schweinhart and Weikart, 1980).

Integration of Curriculum Models

When handicapped and high-risk preschool children have been provided with intervention programs based on each of the curriculum models, they have shown growth and improvement. Most school programs, however, do not follow a single curriculum model. In actual practice, early childhood special education programs are likely to have components of each of these curriculum types. Further, in practical terms, there is a common body of activities that cut across all programs, regardless of their theoretical bases. These activities include language and communication, motor activities, concept and cognitive development activities, and social-affective activities. In addition to the curriculum, there are other characteristics that contribute to the success of a program, for instance the quality of parent interaction and training, the practices for transferring the preschoolers to programs beyond the preschool years, and certain teacher variables.

Summary

• The early preschool years are critical years for an individual. Early detection of high-risk children and the subsequent use of preventative intervention methods are successful in averting or lessening later failure.

• Many early childhood research studies indicate that the child's intelligence, or IQ, score is influenced by environmental conditions and experiences. There were a few early experiments with infants and young children that suggested that early intervention could be successful. The HCEEP (Handicapped Children's Early Education Programs) is a collection of early childhood special education demonstration projects. These model programs have been widely disseminated and they have proved to be effective in improving cognitive, social, and academic skills. Several longitudinal studies of students some fifteen years after they had received early childhood education show that the results are long-lasting and that experimental children retained their advantage over control children. There are only a few programs for infants from birth through age three.

• There are several laws that affect the young handicapped child. PL 94–142 provides for children aged three to twenty-one, unless it is superseded by state law. PL 98- 199 provides additional legislation for the preschool child.

• Head Start programs now must reserve up to 10 percent of their enrollment for handicapped children. The Handicapped Children's Early Education Assistance Act funds HCEEP, model and demonstration programs for handicapped preschool children. The Developmental Disabilities Act can provide assistance for children from birth through two years of age.

• Several types of curriculum models have been used in early childhood special education programs. The traditional, whole-child, approach offers a variety of enrichment activities. The basic skills instruction curriculum focuses on specific preacademic skills. The cognitive development curriculum stresses the teaching of thinking and problem-solving skills. Most programs have elements of each curricular type.

Key Terms

bonding	Handicapped Children's Early Education Program (HCEEP)	cognitive developmental curriculum
screening		direction skills instruction curriculum
Child Find	Developmental Disabilities Act	enrichment curriculum
self-fulfilling prophecy		cost-effective
Head Start		

Chapter Outline

The Learning-Disabled Adolescent

Chapter **9**

Introduction

*T*his chapter focuses on the special problems and programs for the learning-disabled adolescent and adult. Most secondary schools now have programs for the learning disabled, and the amount of research on learning-disabled adolescents is growing. The recognition that for many individuals learning disabilities are a lifelong problem has also spurred concern for the post–high school period and for adults with learning disabilities. The major topics in this chapter are characteristics of learning-disabled adolescents, special considerations and problems at the secondary level, types of learning disabilities programs in the secondary schools, career and vocational education, college and post–high school programs, and learning-disabled adults.

CASE EXAMPLE

Bob, A Learning-Disabled Adolescent

Bob, a fourteen-year-old freshman at Washington High School, is learning disabled. His first-semester grades confirmed what he had feared: he failed three subjects, English, algebra, and history; made only a D in general science; and received a C in physical education and mechanical drawing.

Bob finds that he cannot cope with the assignments, the workload, and the demands of his courses. Even worse, he cannot read the textbooks, he does not understand all that goes on in his classes, and he does poorly on the written exams. He feels as though he is drowning and knows he needs help.

When Bob was in elementary school, he received intermittent help from the learning disabilities resource teacher. Last year, in his eighth-grade class, he was completely mainstreamed without resource help. Although he received no direct special education services, the learning disabilities teacher, his eighth-grade homeroom teacher, and his other subject-area teachers informally discussed Bob's academic progress and planned his program. Bob himself was very involved in these planning sessions. In general, he had a successful year in eighth grade, passing all his subjects with above average grades, although he had to work hard to do it.

Over the summer, Bob grew so much that he had to buy a complete set of new clothes. His voice had changed and he finds that he must shave the dark hair sprouting over his upper lip about once a week. Bob has made new friends at the high school while keeping many of his old friends from eighth grade. He has not told any of his friends about his grades, however. In fact, he is so embarrassed about them that he has stopped seeing his friends.

At this point, he does not know where to turn. His parents are disappointed and angry. In a conference that the school counselor held with him and his parents, they were told that the tests show he has the ability and that he should try harder. Bob is discouraged and depressed. Since the grades were mailed to his parents, he has cut a number of classes. Clearly, without help, there is danger that Bob will become another dropout statistic.

Teen-agers must learn to handle the feelings of insecurity and self-consciousness that are common during adolescence.   *(Alan Carey/The Image Works)*

Characteristics of the Learning-Disabled Adolescent

There are major physical, mental, and emotional differences between the elementary school pupil and the adolescent, and they affect learning. The period of adolescence is well documented as one of turmoil and difficult adjustment. Not only do learning-disabled teen-agers have difficulty in school and social life because of their learning disabilities but they also have the added burden of adolescent change and adjustments. Many of the characteristics of learning disabilities and adolescence overlap. Sometimes it is difficult to determine if a particular behavior is due to the learning disability or to puberty. In most cases, both contribute, and they tend to interrelate with each other, often complicating the problem.

Characteristics of Adolescence

The characteristics of adolescence that may have an impact on learning include the following (Evra, 1983):

1. Adolescents are faced with the task of becoming independent and separating themselves from their families but also need these ties. Thus they must resolve a conflict between a desire for freedom and independence and a desire for security and dependence.

2. Adolescence is a period of rapid changes in physical growth and appearance, including dramatic changes in facial and body structure. Adolescents must develop a new self-image and learn to cope with a different physical appearance, as well as new psychological and biological drives.
3. The adolescent period is also one of developing sexuality—another change that the adolescent must learn to handle. This aspect of adolescence may be very demanding in terms of time, energy, and worry.
4. Peer group pressure and peer values greatly influence adolescents. When peer values differ from those of the parents, family confrontation and conflict may result.
5. Teen-agers tend to be very conscious of themselves—how they look and how they compare with group norms. This self-consciousness can lead to feelings of inferiority and to withdrawal.

Special Characteristics of Learning-Disabled Adolescents

It can be readily seen that all these characteristics of adolescence can have a negative effect on the student's learning. Besides the problems of adolescence, however, other typical characteristics have been noted in learning-disabled adolescents (Wiens, 1983; Deshler & Schumaker, 1983; Kronick, 1981).

1. *Passive learners.* Adolescents with learning disabilities have been characterized as "passive" learners. As a response to problem-solving situations, they have developed an attitude of "learned helplessness" (Torgeson, 1982; Wiens, 1983). Instead of trying to solve a problem, they wait passively until a teacher directs them and tells them what to do.
2. *Poor self-concept.* Poor self-concept and low self-esteem result from years of failure and frustration. Learning-disabled adolescents feel little confidence that they can learn and achieve. Often, too, emotional problems develop due to the lack of experiences of success (Blanton, 1984; Meyer, 1983).
3. *Inept social skills.* Another trait of learning-disabled adolescents is social ineptitude. Often they have difficulty making and keeping friends (Kronick, 1981; see also Chapter 15). During the period when friendships and peer approval are so important, social perception problems create another impediment.
4. *Attentional deficits.* Poor abilities in attention and concentration are another characteristic of the learning-disabled adolescent (Hallahan & Sapona, 1983). Given the long periods of concentration needed for study and for listening in class, these deficits can seriously impede progress in school.

Coping with these problems in addition to those created by puberty can be extremely frustrating and devastating. In addition, of course, the adolescent has to face the various academic learning problems as well. When one considers the combination of academic difficulties, the characteristics of adolescence, and those of learning disabilities, it is small wonder that adolescence is such a trying time for the learning-disabled student.

Juvenile Delinquency and Learning Disabilities

For a few students, the combined problems of adolescence and learning disabilities lead to acts of juvenile delinquency. It must be emphatically stated, however, that this is not the course followed by the great majority of learning-disabled youths. Most learning-disabled adolescents do not encounter problems with the law. On the other hand, research on the linkage between juvenile delinquency and learning disabilities does show that many delinquents manifest symptoms of learning disabilities. Two studies revealed that learning disabilities were twice as prevalent in the delinquent groups as in the nondelinquent groups (Berman, 1981; Keilitz, Zaremba, & Broder, 1979)

An effective approach to treating juvenile delinquency appears to be academic therapy. After a course of academic remediation consisting of fifty-five to sixty-five hours during a school year, one group of juvenile delinquents showed a significant decrease in their delinquent behavior (Crawford, 1984).

Much work still needs to be done in studying the links between learning disabilities and juvenile delinquency. Although a connection appears to exist, causal factors remain unknown. Does the learning disability lead to the delinquent behavior or are there parallel factors that trigger both? More important, we have not yet discovered appropriate treatment for juvenile delinquency or determined how potential delinquents can be prevented from pursuing delinquent behaviors. The study of the connection between learning disabilities and juvenile delinquency has brought new specialists to the learning disabilities team—juvenile court officers and judges. These professionals will strengthen our efforts to understand and help the learning-disabled adolescent.

Special Considerations at the Secondary Level

Meeting the needs of learning-disabled adolescents is a growing area of concern for secondary schools. Programs in the junior and senior high schools are rapidly expanding to meet a demand that stems from students, parents, teachers, and the law. The mandates of PL 94–142 have added urgency to the need for services at the secondary level. An analysis of individualized education programs (IEPs) showed that almost one-half of all handicapped students being served in the public schools are twelve years of age or older (Comptroller General of the United States, 1981). In addition, there is a national resurgence of interest in the high school curriculum. A number of commissions charged with studying high school education in the nation have called for sweeping changes in the high school curriculum (*A Nation at Risk,* 1983). The implementation of a more stringent and demanding high school curriculum will pose additional problems for the learning-disabled student.

At the secondary level, certain problems occur that are not found in elementary school learning disabilities programs.

Wide Range of Student Problems

Learning-disabled adolescents are a diverse population. Their problems range from mild to severe. Their difficulties span the whole secondary curriculum, as well as social, emotional, and behavioral areas. Many of the students who received learning disabilities instruction at the elementary level still need services when they reach junior and senior high school. Other adolescents may not have been identified until they reached the secondary school because of the subtle nature of their problems, the increased demands of the secondary curriculum, or the lack of learning disabilities services at the elementary schools they attended (Lerner, Evans, & Meyers, 1977).

Additional complications at the secondary level stem from the unique characteristics of the learning-disabled adolescent: the turmoil and dissonance that accompanies puberty; the years of failure, low self-esteem, poor motivation, and inadequate peer acceptance; and the disruptive and maladaptive behavior. For the adolescent, behavioral and social problems often take precedence over learning problems. Learning-disabled adolescents are often characterized by avoidance of tasks, impulsivity, emotional swings, overreaction, disorganized study habits, poor use of time, and lack of attention.

Curricular Demands

At the secondary level, too, the problems for the learning-disabled adolescent are magnified by the complex set of curricular demands placed on students. Schumaker, Deshler, and Denton (1984) note that learning-disabled students in high school are typically mainstreamed for four periods a day. In these mainstream classes, they are expected to meet the same curricular demands as all other students, and they are expected to learn, integrate, manage, and express large amounts of content information in spite of their handicaps. Research on learning disabilities in the high school shows that part of the difficulty is due to heavy expectations of reading proficiency that the adolescent cannot meet (Schumaker et al., 1984):

1. *There is a heavy emphasis on reading to obtain information.* Instruction is based on presumed good reading abilities. The learning-disabled students are expected to read large amounts of information, up to fifty pages a week for each mainstreamed class, and they are expected to comprehend and retain this information.

2. *The textbooks used in the content high school courses are generally written above the grade level in which they are used.* For example, if the tenth grade student is reading at fifth grade level and the social studies textbook is written at eleventh grade level, there is a six-year discrepancy. The textbook for the course would be extremely difficult for the student to read and understand. Alley and Deshler (1979) found that the average reading ability for learning-disabled high school students is third to fifth grade.

3. *High school content area teachers generally assume that students have adequate reading ability, and they do not teach reading skills.* There is little emphasis in content courses on teaching students learning aids, such as organization skills or studying the outline.

4. *Learning-disabled students are required to take four classes a semester.* The reading demand from content area classes (for instance, English, science, mathematics, and history) is frustratingly heavy.

Secondary Teachers

Many of the content area secondary school teachers are not oriented to working with learning-disabled students. Their orientation is toward their content specialization, be it mathematics, French, physics, or English literature. They have not been trained to adjust curricula for the student with specific learning deficits. An important function of the learning disabilities teacher in the high school is to help content-area teachers develop a sensitivity to the needs of learning-disabled students and make necessary adjustments in their teaching.

The learning disabilities teacher is the person who has the responsibility of bridging the gap between regular education and special education. This teacher must, of course, be thoroughly familiar with the field of learning disabilities but must also be grounded in the problems of the adolescent and the curriculum of the high school. The responsibilities of the high school learning disabilities teacher may range from helping students with algebra problems or aiding them with a creative writing assignment to helping them with a mechanical drawing lesson or explaining a science experiment. The immediacy and relevancy of the problem is of vital concern to the student, who will not be satisfied unless the help is directly related to that problem. Remediation is most effective when it is closely tied to what is happening in the classroom.

A major task of the high school learning disabilities specialist is to help the content teachers understand the nature of a specific student's problem and the steps needed to help that student. If the student has a severe reading disability, perhaps it would be possible to tape lessons. Certain books have been recorded for the blind and could be made accessible to nonreaders through local libraries. For further information, contact Recording for the Blind (see Appendix D). During examinations, the student with a severe writing problem might be allowed to give answers orally, to tape answers, or to dictate answers to someone else. The students who work very slowly might be allowed additional time. Selling the learning disabilities concept so that high school teachers are willing to make needed modifications is an essential element of the job, and it is one that requires skill in interpersonal relationships.

Another responsibility of the high school learning disabilities teachers is to work with other related personnel. For example, they can plan with guidance counselors to help students prepare for the future. Some learning-disabled students have the desire and ability to prepare for college, but they need careful guidance. Others want specific preparation for vocational careers, and high school counselors can be helpful to these students as well.

Minimum Competency Tests (MCT)

Schools give minimum competency tests to judge whether students have reached a specific skill level. Over three-fourths of the states have passed laws requiring schools to give minimum competency tests. Students must successfully pass these tests to qualify for a high school diploma.

The minimum competency movement has grown out of a demand for accountability on the part of legislatures and concern about the decrease in college entrance test scores such as the Scholastic Aptitude Test (SAT). Supporters of minimum competency tests hope that if minimum standards are set, students will function at higher academic levels, thereby improving overall academic standards. Those who oppose this trend argue that MCT has become another device for discouraging or getting rid of those students who do not conform to the academic norms of our society (Chandler, 1982). In addition, an inordinate amount of time is spent teaching to the test.

A recent federal court decision ruled that competency tests can be used to determine who graduates from high school. The school can present those students who fail the MCT with a "certificate of attendance" instead of the high school diploma.

The MCT requirement raises some serious questions for the learning disabled student. In effect, students with learning disabilities may be denied the high school diploma because of the minimum competency test ruling. In some ways the MCT concept with a preset cutoff point for graduation is in conflict with the basic special education goal of meeting a student's individual needs. Several options have been examined for learning-disabled and other handicapped students. One option is to exempt handicapped students from minimum competency testing; and another, to make modifications in the competency test in terms of format, timing, and so forth. Still another solution is to substitute for the competency test the achievement goals set forth in the IEP, making the IEP serve as the basis for graduation (Ewing & Smith, 1981). How the minimum competency requirements are to be met and how the tests should be administered are critical issues for the learning-disabled adolescents—and these issues are still being debated.

Types of Learning Disabilities Programs in the Secondary Schools

Several different approaches for teaching learning-disabled adolescents are used in junior and senior high schools. A nationwide survey revealed the following predominant program options: (1) the basic skills remedial model, (2) the functional curriculum model, (3) the tutorial model, (4) the work-study model, and (5) the learning strategies model. Table 9.1 shows the five models and the percentage of respondents who reported using the model in the secondary school (Alley and Deshler, 1979; Deshler, Lowrey, & Alley, 1979),

The Basic Skills Remediation Model

The objective of this approach is to improve the students' basic academic skill deficits by providing remedial instruction. The program usually stresses reading and mathematics. Students receive instruction at a level that approximates their achievement or instructional level. For example, if a student appears to be achieving at fifth-grade level, his or her reading instruction will be aimed at that level. The survey showed that 51 percent of the schools responding used this approach. Students received instruction in the categorical (learning disabilities) resource room.

The Functional Curriculum Model

The primary objective of this approach is to equip students to function in society. Students are taught what are often called "survival skills," that is, skills that will enable them to get along in the world outside of school. The curriculum includes subjects such as consumer information, completion of application forms (such as job application forms), banking and money skills (interest rates, installment purchases), and life-care skills (for instance, grooming). Academic content is geared to the students' careers and life needs. For example, reading would be directed toward relevant areas such as directions, want ads, or a driver's instruction manual. Guidance and counseling for self-identity and career identity are often part of the curriculum. Since a regular high school curriculum is usually not consistent with these objectives, educators develop a separate curriculum that is taught in a self-contained classroom. This approach was used by 17 percent of the respondents in the survey.

The Tutorial Model

The objective of this approach is to provide instruction in academic content areas. If Mary experiences failure or difficulty in the American history class, learning disabilities instruction will be focused on the specific material she is

TABLE 9.1   **Learning Disabilities Program Models Used in Secondary Schools**

Model of Teaching	Percentage of Teachers Using Model	Method of Delivering Service
Basic skills remediation	51	Categorical resource room
Functional curriculum	17	Self-contained classroom
Tutorial model	24	Resource room
Work-study model	5	Work-coordinator teacher
Learning strategies model*	——	Resource room

*(limited to the research program)

Source: Data from a survey conducted by G. Alley and D. Deshler, *Teaching the Learning-disabled Adolescent* (Denver, CO: Love, 1979).

studying in the history course. The purpose of the learning disabilities instruction is to help the student meet with success in the regular curriculum. Of course, the learning disabilities teacher must be knowledgeable about the requirements of all academic subjects. The tutorial model was used in 24 percent of the programs surveyed, and the educational service was provided through a resource room.

The Work-Study Model

The objective of this approach is to instruct adolescents in job- and career-related skills, as well as to give them on-the-job experience. Students typically spend half the day on the job and the remainder in school. The Alley and Deshler (1979) survey showed that students in work-study programs studied material compatible with the job experience while in school and usually did so in self-contained settings. It would be possible, however, for the student to take regular courses in the high school during the time spent in school and also work with a learning disabilities teacher. This fresh approach is particularly successful for those students who are turned off by the high school environment. The learning disabilities teacher serves as a work coordinator, obtaining and supervising the jobs in which the student is placed. The survey showed that 5 percent of the respondents used this approach.

The Learning Strategies Model

The learning strategies model is based on the concept that learning-disabled adolescents are "inefficient learners." They do not lack the ability to learn but go about learning in an inefficient manner. For example, their memory may be adequate for remembering the facts in a history lesson, but they have to put the right kind of learning effort into remembering those facts. Knowing how to go about learning is also referred to as "metacognition" (see Chapter 6) or learning strategies (Deshler, Schumaker, & Lenz, 1984).

Learning strategies are techniques, principles, or rules that will facilitate the acquisition, manipulation, integration, storage, and retrieval of information across situations and settings. The objective of a learning strategies approach is to teach adolescents *how* to learn rather than to teach them specific content. For example, if Sam is having difficulty in history, the learning strategies approach would teach Sam techniques of organizing materials for learning rather than history content. The emphasis is on teaching learning-disabled adolescents how to adapt and cope with their changing world. In other words, the focus is on helping them "learn how to learn."

The learning strategies approach appears to benefit learning-disabled adolescents with the following characteristics: (1) above third-grade reading level, (2) ability to deal with symbolic as well as concrete learning tasks, and (3) an average intellectual ability (IQ level of 83–115). The learning strategies can be taught within the resource room (Deshler, Lowrey, & Alley, 1979).

Developing learning strategies for learning-disabled adolescents has been the focus of extensive research at the Kansas University Institute for Research on Learning Disabilities (Deshler, et al., 1984).

Instructional Procedures for Teaching Learning Strategies

The goal of the learning strategies research is to identify specific learning strategies that can be taught to learning disabled students to aid them in coping with the demands of the secondary curriculum. The strategies can be applied to all areas of the curriculum. Researchers at the Kansas University Institute for Research on Learning Disabilities have reported on a number of effective learning strategies (Deshler et al., 1984; Schumaker, Deshler, & Denton, 1984; Schumaker et al., 1982; Deshler, Schumaker, Lenz, & Ellis, 1984; see also Chapter 6 for a full discussion of cognitive learning strategies).

Self-questioning   Students learn to ask themselves questions and find the answers as they proceed through instructional material. In assigned reading material, they may read a paragraph at a time, then ask themselves questions and either answer the questions or find the answers in the paragraph.

Error Monitoring   Students learn to scan material to find errors. They learn how to look over the material of others and their own to detect errors.

Verbal Rehearsal   Students learn to talk to themselves to explain what is happening. This verbalization, or "self-talk," increases the student's understanding of the material.

Self-control Training   Students learn to stop and think before answering. This strategy is designed to reduce impulsive responses.

Organization Strategies   Students learn to group material to facilitate learning. Organizing the material helps students understand and remember what is being learned.

Central to all these learning strategies is a suggested instructional procedure. Students progress through the following instructional procedure for each learning strategy that they are taught (Schumaker, Deshler, & Denton, 1984; Deshler, Alley, Warner, & Schumaker, 1981). The steps described below are for the learning strategy of self-questioning.

Step 1. Test to determine the student's current learning habit. The student is asked to perform a task that requires the target learning strategy. For example, for the target learning strategy of *self-questioning,* the teacher asks the student to read a passage and answer comprehension questions. The teacher discusses the results of the student's performance with the student in order to establish the need for acquiring the learning strategy.

Step 2. Describe the new learning strategy. Next, the teacher explains the steps and behaviors involved in performing the learning strategy. For example, "First, you will read a paragraph. Then you will stop reading and ask youself some questions. As you think of a question, you will answer it yourself or you will go back to the paragraph to find the answer. After you have answered all the questions you can think of, you will read the next paragraph."

Step 3. Model the new learning strategy. In this step the teacher models the strategy. All the steps described in Step 2 are demonstrated. The teacher "thinks aloud" so that the student can witness the entire process.

Step 4. Verbal rehearsal of the strategy. In this step the student rehearses the steps by talking aloud until a criterion of 100 percent correct is reached without prompting from the teacher. The student becomes familiar with the steps through a self-instruction procedure.

Step 5. Practice with controlled materials. In this stage, the teacher provides materials for the student to practice the new learning strategy. By carefully selecting practice materials, the teacher keeps other intervening problems to a minimum. For example, to practice the learning strategy of self-questioning in reading material, the teacher would select material that is easy enough for practicing the target strategy and would not cause the student to get bogged down in very difficult vocabulary.

Step 6. Practice with classroom materials. In this step, once the student has gained proficiency in the strategy with controlled materials, the strategy is applied to materials that are used in the regular classroom. This step is a stage in developing an application and generalization of the learning strategy. After using the strategy successfully in the resource room, the student must learn to generalize the technique to broader learning situations.

Only recently have a small number of colleges begun to respond to the needs of learning-disabled applicants and entrants.   *(Cary Wasserman/The Picture Cube)*

In summary, the goal of the learning strategies approach is to teach learning-disabled adolescents to become involved, active, and independent learners. The focus is on the cognitive aspects of learning rather than on specific subject matter content. Although this is a relatively recent approach to teaching learning-disabled adolescents, research results thus far are promising. They show that it is an effective teaching method, for students learn the strategies and are able to generalize and transfer the new learning style to other situations and settings.

Career and Vocational Education

Learning-disabled adolescents urgently need programs in career and vocational education, since their time remaining in school is usually limited. Although career education is important for all students, it is even more imperative for the handicapped. The nonhandicapped can learn skills more easily from on-the-job training; but without prior preparation, the prospects for success for the handicapped are poor.

Career Education

There is an important distinction between vocational and career education. *Career education* has a broad purpose of preparing students in a general way for the world of work. Although we are discussing it in this chapter on adolescents, the concept should be embedded into the curriculum for elementary students as well. Career education is the totality of all experiences through which students learn about and prepare to engage in work as a part of their way of living.

Career education includes the phases of (1) career awareness (diverse jobs available to adults in modern society); (2) career exploration (skills and competencies are needed in various careers and vocations); and (3) career preparation (more specific training and preparation for the world of work).

Throughout the student's school experience, teachers can stress career education by teaching good work habits and interpersonal skills, by requiring students to complete assignments, meet deadlines, work independently, and be punctual (Cegelka, 1981; Marsh & Price, 1980).

Vocational Training

Vocational training is training for a specific job (such as automechanics or food services). There are several problems related to the vocational training program for the learning disabled. Since the general vocational training program is not designed for the student with learning disabilities, vocational educators may be unaware of, or insensitive to, the particular demands of the learning-disabled adolescent. On the other hand, programs for handicapped adolescents, such as the mentally retarded, orthopedically handicapped, blind, or deaf may be inappropriate for the learning disabled. Therefore, it is usually up to the learning disabilities teacher or a special vocational educator to create a vocational program to meet the needs of the learning-disabled adolescents (Putton, 1981).

Career and Vocational Legislation

The outlook for the handicapped and learning disabled is improving, largely because of several legislative mandates. PL 94–142, the Education for All Handicapped Children Act, extends services to age twenty-one. For the older student, this often means vocational education, which can quite legitimately be regarded as part of the IEP for secondary students. The Vocational Education Act (PL 94–482), as amended in 1976, requires that states spend 20 percent of federal vocational money on disadvantaged pupils and 10 percent on the handicapped. Sections 503 and 504 of the Rehabilitation Act states that institutions receiving federal funds cannot discriminate against the handicapped.

The Rehabilitation Services Administration (RSA) under the Rehabilitation Comprehensive Services and Developmental Disabilities Act (PL 95–602) can now provide services to individuals with severe learning disabilities (Gerber, 1981; the Rehabilitation Services Administration, 1981). Thanks to the diligent work of parent advocate groups (ACLD) and professionals, learning-disabled individuals are eligible for vocational rehabilitation services. To receive services, they must meet the RSA definition and also satisfy the RSA criteria.

The RSA defines severe learning disabilities as individuals who have a disorder in one or more of the psychological processes involved in understanding, perceiving, or expressing language or concepts (spoken or written)—a disorder that may manifest itself in problems related to listening, speaking, reading, writing, spelling, or doing mathematical calculations.

The RSA judges criteria eligibility for services by the following:

1. The individual's psychological processing disorder is diagnosed by a licensed physician and/or licensed or certified psychologist who is skilled in the diagnosis and treatment of such disorders.
2. The disorder results in a substantial handicap to employment.
3. There is a reasonable expectation that vocational rehabilitative services may benefit the individual in terms of employability.

Life Skills

In discussing the educational needs of adolescents, it is also important to consider life skills—those skills that may not be a part of a formal curriculum yet are essential for getting along in the world. The learning-disabled adolescent obviously needs many life skills, such as grooming and interpersonal skills. However, it should be noted that life skills are changing rapidly in our society. The following essential life skills will be needed by all in the next decade (Feirer, 1982), including people with learning disabilities.

Computer literacy. In the next decade almost everyone is going to have to know how to use some type of computer.

Home maintenance. Costs are so great that one cannot afford to hire for everything. Everyone needs to have some basic maintenance skills.

Money management. In this era of inflation and high costs, we all must know how to manage money. Earning a salary is not enough; we must all learn how to manage and build our assets.

Time management. The effective use of time becomes a problem for all.

Skills for employment. This includes many general skills—looking for a job, attitudes about work, ability to handle an interview.

Motivation to continue to learn. We all must face the fact that if we are to grow and develop we must continue to learn. We should know how to keep up with our field and seek new opportunities.

College and Post-High School Programs

Learning-disabled students are frequently excluded from college and post-secondary education because they do not meet the instutition's entrance requirements. In many other cases, students are accepted by a college only to find that because of their learning disabilities they require assistance and modifications that are unavailable at the college. A small number of post-secondary schools are beginning to respond to the needs of the learning disabled (Vogel, 1982).

The process that colleges follow for identifying the learning-disabled college applicant and developing a viable college program for that student is described in detail by Vogel (1982). She found that successful college programs that have been developed were largely due to one dedicated individual at the college who assumed responsibility for the program. A successful college program needs integrated working components. It means training the college staff, identifying resources, and assembling a specific learning disabilities college program staff to work with the students. The staff works in areas such as assessment, academic advising, teaching study skills, enhancing written language skills, and developing social and interpersonal skills.

A survey of college programs for learning-disabled students was made by Cordoni (1982), who observed that a current listing is most difficult because the college programs are continually changing, being created and dropped. Cordoni presents a listing of college programs and related resources for learning-disabled students. One source that attempts to revise and update the information is the *National Directory of Four Year Colleges, Two Year Colleges and Post High School Training Programs for Young People with Learning Disabilities* (Moss & Fielding, 1981).

It should be noted that special accommodations for students with learning disabilities are available for taking both the SAT and the ACT college entrance examinations. Those interested can write to the Scholastic Aptitude Test (SAT) or the American College Testing (ACT) for further information.

Learning-Disabled Adults

The problems created by learning disabilities may not disappear when the individual leaves school. Because of efforts to develop public awareness of learning disabilities through television programs and magazine articles, young adults have recognized that their problems are related to learning disabilities.

What is the life of a learning-disabled adult like? These adults sometimes have great difficulty finding their niche in the world. They have trouble finding and keeping a job, developing a satisfying social life, and even coping with individual daily living.

CASE EXAMPLE

Frank,
A Learning-Disabled Adult

Frank is one example of a learning-disabled adult. A thirty-six-year-old man of average intelligence whose specific difficulty was in reading, he sought help at a university learning disabilities clinic. Employed as a journeyman painter and supporting his wife and two children, he had learned to cope with many daily situations that required reading skills. Although he was unable to read the color labels on paint cans, could not decipher street and road signs, and could not find streets or addresses or use a city map to find the locations of his housepainting jobs, he had learned to manage by compensating for his inability to read. He visually memorized the color codes on the paint cans to determine the color; he tried to limit his work to a specific area of the city because he could not read street signs. When he was sent into an unfamiliar area, he would ask a fellow worker who could provide directions to accompany him, or he would request help from residents of the area to help him reach his destination. He watched television to keep abreast of current affairs, and his wife read and answered correspondence for him. However, inevitably the day came when advancement was no longer possible if he did not learn to read. Moreover, his children were rapidly acquiring the reading skills that he did not possess. His handicap was a continual threat to him and finally led him to search for help. It is remarkable that after so many years of failure and frustration, Frank recognized his problem as that of a learning disability and had the fortitude and motivation to attempt once again the formidable task of learning to read. (Kirk, Kliebhan, & Lerner, 1978)

Blalock (1981) analyzed the records of thirty-eight young adults, aged seventeen to thirty-seven, who were attending a special clinic for learning-disabled adults. All but two demonstrated at least average ability in one or both scores on the Wechsler Adult Intelligence Scale. Their stated purpose for attending the clinic was to understand their problems and get help in learning so that they could move ahead vocationally and educationally. When they applied to the clinic, they identified their problem as reading and written language difficulties. However, the diagnosis of these young adults revealed significant problems in several areas: oral language, reading, written language, arithmetic, and nonverbal abilities. Half of the group reported social problems; they had few friends and felt alone. They also complained of vocational problems, including the inability to keep a job. When they did lose a job, they were uncertain as to what had gone wrong. Blalock noted that many of these young adults had developed amazing strategies for avoiding, hiding, and dealing with their problems.

What is unique about the adult student who is learning disabled? Usually, learning-disabled adults are self-identified and self-referred. They must be intimately involved in both the diagnosis and the remediation process. They are likely to be highly motivated to learn the skills they know that they need in life. They want to know what test results mean and what the goals and purpose of the remediation program are. It is their commitment to the program that enables them to succeed.

Since adults are no longer in school, they usually must find other agencies for services. Most clinics are not geared to serving the learning-disabled adult. Learning disabilities specialists must enlarge their scope to provide service to the adult—a very neglected individual.

The ACLD organization has formed a committee to deal with this problem. Inquiries about joining the Learning-Disabled Adult Committee of ACLD can be sent to ACLD, 4156 Library Road, Pittsburgh, PA 15234. Local groups are also being organized to identify and support learning-disabled adults. One such organization is Time Out to Enjoy, Inc., 715 Lake Street, Suite 100, Oak Park, IL 60301. The Association of Learning Disabled Adults, P. O. Box 9722, Friendship Station, Washington, DC, is another self-help group.

Summary

• There is increasing interest in providing services for the learning-disabled adolescent. Most junior and senior high schools have programs for learning disabilities.

• Learning-disabled adolescents have to cope with the dramatic changes in their lives due to puberty as well as with problems related to their disabilities. Special characteristics of learning disabled adolescents include passive learning styles, poor self-concept, social imperception, and attentional disorders.

• Many juvenile delinquents appear to have learning disabilities. Remedial therapy appears to be an effective way to reduce juvenile delinquency.

• Several special problems occur at the high school level. Students with widely varying needs and with problems ranging from mild to severe, require learning disabilities services. At the high school level, curricular demands are much heavier than at the elementary level, and content area teachers are usually not oriented to the problems of the learning-disabled adolescent. The learning disabilities teacher's role is to initiate the link between regular education and special education.

• Minimum competency tests are being given in many states as a requirement for high school graduation. These tests pose a particular problem for learning-disabled adolescents.

• The types of learning disabilities programs in the secondary schools include basic skills remediation models, functional curriculum models, tutorial models, work-study models, and learning strategies models.

• The learning strategies model teaches students how to learn rather than what to learn. By learning how to learn, the student can apply the learning strategy to all areas of the secondary curriculum.

• A multistep instructional procedure is suggested for teaching learning strategies.

• Another important focus of the high school is career and vocational education. Adolescents need this preparation for life after high school.

• College and post–high school programs for learning-disabled students are growing, and some colleges have developed special services for these students.

• There is growing interest in the learning-disabled adult. We are beginning to recognize that for some individuals learning disabilities do not end with high school graduation but continue as a lifelong problem.

Key Terms

career education
juvenile delinquency
vocational education
life skills

passive learners
learning strategies
work-study program
content area teachers

minimum competency
tests
basic skills remediation

From
Theories to
Teaching
Strategies

PART *4*

Motor and
Perceptual
Development

Chapter **10**

Introduction

*P*art 4 reviews the major areas of learning disabilities: motor and perceptual disabilities (Chapter 10); oral language (Chapter 11); reading (Chapter 12); written language (Chapter 13); mathematics (Chapter 14); and social-emotional disabilities (Chapter 15). Each chapter is divided into two major sections: a Theories section, which presents several of the major theories; and a Teaching Strategies section, which suggests activities for improving skills in that area.

This chapter discusses two closely related areas of human growth, motor development and perceptual development, as they relate to learning disabilities.

■ Theories

When parents, teachers, physicians, or other professionals report their observation of a learning-disabled child or adolescent, they often report traits such as awkwardness in motor skills, unstable balance causing frequent falls, lack of manual dexterity, or a delay in acquiring motor skills, such as riding a bicycle, buttoning a coat, catching a ball, or using eating utensils. Students with such traits are described by Gordon and McKinley (1980) as "clumsy children." Of course, it must be noted that many learning-disabled students do not exhibit these characteristics and some excel in motor and perception skills. Yet motor incoordination and perceptual disturbances are frequently displayed, and they seem to be correlated with certain academic problems. For example, poor handwriting can be due to problems in fine motor and eye-hand coordination, speech and articulation disorders can be caused by motor difficulties in the speech mechanism (control of the tongue, lips, etc.), and arithmetic problems are sometimes linked to perceptual-spatial difficulties. Many special educators think that helping these students improve their dexterity and the effectiveness of their motor performance is just as vital to their prospects of school and social success as the remediation of educational deficits in reading, arithmetic, and study skills (Rosner, 1979).

The pioneers in the field of learning disabilities put much effort into studying the causes, assessment, and treatment of motor and perceptual disorders because motor and perceptual learning provides the foundation for all subsequent learning. But in recent years, this emphasis has decreased. Research suggests that when motor and peceptual training is used in isolation without being integrated into instruction in academic skills, it becomes an indirect and inefficient method for improving the academic achievement of learning-disabled students. (This research is further discussed later in this chapter.) Besides, many learning-disabled students do not have motor or perceptual problems and therefore do not need such training. Today, more emphasis is placed on direct assessment and instruction of academic skills.

Motor Development

Throughout the history of Western civilization, philosophers and educators have written about the apparent relationship that exists between motor development and learning (Mann, 1979). Plato places gymnastics at the first level of education in the training of the philosopher-king. Aristotle writes that a person's soul is characterized by both body and mind. Spinoza advises, "Teach the body to do many things; this will help you to perfect the mind and to come to the intellectual level of thought." Piaget (1936/1952) emphasizes the importances of early sensory-motor learnings as fundamental building blocks for later, more complex perceptual and cognitive development. From the neurophysiological focus, Hebb (1949) stresses the importance of early motor learnings as an integral part of the build-up of brain cell assemblies. Luria (1966), the Russian scholar, writes about the critical relationship between motor learning and cognitive development.

Concern for motor development has also been a recurring theme throughout the history of special education (Itard, 1801/1962; Sequin, 1866/1970; Montessori, 1912). The need for physical education for all exceptional students is emphasized in PL 94–142. It is not surprising, therefore, to find a number of the pioneering theories of learning disabilities focus on sensory-motor and perceptual-motor disorders. Yet, as noted earlier, the field of learning disabilities currently appears to be placing less emphasis on the role of motor development in learning. It is interesting to note that at the same time the rest of the world seems to be embracing the concept that physical fitness, exercise, and motor activities are essential elements for achieving general well-being and improving the life and work of every individual.

CASE EXAMPLE

Motor Coordination Problems

Jim is an example of a student with academic learning problems who also shows signs of immature motor development, laterality confusion, and poor awareness of his own body. Jim was brought to a learning disabilities clinic at age twelve for an evaluation because he was doing poorly in school, particularly in reading and arithmetic. An individual intelligence test indicated that his intelligence was normal, and a screening test for auditory and visual acuity showed no abnormalities. His oral language skills seemed good for his age. At first, Jim's posture gave the impression of being unusually straight, almost military in bearing. During the motor testing, however, it was evident that this seemingly straight posture was actually rigidity. When a change in balance occurred because of a required movement, he was unable to make the correction within his body position and his relationship to gravity. He fell off the balance beam after the first few steps. When a ball was thrown to him, he was unable to catch it, losing his balance. Jim's attempts at catching the ball were similar to those of a child of four or five. He was noted to work at times with his left hand, at other times with his right hand; he had not yet established hand preference. Although he had been given swimming lessons several times, he was still unable to swim. All the children in his neighborhood played baseball after school and on weekends, but Jim could not participate in this sport with children his own age. Consequently, he had no friends, and his teacher identified him as a loner. Evidence of poor motor skills appeared in many academic activities. For example, his handwriting was almost illegible, reflecting his perceptual-motor dysfunction. Jim's father, who had excelled in athletics and had won several sports championships in high school and college, had little patience for working or playing with a son who did not catch on quickly. In fact, because of Jim's abysmal failure in sports, his father was convinced his son was mentally retarded and not "a real boy." For Jim, then, reading was but one part of the difficulty he had in relating to the world; an assessment should take into account his poorly developed motor skills, and an instructional plan should help him establish himself motorically within the world.

For many learning-disabled students, motor incoordination is a serious impediment and does characterize their functioning. They may exhibit motor behaviors that are typical of much younger children. For example, they may display overflow movements (when the individual wishes to perform a movement with the right arm, the left arm involuntarily performs a shadow movement), general poor coordination in gross motor activities, difficulty in fine-motor coordination, poor body image, lack of directionality, and confused laterality. These students are easily spotted in gym class, since they are poor in the physical education activities for their age level. Such students frequently disturb others in the classroom by bumping into objects, falling off chairs, dropping pencils and books, and appearing generally clumsy.

The terms *sensory-motor* and *perceptual-motor* are commonly used in this context. They both refer to an integration of the input of sensations and perceptions and the output of motor activity and reflect what is happening in the learner's central nervous system. The human being has six systems for receiving raw data about the world: the visual (sight), auditory (sound), tactile (touch), kinesthetic (muscle feeling), olfactory (smell), and gustatory (taste). In education emphasis is usually placed on the visual, auditory, kinesthetic, and tactile systems as the most practical approaches for educational instruction.

In the motor learning process, several input channels of sensation or perception are integrated with each other and correlated with motor activity, which in turn provides feedback information to correct the perceptions. Thus, in performing a motor activity such as a somersault, the learner *feels* the surface of the floor; has a *body awareness* of space, changing body position, and balance; *sees* the floor and other objects in relation to changing positions; *hears* the body thump on the floor; and *moves* in a certain fashion.

Several theories of motor development and disabilities are reviewed in the following sections. Each represents a theory of motor development from the perspective of a different discipline: (1) *adaptive physical education* (the physical education theory of Cratty), (2) *psychology* (the perceptual-motor theory of Kephart), (3) *developmental optometry* (the visuomotor theory of Getman), (4) *occupational therapy* (the sensory-integration theory of Ayres), and (5) *physical therapy* (the patterning theory of neurological integration of Doman and Delacato). These particular theories have been selected for review because they represent different disciplines, and they serve as vehicles for the discussion of key concepts of motor disorders and their relationship to learning disabilities.

Adaptive Physical Education and Motor Learning: Cratty

Cratty (1971, 1973), a physical educator, emphasizes the importance of movement games as a way of helping students with learning problems. Although Cratty is cautious about the academic benefits of motor training, he believes that gross movement activities can provide a sensory experience that will enhance general classroom learning.

Cratty provides numerous examples of how physical education can be related to classroom learning. For example, the student's attention span can be lengthened through games and physical activities in the hope that the increased ability to pay attention can be transferred to academic learning. The learning of letters can be a physical activity if large letters made of rope are placed on a playground and games devised in which the student runs or walks over the shape of letters. Activities that involve the total body may also serve to focus the attention of the hyperactive child.

Cratty notes that the ability to play games can serve to enhance self-concept, social acceptance by peers, and academic performance. Motor activities—such as riding bicycles, playing games, and dancing—signal the emergence of various developmental levels. Inability to accomplish these activities with reasonable proficiency may precipitate a chain of failure.

Cratty (1971) has developed a motor program designed to use games for enhancing academic learning.

Adaptive physical education programs are physical education programs that have been modified to meet the needs of exceptional students. Their goal is to help handicapped students take advantage of the same physical, emotional, and social benefits of exercise, recreation, and leisure activities that the nonhandicapped enjoy. In some cases, learning-disabled students receive motor training and physical education through an adaptive physical education program. Helping learning-disabled students take part in physical education in the school can be an important step in integrating them into the

Source: © 1974 United Feature Syndicate, Inc. Reprinted with permission.

mainstream of school life (Heward & Orlansky, 1984; Reid, 1982; Sherrill, 1976). As noted earlier, PL 94–142 has underscored importance of physical education in educating the handicapped students. The intent of the law is to provide physical education instruction for all handicapped students in the schools.

Perceptual-Motor Theory: Kephart

The perceptual-motor theory of learning disabilities put forth by Kephart (1963, 1967, 1971) was a major force in the development of the field of learning disabilities. According to this theory, normal perceptual-motor development helps establish a solid and reliable concept of the world. In Kephart's terms, the student establishes a stable *perceptual-motor world*. This approach examines the normal sequential development of motor patterns and motor generalizations and compares the motor development of students with learning problems to that of normal students.

Normal children are able to develop a rather stable perceptual-motor world by the time they encounter academic work at the age of six. For many children with learning disabilities, however, their perceptual-motor world is unstable and unreliable. These children encounter problems when confronted with symbolic materials because they have an inadequate orientation to what Kephart calls the basic realities of the universe that surrounds them— specifically the dimensions of space and time. To deal with symbolic materials, the student must learn to make some rather precise observations about space and time and relate them to objects and events.

Most educational approaches assume that these relationships have already been established and therefore build on presumed competencies in programs designed to develop conceptual and cognitive abilities. The perceptual-motor theory suggests that for many students such assumptions cannot be made, for these students have not had the necessary experiences to internalize a comprehensive and consistent scheme of the world. They have been unable to adequately organize their information-processing systems to the degree necessary to benefit from such a curriculum. As a consequence, they are disorganized motorically, perceptually, and cognitively.

Development of Motor Patterns

An individual's first learnings are motor learnings—muscular and motor responses. Through motor behavior the child interacts with and learns about the world. According to Kephart, learning difficulty may begin at this stage because the child's motor responses do not evolve into motor patterns. The differentiation between a *motor skill* and a *motor pattern* is an important element of this theory.

A *motor skill* is a motor act that may have a high degree of precision, but it has a purpose of performing a specific act or the accomplishment of a

**Learning-disabled students' taking part in physical education activities can be impor-
tant in their integration into the mainstream of school life.**

(Paul S. Conklin/Monkmeyer)

certain end. The *motor pattern* may be less precise, but it is more variable.
The purpose of the motor pattern goes beyond mere performance; it provides feedback and more information to the individual. For example, throwing a ball at a target may be a motor skill, but the ability to utilize this skill as
part of a baseball game may be called a motor pattern. Another illustration is
the trampoline. Kephart is not trying to develop expertise in trampoline but
rather, using the activity to develop certain motor patterns.

When outside pressure is exerted on the student to perform a certain
motor act not within the student's current sequential development, such a
skill may be acquired; but it becomes a *splinter skill.* Splinter skills are not an
integral part of the orderly sequential development. Kephart illustrates a
splinter skill with the example of a student who was required to learn to write
even though he had not developed the physiological readiness to perform
this act. The student acquired a splinter skill permitting him to write his name
by memorizing a series of fine finger movements that were unrelated to the
wrist or other parts of the arm or of the body (Kephart, 1963). Some people
dance as though it were a splinter skill, and the movement of their legs seems
unrelated to the rest of their bodies. Barsch (1966) takes a similar approach in
his discussion of movement training: "Movement training is not for the arms
and legs; it is for alignment and balance. Movement training is not for muscle
development but rather for kinesthetic awareness."

Motor Generalizations

Extensions and combinations of motor patterns lead to motor generalizations. *Motor generalizations* are the integration and incorporation of motor patterns into broader motor tasks. In the realm of intellectual development, generalizations are formed by combining concepts into higher abstractions of thought. Similarly, in motor learning, motor generalizations are the result of combining and integrating many motor patterns.

Four motor generalizations are discussed by Kephart as important to success in school: balance and maintenance of posture, contact and release, locomotion, and receipt and propulsion. The relationship of each of these generalizations to learning is discussed in the following paragraphs.

Balance and Maintenance of Posture   This motor generalization involves activities by which children become aware of and maintain a relationship to the force of gravity. Gravity is a basic force and the point of origin of the exploration of space, so it is very important that children learn to be aware of the pull of gravity and learn to manipulate their bodies accordingly. Children grope with gravitational forces in almost all situations—for example, when they first lift their heads against the gravitational pull; stand in an erect position; or keep their balance in walking, going across a balance beam, or tandem (heel-to-toe) walking.

Contact and Release   Through the motor generalization of contact, children obtain information about things in the world by manipulating objects. The activities of reaching for, grasping, and releasing objects enable children to investigate the objects through many sensory avenues, including looking, tasting, mouthing, listening, feeling, and even smelling. Through such extensive sensorimotor activities, children observe the attributes and characteristics of objects and eventually develop skill in form perception, figure-ground relationships, and others.

Locomotion   A third kind of motor generalization is locomotion, which enables children to observe relationships between one object and another in space. The motor patterns of crawling, walking, running, jumping, and hopping permit children to move through space to investigate the properties of surrounding space and the relationship between objects. They now move their bodies to explore "out there."

Receipt and Propulsion   The first three generalizations are static; objects remain in a place in space. *Receipt and propulsion* are dynamic; now children learn about the movement of objects in space through motor activities such as catching, pushing, pulling, throwing, and batting. According to Kephart, children are at first egocentric, seeing their own bodies as the center of the universe and the point of origin. All directions are interpreted in terms of movements away from or toward themselves: a ball rolling past them at first appears to be approaching them; but as it crosses the midline or center of their bodies, it appears to be going away from them. The concept of the midline plays an important part in Kephart's framework of laterality and directionality. He suggests that children must learn to deal with three midline planes within their bodies: (1) the lateral, or side-to-side midline; (2) the forward and backward midline; and (3) the vertical, or upper-to-lower midline. *Receipt* refers to those activities in which children make observations of objects coming toward them; *propulsion* refers to activities and observations concerning objects pushed away from their bodies. By combining these movements and observations, they also investigate movements lateral to themselves up and down, back and forth, and left and right.

It is through the four motor generalizations that children gain information about the space structure of their world.

Perceptual-Motor Match

As children gain information through motor generalizations, they also begin to note perceptual information. Since they cannot investigate all objects in motor fashion, they begin to learn to investigate them perceptually. Perceptual data only become meaningful when they are correlated with previously learned motor information; thus, perceptual information must be matched or aligned with the built-up body of motor information. Kephart terms the process of comparing and collating the two kinds of input data *perceptual-motor match*.

We know that the perceptual world is one of many seeming distortions. For example, when a circle is seen from certain angles, it looks like an ellipse or even a straight line. A rectangle from an angle may look like a trapezoid. This distortion of perception is utilized by the artist in creating perspective. In the process of perceptual-motor match, the distorted perceptions are equated to the stored information developed through motor generalizations, and the distorted perceptions are thereby adjusted.

If the perceptual-motor match is not properly made, the child lives in two conflicting worlds—a perceptual world and a motor world. The child cannot trust the information being received because the two kinds do not match and cannot be collated. The world for such children is indeed an uncomfortable, inconsistent, and unreliable place, and since they are unsure of what reality is, their behavior frequently becomes bizarre. Children who constantly touch objects may do so because they are not sure what they are seeing. One teacher of children with learning disabilities reported that whenever she wore a certain polka-dot dress the children wanted to touch the dots because they did not understand what they saw. Figure 10.1 illustrates the match that must be made between the motor information of what a tabletop looks like and the perceptual information of what one actually views. The perceptual view of the table is distorted and must be matched to the motor information. The child who has not developed perception of shapes, such as squares and rectangles, will have many difficulties in school subjects that assume such perceptual ability.

FIGURE 10.1
Two Views of a Tabletop

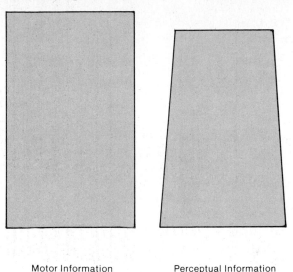

Motor Information   Perceptual Information

Since the child learns to explore objects by eye that previously had to be explored by hand, vision is the sensory avenue that gives the greatest amount of information. Ocular control, therefore, is important in the establishment of perceptual-motor match.

Purdue Perceptual-Motor Survey

One test based on Kephart's theory is the *Purdue Perceptual-Motor Survey* (Roach & Kephart, 1966). It includes such tasks as walking a board or balance beam, jumping and hopping, identification of body parts, imitation of movement, ability to move through an obstacle course, movement of arms and legs (angels in the snow), steppingstones, chalkboard drawing, ocular pursuits, and visual achievement forms (copying geometric shapes).

Visuomotor Theory: Getman

Another influential theory of the development of the motor system and its interaction with learning was presented by Getman (1965), a developmental optometrist. His approach reflects a key interest in the development of vision, which is equated with perception. Perception within this framework is a learned skill and refers to the learner's ability to interpret data coming into the senses.

Getman stresses the developmental sequence of the acquisition of motor and perceptual skills. Each successive stage of motor development depends on an earlier stage of learning. The sequential stages of visuomotor development in this theory are as follows:

Level 1. The Innate Response System   The infant is born with an innate response system, which is the basis of all learning. The motor responses within this system are unlearned and must be reasonably intact and operable at birth. They include the *tonic neck reflex*, which is the basic position or starting point from which the child moves; the *startle reflex*, which is a bodily reaction to a sudden loud noise and sudden flash of light; the *light reflex*, at first as a tightening of the eyelids and later as a reduction in the size of the pupil during exposure to bright light; the *grasp reflex*, which is a grasping of objects and is related to attention span; the *reciprocal reflex*, which refers to the facility of thrust and counterthrust of bodily movements; the *stato-kinetic reflex*, the state of relaxed attentiveness or a readiness to act; and the *myotatic reflex*, a stretch reflex system that provides the body with information concerning its own status. The innate response system, then, becomes the basis for all further learning.

Level 2. The General Motor System   The next level of learning, according to Getman, is the general motor system of locomotion or mobility skills: *creeping, walking, running, jumping, skipping, hopping*. Through such activities the child is able to build on information obtained in the innate response system, thus acquiring skills of mobility, reciprocity, and coordination. The child who does not master these skills may be awkward and lacking in coordination. Moreover, the child who does not perfect the general motor skills at this level will not be able to build the solid base needed to continue building the pyramid of learning. For this reason, children need the physical activities that will permit the development of general, or gross, motor skills.

Level 3. The Special Motor System   The special motor system builds on the first two levels toward more selective and elaborate combinations of motor skills: *eye-hand* relationships, *combinations of two hands* working together, *hand-foot* relationships, *voice* and *gesture* relationships. Too often children are required to perform these fine-motor tasks before they have facility with earlier and more basic skills. Getman observes that the child who cannot color a square or cut corners may not have learned to manipulate or move around corners using the entire motor system.

Level 4. The Ocular Motor System   The ocular motor system, the movement of the eyes, must be developed and controlled in a special manner for success in classroom tasks. The ocular system has two information-receiving, processing, and effector circuits—one for each eye—that have to be constantly matched and balanced. Getman contends that skills of eye movement are often taken for granted. Students may test out with perfect 20/20 eyesight, yet have an inadequacy in the bilateral relationships, creating stress or even double vision when doing close academic work. The student must learn to control and team the eyes across the lines of print. The ocular skills include *fixation*, the ability to visually locate a target; *saccadics*, the visual movement from one target to another; *pursuits*, the ability to have both eyes follow a moving target; and *rotation*, free movement of both eyes in any and all directions.

Level 5. The Speech Motor System   The speech-motor and the auditory integration system includes the skills of *babbling, jargon, imitative speech*, and *original speech*.

Level 6. The Visualization System   The term *visualization* refers to the ability to remember not only what has previously been seen by the eye, but also what has been heard, touched, or felt. It is the ability to recall a response when the original sensory stimulus is not present. All senses (tactile, auditory, sight, kinesthetic, and so forth) contribute to this ability. This level of learning is also called imagery or memory.

Two kinds of visualization are considered: *immediate*, whereby one can "see" a coin felt in one's pocket; and *past-future*, whereby one can review an event that happened yesterday or preview an event that will occur tomorrow.

Level 7. Perception   *Perception* is the next level of learning. All the experiences, skills, and systems represented by the underlying levels contribute to perception. Perception is the result of intact and complete learning in the supporting developmental levels.

In summary, then, the Getman visuomotor theory proposes that cognitive learning is built on a foundation of successful motor and perceptual learning at each level. The salient point is that cognitive and intellectual thought must have a solid base of extensive and successful motor learning. Since each level of learning is more precise and exacting than the preceding one, a base of successful learning should be obtained before moving to the next level with security. Students may fail in an academic cognitive program because they do not have the underlying motor foundation. The recommendation is that many students need more experiences in the base levels of motor development.

Several teaching programs deriving from this model have been designed. One, *Developing Learning Readiness: A Visual-Motor Tactile Skills Program* (Getman, Kane, & McKee, 1968), has activities for six areas of development: general coordination, practice in balance, practice in eye-hand coordination, practice in eye movement, practice in form recognition, and practice in visual memory.

Sensory-Integration Theory: Ayres

Ayres (1978, 1981) presents a theory of motor learning from the perspective of occupational therapy. The field of occupational therapy recognizes complex principles of brain physiology and function, and it prescribes specific physical therapy and exercises designed to modify the brain function of individual patients with various kinds of debilitating motor problems. Ayres has applied these theories and treatment procedures to learning-disabled children.

Learning is seen as a highly complex function of the central nervous system. The human brain, which has evolved over millions of years, is adaptable and developed in response to the complex cognitive needs of the human being. The brain's ability to function effectively, however, is dependent on lower neural structures. Since the child's brain has the quality of plasticity or adaptability, the assumption is that it can be reorganized through movement activities.

Thus, Ayres suggests that brain function in learning-disabled children can be modified through therapy that stimulates sensory integration within the brain and thereby normalizes behavior and enhances learning. Three systems are important in sensory integration: the vestibular system, the tactile system, and the proprioceptive systems. The *vestibular* system enables one to detect motion; the *tactile* system involves the sense of touch and stimulation of skin surfaces; the *proprioceptive* system involves the stimulation from within the body itself (the digestive system, nerves, joints, ligaments, and bone receptors).

Methods of therapy include activities that stimulate these three systems, for instance, *tactile* stimulation through touching and rubbing skin surfaces; *vestibular* stimulation through activities such as swinging, spinning, and being rolled on a large ball; and *proprioceptive* stimulation through scooter board activities.

Ayres strongly warns that these techniques require a highly trained therapist and that damage could occur by using the techniques without sufficient knowledge about the relationship between these exercises and brain structure. Both Ayres (1978) and deQuiros (1976) describe studies of learning-disabled students who have responded to sensory-integration therapy.

Ayres developed the *Southern California Test Battery for Assessment of Dysfunction*, which includes tests in motor accuracy, perceptual-motor skills, figure-ground visual perception, kinesthetic and tactile perception, and space perception.

Patterning Theory of Neurological Organization: Doman and Delacato

Perhaps the most controversial of the motor approaches to learning problems, the "patterning" theory of neurological organization was developed by a physical therapist, Glenn Doman, and an educator, Carl Delacato (Delacato, 1966). Its goal, according to its authors, is to establish in brain-injured, mentally retarded, and reading-disabled children the neurological developmental stages observed in normal children. The authors also suggest that the procedures benefit normal children as well.

Patterning Concepts

The concept underlying the methods advocated is that the well-functioning child develops what the authors call "full neurological organization." The theory assumes that "the ontogeny recapitulates the phylogeny," or that the process that an individual member of the human species goes through in maturing follows the same developmental stages of the entire species in the long process of evolution. Thus, in the progression toward full neurological organization, the human being proceeds in an orderly way anatomically in the central nervous system, progressing sequentially through higher levels of the nervous system: (1) spinal cord medula, (2) the pons, (3) the midbrain, (4) the cortex, and finally (5) full neurological organization, or the establishment of cortical hemispherical dominance.

Doman and Delacato maintain that there are six functional attainments of the human being: motor skills (mobility in walking upright and in cross-pattern fashion), speech, writing, reading (visual skills), understanding speech (auditory skills), and stereognosis (tactile skills). The attainment of these six skills is related to and dependent on the individual's anatomical progress toward neurological organization.

The failure to pass through a certain sequence of development at any stage indicates poor neurological organization and will result in problems in mobility or communication. The authors maintain that by measuring the level of neurological organization it becomes theoretically possible to prescribe activities that will improve neurological development and thereby eliminate or prevent learning disorders.

The underdeveloped neurological stages are overcome by engaging the child in activities designed to develop those levels of neurological growth. For children who are physically unable to perform the prescribed motor activities, the activities are passively imposed on their nervous systems by moving their limbs. According to the theory, when the neurological organization is completed, the problem in learning is overcome. The sequence of stages toward the attainment of mobility is (1) rolling over; (2) crawling in a circle or backward; (3) crawling without a pattern; (4) crawling homologously (with both arms or legs together); (5) crawling homolaterally (with arm and leg on one side of body together); (6) crawling cross-pattern; (7) creeping without pattern; (8) creeping homologously; (9) creeping homolaterally; (10) creeping cross-pattern; (11) cruising (walking holding); (12) walking without pattern; (13) walking cross-pattern (Doman, Spitz, Zuchman, Delacato, & Doman, 1967).

The treatment requires children to pass through the above sequential stages to develop neurological organization. In severe cases of brain damage, the patterning is imposed by adults who manipulate the limbs and head of the child in prescribed positions determined by the authors. This "patterning" is to be carried out in strict observance of the plan for five minutes at least four times a day, seven days a week (Doman et al., 1967). Other techniques include sensory stimulation; breathing exercises; restriction of fluids, salt, and sugar; early teaching of reading; sleeping in prescribed body positions; elimination of exposure to music; and training of eye and hand use. The goal of all these activities is the establishment of hemispheric dominance and thereby full neurological organization.

The approach and techniques suggested in this program have been used in many types of cases, including individual therapy with severely retarded and brain-injured children as well as group classroom instruction with normal children. Through the patterning approach, children must relearn and perform each stage of motor learning identified by the developers of the theory to overcome their problems. They must relearn to properly creep, crawl, walk, and so forth, since these motor activities are presumed to have an effect on reorganizing the structure of their brains.

Some reports of the success of the method have been presented in the literature (Delacato, 1966). However, other writers (Robbins, 1966; Glass & Robbins, 1967; Freeman, 1967) have found the theory, approach, treatment, and research to be inadequate. Medical, health, and educational organizations have expressed concern about the Doman-Delacato treatment of neurologically handicapped children (Cruickshank, 1968; American Academy of Pediatrics, 1982).

In spite of strong opposition from doctors and educators to the patterning method, many parents have become ardent advocates of the theory and techniques. In severe cases where all other professionals had counseled parents that there was no hope, patterning was the one avenue of action open. Many of these parents claim the method was successful and are enthusiastic supporters of the technique. The question is whether improvement is due to the technique or to other factors.

An Appraisal of Motor Theories

Although there are many differences among the theories of motor development described above, certain common principles and assumptions are evident:

1. Human learning begins with motor learning; as human beings move, they learn. An understanding of the dynamics of learning necessarily involves an understanding of movement and motor development.
2. There is a natural sequence of developmental motor stages; each stage must be successfully acquired by the child before the next stage is added.
3. Academic and cognitive learning is based on successful motor learning experiences. A student's school problems may be due to insufficient motor experiences and gaps in motor learning.
4. Intervention methods in motor training can provide students with missing motor experiences, build motor skills, and thereby prepare the student for more advanced academic and cognitive learning.

Most of the motor theories and motor training programs were developed early in the history of the field of learning disabilities and were often part of the teaching curriculum. Today there is more emphasis on direct instruction of academic and cognitive skills and less on building prerequisite learnings. We find few motor-training activities in the curriculum of current learning disabilities programs, although they are usually part of the curriculum of early childhood special education and adaptive physical education programs.

In general, research studies suggest that motor-training programs used in isolation without accompanying instruction in academic skills are not efficient methods for improving academic achievement (Goodman & Hammill, 1973; Hammill, Goodman & Wiederholt, 1974; Robertson, 1981; Meyers and Hammill, 1982). A recent research analysis of motor-training programs, using a sophisticated statistical technique, meta-analysis, supported the earlier findings (Kavale & Mattson, 1983).

Despite these research results, we cannot conclude that motor development is unimportant or that this aspect of learning should be disregarded. Movement and motor experiences are crucial to human development, and most theories of child development recognize the significance of such experiences for human growth. The major role of physical exercise in fostering general well-being is also acknowledged today. However, better plans and theories are needed for building the bridge between motor experiences and academic learning. Training in motor skills is insufficient; we still must teach academic skills. Motor training alone will not teach a child to read, any more than eyeglasses alone will instantly transform a nonreader into a bookworm. If a teacher ascertains that a student has a deficit in motor development, the teacher should not necessarily delay academic instruction.

Providing motor experiences can bring about many unanticipated and probably unmeasurable improvements. It can help a student become happier, more confident, and more available for learning. When the motor training requires the student to go *through, under, over, between*, and *around* obstacles, the student is also learning important language concepts. Simultaneous work in motor development and academic skills can be designed to reinforce and enhance each other. For example, in one summer camping and academic program for students with learning disabilities, the campers were noted to have a breakthrough in reading the same time they learned to swim (Lerner, Bernstein, Stevenson, & Rubin, 1971).

Finally, it should be reiterated that many learning-disabled students do not have underlying motor disabilities, and such disabilities should not be considered as a factor in planning instruction for these students.

Tests of Motor Development

Among the tests available to measure motor development and screen for motor deficits are the *Purdue Perceptual Motor Survey, Lincoln-Oseretsky Motor Development Scale*, and the *Southern California Test Battery for As-*

sessment of Dysfunction (which includes the *Southern California Kinesthesia and Tactile Perception Tests*, the *Southern California Figure-Ground Visual Perception Test*, the *Southern California Motor Accuracy Test*, the *Southern California Perceptual-Motor Tests*, and the *Ayres Space Test*). Descriptive data concerning these tests appear in Appendix C.

Perceptual Development

Perception is the term applied to the recognition of sensory information, the intellect's ability to extract meaning from the data received by the senses. Perception is a learned skill, so the teaching process can have a direct impact on a perceptual facility. We shall explore several constructs of perception that have implications for teaching students with learning disabilities: the perceptual-modality concept, overloading of the perceptual systems, whole and part perception, visual perception, auditory perception, haptic perception, cross-modal perception, form and direction perception, and social perception. In addition, we shall examine the research, criticism, and implications of theories of perception. Teaching strategies for perception are contained in the last section of this chapter.

CASE EXAMPLES

Perceptual Problems

A Visual Learner

Eight-year-old Sandra failed many tasks that involved learning through the auditory modality. She could not learn nursery rhymes, was unable to get messages straight over the telephone, forgot spoken instructions, could not discriminate between pairs of spoken words with minimal contrast or a single phoneme difference (cat-cap), and found phonics instruction baffling. Sandra was failing in reading; yet she had passed the reading readiness test with ease because it tested performance requiring skills within the visual modality. At first, Sandra could not remember the arithmetic facts, but there was a sudden spurt in arithmetic achievement during the second half of first grade. She explained that she solved her arithmetic problems by putting the classroom clock in her head. By "looking" at the minute marks on the clock to perform arithmetic tasks, Sandra was using her superior visual modality to compensate for her deficit in auditory processing.

An Auditory Learner

In contrast, John, at age eight, performed several years above his age level on tasks requiring auditory processing. He had easily learned to say the alphabet letters in sequence. He also learned poems and nursery rhymes, remembered series of digits, phone numbers, and verbal instructions, and quickly learned to detect phoneme differences in words. Visual tasks, however, were difficult for John. He had trouble putting puzzles together, seeing and remembering forms in designs, doing block arrangements, remembering the sequence and order of things he saw, and recalling what words looked like in print.

Perceptual-Modality Concept

The concept of perceptual modality as it relates to learning disabilities was introduced in Chapter 6, in the discussion on psychological processing. Students learn in different ways. Some learn best by listening (auditory modality), some by looking (visual modality), and some by touching (tactile modality) or by performing an action (kinesthetic modality). Adults, too, have individual learning styles. Some learn best by listening to an explanation; others know that to learn something they must read about it or watch it being done; and still others learn best by writing it down or going through the action themselves. Each of these ways of learning and receiving information is called a perceptual modality. The concept was proposed as early as 1886, when Charcot observed that individuals have a predilection for one perceptual input avenue over others and categorized people as "audile," "visile," and "tactile" learners (Charcot, 1886/1953). Many students with learning problems have a much greater facility in using one perceptual modality than another; in addition, a particular perceptual modality may be so inefficient for certain individuals that it is an unproductive pathway of learning (Wepman, 1968). As noted in Chapter 6, the theory suggests that teachers assess strengths and weaknesses in learning through visual, auditory, or tactile modes, and then use this information to select an appropriate teaching approach. The three alternative methods of instruction are (1) strengthening the deficit modality, (2) teaching through the intact modality, and (3) combining both methods. The utility of the perceptual-modality concept is controversial, and an appraisal of its application appears at the end of this section and in Chapter 6.

Overloading Perceptual Systems

Overloading the perceptual systems means that the reception of information from one modality interferes with information coming from another input modality. The learning-disabled student may have a lower tolerance for receiving and integrating information from several input systems at the same time. An analogy might be made to an overloaded fuse that blows out when it cannot handle any more electrical energy. Unable to accept and process an excess of data, the perceptual system becomes overloaded and breaks down. Overloading symptoms include confusion, poor recall, retrogression, refusal of the task, poor attention, temper tantrums, or even seizures (Johnson & Myklebust, 1967). Strauss and Lehtinen (1947) called such reactions "catastrophic responses."

The implications for teaching is that teachers should be cautious in using multisensory techniques and that they should evaluate the student before selecting methods that stimulate several perceptual modalities. Such recommendations differ substantially from teaching plans stemming from certain other theories. Some methods use a simultaneous stimulation of all input modalities to reinforce learning (Fernald, 1943; Gillingham & Stillman, 1966). Such methods advocate that when a student is learning to read a word, stimulating the eye, ear, touch, and motor avenues simultaneously will aid in the learning process. The student will hear the word, say the word, see the word, feel the word, write the word, and perhaps spell the word. In contrast, the concept of overloading implies that for certain students, multisensory teaching procedures may cause a breakdown of learning by overstimulating the brain.

Students sometimes learn by themselves to adapt their behavior to avoid overloading perceptual input. One boy was observed to avoid looking at an individual's face whenever he was engaged in conversation. When asked about this behavior, the boy explained that he found he could not understand what was being said if he watched the speaker's face while listening. The visual stimuli, in effect, interfered with the ability to comprehend through the auditory modality.

Whole and Part Perception

In addition to differences in perceptual modalities of learning, another difference in perceptual styles has been observed—that there are "whole perceivers" and "part perceivers" (Goins, 1958). Some learners apparently perceive an object in its entirety—its entire gestalt—while others tend to focus on minute details, missing the gestalt. This perceptual characteristic is similar to the background-foreground confusion noted by Strauss and Lehtinen (1947). Both the ability to see the whole and the ability to see parts are needed for effective learning. In a task such as reading, learners must be able to move flexibly from whole to parts as their purpose dictates. At times they must see the word in its entirety, and at other times see a small detail that differentiates it from another word. For example, to differentiate between *house* and *horse* the reader must be able to note details in words. The word *elephant*, however, is likely to be recognized as a whole or as a sight word. Students who rely on only one of these perceptual styles appear to have difficulty learning to read.

Students with learning disabilities often manifest this characteristic in their coloring of pictures. The sleeve may be colored red, while the body of the shirt is blue, and the other sleeve is yellow. One girl colored each side of the crease in the trousers a different color. She saw the parts but not the whole. Jerry, another "part perceiver," identified a tiny difference that the artist had made in two illustrations of an automobile that accompanied a story. Jerry was so concerned with the suspicion that it was a different automobile that he could no longer concentrate on the story. Students with such atypical styles of perception may be noted by teachers, but frequently such behavior is misinterpreted. One kindergarten teacher described a child who was subsequently found to have severe learning and perception problems as follows: 'Paul has a good deal of ability; he shows originality; and he has a knack for describing in detail. He is unusually perceptive."

Visual Perception

Visual perception plays a significant role in school learning, particularly in reading. Some students have difficulty in tasks requiring the visual discrimination of geometric designs and pictures. Others succeed at this task but fail in the visual discrimination of letters and words.

Within the broad scope of visual perception, several component skills of visual perception can be identified:

Spatial relations refers to perception of the position of objects in space. This dimension of visual functioning implies the perception of the placement of an object or a symbol (pictures, letters, numbers) and the spatial relation of that entity to others surrounding it. In reading, words must be seen as separate entities surrounded by space.

Visual discriminaion refers to the ability to differentiate one object from another. In a readiness test, for example, the child may be asked to find a rabbit that is different—to discover the rabbit with one ear in a row of rabbits with two ears. When asked to visually distinguish between the letters *m* and *n*, the child must perceive the number of humps in each letter. The skill of matching identical pictures, designs, shapes, letters, and words is another visual discrimination task. Objects may be discriminated by color, shape, pattern, size, position, or brightness. The ability to visually discriminate letters and words becomes essential in learning to read (Barrett, 1965).

Figure-ground discrimination refers to the ability to distinguish an object from the background surrounding it. The student with a deficit in this area cannot focus on the item in question apart from the visual background. Consequently, the student is distracted by irrelevant stimuli.

Visual closure is a task in which the subject is asked to recognize or identify an object, despite the fact that the total stimulus is not presented. For example, a competent reader can read a line of print when the top half of the print is covered. There are enough letter clues in the remaining bottom portion for the reader to provide visual closure to read the line.

Object recognition refers to the ability to recognize the nature of objects when viewing them. This includes recognition of geometric shapes, such as a square; of objects, such as a cat, a face, or a toy; of alphabetic letters and numbers; and of words. The kindergartener's ability to recognize geometric patterns, letters, and numbers has been found to be a good predictor of reading achievement (Richek, List, & Lerner, 1983).

The *Frostig Developmental Test of Visual Perception* evaluates five components of visual perception:

1. *Visual-motor coordination*—the ability to coordinate vision with the movements of the body or parts of the body.
2. *Figure-ground perception*—the ability to attend to one aspect of the visual field while perceiving it in relation to the rest of the field
3. *Perceptual constancy*—the ability to perceive objects possessing invariant properties such as shape, position, size, and so forth, in spite of the variability of the impression on the sensory surface

4. *Perception of position*—the perception in space of an object in relation to the observer
5. *Perception of spatial relationships*—the ability to perceive the positions of two or more objects in relation to each other.

The ITPA has several subtests that assess aspects of visual perception: *Visual Reception, Visual Association, Visual Closure*, and *Visual Sequential Memory*. Subtests of the *Detroit Tests of Learning Aptitude* that sample aspects of visual perception include *Design Reproduction* and *Object Sequences*. The K-ABC has several tests in the *sequential processing* and the *simultaneous processing* components that assess visual perception.

Other tests of visual perception are the *Bender Visual-Motor Gestalt Test* (Koppitz, 1964); the *Developmental Test of Visual-Motor Integration*; the *Motor-Free Test of Visual Perception*; and the *Southern California Figure-Ground Perception Test*. Clues to the child's skills in visual perception tasks can be obtained from subtests of the *Wechsler Intelligence Scale for Children-Revised* (WISC-R): *Picture Arrangement, Block Design, Object Assembly*, and *Coding*. Descriptive data about these tests appear in Appendix C.

Several illustrative items used in exercises to test or improve visual perception are shown in Figure 10.2.

Auditory Perception

Auditory perception provides another pathway for learning. Many students who have difficulty learning phonics are found to have poor auditory processing skills. This is not a problem of hearing or auditory acuity, but a disability in auditory perception—the ability to recognize or interpret what is heard. The auditory mode of perception can be divided into the following subskills to differentiate more specific auditory functions: (1) auditory discrimination, (2) auditory memory, (3) auditory sequencing, and (4) auditory blending.

Auditory discrimination refers to the ability to recognize a difference between phoneme sounds and to identify words that are the same and words that are different. In the *Wepman Test of Auditory Discrimination*, the student must decide whether two words are the same or different. The different words have a minimal sound difference or contrast of a single phoneme sound. The student is faced away from the examiner—so there is no visual cue of watching the speaker's mouth—and is asked whether two words in a pair are the same or different, for example, "mit-mat" or "big-pig." The *Goldman-Fristoe-Woodcock Test of Auditory Discrimination* includes tests of auditory discrimination of phonemes against a quiet and noisy background.

Auditory memory is the ability to store and recall what one has heard. For example, the student could be asked to do three activities, such as close the window, open the door, and place the book on the desk. Is the student

FIGURE 10.2
Examples of Visual Perception Tasks

WHOLE AND PART PERCEPTION: VISUAL CLOSURE

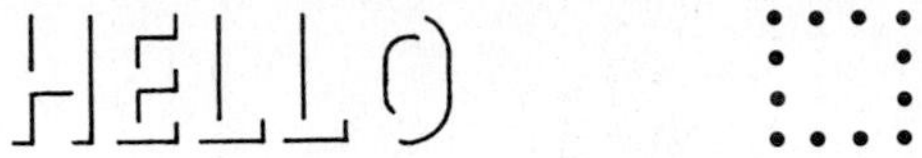

If one sees the parts, there are no letters here — only straight and curved lines. By looking at the whole, the letters are perceived.

To perceive a square, one must see this form as a whole.

VISUAL-MOTOR PERCEPTION.

Copy these patterns

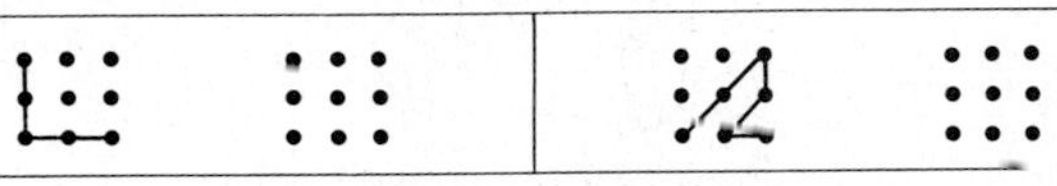

This task is a visual-motor task. The child must receive the information through the visual modality and then transfer to a motor movement.

FIGURE-GROUND PERCEPTION

Find the football.

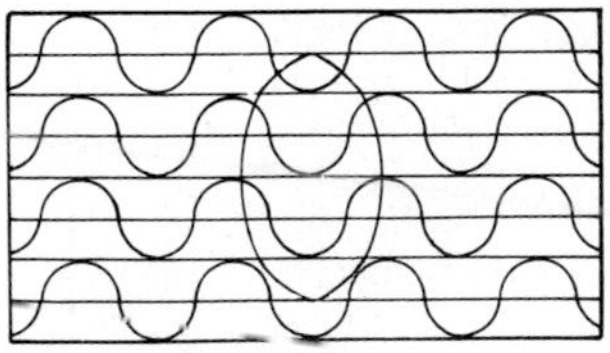

In this task the child is required to visually perceive a foreground figure against the background stimuli.

VISUAL FORM PERCEPTION: PERCEPTUAL CONSTANCY.

Find the form like the first one.

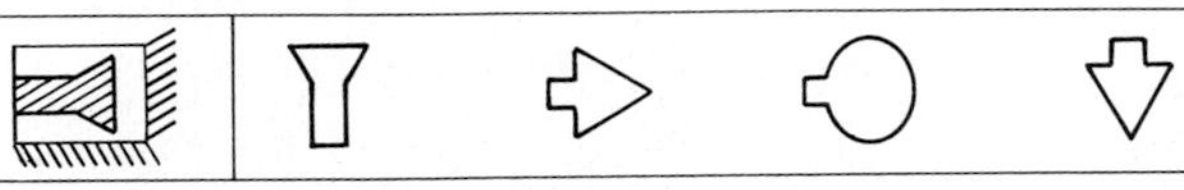

The child must maintain visual form constancy to find the shape when the position is changed.

VISUAL DISCRIMINATION: LETTERS
Find the form like the first one.

| D | F | D | M | P | L |

The child is required to visually discriminate and match identical letter shapes.

VISUAL DISCRIMINATION: WORDS
Find the form like the first one.

| horse | house | hose | horse | enough |

The child is required to visually discriminate and match identical words.

"LISTEN! WHAT WAS THAT? MY BEEPER,
MY WRISTWATCH ALARM, YOUR MICROWAVE,
OUR TELEPHONE OR A TELEPHONE ON TV?"

Source: From *The Wall Street Journal.* Reprinted by permission of Cartoon Features Syndicate.

able to store and retrieve through listening to such directions? One subtest of the *Detroit Tests of Learning Aptitude—Oral Directions*—is designed to assess such functions.

Auditory sequencing is the ability to remember the order of items given orally in a sequential list. For example, the alphabet "A, B, C . . ." and the months of the year "January, February, March . . ." are learned as an auditory sequence. Tests of auditory sequencing are found in the ITPA, *Auditory Sequential Memory*; WISC-R, *Digit Span; Detroit Tests of Learning Aptitude, Word Sequences;* and the *Kaufman-Assessment Battery for Children* (K-ABC), *Number Recall.*

Auditory blending is the ability to blend single phonic elements or phonemes into a complete word. Students with such disabilities are not able to blend the phonemes "m-a-n" to form the word *man.* Tests of this auditory skill include the ITPA subtests. *Sound Blending* and *Auditory Closure*, and the *Roswell-Chall Auditory Blending Test.*

All of the auditory subskills can be sampled through clinical observations during teaching sessions, through informal tests, or through formally designed standardized tests. The *Goldman-Fristoe-Woodcock Auditory Skills Test Battery* assesses several auditory perception skills.

Haptic Perception: Tactile and Kinesthetic Abilities

Haptic perception refers to information received through two modalities, the tactile and the kinesthetic. The term *haptic* is used to refer to both systems.

Tactile perception is obtained through the sense of touch via the fingers and skin surfaces. The ability to recognize an object by touching it, to identify a numeral that is drawn on one's back or arm, to discriminate between smooth and rough surfaces, to identify which finger is being touched—all are examples of tactile perception.

Kinesthetic perception is obtained through body movements and muscle feeling. The awareness of positions taken by different parts of the body, bodily feelings of muscular contraction, tension, and relaxation are examples of kinesthetic perception. The earlier discussion of body image and motor information in the "Motor Development" section of this chapter provides a broader view of the kinesthetic system.

Both dimensions of the haptic system are important for obtaining information about object qualities, bodily movement, and their interrelationships. Most school tasks, as well as most acts in everyday life, require both touch and body movement. Tactile and kinesthetic perception play important roles in learning. There is a need to know more about dysfunctions in the haptic areas and their relationship to other areas of learning.

One test designed to assess haptic functions is the *Southern California Kinesthetic and Tactile Perception Test.*

Cross-Modal Perception

Another theory suggests that a major difficulty in learning is the inability to integrate one modality of function with another (Chalfant & Scheffelin, 1969). The neurological process of converting information within the brain from one modality to another has been referred to as *cross-modality perception*, as well as *intersensory integration.* In many types of learning, information received through one sensory input system must be transferred to or integrated with another perceptual system; and the learner must be able to shift, or cross, from one to the other, integrating the two systems. Some students appear quite adequate in both visual and auditory systems when they are assessed alone, but the deficit appears when a task requires the integration of the two systems.

An example of cross-modal perception is found in the reading process, where the reader must integrate visual symbols with their auditory equivalents. Johnson and Myklebust (1967) propose that some reading disorders are due to an inability to make such conversions. Thus the student who cannot convert from the visual modality to the auditory modality is able to learn what letters look like but cannot associate these visual images with their sound equivalents. Conversely, the student who cannot convert from the auditory modality to the visual learns what letters sound like but cannot associate the sound with the visual form of the letters. Another illustration of a deficit in cross-modal perception is the student who has difficulty planning and executing motor movements. For example, to speak the student must convert an auditory memory of a word to a motor plan in order to say the word (auditory system to motor system).

Although there is as yet little information concerning the development of the integration of perceptual systems, some researchers believe that more complex learning is dependent on the gradual integration of the modality systems. Research studies of cross-modality integration that have been conducted thus far suggest that there are differences in intersensory integrative ability between normal children and neurologically impaired children. Individuals who apparently function normally with a task requiring a single perceptual modality have difficulty when the task involves simultaneous or successive functioning of several modalities. The breakdown occurs in tasks requiring cross-modal perception and has been referred to as an integrative disorder (Ayres, 1981; Chalfant and Scheffelin, 1969; Birch and Belmont, 1964; Birch and Lefford, 1963; Belmont, Birch, and Karp, 1965).

Frostig and Maslow (1973) advocate exercises in cross-modality associations for children found to have difficulty with the cross-modal process. Examples of such activities are: following spoken directions (auditory-verbal to motor); describing a picture (visual to auditory-verbal); finding certain objects in pictures (auditory-verbal to visual); feeling objects through a curtain and drawing their shapes on paper (tactile to visual-motor); determining whether two objects are the same or different when one is touched while the other is seen (tactile to visual); determining whether two patterns are the same or different when one is touched and the other heard—for example, *dot-dot-dash* patterns (tactile to auditory). Activities designed to have the child perform cross-modal functions are suggested later in this chapter.

Probably many tests that purport to be testing a single perceptual modality actually require the integration of two or more perceptual modalities. That is, a visual perception test may actually require integration of the visual, motor, and auditory functions. Although many tests require cross-modal functions in performance, at the present time few tests, if any, are available that have been designed specifically to assess cross-modal perception.

Form and Directional Perception

An interesting analysis of perception has been made by Money (1966), in regard to the relationship of the perceptual world of objects and the perceptual world of letters and words. A perceptual generalization made by children in the prereading stage of development is the "law of object constancy." A child concludes that an object retains the same name or meaning regardless of the position it happens to be in, the direction it faces, or the modification of slight additions or subtractions. A chair, for example, is a chair regardless of whether it faces left or right, back or front, upside down or right side up, or whether it is upholstered or has additional cushions, or even if it has a leg missing. It is still called a chair. The child has made similar generalizations about dogs; no matter what its position, size, color, or quantity of hair, a dog is still called a dog.

When beginning to deal with letters and words, however, the child finds that this perceptual generalization no longer holds true. The placement of a circle on a stick from left to right, or top to bottom, changes the name of the letter from *b* to *d* to *p* to *q*, and the addition of a small line changes *c* to *e*. The direction the word is facing changes it from *was* to *saw*, or *no* to *on*, or *top* to *pot*. One incident of such confusion happened during a teachers' strike. A boy with directional perception difficulties looked at the picket signs and asked why they were picketing if the strike was called off. The sign, lettered *ON STRIKE*, was read by the youngster as *NO STRIKE*. Another example is the student who reversed the letters in the word in making a Christmas card. He printed LEON instead of "NOEL."

The implication, then, is that some students with reading disabilities fail to make the necessary amendments to an earlier perceptual generalization they have formulated

Social Perception

Thus far, we have considered disturbances in the perception of physical objects and events. Psychologists have recently turned their attention to another dimension of perception—that of *social perception*, the skill of interpreting stimuli in the social environment and appropriately relating such interpretations to the social situation. Some students appear to have difficulty perceiving social data, and they consequently have trouble learning how to make social judgments and how to adapt their behavior to the social situation. The problems of poor social perception are discussed further in Chapter 15.

An Appraisal of Perceptual Theories

A detailed account of the criticism of theories of psychological processing as factors in learning disabilities appears in Chapter 6, so it will not be repeated here. To review, the criticism relates to (1) the inadequacy of tests of perception, (2) the low correlation between teaching methods based on perceptual information and academic improvement, and (3) unproven assumptions about the existence of perceptual deficits. We can conclude that perceptual processes exist but that we need a more encompassing theoretical framework to explain how information is processed.

Sensitive teachers use information about a student's style of learning (perceptual strengths and weaknesses) in teaching academic skills. They move as quickly as possible into the academic area they are trying to improve. If possible, they will teach visual discrimination of letters and words instead of symbols.

Current thought on the implications of perceptual development theories for teaching the learning disabled can be summarized as follows: (1) tests for assessing perceptual modalities are still imprecise and need improvement; (2) the goal of teaching the learning disabled is to impart academic skills and so perceptual training alone is insufficient and the teacher must also teach academic skills; and (3) more research is needed to understand how the components of perception relate to the total learning process.

Tests of Perceptual Processes

Some tests or subtests that can be used to measure specific perceptual areas were mentioned throughout this section. The widely used perceptual tests include *K-ABC; Illinois Test for Psycholinguistic Abilities; (Wepman) Auditory Discrimination Test; Goldman-Fristoe-Woodcock Test of Auditory Discrimination; Bender Visual Motor Gestalt Test; Motor Free Visual Perceptual Tests; Southern California Figure-Ground Visual Perception Test; Detroit Tests of Learning Aptitude; (Benton) Visual Retention Test; (Beery-Buktenica) Developmental Test of Visual Motor Integration;* and the *(Frostig) Developmental Test of Visual Perception.* Additional information concerning these tests appears in Appendix C.

■ Teaching Strategies

The rest of this chapter lists some representative activities for teaching motor and perceptual skills. These activities are not organized to implement any particular theory, nor do they represent any particular curriculum. They are a collection of activities designed to give the reader an idea of the possibilities that exist.

Activities for Motor Development

Many of these activities are similar to those used in a regular or adaptive physical education program. When learning disabilities teachers have been able to obtain the cooperation of physical educators in the school, these specialists become ardent team members, taking the responsibility for developing and implementing a motor development curriculum for children with learning disabilities. Utilization of such personnel has proved beneficial to both the academic and physical education programs.

Teaching strategies are subdivided into three areas: gross motor skills, body awareness and body-image development, and fine motor skills.

Balance and depth perception are important perceptual-motor skills, which a child begins to develop from an early age.   *(Robert V. Eckert, Jr./EKM-Nepenthe)*

Gross Motor Activities

Gross motor activities involve the total musculature of the body and the ability to move various parts of the body on command, controlling body movements in relationship to various outer and inner elements, such as gravity, laterality, and body midlines. The purpose of these activities is to develop smoother, more effective body movements and also to increase the student's sense of spatial orientation and body consciousness. Activities of gross motor movement are grouped as walking activities, floor activities, balance beam activities, and other gross motor activities.

Walking Activities

1. ***Forward Walk.***   Have the student walk on a straight or curved path marked on the floor to a target goal. The path may be wide or narrow, but the narrower the path, the more difficult the task. A single line requiring tandem walking (heel-to-toe) is more difficult than a widely

spaced walk. A slow pace is more difficult than a running pace. Walking without shoes and socks is more difficult than walking with shoes.

2. **Backward walk.**   Have the student walk through the same course backward.

3. **Sideways walk.**   The student should walk a predetermined course sideways to the right one step at a time; then to the left one step at a time; finally, walk sideways with one foot crossing over the other.

4. **Variations.**   Have the student walk the above with arms in different positions, carrying objects, dropping objects along the way, such as balls into containers, or with eyes focused on various parts of the room.

5. **Animal walks.**   Have the student imitate the walks of various animals: elephant walk (bend forward at the waist, allowing arms to hang down, taking big steps while swaying from side to side); rabbit hop (placing hands on the floor, do deep knee bends, and move feet together between hands); crab walk (crawl forward and backward face up); duck walk (walk with hands on knees while doing a deep knee bend); worm walk (with hands and feet on the floor, take small steps first with feet, then with hands).

6. **Moon walk.**   Ask the student to imitate the leaping kangaroo-like steps of the astronauts on the moon.

7. **Cross-pattern walking.**   Have the student step off with one foot and the opposite hand pointed to the foot. Eyes and head follow the hand.

8. **Steppingstones.**   Put objects on the floor for steppingstones identifying placement for right foot and left foot by color or the letters R and L. The student is to follow the course by placing the correct foot on each steppingstone.

9. **Box game.**   The student has two boxes (the size of shoe boxes), one behind and one in front. The student steps into the front box with both feet, moves the rear box from behind to the front and then steps into that. The student can use different hands to move boxes and use alternating feet. The student should be moving toward a finish line.

10. **Line walks.**   Draw lines in colors on the floor. Lines can be curved, angular, or spiral. Also use a rope placed on the floor and have the student walk along the side of the rope.

11. **Ladder walk.**   Place a ladder flat on the ground. Have the student walk between the rungs forward, backward and then hop through the rungs.

Floor Activities

1. **Angels in the snow.**   Have the student lie down with back on the floor and move limbs on command. Begin with bilateral commands: for example, move feet apart as far as possible, move arms along the floor until they meet above the head. Follow with unilateral commands: move left arm only, move left leg only. Finally, give cross-lateral commands: move left arm and right leg out.

2. ***Crawling.***   Since the student's first developmental motor activities are on the floor, some authorities feel it is important to have the student re-experience such movements as creeping (with stomach touching the floor), unilateral crawl (moving arm and leg on one side of the body together), and cross-lateral crawl (moving left arm with right leg and right arm with the left leg while crawling).

3. ***Obstacle crawl.***   Create an obstacle course with boxes, hoops, tables, barrels, chains, and so on, and have the student cover a predetermined course, going *through, under, over,* and *around* various objects.

Balance Beam Activities

The balance beam can be a flat board, either purchased or made from a two-by-four. It can be of various widths; the narrower the width, the more difficult the activities. Kephart (1971) suggests a section of two-by-four measuring eight to twelve feet long. Each end of the board is fitted into a bracket that serves as a brace and prevents the board from tipping over. The board can be set flat with the wide surface up or set on its edge with the narrow surface up.

1. ***Walking forward.***   Have the student walk forward slowly across the board with a normal stride or a tandem walk (heel to toe). The task is more difficult with bare feet than with shoes on.

2. ***Walking backward.***   Have the student walk backward while keeping balance.

3. ***Sideways walking.***   Ask the student to walk across the board sideways starting with the left foot, then using the right. One foot could slide to the other or cross over the other.

4. ***Variations.***   Variations and more complex activities for the balance beam can be devised by adding activities such as turning, picking up objects on the board, kneeling, dropping objects such as balls or bean-bags into containers while going across, following oral or recorded commands while on the board, walking while blindfolded or with eyes focused on an object.

Other Gross Motor Activities

1. ***Skateboard.***   The skateboard provides another technique for gross body-movement activities. The student can ride the skateboard lying on the stomach, kneeling, or standing; and the surface can be flat or a downhill slope. The *balance board* is another variation. This is a square board placed on a block-shaped piece of wood. Unless the weight of the body is correctly distributed, the board will tilt to one side.

2. ***Stand-up.***   Have the students sit on the floor with their knees bent and feet on the floor. Ask them to get up and sit down again. Vary this exercise by having them do it with or without using their hands, with the eyes closed, and with the eyes open.

3. *Jumping jacks.*   Have students jump, putting feet wide apart, while clapping hands above the head. To vary this activity, the student can make quarter turns, half turns, and full turns, or jump to the left, right, north, or south.

4. *Hopping.*   The students should hop on one foot at a time and alternate feet while hopping. They should hop in rhythmical patterns; left, left, right, right; or left, left, right—right, right, left.

5. *Bouncing.*   Have the students bounce on a trampoline, bedsprings, mattress, or on a large truck tire tube.

6. *Galloping steps.*   These can be done to the accompaniment of rhythmic clapping or music. The speed can be regulated and changed from fast to slow.

7. *Skipping.*   A difficult activity for students with poor motor coordination, it combines rhythm, balance, body movement, and coordination. Many students need help to learn to skip.

8. *Hopscotch games.*   Hopscotch games can be made on the concrete outdoors or put on plastic or oilcloth for indoor use.

9. *Hoop games.*   Hoops of various sizes from the hula hoop down can be used to develop motor skills. Have students twist them around the arms, legs, waist; bounce balls in them; toss beanbags in them; or step in and out of them.

10. *The stegel.*   The stegel is a multiuse piece of equipment for outdoors. Consisting of a balance board, a ladder, a springboard, and sawhorses, this apparatus, adapted from Germany, has proved useful for a wide variety of motor activities. Some exercises to use with the stegel are to have students weave in and out of the ladder rungs, reverse the direction of an exercise, jump off the springboard, or go forward and backward on the individual beams.

11. *Rope skills.*   A length of rope can be used in a variety of exercises. Have the student put the rope around designated parts of the body (knees, ankles, hips) to teach body image. Have the student follow directions, put the rope around chairs, under a table, through a lampshade, jump back and forth or sideways over the rope, or make shapes, letters, or numbers with the rope.

Body Image and Body Awareness Activities

The purpose of these activities is to help the student develop accurate images of the location of the parts of the body and function of these body parts.

1. *Pointing to body parts.*   Ask the student to point to the various parts of the body: nose, right elbow, left ankle, and so forth. This activity is more difficult with the eyes closed. Students can also lie down on the floor and be asked to touch various parts of their bodies. This activity is more difficult if done in a rhythmic pattern—use a metronome, for example.

2. ***The robot.*** A robot made from cardboard, held together at the joints with fasteners, can be moved into various positions. The students can move the limbs of the robot on command and match the positions with their own body movements.

3. ***Simon Says.*** This game can be played with eyes open and with eyes closed.

4. ***Puzzles.*** Puzzles of people, animals, objects, and so forth can be cut to show functional portions of the body.

5. ***What is missing?*** Use pictures with body parts missing. Have the student tell or draw what is missing.

6. ***Life-size drawing.*** This can be made by having students lie down on a large sheet of paper and tracing an outline around them. They fill in and color the clothes and the details of the face and body.

7. ***Awareness of the body parts through touch.*** Touch various parts of the students' bodies while their eyes are closed and ask them which part was touched.

8. ***Games.*** Games such as Lobby Loo, Hokey-Pokey, and Did You Ever See a Lassie help develop concepts of left, right, and body image.

9. ***Pantomime.*** The students pantomime actions that are characteristic of a particular occupation, such as a bus driver driving a bus, a police officer directing traffic, a mail carrier delivering a letter, or a chef cooking.

10. ***Following instructions.*** Instruct students to put their left hands on their right ears, and right hands on their left shoulders. Other instructions might be to put the right hand in front of the left hand; or turn right, walk two steps, and turn left.

11. ***Twister.*** Make rows of colored circles on the floor, or use an oilcloth or plastic sheet, or use the commercial game. Make instruction cards: put left foot on green circle and right foot on red circle.

12. ***Estimating.*** Have the student estimate the number of steps it will take to get to a goal.

13. ***Facial expression.*** Have the student look at pictures of people and tell if a person is happy, sad, or surprised. Tell a story and ask the student to match the appropriate facial expression to the story. How does the person in the story feel?

14. ***Water activities.*** Gross motor movements done in a pool or lake allow the student some freedom from the force of gravity. Some activities are easier for the student to learn in the water, since it affords greater control and can be done at a slower pace. Swimming is also an excellent activity to strengthen general motor functioning.

Fine Motor Activities

Although some students may do well at gross motor activities, their performance may be poor when it comes to fine motor activities. Teaching strategies in this section are grouped as follows: (a) throwing and catching activities, (b) eye-hand coordination activities, (c) chalkboard activities, and (d) eye movement.

Throwing and Catching Activities

1. **Throwing.**   In throwing objects at targets or to the teacher or to each other, students can use balloons, wet sponges, beanbags, yarn balls, and rubber balls of various sizes.
2. **Catching.**   Catching is a more difficult skill than throwing and the student can practice catching the above objects thrown by the teacher or other students.
3. **Ball games.**   Many ball games help in the development of motor coordination. Balloon volleyball, rolling ball games, bouncing balls on the ground, and throwing balls against the wall are some examples.
4. **Tire-tube games.**   Old tire tubes provide good objects for games of rolling and catching.
5. **Rag ball.**   Many students find that throwing and catching a rubber ball is too difficult a task. Initially, a rag ball can be used. It can be made by gathering rags or discarded nylon hosiery and covering them with cloth.

Eye-Hand Coordination Activities

1. **Tracing.**   Have the student trace lines, pictures, designs, letters, or numbers on tracing paper, plastic, or stencils. Use directional arrows, color cues, and numbers to help the student trace the figures.
2. **Water control.**   Ask the student to carry and pour water into measured buckets from pitchers to specified levels. Use smaller amounts and finer measurements to make the task more difficult. Coloring the water makes the activity more interesting.
3. **Cutting with scissors.**   Have students cut with scissors, choosing activities appropriate to their needs. The easiest task is cutting straight lines marked near the edges of paper. The students should cut along straight lines across the center of the paper. Some might need a cardboard attached to the paper to help guide the scissors. Have students cut out marked geometric shapes, such as squares, rectangles, and triangles. You can draw lines in different colors to indicate change of direction in cutting. Have students cut out curving lines and circles, then cut out pictures, and also cut out patterns made with dots and faint lines.
4. **Stencils or templates.**   Have the student draw outlines of patterns of geometric shapes. Templates can be made from cardboard, wood, plastic, old x-ray films, or containers for packaged meat. Two styles can be made: a solid shape or frames with the shape cut out.
5. **Lacing.**   A cardboard punched with holes or a pegboard can be used for this activity. A design or picture is made on the board and the student follows the pattern by weaving or sewing through the holes with a heavy shoelace, yarn, or cord.

6. *Rolling-pin game.*   Place colored strips on a rolling pin. Hang a ball from a string at eye height and place a cardboard with stripes behind it. The ball is hit with a rolling pin at a place of a particular color and aimed to hit a designated color stripe on the cardboard. For example, hit the ball with the red stripe of the rolling pin and have the ball hit the cardboard on the green stripe.

7. *Primary games.*   Many primary and preschool games and toys, such as pounding pegs with a hammer, hammer and nail games, and dropping forms into slots, can be useful to practice fine motor control.

8. *Paper-and-pencil activities.*   Coloring books, readiness books, dot-to-dot books, and kindergarten books frequently provide good paper-and-pencil activities for fine motor and eye-hand development.

9. *Jacks.*   The game of jacks provides opportunity for development of eye-hand coordination, rhythmical movements, and fine finger and hand movements.

10. *Clipping clothespins.*   Clothespins can be clipped onto a line or a box. Students can be timed in this activity by counting the number of clothespins clipped in a specified time.

11. *Copying designs.*   Students look at a geometric design and copy it onto a piece of paper.

12. *Paper folding or Japanese origami.*   Simple paper-folding activities are useful for the development of eye-hand coordination and fine motor control, and for learning to follow directions.

Chalkboard Activities

Kephart (1971) suggests that chalkboard activities should be tackled before paper-and-pencil work. Chalkboard work encourages a freer use of large muscles of the shoulder and elbow rather than the tight, restricted "splinter" movement of the fingers that students often develop in paper-and-pencil tasks.

1. *Dot to dot.*   The student connects two dots on the chalkboard with a line. Dots can be placed in various positions and in varying numbers, and the student must plan the lines of connection.

2. *Circles.*   The student can practice making large circles on the board with one hand and with two hands, clockwise and counterclockwise.

3. *Geometric shapes.*   Have the student do similar activities to those described above with lines (horizontal, vertical, and diagonal), triangles, squares, rectangles, and diamonds. At first the student can use templates to make these shapes at the board; later the shapes can be copied from models.

4. *Letters and numbers.*   The student can practice making letters and numbers on the chalkboard. Letters can be written in either manuscript or cursive style.

Eye-Movement Activities

One of the most controversial areas of motor training is that of eye-movement training. While some eye specialists discount it entirely, others believe it to be beneficial in certain cases. Kephart (1971) states that children must have a reasonably solid motor functioning and eye-movement pattern before training in ocular control can improve the child's ability to gain spatial and orientational information. Therefore, ocular pursuit training should be started only after the child has developed sufficient laterality and directionality to form the basis for adequate matching. Activities for eye-movement training are presented in detail by Kephart (1971) and Getman et al. (1968).

1. ***Ocular-pursuit training.*** In this activity students are to follow a moving target with their eyes. The target could be the eraser end of a pencil, a penlight, or the examiner's finger. The target is moved in a horizontal arc, eighteen inches to the left and to the right; the target is moved in a vertical arc up and down; it is moved in a diagonal movement and in a rotating movement. Similar activities can be done with one eye covered.

2. ***Finger and penlight.*** Students can follow the light of a penlight or flashlight with their eyes and with their fingers and eyes. They can also try to follow the teacher's light with their own.

3. ***Moving ball.*** Have the student follow the motions of a ball. The teacher can hold a large ball, then smaller balls, or a ball can be hung from a hook in the ceiling or wall.

4. ***Quick focus.*** Have students look at a pencil about a foot in front of them and then look to a target on the wall as quickly as possible, then back to the pencil, then to the target. Repeat a dozen times. Change targets, using other points of reference in the room.

5. ***Visual tracking.*** Have students trace pathways on paper using crayon, then the finger, finger above the paper, and follow the line with only the eye. These pathways can become increasingly complex as they cross and overlap each other and change directions.

Activities for Perceptual Development

Many students with learning disabilities live in a warped perceptual world. Although they have no basic impairment in their sensory organs, they cannot interpret sensations in a normal manner. They do not hear, see, feel, or integrate sensory stimuli in their environmental surroundings the way others do. The abnormality is not in the sensory organ itself but in perception resulting from stimulation to the sensory organ. Auditory perception takes place in the brain, not in the ear; similarly, visual perception takes place in the brain, not in the eye. Perceptual disturbances are important factors in the failure to learn, particularly at the early stages of academic instruction.

The perceptual activities suggested in this section are divided into the following categories: visual perception, auditory perception, haptic perception, and cross-modal perception. The teaching strategies are representative of activities stemming from perceptual theories of learning disabilities. The classification of these activities is somewhat arbitrary, since many overlap with other processes and other areas of learning. The activities presented here are representative of activities from many sources and learning disabilities programs.

Visual Perception Activities

Numerous studies have established that visual perception is highly related to academic performance, particularly reading. Various authors and studies have found a number of visual perception subskills to be essential. Frostig (1968) identifies *five visual perception functions*: visual-motor coordination, figure-ground perception, perceptual constancy, perception of position in space, and perception of spatial relationships.

In a study of visual discrimination tasks as a predictor of first-grade reading achievement, Barrett (1965) concluded that *three visual discrimination tasks* make the strongest contribution to such a prediction: the ability to read letters and numbers, the ability to copy geometric patterns, and the ability to match printed words. DeHirsch's study (1966) similarly indicated that a number of visual perception tasks significantly contribute to a predictive reading index. They include the Bender *Visual Motor Gestalt Test*, word matching, letter matching, and word recognition. It is interesting to note that some of these highly predictive tasks are closer to the category of reading skills than to basic visual perception skills. These techniques are designed to improve visual perception:

1. **Pegboard designs.** Have the student reproduce colored visual geometric patterns to form the design on a pegboard using colored pegs.
2. **Parquetry blocks.** Have them copy patterns using parquetry blocks.
3. **Block designs.** Using wood or plastic blocks that are all one color or have faces of different colors, have the student match geometric shapes and build copies of models.
4. **Finding shapes in pictures.** The student is asked to find all the round objects or designs in a picture, all the square objects, and so forth.
5. **Bead designs.** Ask the student to copy or reproduce designs with beads on a string, or simply place shapes in varying patterns.
6. **Puzzles.** Have the student put together puzzles that are made by the teacher or commercially. Subjects such as people, animals, forms, numbers, or letters can be cut in pieces to show functional parts.
7. **Classification.** Have the student group or classify geometric shapes of varying sizes and colors. The figures may be cut out of wood or cardboard or be placed on small cards.

8. **Rubber-band designs.** Have the student copy geometric configurations with colored rubber bands stretched between rows of nails on a board.

9. **Worksheets.** Ditto sheets designed to teach visual perception skills can be purchased or made by the teacher. The student should find the objects or shapes that are different, match the same objects, find objects in varying spatial positions, and separate the shapes and figures from the background. Some publishers put this material into workbooks. If the workbook is to be reused, it will last longer if put in a clear plastic cover.

10. **Matching geometric shapes.** Place shapes on cards and have the student play games requiring the matching of these shapes. Collect different-sized jars with lids. Mix the lids and have the student match lids with jars.

11. **Dominoes.** Make a domino-type game by making sets of cards using sandpaper, felt, self-adhesive covering, or painted dots to be matched.

12. **Playing cards.** A deck of playing cards provides excellent teaching material to match suits, pictures, numbers, and sets.

13. **Letters and numbers.** Visual perception and discrimination of letters is an important reading readiness skill. Games that provide opportunities to match, sort, or name shapes can be adapted to letters and numbers.

14. **Letter bingo.** Bingo cards can be made with letters. As letters are called, the student recognizes and covers up the letters.

15. **Finding missing parts.** Use pictures from magazines and cut off functional parts of the pictures. The student should find and fill in the missing parts from a group of missing parts.

16. **Visual perception of words.** The ability to perceive words is, of course, highly related to reading. Games of matching, sorting, grouping, tracing, and drawing geometric shapes and letters could be applied to words.

17. **Rate of perception.** Use a tachistoscope or flash card to reduce the length of time that the student has to recognize pictures, figures, numbers, words.

18. **Far-point visual perception.** Use the overhead projector and a screen for far-point practice in visual perception. Shapes and letters can be cut out of colored transparencies. Overlays of background designs can be placed over shapes for background-foreground practice.

Visual Memory

1. **Identifying missing objects.** Expose a collection of objects. Cover and remove one of the objects. Show the collection again, asking the student to identify the missing object.

2. **Finding the right design.** Expose a geometrical design, letters, or numbers. Have the student select the appropriate one from several alternatives or reproduce the design on paper.

3. ***Ordering from memory.***   Expose a short series of shapes, designs, or objects. Have the student place another set of these designs in the identical order from memory. Playing cards, colored blocks, blocks with designs, or Mah-Jongg tiles are among the materials that might be used for such an activity.

4. ***Recalling seen objects.***   Tachistoscopic exposure or flash cards can be used for recall of designs, digits, letters, or words that have been seen.

5. ***Stories from pictures.***   Place pictures of activities that tell a story on a flannel board. Remove the pictures and have the pupils tell the story depending on visual memory of the pictures.

6. ***Enumerating seen objects.***   Have the student look out the window, and then tell how many things were seen.

7. ***Recalling missing parts.***   Use an overhead projector to show numbers, pictures, or letters. Have the student look and then cover one. Ask which is missing.

8. ***Repeating patterns.***   Make a pattern of wooden beads or buttons. Have the student look for a few seconds; then ask for repetition of the pattern. Arrange blocks to show a pattern or use drawings of blocks to show the pattern. Have the student reproduce the pattern from memory with actual blocks.

Auditory Perception Activities

Although traditionally more emphasis has been given to visual perception in building readiness skills, we now realize the crucial role auditory perception plays in learning (Wiig & Semel, 1984). Before designing teaching strategies for building perception skills, it is necessary to identify the subskills constituting auditory perception (Valett, 1983). These subskills include auditory sensitivity, auditory attending, auditory discrimination, auditory awareness of letter sounds, and auditory memory. Such a hierarchy of auditory perception subskills presents certain inherent difficulties for designing tests and teaching methods.

First, in both testing and teaching, each auditory subskill becomes contaminated with demands of other learning processes. A second difficulty has been that some students who are successful in academic performance fail certain auditory subtests. Third, the relationship between training in an auditory subskill and academic improvement has not yet been clearly established.

What has research shown about the relationship between deficits in auditory perception and academic achievement? DeHirsch's research (1966) revealed that two auditory perception tasks made a significant contribution to the predictive reading index: the *Wepman Auditory Discrimination Test* and the *Imitation of Tapped-out Patterns Test*. However, these tests do not assess only auditory perception but also other learning processes, such as short-term memory. Dykstra (1966) found that five auditory discrimination measures made a significant contribution to a prediction of reading achievement:

(1) discriminating between spoken words that do or do not begin with identical sounds, (2) detecting rhyming elements at the ends of words, (3) identifying the correct pronunciation of words, (4) using auditory clues with context clues to identify strange words, and (5) recognizing similarities and differences in final consonants and rhymes. Again, these tests require other processes besides pure auditory perception. Research with the *Illinois Test of Psycholinguistic Abilities* indicates that reading disability cases do poorly in the subtests of auditory short-term memory and grammatic closure.

In spite of the lack of clear-cut evidence showing cause-effect relationships and the imprecision of our knowledge of the subskills that make up auditory perception, most authorities agree that auditory perception is an essential factor in learning and that students should be helped to acquire these skills. The teaching strategies that follow are designed to help students improve their auditory perception.

Auditory Sensitivity to Sounds

1. ***Listening for sounds.***   Have the students close their eyes and become auditorily sensitive to environmental sounds about them. Sounds of cars, airplanes, animals, other outside sounds, sounds in the next room, and so forth, can be attended to and identified.
2. ***Recorded sounds.***   Sounds of planes, trains, animals, and typewriters can be taped or recorded, and then played back to the students, who would be asked to identify them.
3. ***Sounds made by the teacher.***   Have the students close their eyes and identify sounds the teacher makes. Examples of such sounds include dropping a pencil, tearing a piece of paper, using a stapler, bouncing a ball, sharpening a pencil, tapping on a glass, opening a window, snapping the lights, leafing through a book, cutting with scissors, opening a drawer, jingling money, or writing on a blackboard.
4. ***Food sounds.***   Ask the students to listen for the kind of food that is being eaten, cut, or sliced: celery, apples, carrots.
5. ***Shaking sounds.***   Place small hard items such as stones, beans, chalk, salt, sand, or rice into small containers or jars with covers. Have the students identify the contents through shaking and listening.

Auditory Attending

1. ***Attending for sound patterns.***   Have the students close their eyes or sit facing away from the teacher. Clap hands, play a drum, bounce a ball, etc. Ask how many counts there were, or ask that the patterns made be repeated. Rhythmic patterns can be made for students to repeat. For example: slow, fast, fast.
2. ***Sound patterns on two objects.***   This is a variation on the above suggestion; for example, use a cup and a book to tap out sound patterns.

Discrimination of Sounds

1. ***Near or far.*** With eyes closed, students are to judge what part of the room a sound is coming from, and whether it is near or far.
2. ***Loud or soft.*** Help the students to judge and discriminate between loud and soft sounds as the teacher produces these sounds.
3. ***High and low.*** Students learn to judge and discriminate between high and low sounds as the teacher produces these sounds.
4. ***Find the sound.*** One student hides a music box or ticking clock and the others try to find it by locating the sound.
5. ***Follow the sound.*** The teacher or a student blows a whistle while walking around the room. Through listening, other students should try to follow the route taken.
6. ***Blindman's buff.*** One student in the group says something or makes an animal sound. The blindfolded student tries to guess who it is.
7. ***Auditory figure-background.*** To help students attend to a fore-ground sound against simultaneous irrelevant environmental noises, have them listen for pertinent auditory stimuli against a background of music.

Awareness of Phonemes or Letter Sounds

For success at the beginning stages of reading, the child must perceive the individual phoneme sounds of the language and must learn to discriminate from other sounds each language sound that represents a letter shape. Such abilities are essential for decoding written language.

1. ***Initial consonants.*** Have the student tell which word begins like *milk.* Say three words like "astronaut, mountain, bicycle." Ask the student to think of words that begin like *Tom,* to find pictures of words that begin like *Tom,* or to find pictures of words in magazines that begin with the letter *T.* Ask the student which word is different at the beginning: *"paper, pear, table, past."*
2. ***Consonant blends, digraphs, endings, vowels.*** Similar activities can be devised to help the student learn to perceive auditorily and discriminate other phonic elements.
3. ***Rhyming words.*** Learning to hear rhyming words helps the student recognize phonograms. Games similar to those for initial consonants can be used with rhyming words. Experience with nursery rhymes and poems that contain rhymes is useful.
4. ***Riddle rhymes.*** Make up riddles that rhyme. Have the student guess the last rhyming word. For example: "It rhymes with book. You hang your clothes on a _____ ."

Additional activities for the development of auditory perception of letter sounds and words are represented in Chapter 11 under listening skills.

Auditory Memory

1. ***Do this.***   Place five or six objects in front of the student and give a series of directions to follow. For example: "Put the green block in Jean's lap; place the yellow flower under John's chair; and put the orange ball into Joe's desk." The list can be increased as the student improves in auditory memory.

2. ***Following directions.***   Give the student several simple tasks to perform. For example: "Draw a big red square on your paper, put a small green circle underneath the square, and draw a black line from the middle of the circle to the upper right-hand corner of the square." Such activities can be taped for use with earphones at a listening center.

3. ***Lists of numbers or words.***   Help the student hold in mind a list of numbers or single words. Start with two and ask for repetition. Gradually, add to the list as the student performs the task. At first a visual reminder in the form of a picture clue may be helpful.

4. ***Nursery rhymes.***   The learning of nursery rhymes, poems, finger plays, and so forth, may be useful in developing auditory memory.

5. ***Number series.***   Give a series of numbers and ask the student to answer questions about the series. For example. "Write the fourth one: 3, 8, 1, 9, 4." Other directions could include the largest, smallest, closest to five, last, the one nearest your age, and so on.

6. ***Television programs.***   Ask students to watch a television program and remember certain things. For example: "Watch *The Wizard of Oz* tonight and tomorrow tell me all the different lands that Dorothy visited."

7. ***Going to the moon.***   Update the game of "Grandmother's Trunk" or "Going to New York." Say "I took a trip to the moon and took my space suit." The student repeats the statement but adds one item, for example, "helmet." Pictures may be used to help with auditory memory.

8. ***Repetition of sentences.***   Dictate sentences and have the student repeat them. Start with short simple sentences; then add compound sentences and complex clauses.

9. ***Serial order of letters and numbers.***   Say several letters in alphabetical order, omitting some. Ask the pupil to supply omitted numbers or letters: d, e, f (pause or tap) h; 3, 4 (pause or tap) 6, 7.

10. ***Ordering events.***   Read a selection that relates a short series of events. Have the students retell the story mentioning each event in order.

Haptic Perception Activities: Tactile and Kinesthetic Skills

For students who do not learn easily through the visual modality or the auditory modality, haptic perception provides an avenue for learning. The following activities are representative of activities designed to stimulate tactile and kinesthetic perception.

1. *Feeling various textures.* Have the student feel various textures, such as smooth wood, metal, sandpaper, felt, flocking, sponge, wet surfaces, foods, and so forth.
2. *Touching boards.* These boards are made by attaching different materials to small pieces of wood. The student touches the boards without looking and learns to discriminate and match the various surfaces.
3. *Feeling shapes.* Various textures cut in geometric patterns or letters can be placed on boards and felt, discriminated, matched, identified through tactile perception. These shapes can also be made of plastic, wood, cardboard, clay, etc.
4. *Feeling temperatures.* Fill small jars with water to touch as a way of teaching warm, hot, and cold.
5. *Feeling weights.* Fill small cardboard spice containers with beans, rice, and so on, to different levels. Have the child match weights through shaking and sensing the weights.
6. *Smelling.* Put materials of distinctive scents in bottles (cloves, cinnamon, vinegar, and so forth). Have the student match the smells.
7. *Recognizing by touch.* Trace designs, numbers, or letters on the student's palms. Ask them to reproduce or to identify the shape they felt.
8. *Identifying letters by feeling.* Have the student learn to identify shapes, numbers, and letters by feeling them.
9. *Grab bag.* Put various objects in a bag or box. Have the student recognize the object through the sense of touch.
10. *Arranging sizes by feeling.* Have the students arrange geometric shapes of varying sizes according to size while blindfolded.
11. *Feeling and matching.* Ask students to match pairs of objects by feeling their shape and texture. Use a variety of textures pasted on pieces of wood, masonite, or plastic.

Additional ways of developing kinesthetic perception can be found earlier in this chapter, in the body image and body awareness activities.

Cross-Modal Perception Activities

Many students have difficulty learning because they cannot transfer information from one perceptual modality to another or they cannot integrate two perceptual modalities. Most academic tasks involve such intersensory or cross-modal perception. Below are some activities that require two or more perceptual modalities to function jointly.

1. *Visual to auditory.* Have the student look at a pattern of dots and dashes and then translate it into a rhythmical form on a drum.
2. *Auditory to visual.* Have the student listen to a rhythmical beat and select the matching visual pattern of dots and dashes from several alternatives.

3. **Auditory to motor-visual.** Have the student listen to a rhythmical beat and transfer it to a visual form by writing out matching dots and dashes.

4. **Auditory-verbal to motor.** Play a game similar to Simon Says. The student listens to commands and transfers commands to movements of body parts.

5. **Tactile to visual motor.** Have the student feel shapes in a box or under a covering and draw the shapes that are felt on a piece of paper.

6. **Auditory to visual.** Record and play sounds of common objects, pets, household appliances, and so forth, and ask the student to match the sounds with the appropriate picture from several alternatives.

7. **Beat out names.** Beat the syllables in the rhythm and accent of names of the students in the group. For example: Marilyn McPhergeson.

> **Drumbeat:**   LOUD-soft-soft   soft-LOUD-soft-soft
>   1 2 3   4 1 2 3

Have the students guess the name being drummed out. Holidays or songs can also be used.

8. **Visual to auditory-verbal.** Have the student look at pictures. Ask "Which begins with *F*?" Which rhymes with *coat*? Which has a short *O* sound?"

9. **Auditory-verbal to visual.** Describe a picture. Then have the students choose the picture you were describing from several alternatives.

Summary

- This chapter reviewed motor and perception theories of learning disabilities and presented teaching strategies for developing motor and perception skills.

- Several theories of motor development have influenced the field of learning disabilities. Each is derived from a different discipline.

- Cratty discusses the importance of movement and games from the physical educator's perspective.

- Kephart, a psychologist, developed the perceptual-motor theory, which has become the basis for much of the thinking about motor development in learning disabilities.

- The visuomotor theory of Getman is an example of a developmental optometrist's view of motor learning. It emphasizes the role of vision. The model suggests that there are several sequential levels of motor learning and each is dependent on learning achieved at earlier stages.

- Representing the discipline of occupational therapy, Ayres theorizes that sensorimotor learning relates to basic neurophysiological integration.

- The patterning theory of neurological organization of Doman and Delacato is based on the presumption that the well-functioning child develops full neurological organization. These writers counsel that when a child with learning problems performs a certain sequence of patterning and motor activities, the child's neurological organization will improve and promote academic gains.

- Perception refers to the recognition of sensory information or the ability by which the intellect extracts meaning from sensory stimulation.

- The perceptual-modality concept suggests that each student has a preferred perceptual modality for learning and that individual learning styles can be matched to appropriate teaching methods.

- Constructs of perception that have implications for learning disabilities include the perceptual-modality concept, overloading the perceptual modalities, whole and part perception, visual perception, auditory perception, tactile perception, kinesthetic perception, cross-modal perception, form and directional perception, and social perception.

- Perception is a learned skill. Environmental influences, including teaching procedures, can modify and strengthen perceptual learning.

- The Teaching Strategies section of this chapter offers a sampling of activities used in motor and perception programs.

Key Terms

visual discrimination	vestibular system	perceptual-motor skill
haptic learning	sensory integration	auditory perception
perceptual-motor match	perceptual modality con-	tactile learning
sensory-motor	cept	auditory blending
splinter skill	cross-modality perception	kinesthetic learning

Oral
Language:
Listening
and
Speaking

Chapter **11**

Introduction

*I*n spite of our awareness of its importance to humanity, many aspects of language remain mysterious. How is it acquired by the child? What is the connection between symbolic language and the thinking process? What are the links between language and other components of human development, such as motor, perceptual, conceptual, and social learnings? How does a language impairment affect learning? What universals exist among the various languages of our world?

This chapter examines such issues and describes the views of four language-related professions—*language arts, language pathology, linguistics, and psycholinguistics*—and discusses several ways of assessing language abilities. The Teaching Strategies section of this chapter provides instructional methods for the two modes of oral language—listening and speaking.

■ Theories

Language is a wondrous thing. It is recognized as one of the greatest of human achievements—more important than all the physical tools invented in the last two thousand years. The acquisition of language is unique to human beings. Although lower animals have communication systems, only humans have attained the most highly developed system of communication—speech. Language fulfills several very human functions: it provides a means for communicating and socializing with other human beings, it enables the culture to be transmitted from generation to generation, and it is a vehicle of thought.

A language deficit, then, may diminish an individual's capacity to function as a whole person. The intimate relationship between a language deficit and learning disabilities is apparent when we realize that most learning-disabled individuals manifest some aspect of language inadequacy. Unlike a crippling defect of the body, a language disorder cannot be seen. Yet its effects are often more pervasive and insidious than other acute organic defects.

Language and Learning

Language plays a vital role in learning. Many kinds of learning are dependent on the individual's mastery of language and facility with verbal symbols. Although the relationship of language to thinking has been studied by such eminent scholars as Vygotsky (1962), Piaget (1952), and Luria (1961), the exact nature of this relationship is still not fully understood. We do know, however, that as language develops it plays an increasingly important part in the thinking processes. The ability to grasp abstract concepts appears to be highly related to one's mastery of language. Words become the symbols for objects and classes of objects, and for ideas. Thus, language permits human beings to speak of things unseen, of the past, and of the future. It is a tool that helps us learn, retain, recall, and transmit information and control our environment.

CASE EXAMPLES

Language and Learning

Helen Keller

One of the most dramatic illustrations of the dependency of thought on language is the experience of Helen Keller as she became aware that things have symbolic names that represent them. The impact of this discovery, made at age seven, changed her behavior from that of an intractable, undisciplined animal-like child to that of a thinking, language-oriented human being. Her teacher Anne Sullivan described the events (Keller, 1961):

> I made Helen hold her mug under the spout while I pumped. As the cold water gushed forth, filling the mug, I spelled "w-a-t-e-r" in Helen's free hand. The word coming so close upon the sensation of cold water rushing over her hand seemed to startle her. She dropped the mug and stood as one transfixed. A new light came into her face. She spelled "water" several times. Then she dropped to the ground and asked for its name and pointed to the pump and the trellis and suddenly turning around she asked for my name. . . . All the way back to the house she was highly excited, and learned the name of every object she touched, so that in a few hours she had added thirty new words to her vocabulary. (pp. 273–274)

Helen Keller also described the transformation caused by her own awareness of language

> As the cool water gushed over one hand she spelled into the other the word *water,* first slowly, then rapidly. I stool still, my whole attention fixed upon the motion of her fingers.
>
> Suddenly I felt a misty consciousness as of something forgotten—a thrill of returning thought; and somehow the mystery of language was revealed to me. I knew then that "w-a-t-e-r" meant the wonderful, cool something that was flowing over my hand. That living word awakened my soul, gave it light, hope, joy, set it free. . . . I left the wellhouse eager to learn. Everything had a name, and each name gave birth to a new thought. (p. 34)

Helen Keller had learned that a word can be used to signify objects and to order the events, ideas, and meaning of the world about her. Language had become a tool for her to use.

Victor: The Wild Boy of Aveyron

One other dramatic illustration of the effects of the lack of language development is the case of Victor, the "wild boy of Aveyron" (Itard, 1801/1962). Victor was captured in southern France in 1800 at about the age of twelve, after living alone as an animal in the forest of Aveyron. He had no concept of language and his behavior was totally uncontrolled and animal-like. Itard, a physician and one of the early workers interested in special education, tried to humanize Victor by teaching him language skills. Although some minimal learning took place after Itard had worked with him for five years, Victor was never able to develop language skills and did not reach a level of behavior that could be termed "human." Many explanations of Victor's inability to learn have been suggested, but the lack of language acquisition undoubtedly was an important element.

The intricate and reciprocal relationship that exists between language and learning becomes evident in two groups in our schools: students with *language disorders* and students with *language differences*.

Language Disorders

Many students with learning disabilities have an underlying language disorder. Language pathologists use the term *language disorder* to refer to children with a *language delay* or a *language deficit.* The language-delayed child may not be talking at all or may be using very little language at an age when language normally develops. The child with a language deficit may be talking, but using strange syntactical patterns, confused word order, or inappropriate words. Thus, the child who is not speaking at age four is language-delayed; the child with a language deficit may be saying at age five, "Why not don't he eats?" Such disorders occur in spite of the fact that these children have encountered a rich language environment and ample opportunity to hear and participate in standard English. Problems of language disorders are sometimes referred to as childhood aphasia or developmental aphasia. *Acquired aphasia* is a medical term used to identify adults who lose the ability to speak because of brain damage due to a stroke, disease, or accident. *Childhood* or *developmental aphasia* refers to the condition in children who have not yet learned to speak; a neurological dysfunction is suspected.

Recent work in language research by linguistics experts and speech pathologists has given educators further insights into language disorders and their relationship to learning disabilities. New techniques for measuring and describing a child's language have become available through advances in linguistics that have enabled professionals to discover that not all children are sophisticated users of their native language (Wiig & Semel, 1984; Wallach & Goldsmith, 1977). Speech pathologists have broadened their interests to the study of language disorders (in addition to speech disorders) and have found that many young children have disorders in vocabulary, word meanings, concept formation, and the learning of grammatical rules (Lee, 1974; Lee, Koenigsnect, & Mulhern, 1975). Further studies have shown that students with various kinds of language disturbances as preschoolers seem to be handicapped in later years by a variety of language disorders in reading, writing, and speaking. There is growing evidence that severe reading problems are associated with language difficulties in both elementary-age children and adolescents. Compared to normal readers, the poor readers have less verbal fluency, smaller speaking vocabularies, poorer organizational and integrative skills, and inferior syntactic ability. Disabled readers differ from normal readers in their abilities in three major segments of language: semantics, syntax, and phonology (Vogel, 1975, 1977; Wong & Roadhouse, 1978).

Perhaps the most severe type of language disorder is found in deaf students. Students with a profound hearing loss are unable to develop speech and language through the normal means of casual listening. Consequently, their ability to develop many kinds of concepts is substantially impaired. Research shows that the educational achievement level of deaf adolescents is three or four years below that of hearing students. As a result of the deficiency in development of verbal language functions, the intelligence quotient (IQ) of the average deaf student is about ten points lower than that of the hearing student. These scores reflect disabilities in language facility, not basic intelligence.

As noted in Chapter 7, there is increasing evidence that the relatively common childhood condition, *otitis media,* can seriously impair language learning in children (Hutton, 1984; Reichman & Healey, 1983). This condition, which involves an infection of the middle ear, can cause hearing loss. Even if the hearing loss is temporary and mild, it can lead to a language delay if it occurs at ages that are critical for language learning in young children.

CASE EXAMPLE

Language Delay

Noah G., aged five years and six months, was in kindergarten when his parents were contacted about problems he was having in school. The kindergarten teacher said that Noah did not seem to get along with the other children in class. He had no friends, would often "strike" out and hit his classmates, and was especially disruptive during the "conversation time" and story periods. He refused to participate in class activities such as the puppet show that was being prepared for presentation to the parents. The kindergarten teacher said that at times she did not know what Noah wanted, and this seemed to provoke a tantrum.

Mrs. G. said that Noah does not want to go to school and that it is sometimes difficult to get him to go to his class. In relating his developmental history, Mrs. G. said that Noah was born six weeks

prematurely, weighing four pounds and five ounces, and was placed in an incubator for a short period of time. He was a colicky baby and had difficulty nursing. His motor development was average; he crawled at eight months and walked alone at twelve months. Language development was slow. He spoke his first word at twenty-four months and did not begin speaking in sentences until age three. Since he could not communicate with others, he often resorted to pointing and grunting to make his wants known and frequently had temper tantrums when others did not understand what he wanted. Noah does not get along well with his two sisters who are older. Both of his sisters are very verbal and do not give Noah much chance to say anything. When Noah is asked a question, his sisters answer before he can respond. Mrs. G. said that the doctor suspected a hearing loss when Noah was younger. He had many colds as a toddler and had a condition the doctor called otitis media, with fluid behind the eardrums. The doctor put tubes in his ears when he was four and his hearing tested as normal after this procedure.

The speech teacher observed Noah during class and reported that he played alone most of the time. During the storytelling period and show-and-tell time, he wandered about the room. Often when another child was playing with a toy, Noah would grab it. If the other child did not give it up readily, Noah would hit his classmate until he got it. He listened very little and did not talk to other children in the class. He seemed to tire of one activity very quickly, moving on to another.

During the multidisciplinary evalua-tion, the speech teacher checked his hearing with an audiometer, and his auditory acuity was normal. The school psychologist tested Noah with an IQ test (Wechsler Preschool and Primary Scale of Intelligence). His full scale IQ score was in the normal range (FSIQ 101), with his performance IQ score (PIQ 119) substantially higher than his verbal IQ score (VIQ 84).

The case conference team recommended that Noah be placed in a developmental kindergarten and receive language therapy from the speech-language pathologist in the school. The speech-language pathologist would also work with parents and the kindergarten teacher to develop language activities for the home and mainstream setting.

Language Differences

A *language difference* (in contrast to a *language disorder*) is another language problem that may affect school learning. American society has been described as one of *cultural pluralism*; many students come from cultures where a language or dialect other than standard English is spoken. Language differences can interfere with school learning for students who use nonstandard English and those whose native language is not English.

For example, the student's native language may be a dialect of standard English, such as black English or an Appalachian dialect. The student's language is similar to that of others in the immediate environment, is appropriate for the surroundings, and causes no difficulty in communicating with others within this environment. Although such youngsters do not have a language disorder, their language or dialect differences interfere with learning in standard English, and as a result they often have difficulty learning to read (Shuy, 1972). Similar observations concerning the relationship between language differences and language learning have been made about bilingual youngsters (Hoffer, 1983). For the student whose native language is not English, learning skills in English may impose a real challenge. It should be emphasized that a language difference is not a language disorder. However, teachers who work with these students suspect that some of the youngsters have a language disorder in addition to their language difference.

Nonstandard English

Though the language system referred to as nonstandard English is a version of standard English, it is significantly different. Linguists have observed and systematically analyzed major differences in vocabulary, dialect, and grammatical structures between standard and nonstandard English. Many linguists stress that although nonstandard languages are different, they are substantially equal language systems. That is, they consist of a fully developed language that is functionally adequate and structurally systematic, and they meet the needs of its users (Labov, 1973). Even though nonstandard language reflects a language difference rather than a language deficiency, there frequently is a mismatch between the pupil's language system and the language system employed by the school. Thus, some linguists suggest that the use of nonstandard English becomes an impediment to school learning because the pupil is not equipped for the kind of language proficiency required in the classroom or for many other challenges of life For example, Bernstein (1964) analyzes nonstandard English as a "restricted code," one that impedes school learning because the student's limited vocabulary is insufficient for the kinds of thinking required in school. In a recent analysis of nonstandard English, Honey (1983) maintains that abstract concepts, scientific analysis, and logical thinking, and the communication of these subtle ideas require a mastery of a complex, sophisticated language system. Standard English provides the tools for these activities of modern life. Consequently, if students are not verbally equipped for the kind of language proficiency required in the classroom, they cannot do well in school. For example, nonstandard speakers tend to score lower on reading tests than pupils who are proficient in standard English. One effect of the mismatch between a student's nonstandard language and the standard language basis of schooling is that the student falls further and further behind. Such students need a secure and broad oral language base before being introduced to more complex written language skills and reading.

Bilingual Students

In our pluralistic society, an increasing number of students in our schools come from homes where a language other than English is spoken. These students often have limited English proficiency; they have difficulty understanding and using the English language. Some of these students speak only their native tongue; others use both English and their native language but still have great difficulty with English. Many of these students have learning disabilities in addition to their language problem. They must cope not only with learning English, but with their learning disabilities as well (Poplin & Wright, 1983; Ochoa, Pacheco, & Omark, 1983).

Three approaches to learning a second language are (1) the *ESL* approach, (2) the *bilingual* approach, and (3) the *immersion* approach. Each is based on different assumptions, and we can expect each to have different effects on the learning-disabled student (Richek, List, & Lerner, 1983).

ESL stands for "English as a second language." In this method, students learn through carefully controlled oral repetitions of selected second-language patterns. If students come from many different language backgrounds, this approach might be selected.

In the *bilingual* approach, students use their native language for part of the school day and a second language (English) for the other portion of the school day. The objective of the bilingual program is to strengthen school learning through the native language and gradually add the second language. The underlying philosophy is that students will recognize and respect the importance of their native culture and language in American society. In the bilingual method, then, schooling is provided in two languages. Academic subjects are usually taught in the native language and the student receives oral practice in English. For bilingual students with underlying basic language disorders and learning disabilities, however, learning two languages simultaneously may be confusing.

In the *immersion* method, students are "immersed" in, or receive extensive exposure to, the second language. In fact, where there is no formal instruction for a person learning a second language, this is essentially what occurs. Individuals simply learn through this type of repeated exposure as they live daily in the mainstream of the dominant language society. Immersion is the instructional method for schoolchildren in Quebec, where it is used to teach French to English-speaking children by enrolling them in French-speaking schools.

There is limited research evidence as to how these various instructional methods affect the learning-disabled student who speaks a foreign language or who is bilingual. However, it is evident that teachers must be particularly sensitive to the needs of these students, and some bilingual students require learning disabilities instructional services (Cummins, 1983; Bernal, 1983; Ochoa et al., 1983). Research is still needed on ways of identifying the learning disabled among bilingual students and on developing appropriate intervention methods for them.

Language Problems and Learning Disabilities

As noted earlier, language problems of one form or another are the underlying basis for many learning disabilities. Oral language disorders include delayed speech, disorders of grammar or syntax, deficiencies in vocabulary acquisition, and poor understanding of oral language. Research shows that many learning-disabled students do not do well in situations requiring extensive language interactions and conversations, and they are less skillful than non-learning-disabled peers in maintaining a conversation (Pearl, Bryan, & Donahue, 1983; Bryan, Pearl, Donahue, & Bryan, 1983). There is also abundant evidence that learning-disabled adolescents and adults have poorer language and communication skills than counterparts who are achieving normally (Olsen, Wong, & Marx, 1983; Blalock, 1982).

Language disorders may also take the form of written language disabilities in reading, writing, or spelling. Many students with severe reading problems have underlying disabilities in oral language. We find that young children who display oral language disorders as preschoolers may eventually acquire oral language skills only to have their basic language disability reappear several years later as a reading disability (Rubin & Liberman, 1983).

The theoretical concepts of four language-related disciplines contribute to our understanding of the role of language in learning disabilities. Some of the viewpoints of *language arts, language pathology, linguistics,* and *psycholinguistics* are briefly discussed in the following sections.

Language Arts

Within the school setting, language arts specialists are concerned with all currriculum areas related to language: listening, oral language, reading, writing, and spelling. Their responsibilities include materials, methods, and the organization of these curriculum areas for all students in the school. Although concerned primarily with the developmental language arts program of the entire school, the language arts specialist also has rich contributions to make to the understanding of students with language and learning disabilities and to the development of programs for atypical students. Analysis of the relationship of the various areas of the language arts is one such contribution.

Elements of Language

The *language arts* encompass the curriculum activities that utilize language—listening, speaking, reading, and writing. Some writers also add the communication elements of gesturing to this list. The interrelation of these elements of the language arts has many implications for teaching children with learning disabilities.

For most people the acquisition of these skills follows a hierarchy of development: (a) listening, (2) speaking, (3) reading, and (4) writing (Figure 11.1). A firm foundation is required at each level before the next skill level can be effectively added or integrated. In the historical development of communication skills, the oral language skills of listening and speaking were developed hundreds of thousands of years before the development of the written skills of reading and writing. The written form of language is relatively recent, and many civilizations, even today, have only a spoken language and no written form.

Since people develop the *oral* language skills of listening and speaking first, these skills are referred to as the primary language system; reading and writing are referred to as a secondary language system. In reading, we are dealing with a symbol of a symbol. While the spoken word is a symbol of an idea, the written word is a symbol of the spoken word. Helen Keller is said to have considered finger spelling as her primary language system because she learned it first, and Braille as a secondary system.

Two of the four elements of the language arts can be categorized as

FIGURE 11.1
The Elements of Language: A Developmental Hierarchy

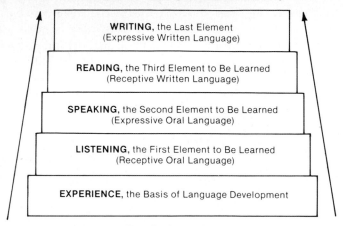

Source: Adapted from R. Kellogg, "Listening," in Pose Lamb (Ed.), *Guiding Children's Language Learning* (Dubuque, IA: Wm. C. Brown, 1971), p. 118.

input, or *receptive,* skills, while the other two elements are *output,* or *expressive,* skills. Listening and reading are input, or receptive, skills, feeding data into the central nervous system. Speaking and writing, which are output, or expressive, skills, originate data in the brain and send them out.

One implication of these categories for teaching is that a large quantity of input experience and information is necessary before output skills can be effectively executed. This principle has been concisely stated as *"intake* before *outgo,"* or input precedes output. Language arts specialists warn against assigning students to produce output, such as a written theme, before they have been exposed to adequate input experiences—such as discussions, field trips, reading, and other media. These experiences will enhance the productivity of the output, the written composition. The integrating mechanism between the input and output is the brain or central nervous system. The integrating process is often referred to as "the black box." The relationship between input and output skills is diagrammed in Figure 11.2.

Communication Process

In terms of a communication model, as shown in Figure 11.3, the skills of listening and reading are described as *decoding* functions whereas speaking and writing are seen as *encoding* functions. In the model, individual A is transmitting an idea to individual B. Individual A must convert her idea into language symbols. She puts it into a coded form; that is, she *encodes* the message into sound symbols (speaking) or visual graphic symbols (writing). Individual B, who receives the message, must then convert the symbols back

FIGURE 11.2
Relationship of the Four Elements of Language

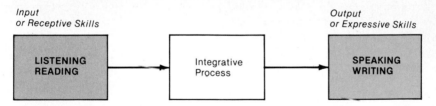

into an idea. He *decodes* the sound symbols (listening), or decodes the visual symbols (reading).

The implications of this communication model for language and learning disorders are great. A breakdown could occur anywhere in this process. For example, in the encoding portion of the communication process, the impairment could be in the stage of formulating the idea, in encoding it into spoken and written language symbols, in the memory of sequences of previous symbolic experiences, or in the brain signals to the motor mechanism used in speaking or writing. In the decoding portion of the communication process, the impairment could be in the reception and perception of the symbols through the eye or the ear, in the integration of these stimuli in the brain, or in the recall or memory as it affects the ability to translate the sensory images into an idea.

The focus of the language arts specialist, then, is upon the normal language development of the student and the language curriculum of the school. The purpose of analyzing the relationship of various elements of the language arts and communication is to enhance the language arts program and language development in the regular curriculum for all the students in the school.

Language Pathology

The language pathologist is concerned with atypical language development. *Language pathology* is the study of the causes and treatment of disorders of symbolic verbal behavior.

It is important to differentiate between a speech disorder and a language disorder. A *speech disorder* refers to abnormalities of speech, such as articulation, voice, or fluency difficulties. The child who lisps, cannot pronounce the "r" sound, or stutters has a speech disorder. A *language disorder* is much broader, encompassing disorders of the entire spectrum of communication and verbal behavior, including such problems as delayed speech, disorders of vocabulary, word meanings or concept formations, the misapplication of grammatical rules, and poor language comprehension. Because the experience and education of language pathologists are likely to be rooted in the

FIGURE 11.3
A Model of the Communication Process

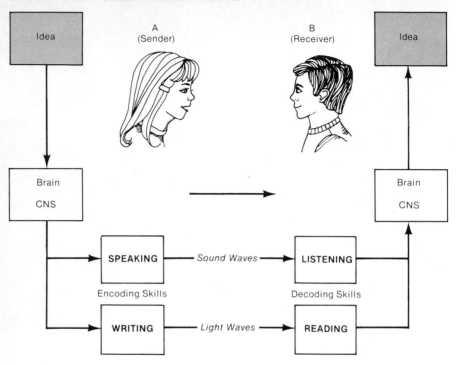

field of speech, their areas of expertise also include knowledge of normal developmental speech, the kinds and degrees of hearing and speech disorders, the pathology of the ear and speech organs, and the fields of acoustics and phonetics.

Humans have developed two forms of communication through language symbols: oral language and written language. The chief interest of the language pathologist is disorders of oral language. The term *developmental aphasia* is sometimes used to describe the child who has severe difficulty in acquiring oral language, implying that the disorder is caused by a central nervous system dysfunction (Eisenson, 1972; Geschwind, 1979). Many authorities, however, prefer the term *language disorders* to describe a variety of language problems, such as delayed speech, paucity of vocabulary, and syntax abnormalities.

The language pathologist warns that many students in our schools probably suffer from some form of language disorder. The problem of some students is in receiving symbolic auditory information or in listening; others have difficulty using auditory verbal symbols or speaking; and others have difficulty reading or writing language. The three-year-old who does not appear to understand simple directions, the four-year-old who has not yet learned to speak, or the ten-year-old who cannot read or write may have a language disorder. There is growing evidence that auditory and language deficiencies are extremely important factors in learning difficulties, and these factors have been neglected in comparison to the emphasis given to visual aspects of learning.

One way of classifying the stages of oral language development—as *inner language, receptive language,* and *expressive language*—has proved to be particularly useful for discussing different types of language disorders (Myklebust, 1965). The language disorder has different characteristics in each of these three stages.

Inner Language Disorders

The first level of linguistic learning refers to the preverbal ability to internalize and organize experiences, the antecedents of language and speaking. This process has been referred to as "inner speech" by Vygotsky (1962), "preoperational thought" by Piaget (1952), and "inner language" by Myklebust (1964). A disorder at this level refers to the inability to assimilate experiences. For example, the child may not be able to organize doll furniture or doll families into a meaningful play situation or may be unable to associate the sound of a bark with a dog. A disorder at this level is the most severe form of language disturbance.

Receptive Language Disorders

The process of understanding verbal symbols is called *receptive language,* and a disorder of this process may be termed *receptive aphasia.* It is thought that language reception is a prerequisite for the development of expressive language.

A child may be deficient in any of the subskills of receptive language. Some children are unable to discriminate between the pitch levels of two tones (tone discrimination), and others cannot discriminate or blend isolated single letter sounds (phonemic discrimination). Another type of receptive language skill that some children lack is the ability to discriminate small word parts within a sentence (morphemic discrimination)—such as the "z" sound difference between "the cows ate grass" and "the cow ate grass."

Some children are unable to understand the meaning of even a single word. Others have difficulty with more complex units of speech, such as sentences or longer speech units. A child with receptive language problems may be able to understand single words such as *sit, chair, eat,* and *candy* but have difficulty understanding sentences using those words, for example, "Sit on the chair after you eat the candy." Some children understand a word in one context but are unable to relate it to another context. The word *run* may be understood as a method of locomotion; but the child may not get the meaning when it is used in reference to something in baseball, a faucet, a woman's stocking, or a river. *Echolalia,* the behavior of repeating words or sentences in parrot-like fashion, without understanding the meaning, is another form of a receptive language disorder.

Expressive Language Disorders

The process of producing spoken language is called *expressive language,* and a disorder in this process may be called *expressive aphasia* (Johnson & Myklebust, 1967). Children with this disorder depend on pointing and gesturing to make their wants known. The child with an expressive language disorder can understand speech and language, does not have a muscular paralysis that prevents speaking, and even may do well on nonverbal tasks; yet this child is poor in the skill of speaking.

There are a number of clinical conditions of expressive language that concern language pathologists. *Dysnomia* refers to a deficiency in remembering and expressing words. Children with dysnomia may substitute a word like *thing* for every object they cannot remember, or they may attempt to use other expressions to talk around the subject. For example, when asked to list the foods she ate for lunch, one ten-year-old girl used circumlocution in describing a "round red thing that rhymed with potato," but she was unable to remember the word *tomato.* Some children remember the sound of the word, but they cannot at will move or manipulate their speech musculature to make the appropriate sounds, even though they do not have a paralysis. The condition is described as a type of *apraxia.* In another type of expressive aphasia, a child is able to speak single words or short phrases but has difficulty formulating complete sentences. Many of the children in our schools who speak in single words or short phrases are not recognized as having a language disorder.

In summary, language pathologists study the nature, causes, and treatment of all language disorders in both children and adults. They analyze normal language development in order to better understand and treat abnormalities in language function.

Linguistics

Another group of scientists, linguists, study the problem of language from a different perspective. *Linguistics* can be defined as the scientific study of the nature and function of language. Concepts from the field of linguistics are being applied to every area of the language arts. The application of linguistics is seen in the teaching of listening, speaking, reading, writing, spelling, grammar, and usage.

Linguists are primarily interested in the study of aspects of language itself. Their prime concern is *not* in education or teaching, nor is it in the application of linguistic findings to the school curriculum. Therefore, educators who wish to incorporate linguistics in educational programs must be knowledgeable in both linguistics and education in order to design and implement workable programs. It seems axiomatic that any professional concerned with language learning or disorders must be well acquainted with the discipline that studies language.

Linguists use the methodology and objectivity of the scientist in their investigation and analysis of linguistic phenomena. Early linguists were anthropologists who found that to make an intensive study of a particular culture they needed to understand the language of that culture. The anthropological linguists devised systems such as the International Phonetic Alphabet (IPA) to permit phonetic transcriptions of languages under investigation. Historical and comparative linguists played important roles in the study of language by tracing the historical development of language and by comparing common elements of various languages. Later, American linguists directed their attention toward the scientific study of American English. Using the tools and technology of earlier linguistic scholars, they developed a framework to describe the structure of the American forms of the English.

Linguistics, then, is the study of the patterns of language systems, the nature of language, its development, its function, and the way it is manipulated. One should not look at linguistics as a method of teaching, but rather as a scientific approach to the understanding of all language in all its forms.

Attitudes Toward Language

For the teachers of students with learning disabilities, a number of linguistic attitudes and perspectives are pertinent. The linguist urges that teachers develop a fresh attitude toward language. Language should be viewed as a dynamic, living, changing tool, responsive to the needs and circumstances of the people using it, rather than as a static, unchanging, prescribed set of rules. The American branch of the English language, which we use in this country, has many variations. The linguist encourages a new respect for various dialects and an acceptance of a variety of language forms. A student's own language is one of the most important links with the outside world. The significance of this can be appreciated when we realize that language provides one of the starting points in the educative process. Linguistic science is forcing us to question many of our traditional values and assumptions about language and the teaching of language—assumptions held for so long that they have been placed in the category of principles, truths, and rules.

Linguistic Concepts

A few basic linguistic concepts and terms are essential for today's teacher. Linguists have thought of language as having a number of systems: *phonology, morphology, syntax, semantics,* and *pragmatics.*

Phonology is the system of speech sounds in a language. The smallest unit of sound is a *phoneme*. Different languages and dialects utilize different phonemes. For example, the word *cat* contains three phonemes: *k/æ/t.* Phoneme recognition is important in learning to read as well as in oral language. The recognition, analysis, and synthesis of phoneme elements in written words, often referred to as *phonics,* is difficult for some children.

Morphology is the system of meaning units in a language. The smallest unit of meaning is a *morpheme.* Different languages indicate meaning changes through different morphological forms. In standard English, for example, the word *boy* is one morpheme or meaning unit; and the word *boys* contains two morphemes or meaning units (*boy* plus plurality). The child who does not internalize the morphemic structure of standard English might say, "There are three boy."

Children who are unaware of exceptions to morphemic rules may overgeneralize. For example, the past tense form of *fight* and *go* might be formulated as *fighted* and *goed.* Berko (1958) surmised that normal preschool and first-grade children have well-established rules of morphology. In a study she conducted, children applied their morphological rules to nonsense words. For example, she showed each child a drawing of a birdlike creature and said, "This is a *wug.*" Next she pointed to a drawing with two of these creatures and asked the child to complete the sentence, "There are two _____." By applying the morphological rule for plurals, the child gives the answer of *wugs* by adding the phoneme /z/.

Syntax refers to the grammar system of language—the way the words are strung together to form sentences. Different languages have developed different syntactic or grammatical systems. In the English language (unlike some other languages), word order is extremely important to convey meaning. Thus, "John pushes a car" has a different meaning from "A car pushes John." A child with a syntactic language disorder may not have learned how to order words in a sentence. Further, in English we can transform the order of the words—still keeping the same subject—to generate a new meaning: the sentence "Mother is working" can be transformed to generate "Is Mother working?" The child with a syntactic language disorder may be unable to generate such sentence transformations. In one research study (Spradlin, 1967), when children with language disorders were asked to repeat the question form of "Is the boy running?" many repeated the simple declarative form, "The boy is running."

When first graders were shown two pictures, one of a cat chasing a dog and the other of a dog chasing a cat, and were asked to point to the picture called "The cat is chased by the dog," many children chose the incorrect picture. At their developmental level, they did not understand the meaning of the passive form of the sentence (Gleason, 1969).

Semantics is the study of meaning in language. Pupils with meager vocabulary understanding or usage and youngsters who have difficulty relating a string of words to a meaningful association may have a semantic language disorder. Unlike the morphology, phonology, and syntax systems, which normally become firmly established when the child is very young, the development of vocabulary, or the semantic system, continues through life.

A student with a semantics disorder may have the concept but not the appropriate word to express it. For example, one adolescent talked about the "two girls with the same face." She did not have the word "twin" to communicate the idea.

Pragmatics, the most recent area of linguistic study, is the social side of language, dealing with the relationship between the speaker and the context. Pragmatics takes into account the relationship between speaker and listener, the degree of knowledge of the listener as assessed by the speaker, and behaviors such as taking turns in conversations, staying on the topic, and asking pertinent questions, as well as general appearance, involvement in the conversation, and eye contact (Simms & Crump, 1983). The poor ability of learning-disabled students to interpret, infer, compare, and respond to the speech of others may be the cause of many of their social difficulties (Bryan, Pearl, Donahue, & Bryan, 1983; Bryan, Donahue, & Pearl, 1981; Donahue, Pearl & Bryan, 1983).

Another element of the language system is *intonation,* the sound patterns of language, including *pitch* (melody), *stress* (accent), and *juncture* (pauses) of a spoken language. The intonation system of each language is different. An example of intonational differences is the contrast between the sound of "White House cat" (a certain cat that lives in the residence of the president of the United States) and "white house-cat" (a domesticated cat with white fur). Students who have been unable to capture the intonation system of English may speak in a monotone and their speech may be without expression.

When listening to the intonation pattern of infants, it is impossible to distinguish the babbling of a three-month-old Chinese child from that of a Dutch or an American baby. By the age of six months, however, the intonation of the babbling is similar to the intonation of the language in the infant's immediate environment; the babbling is in Chinese, Dutch, or English. Experimental evidence indicates that the "native language" of a six-month-old baby can be identified through tape recordings of the baby's babbling (Smith, 1972). The baby is demonstrating the acquisition of rules for intonation patterns and has begun to produce phonemes of the native language.

In summary, the study of linguistics has brought a better understanding of the nature of language and a useful framework for analyzing language deviations found in learning-disabled students.

Psycholinguistics

Psycholinguistics, as the name implies, is a field of study that blends aspects of two disciplines, psychology and linguistics. In a sense, these two disciplines view opposite ends of the language, or communication, process. Whereas the linguist studies the *output* of the process, the language itself, the psychologist is interested in the *input,* the factors causing the speaker to say certain words

at a particular time. The cross-fertilization between linguistics and psychology
was needed because neither discipline by itself was able to develop a complete perspective of the language-learning process. Psycholinguistics is a field
of study that attempts to look at the total picture of the language process
rather than at only one facet of it.

Because psycholinguistics encompasses many points of view, it serves as
a discipline that brings together the many segmented fields studying various
aspects of language and learning. The goal of psycholinguistics is to develop
an understanding and explanation of language processing. Several promising
developments have a bearing on learning disabilities.

A major contribution of psycholinguistics has been a theory about how
language develops in children. There are several competing explanations of
language learning. Behavioral psychologists say that language is learned according to the same principles as other kinds of behavior (Skinner, 1957);
that is, language is learned through imitation and reinforcement. The infant
begins with no knowledge of language but gradually acquires language skills,
largely through reinforced imitation of models. For example, the parents are
likely to show delight and approval (reinforcement) when the baby's vocalizations resemble adult speech; the child is thought to have said the first word.
The infant likes the attention and, with such positive reinforcement, tends to
repeat those sounds. Consequently, behaviorists have concluded that language is learned through the principles of imitation and reinforcement.

The psycholinguistic theory of language learning offers an alternate view
of the mechanism of language development—a view based on the biological
and genetic foundations of language as proposed by Lenneberg (1967).
Psycholinguists believe that children are predisposed biologically both to
learn and use language. Chomsky (1965) argues that the human being has
developed an innate capacity for dealing with the linguistic universals common to all languages. What is learned is not a string of words but transformational rules that enable the speaker to generate an infinite variety of novel
sentences and enable a listener to understand the infinite variety of sentences
heard.

Psycholinguists have recently focused attention on the mystery of the
acquisition of language. The work of the generative-transformationalists
(Chomsky, 1965) has touched on topics that also concern specialists in
learning disabilities. Two important problems for the generative-
transformationalists are: what is it about language that enables a child to learn
it, internalize it, and use it, and what is it about a child that permits him or her
to learn the language? To quote Chomsky (1965), "What are the initial assumptions concerning the nature of language that the child brings to language learning, and how detailed and specific is the innate scheme (the
general definition of "grammar") that gradually becomes more explicit and
differentiated as the child learns the language?" (p. 27).

In the process of learning a language, the child has a limited number of

primary linguistic experiences. At a rather young age, the child hears speech and begins to understand and repeat certain words and sentences. These definite and limited experiences produce an ability to understand and produce new sentences that may never have been heard before. To add to this mystery, children in all cultures have the ability to perform this feat in their native language at about the same chronological and developmental stage. When it is time to enter school, the child who has developed along a normal linguistic pattern uses language nearly as well as the adults in the immediate environment, using and understanding almost all the common sentence patterns. Carroll (1966) notes this fascinating characteristic of language learning:

> The process by which children learn their native language is in many aspects a mystery. . . . The "average" or "normal" child who is reared in a sufficiently rich linguistic environment has usually mastered all the essential parts of the system by the time he is six or seven. The fact that he is able to utter and comprehend thousands of sentences that he has never heard before is evidence of this accomplishment. (p. 577)

As the psycholinguist views language acquisition, the child learning a language does not merely learn a set of sentences but rather learns to internalize the total language system in understanding and making new sentences. The task of the psycholinguist is to analyze the process of language learning and producing. Such knowledge should be of great value to teachers of learning-disabled students.

Chomsky suggests that the transition in language learning from the simple stages of comprehension and expression to the stage at which the child uses a complex mechanism of language is so rapid that accurate notation of the child's language acquisition and development by observation alone is virtually impossible; and the little that can be observed is not very enlightening. In that brief period of transition, the child suddenly learns to use the mechanisms of grammar. According to Chomsky, the task of learning human language is so complex that some important aspects of language cannot be learned but are innate within the brain. This theory views language learning as similar to learning to walk; rather than being completely acquired, some aspects of spoken language "unfold" or "flower" under appropriate developmental and environmental circumstances.

Significant research on the acquisition and development of language by children has emerged from Chomsky's conclusions and psycholinguistic theories (Menyuk, 1969; Berko, 1958; Brown, Cazden, and Bellugi-Klima, 1971; Bloom & Lahey, 1983). As psycholinguists investigate child language development, they try to understand what the child already knows. Children without language problems learn to understand the verbalization of others and to respond in a meaningful way by internalizing these language systems before they reach school age. Research techniques devised to analyze language de-

velopment provide valuable data concerning the language of children who develop in a normal fashion, as well as information about children who develop language in a deviant manner. Such knowledge should be invaluable to the learning disabilities specialist.

Language Tests: Listening and Speaking

Listening Tests

Relatively few listening tests are available to evaluate a child's development in receptive oral language skills, compared to the tests available in the field of reading. Among the tests of listening are the *Peabody Picture Vocabulary Test,* the *Ammons Full Range Vocabulary Test, Listening Comprehension Test* (a portion of the *Sequential Tests of Educational Progress*), *Brown-Carlsen Listening Comprehension Test, Durrell Listening-Reading Test,* the *Auditory Reception* and *Auditory Memory* tests (subtests of the *Illinois Test of Psycholinguistic Abilities*), the receptive language portion of the *Northwestern Syntax Screening Test,* the *Carrow Test for Auditory Comprehension of Language,* and the *Test of Language Development* (TOLD). Descriptive information concerning these tests can be found in Appendix C.

Oral Language Tests

Several methods are used to assess language development. One way is to give the child a *standardized normed test,* wherein the child is presented with a stimulus and asked to answer with a word. A second is to obtain a *language sample* and analyze that sample using techniques of linguistic analysis.

Most of the oral language tests are standardized normed tests. Some oral language tests of the standardized normed type include the *Verbal Expression* and *Grammatic Closure* tests (subtests of the *Illinois Test of Psycholinguistic Abilities*), the *Vocabulary* test (subtest of the WISC-R), and *Word Opposites* and *Sentence Imitation* (of the *Detroit Tests for Learning Aptitude*). Other tests that assess language are the *Test of Language Development* (TOLD), the *Clinical Evaluation of Language Functions* (CELF), the *Houston Test of Language Development,* the *Mecham Verbal Language Development Scale,* the *Northwestern Syntax Screening Test,* the *Utah Tests of Language Development,* and the *Peabody Picture Vocabulary Test.*

Descriptive information concerning these tests can be found in Appendix C.

The analysis of a language sample approach is used in the *developmental sentence analysis* (DDS) (Lee, 1974), which is based on a transformational-generative grammar analysis. The DDS technique scores a corpus of fifty sentences that are obtained by presenting stimulus materials such as interesting pictures to encourage the child to produce language. The language

sample produced is put on tape. The child's language is reviewed and scored on eight categories of grammatical forms: (1) indefinite pronouns or noun modifiers, (2) personal pronouns, (3) main verbs, (4) secondary verbs, (5) negatives, (6) conjunctions, (7) interrogative reversals, and (8) "wh" questions. Scores for ages two to seven are given in the scoring tables. A follow-up to this assessment method for teaching language through story-telling is presented by Lee et al. (1975). Another example of the language sample approach to testing is the *Carrow Elicted Language Inventory.*

All of these tests are described in Appendix C.

■ Teaching Strategies

The normal sequence of the development of language skills is (1) listening, (2) speaking, (3) reading, and (4) writing. Spelling and handwriting can be considered part of writing. We shall discuss teaching strategies for the development of the oral language skills of listening and speaking in the following section. A discussion of reading is presented in Chapter 12 and the written language skills of writing and spelling are dealt with in Chapter 13.

Oral language has two contrasting sides: understanding oral language, or input, and producing oral language, or output. The two functions may be referred to by language arts specialists as listening and speaking; by language pathologists as receptive language and expressive language; and by psycholinguists as auditory decoding and verbal encoding. Disorders of these functions are referred to by language pathologists as receptive aphasia and expressive aphasia. The child with "delayed speech" is one who has not developed language and speech skills at the appropriate chronological stage. This child could have a problem in either or both aspects of oral language— in reception and in expression. Although it is often impossible to draw a definite line between experiences in listening and speaking, the ability to listen and understand is generally considered a basis for speaking.

Listening

Listening as an element of the language arts and as a specific language skill has been neglected. Although concern for the instruction of speaking and reading is common, the child is typically expected to acquire the ability to listen without special instruction. The fact is that many children do not acquire functional skills in listening by themselves. According to medical hearing specialists, over half the cases referred to them for suspected deafness do not have any defect in hearing acuity or any organic pathology causing their seeming deafness.

The child's ability to listen, it seems, has been taken for granted. We are finally beginning to realize that listening is a basic skill that can be improved

This teacher is developing listening comprehension skills in her students by reading aloud to them.   *(Alan Carey/The Image Works)*

through teaching and practice. Compared to the quantity of research in reading, the research and study that has been conducted in listening is miniscule. One explanation for poor listening skills is that children of today are so bombarded with constant sound that many have actually learned to "tune out" what they do not wish to hear, and many children have become skillful at *not* listening. It is the task of the teacher, particularly the teacher of children with learning disabilities, to help those who have learned not to listen to become auditorily perceptive and to "tune in."

Some children have a learning problem that stems from their inability to comprehend speech. Such a condition is often termed a receptive language disorder, and the child with such a condition may avoid language activities because listening is so painful.

Listening differs from hearing, which is a physiological process that does not involve interpretation. One can hear a foreign language with good auditory acuity but be unable to listen to what is being said. In contrast to hearing, listening demands that one select appropriate meanings and organize ideas according to their relationships. In addition, listening calls for evaluation, acceptance or rejection, internalization, and at times appreciation of the ideas expressed. Listening is the foundation of all language growth, and the child with a deficit in listening skills has a handicap in all the communication skills.

Relationship Between Listening and Reading

The two language modes of receiving information and ideas from others are listening and reading. There are many similarities between these two modes of decoding symbolic language. Both require sensory stimulation, one to the eye and one to the ear. Both require the ability to receive, make sense out of, and organize the sensory stimuli. Both need a memory bank of vocabulary to relate the words that are read or heard. Both need a grasp of the various linguistic systems of the language being used, that is, phonology, morphology, syntax, and semantics. Both require an attentive attitude, for without close attention, half-listening or half-reading results. Finally, both demand the application of specific thinking skills for comprehension of the ideas being listened to or read. It is not surprising, therefore, that research studies show a high correlation between the receptive language skills of listening and reading, and that instruction in listening comprehension is likely to result in improvement in reading comprehension (Berger, 1978).

There are, however, important differences between listening and reading. The reader can reread and study the material, but the listener can hear the material only once and then it is gone. Of course, the use of a tape recorder modifies that difference somewhat, but a tape recorder can be used in relatively few of the situations that demand careful listening. Readers can regulate their speed, going slower or faster as their purpose and the difficulty of the material dictate, but the listener's speed of listening is set by the speaker. The listener has additional clues of voice, gesture, appearance, and emphasis of the speaker, but the reader cannot derive such supporting information from the printed page. In the listener-speaker combination, there is more opportunity for feedback, questioning, and for a two-way discussion than in reading.

The term *reading* implies comprehension in the reading act; thus the term *auding* can be used to refer to comprehension in the listening act. In reading, it is useful to classify skills at the level of decoding skills and at the level of comprehension skills; so, too, in listening one can speak of a level of decoding or perception of sounds and words and a level of comprehending what is heard, or auding. Table 11.1 illustrates the similarities between the levels of the two receptive language skills of listening and reading.

When teachers ask students "to listen," they do not mean they should simply *hear,* nor do they mean they should just recognize the words being spoken. When students are directed to listen, they are expected to comprehend, the communication message being sent. Just as reading is made up of many substrata abilities, so listening contains many component abilities and skills.

TABLE 11.1   **Similarities Between the Levels of Listening and Reading**

Receptive Language Skills	Reading (Visual)	Listening (Auditory)
Sensory stimulation	Seeing (eyes)	Hearing (ears)
Decoding skills	Visual perception	Auditory perception
	Recognition of words in print	Recognition of words and sounds heard
Comprehension	Reading	Listening (auding)

Activities for Teaching Listening

The following paragraphs suggest some techniques that have been used to develop, train, and strengthen the subabilities of listening. The optimal sequence of teaching listening, or auditory receptive, skills has not as yet been clearly specified by research (Valett, 1983). Therefore, the techniques presented are a collection of methods from authorities in a number of language-related fields.

Listening skills can be categorized into successive levels that require increasingly complex abilities.

1. Auditory perception of nonlanguage sounds
2. Auditory perception and discrimination of isolated single language sounds
3. Understanding of words and concepts, and building of a listening vocabulary
4. Understanding sentences and other linguistic elements of language
5. Auditory memory
6. Auding, or listening comprehension

   a. Following directions
   b. Understanding a sequence of events through listening
   c. Recalling details
   d. Getting the main idea
   e. Making inferences and drawing conclusions

7. Critical listening

   Some strategies for each of these levels of listening are suggested below.

Auditory Perception of Nonlanguage Sounds

These sounds are the environmental sounds around us. Many of the techniques for teaching auditory perception are included in Chapter 10, in "Auditory Perception Activities." The student is helped to be aware of sounds, to contrast sounds, to locate the direction of sounds, and to associate sounds with objects.

Auditory Perception and Discrimination of Language Sounds

An important factor in reading readiness is the ability to perceive and recognize the phoneme sounds of our language. Without such a skill, the learning of phonics is impossible (Liberman, 1973; Rubin & Liberman, 1983).

1. ***Initial consonants—auditory recognition.*** Use real objects or pictures of objects. Say the name of the object and ask the student to tell which pictures or objects begin with the same sound. The student may group those objects whose names have the same initial sound in one place, may put all objects whose names begin with that sound in one container, or may paste pictures of these objects on a chart. For example, the initial consonant "m" may be presented with "milk, money, missile, moon, man, monkey."

2. ***Sound boxes.*** A box, approximately the size of a shoe box, can be used for each sound being taught. Put the letter representing the sound on the front, and collect toys, pictures, and other objects for the students to place in the appropriate box.

3. ***Initial consonants—same or different.*** Say three words, two of which have the same initial consonant. Ask the student to identify the word that begins with a different sound. For example: Car—dog—cat.

4. ***Consonant blend bingo.*** Make bingo cards with consonant blends and consonant digraphs in the squares. Read words and ask the student to cover the blend that begins each word.

5. ***Hear and write.*** Read words that begin with initial consonants, consonant blends, or consonant digraphs. Ask the student to listen and write the blend that begins each word.

6. ***Substitutions.*** Help the student learn to substitute one initial sound for another to make a new word. For example: "Take the end of the word *book* and put in the beginning of the word *hand,* and get something you hang coats on" (hook).

7. ***Auditory blending game.*** Have the student identify objects or answer questions after you speak the name of an object by separating the individual phonemes. For example: "p-e-n" or "f-u-n." "What is your n-ā-m?"

8. ***Hearing vowels.*** Vowels are more difficult than consonants for many children to hear. Begin by listening for and identifying the short vowels. The use of key words for the student to refer to is helpful. For the short "a" for example, use a picture of an astronaut. After the student recognizes the short vowel, you can help by identifying the long vowel sound. Then contrast the sound of the short vowel with that of the long vowel. The techniques used for the initial consonants and consonant blends may be adapted for the vowel sounds.

9. ***Riddle rhymes.*** Make up riddle rhymes and encourage the students to make up others. For example: "I rhyme with *look.* You read me. What am I?"

10. ***Awareness of rhyming sounds.***   Have the student listen to a series of three words and tell which two of the words rhyme: ball—sit—wall; hit—pie—tie.
11. ***Same or different.***   Say pairs of words or pairs of nonsense words and ask the student to determine if they are the same or different. For example: tag—tack; big—beg; singing—sinking; shin—chin; lup—lub.
12. ***Hearing syllables.***   Have the student listen to the pronunciation of multisyllabic words and determine the number of syllables in each word. Clapping or identifying the vowel sounds heard helps the students determine the number of syllables.

Understanding Words

The development of a listening vocabulary is a basic requirement in listening. Students must understand the names of objects, the names of actions, the names of qualities, and the names of more abstract concepts. It is easier to teach what linguists call form class words, those that carry primary lexical-meaning (such as nouns, verbs, adjectives, adverbs), than to teach the structure or function words that indicate relationships within sentences.

1. ***Names of objects.***   To help students understand names, use actual objects, such as a ball, pencil, or doll. Sometimes exaggeration and gesture are needed to help the student who has a severe receptive disorder understand the meaning of the word that symbolizes the object.
2. ***Verb meanings.***   It is more difficult to teach the concept of a verb than the name of an object. Verbs such as hop, sit, walk can be illustrated with the performance of the activity.
3. ***Pictures.***   Pictures are useful in reinforcing and reviewing the vocabulary that has been taught.
4. ***Concepts of attributes.***   Words that describe the attributes of objects can be taught by providing contrasting sets of experiences that illustrate the attributes. For example: rough—smooth; pretty—ugly; little—big; hot—cold. Both concrete objects and pictures are useful in teaching attributes.
5. ***Development of concepts.***   By combining experiences with particular objects, the student is helped to understand the concept beyond the object itself. For example, in learning about the concept of a chair, the student is shown a kitchen chair, an upholstered chair, a folding chair, a lawn chair, a doll chair, and a rocking chair. Through experiences with many objects, the student develops the concept of chair.
6. ***Classes of objects.***   An even broader classification of objects must be made and labeled with a word. For example, the word *food* refers not to any single type of food but to all foods. Students, therefore, could be taught objects that "are food" and could be asked to remove from a display any objects "that are not food."

Understanding Sentences and Other Linguistic Units

We are all expected to comprehend language within the linguistic structure of the sentence rather than in single words. As the linguists and educators develop methods to help students learn the linguistic systems of the American English language, these methods should also prove useful to the teacher who helps students with language disabilities. Some students with a receptive language difficulty need structured practice in understanding sentences.

1. ***Directions.*** Simple directions given in sentences can provide the student with needed experiences in understanding sentences. For example, "Give me the blue truck," or "Put the book on the table" are directions that could be included.

2. ***Finding the picture.*** Line up several pictures. Give a sentence about one picture and ask the student to point to the correct picture. This exercise can be made harder by adding more sentences to describe the picture.

3. ***Function words.*** Linguists refer to function or structure words as the words that show structural relationship between parts of a sentence and grammatical meaning. They include noun determiners, auxiliary verbal forms, subordinators, prepositions, connectors, and question words. These words cannot be taught in isolation; they must be taught within a sentence or phrase. For example, words such as *on, over, under, behind, in front of, beneath, inside,* and *in* can be taught by placing objects *in* a box or *under* a chair while saying the entire phrase to convey the meaning.

4. ***Riddles.*** Have the student listen to the sentence and fill in the word that fits. For example: "I am thinking of a word that tells what you use to go down a snowy hill" (sled).

Auditory Memory

The student must not only listen and hear but must also store auditory experiences and be able to retrieve them and relate them when desired. Several teaching strategies for improving auditory memory are presented in Chapters 6 and 10.

Listening Comprehension

This skill is similar to what has been called reading comprehension; however, intake is through hearing language rather than reading it. Auding combines listening skills with thinking skills.

1. ***Listening for details.*** Read a story to the child and ask questions about the story that are detailed in nature: true-false, who, what, when, where, and how questions. In another type of detail exercise, a manual on a subject such as how to take care of a new pet is read to the student, who is then asked to list all the things to do.

2. ***Sequence of events.***   Read a story and ask the student to picture the different events in the order that they happened. The use of a pictorial series, such as a comic strip, to illustrate the events of the story is helpful; the pictures are mixed and the student is asked to place the series in the proper chronological order.

3. ***Following directions.***   Read directions on making something. Have the materials ready and ask the student to follow the directions step by step.

4. ***Getting the main idea.***   Read a short but unfamiliar story and ask the student to make up a good title for the story. Read a story and ask the student to choose the main idea from three choices.

5. ***Making inferences and drawing conclusions.***   Read a part of a story that the student does not know. Stop at an exciting point and ask the student to guess what happens next. In another approach, the teacher reads a story that another student started and explains that the author did not know how to finish it. Now that the dog, Red, is in trouble, can the student suggest an ending?

Critical Listening

Good listening means not only understanding what is said but also the ability to listen critically, to make judgments and evaluations of what is being said.

1. ***Recognizing absurdities.***   Tell a short story with a word or phrase that does not fit the story. Ask the student to discover what is funny or foolish about the story. For example, "It rained all night in the middle of the day," or "The sun was shining brightly in the middle of the night."

2. ***Listening to advertisements.***   Have the student listen to advertisements and determine *how* the advertiser is trying to get the listener to buy the products. Adolescents enjoy detecting propaganda techniques.

3. ***Correct me.***   Use flannel board figures while telling a story. Plan obvious errors through discrepancies between what is said and what is placed on the board. Have the student listen for and correct the mistakes.

Speaking

Oral language, including listening and speaking, is identified as the primary form of language; written language is only a secondary form. In spite of the recognition and acceptance of the primacy of oral language, instructional practices in both regular classrooms and remedial work do not always reflect this relationship between oral and written language. Emphasis in teaching is too frequently focused on the written forms of communication—reading and writing.

Sequential Acquisition of Language

A general overview of the student's language development may provide a perspective for viewing language abnormalities. The child's first attempt to use vocal mechanisms is the birth cry. Through longitudinal and behavioral studies, researchers have observed and categorized the stages that the individual goes through in the short span of time from the birth cry to the full acquisition of speech (McCarthy, 1954).

Vocalization during the first nine months of life is called *babbling*. During this stage children produce many sounds, those in their native language as well as those found in other languages. Infants derive pleasure from hearing the sounds they make and such sound making gives them the opportunity to use the tongue, larynx, and other vocal apparatus and to respond orally to others. Deaf children have been observed to begin the babbling stages, but because they receive no feedback or satisfaction from hearing the sounds, they soon stop. Some children with language disorders are reported by parents not to have engaged in activities of babbling, gurgling, or blowing bubbles. Encouragement of such oral play becomes one technique by which the teacher can help these children recapitulate the normal states of language acquisition.

By about nine months, the babbling softens and becomes what is called *jargon*. Children retain the phoneme sounds that are used in the language they hear. The rhythm and melody of oral speaking patterns of others around them are reflected in their vocalizations. Although intonational patterns may be similar to those of adults, children do not yet use words. It is as though they are pretending to talk. Chinese children, for example, have been observed to have mastery of basic Chinese intonation patterns by twenty months of age, a feat that is very difficult for an English-speaking adult to accomplish. The parents of children who are diagnosed as having language disabilities often report that their children had missed this stage of development.

Single words, such as *mama* and *dadda,* normally develop between twelve and eighteen months of age. The ability to *imitate* is evident at this stage, and children may well imitate sounds or words that they hear others say or that they themselves produce. Children with language disabilities are frequently reported not to have engaged in verbal imitation and repetition activities.

Two- and three-word sentences follow the use of single words, for example, *Baby eat, Daddy home, Coat off.* Once children begin to use language, their skill in speech increases at a remarkably rapid pace. Between eighteen months, when a baby first produces a two-word utterance, and age three, many children learn the essentials of English grammar and can produce all linguistic types of sentences. The child's oral language development at age three appears to be almost abrupt; the child has an extensive vocabulary and uses rather complex sentence structures. During this stage, reports become rather hazy—partly because things develop so rapidly and partly because, as observers, we do not understand the underlying mechanism of language acquisition. By the time children enter school at age six, they are said to have completely learned the grammar of their native language, and their understanding vocabulary is large. Speaking vocabulary is, of course, smaller.

As already noted, it appears to be impossible to observe accurately the development in language from the beginning simple stages to the quickly following stage at which children become adept with the complex structure of language (Chomsky, 1965). It is in that brief period that children who are developing normally in language suddenly learn to use the mechanisms of grammar; they are able to formulate unique and original sentences.

As our knowledge of normal language acquisition accrues, we are discovering that many children with learning disabilities do not follow a normal developmental language pattern. Although language for the normal child seems to be acquired in a relatively natural and easy manner, without a need for the direct teaching of talking, some children have difficulty in acquiring one or several properties of language. Some have difficulty with the phonology of language—in differentiating and producing the appropriate sounds; others have difficulty in remembering words or in structuring morphological rules; some children have difficulty with grammar or syntax of the language and in putting words together to formulate sentences; still others have a semantic difficulty in vocabulary development.

Experiences in listening (the input, or receptive, side of language) precede speaking (the output, or expressive, side of language). Listening alone does not produce the ability to speak, but a looping or feedback process must be created in which the child both listens and speaks. The interrelationship of input and output activities provides immediate reinforcement that shapes speaking behavior. For example, teachers have noted that listening to television does not seem to have an impact on the basic language patterns of the viewer. Although the speech on television may be a model of standard American English, the speech patterns of viewers reflect those of their home and peer group rather than that of television performers.

Natural Language Stimulation Activities for Language-delayed Children

Teachers and parents can take advantage of many opportunities in the daily life of a child in school or home to provide natural language stimulation (Lowenthal, 1984).

1. **Expansion.**   This is a technique to enlarge and enhance the child's language. In the conversation below, the adult expands a child's limited utterance.
   Child: "Cookie."
   Teacher or Parent: "Cookie? I want cookie. Well, here it is!"
2. **Parallel talk.**   In this technique, the adult tries to help language develop by supplying language stimulation even when no speech is heard. As the child plays, the teacher or parent guesses what the child is thinking and supplies short phrases describing the actions, thereby placing words and sentences in the child's mind (inner language) for future reference. For example, if the child is banging on a block on the floor, the teacher might say: "There's the block. If I hit the block on the floor, it

makes a noise. A big noise. Bang, bang, bang. Block. My block. Bang the block."

3. **Self-talk.**   In this technique, teachers engage in activities that do not directly involve the child. As teachers complete their own tasks and are working in close proximity to the child, they can capitalize on opportunities to use meaningful language stimulation that the child can hear. For example, the teacher might say while cutting some paper, "I have to cut the paper. Cut the paper. I need scissors. My scissors. Open, shut the scissors. Open, shut. I can cut, cut, cut."

Activities for Teaching Oral Expression

Below are listed a number of activities to improve skills in verbal expression. These techniques are not intended to be inclusive but are merely representative of activities designed to advance skills in speaking.

Building a Speaking Vocabulary

Some children with language disorders have an extremely limited vocabulary and a very specific, narrow, and concrete sense of the meaning of words. Throughout their lives, people have a much larger listening vocabulary than speaking vocabulary. Young children are able to understand words long before they are able to produce and use them. A child with a language disorder may be able to recognize words when they hear them but cannot initiate the use of those words. Adults with known brain injuries may lose their ability to remember words easily as a result of damage to the language area of the brain. Such a condition is referred to as *dysnomia,* meaning the inability to remember the names of objects. Children may substitute another referent like "thing" or "whatsit" or "that" or a gesture or pantomime for the word they cannot bring to mind. The following ways are suggested to help students use words and build an accessible speaking vocabulary.

1. **Naming.**   Have the student name common objects in the room or outside (chair, door, table, tree, stone). Have a collection of objects in a box or bag. As each is removed, have the student name it. Have the student name colors, animals, shapes, and so forth. Use pictures of objects. A collection or a file of good pictures provides excellent teaching material. Pictures can be made more durable and washable by backing them with cardboard and covering them with a self-adhesive transparent material.

2. **Department store.**   The game of department store (or hardware store, supermarket, restaurant, shoe store, and so on) gives the student the opportunity to use naming words. One student plays the role of the customer and gives orders to another, who is the clerk. The clerk collects pictures of the items ordered and gives the orders to his or her customer while naming them.

3. **Rapid naming.**   Give the student a specified length of time (one min-

ute) to name all the objects in the room. Keep a record of the number of words named to note improvement. Pictures can be used and the student asked to name objects in the pictures. Another variation could be related to sports, the outdoors, pets, and so forth.

4. ***Missing words.*** Have the student say the word that finishes a riddle. Who delivers the mail? (mail carrier). I bounce a _____ (ball). Read a story to the children, pausing at certain places leaving out words; the child is to supply the missing word. The use of pictures helps in recall and naming of the object.

5. ***Word combinations.*** Some words can best be learned as part of a group. When one member of the group is named, the child may be helped to remember the second, for example, paper and pencil, boy and girl, hat and coat, cats and dogs. Series may also be learned in this fashion: days of the week, months of the year.

6. ***Troublesome words.*** The teacher should be alert for troublesome words. It may be possible to have an immediate lesson when such a word is noted, then plan for future exercises using that word.

Producing Speech Sounds

Some children have difficulty in initiating the motor movements required to produce speech. Such children may be able to remember the words but cannot activate the appropriate speech musculature, although they do not have a paralysis. Such a condition has been referred to as a speech *apraxia.* The techniques of the speech specialist in working with problems of articulation may be helpful in this condition.

1. ***Exercising speech muscles and organs.*** The child is encouraged to use the various muscles used in speaking for nonspeech activities: smiling, chewing, swallowing, whistling, yawning, blowing, laughing, and various tongue movements.

2. ***Feeling vibrations and observing sounds.*** As the teacher makes sounds, the student feels the vibrations of the sounds by touching the teacher's face or throat and observing the mouth movements and shaping during the production of sounds. The use of a mirror is helpful to enable students to observe themselves in producing sounds.

Learning Linguistic Patterns

1. ***Morphological generalizations.*** Some children have difficulty learning to internalize and use the morphological structure of the language. For example, one must make generalizations concerning the system of forming plurals, showing past tense, forming possessives. One must also learn the exceptions where generalizations do not hold true. For example, the phoneme /s/ or /z/ is usually added to a word in English to show plurality: "three cats" or "two dogs." In some cases the sound of

By recounting a story aloud and having her words written down by the tutor, this girl is practicing oral language skills. *(Paul Conklin/Monkmeyer)*

/ez/ is added, as in "two dresses," or the root word is changed, as in "two men." In a few cases the word is not changed, as in "four fish." For the child unable to formulate such generalizations, games in making plurals can be helpful. It is interesting to note that the morphemic rules of standard American English do not always hold in dialectical variations. The morphemic generalization in a non-standard English dialect (as well as in certain other languages) is to use the appropriate quantitative adjective but not pluralize the noun: *"That cost two dollar."*

2. *Use pictures to build morphological generalizations.* Point to the picture that describes each sentence.

> Picture 1 shows: The boy is *painting* a picture.
> Picture 2 shows: The picture is now *painted*.
> Picture 1: The *dog is* running.
> Picture 2: The *dogs are* running.

Formulating Sentences

Some children are able to use single words or short phrases but cannot generate longer syntactic units or sentences. Linguists hypothesize that children, in acquiring language, must learn to internalize sentence patterns so that they can "generate" new sentences. Some linguists have said that the child becomes a sentence-producing machine. To achieve this state, many skills are required—including the ability to understand language, to remember word sequences, and to formulate complex rules of grammar.

1. **Experiences with many kinds of sentences.**   Start with the basic kernel sentence and help the child to generate transformations of the kernel sentence. For example, two kernel sentences can be combined in various ways.

> Kernel sentence: The children play games.
> Kernel sentence: The children are tired.
> Transformation: The children who are tired play games.
>   The children who play games are tired.

Sentence pattern variations:

Statements	Questions
Children play games.	Do children play games?
Games are played by children.	Are games played by children?
Children do not play games.	Don't children play games?
Children do play games.	Do children play games?

2. **Structure words.**   These are the function words that show the relationship between parts of the sentence. Words such as *on, in, under,* and *who* are best taught within the sentence. Close observation reveals that many children have hazy concepts of the meaning of such words. Students can be asked to put blocks *in, on,* or *under* a table or chair, and then to explain what they did. Words such as *yet, but, never,* and *which* often need clarification. The teacher can give a sentence with only the key or class words and then ask the student to add the structure words. For example: "Jack—went—school—sweater."

3. **Substitution to form sentences.**   Form new sentences by substituting a single word in an existing kernel sentence. "I took my *coat* off. I took my *boots* off." "The child is *reading.* The child is *running.* The child is *jumping.*"

4. **Detective game.**   To help in formulating questions, have the student ask questions concerning the location of a hidden object until it is found.

Practicing Oral Language Skills

Reading specialists assert that much practice is needed in using and stabilizing newly learned reading skills; they frequently say, "You learn to read by reading." Practice is needed, too, for students with a deficiency in verbal expression skills, who need much opportunity in using words and in formulating sentences. Plans must be made to enable them to practice their speaking skills.

1. **Oral language activities.**   A number of activities can be used to promote practice in the use of oral language and speaking. These include conversations, discussions, radio or television broadcasts, show and tell

sessions, puppetry, dramatic play, telephoning, choral speaking, report-ing, interviewing, telling stories, riddles, or jokes, giving book reports, and role playing.

2. **Discussion of objects.**   Help the student tell about attributes of an object—its color, size, shape, composition, major parts—and compare it with other objects.

3. **Categories.**   Place in a box items that can be grouped to teach catego-ries, for example, toys, clothes, animals, vehicles, furniture, fruit. Ask the student to find the ones that go together and tell what they are. Or teachers can name the category while the students find and name the items. Put items together and ask which do not belong.

4. **Comprehension.**   Ask questions that require students to think and for-mulate responses. What would you be if you dressed funny and were in a circus? Why is it easier to make a dress shorter than it is to make it longer? Why should you put a goldfish in a bowl of water?

5. **Tell me how** . . . you brush your teeth, go to school, and so forth. Also, tell me why . . . . Tell me where do we . . . .

6. **Finishing stories.**   Begin a story and let the student finish it. For ex-ample: Betty went to visit her aunt in a strange city. When the plane landed, Betty could not see her aunt at the airport. . . .

7. **Peabody Language Kits.**   These kits are boxes containing puppets, pictures, and language lessons, all designed to develop oral language abilities.

Improving Oral Language of Adolescents

Direct instruction in language also helps improve the oral language and communication skills of learning-disabled adolescents. Because secondary students at first appear to have adequate oral language skills, their needs are often overlooked. In addition, the secondary curriculum emphasizes perfor-mance in written language more than oral language, so their deficiencies may go undetected. Upon closer observation, however, we find that the oral lan-guage of many learning-disabled secondary students is very meager. Many of the methods described earlier work for adolescents, and the following are also useful.

1. **Cognitive strategies.**   Methods that emphasize cognitive strategies work particularly well in teaching adolescents. It is especially important that the adolescents be involved in setting the goals they are trying to reach and in developing learning strategies to reach these goals. Self-monitoring, verbal rehearsal, and error analysis are the kinds of strate-gies that have been helpful in reading, and they can also be used for improving oral language.

2. **Vocabulary building through classification.**   Oral vocabulary can be expanded by helping adolescents classify and organize words. For example, they can build lists or hierarchies of words on a topic; for the

topic of space exploration, they might use words that classify space vehicles, space inventions, first events that occurred in space, and so on. There
are several approaches to this activity. The teacher can supply the words
for classifying, the students can supply the words, or the teacher can
provide a partial classification system and the students can complete it.

3. *Listening in stages.*   The teacher reads the beginning of a selection to
the students. After listening to several paragraphs, the teacher stops and
asks questions. "By now you should be able to answer. . . ." This activity,
in turn, provides a set for the next portion of listening.

4. *Reciprocal questioning.*   This is a reverse of the previous technique.
However, instead of the teacher asking the questions, the students ask
the questions. The technique encourages the development of questioning skills.

5. *Sentence combining.*   The teacher gives the students two short sentences orally. The task for the student is to think of how many ways the
sentences can be combined into one sentence.

6. *Review of a group discussion.*   Students hold a short discussion on
an assigned topic. After the discussion, the students analyze the effectiveness of the discussion. Did they keep on the topic? Did they allow
others to talk? Did they direct the conversation to the right people? Did
they follow through when a point was made?

7. *Explaining how to play a game.*   Many learning-disabled students
have difficulty in giving explanations and need practice in this activity.
For example, students can explain how to play a game, how to make
something, or how to do something. It is helpful to follow an exercise in
explaining with a self-monitoring session of the effectiveness of the explanation. The recipient of the explanation can be a peer or a younger
child. The student could first engage in verbal rehearsal to practice the
explanation and then try to be sensitive to whether the listener understands and is able to respond to questions. Examples of subjects for
explanation include the rules of a video game, how to cook and peel a
hard-boiled egg, or how to play checkers or bingo.

Summary

- Language is perhaps the most important accomplishment of the human
being. It is intimately related to all kinds of learning.

- Language plays a vital role in learning. It enhances thinking, permits us to
speak of things unseen, of the past, and of the future. It also serves to transmit
information and control the environment.

- The close relationship between language deficits and learning can be
seen in the examples of two groups of students—those with language disorders and those with language differences.

- Speech pathologists refer to a language disorder as a language delay or a language deficit. This includes children who learn to speak late and children whose language pattern is atypical. Language differences are found in students who have a language system that differs from standard English. Students who use nonstandard English may have great difficulty in school because school instruction is based on standard English. Bilingual students have a native language that is not English. Some bilingual students have both a language problem and a learning disability.

- Four disciplines contribute to our understanding of language as it relates to the learning disabled: language arts, language pathology, linguistics, and psycholinguistics.

- The language arts specialist is concerned with the creation of academic language programs that develop the four elements of language—listening, speaking, reading, and writing. Written language skills depend on a firm foundation in oral language. Language disorders affect children when they are learning to speak. The language ability of poor readers is often inferior to that of good readers. The contribution and expertise of the language arts specialist is important for working with the learning-disabled student.

- The language pathologist studies the causes and treatment of disorders of symbolic verbal behavior. The several kinds of language disorders among children with learning disabilities have been characterized as inner language disorders, receptive language disorders, and expressive language disorders.

- The linguist undertakes the scientific study of the nature of language. The important linguistic concepts include phonology, morphology, syntax, semantics, and pragmatics.

- The psycholinguist is interested in the complete communication process—the underlying psychology of language, as well as the nature of language itself. Psycholinguists are developing ways of analyzing the thinking processes fundamental to language and are studying language acquisition.

- In spite of the differences of focus among these professions, there is much agreement in their analyses of language problems and each can enhance the work of the others.

- The *Teaching Strategies* section suggests activities for teaching listening and oral language.

Key Terms

language delay	syntax	receptive oral language
childhood aphasia	dysnomia	linguistics
semantics	language pathology	expressive oral language
phonology	language difference	
morphology	bilingual	

Reading

Introduction

*T*he teaching of reading historically has been considered a prime responsibility of the schools. Yet reading scholars are still plagued by the question "What is reading?" Does reading mean those skills that enable one to decode the black squiggles called print? Is reading a symbol of spoken language, a visual receptive form of language? Is it the integration of visual and auditory stimuli? Is reading a visual process, determined by certain kinds of eye movements? Is reading a cognitive and psycholinguistic activity? Is reading thinking? Is it a means of enjoyment, escape, and vicarious experience? Is it a tool of learning? Is reading a subject taught in school? Is it a way of bridging time and space? In truth, depending on the situation, reading fits all these descriptions. We must recognize that reading is not a single task or one set of activities but comprises a variety of complex behaviors and processes. Reading serves many functions for both the individual and society.

In today's world increasing quantities of sensory data and information come to us through nonprint media. For many purposes, the global environment of television has replaced the world of print. Some educators have even suggested that a "bookless curriculum" be established in our schools—one that presents instruction through the use of nonprint media designed to relate information and to create appropriate learning experiences (Wiseman, 1981). Despite such signs of the declining value of reading in contemporary life, there is contrasting evidence that reading is assuming a greater role. For example, although millions of Americans watched television to view momentous occurrences, such as tragic assassinations, special sports events, critical political happenings, the awe-inspiring moon walk and space trips, these television viewers were eager to read the newspapers the next day to make the events they had witnessed more coherent, detailed and comprehensible.

In spite of the new role that nonprint media play in providing a message, illiteracy has become a more debilitating handicap than ever. A few generations ago, people managed to get along quite well in the business and social worlds without the ability to read, but they can no longer do so. Lengthier periods of compulsory education, minimum competency tests, the requirement of diplomas and degrees for jobs, more comprehensive school testing programs, the necessity of filling out application forms and taking licensing examinations—all make life for the nonreader uncomfortable and full of impassable barriers. Reading teachers have a quotable saying: "Children must learn to read so that they can later read to learn." Indeed, since reading is the basic tool for all academic subjects, failure in school is frequently due to inadequate reading ability.

The increase in high technology and automation has spurred a demand for highly trained people. In today's world, old jobs rapidly become obsolete, making the process of retraining a necessity. It is predicted that workers in every occupation will have to retrain themselves to prepare for new jobs many times during their work careers. A key tool for retraining and maintaining employable skills is the ability to read efficiently. Even the criminal world wants literate workers. According to a sociology research study, crime organizations have gone through an innovative stage and upgraded literacy requirements. As a result, "as criminal jobs become increasingly complex," there will be "no place in the higher levels of organized crime for high school dropouts" (*Chicago Tribune*, May 15, 1967).

Many of the ills of our society have been related to reading disabilities. The ranks of the unemployed, school dropouts, and juvenile delinquents tend to have very poor reading skills. Upon examination, the problems of our schools, of poverty, of the concerns of troubled parents, as well as the plight of most learning-disabled students, all show an association with poor reading. The overall literacy problem that confronts our nation is serious. According to a recent national survey, 10 percent of the nation's seventeen-year-olds are unable to read even simple materials (the *National Assessment of Educational Progress*, 1981).

Although students with learning disabilities have difficulties in many areas of learning, poor reading is the most frequently reported academic problem (Kirk & Elkins, 1975; Lewis, 1983; Deshler, Schumaker, Lenz, & Ellis, 1984). It is important, therefore, that teachers of learning-disabled students be well grounded in the concepts and methodologies of the field of reading (Richek, List, & Lerner, 1983).

■ Theories

Dyslexia

The term *dyslexia* is frequently used to refer to a condition causing those afflicted to have extreme difficulty in acquiring reading skills. As one type of learning disability, this unusual malady continues to challenge researchers, mystify clinicians, and cause great emotional distress to dyslexic individuals.

CASE EXAMPLES

Dyslexia

Adults who have suffered from dyslexia can long recall the anguish of trying to cope with this mysterious condition in a world that requires people to read.

I remember vividly the pain and mortification I felt as a boy of 8 when I was assigned to read a short passage of a scripture with a community vesper service during the summer vacation in

Maine—and did a thoroughly miserable job of it.

Nelson Rockefeller
TV Guide, *October 16, 1976*

A bride of six months wrote that she had just discovered her husband could not read and had dyslexia. She wrote: "Yesterday, John admitted the truth. He can't read. He was so ashamed he cried when he told me."

Letter to Ann Landers
Miami Herald, *October 9, 1979*

The first time I remember shame was when I used the wrong word or got words in the wrong order. Everyone always laughed at me. Perhaps I could have laughed too if I had been able to see the mistakes I had made. But I couldn't. What I had said sounded quite logical to me. I would sit there trying hard to think what I had said then burst out crying. . . . my lack of reading and writing ability became noted, not only by the teachers, but by the children, too. There was no help or even understanding. Just impatience on the teacher's part.

I can still remember the terror as the class stood up in turn to read aloud. I would start to read with sweaty hands as the print danced before my eyes. I would stammer and sputter in an effort to start. The teacher would look up, see it was me and say crossly, "Oh, for goodness sake; sit down and shut up." . . . I would do anything rather than go to school; powder my face with talcum to make me look pale; scream; have hysterics; be doubled up with pain, be sick.

Sue Loftus-Brigham
Dyslexia Need Not Be a Disaster
*London: London Dyslexia
Association, 1983*

There was something wrong with my brain. What had previously been a shadowy suspicion that hovered on the edge of consciousness became certain knowledge the year I was nine and entered fourth grade. I seemed to be like other children, but I was not like them: I could not learn to read or spell.

Eileen Simpson
Reversals: A Personal Account
of Victory over Dyslexia
Boston: Houghton Mifflin, 1979.

The word *dyslexia* is derived from two Greek roots, *dys* ("not") and *lexia* ("read"). Thus, it simply means an inability to read. In the medical field, when an adult patient loses the ability to read because of brain damage caused by a stroke, an accident, or organic brain disease, neurologists call the disorder *acquired alexia*. When a child is unable to learn the skill of reading and the cause is ascribed to brain pathology, the condition is sometimes called *developmental alexia* or *dyslexia*. Neurological research on this condition suggests that dyslexia has a biological basis; that within the community of poor readers there is a hard core of cases in which the learning defect is inborn, caused by neurobiological factors (Geshwind, 1982; Galaburda, 1983; Duane, 1983). The condition occurs in a small percentage of people with reading problems and the disability is extremely severe, persistent, and very resistant to treatment (Richek et al., 1983). Most individuals who encounter reading problems do not have dyslexia.

Individuals with this unusual reading disorder have puzzled the medical and educational communities for many years. As early as 1896, an English physician published a description of a case of a fourteen-year-old boy who could not read in spite of the fact that he appeared to be intelligent (Morgan, 1896). A few years later, another English ophthalmologist, Hinshelwood (1917), reported on a condition he called, "congenital word blindness," a pathological condition due to a disorder of the visual centers of the brain producing difficulty in interpreting written language. Later, an American neurologist, Orton (1937), pioneered research on the relationship of brain anomalies to dyslexia, analyzing its cause as a lack of cerebral dominance. The Orton Dyslexia Society was organized to continue Orton's research on the biological bases of dyslexia and to promote its treatment (Geshwind, 1982).

With the advent of new brain examination tools, research on dyslexia has continued and increased in recent years (Kinsbourne, 1983). In a promising genetic study, researchers traced dyslexia through several generations and discovered a linkage to a defective gene located on chromosome 15 (Smith, Kimberling, Pennington, & Lubs, 1983). In another fascinating ongoing brain research project on dyslexia, at Harvard Medical School, researchers are conducting autopsies to study the brain tissues of young dyslexics who died in accidents (mostly motorcycle accidents). The analyses of the brain tissues in the few postmortem cases examined thus far show that these dyslexics had abnormalities among cells in the language area of the left hemisphere (Galaburda & Kemper, 1979; Galaburda, 1983; Geshwind, 1983). Interestingly, the abnormalities were located in the same area of the brain in which adult patients with acquired alexia suffer damage and which Orton had hypothesized as the location of abnormality in children with developmental dyslexia (Geshwind, 1982). Thus, accumulating biological evidence supports the concept that dyslexia has a biological and organic basis.

Misunderstanding and confusion about dyslexia continues among professionals in education, reading, psychology, learning disabilities, and medicine because the term is used in so many ways. It has been variously viewed as a set of reading problems related to (1) diagnosed organic brain damage, (2) behavioral manifestations of central nervous system dysfunction, (3) a genetic or inherited reading disability, (4) general reading retardation, and (5) the inability to learn to read through regular classroom methods (Richek et al., 1983; Lerner, 1975). It seems advisable, however, to reserve the term dyslexia for those unusual cases of very severe and persistent reading difficulty.

Dyslexia continues to be an intriguing challenge for researchers and clinicians. Perhaps continuing brain research will bring a better understanding of this puzzling condition. Some of the teaching methods that are successful with more common types of reading disability can also be used for treating dyslexia, but the teacher needs even greater sensitivity, understanding, and ingenuity in the diagnostic and clinical teaching process. Some of the methods described as remedial approaches in the Teaching Strategies section of this chapter can be useful in helping dyslexic students.

If students have been progressing normally with the development of reading skills, they begin—during the intermediate school years—to seek out favorite authors and to read widely for pleasure.   *(Sybil Shackman/Monkmeyer)*

Sequential Development of Reading Ability

Teachers of students with reading problems should have an understanding of developmental reading programs and normal reading growth. The sequence of stages that the child normally goes through in acquiring reading skills is commonly divided as (1) the development of reading readiness, (2) the initial stage of learning how to read, (3) the rapid growth of reading skills, (4) the stage of wide reading, and (5) the refinement of reading skills (Harris & Sipay, 1980). For the learning-disabled student, the reading problems snowball. If normal reading growth is missed at any one stage, the student will also miss the reading growth at subsequent stages. As a result, the student falls further and further behind.

Stage 1: Development of Reading Readiness   This stage begins at birth and continues through the beginning stages of reading. It encompasses the development of language skills of listening and speaking, of motor development, auditory and visual discrimination, concept and cognitive thinking, and of the ability to attend to and concentrate on activities. The role of kindergarten has traditionally been to build such reading readiness skills, sometimes referred to as *prerequisites* of reading.

Stage 2: Initial Stage of Learning to Read   This stage, the start of the formal reading program, has traditionally occurred in first grade; but reading may begin in kindergarten, second grade, or even later. This beginning-to-read stage has been the most researched and the object of the greatest number of innovations and changes.

Great controversies about the teaching of reading have also revolved about the beginning stage of reading instruction. One often quoted investigation of different approaches to beginning reading, *Learning to Read: The Great Debate*, concluded that beginning reading is primarily a decoding process and that code-emphasis methods at this stage produce the best results (Chall, 1967). The phonics emphasis was also recommended more recently for beginning readers by Chall and Stahl (1982) and for beginning reading for learning-disabled children (Lewis, 1983; Jenkins, Stein, & Osborn (1981). Another comprehensive investigation of beginning reading, the *Cooperative Research Program in First-Grade Reading Instruction* (Bond & Dykstra, 1967), came to somewhat different conclusions. This large-scale cooperative research found that no one method is so outstanding that it should be used to the exclusion of others. Moreover, the researchers discovered greater variation among the teachers within a method than among the methods.

Educators use a variety of methods to introduce children to the initial stage of reading. Some children begin reading with the language experience approach; others start with the first preprimer of the basal reader or with a phonics method or with other methods, such as linguistics, programmed reading, or computer instruction. At this initial stage, students typically begin to develop a sight vocabulary, start to associate sound with the visual symbols of the letter, learn to follow a line of print from left to right across a page and begin learning functional comprehension skills. Much of the reading at this stage is oral, and students realize that reading is "talk written down."

Stage 3: Rapid Development of Reading Skills   This phase normally takes place in the second and third grades. It is an extension, refinement, and amplification of the previous stage. The student proceeding normally in reading now rapidly develops advanced word recognition skills, builds a substantial sight vocabulary, becomes adept at using various types of context clues, and establishes skill in phonic and structural analysis. The bulk of the phonics program is presented by the end of third grade. Thus, the student developing normally has learned phonic generalizations and makes effective application of them by the end of the primary years. This stage lays the foundation for later reading development.

Stage 4: Stage of Wide Reading   The program of the intermediate grades emphasizes extensive reading and broadens and enriches the student's reading experiences. The basic skills of the primary grades are improved and strengthened. Now the student progressing normally can read for pleasure. Voluntary reading reaches a peak in these years. Librarians report more enthusiasm for reading among students at this stage than perhaps at any other. During this period students discover a favorite series, such as *Choose Your Own Adventure* by Edward Packard, the *Soup Series* by Robert Newton Peck, *Encyclopedia Brown* by Donald Sobal, the *Hardy Boys*, or the *Nancy Drew* mysteries. At this stage, too, students may read all the books of a favorite author, such as Judy Blume, Betsy Byars, Marguerite Henry, Lois Lenski, or Beverly Cleary. Youngsters like to share the discovery of a good book, and students from the classroom may soon have their names on a waiting list to read the new favorite of one of their classmates. Book clubs are popular at this age and librarians report that there is often a run on a book after it is dramatized on television. Students developing normally in reading enjoy the process of reading for fun at this stage, although they still need help in developing skills in reading factual materials. At this stage also, they begin to learn study skills.

Stage 5: Refinement of Reading   Schools are beginning to realize that reading development is not completed by the end of elementary school, even for students who do not have special reading problems. During junior and senior high school, students need continued guidance for effective reading growth. In fact, reading skills are never completely perfected; even in college and during adult life, one is still developing advanced reading abilities. The development of more advanced comprehension skills, the refinement of study skills, an increase in reading rate, and the achievement of a flexibility in reading for different purposes are the responsibility of secondary schools. It is at this point, when longer periods of concentrated reading are required, that some students who *had* been progressing apparently well begin to fail in reading. The reading problem at this stage is quite different from that of the child who is unable to learn to decode a graphic symbol at the beginning stage of reading.

Components of Reading: Word Recognition and Comprehension

The process of teaching reading can be divided into two components: (1) teaching word recognition and (2) teaching reading comprehension. The reader needs word recognition to decode printed letters, to match letters and words with sounds, and to have a means for figuring out, or unlocking, unknown words. Comprehension, however, allows the reader to understand the meaning of what is being read. Word recognition is a necessary prerequisite for comprehension, but if the student says the words in a passage without gathering their meaning, one would hesitate to call that reading. Both are needed if the student is to learn to read and function as a reader. Usually, word recognition receives more emphasis in the beginning stages and comprehension receives emphasis in the later stages of reading instruction.

Word Recognition

Word recognition abilities comprise a cluster of strategies or clues for recognizing words. Word recognition strategies include *sight words, context clues, phonics*, and *structural analysis*. Because readers should be encouraged to use all these strategies to figure out a word, teachers should be familiar with the value and methods of teaching each type.

Sight words refer to the words that are to be recognized instantly, without hesitation or further analysis. Table 12.1 illustrates 220 basic sight words that students should know automatically. The sight words are divided into groups according to their difficulty.

Context clues means recognizing a word through the context or meaning of the sentence or paragraph in which it appears. Students should be strongly encouraged to use the redundancy of the language, which gives hints about an unknown word; and they should learn to make intelligent guesses about unknown words.

Phonics is the word-recognition skill in which the reader matches the sound of a letter to a specific written symbol. Many of the materials and methods of reading instruction emphasize this approach. It is, however, only one of the word-recognition skills and should be placed in proper perspective. *Decoding* is another term used to describe making the connection between the sound and letter symbol. To "break the code," a reader must become aware of each phoneme within a word. Liberman (1982) has found that students with reading disabilities have trouble analyzing the phonemic structure of the written word and matching it with the phonemic structure of the spoken word they already know.

The written form of English has an inconsistent phoneme-grapheme relationship; that is, the relationship between the letter and its sound equivalent is not always predictable. Some authorities feel that printed English is difficult for many children to decipher because of the irregular spelling pattern of the English language. The letter *a*, for example, is given a different sound in each of the following typical first-grade words: *at, Jane, ball, father, was, saw, are*. Another example of this complexity is the phoneme of long *i*, which has a different spelling pattern in each of the following words: *aisle, aye, I, eye, ice, tie, high, choir, buy, sky, rye, pine, type*. To further complicate the problem of learning to read English, many of the most frequently used sight words in first-grade books have irregular spelling patterns. A few of these words are shown in column A of Table 12.2; column B shows the way they would be spelled with a dependable phoneme-grapheme relationship, so that readers could "sound them out."

TABLE 12.1   **220 Basic Word Sight Vocabulary**

Preprimer	Primer	First	Second	Third
1. the	45. when	89. many	133. know	177. don't
2. of	46. who	90. before	134. while	178. does
3. and	47. will	91. must	135. last	179. got
4. to	48. more	92. through	136. might	180. united
5. a	49. no	93. back	137. us	181. left
6. in	50. if	94. years	138. great	182. number
7. that	51. out	95. where	139. old	183. course
8. is	52. so	96. much	140. year	184. war
9. was	53. said	97. your	141. off	185. until
10. he	54. what	98. may	142. come	186. always
11. for	55. up	99. well	143. since	187. away
12. it	56. its	100. down	144. against	188. something
13. with	57. about	101. should	145. go	189. fact
14. as	58. into	102. because	146. came	190. through
15. his	59. than	103. each	147. right	191. water
16. on	60. them	104. just	148. used	192. less
17. be	61. can	105. those	149. take	193. public
18. at	62. only	106. people	150. three	194. put
19. by	63. other	107. Mr.	151. states	195. thing
20. I	64. new	108. how	152. himself	196. almost
21. this	65. some	109. too	153. few	197. hand
22. had	66. could	110. little	154. house	198. enough
23. not	67. time	111. state	155. use	199. far
24. are	68. these	112. good	156. during	200. took
25. but	69. two	113. very	157. without	201. head
26. from	70. may	114. make	158. again	202. yet
27. or	71. then	115. would	159. place	203. government
28. have	72. do	116. still	160. American	204. system
29. an	73. first	117. own	161. around	205. better
30. they	74. any	118. see	162. however	206. set
31. which	75. my	119. men	163. home	207. told
32. one	76. now	120. work	164. small	208. nothing
33. you	77. such	121. long	165. found	209. night
34. were	78. like	122. get	166. Mrs.	210. end
35. her	79. our	123. here	167. thought	211. why
36. all	80. over	124. between	168. went	212. called
37. she	81. man	125. both	169. say	213. didn't
38. there	82. me	126. life	170. part	214. eyes
39. would	83. even	127. being	171. once	215. find
40. their	84. most	128. under	172. general	216. going
41. we	85. made	129. never	173. high	217. look
42. him	86. after	130. day	174. upon	218. asked
43. been	87. also	131. same	175. school	219. later
44. has	88. did	132. another	176. every	220. knew

Source: Dale D. Johnson, "The Dolch List Reexamined," *The Reading Teacher* 24 (February 1971): 455–456. The 220 most frequent words in the Kucera-Francis corpus. Reprinted with permission of Dale D. Johnson and the International Reading Association.

TABLE 12.2   **Typical First-Grade Sight Words**

A. English Spelling	B. Phonic Spelling
of	uv
laugh	laf
was	wuz
is	iz
come	kum
said	sed
what	wut
from	frum
one	wun
night	niet
know	noe
they	thai

There are several ways of meeting the problems of the undependable written form of English.

1. The basal reader solution is to introduce only a small number of words at a time, selecting words on the basis of frequency of use. Some beginning reading words are regularly spelled and some have irregular spellings. Words are learned visually through much review and through context, meaning and language. In addition, basal readers provide some phonics instruction using words that have regular spellings.
2. The approach of phonics and linguistics methods is to simplify the initial learning phase by selecting only words that have a consistent sound-symbol spelling relationship. Thus, children learn phonics and are exposed to carefully selected words with dependable spellings.
3. Another approach is to simplify beginning reading by changing the written symbol or by modifying the written alphabet for initial learning. This is the approach used by the *initial teaching alphabet* (i.t.a.). This approach to beginning teaching is no longer as widely used as it was some years ago.

In effect, approaches 2 and 3 do not solve the problem; they merely delay the student's contact with the undependable spelling of many common English words. Students are kept from learning the "awful truth about spelling" until second grade or later. Inevitably the undependable written form of English must be confronted by the reader.

Many teachers are not well grounded in phonics and phonic generalizations (Lerner & List, 1970; Horne, 1978). Some teachers do not remember learning phonics when they learned to read, and many teachers have not received adequate phonics instruction in their preservice teacher education. The reader may wish to take the *Foniks Kwiz*, Appendix B. A brief review of phonic generalizations follows the quiz.

Structural analysis refers to the recognition of words through the analysis of word units. For example, prefixes, suffixes, root words, compound words, and syllables often provide useful ways to figure out unknown words.

Other *word recognition strategies* may be used, although they may not be as dependable as those listed above. They include *configuration* (seeing the shape of a word), *dictionary* skills, and the analysis of the *accents* in words.

Although reading specialists continue to debate which of these word recognition strategies is the best (sight words, context clues, phonics, structural analysis), actually readers need to use them all in reading. At different times the reader needs different approaches to word recognition. Most often, however, several are used together. Learning-disabled students need practice in each of these word recognition strategies to achieve independence and flexibility (Richek et al., 1983).

Reading Comprehension

The purpose of reading, of course, is to gather meaning from the printed page. Since comprehension is the heart and purpose of reading, every reading program should provide for the development of reading comprehension abilities.

Much attention and debate concerning reading methods have been directed to word-recognition problems; yet the problems related to teaching reading comprehension are far more important and difficult. The major problem for many learning-disabled students lies in reading comprehension. Recognizing this fact, the developers of Public Law 94–142 wisely wrote into law that a learning disability can be in the area of "basic reading skill" (word recognition) or in "reading comprehension."

Levels of Reading

Reading comprehension can take place on four levels: (1) the literal level, (2) the organizational level, (3) the inferential level, and (4) the critical level. Each level deepens one's understanding of the material, and each level requires increasingly complex thinking skills.

The *literal level* of comprehension refers to the skills at the least complex level of reading comprehension. It is the ability to recognize and understand the directly stated ideas of the author. This level is sometimes referred to as "reading the lines" of print.

The *organizational level* of comprehension requires the reader to do more than understand the stated facts. It requires the ability to see relationships within the material and to determine what is important and significant and what is supporting detail. For example, can the reader state the key idea or main point from an entire paragraph or selection?

The *inferential level* refers to the kind of reading needed to grasp not only overt meanings and the organization, but also the meanings that are implied. The reader must think of more than the words and symbols themselves to supply the meanings intended to interpret the passage. This level of reading has also been referred to as "reading between the lines."

The *critical level* of reading refers to the kind of reading that requires personal judgment and evaluation. At this level the reader forms generalizations, draws conclusions, compares, analyzes, and applies ideas gained in reading. This level is often referred to as "reading beyond the lines."

The goal in teaching learning disabilities students is first to help them gain the control of the literal level and then gradually increase their levels of understanding.

At times effective reading of even a single selection requires readers to perform at all these levels. Adler (1956) describes such an occasion in *How to Read a Book.*

> When [people] are in love and are reading a love letter, they read for all they are worth. They read every word three ways; they read the whole in terms of the parts, and each part in terms of the whole; they grow sensitive to context and ambiguity, to insinuation and implication; they perceive the color of words, the order of phrases, and the weight of sentences. They may even take punctuation into account. Then, if never before or after, they read. (p. 4)

Two Views of Reading Comprehension: Specific Skills and a Holistic Process

Reading comprehension has been viewed in terms of two distinct theoretical frameworks: (1) *as a set of specific, separate, identifiable, and observable reading skills,* and (2) *as a holistic process,* or a unified whole dependent on the personal experiences and the knowledge of language that the reader brings to the printed text. Each of these two views is based upon a different theory of learning and each leads to different methods of teaching (Richek et al., 1983).

The Specific Skills View of Reading Comprehension

Traditionally, reading comprehension has been linked with a set of identifiable and teachable skills, such as noting important facts and details, finding the main idea, and following directions. A major advantage of identifying discrete comprehension skills is that the teacher can easily divide the very general concept of reading comprehension into smaller units that are manageable for instruction. Consequently, the student's attention can be directly focused on reaching specific and definable goals. The diagnosis involves determining which specific reading skills the student has already ac-

quired and which must still be taught. Remedial instruction involves the direct teaching of those discrete comprehension skills yet to be learned.

The specific skills approach to reading first requires identification of the essential skills. Once identified, the skills can be placed in a logical sequence (or taxonomy) for teaching (Bloom, ed. 1956; Otto & Askov, 1972). The specific skills approach can be used for teaching both word recognition and comprehension. Samuels (1981) reported that the skills-centered approach was successful with poor readers.

Although reading authorities do not all agree on which comprehension skills are important and how they should be sequenced, the comprehension skills that are commonly identified are described as follows, in a sequence from the easier to the more difficult (Richek et al., 1983):

1. *Noting clearly stated facts and important details of a selection.* This skill is considered one of the easiest comprehension skills. Most of the questions asked on reading tests and by teachers are questions of detail. For example: "What color was Jane's new dress?" "What is the largest city in Montana?" "In what year was the treaty signed?" This skill requires memory; if the detail can be related to a main idea, it is easier to remember.

2. *Grasping the main idea.* This skill entails the reader's ability to get the

nucleus of the idea presented or to capture the core of the information. It is much harder than finding details, and many readers are unable to see through the details to get the central thought of a selection. Teachers can help students develop this skill by asking them to select the best title for a selection from several alternatives, by having them make up a title for a selection, or by asking them to state in one sentence what a short selection is about.

3. *Following a sequence of events or steps.* This skill is one of organizing— being able to see the steps of a process or the events in a story. Seeing such order is important to thinking, understanding language, and reading. To provide practice in this skill, the teacher can give the events in scrambled order and ask the student to sort them into the correct order. The ability to follow printed directions is closely allied to this skill, and the reader proceeds step by step to carry out a project. The *Boy Scout Handbook*, model plane directions, a cookbook, or directions for playing a game provide practical material for teaching this skill.

4. *Drawing inferences and reaching conclusions.* This skill requires great emphasis on thoughtful reading and interpretation. Here the reader must go beyond the lines and the facts given in order to reach a conclusion. Questions such as "What does the author mean?" or "Can you predict or anticipate what will happen next?" are geared to encourage such thinking. The reader who can do this is thinking along with the author.

5. *Organizing ideas.* This skill refers to the ability to see interrelationships among the ideas of a reading selection. It involves sensing cause and effect, comparing and contrasting relationships, and seeing the author's general plan for structuring the material. Studying the table of contents, looking at topic headings and outlining are techniques to help the student see how the ideas are organized.

6. *Applying what is read to solve problems and verify statements.* If reading is to be a functional skill, the material must be adapted to new situations and integrated with previous experiences. The ability to transfer and integrate the knowledge and skills gained in reading is a difficult skill for many students to acquire. Information gained through reading a story about a boy in Mexico might be applied to a lesson in social studies. Or a problem can be formulated and the answer found through reading a selection.

7. *Evaluating materials for bias, relevance, and consistency.* This skill is sometimes referred to as critical reading. Making judgments about the author's bias, comparing several sources of information, detecting propaganda techniques, and determining the logic of an argument or approach are all included in this skill. Even students who are capable readers are likely to need help with this comprehension skill. Students enjoy the critical examination of advertisements for the detection of propaganda techniques. The comparing of editorials on the same subject or of two new reports of a single event provides good material for developing this skill.

The advantage of a skills approach is that it facilitates testing and instruction. A number of methods of reading instruction are based on the specific skills theory; two are discussed here.

Mastery Learning   A theory of instruction called *mastery learning* was developed by Bloom (1976). This approach provides a basis for teaching all students, including those who have difficulty learning to read. The basic hypothesis of mastery learning is that all of the content that students should learn can be broken into an ordered sequence of skills. Further, every student can acquire this content if he or she masters each of these skills through carefully sequenced instruction.

Skills Management Systems   A related application of the specific skills approach to reading, which is often used with learning-disabled students, is the criterion-referenced, or skills management, system. The current skills of the student are assessed through *criterion-referenced testing* (CRT). CRT is a testing method designed to enable the teacher to pinpoint which reading skills a student knows, which the student does not know and should be taught, and when these skills have been learned. The authors of criterion-referenced materials, in effect, establish what they believe to be the specific sequence of reading skills. The student is tested for each skill; if achievement does not reach a pre-established criterion of success, teaching is provided specifically for that student. When the student learns the skill at the proficiency of the established criterion, instruction for the student is focused on the next skill in the hierarchy. For example, when Frank learns skill number 25 (the *bl* blend at a 90-percent level of proficiency), he moves on to learn skill number 26. The number of specified skills identified in criterion-referenced reading programs ranges to 450 (Thompson & Dziuban, 1973).

The CRT (criterion-referenced testing) approach has been proposed as an alternative to the NRT (norm-referenced testing) approach. To illustrate the difference between CRT and NRT, Frank's reading performance on a standardized *norm-referenced reading test* shows he performed at a 4.7 grade level. Frank's performance on a *criterion-referenced test* shows he has mastered reading for facts, but he lacks the skill of finding the main idea. Thus, CRT is used to identify an individual student's performance in very specific skills. In contrast, NRT is used to identify an individual's general performance in comparison to that of peers on the same standardized test. To use another illustration, the measured system in CRT tells you that Mary has the skills to swim a mile or that Jack has achieved an acceptable criterion level of 85 percent in reading skill number 12. The NRT measurement system tells you that Mary is an average swimmer for her age or that Jack has reached a reading grade level of 3.6. CRT has been compared to climbing a ladder; each rung (skill) must be touched (learned) or the climber will fall off.

Some of the commercial skills management programs based on the specific skills approach to reading are listed below; the publishers are mentioned in parentheses.

SCORE (Westinghouse Learning)
Fountain Valley Teacher Support System in Reading (Zweig)
Individual Pupil Monitoring System (Houghton Mifflin)
Prescriptive Reading Inventory (CTB/McGraw-Hill)
High Intensity Learning System (Random House)
Reading Mastery (SRA)
Wisconsin Design for Reading Skill Development (Learning Multi-Systems)
Classroom Management System (Harper & Row)

The Holistic View of Reading Comprehension

A growing number of influential reading scholars conceptualize reading as a unitary, whole process, entailing cognitive and psycholinguistic behavior. Rejecting the notion of reading as discrete specific skills, the holistic approach offers a fresh insight into how readers go about understanding printed text material. This view emphasizes that all readers must be able to bridge the gap between the information presented in the written text and the knowledge in their heads in order to understand and remember what is read (Goodman, 1969; Goodman & Burke, 1980; Smith, 1982; Anderson, Reynolds, Schallert, & Goetz, 1977; Rumelhart, 1981; Pearson & Spiro, 1980). What are some of the major ideas supporting the holistic view of reading comprehension?

1. *Specific skills do not exist in reality.* The obvious underlying assumption of the specific skills approach to reading is that specific subskills of reading do exist and that they can be identified, classified, tested and taught. Do these specific skills of reading actually exist, or are they merely a pedagogical convenience created by reading scholars? The proponents of the holistic view of reading argue that the whole notion of a sequence or hierarchy of skills is only an artifact that appeals to our sense of logic but does not exist in reality.

   Research on specific skills is inconclusive. Davis (1968) demonstrated that comprehension material could be factored into independent subskills. Farr (1969), however, found little evidence showing that reading tests effectively measure specific subskills. Guthrie's (1973) research revealed differences between good and poor readers in terms of possessing specific skills. For good readers, comprehension appears to be a single, or unitary, process because they have learned to integrate subskills into a whole reading act. For poor readers, however, specific subskills of reading appear to exist because the poor readers have not as yet integrated subskills into a whole reading act. Samuels (1981) found that most of the successful reading programs designed for low-achieving students use the skills approach, incorporating a skills-centered curriculum and specific reading objectives. Thus, answers to the basic question about the existence of specific skills are still inconclusive, although a

It is important that reading instruction for learning-disabled students include methods of transferring and integrating specific reading skills into the whole reading act.   *(Elizabeth Crews)*

skills approach does appear to be more effective with poor readers (Chall & Stahl, 1982).

2. *Reading comprehension depends on what the reader brings to the written material.* Reading comprehension depends on the reader's experience, knowledge of language, recognition of syntactic structure, and the redundancy of a printed passage (Goodman, 1969; Smith, 1982). In fact, Smith (1982) believes that the reader's knowledge is more important for reading comprehension than the text itself.

An excellent illustration of the importance of the reader's knowledge in reading comprehension is presented by Aulls (1982). First read the following paragraph.

A newspaper is better than a magazine, and on a seashore is a better place than a street. At first it is better to run than to walk. Also you may have to try several times. It takes some skill but it's easy to learn. Even young children can enjoy it. Once successful, complications are minimal. Birds seldom get too close. One needs lots of room. Rain soaks in very fast. Too many people doing the same thing can also cause problems. If there are no complications, it can be very peaceful. A rock will serve as an anchor. If things break loose from it, however, you will not get a second chance. (Bransford & Johnson, 1972), cited by Aulls, 1982, p. 52)

As a mature reader, you were able to understand every word of this paragraph, yet you probably did not understand the passage and cannot explain what it is about. The reason you had difficulty is that you did not have the appropriate background knowledge to bring to the printed text. Now, we expand your background knowledge by telling you that the passage is about *kites*. If you reread the paragraph now, you will find a marked improvement in your reading comprehension. The implication for teaching is that when the reader has limited prior knowledge to relate to the text content, no amount of rereading will increase comprehension. What the learning-disabled student needs in many cases is more background knowledge to improve comprehension.

3. *Reading is a language process.* Any system of teaching reading must recognize that reading is a process for obtaining meaning through language, that is, a psycholinguistic process. Consequently Goodman (1972) recommends that reading be taught as an extension of natural language learning. This can happen if teachers understand the language processes underlying reading.

During the reading process, the reader cannot complete the thought until the final word or phrase. For example, in the two phrases, "the little white pebble" and "the little understood theory," the word, *little*, connotes something quite different in each phrase. The reader cannot know the meaning of the word, or sometimes even the pronunciation, until the end of the phrase or sentence. In English, the meaning of the beginning is dependent on the end. The flow of thought in English is not left to right, but in many cases circular. Although the eye goes from left to right, the mind does not. Certain ideas and words must be held until some part of the sentence permits the completion of the thought. For example, "When *Lee* looked at the *note* again, she realized that she should have played A sharp." The meaning of *note* and Lee's gender must be kept in abeyance until the end of the sentence provides the clarification. In the following example, a decision about the pronunciation of "tears" cannot be made until the end of the sentence: "John had *tears* in his shirt."

Other clues for understanding both oral and written language are the *redundancies* in language. Redundancy means sending the same message in other forms. That is, information from one source supports information from another source, reinforcing and enhancing the intended message. Such cues therefore help readers construct the meaning in a written text. The following sentences are examples of redundancies:

- "Would you reiterate that? Please say it again." (The second sentence explains the first.)
- "Do you want a piece of cake?" (Both the structure of the sentence and the question mark show that the sentence is an interrogative.)
- "The girl wore her plaid skirt." (We know the sentence is about a female person from the words, *girl, her,* and *skirt.*)

In remediating reading problems, students should be taught to look for and make use of the redundancies in language.

4. *Reading comprehension requires active interaction with the text.* To comprehend reading material, the reader must be an "active" participant, interacting with the text material. The research of Anderson et al. (1977), Rumelhart (1981), and Torgesen (1980) suggests that to truly read, readers must actively combine their existing *schema* (conceptual structure and knowledge that the reader already possesses) with the new information of the printed text. Many learning-disabled students are passive readers; that is, they do not know how to effectively interact with the text in the reading process and merge the information with what they already know. The instruction for these students must be geared to getting them actively involved in the reading to try to reconstruct the author's message.

There is evidence that good readers generally do not read every word of a passage; instead they "sample" certain words to determine the meaning of the passage and skip many others. They go back and read every word only when they encounter something unexpected.

5. *Reading is a thinking process.* The relationship between reading and thinking has been noted for a long time. In 1917, Thorndike likened the thinking process used in mathematics to that of reading.

> . . . understanding a paragraph is like solving a problem in mathematics. It consists in selecting the right elements of the situation and putting them together in the right relations, and also with the right amount of weight or influence or force for each. . . . all under the influence of the right mental set or purpose or demands. (p. 329)

Defining reading as thinking, Stauffer (1975) perceives reading as something akin to problem solving. As in problem solving, the reader must employ concepts, develop hypotheses, test them out, and modify those concepts. In this way, reading comprehension is a mode of inquiry, and methods that employ discovery techniques should be used in the teaching of reading. The key to teaching from this perspective is to guide students to set up their own questions and purposes of reading. Students then read to solve problems that they have devised for themselves. For example, a student is first encouraged to guess what will happen next in the story and then read to determine the accuracy of those predictions. This approach is called a *directed reading-thinking activity* and is described in the Teaching Strategies section of this chapter.

Integrating Specific Skills and Holistic Reading Approaches

The two approaches to teaching reading comprehension are complementary and must be combined for effective reading. Specific skills give direction to remedial instruction. The holistic approach stresses the reader's experience, motivation, and participation in reading. Eventually, the specific reading skills must be transferred and integrated into the whole reading act for effective reading (Jenkins & Pany, 1981). While good readers readily learn the subskills and then intuitively combine and integrate them, less accomplished readers may be still struggling to acquire specific reading skills and therefore using them in an unintegrated, splintered manner. It is important that reading instruction for learning-disabled students include methods of transferring and integrating specific reading skills into the whole reading act (Richek et al., 1983).

Assessing Reading

There are more methods and tests for assessing reading than for any other area of the curriculum. Reading can be assessed through formal tests (survey tests, diagnostic reading tests, and comprehensive test batteries) or by informal measures, such as the informal reading inventory, miscue analysis, word-list tests, teacher-made tests, and diagnostic teaching.

Formal Reading Tests

Many of the tests available for testing reading achievement are described in Appendix C. The following are among the most widely used reading tests:

Survey Tests   These are group tests that give an overall reading achievement level. These tests generally give at least two scores: word recognition and comprehension. *Gates-MacGinitie Reading Tests, Metropolitan Achievement Tests, SRA Achievement Tests.*

Diagnostic Reading Tests   These are individual tests that provide more in-depth information about the student's strengths and weaknesses in reading skills. *Durrell Analysis of Reading Difficulty, Gates-McKillop-Horowitz Reading Diagnostic Test, Spache Diagnostic Reading Scales, Woodcock Reading Mastery Test, Gray Oral Reading Test, Test of Reading Comprehension (TORC).*

Comprehensive Batteries   These are test batteries that measure several academic areas, including reading. *Peabody Individual Achievement Test (PIAT), Woodcock-Johnson Psychoeducational Battery: Reading, Wide-Range Achievement Tests (WRAT),* (Brigance) *Inventory of Basic Skills.*

Informal Reading Tests

Observation

One of the simplist methods of assessing reading is to observe informally as the student reads aloud. The teacher can readily detect the student's general reading level, word recognition abilities, the types of errors that are made, and whether the student seems to understand the material. This method is very practical and can be as informative as elaborate test batteries.

Informal Reading Inventory

The informal reading inventory (IRI), which can be quickly and easily administered, provides a wealth of information concerning reading skills, reading levels, types of errors, the student's techniques of attacking unknown words, and related behavioral characteristics (Johnson & Kress, 1965).

Briefly, the procedure of the informal reading inventory is as follows. The examiner chooses selections approximately one hundred words in length from a series of graded reading levels (or a commercial standard reading inventory can be selected). The student reads aloud from several graded levels while the teacher records the errors in a systematic manner. If more than five errors per hundred words are made, the student is given progressively easier selections until a level is found at which there are no more than two errors per hundred words. The student is asked four to ten questions about each selection to check comprehension. Using the following criteria, three reading levels can be determined through the use of an informal reading inventory.

1. *Independent reading level.* Criteria: The student is able to recognize about 95 percent of the words and answer 90 percent of the comprehension questions correctly. This is the level at which students are able to read library books independently or do reading work by themselves.
2. *Instructional reading level.* Criteria: The student is able to recognize about 90 percent of the words in the selection, with a comprehension score of about 70 percent. This is the reading level at which the student will profit from teacher-directed reading instruction.
3. *Frustration reading level.* Criteria: The student is able to recognize less than 90 percent of the words, with a comprehension score of less than 70 percent or less. This reading level is too difficult for the student who does not understand the material. It should not be used for instruction.

In addition to informal reading inventories developed by teachers, several commercial standard reading inventories are available and offer a convenient way to administer the reading inventory. They include the *Classroom Reading Inventory*, the *Standard Reading Inventory, Sucher-Allred Reading Placement Inventory*, and the *Spire Individual Reading Evaluation*. They are described in Appendix C.

A flow chart of the steps for administering and scoring the informal reading inventory (IRI) is shown in Figure 12.1. *The Informal Reading Inventory* (Richek et al., 1983, pp. 396–425) follows these steps and can also be used by teachers.

FIGURE 12.1
Flow Chart of the Steps in the Informal Reading Inventory (IRI)

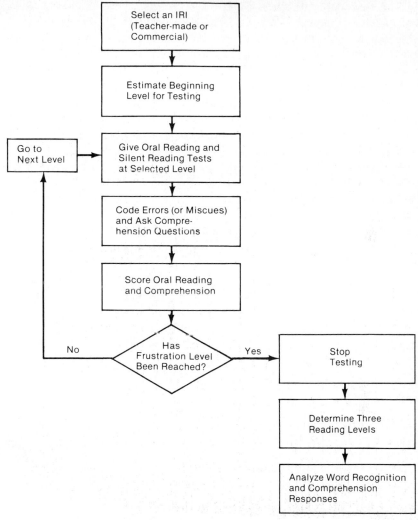

Source: Adapted from M. Richek, L. List, and J. Lerner, *Reading Problems: Diagnostic and Remediation* (Englewood Cliffs, NJ: Prentice-Hall, 1983).

Miscue Analysis of Oral Reading

Miscue analysis is a psycholinguistic approach to assessing oral reading. It was first suggested by Goodman (1967), who views reading as a psycholinguistic guessing game in which the reader's thought and language ability interact in anticipating what is to come. Miscues are the deviations from the printed text that the student makes while reading orally. These miscues (sometimes called errors) should be viewed as diagnostic opportunities because through them readers reveal their underlying language processes. In effect, the student's own underlying language patterns and structure may give rise to the deviation. The miscue may be a positive effort to preserve comprehension (Goodman, 1969; Goodman & Gollasch, 1980–81; Goodman, 1976).

Research with miscue analysis assessment shows that while more proficient readers do not necessarily make fewer oral reading deviations (or errors) than other readers, their miscues are of a different kind. The miscues of less proficient readers typically reflect errors of graphic information (for example, *want* for *what* but make little sense in the context of the passage as a whole. More accomplished readers, however, tend to make miscues that appear quite gross visually (for example, *car* for *automobile*) but retain the underlying meaning of the passage.

An interesting study of the psycholinguistic processes underlying reading was made by Beaver (1968). In this study, children were given material to read orally, and their errors in reading were carefully noted. Psycholinguistic analysis of the errors revealed that many were not phonic or phonological shortcomings. Most of the errors (about four-fifths of his sample) were other kinds of linguistic errors, such as morphological or syntactic errors. Beaver reasoned that the process going on when a person reads is not only decoding, but also a kind of retroactive encoding. A reader scans the syntactic structure of the sentence, passes the whole back through his or her own grammar or language rules, and then interprets it within his or her own grammar or language system. However, the reader's own language system may not correspond to the actual syntactic system of the text. Below are some examples of such errors.

> Text: I am Tiphia, servant *to* Mighty Gwump.
> Reader: I am Tiphia, servant *of* Mighty Gwump.

> Text: Now he had been *caught*.
> Reader: Now he had been *catched*.

> Text: Bobby's team *was* the Wildcats.
> Reader: Bobby's team *were* the Wildcats.

> Text: I *have taken* the book.
> Reader: I *has took* the book.

Such studies suggest that a reader not only must decode the words and language of the writer, but also *re*code the ideas into his or her own language pattern to get meaning. The errors are not in decoding the author's language but in recoding it into the reader's linguistic patterns.

A commercial instrument, the *Reading Miscue Inventory* (Goodman & Burke, 1972), contains passages and scoring sheets to help teachers use miscue analysis assessment procedures for analyzing a student's oral reading (see Appendix C).

■ Teaching Strategies

This section, presenting reading methods and materials for teaching students with learning disabilities, is organized as follows: (1) *adaptations of standard reading methods*, which can be very effective if appropriate modifications are made; (2) *special remedial approaches*, or methods designed especially for students with reading difficulties; (3) *methods for teaching reading comprehension*, which include comprehension strategies from several perspectives of reading; and (4) *methods for dealing with special reading problems.*

Teachers of learning-disabled students should be familiar with the standard reading methods, know how to modify them, and be competent in special remedial strategies (Richek et al., 1983).

Adaptations of Standard Approaches to the Teaching of Reading

Methods and materials intended for students progressing normally in reading can be successfully adapted for learning-disabled students. Such adaptations include increasing the amount of repetition, allotting more time for the completion of work, providing more examples or activities, providing more review, introducing the work more slowly, expanding the background information, providing more work on vocabulary development, and using different standard books and materials than the student has previously used. Sometimes a standard method seems to work because it is taught at another time, in another place, or by a different teacher—perhaps one who has the magic clinical touch. In general, the standard approach with appropriate changes should be tried first (Richek et al., 1983; Kirk, Klieban & Lerner, 1978). Several standard methods are reviewed below—basal readers, phonics, linguistics, the language experience approach, and individualized reading—and the use of computers for teaching reading is also discussed.

Basal Reading Series

Basal readers are a sequential and interrelated set of books and supportive materials intended to provide the basic material for the development of fundamental reading skills. A basal reading series consists of graded readers that gradually increase in difficulty, typically beginning with very simple readiness and first-grade books and going through the sixth- or eighth-grade level. The books increase in difficulty in vocabulary, story content, and skill development. Most basal reading series assume an eclectic approach to the teaching of reading, incorporating *many* procedures to teach readiness, vocabulary, word recognition, comprehension, and the enjoyment of literature.

The basal reader, as the major tool of reading instruction for the past forty years, has been the target of continual criticism from diverse groups, including professors of education, scholars from other academic disciplines, the popular press, parent groups, political observers, moralists, and, most recently, ethnic and women's groups. Critics have scoffed at and satirized the language, phonics presentation, story content, class appeal, pictures, qualities, and environment of the characters of the basal reader. In spite of this highly vocal and severe criticism of the basal reader, its acceptance in the classroom has been widespread. Surveys have found the basal reader to be the major tool for reading instruction in most of the elementary classrooms throughout the country (Harris & Sipay, 1980).

Because most basal readers are not committed to any one teaching procedure, changes can occur readily. Publishers are continually making modifications in response to the demands of the times and their consumer market. Recent trends in basal readers have been to introduce phonics earlier and to make the teaching of phonics more obvious; to introduce formal reading earlier; to have readiness and kindergarten books introduce more formal aspects of the reading program than they once did—such as letters and sight words; to make stories longer and more sophisticated; and to have the stories describe many ethnic groups and ways of life.

There are also series of readers especially produced for remedial instruction. The following sets of books are designed for high interest but easier reading level. The names of the series and their publishers, as well as the reading levels (RL), are listed below:

> Alike but Different (Learning Trends, Globe), RL 1–2
> Getting It Together (Science Research Associates), RL 2–6
> High Action Reading Series (Modern Curriculum Press), RL 2–6
> Intrigue Series (Benefic Press), RL 2–4
> Key Text (The Economy Company), RL 1–8
> McCall-Crabbs Standard Test Lessons in Reading, RL 3–8
> Mini Units in Reading (Globe), RL 4–6
> Moving Along Series (Benefic Press), RL 1.5–4.5
> The New Cornerstone Readers (Addison-Wesley), RL 1–4
> The New Kaleidoscope Readers (Addison-Wesley), RL 2–7
> The New Open Highways Program (Scott, Foresman), RL 1–8
> New Practice Readers (Webster/McGraw-Hill), RL 2–6
> Reader's Digest New Reading Skill Builders (Reader's Digest Services), RL 1–6
> Reading for Concepts (Webster/McGraw-Hill), RL 1.6–6.7
> Spanish Reading Keys (The Economy Company), RL 1–3
> Sprint Reading Skills Program (Scholastic Book Services), RL 2.0–4.0
> SRA Reading Laboratories (Science Research Associates), RL 1–9
> Triple Take (Reader's Digest Services), RL 3–8

FIGURE 12.2
Example of Phonics Exercises

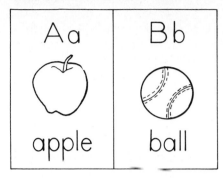
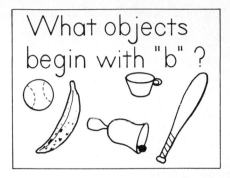

Phonics Methods

Phonics systems and phonics books have also been on the market for over fifty years. The availability of multimedia has enabled old wine to be put into new bottles. Old phonics materials are being reproduced as transparencies, preprinted duplicating masters for duplication, filmstrips, charts, recordings, audiotapes, and computer software packages. Typically, the phonics method is synthetic rather than analytic. First, students learn isolated letters and their sound equivalents; then they blend, or synthesize, these individual elements into whole words. Typical exercises in phonic materials appear in Figure 12.2. Some of the widely used phonics programs are listed below.

> *Keys to Reading* (The Economy Company)
> *Phonovisual Program* (Phonovisual Products, Inc.)
> *Building Reading Skills* (McCormick Mathers Publishing)
> *New Phonics Skilltexts* (Charles E. Merrill)
> *Phonics We Use* (Riverside Publishing Co.)
> *Learning About Words Series* (Bureau of Publications, Teachers College, Columbia University)
> *Speech-to-Print Phonics* (Harcourt Brace Jovanovich)
> *Breaking the Code* (Open Court)
> *Wordland Series* (Continental Press)

Linguistic Approach

The linguistic approach to reading defines learning to read as essentially a decoding process. This view assumes that children coming to school have already mastered oral language; their reading task is learning to decipher the relationship between the written letter and the phoneme sound in order to respond to the printed marks with the appropriate sounds of speech. Reading, then, within this framework, is decoding the phoneme-grapheme relationship. The linguistic approach to reading emphasizes phonology, or the sound system of the English language. Morphology, syntax, and semantics are considered less critical.

The developers of the linguistic approach to reading reason that children who have already learned to make generalizations about the phonemes or sound elements of oral language should, in a similar way, learn to make generalizations about the written letter symbols that represent speech sounds. Reading is introduced by carefully selecting for the initial reading experiences only those words having a consistent and regular spelling pattern. Words that use a consonant-vowel-consonant (CVC) pattern are presented as whole words, and students are expected to learn the code by making generalizations through minimal contrasts of sounds in the words selected. For example, the student is to make a generalization concerning the short "a" sound by learning words in print such as:

can	Nan	van
fan	Dan	pan
man	tan	ran

These carefully selected, regularly spelled words are then strung together to make sentences. For example (Bloomfield & Barnhart, 1963, p. 22):

Nan can fan Dan.
Can Dan fan Nan?
Dan can fan Nan.
Nan, fan Dan.
Dan, fan Nan.

This linguistic approach differs from the phonics method in that the letters and sound equivalents are not presented in isolation to be blended into whole words, but the letters are embedded in words with regular spelling patterns so that the learner can make generalizations about minimal contrast elements. Some materials based on this linguistic approach are

The Palo Alto Reading Program (Harcourt Brace)
Merrill Linguistic Readers (Charles E. Merrill)
SRA Basic Reading Series (Science Research Associates)
Visual-Linguistic Basic Reading Series (Educational Services Press)
The Structural Reading Series (L. W. Singer)
Miami Linguistic Readers (D. C. Heath)
Linguistic Readers (Harper & Row)
Let's Read (Clarence L. Barnhart)

Language Experience Approach

The language experience method is based on a view of reading as an integrated extension of language arts. The development of reading skills is linked with the development of the skills of listening, speaking, and writing. The raw

FIGURE 12.3
Language Experience Chart

We went to the circus.
We saw a lion.
We saw a monkey.
We saw a clown.

materials are the experiences and language of the student. The student begins by dictating stories to the teacher. These are written down by the teacher, and they become the basis of the student's first reading experiences. According to Allen (1976), the language experience approach to reading permits the student to conceptualize as follows about written material:

What I can think about, I can talk about.
What I can say, I can write (or someone can write for me).
What I can write, I can read.
I can read what others write for me to read.

There is no predetermined, rigid control over vocabulary, syntax, or content, and the teacher uses the raw materials of the reading matter that the student composes to develop reading skills. This approach to reading has a vitality and immediacy, as well as an element of creativity, that have proven useful both in the beginning-to-read stage with young children and in corrective work with older pupils. The interest of the student is high because the emphasis is on reading material that grows out of the student's experiences and the student's natural language in expressing these experiences. This approach is initially very dependent on the visual modality and visual memory for words, de-emphasizing the structured development of phonological skills.

An example of a language experience chart is shown in Figure 12.3.

Individualized Reading

The goal of the individualized reading program is to assure that each student within the classroom is reading in books suited to individual needs. No one set of instructional material is likely to work well for an entire class or even for all members of a reading group within a class. With this method, each student selects his or her personal interests and level and has the opportunity to read at the appropriate rate.

An important feature of the method is the individual conference between the student and the teacher. At this conference, the student reads aloud and discusses the book with the teacher. Records concerning the student's reading material, level of performance, and strengths and weaknesses in reading skills are kept by the teacher from information gathered at the conference. The teacher can then plan activities to build and develop the skills the student lacks.

Individualized reading builds on the student's own interests and enthusiasm. This method has proved to be particularly successful with those who do not do well in a group situation and promotes an unmeasurable, but highly desirable, positive attitude toward reading.

In addition to reading library books and trade books in individualized reading programs, buying one's own paperback books and membership in paperback book clubs have both proved to be fruitful approaches to individualized reading programs. Fader and Schaevitz (1966) described one such program, in which paperback books were used to bring the pleasure of reading to delinquent boys.

Computer Instruction in Reading

Computers as an aid in teaching learning-disabled students are discussed in several contexts in this book (Chapters 2, 6, 14); the discussion here focuses on the computer's use in reading. The first computer-assisted instruction programs tried in the schools were developed by Atkinson and Fletcher (1972) to teach beginning reading skills. These computer programs were designed for use with the large mainframe computers and intended to supplement classroom instruction. When first graders used them for about twelve minutes a day for five months, they achieved significantly higher reading scores, according to the research reports. Some schools today still rely on these computer-assisted reading programs.

However, since most teachers did not have access to expensive large mainframe computers, the use of the programs was limited. The rapid development of the microcomputer in the last few years changed the situation. Most of the schools now have some microcomputers available and their use for teaching reading is increasing. Kuchinskas (1983) suggests that microcomputers have the following applications in the reading program:

> *Drill and practice programs*   Computers have the patience and endurance to offer repeated drill and practice sessions. For these programs, the student should have already been taught the basic concept or skill; the computer is then an excellent tool to provide review, reinforcement, and practice.

Tutorial programs   These computer programs provide instruction of specific skills, giving students who need repeated instruction the opportunity to have a skill re-taught several times. These programs will typically provide constant feedback so that the students will know how they are doing.

Testing programs   Some computer programs are essentially testing programs and do not include any instruction. An assessment may be made after a certain unit of work is completed. In some of these programs, the assessment results are known to the teacher but not to the student.

Generation of cloze passages   Microcomputers have the capability of producing passages with a variety of types of deletions. Such programs could help the teacher develop cloze material for the student with designated deletions.

Vocabulary lists   The computer could be programmed to generate vocabulary lists based on designated parameters. For example, it could generate lists of words at a specified difficulty level, or on a certain subject area, or on a particular reading selection.

The full potential of the microcomputer is still unknown because it is so new. At present, we do know that many students enjoy working with the machine, schools are rapidly purchasing equipment, and software programs are mushrooming. Learning disabilities teachers certainly should become aware of this new teaching tool.

Teachers do not have to understand programming or the computer's inner workings to be able to use easily commercially prepared programs (software packages). Many learning-disabled students enjoy practicing reading skills with the microcomputer because (1) it provides individual instruction; (2) it provides nonthreatening feedback and corrective procedures immediately and continually; (3) it has infinite patience, providing the opportunity for as much drill and repetition as the student needs and wants; and (4) it can provide large amounts of skills-oriented practice.

There are several types of software that can be purchased (Indiana Department of Public Instruction, 1984):

Ready-to-run programs. These commercial programs are complete and ready to use. All the teacher or student has to do is insert the diskette into the drive and turn on the machine, and the lessons appear on the monitor. Many companies are developing commercial ready-to-run software packages, and selecting good programs is not easy. Journals such as the *Reading Teacher* and the *Journal of Learning Disabilities* review microcomputer ready-to-run software packages for teaching reading. Also, it is useful to attend computer conferences to learn about software packages. Some teachers have organized computer users groups to share information about good software packages. Before selecting a program, it is necessary to know whether the software package will run on the kind of computer that is in the school (i.e., Apple II, II +, IIe; TRS-80; Commodore 64; Atari 400 or 800; IBM PC, Jr.).

Shell programs. These programs provide a framework within which the teacher can add a customized curriculum. For example, teachers can write in the vocabulary words they want the students to learn. These programs are more personalized and can be made to individually fit a student or class. One shell program available is *Wizworks* (DLM). This can be used in reading and mathematics and is particularly useful with adolescents.

Authoring programs. These programs allow the teacher to write instructional programs. Though they are the most difficult to use, they can be tailored to the specific needs of a student or a class.

Special Remedial Approaches to the Teaching of Reading

The methods discussed in this section are considered special approaches that are not typically used in the regular class but have been designed for the student with reading problems. The methods we shall describe are VAKT, represented by the Fernald method and the Gilligham method, Distar, Rebus, programmed reading, Glass Analysis, the neurological impress method, repeated readings, the Hegge-Kirk-Kirk Remedial Reading Drills, and the initial teaching alphabet.

VAKT

Several methods of teaching reading are built on the premise that stimulation of several avenues of sensory input reinforces learning. In these methods, kinesthetic and tactile stimulation is emphasized along with the auditory and visual modalities. These methods utilize tracing in teaching and are often referred to as VAKT (visual-auditory-kinesthetic-tactile) methods. The tracing is usually performed by having the student trace a word or letter that has been written on a strip of paper about four inches by ten inches in large script and printing. The student traces the word with a finger in contact with the paper. To increase the tactile and kinesthetic sensation, sandpaper letters, sand or clay trays, or fingerpaints have been used for tracing activities.

In learning a word in the VAKT technique, students (1) see the word, (2) hear the teacher say the word, (3) say the word themselves, (4) hear themselves say the word, (5) feel the muscle movement as they trace the word, (6) feel the tactile surface under their fingertips, (7) see their hands move as they trace, and (8) hear themselves say the word as they trace it.

Two methods of teaching reading that emphasize the tactile and kinesthetic modalities are the *Fernald method* (Fernald, 1943) and the *Gillingham method* (Gillingham & Stillman, 1966). Although both of these methods stress tracing, they are quite different in their approach to teaching. In the Fernald method the student learns a word as a total pattern, tracing the entire word, and thereby strengthening the memory and visualization of the entire word. The Gillingham method, in contrast, uses the tracing technique to teach individual letters.

The Fernald Method

Fernald (1943) developed a multisensory approach to reading that simultaneously involves four sensory avenues: visual, auditory, kinesthetic, and tactile. The words to be learned are selected from stories that the student has dictated. The method consists of four stages.

In Stage 1, the teacher writes the word to be learned on paper with a crayon. The student then traces the word with his or her fingers making contact with the paper (using both tactile and kinesthetic senses). As the student traces it, the teacher says the word so that the student hears it (thus using the auditory sense). This process is repeated until the student can write the word correctly without looking at the sample. When that task is accomplished, the word is placed in a file box. Words thus learned are accumulated in the box until the student writes a story using the words. The story is then typed so the student can read his or her own story. In Stage 2, the student is no longer required to trace each word, but learns each new word by looking at the teacher's written copy of the word, saying it to himself or herself, and writing it. In Stage 3, the student learns new words by looking at a printed word and repeating it internally before writing it. At this point, the student may begin reading from books. Finally, in Stage 4, the student is able to recognize new words from their similarity to printed words or parts of words previously learned. Thus, the student can generalize the knowledge acquired through the reading skills. The uniqueness of the Fernald method is most evident in Stage 1.

The Gillingham Method

The Gillingham method is an outgrowth of the Orton theory of reading disability (Orton, 1937). It is a highly structured approach requiring five lessons a week for a minimum of two years. The initial activities focus on the learning of individual letter sounds and blending. The student uses a tracing technique to learn single letters and their sound equivalents. These single sounds are later combined into larger groupings and then into short words.

Simultaneous spelling tasks are also part of this technique; while writing the letters, the students say both the sounds of the letters in sequence and the letter names. The method emphasizes phonics and depends on a formal sequence of learning. Independent reading is delayed until the major part of the phonics program has been covered. A variation of the Gillingham method is offered by Slingerland (1976), who provides an extensive set of materials. Another adaptation is the *Recipe for Reading* (Traub & Bloom, 1970), which is accompanied by twenty-one supplementary readers.

Reading Mastery: DISTAR

The *Reading Mastery: DISTAR* Reading Program (Englemann & Bruner, 1984) consists of Books I and II of the SRA Reading Mastery basal reader series. It is a highly structured decoding program that requires following a very specific step-by-step procedure. It emphasizes directed instruction, drill, and repetition. There are three types of Distar programs: one for language, one for arithmetic, and one for reading.

In *Reading Mastery: DISTAR*, the teacher is given specific procedures and oral instruction to say throughout each step of the program. Pupil instruction is given in small groups for thirty-minute periods, five times per week. Skill mastery in the program is measured by criterion-referenced tests. If a student has not mastered the skill, special additional lessons are provided. The *Reading Mastery: DISTAR* Reading Program uses a synthetic phonics approach, and the students are first taught the prerequisite skill of auditory blending to help them combine isolated sounds into words. In addition, the shape of some alphabet letters is modified so that they provide clues to the letter sounds. For example, the letters of the digraph "th" are connected so that it is clear to the student that they are one sound. The silent "e" at the end of a word is written smaller than the rest of the letters to emphasize that it is not pronounced. The special alphabet of Distar is gradually phased out as the student progresses.

The *Reading Mastery: DISTAR* Reading Program is a complete reading program, contains both isolated drills and instructional reading. It follows a behavioral management approach, progressing in small steps, and uses specified teacher praise as reinforcement. Criterion-referenced tests monitor progress. The teacher is guided in specific procedures and oral instructions through each step of the program. Research reviews on *Reading Mastery: DISTAR* are reported by Bateman (1979) and Becker and Carnine (1980).

A sample *Reading Mastery: DISTAR* Reading Program page is shown in Figure 12.4.

The *SRA Corrective Reading Program, Decoding* (Englemann, Becker, Hanner, & Johnson, 1980) is based on the Distar concepts but is geared toward the older student (grades four through twelve). The program develops primary and intermediate reading skills using material of interest to the older student. As with the *Reading Mastery: DISTAR* Reading Program, instruction is constructed and guided very carefully. Materials include a teacher's management and skill manual, presentation books, and assessment materials. Students use stories, student contracts, and progress charts. There is a companion SRA Corrective Reading Program, which concentrates on comprehension.

FIGURE 12.4
Sample *Reading Mastery*: DISTAR Reading Program selection

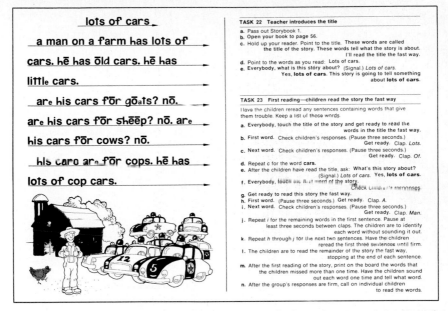

Source: From the *Reading Mastery Series Guide*, by Steve Osborn, for the *Reading Mastery Series* program by Seigfried Engelmann, et al. Copyright © Science Research Associates, Inc. 1984. Reprinted by permission of the publisher.

The Rebus Approach

Another attempt to simplify the initial stages of learning to read relies on rebus symbols. A rebus is a picture or a symbol that suggests the word it represents and is used in reading material in place of certain printed words. For example, in the Peabody Rebus Reading Program, the printed word *be* is represented by a picture of a bumblebee. As the program progresses, the symbols are gradually replaced with printed words. An illustration from the Peabody Reading Program is shown in Figure 12.5.

Programmed Reading Instruction

A few programmed materials are available for teaching reading. These materials are designed to be self-instructional and self-corrective. The concept behind the programmed materials is that the learning process is enhanced because the material is individualized and self-teaching and provides instant reinforcement. The subject matter is presented in small, discrete, sequential steps, or "frames," containing a single question or instruction. The student responds to the question and then checks the answer to see if it is correct before proceeding to the next frame. Programmed reading series include

FIGURE 12.5
Example of Rebus Reading

THE   DOG   CAT   TABLE   BOX   ON   IN   UNDER   IS

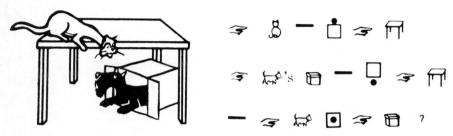

Source: Sample rebus vocabulary and passage from *Peabody Rebus Reading Program* (Circle Pines, MN: American Guidance Services, Inc.).

Sullivan Reading (Behavioral Reading Laboratories) and *Programmed Reading* (Webster/McGraw-Hill).

Glass Analysis

Glass Analysis is a method for teaching reading through the decoding of letter clusters within words (Glass, 1973). The method makes certain assumptions about the function of decoding in reading. First, the processes of decoding and reading are clearly separated. *Decoding* is defined as the act of correctly determining the accepted sound connected with a printed word. *Reading*, on the other hand, is defined as the act of deriving meaning from the printed word. Second, decoding precedes reading. If the student does not learn to decode efficiently, the student will not learn to read.

Through *Glass Analysis*, the student is guided to recognize common letter clusters easily and quickly while looking at the whole word. The method concentrates on intensive auditory and visual training focused on the word being studied (Glass, 1973; Glass & Burton, 1973). The materials needed to teach recognition of letter clusters can be made by the teacher. Essentially, they consist of flash cards about three inches by six inches in size. Commercially published materials are available from Easier-to-Learn Materials (see Appendix D). On each card, the teacher prints a carefully selected word within the student's vocabulary. *Letter clusters* are defined as two or more letters that, in a whole word, represent a relatively consistent sound.

For example in the word *catch*, the clusters are *at* and *ch*; in *play*, the clusters are *pl* and *ay*; in *standard*, the clusters may be *st, an*, or *and*, and *ar* or *ard* (Glass, 1973).

Glass specifies four steps to teach each word:

1. Identify the whole word and the letters and sound of the target clusters.
2. Pronounce the sound or sounds, and ask the child for the letter or letters.
3. Give the letter or letters, and ask for the sound or sounds.
4. Take away letters, and ask for the remaining sound.

The teacher is advised not to separate letters in a blend, digraph, or vowel cluster; to avoid covering up any part of the whole word; and to make sure that the student never sees less than the entire word.

The following is an example of specific instructions recommended to teach the word *song* (Glass, 1973):

> The child is shown the word *song* on the card.
> The teacher asks, "In the word *song*, what sound does the letter *s* make? What sound does the *ong* make? If I took off the *s*, what sound would be left? What is the whole word? (p. 27)

According to Glass, this method shapes perception by studying and teaching whole words in a way that will help the students when they see other words containing the same letter clusters. The students respond visually as well as auditorily to letter clusters. Glass suggests that this is what all successful decoders do—recollect how letters cluster into whole words. The method is firmly based on the concept of clustering.

Neurological Impress Method

The *neurological impress method* is an approach to the teaching of reading for students with severe reading disabilities (Heckelman, 1969; Langford, Slade, & Barnett, 1974). It is a system of unison reading by the student and the instructor at a rapid pace. The student sits slightly in front of the instructor and both read together, the voice of the instructor being directed into the ear of the student at a fairly close range. The student or teacher uses a finger as a locator as the words are read, and the finger should be at the location of the spoken word. At times, the instructor may be louder and faster than the student and at other times the instructor may read more softly than the reading voice of the student, who may lag slightly behind. No preliminary preparations are made with the reading material before the student sees it. The object is simply to cover as many pages of reading material as possible within the time available without causing fatigue to the student. The theory underlying the method is that the auditory process of feedback from the reader's own voice and the voice of someone else reading the same material establishes a new learning process.

Repeated Readings

This method provides repeated practice in oral reading to improve reading fluency. It is a supplementary technique to use with slow, halting readers who identify most words in a passage accurately. The method involves the selection of passages fifty to two hundred words long at a difficulty level that enables the reader to recognize most of the words. The student then reads the selection orally three or four times before proceeding to a new passage. Word accuracy rates and reading speed are usually reported to the student after each reading, and daily practice is recommended. Moyer (1983) reports that the method seems to be effective in increasing fluency for some slow readers. According to one study, learning-disabled students enjoy doing repeated reading when the passages are displayed on a microcomputer screen. The computer program generated the reading passages from a large selection placed in memory (Indiana Department of Public Instruction, 1984).

Hegge-Kirk-Kirk Remedial Reading Drills

These reading drills consist of words with a consistent phonic pattern for the student to read (Hegge, Kirk, & Kirk, 1965). The child simply reads across the page words that have been arranged in four parts. Part I introduces the most frequent sounds, including short vowels and consonants; Part II consists of certain combinations of the previously learned sounds; Part III presents less frequently used sounds in whole words; and Part IV provides supplementary exercises. The drills are based on the principles of minimal change, one response to one symbol, repetition, and social reinforcement. This method has proved successful with students who had failed to profit from various conventional school methods. Figure 12.6 shows a sample page from the Hegge-Kirk-Kirk Remedial Reading Drills.

Initial Teaching Alphabet (i.t.a.)

The initial teaching alphabet is an attempt to provide a medium that will make spelling as regular as possible. The i.t.a. alphabet consists of forty-four characters, each representing a different phoneme. The symbols of the conventional alphabet have been augmented for those phonemes having no letters of their own in traditional orthography, for example, *sh, ch, th*. Certain letters of the alphabet, such as *q* and *x*, have been eliminated because they have sound equivalents represented by other letters. Capital letters, or uppercase letters, have been eliminated to reduce confusion (Tanyzer & Mazurkiewicz, 1967). A sample selection written in i.t.a. is shown in Figure 12.7.

With normal reading growth, the transition to the conventional alphabet (traditional orthography, or t.o.) is planned for the beginning of the second year in the i.t.a. basal series.

FIGURE 12.6
Sample Remedial Reading Drill

PART I.   Introductory Sounds

Drill 1

a

s a t	m a t	r a t	b a t	c a t	f a t
c a p	s a p	m a p	t a p	l a p	r a p
a m	r a m	S a m	h a m	d a m	j a m
r a g	b a g	t a g	w a g	h a g	l a g
c a n	m a n	r a n	t a n	f a n	p a n
s a d	m a d	h a d	l a d	p a d	d a d

s a t	s a p	S a m	s a d
m a p	m a n	m a d	m a t
t a n	t a p	t a g	t a x
c a b	c a t	c a p	c a n
b a g	b a d	b a n	b a t
h a t	h a m	h a g	h a d
r a p	r a t	r a n	r a g
l a d	l a p	f a n	f a t

s a t	m a n	f a t	t a n	p a t	b a n
m a p	c a n	m a d	c a t	m a n	c a b
r a g	c a t	l a p	h a m	b a t	t a p
j a m	f a n	d a m	h a d	t a g	r a p

sat	cap	rag	can	sad	mat	sap
ram	bag	man	mad	rat	map	Sam
tag	ran	had	bat	tap	ham	wag
tan	lad	cat	lap	dam	hag	fan
pad	fat	rap	jam	lag	pan	dad

Source: From T. G. Hegge, Samuel A. Kirk, and Winifred Kirk. *Remedial Reading Drills* (Ann Arbor, MI: George Wahr Publishing Co., 1965).

FIGURE 12.7
Sample Selection Written in i.t.a.

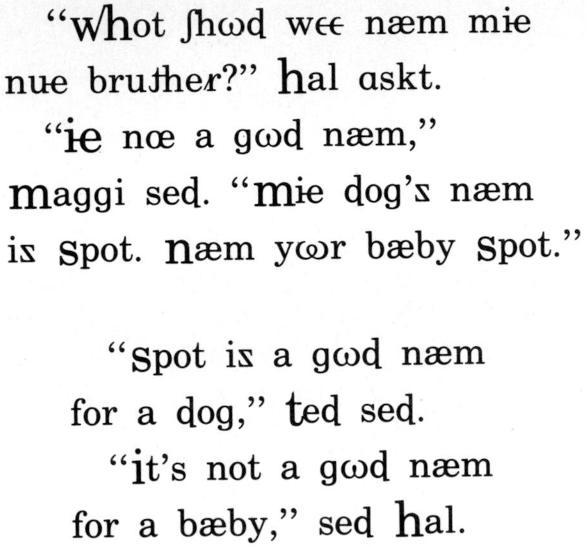

"whot ʃhɷd wee næm mie
nue bruⱦheɾ?" hal ɑskt.
"ie nœ a gɷd næm,"
maggi sed. "mie dog'ꝛ næm
iꝛ Ʂpot. næm yɷr bæby Ʂpot."

"Ʂpot iꝛ a gɷd næm
for a dog," ted sed.
"it's not a gɷd næm
for a bæby," sed hal.

Source: From *Pitman i/t/a Early-to-Read Program* by Mazurkiewicz and
Tanzer. Copyright © 1967 by Pitman Learning, Inc. Reprinted by permission of the publisher.

Teaching Reading Comprehension

Many of the standard and remedial methods already discussed teach reading
comprehension, and this section presents some additional instruction strategies.

Meaning Vocabulary and Concepts

The student's knowledge of vocabulary and ability to understand the concepts
of words are closely related to reading achievement, and limited vocabulary
development can seriously hamper reading comprehension (Anderson &
Freebody, 1981). As words become more abstract, the concepts become
more difficult to grasp for some learning-disabled students.

Concepts are commonly explained as ideas, abstractions, or knowing the
essence of things. For example, the concept of *chair* refers to an idea, an
abstraction, or a symbol of concrete experiences. A person's experiences
may have included exposure to a specific rocking chair, an upholstered chair,
and a baby's high chair, but the concept *chair* symbolizes a set of attributes
about "chairness." The word *chair* allows a person to make an inference

about new experiences with chairs, such as a lawn chair, observed for the first time. The word or concept of *chair*, by itself, does not have an empirical reference point.

At a still more abstract level, words become further removed from concrete referents. The concept *chair* is part of a broader concept of *furniture*. Concepts even more removed from the sensory world are ideas such as *democracy, loyalty, fairness,* or *freedom.*

A further confusion in school learning is related to the fact that important concepts are presented as technical terms in textbooks: *plateau, continental divide, density of population, pollution, the law of gravity, monopoly.* Problems in reading in the content areas are frequently due not to the difficulty of the words, but to the concentration and compactness of the presentation of the concepts.

Although it is possible to form concepts without words, language plays an important role in concept development, and a language problem is likely to be reflected in faulty conceptual abilities, limiting vocabulary development. When a student's concepts are meager, imprecise, or inaccurate, it becomes difficult to comprehend a reading passage. Illustrations of the consequences of imprecise concept development are given in the "Case Examples–Misunderstanding of Concepts."

CASE EXAMPLES

Misunderstanding of Concepts

• Some students confuse one attribute of an object with the concept of the object. For example, Paula could not understand the circular concept of the roundness of a plate. When told that the plate was "round" and asked to circle along its edges, Paula said. "That's not round; that's a dish." Some students confuse the concept of an object with its name. When Paula was asked if the moon could be called by another name, such as "cow," she responded, "No, because the moon doesn't give milk."

• The following example illustrates the consequences of the misunderstanding of a symbol that conveys multiple concepts. Nine-year-old Susie came home from school in tears with a medical form from the school nurse advising her parents to take their daughter for an eye examination. The child sobbed that the cause of her anguish was not that she needed eyeglasses, but that the blank next to the word SEX on the examination form had been filled in by the nurse with an "F." That symbol "F" conveyed the concept of a grade, and Susie feared she had failed sex.

• Often, students will deal with their inability to understand a concept by ignoring it. By failing to read a word they do not know, they may change the entire meaning of a passage. One high school student thought the school was using pornographic material because the people described in the following passage were nude: "The pilgrims did not wear gaudy clothes." Since the boy did not know the meaning of the word *gaudy*, he simply eliminated it from the sentence.

• A small group of learning-disabled adolescents who made cookies in a home economics class were puzzled when their cookies stuck to the baking pan. They explained to their teacher that they had followed instructions by greasing the "bottom" of the pan. The concept of "bottom" meant underside to them, and the part of the pan on which they put the cookies seemed to them to be the "top" of the pan.

Strategies for Expanding Vocabulary

1. ***Multiple word meanings.*** Multiple meanings of words often cause confusion in reading. For example, there are many meanings of the word *note*. In music, *note* means the elliptical character in a certain position on the music staff. In arithmetic or business, a *note* might mean a written promise to pay. In English or study hall, a *note* might refer to an informal written communication. In social studies, a *note* might refer to a formal communiqué between the heads of two nations. In science, one might be able to *note* results of an experiment, meaning to observe them. In English class, the selection of literature might discuss an individual who was a person of great *note*, or importance, in the community. In any lesson, the student could be asked to make *note* of an examination date, meaning to remember it. The teacher could make a *note*, meaning a remark, in the margin of the paper. In material on England, paper money may be called a *bank note*. The student who could not hold the various concepts of this word in mind would have trouble understanding many areas of the curriculum. Highlighting multiple meanings through dictionary games, sentence-completion exercises and class discussion can be important in helping students develop an awareness of one word's different meanings.

2. ***Providing concrete experiences.*** To build vocabulary and develop concepts for reading, students need concrete experiences with words. A first step is to provide students with primary experiences with actual referents. The next step is to encourage and assist students to draw conclusions from their experiences. As they progress to more advanced stages, teachers can foster skills of classifying, summarizing, and generalizing.

3. ***Sources for vocabulary.*** Since vocabulary is woven into every phase of our lives, new words can be drawn from any aspect of a student's experience: television, sports, newspapers, advertising, science, and so on. Many students enjoy keeping lists of new words learned and developing word books.

The Now Society

©Chronicle Publishing Co. 1974

5-22

"It burn. It bright. I call it 'wheel.' "

Source: Reprinted by permission of Chronicle Features.

4. ***Vocabulary through classification.*** Another way to learn new words is to attach them to known words. Much vocabulary growth takes place in this manner. Vertical vocabulary expansion involves taking a known word and breaking it down into categories. For example, students take the concept *dog* and break it into many species (*collie, terrier, cocker spaniel*). Horizontal vocabulary growth refers to enrichment and differentiation. Children may first call all animals "dogs." Then they learn to distinguish cats, horses, and other creatures.

Language Emphasis Strategies

The following methods emphasize the holistic, language, and meaning aspects of reading.

1. ***The directed reading-thinking activity.***   Stauffer (1975) asserts
   that the cognitive processes in reading are best taught through the directed reading-thinking activity (DR-TA). Pointing to the many similarities between reading and thinking, he concludes that reading
   should be taught as a thinking activity. Both reading and thinking require
   a context to be read or thought about, both embody the dynamics of
   discovery, and both entail a systematic examination of ideas.

   Reading, like thinking is in continual change. At every turning of a page, or
   even a phrase, the reader has to take into account the context—its parts, its
   problems, its perplexities. From these he must be able to follow the threads of
   a plot that point the way toward the plot end. Or, he must follow the course of
   ideas in nonfiction that lead to an outcome or solution. He must assess what
   he finds, weigh it, accept or reject it, or alter his objectives.
       It is apparent, therefore, that both reading and thinking start with a state
   of doubt or of desire. It is apparent also that the process of reconstruction
   goes on as inquiry or discovery, until the doubt is resolved, the perplexity
   settled, or the pleasure attained. (Stauffer, 1969, p. 38)

       Within such an approach, teaching reading becomes a way of teach-
   ing thinking. The important questions the teacher asks in directing the
   process are what do you think, why do you think so, and can you prove
   it? The emphasis in the DR-TA is on pupil thinking. The goals are to teach
   pupils (a) to examine, (b) to hypothesize, (c) to find proof, (d) to sus-
   pend judgment, and (e) to make decisions.
2. ***Written conversations.***   Instead of saying what they wish to communicate, students can write it and then read what they have written, sharing
   it with the teacher or other students. The responses should also be
   written (Goodman & Burke, 1980). People who surreptitiously sent small
   folded notes to their friends when they were adolescents in junior high
   school will remember what fun that was.
3. ***Listening opportunities.***   By listening to the teacher reading or to an
   audiotape, students can learn the structure of language, build vocabulary,
   and learn about books and stories. They can also follow the text in the
   book while listening.
4. ***Using themes.***   The theme approach requires the teacher to find a topic
   that interests the student and then gather reading material on that topic.
   By capturing the student's interest, the teacher encourages an active
   involvement in the reading, and lessons can build on the student's background knowledge and experience.
5. ***Providing extensive reading practice.***   Often so much time is
   spent on remedial lessons, learning skills, drill, and practice, that not
   enough time is devoted to reading itself. Students cannot learn to read by
   using a paper and pencil. Time must be planned for sustained reading
   and for reading for enjoyment.

6. **Using materials without words.** To foster the comprehension in reading, the teacher can use materials that do not have words, such as comic books without captions, silent films, and books of photographs. The students first figure out the story content from the pictures and films; then they make the transition to printed words. Once the students understand the material, words become meaningful. The students could even write their own dialogue.

7. **Cloze procedure.** A technique called the "cloze procedure" has been used by some reading researchers to discover the psycholinguistic processes underlying the reading act (Jongsma, 1971; Bormuth, 1968). The cloze procedure is based on the Gestalt idea of closure—the impulse to complete a structure and make it whole by supplying a missing element. The procedure is applied to the reading process as follows. Every "nth" word in a printed passage is omitted and the reader is asked to make closure by supplying the missing words. Because words are deleted at random, both *lexical* words and *structural* words are omitted. In the linguistic framework, lexical words carry primary meaning and are roughly similar to the verbs, nouns, adjectives, and adverbs. The structural words consist of those words that indicate relationships, such as articles, prepositions, conjunctions, and auxilliary verbs. Thus, reader's closure must bridge gaps in both language and thought. What the reader supplies gives clues to his or her underlying psycholinguistic processes.

The procedure has been used successfully as a test of reading comprehension, as a measure of readability or assessment of the difficulty level of a reading selection, and as a method of improving reading. Bormuth (1968, p. 435) described the following steps for the cloze procedure in measuring readability of a reading selection:

a. Passages are selected from the material which is being evaluated.
b. Every fifth word in the passage is deleted and replaced by an underlined blank of a standard length.
c. The tests are duplicated and given, without time limits, to students who have *not* read the passages from which the tests were made.
d. The students are instructed to write in each blank the word they think was deleted.
e. Responses are scored correct when they exactly match the words deleted (minor misspellings are disregarded).

This technique has been reported to be a valid means of measuring the readability level (comprehension difficulty) of passages as well as a reliable measure of reading comprehension. One advantage of the cloze test over the conventional reading test or other fill-in-the-blank tests is that the words deleted are randomly selected; therefore, they may represent either lexical words or structural words.

The cloze procedure may have possibilities in probing other psycholinguistic abilities. An analysis of why an individual fails to supply the missing words may be used to measure listening ability, to analyze the role of reasoning in reading, to diagnose the student's skills with both structural and lexical linguistic components, to gather information on cognitive styles, and to supply information on the human brain as an information storage and retrieval system.

The cloze procedure can be used for teaching reading comprehension, as well as for judging the difficulty of reading material. Exercises such as the one below can be devised. In this case, the reading material was retyped with every tenth word deleted and replaced by a standard-sized line. The student supplies the missing words. A sample selection of a cloze passage is shown below.

Farming in Switzerland

Switzerland is a country of very high, steep mountains _____ narrow valleys. In the valleys are the farms where _____ farmers raise much of the food they need for _____ and their animals. Because the valleys are tiny, the _____ are small. There is no room on them for _____ grassland that is needed for pasturing cows or goats _____ sheep during the summer.

(Answers: and, the, themselves, farms, the, or)*

Metacognitive Learning Strategies

Learning-disabled students have been characterized as "strategy deficient," that is, they do not spontaneously employ or generate the kinds of strategies of learning that non-learning-disabled students use (Deshler et al., 1984). However, once taught a specific strategy, many learning-disabled students can and do use the strategy effectively. As noted earlier, the learning strategies approach is designed to teach students how to learn rather to teach specific content. Several of the learning strategies methods are particularly useful for improving reading comprehension (see also, Chapters 6 and 8).

1. **Advance organizers.** This technique is used to establish a mind set for the reader, relating new material to previously learned information before the material is read (Good & Brophy, 1978). Advance organizers could take several forms: introduction of general concepts, a linkage to previously learned materials, or a study of a complex introductory passage.

2. **Search strategies training.** In this strategy, students are taught how to scan the material before answering a question. They are taught to stop,

*From P. McKee, M. Harrison, A. McCowen, and E. Lehr, *High Roads*, fourth-grade reader (Boston: Houghton Mifflin, 1962), p. 34.

listen, look, and think—to systematically consider alternative approaches and answers before responding to a problem. The aim is to reduce impulsive, thoughtless answers and to delay a response until a systematic search for the right one has been made.

3. ***Verbal rehearsal.*** In this strategy, students learn to verbalize a problem encountered in reading comprehension. They state the problem to themselves as a planned approach for clarifying the problem. There are three stages for teaching this strategy: (1) the students observe the instructor's modeling of verbalization of the problem, (2) the students instruct themselves by verbalizing aloud or in a whisper, and (3) the students verbalize silently.

4. ***Self-monitoring.*** In this strategy, students learn to monitor their own mistakes. Learning-disabled students need training in the strategy of checking their own responses and becoming conscious of errors or answers that do not make sense. To reach this stage requires active involvement in the learning process rather than passive learning, in which students are not conscious of incongruities.

5. ***Questioning strategies.*** The types of questions teachers ask stimulate the various types of thinking that students engage in during reading. Many of the questions teachers use demand recall of details. Questions that provoke conjecture, explanation, evaluation, and judgment must also be planned. The four types of comprehension questions are:

   a. Literal Comprehension: What did little brother want to eat?
   b. Interpretation: Why was the cooky jar kept on the basement steps?
   c. Critical Reading: Did mother do the right thing in leaving the children alone?
   d. Creative Reading: How would you have solved this problem?

   In the *self-questioning* learning strategies approach, students develop their own comprehension questions. Through direct instruction learning-disabled students have been trained successfully to use self-questioning strategies while reading. They asked themselves such questions as what am I reading this passage for? what is the main idea? what is a good question about the main idea? The students learn to monitor their reading, and their comprehension improves significantly (Wong & Jones, 1982).

Methods for Dealing with Special Reading Problems

Students who have great difficulty in acquiring reading skills often encounter special types of problems, such as reversals, finger pointing, lip moving, halting oral reading, and poor silent reading. The methods discussed in this section are strategies for these very specific problems (Richek et al., 1983).

Reversals

Reversals are the tendency to reverse letters or words that are different only in direction, such as *b* for *d*, *no* for *on*, or *saw* for *was*. Inversions are another common type of error, such as *u* for *n*. Poor readers with this problem may even write backwards producing "mirror writing."

It is very common for beginning readers to make reversals. At the beginning stages of reading, such errors merely indicate a lack of experience with letters and words. Reversals typically disappear as the student gains experience and proficiency in reading. Therefore, teachers must decide if the reversals are merely a normal developmental stage (in which case they should be ignored) or if they indicate a problem interfering with reading progress and need specific remediation. The following remedial methods are suggested:

1. Concentrate on one letter at a time. For example, start with the letter *b*, make a large chart, and use a memory word, such as *bicycle*.
2. Trace the confusable word or letter on a large card or on the blackboard, or use felt letters so that the student has kinesthetic reinforcement.
3. Underline the first letter of a confusable word or write the first letter in a color.
4. Use phonics instruction to reinforce the pronunciation of the confusable word.
5. Write the confusable word and say it while writing.
6. Use memory devices. For example, show that the lower case *b* goes in the same direction as the capital *B* and that one can be superimposed on the other.

Finger Pointing and Lip Moving

Both these behaviors are characteristic and normal behaviors in the early stages of reading. Moreover, when material becomes difficult, even the mature and efficient reader will fall back on these habits because they do help the reader understand difficult and frustrating material. Some learning-disabled students may need these aids to understand what they are reading.

However, finger pointing and lip moving inhibit fluent reading and should be discouraged when no longer needed. Both habits encourage word-by-word reading, vocalization or subvocalization, inhibit speed, and reduce comprehension.

1. Material selected should not be so difficult that it forces the student to use these behaviors.
2. Extensive finger pointing may be a symptom of visual difficulties. In some cases, the student may need a visual examination.
3. Students should be made aware of their habits and made to understand how they inhibit reading progress.

4. A first stage in eliminating finger pointing can be the use of markers to replace the finger, and then the elimination of the marker.
5. Students may need to be reminded that they are moving their lips. Increasing the speed of reading also acts to eliminate lip moving.

Disfluent Oral Reading

A technique known as *repeated readings* has been found to effectively improve fluency (Moyer, 1983). Poor readers often read in a very hesitant, nonfluent, halting manner. Research studies show that teachers have a tendency to interrupt poor readers much more often than good readers, thereby discouraging oral reading fluency (Allington, 1978). To improve oral reading, students need more practice in reading orally. Make sure the material is not too difficult, have the students read the material silently first, and tell them you will not interrupt while the reading is in progress.

Inability to Read Silently

Most purposeful reading for adults is silent. Therefore, remedial instruction should include opportunities for the student to read silently. To stress the importance of silent reading, it should be done before oral reading. Students need direct motivation for reading silently. For example, stress the information that the student should find in the text. Follow the silent reading with questions and discussion so that the students will see it as a meaningful activity. Gradually increase the quantity of silent reading that is expected.

Tape-recorded Textbooks for Handicapped Students

There are several sources for obtaining tape recordings of books available to handicapped students. Students identified as learning disabled are among those eligible to obtain books recorded for the blind. These recorded textbooks are available at no cost. In addition, new titles can be recorded if needed. For students with severe reading problems, recorded textbooks can be a real boon for grasping content. For further information contact Recording for the Blind, 215 E. 58th Street; New York, NY 10022.

Summary

• Reading is one of the major academic difficulties for students with learning disabilities. Inability to read has detrimental consequences for society as well as for the poor reader.

• Dyslexia is one form of learning disabilities in which the individual encounters extreme difficulty in learning to read. The problem is thought to be related to abnormalities in brain structure or function.

• To best assist students with reading problems, it is important for teachers to understand the normal developmental sequence of reading acquisition: (1) reading readiness, (2) initial stage of reading, (3) the rapid development of reading skills, (4) wide reading, and (5) refinement of reading.

• There are two major components to consider in teaching reading: (1) word recognition, and (2) reading comprehension. The word recognition clues include sight words, context clues, phonics, and structural analysis. The ability to recognize words is prerequisite to reading comprehension.

• The four levels of reading are the literal, organizational, inferential, and critical levels.

• Two theoretical frameworks applied to reading comprehension view it, respectively, as (1) specific skills, and (2) a holistic process. The specific skills theory requires that each discrete comprehension skill be identified and taught. When the holistic approach is used, reading is taught as a whole process involving cognitive and psycholinguistic behavior. The two components of reading comprehension can be integrated in instruction.

• There are many ways to assess reading ability. Formal tests include survey tests, diagnostic tests, and comprehensive batteries. Informal tests include informal reading inventories, miscue analysis, and teacher-made tests. Each type of test assesses a different kind of information about the student's reading.

• Teaching strategies are organized into (1) adaptations of standard reading methods, (2) special remedial reading methods, (3) reading comprehension methods, and (4) techniques for dealing with special reading problems.

• If appropriately modified, the standard or developmental methods can be very effective in helping students with learning disabilities.

• A number of special methods are used for students with reading problems, and teachers of learning-disabled students should be competent in them.

• The section on the teaching of reading comprehension suggests ways of building meaning vocabulary, language emphasis methods, and learning strategies methods. Methods for special reading problems include reversals, finger pointing, lip moving, oral and silent reading, and Talking Books for the Blind.

Key Terms

sight words
language-experience
  method
context clues
phonics
structural analysis
word recognition skills
VAKT
dyslexia

reading comprehension
holistic view of reading
reversals
basal reading series
programmed reading
  instruction
psycholinguistic view of
  reading
linguistic readers

neurological impress
  method
cloze procedure

Chapter Outline

Written Language: Handwriting, Spelling, and Written Expression

Chapter **13**

Introduction

*T*his chapter considers written language learning disabilities in three areas of the curriculum: (1) handwriting, (2) spelling, and (3) written expression. The Theory section discusses the major theoretical concepts of each of these areas, and the Teaching Strategies section presents specific instructional techniques that have been found useful in helping learning-disabled students in each area. It is important to note that writing tasks are required in all subjects of the curriculum, not only when written language is the focus of instruction. The instructional concept of "writing across the curriculum" has become a persuasive force in the teaching of writing (Emig, 1982).

■ Theories

Many people dislike writing, and their disdainful attitude toward writing is illustrated by the story of the New York City taxicab driver who skillfully guided his cab past a pedestrian. In explaining to his passenger why he was so careful, the cabbie said, "I always try to avoid hittin' 'em because every time ya hit one, ya gotta write out a long report about it."

Words are the primary means of communication for human beings. It is the way we tell each other what we want and what we don't want, what we think, and how we feel. When words are spoken, they are a wonderful asset—quick, direct, and easy. But when words must be written, they become burdensome—a slow and laborious task. Many learning-disabled students have significant problems in the acquisition and use of written language, and these problems often continue to adversely affect their lives as adults (Poplin, 1983).

The written form of language is the highest and most complex type of communication. In the hierarchy of the development of language skills, it is the last to be learned. But before we can write, we need a foundation of previous learnings and experiences in listening, speaking, and reading. Besides an adequate basis of oral language skills, proficiency in using written language requires many other competencies. These include the ability to keep one idea in mind while formulating the idea in words and sentences; skill in planning the correct graphic form for each letter and word while manipulating the writing instrument; and sufficient visual and motor memory to integrate complex eye-hand relationships.

CASE EXAMPLE

A Written-Language Disability

The following news event illustrates the importance of writing skills for successful communication. In an attempted burglary, a would-be robber handed this handwritten note to the bank teller:

I GOT A BUM. I ALSO HAVE A CONTOUR. I'M GOING TO BLOW YOU SKY HEIGHT. I'M NO KILLEN. THIS IS A HELD UP.*

   Unable to decipher the note, the teller asked the robber for help in reading the message. By the time the robber deciphered the words for the teller, the police had arrived and arrested him. To make the matter worse for the robber, the police were also able to trace him to other bank holdups in which the same spelling and writing errors were made in the burglary note. This case of a thwarted bank holdup illustrates the point that written language skills are required in most occupations today— even to be a successful bank robber. (*Miami Herald,* 1980)

*Translation: I got a bomb. I also have a control. I'm going to blow you sky high. I'm no killer. This is a holdup.

Handwriting

Even in these days of self-correcting typewriters and the magic of computer word processing, handwriting is a necessary competency. In school, it is the usual medium through which students convey to teachers what they have learned. In many situations, adults also find writing a necessity that they cannot avoid (Hagin, 1983).

   Handwriting is the most concrete of the communication skills. The student's handwriting can be directly observed, evaluated and preserved. It differs from the receptive skill of reading in that the measurement of the reading comprehension skill must necessarily be indirect, through the asking of questions; students must verbalize in some way to let you know what they have read. Handwriting also differs from the expressive skill of speaking, since it provides a permanent record of the output and since it requires visual and motor skills.

   Difficulty in handwriting, sometimes referred to as *dysgraphia,* may reflect the underlying presence of many other deficits. Students with handwriting problems may be unable to execute efficiently the motor movements required to write or to copy written letters or forms; they may be unable to transfer the input of visual information to the output of fine motor movement; or they may be poor in other visual-motor functions and in activities requiring motor and spatial judgments. The intricacy of the psychomotor process involved in handwriting has long been recognized.

   Learning to write is not a mechanical, lower-level reflex response, but a thinking process, entailing activity of the cortical nerve areas. Smooth motor coordination of eye and hand, control of arm, hand, and finger muscles are acquired in the process of learning to write and are needed for legible results. Learning to write also requires maturity adequate for accurate perception of the symbol patterns. Writing from memory demands the retention of visual and kinesthetic images of forms, not present to the senses, for future recall. . . . The capacity for graphic representation, such as writing requires, depends on the motor function of the eye and its coordination with eye movements. (Hildreth, 1947)

Some of the underlying shortcomings that interfere with handwriting performance are (a) poor motor skills, (b) unstable and erratic temperament, (c) faulty visual perception of letters and words, and (d) difficulty in retaining visual impressions. The student's difficulty may also be in cross-modal transfer from the visual to motor modalities. Left-handedness provides an additional obstacle to learning to write. Another cause of poor writing is poor instruction in handwriting skills.

Figure 13.1 illustrates the attempts of two ten-year-old boys with handwriting disorders to copy some writing materials.

Cursive Versus Manuscript Handwriting

There is some difference of opinion as to whether writing instruction for the learning disabled should begin with manuscript or cursive writing. The developmental handwriting curriculum in most schools begins with manuscript writing (sometimes called *printing*) in first grade; the transfer to cursive writing (sometimes called *script*) is typically made somewhere in the third grade.

The arguments for beginning with cursive writing are that it minimizes spatial judgment problems for the student and that there is a rhythmic continuity and wholeness that is missing from manuscript writing. Further, errors of reversals are virtually eliminated with cursive writing; and if instruction begins with the cursive form, the need to transfer from one form to another is eliminated. Many students with learning disabilities find it difficult to make the transfer to cursive writing if they have first learned manuscript writing (Thurber, 1983).

The advantages of manuscript writing are that it is easier to learn since it consists of only circles and straight lines; the manuscript letter form is closer to the printed form used in reading; and some educators feel it is not important to transfer to cursive writing at all since the manuscript form is legal, legible, and thought by some to be just as rapid. (Barbe, Milone, & Wasylyk, 1983)

Good results have been obtained with instruction in both symbolic forms. Reinforcing the system the student is using in the classroom seems to be a wise strategy, if all other things are equal. For young children, this is likely to be the manuscript form, and for pupils in the intermediate grades

FIGURE 13.1

Illustrations of the Handwriting of Two Ten-year-old Boys with Handwriting Disabilities (In both cases the boys were asked to copy from a sample.)

Handwriting of Mike: 10 years old

Handwriting of Allen: 10 years old

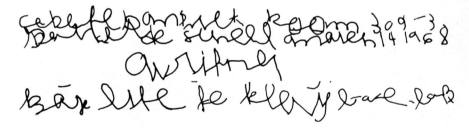

the cursive form is likely to be used. Samples of manuscript and cursive letters are shown in Figure 13.2.

Hagin (1983) suggests that some students who have great difficulty making the transfer from manuscript writing to cursive writing because of lags in visual-motor control do better with a writing style that is in between cursive and manuscript writing. Hagin calls this style *write right—or left*. It is a simplified cursive writing style in which letters are written with a vertical stroke rather than the diagonal slant of typical cursive writing. It is actually a kind of connected manuscript writing. Instead of slanting the paper and the stroke of the letter, both are kept straight as is done in manuscript letters. The letters, however, are connected so that the student does not have to lift

FIGURE 13.2
Sample Manuscript and Cursive Alphabets

MANUSCRIPT ALPHABET

ABCDEFGHIJKLMNOPQR
STUVWXYZabcdefghijklm
nopqrstuvwxyz 1234567891O

CURSIVE ALPHABET

Aa Bb Cc Dd Ee Ff
Gg Hh Ii Jj Kk Ll
Mm Nn Oo Pp Qq Rr
Ss Tt Uu Vv Ww Xx
Yy Zz 1 2 3 4 5 6 7 8 9 10

Source: From the *Sample Manuscript Alphabet*, Grade 3, and the *Sample Cursive Alphabet*, Grade 3 (Columbus, OH: Zaner-Bloser, 1958).

the pencil. Hagin found that students with handwriting learning disabilities can more easily transfer from manuscript writing to this modified form of cursive writing.

The Left-handed Student

Left-handed people encounter a special problem since their natural tendency is to write from right to left on the page. In writing from left to right, left-handers have difficulty seeing what they have written because the hand covers it up, and there is a tendency to smudge the writing as the left hand moves. To avoid the smudging, some left-handed students begin "hooking" the hand in writing when they start using ball-point pens.

Left-handedness today is accepted as natural for some people. The student who has not yet stabilized handedness should be encouraged to write with the right hand. However, the student with a strong preference for the left hand should be permitted to write as a "lefty," even though this creates some special problems in writing and requires special instruction.

For manuscript writing, the paper should be placed directly in front of the left-handed pupil, without a slant. However, for cursive writing, the top of the paper should be slanted north-northeast, opposite to the slant used by the right-handed student. The pencil should be long, gripped about one inch from the tip, with the eraser pointing to the left shoulder. The position of the hand is curved, with the weight resting on the outside of the little finger, and "hooking" should be avoided. Research shows that left-handers can learn to write just as fast as right-handers.

Typewriting

Students with severe problems in handwriting who do not make progress with instruction, or students who write very slowly may find a typewriter a more effective means of written communication. The electric typewriter has proved to be useful for those with severe motor difficulty. Special instruction in typing will be required to help the student learn to use the typewriter. Not only can students with handwriting problems learn to type reasonably well, but as they learn to type, they appear to develop a better awareness of the sequences of letters in words.

Microcomputers and Writing

The technology of the microcomputer has the potential of revolutionizing the way all components of the written language curriculum (handwriting, spelling, and written expression) are taught and learned. Learning typewriting skills using the microcomputer make a great deal of sense. In just terms of the mechanics of typing, the microcomputer has all the advantages of the typewriter, plus the ease of making corrections on a screen before the passage is printed on paper. Simply backspacing to correct errors eliminates the need for frustrating erasers, holes in the paper, and messy crossouts. Even after the material is printed on paper, the user can quickly make corrections without rewriting or retyping the entire product. The microcomputer becomes a tool for simplifying the mechanics of both handwriting and typing.

The advent of the computer and its anticipated increased use in the near future make typing ability a survival skill that will be needed to function in society. Software programs to teach keyboard typing skills are useful. One such program, *MasterType* (Lightning Software, Inc.) teaches students to develop mastery of the computer keyboard through a game format, using seventeen progressive lessons.

Worthy of mention is the *KoalaPad*. This is a computer peripheral that allows the student to perform visual-motor functions on a special pad to create letters, shapes, lines, artwork, and graphics on the computer screen.

Spelling

Spelling has been called "the invention of the devil." To continue with this spiritual analogy, the ability to spell well, someone once quipped, is "a gift from God." Spelling is one curriculum area in which neither creativity nor divergent thinking is encouraged. Only one pattern or arrangement of letters can be accepted as correct; there is no compromise or leeway. What makes spelling so difficult is that the written form of the English language has an inconsistent pattern; there is not a one-to-one correspondence between the spoken sounds of English and the written form of the language. Therefore, spelling is not an easy task, even for those who are not afflicted with learning disabilities.

Spelling a word is much more difficult than reading it. Several clues aid the reader in recognizing a word in print: context, phonics, structural analysis, and configuration. There is no opportunity, however, to draw on peripheral clues in reproducing a word. Many students who are poor in the ability to reproduce words in spelling are skilled in the ability to recognize them in reading. However, the student who is poor in decoding words in reading is almost always poor in spelling as well.

Two Theories of Word Selection for Teaching Spelling

There are two alternatives for selecting words to teach spelling. One is a *linguistic* orientation; the other is a *frequency-of-use* approach.

Linguistic Approach to Spelling

The linguistic theory is based on the belief that the spelling of American English is sufficiently rule-covered to warrant an instructional method that

Visual memory is one of the abilities necessary for good spelling, and if a weakness exists in this area, games and activities that stress visual sequential memory are often very helpful.   *(Teri Leigh Stratford/Monkmeyer)*

stresses phonological, morphological, and syntactic rules or word patterns. This might also be called a phonics approach to spelling, since it selects words in order to teach phonics generalizations, structural analysis, or linguistic patterns.

In spite of the seemingly numerous exceptions to the rules, basic research in linguistics has indicated that there are predictable spelling patterns and an underlying system of phonological and morphological regularity. Hanna, Hodges, & Hanna (1971) reported that an in-depth analysis of seventeen thousand words showed that the correct spelling pattern can be predicted for a phoneme sound 90 percent of the time when the main phonological facts of position in syllables, syllable stress, and internal constraints underlying the orthography are taken into consideration. A linguistic approach to the teaching of spelling capitalizes on the underlying regularity that exists between phonological and morphological elements in the oral language and their graphemic representation in orthography.

What linguists suggest is that students be helped to discover the underlying linguistic patterns and that words for spelling instruction be selected on the basis of demonstrating the underlying linguistic patterns. Linguists maintain that the spelling curriculum should be organized to encourage such linguistic discovery. When teaching a spelling pattern of the phoneme "oy," for example, the teacher should include in the spelling lesson words like: *boy, joy, Roy,* and *toy,* to help learners form a linguistic or phonological generalization.

Similar proposals have been made by authorities in reading, who suggest that spelling programs be merged with phonics instruction. They argue that the phonics and word-analysis skills be practiced not in the reading class but during the spelling class.

Word-Frequency Approach to Spelling

This alternative approach to spelling suggests that students should learn the words that are used in written language most frequently. These spelling programs select words for spelling instruction on the basis of "frequency-of-use" word lists rather than on the basis of "linguistic patterns." A common core of spelling words that are most frequently used in writing was determined through extensive investigations of the writing done by children and adults. Spelling programs that select words on the basis of their utility in writing use the studies of writing vocabularies conducted by spelling authorities such as Fitzgerald (1951). A relatively small number of words do most of the work. The following estimate of needed spelling words is given by Rinsland (1945):

> 100 words make up more than 60% of elementary children's writing
> 500 words make up more than 82% of elementary children's writing
> 1,000 words make up more than 89% of elementary children's writing
> 2,000 words make up more than 95% of elementary children's writing

Fitzgerald (1955) suggests that 2,650 words and their repetitions in derivative forms make up about 95 percent of the writing of elementary school children. He recommends a basic list of 3,500 words for children in elementary school. The criteria for word selection in the traditional spelling curriculum, then, are frequency of use, permanency, and utility.

All these studies show that a few words of our language are used over and over again. Sixty percent of our writing consists of the one hundred words shown in Table 13.1.

The word-frequency approach to spelling also assumes that there are many exceptions to spelling and phonics rules in our language, and that these exceptions often occur in the most frequently used words. Because of such irregularities, it is difficult to convey patterns and rules to beginning spellers. Examples of the irregular relationship between phonemes (the spoken sound) and graphemes (the written symbol) are easy to cite. George Bernard Shaw, an advocate of spelling reform, is credited with the suggestion that the word "fish" be spelled *ghoti*: *gh* as in "cough"; *o* as in "women"; *ti* as in

TABLE 13.1 **One Hundred Most Common Words in Written Language**

a	eat	in	our	there
all	for	is	out	they
am	girl	it	over	this
and	go	just	play	time
are	going	know	pretty	to
at	good	like	put	too
baby	got	little	red	tree
ball	had	look	run	two
be	has	made	said	up
big	have	make	saw	want
boy	he	man	school	was
but	her	me	see	we
can	here	mother	she	went
Christmas	him	my	so	what
come	his	name	some	when
did	home	not	take	will
do	house	now	that	with
dog	how	of	the	would
doll	I	on	then	you
down	I'm	one	them	your

"nation." Following phonic generalizations, the word *natural* could be spelled *pnatchurile*. The many inconsistencies that exist in English spelling are illustrated in the following limericks.

> A king, on assuming his reign,
> Exclaimed with a feeling of peign:
> "Tho I'm legally heir
> No one here seems to ceir
> That I haven't been born with a breign."

> A merchant addressing a debtor,
> Remarked in the course of his lebtor
> That he chose to suppose
> A man knose what he ose
> And the sooner he pays it, the bedtor!

> A young lady crossing the ocean
> Grew ill from the ship's dizzy mocean,
> She called with a sigh
> And a tear in her eigh,
> For the doctor to give her a pocean.

> And now our brief lesson is through—
> I trust you'll agree it was trough;

For it's chiefly designed
To impress on your migned
What wonders our spelling can dough!*

One teacher found that pupils' spelling of the word "awful" was varied, including: *offul, awful, offel,* and *offle.* Each is an accurate phonetic transcription of the oral sounds of the word.

Problems Related to Spelling

There are many subskills and abilities demanded in the act of spelling. Individuals must be able, initially, to read the word; they must be knowledgeable and skillful in certain relationships of phonics and structural analysis; they must be able to apply appropriate phonic generalizations; they must be able to visualize the appearance of the word; and, finally, they need to have the motor facility to write the word. Difficulties in spelling may be due to a deficit in any or a combination of the above skills.

In addition to phonological generalizations, the ability to spell appears to be related to visual sequential memory. The student who is unable to remember or visualize the letters and order of the letters in words will be poor in spelling. Many of the techniques that have been successful in teaching spelling have, in effect, been ways to strengthen visual sequential memory. Fernald (1943), for example, developed a tracing technique to teach spelling that reinforced the visual image of the word by using the tactile and kinesthetic modalities. To spell a word correctly, the individual must not only have stored the word in memory, but also be able to retrieve it completely. Unlike recognizing a word in reading, there are no visual clues.

If visual memory is a problem, activities to help strengthen and reinforce the visual memory of the spelling words are suggested. If deficits in auditory perception of letter sounds or auditory memory problems makes it difficult to hold the sounds or syllables in mind, the teaching plan should take these factors into account. Motor memory is also a factor in spelling, for the speller must remember how the word "felt" when it was previously written. In addition, intersensory transfer probably plays a crucial role in developing efficient spelling ability. A crossing and integrating of visual, auditory, and kinesthetic functions must take place before the spelling of a word becomes a subconscious, automatic process.

Intersensory transfer is needed for efficient spelling behavior. According to Personke and Yee (1966), no one channel is correct for spelling a word each time it is met. Memory of the word's spelling is reinforced when the word is correctly spelled. Brothers and Holsclaw (1969) suggest that a spelling program should fuse five spelling behaviors: (1) copying, (2) proofread-

---

* Reprinted by special permission of Dr. Emmett Albert Betts, *Phonemic Spelling Council.*

ing, (3) rewriting, (4) writing from memory consciously, and (5) spelling automatically without conscious thought.

Microcomputers and Spelling

A variety of microcomputer programs are being developed to test and to teach spelling. Also, some microcomputer software packages have a built-in spelling scanner permitting the checking for misspelled words. The computer spots misspelled words as words that do not match the words in a predetermined file of common words. Such programs also aid in finding typographical errors. One such program, *Sensible Speller IV,* contains a file of eighty thousand words and allows the user to add more words.

Some software packages have spelling games, such as crossword puzzles and hangman. Audio cassettes and speech synthesizers provide audiovisual capabilities, allowing for a variety of testing and teaching spelling activities. With the speech synthesizer, the computer actually produces the spelling words orally. The student types the words and the computer then checks the spelling. One spelling program with a speech synthesizer is ECHO II. Still other software packages are designed to analyze spelling errors (Hasselbring & Owens, 1983). The microcomputer has the potential for drastically changing the way we teach and assess spelling.

Assessment of Spelling

Formal Tests

Some tests of spelling are part of a comprehensive academic achievement battery; others are individual spelling tests. Among the most widely used spelling tests are

> *Test of Written Spelling* (TWS)
> *Test of Written Language* (TOWL)
> *Peabody Individual Achievement Test* (PIAT)
> *Wide Range Achievement Test* (WRAT)
> *Durrell Analysis of Reading Difficulty*
> *Diagnostic Screening Test for Developmental Dyslexia* (Boder)

These tests are described more fully in Appendix C.

Informal Tests

Teachers may wish to develop their own informal spelling test. Mann and Suiter (1975) recommend a simple procedure to assess a child's spelling. First, obtain a basal spelling series. Select at random fifteen words from the Grade 1 spelling book and twenty words each from the grades 2 through 6 spelling books. Ask the student to spell the words on paper as they are dictated from each successive list until the student misses seven words on a

TABLE 13.2   **Informal Spelling Test**

Grade 1	Grade 2	Grade 3	Grade 4	Grade 5	Grade 6	Grade 7
all	be	after	because	bread	build	although
at	come	before	dinner	don't	hair	amount
for	give	brown	few	floor	music	business
his	house	dog	light	beautiful	eight	excuse
it	long	never	place	money	brought	receive
not	must	find	sent	minute	except	measure
see	ran	gray	table	ready	suit	telephone
up	some	hope	town	snow	whose	station
me	want	live	only	through	yesterday	possible
go	your	mother	farm	bright	instead	excuse

level. This constitutes failure at that level. The format for dictating this is: the teacher (1) says the word, (2) uses the word in a sentence, and (3) repeats the word.

To obtain a random selection, divide the total number of words at a level by twenty. For example, if there are five hundred words at a grade level, the quotient would be twenty-five. Therefore, select for the list every twenty-fifth word in the book.

A short form of an informal spelling test was developed by selecting ten words from a frequency-of-use word list (Durrell, 1956), as shown in Table 13.2. Have the student spell on paper from each list until he or she misses three words at a level. The student's spelling level can be estimated as that at which two words are missed.

Analysis of Spelling Errors

Analysis of errors gives more information than grade level test scores. Boder (1973, 1976) proposes that an analysis of spelling error pattern can help in understanding a student's approach to spelling, as well as be a way of classifying students into one of three types of dyslexia. She suggests looking for three types of reading-spelling error patterns:

> *Group 1. Dysphonetic dyslexia* (phonetically inaccurate spellings). These errors include some of the correct letters but the letters are placed in bizarre positions: *ronaeg* (for *orange*); *lghit* (for *light*); *heows* (for *whose*). They may also involve semantic substitutions, such as *funny* for *laugh*, or *airplane* for *train*. This type of error reflects a primary deficit in sound-symbol integration. Students with this problem read and spell primarily through visualization.
>
> *Group 2. Dyseidetic dyslexia* (phonic-equivalent errors). The misspellings range from *lisn* for *listen* and *atenchen* for *attention* to *pese* for *peace*, *det* for *debt*, and *shofer* for *chauffeur*. This type of error reflects a

primary deficit in the ability to perceive and recall whole words as a gestalt. Students with this problem read and spell primarily through the process of phonic analysis.

Group 3. Dysphonetic-dyseidetic dyslexia (mixed type, both kinds of errors). Students with these error patterns make both types of errors, and they are considered the most severe cases.

Boder (1973, 1976) analyzes students in group 1 as visual spellers, and students in group 2 as auditory spellers. The *Diagnostic Screening Test for Developmental Dyslexia* (Boder, 1982) is designed to test and classify the types of errors that the student is making. Research using the Boder analysis of spelling errors was conducted by Moats (1983) and Camp and Dolcourt (1977) to study the spelling error patterns of dyslexic pupils.

Written Expression

Lack of facility in expressing thoughts through written language is probably the most prevalent disability of the communication skills. Many adults, as well as children, are unable to communicate effectively and to share ideas through writing. The ability to write down ideas requires many underlying prerequisite skills: facility in oral language, ability to read, some skill in spelling, a legible handwriting, and some knowledge of the rules of written usage.

Problems Related to Writing

In addition to the preceding requirements, the student must have something to write about. Writing is a means of producing an output of ideas; obviously, there can be little output without an abundance of input. Because a strong relationship exists between the quantity of input experiences and the quality of output in the form of writing, the teacher must provide rich input experiences, such as trips, stories, discussions, and oral language activities. A written assignment that is given without first supplying a receptive build-up (such as "Write a five hundred-word theme on spring") is not likely to yield rich written productions. Writing needs prior sufficient input experiences to create and stimulate ideas students can write about.

Another possible detriment to writing is the teacher's response to the student's writing, if it takes the form of excessive correction. Students can be discouraged from trying if they attempt to express ideas only to have their papers returned full of grammatical, spelling, punctuation, and handwriting corrections in red ink with heavy penalties for mistakes. As one pupil remarked, "An 'F' looks so much worse in red ink." From the behavior modification viewpoint, the student is receiving negative reinforcement. Such students soon learn to beat the game by limiting their writing vocabulary to words they know how to spell, by keeping their sentences simple, by avoiding complex and creative ideas, and by keeping their compositions short.

Writing as a Cognitive Process

Current research on the teaching of writing suggests the need for a major shift in the instruction of written expression. The recommended shift changes the emphasis from the *product* of writing to the *process* of writing (Smith, 1982; Martin, 1983; Nodine, 1983). In the traditional approach of the past, the focus was on the final product (or written assignment) created by the student. The teacher checked and graded this product, based on certain expectations of perfection. Students were expected to spell correctly, use adjectives, and compose topic sentences, and they were also graded on word choice, grammar, organization, and ideas. The paper was then returned to the student with corrections (often in red ink) and students were expected to learn and improve their writing skills from these grades and corrections. The more conscientious the teacher, the more conscientiously the corrections filled the student's papers. The result of this type of writing instruction was that most people learned to dislike writing.

In contrast, the *process* approach to writing emphasizes the cognitive process the writer engages in during writing. Teachers are encouraged to understand the complexity of the writing task and help students in the many thinking, selecting, and organizing tasks required. Students should ask themselves these questions: who is the intended audience? what is the purpose of the writing? how can I get ideas? how can I develop and organize the ideas? how can I translate and revise the ideas so that the reader will understand them?

Also important is the teaching of writing as a recursive and progressive process. The first draft of a piece of writing is not for the reader but for the writer. As the writer jots down words and paragraphs, they give rise to new ideas or sometimes to revisions of ideas already written. At this stage there may be an overflow of ideas with little organization or consideration of prose, grammar, and spelling.

Subsequent drafts involve the procedures of taking the ideas of the initial draft and organizing and refining them. In the final draft, the reader must be considered. Thus, writing is a cognitive process, consisting of prewriting, writing, and rewriting. The amount of rewriting to be done depends on the intended audience. Specialists in the area of writing emphasize that writing is a learned skill that can be taught in a school setting. Further, writing should be taught as a thinking-learning activity (Alexander, 1983).

Microcomputers and Word Processing

The microcomputer and a word-processing software package serve as a tremendous boon to the teaching of writing. Word processing is designed to make the revising, rewriting, and correcting process easier. In word processing, the words are electronically stored on computer disc or tape, and kept in a state that the writer can easily change. The writer can add, correct, delete,

Source: © 1984 United Feature Syndicate, Inc.

revise, and freely experiment until the display screen shows exactly what the user wants to write. At that point, by pushing "print," the writer receives a printed copy. The printed copy can be further revised, corrected, re-edited. The new changes and corrections are typed and shown on the video screen. When satisfied with the corrected version, the writer pushes "print" again and in a few minutes has a new printed copy with the revisions. Word processing eliminates the arduous rewriting or retyping and encourages the important cognitive process of writing—thinking about editing and revising.

A widely used word-processing language that has proved to be easy and successful for children is the *Bank Street Writer,* designed for grades 4–12.

Tests of Written Expression

Although written expression is specified in PL 94–142 as one of the areas in which a pupil can have a learning disability, relatively few tests are available for assessing problems in this important academic area. Formal and informal assessment instruments are briefly described below. Additional information on these instruments appears in Appendix C.

The Picture Story Language Test (PSLT) is an individualized, standardized instrument for diagnosing a student's product of written expression. In the PSLT, the student is shown a stimulus picture and asked to write a story about the picture. Three types of scores are determined: (1) productivity (how many words and sentences were produced), (2) syntax (word usage), and (3) abstract-concrete scale (conceptual quality).

Test of Written Language (TOWL) is a standardized instrument for measuring written-language performance. It includes measures of syntax, spelling, production, handwriting, punctuation, and capitalization. It also produces measures of Vocabulary and Thematic Maturity that are devised from a student's natural writing product, a story written from a picture stimulus.

Test of Adolescent Language (TOAL) includes subtests on writing, grammar, and written vocabulary.

Woodcock Johnson Psycho-Educational Battery (WJ Battery) includes Written Language Cluster and Written Language Aptitude Cluster scores.

Checklist of Written Expression (Poteet, 1980) is a useful informal assessment device for evaluating written products of learning-disabled students. It is designed to measure penmanship, spelling, grammar, and ideation.

Diagnostic Evaluation of Written Skills (Weiner, 1980) is an informal scale to evaluate graphic, orthographic, phonological, and syntactic components of written language.

Diagnostic Evaluation of Expository Paragraphs (Moran, 1981) is an informal evaluation device for analyzing themes of adolescents. It measures syntactic maturity, percentage of correct conventions, spelling, and mechanics.

■ Teaching Strategies

The rest of this chapter presents specific instructional strategies for the curriculum areas of written language: handwriting, spelling, and written expression.

Activities for Teaching Handwriting

The following activities are representative of methods that have been useful in teaching handwriting.

1. ***Chalkboard activities.*** These provide practice before writing instruction is begun. Circles, lines, geometric shapes, letters, and numbers can be made with large free movements using the muscles of the shoulders, arms, hands, and fingers. For additional suggestions, see Chapter 10, "chalkboard activities," in the section on fine motor activities.

2. ***Other materials for writing movement practice.*** Finger painting or writing in a clay pan or a sand tray gives the student practice in writing movements. Put a layer of sand, cornmeal, salt, or nondrying clay on a cookie sheet. Use commercial or homemade finger paints for the painting practice. The finger or a pointed stick can be used to practice writing

Many aspects of handwriting instruction—such as position and comfort of the student, type of lined paper used, and manner in which the pencil is held—can influence a student's success in learning to write.   *(Alan Carey/The Image Works)*

shapes, forms, letters, and numbers. A small wet sponge could be used on a chalkboard to draw shapes.

3. **Position.**   To prepare for writing, have the student sit in a comfortable chair, have the table at the proper height, feet flat on the floor, both forearms on the writing surface. The nonwriting hand should hold the paper at the top.

4. **Paper.**   For manuscript writing, the paper should be placed without a slant, parallel with the lower edge of the desk. For cursive writing, the paper is tilted at an angle approximately 60 degrees from vertical—to the left for right-handed students and to the right for left-handed students. To help the student remember the current slant, a strip of tape parallel to the top of the paper may be placed at the top of the desk. To keep the paper from sliding, it may be necessary to attach the paper to the desk with masking tape.

5. ***Holding the pencil.***   Many children with writing disorders do not know how, or are unable, to hold a pencil properly between the thumb and middle finger with the index finger riding the pencil. The pencil should be grasped above the sharpened point. A piece of tape or a rubber band can be placed around the pencil to help the student hold it at the right place.

   For the child who has difficulty with the grasp, the pencil can be put through a practice golf ball (the kind with many holes). Have the pupil place the middle finger and thumb around the ball to practice the right grip. Large, primary-size pencils, large crayons, and felt-tip pens are useful for the beginning stages of writing. Clay might be placed around the pencil to help the student grasp it. Short pencils should be avoided, as it is impossible to grip them correctly.

6. ***Stencils and templates.***   Geometric forms (squares, circles, and so forth), letters, and numbers can be represented in stencils made from cardboard or plastic. Clip the stencil to the paper to prevent it from moving. Have the student trace the form with a finger or with a pencil or crayon. Then remove the stencil and reveal the figure that has been made. The stencil can be made so that the hole creates the shape, or, in reverse, so that the outer edges of the stencil create the shape. Discarded hospital x-ray films and packaged-meat trays have proved to be useful materials for making templates.

7. ***Tracing.***   Make heavy black figures on white paper and clip a sheet of onionskin paper over the letters. Have the student trace the forms and letters. Start with diagonal lines and circles, then horizontal and vertical lines, geometric shapes, and finally letters and numbers. The student may also trace with a crayon or felt-tip pen over a black letter on paper or may use a transparent sheet. Another idea is to put letters on transparencies and project the image with an overhead projector onto a chalkboard or a large sheet of paper. The student can then trace over the image.

8. ***Drawing between the lines.***   Have the student practice making "roads" between double lines in a variety of widths and shapes. Then the student can write letters by going between the double lines of outlined letters. Use arrows and numbers to show direction and sequence of the lines.

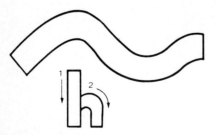
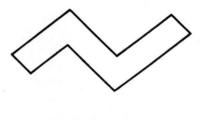

9. ***Dot-dot.***   Draw a complete figure and then an outline of the same figure using dots. Ask the student to make the figure by connecting the dots.

10. ***Tracing with reducing cues.***   Write the complete letter or word and have the student trace it; then write the first part of the letter or word and have the student trace your part and then complete the letter. Finally, reduce the cue to only the upstroke and have the student write the entire letter or word.

11. ***Lined paper.***   Begin by using unlined paper. Paper with wide lines may be used later to help the student determine placement of letters. It may be helpful to use specially lined paper that is color-cued to aid in letter placement. Regular lined paper can also be color-cued to help the student in making letters. Paper of this type is marketed by DLM-Teaching Resources (Appendix D).

12. ***Template lines.***   For students who need additional help in stopping at lines, tape can be placed at bottom and top lines. Windows can be cut out of shirt cardboard to give further guidance for spacing letters. Below is a picture of a cardboard with three window slots for one-line, two-line, and three-line letters

One-line letters are those that fit in a single-line space: a, c, e, i, m, n. Two-line letters are considered to be those with ascenders only: b, d, h, k, l, t. And three-line letters are those with descenders: f, g, j, p. q, z, y.

13. **Letter difficulty.**   Larson (1968) suggests teaching the cursive letters in the following order: beginning letters—m, n, t, i, u, w, r, s, l, e; more difficult letters—x, z, y, j, p, h, b, k, f, g, q; and combinations of letters— me, be, go, it, no, and so forth.

14. **Verbal cues.**   Students are helped in the motor act of writing by hearing the directions, for example, "down-up-and-around." Care must be taken when using this technique that the student is not distracted by these verbal instructions.

15. **Words and sentences.**   After the student learns to write single letters, instruction should proceed to the writing of words and sentences. Spacing, size, and slant are additional factors to be considered.

Activities for Teaching Spelling

1. **Auditory perception and memory of letter sounds.**   Provide practice in auditory perception of letter sounds, strengthen knowledge of phonics and structural analysis, and develop skills in applying phonic generalizations. See Chapter 10 for specific techniques.

2. **Visual perception and memory of letters.**   Help the student strengthen visual perception and memory so that the visual image of the word can be retained. Materials should be clear and concise, and the student should be helped to focus attention on the activity. Letting the student use a pocket flashlight might be helpful as an aid in focusing attention. To develop speed of visual recognition, a tachistoscope can be used to expose material from 1½ seconds to 1/100 second. Flash cards can also be used as an aid in developing speed. See Chapter 10 for specific methods to develop visual perception and memory.

3. ***Multisensory methods in spelling.*** When students are asked to study spelling lessons, they are frequently at a loss as to what to do. Fitzgerald (1955) suggests the following five steps as a multisensory approach that utilizes the visual, auditory, kinesthetic, and tactile modalities.

   a. *Meaning and pronunciation.* Have students look at the word, pronounce it correctly, and use it in a sentence.
   b. *Imagery.* Ask students to "see" the word and say the word. Have them say each syllable of the word, say the word syllable by syllable, spell the word orally, and then trace the word in the air or over the word itself with a finger.
   c. *Recall.* Ask students to look at the word and then close their eyes and see the word in their mind's eye. Have them spell the word orally. Ask them to open their eyes to see if they were correct. (If they make an error, they should repeat the process.)
   d. *Writing the word.* Students write the word correctly from memory, check the spelling against the original, and then check the writing, to make sure every letter is legible.
   e. *Mastery.* Students cover the word and write it. If they are correct, they should cover and write it two more times.

4. ***The Fernald method*** (Fernald, 1943).   This method is a multisensory approach to teaching reading and writing as well as spelling. Very briefly, the following steps are involved:

   a. Students are told that they are going to learn words in a new way that has proved to be very successful. They are encouraged to select a word that they wish to learn.
   b. The teacher writes that word on a piece of paper, four inches by ten inches, as the students watch and as the teacher says the word.
   c. The students trace the word, saying it several times, then write the word on a separate piece of paper while saying it.
   d. The word is then written from memory without looking at the original copy. If it is incorrect, the tracing and saying steps are repeated. If it is correct, it is put in a file box. The words in the file box are used later in stories.
   e. At later stages, this painstaking tracing method for learning words is not needed. Now the students learn a word by *looking* as the teacher writes it, *saying* it, and *writing* it. At a still later stage, the students can learn by only looking at a word in print and writing it, and, finally, by merely looking at it.

5. ***The "test-study-test" versus the "study-test" method.***   In teaching spelling to a classroom, there are two common approaches: the "test-study-test" and the "study-test" plans. The test-study-test method uses a pretest, which is usually given at the beginning of the week. The student

then studies only those words that were missed on the pretest. This method is better for older students who have fairly good spelling abilities, since there is no need to study words they already know. The study-test method is better for young pupils and those with poor spelling abilities. Since too many words would be missed on a pretest, this method permits the study of a few well-selected words before the test is given.

6. *Spelling words on the filmstrip projector.* Put spelling words on transparencies. Cut strips to widths that fit into the projector. Push the strip through to show spelling words on the screen. Cover and show quickly for tachistoscopic use. Words can also be written with certain letters left out, to be completed by the child (Lerner & Vaver, 1970).

7. *Listening centers and tapes.* Spelling lessons can be easily put on tape. After pupils have advanced to a level that enables them to work by themselves, spelling lessons can be completed in a listening laboratory. The use of earphones allows for individualization of instruction, and for many students the earphones provide an aid to block out distracting auditory stimuli.

8. *Programmed spelling.* Some of the new materials in spelling are designed as programmed materials. The material is given in small steps, providing immediate reinforcement, and the programs are designed to be self-instructional.

9. *The Bad Speller's Dictionary.* This dictionary (Krevisky & Linfield, 1963) is useful for poor spellers. Words are arranged alphabetically according to their common misspellings.

10. *Imitation of children's errors.* A study by Kauffman, Hallahan, Haas, Brame, and Born (1978) showed that it was beneficial to imitate the student's spelling error before presenting the correct model, especially in the case of words that are not spelled phonetically. This method gives the student the opportunity to see correct and incorrect responses, and helps to focus attention on the specific ways the incorrect response differs from the correct one.

11. *Shorthand Dictionaries.* Adult dyslexics have found the dictionaries designed for secretaries who use shorthand transcriptions a useful spelling tool. This is because the shorthand dictionary (unlike most regular dictionaries) contains the word with its various endings, which are so troublesome in spelling (for example, *ence, ance*).

12. *Follet's Vest Pocket Word Divider.* This is another useful spelling aid, containing fifty thousand words.

Activities for Teaching Written Expression

1. *Developmental instructional sequence.* The following sequence is useful in planning the teaching of written expression.

a. *Composing and dictating to the teacher.* Before pupils begin to write by themselves, they can develop skills in organizing ideas through language by dictating compositions. The teacher writes down the story; the student gets the idea that thoughts can be expressed in oral language and written down. These experiences are then permanent, and they can be reviewed by the student and read by other people. The student also sees how capital letters, spelling, and punctuation are used to clarify the thoughts expressed.

b. *Copying.* The next step in learning to write is to copy the ideas the teacher has put in written form. Now the student needs the visual-motor skills and handwriting skills. Copying may be very tiring for some students, and it needs close supervision to be of value.

c. *Dictation.* After studying an experience story that the student has written and copied, the teacher helps the student recall the story, and then the teacher dictates the entire story or parts of the story for the student to write. At first the student will need to study the story carefully, but later he or she will be able to write as the teacher dictates, without previous study.

d. *Rewriting.* Have the student rewrite the story independently, without dictation by the teacher.

e. *Practice.* Like any other skill, much practice is needed in learning to write. Give the student many experiences in writing. Difficult spelling words can be anticipated and listed on the board, or the student may simply ask for the spelling of difficult words.

2. ***Providing motivation through grading.*** Avoid discouraging the pupil through grading procedures. Teachers may grade only ideas, not the technical form, for some assignments. Or the teacher may give two grades: one for ideas and one for technical skills. For the pupil who makes errors in many areas, the teacher might select only one skill at a time for correction, such as capitalization.

3. ***Personal and functional writing.*** It is useful to make a differentiation between *personal* writing lessons and *functional* writing lessons. In personal writing, the goal is to develop ideas and express them in written form. The *process* rather than the *output* itself is important, and there is less need for technical perfection. In contrast, the goal of functional writing is to learn the form of the output. In this case, the final product, such as a business letter, will be read by another individual and certain standards and structure are essential. By separating the goals of these two types of lessons, one can develop different kinds of writing skills in each.

4. ***Providing abundant input.*** Students need something to write about. Before asking students to write, make sure that they have enough firsthand experiences. Trips, creative activities, television shows, movies and sports events can be exploited for writing material. Talking about the experiences is also helpful.

5. *Frequent writing.*   Frequent writing has been recommended as help-ful in developing written expression skills. Fader and Schavitz (1966) found that the assignment of a certain number of pages per week in a personal journal that was uncorrected, and even unread, by the teacher was an excellent technique to provide needed practice and to improve the quality of writing.

6. *The cloze procedure.*   The cloze method (discussed in Chapter 12) can also be used to teach written expression. Write a sentence with a word deleted and have pupils try to insert as many words as possible. For example: John _____ the ball. Sentences can be taken from reading material.

7. *Combining sentences.*   This approach to teaching written expression is especially useful for adolescents and adults. Several separate kernel sentences are written. The student must combine the kernel sentences into a more complex sentence by adding clauses and connectors.

Summary

• This chapter examined theories and teaching strategies for the three areas of written communication: handwriting, spelling, and written expres-sion.

• Handwriting is a fine motor skill and one with which many learning-disabled individuals have difficulty. Special consideration must be given to the decision to teach either cursive or manuscript writing, to techniques that can help the left-handed student, and to the efficacy of typewriting for se-verely disabled students. Handwriting difficulties for some students may be eased by having them use a microcomputer for writing.

• Spelling is particularly difficult in English because of the irregularity between spoken and written forms of language. Two choices are available for selecting words to use in spelling instruction: the linguistic approach empha-sizes phonic patterns and underlying rules; the frequency-of-use approach focuses on teaching the spelling of words found most often in the students' reading materials. Spelling requires many intact skills: reading, knowledge of phonics rule, visual memory, and the motor facility to write.

• Written expression is the most difficult of the language skills to achieve and the most common communication disability. Students with underlying oral language difficulties are also likely to experience difficulty in written communication. Teaching writing as a cognitive process emphasizes the thinking process involved in writing rather than the correctness of the written product. It is important to help students develop a rich background of experi-ences in order to encourage them to express those experiences.

• This chapter presented specific teaching strategies for the three areas of the written language curriculum: handwriting, spelling, and written expression.

Key Terms

dysgraphia

dysphonetic dyslexic spelling errors

dyseidetic dyslexic spelling errors

speech synthesizer

upper case letters

manuscript writing

cursive writing

kinesthetic memory

personal writing

functional writing

word processing

word-frequency approach to spelling

ASIA

Chapter Outline

Introduction   Theories

Characteristics of Students with Mathematics Disabilities

Early Indications of Mathematics Problems/
Disturbances of Spatial Relationships/
Disturbances of Motor and Visual-Perception
Abilities/Language and Reading Problems/Poor
Concepts of Direction and Time/Memory
Problems/Other Characteristics

Changing Ideas About Mathematics Education

Learning Theories as a Basis for Teaching Mathematics

Developmental Learning Hierarchies/Mastery
Learning/Cognitive Learning Strategies and
Information Processing/Implications for Learning
Disabilities

Using Technology

Calculators/Computers in Mathematics Education

Assessing Mathematics Proficiency

Informal Inventories/Analyzing Mathematics
Errors/Standardized Survey Tests/Individual
Clinical Tests

Teaching Strategies

The Mathematics Curriculum

The Sequence of Mathematics Through the
Grades/Mathematics Learning Disabilities at the
Secondary Level

Principles of Remedial Instruction in Mathematics

Establish Readiness for Mathematics Learning/
Progress from the Concrete to the Abstract/
Provide Opportunity for Practice and Review/
Teach Students to Generalize to New
Situations/Consider the Student's Strengths and
Weaknesses/Build a Solid Foundation of
Mathematics Concepts and Skills/Provide a
Balanced Mathematics Program

Activities for Teaching Mathematics

Teaching Mathematics Concepts/Teaching
Mathematics Skills/Teaching Applications for
Problem Solving

Summary

Mathematics

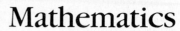

Parallel

Chapter 14

Introduction

$\mathbf{A}$s noted in Chapter 1, Public Law 94–142 identifies two mathematics problem areas in which a student can have a learning disability, *mathematics calculation* and *mathematics reasoning*. This chapter considers both types of problems, as they occur within the three major elements of the mathematics curriculum: (1) concepts, (2) skills, and (3) problem solving. In the Theories section of this chapter, we examine the characteristics of students with learning disabilities in mathematics, the changing ideas about the teaching of mathematics, the learning theories that set the foundation for mathematics education, and assessment methods. In the Teaching Strategies section, we discuss the overall mathematics curriculum, principles of mathematics remedial teaching, and activities for teaching concepts, skills, and problem solving.

■ Theories

Mathematics has been called a universal language. It is a symbolic language that enables human beings to think about, record, and communicate ideas concerning the elements and the relationships of quantity. The scope of mathematics includes the operations of counting, measurement, arithmetic, calculation, geometry, and algebra, as well as the ability to think in quantitative terms. The term *mathematics* encompasses more than the term *arithmetic*. Mathematics is the study of the whole fabric of numbers and their relationships; arithmetic is simply the computational operations taught in the schools (Laycock & Watson, 1975).

Characteristics of Students with Mathematics Disabilities

The subject of remedial mathematics has received much less attention than other areas of remedial education. Yet for many youngsters with learning disabilities, mathematics is the major area of learning difficulty. A severe mathematics learning disability and related conceptual disturbances in learning quantitative elements are sometimes referred to as *dyscalculia*. As with the term *dyslexia* in relation to a severe reading disability (see Chapter 12), dyscalculia has a medical connotation suggesting a central nervous system involvement. Whatever it is called, severe difficulty in learning mathematics can be a debilitating problem in school and in later life. Not all students with learning disabilities have difficulty with number concepts. In fact, some students with severe reading disability have strong mathematics skills. Yet math-

Although they have received far less attention than learning disabilities in reading, specific problems in learning mathematics can be a major and debilitating frustration for many students. *(Peter Vandermark/Stock, Boston)*

ematics disorders do affect a significant portion of the learning disabilities population.

Many of the symptoms of learning disabilities can be linked to mathematics difficulties. Difficulties in spatial relationships, visual-perceptual disturbances, problems with symbols, language disorders, and cognitive abnormalities all have obvious implications for number learning. It must be remembered, however, that each student is unique, and not all who have a mathematics problem will exhibit these characteristics. Nor will any one student be likely to have all these traits.

Early Indications of Mathematics Problems

For some students, difficulties with numerical relationships begin at an early age. The ability to count, to understand the one-to-one correspondence, to match, to sort, and to compare hinges on the student's experiences in manipulating objects. The student with a short attention span, with disturbed perceptual skills, or with inadequate motor development may not have had sufficient or appropriate experiences with activities of manipulation—experiences that would prepare for understandings of space, form, order, time, distance, and quantity.

A child's early concepts of quantity are evidenced in early language in such phrases as "all gone," "that's all," "more," "big," and "little." Normally, young children learn by playing with objects, such as pots and pans, boxes that fit into each other, and objects that can be put into containers. All these activities help develop a sense of space, sequence, and order. Students with mathematics learning disabilities may have missed these essential experiences in their childhood. Parents often report that as young children these students did not enjoy or engage in play with blocks, puzzles, models, or construction-type toys.

Disturbances of Spatial Relationships

Many concepts of spatial relationships are normally acquired at the preschool level. Concepts such as *up-down, over-under, top-bottom, high-low, near-far, front-back, beginning-end,* and *across,* are often confusing to children with mathematics disabilities. A disturbance in spatial relationship can interfere with the visualization of the entire number system. For example, the child may be unable to perceive distances between numbers, on number lines or rulers, and may not know if the number three is closer to four or six (Strauss & Lehtinen, 1947; Bley & Thornton, 1981).

Disturbances of Motor and Visual-Perception Abilities

Students with mathematics disabilities have been observed to have difficulty with activities that require visual perception and visual-motor association. Strauss (1951) noted that some children are unable to count objects in a series by pointing to each of them and saying "One, two, three, four, five." Children with this difficulty must first learn to count by grasping and physically manipulating objects. Grasping the objects appears to be an earlier development in the neuromotor and perceptual developmental hierarchy than pointing to objects.

Many students with a basic mathematics disability are unable to see objects in groups (or sets)—an ability needed to quickly identify the number of objects in a group. Even when adding a group of three with a group of four objects, some students with mathematics disability persist in the behavior of counting the objects one by one to determine the total number in the two groups, far beyond the age that this behavior is considered normal (Thornton, Jones, & Toohey, 1983).

Some students are unable to perceive visually a geometric shape as a complete and integrated entity. A square may not appear as a square shape but as four unrelated lines, as a hexagon, or even as a circle.

Other youngsters have difficulty in learning to perceive number symbols visually. They might confuse the vertical stroke of the number **1** and the number **4**, or they may confuse the upper half of the number **2** and portions of the number **3**.

Students with poor mathematics abilities frequently perform inadequately in visual-motor tasks. Because they cannot capture the gestalt of a shape and because they have a disturbance in perceiving spatial relationships and in making spatial judgments, they may not be able to copy geometric forms, shapes, numbers, or letters adequately. (Consequently, they are likely to perform poorly in handwriting as well as arithmetic.) When students cannot write numbers easily, they also cannot read their own numbers, and they cannot align them properly. As a result, they make errors in computation (Bley & Thornton, 1981). Students must learn to copy and line up numbers accurately in order to calculate problems in addition and subtraction, in place value, and in multiplication and division, where more complicated alignments are needed (Thornton, Tucker, Dossey, & Edna, 1983).

Language and Reading Problems

Some students with a mathematics disability have good verbal and auditory skills. In fact, they may be highly verbal and even be excellent readers. However, for other youngsters with a mathematics disability, the problems are compounded by handicaps in language and reading. Because of the language disorder, the student may confuse the meaning of mathematics terms—*plus, take away, minus, carrying, borrowing, place value*. Arithmetic word story problems are particularly difficult for the student with an underlying language disorder. In many cases, the source of the difficulty is that the student does not understand the language structures of the word story problem (Resnick, 1982; Nesher, 1982). If the student is unable to read and comprehend the word story problem, he or she would not be able to perform the mathematics tasks required to solve it (Cawley, Fitzmaurice, Shaw, Kahn, & Bates, 1979; McLeod & Crump, 1978).

Poor Concepts of Direction and Time

Students with mathematics disabilities often have a poor sense of direction and time. They become lost easily and cannot find their way to a friends' house or home from school. They sometimes forget if it is morning or afternoon and go home during the recess period thinking the school day has ended. They have difficulty estimating the time span of an hour, a minute, several hours, or a week; and they cannot estimate how long a task will take.

Many basic concepts of time are normally learned during the preschool years. Expressions such as "ten minutes ago," "in a half-hour," and "later" are normally part of the preschooler's understanding and speaking vocabulary. By the end of first grade, the students are expected to tell time to the half-hour; by the middle grades, to the nearest minute. Learning-disabled students, however, often have great difficulty with the time concept. They may not be able to judge and allocate the time needed to complete an assignment. In addition, their perceptual problem may keep them from accurately seeing the numbers on a clock face (Bley & Thornton, 1981).

Memory Problems

An understanding of the underlying number system is important for success in mathematics, but of equal importance is the development of skills in the computational operations of arithmetic. For efficient learning, the computational facts of adding, subtracting, multiplying, and dividing must become automatic. Often the student with a severe memory deficit understands the underlying number system but is unable to quickly recall the number facts. With older students, visual memory is also important in learning geometry. The student must remember different geometric shapes and the number of angles on a figure (Thornton, Tucker, Dossey, & Edna, 1983; Torgesen, 1980).

Other Characteristics

Lack of *prerequisite* skills is another consideration. Students may be introduced to a mathematics skill before they are ready for such instruction. Attempts at teaching only confuse them. These students need more experiences with prenumber concepts and skills.

Pupils with poor number sense have been observed to have an inaccurate or imprecise notion of *body image*. They may be unable to understand the basic relationship of the body parts. When asked to draw a picture of a human figure, they may draw the body parts as completely unrelated or misplaced, or with stick legs coming from the head, or with no body at all.

Poor *social maturity* has been noted among many students with mathematics disabilities. Badian and Ghublikian (1983) found poor social-personal characteristics in this group. Johnson and Myklebust (1967) reported that the mean social quotient of a group of dyscalculic children was substantially below their mean verbal intelligence quotient. Further, the performance scores on an intelligence test for this group were far below the scores obtained on the verbal portions of the test.

Changing Ideas About Mathematics Education

We have witnessed wide swings in the philosophy of teaching mathematics over the past thirty years. Mathematics education seems to be particularly prone to the vagaries of international events and national political pressures. Some thirty years ago, the nation's concern about the mathematics knowledge of our students was triggered by the Soviet Union's launching of sputnik, thereby beating the United States into space. The "modern math" curriculum was a response to the call for a more sophisticated mathematics education. Spearheaded by eminent mathematicians, "modern math" had as its goal to help students develop an understanding of the basic structure of the number system rather than learn skills and facts by rote. The emphasis was on teaching the *why,* as well as the *how,* of mathematics through the process of discovery and exploration. However, the "modern math" approach neglected some of the psychological aspects of learning. For many students with mathematics learning disabilities, "modern math" proved to be an inappropriate method, one that compounded their mathematics problems (Wood, 1980).

A more recent event that also prompted mathematics reform was the observation that mathematics scores of the nation's students were declining each year as revealed in tests such as the SAT. (This decline has now begun to level off and the scores have improved, according to the most recent test data.) The annual decline in these scores was highly publicized, leading to new calls for changes in mathematics education. The "basic skills movement" reflected a disillusionment with modern math instruction and a mandate for more emphasis on mathematics calculation skills. The back-to-basics movement advocates the return to the intensive teaching of computation facts. In tune with the times, some of the very early ideas on teaching arithmetic and remediating arithmetic difficulties have reappeared (Brueckner & Bond, 1955; Buswell & John, 1925; Brueckner, 1955). Although many learning-disabled pupils seem to benefit from programs geared to the direct teaching of calculation skills, these skills are only a portion of mathematics education. Concepts, skills, and problem-solving applications are all essential elements of mathematics learning and must be incorporated in the curriculum.

The National Council for Teachers of Mathematics (1980) recommended that the mathematics curriculum include ten basic skills areas:

1. Problem solving
2. Applying mathematics in everyday situations
3. Alertness to the reasonableness of results
4. Estimation and approximation
5. Appropriate computational skills
6. Geometry
7. Measurement
8. Reading, interpreting, and constructing tables, charts, and graphs
9. Using mathematics to predict
10. Computer literacy

Most recently, several commissions have been charged with the task of investigating public education. One influential report, *The Nation at Risk*

(The National Commission on Excellence in Education, 1983), warned that "the educational foundations of our society are presently being eroded by a rising tide of mediocrity that threatens our very future as a Nation and a people" (p. 5). Among other recommendations, the commission called for improvements in teaching mathematics and for computer literacy. Specifically, it called for the high school curriculum to require three years of mathematics and one semester of computer science for graduation. As the new recommendations for mathematics reform are implemented, they will translate into a more stringent high school mathematics program and will certainly have ramifications for students with mathematics learning disabilities.

Unfortunately, students with mathematics disabilities are subjects of wide swings in the philosophy of teaching mathematics. We must make sure that the recommended mathematics curriculum is appropriate for the individual student. In teaching mathematics to learning-disabled students, we must take into account the specific needs of each student, the requirements of the mathematics curriculum of the school, and theories of learning and teaching.

Learning Theories as a Basis for Teaching Mathematics

There are several learning theories that provide the underpinnings of mathematics education today. The three most influential ones are briefly reviewed: (1) *developmental learning hierarchies,* leading to concern about student readiness, providing basic experiences, and teaching prerequisite mathematics skills; (2) *mastery learning,* leading to an emphasis on direct and structured teaching methods; and (3) *information processing and cognitive learning strategies,* leading to emphasis on problem solving and the encouragement of student thinking about the processing of information in mathematics.

Developmental Learning Hierarchies

The writings of Piaget have greatly influenced the teaching of mathematics. Piaget's ideas are discussed in Chapter 6, but the notion that the child goes through a series of intellectual developmental stages has direct implication for mathematics teaching. Since the cognitive abilities and the kinds of thinking that occur are different at each stage, the teacher must consider whether the student's stage of growth make it possible to learn the mathematics of the particular lesson. As noted in Chapter 6, Piaget's stages of cognitive development are *sensorimotor stage* (birth to age two), *preoperational stage* (ages two to seven), *concrete operational stage* (ages seven or eight to eleven), and *formal operational stage* (ages eleven to fourteen).

Piaget's views, according to Reisman (1981, p. 5), have these implications for mathematics instruction:

1. Intellectual development takes place through a series of stages that must always occur in the same order.
2. Stages are defined by clusters of mental operations (seriating, conserving, classifying, hypothesizing, inferring) that underlie intellectual behavior.
3. Movement through the stages is accomplished by equilibration, the process of development that involves the interactions between experience (assimilation) and growing cognitive structures (accommodation).

This means that it is fruitless to attempt to teach a mathematics skill or concept before the appropriate cognitive development has occurred in the learner. For example, if the mathematics lesson requires formal operations (abstract reasoning) and the student has not reached that stage of development, the learning will not be successful. Piaget made many other important contributions to mathematics education. For example, Thornton, Tucker, Dossey & Edna (1983) point out that Piaget's theories explain the importance of using concrete materials to facilitate mathematics learning.

Mastery Learning

Mastery learning (Bloom, 1976), discussed in Chapter 6, is another learning theory with implications for the teaching of mathematics (Underhill, Uprichards, & Heddens, 1980). The mastery learning approach is compatible with instructional methods advocated by behavioral psychologists, such as Gagne (1984). The steps in mastery learning for teaching mathematics are as follows:

1. *Target a specific objective to be accomplished.* This goal must be measurable and observable. For example, the student will write the answers to twenty multiplication problems (numerals 1 through 7) in ten minutes with 90 percent accuracy.
2. *Outline the steps needed to reach that objective.*
3. *Determine which of these steps the student already knows.* For example, does the student already know the numerals 1 through 5 easily in multiplication? Can the student already do the task accurately, but very slowly?
4. *Sequence the steps needed to reach the objective.* If the student already knows 1 through 5, then the steps for teaching multiplication of the 6 and 7 will be needed. If the student already knows 1 through 7 but does the problems very slowly, then teaching to provide drill and practice to speed the computations will be needed.

Mathematics programs based on this approach are highly structured and carefully sequenced; they require very directive teaching. The sequential nature of mathematics makes the mastery learning approach particularly adaptable to this content. Examples of mathematics programs based on this philosophy include *DISTAR Arithmetic* (Science Research Associates); *Sullivan Programmed Math* (Webster/McGraw-Hill); *Sequential Mathematics* (Harcourt Brace Jovanovich); and *Criterion-referenced Measurement Program/Mathematics* (Science Research Associates).

Cognitive Learning Strategies and Information Processing

The cognitive learning strategies approach to teaching, discussed in Chapter 6, also has useful applications for the teaching of mathematics. From this perspective, the student learning mathematics is viewed as a problem solver. What is emphasized is the use of cognitive strategies and the processing of information as students to go about learning mathematics. Students, in effect, learn to monitor their own thinking. They are encouraged to talk to themselves, asking themselves questions, as a method of learning and promoting thinking and information processing (Deshler, Schumaker, & Lenz, 1984; Carpenter, Moser, & Romberg, 1982; Reisman, 1981; Resnick & Ford, 1981). Examples of this kind of thinking and self-questioning are: "What is missing?" or "Do I need to add or subtract?" Or they can comment, "Oh, I've had this same kind of problem wrong before," or "I need to draw this on paper in order to see what is missing."

Carpenter and Moser (1982) conducted research on the cognitive strategies children use in mathematics, and they found that in grades 1 and 2 children invent their own strategies to solve simple word problems. By the middle grades, however, they stop their personal cognitive analysis and rely on rote procedures they have learned. They tend merely to compute with whatever numbers are in the problem. The researchers suggest that students in the middle grades be encouraged to continue to create and use cognitive strategies for problem solving in mathematics. Collis (1982) recommends that the mathematics teacher should help structure the student's response to a mathematics problem, by beginning a dialogue about that response for the purpose of raising the level of the student's answers.

Mathematics programs stressing cognitive problem-solving include *Stern Structural Arithmetic* (Houghton Mifflin); *Project MATH* (Educational Development Corp.); and *Nuffield Mathematics* Project (Nuffield Foundation).

Implications for Learning Disabilities

All three theories apply to the teaching of mathematics to students with learning disabilities. First, teachers should consider the developmental stage of the student. In many cases, students need more experience with prenumber learnings to provide the foundation for mathematics learning. Students cannot be expected to do abstract reasoning without the prerequisite development and experiences.

In addition, the learning disabled-student needs carefully structured and planned instruction in mathematics. The process of task analysis, setting specific objectives, and planning the sequences is essential. Of extreme importance, too, is the allocation of sufficient time for learning each step of the sequence.

Finally, the teaching of cognitive learning strategies has been found effective in helping learning-disabled students learn mathematics (Deshler, Schumaker & Levy 1984; Carpenter et al., 1982; Resnick & Ford 1981; Hallahan, 1980; Torgesen, 1980; Cawley, Fitzmaurice, Shaw, Kahn, & Bates, 1979). Students must be encouraged to ask themselves questions, to cognitively process information as a problem solving strategy, and to develop their own approach to learning and thinking about mathematics.

Using Technology

Two products of high technology have particular significance for the teaching of mathematics: the calculator and the microcomputer. Students often have access to these devices outside of the school setting as well as within the classroom.

Calculators

The calculator is widely recognized as having revolutionized functional arithmetic. Calculators are being used everywhere — grocery stores, restaurants, real estate firms, used car salesrooms, and college classes. The question one must ask is "Should pupils in school be taught how to make efficient use of the calculator in today's world?" There is undoubtedly a place for the calculator in our instructional planning, but students should be required to learn the computation facts. However, there are times for using the calculator as well. Calculators have been suggested for lessons that aim to teach mathematics reasoning, not calculation skills per se. Students often become so bogged down in computation that they never get to the mathematics-reasoning aspects of the lesson; the use of calculators can free them for understanding the mathematical concept underlying the calculation.

A low-cost pocket calculator is easily accessible, handy, can be used to compute basic facts as well as more complicated math processes, and can be used for drill and for self-checking. It is particularly helpful for the adult who has not memorized basic computation facts, since it is more socially acceptable than other counting systems.

Computers in Mathematics Education

Ready or not, the schools have to cope with the computer age that has burst upon them. Although computers are used in various parts of the curriculum, as has already been discussed (IEPs, reading, and writing), the mathematics program appears to have the main responsibility for computer education. Often computer education is part of the mathematics curriculum in the schools, the microcomputer may be located in the math lab, and the mathematics teacher is likely to be the staff member expected to teach computer literacy courses.

More than 60 percent of the elementary schools and 86 percent of the secondary schools now have microcomputers, and they possess a variety of hardware. One survey showed that about 40 percent of the schools have Apples, 35 percent have Tandys, 20 percent have Commodores, and the balance is divided among several different other brands (Ingersoll, Smith, & Elliot, 1983). The IBM PC jr. is likely to take a chunk of this market in the near future. The computer programs—the software—must be adapted for the particular hardware with which it will be used.

In mathematics, especially on the elementary school level, computers have been used mostly with the *drill-and-practice* software packages, which offer students additional review of computation facts. Programs are coming out so fast that it is difficult to keep up with them. Many are excellent teaching tools, but some fall short of expectations. Teachers will have to read software reviews, go to computer conferences, and try out software programs to sort out the good software packages for mathematics drill and review. One arithmetic drill program students seem to like is *Alligator Alley* (DLM).

Another use of the computer for mathematics is *computer-managed instruction*. These programs are designed for prescriptive teaching, assessment, and keeping records. One computer-managed instruction program is CADPP, which is designed to teach reading and mathematics. This program has been used in more than 210 classrooms in sixty-nine Chapter I projects (special remedial programs funded by the Department of Education) and has been judged by a Department of Education panel to be effective (Anderson & Glowinski, 1982). The computer is also excellent for practice in problem-solving skills. The programs *Gertrude's Secrets* and *Gertrude's Puzzles* (The Learning Company) have proved popular and require limited reading skills.

The full potential of the microcomputer, however, goes beyond the drill-and-practice programs or managing instruction. Perhaps its most exciting and creative use for learning-disabled students is learning and programming with the computer language known as LOGO. Developed at the Massachusetts Institute of Technology by Seymour Papert (1980) after five years of study with Piaget, LOGO is consistent with what is known about cognitive development in children. It can be learned and used at many levels of complexity. A young child can do some fascinating graphics programmed within a few minutes of being introduced to LOGO (Maddux, 1984; Gray, 1984).

LOGO graphics employ a "turtle," a small shape that can be moved about the screen, leaving a line in its path. The turtle can be used to create colorful and complex designs. The student moves the turtle by entering simple commands one at a time, or a program can be written and later carried out all at

If learning-disabled students are encouraged to attempt simple computer programming, they may experience success and build confidence in a new and prestigious part of the school environment.   *(Jerry Howard/Positive Images)*

once. Students learn single words, problem-solving skills, right and left, basic elements of programming, and geometric concepts that they would not normally learn until junior high school. The graphics enhance student learning, and quick visual feedback lets student programmers know whether they made the right decisions.

Maddux (1984) believes that LOGO is particularly suited for learning-disabled students for several reasons:

1. LOGO offers the learning-disabled student success, instead of failure, with prestigious technological equipment in the school setting. Students become more willing to try new things and not so frightened to use their abilities.
2. LOGO can be highly motivating because the complex graphics can be created immediately, encouraging learning-disabled students to continue to learn in order to master LOGO.
3. LOGO is self-correcting, and so the student is not subject to adult criticism or correction.
4. Work with LOGO provides practice with spatial relations and abstract concepts.
5. Teachers have reported that social interactions increase when students

use LOGO. Students share their experiences and solve problems together.

6. LOGO helps to reduce impulsivity and increase attention span.
7. LOGO gives students a chance to use numbers and mathematics in an interesting setting that is relevant, novel, and free from unpleasant associations.

The following original case describes a learning-disabled student who took part in a LOGO instruction program. It was suggested by an article in *Educational Computer* (1984) by L. Gray.

CASE EXAMPLE

A Learning-Disabled Computer Programmer

Max was one of several students at the Sloan School who attended a series of LOGO classes during the school year. Classified as a case of severe learning disabilities, Max's evaluation showed he had auditory difficulties and poor visual memory. Large for his age, he had problems with motor coordination and lacked social skills, and so made few friends in class.

Max enjoyed working on the computer right from the start. It gave him a sense of control. At first Max needed help to use the keyboard and spell the various commands. Very soon, however, he developed a logical and organized way to plan and correct his work. He learned to command the computer to draw a series of rectangles and circles and tell his turtle to spin in repetitive patterns. Max became fascinated with the activities on the screen that he created by himself.

As Max became more deeply involved with LOGO, his personality seemed to change. As he met with the initial success in using LOGO, he became more active and assertive and soon learned to comprehend the different error messages and to use new commands.

The LOGO teacher observed that Max displayed more purposeful, problem-solving behavior when using the computer. His social skills improved, too, as he began to express interest in the work of other students and to show them his work. His face became more expressive; his posture was more relaxed. His resource teacher reported that Max had learned how to concentrate on his lessons. His sixth-grade teacher said that Max was beginning to show he really cared about his school work and seemed more confident in his academic abilities. All of Max's teachers believed these changes were directly due to the successful experiences in the LOGO class.

Assessing Mathematics Proficiency

Information about a student's abilities and proficiency in mathematics can be gathered in several ways. The teacher can (1) give informal inventories and tests, (2) conduct an analysis of the errors being made by the student, (3) administer standardized survey tests, or (4) use individual clinical tests designed for diagnosis. An extensive and comprehensive evaluation would probably involve all four types of assessment. In other cases, only one or two of the assessment methods may suffice.

Informal Inventories

Many learning disabilities specialists believe that informal measures are the best way of obtaining information about a student's performance and abilities in mathematics (Zigmond, Vallecorsa, & Silverman, 1983; Guerin & Maier, 1983). Observations of a student's daily behavior, the student's performance on homework assignments, and teacher-made tests or tests that accompany the mathematics textbook can provide information for basic assessment decisions.

Zigmond et al. (1983) recommend a twelve-step informal assessment strategy, which leads the teacher from the decision to assess to the instruction plan based on that assessment.

1. Decide what to assess.
2. Select or develop a skill hierarchy.
3. Decide where to begin.
4. Select or develop survey instrument.
5. Get ready to test.
6. Administer the survey.
7. Note errors and performance style.
8. Analyze findings and summarize outcomes.
9. Hypothesize reasons for errors and determine areas to probe.
10. Probe.
11. Complete record-keeping forms and generate teaching objectives.
12. Start teaching; update assessment information.

A key factor in this method is the probe. First, the teacher gives a general informal survey test to assess the student's overall mathematics proficiency. Then the teacher designs an informal probe, a much more specific and precise measure of the area of difficulty. For example, the mathematics survey test could have a few addition, subtraction, multiplication and division problems using whole numbers, fractions, and decimals. If the student began to show difficulty with division problems in the survey, then the probe would examine this specific area of mathematics more closely. Thus, the informal assessment is tailored for the individual student.

An informal mathematics test can be devised by the teacher to obtain a fast assessment of the student's skills (Zigmond et al., 1983; Underhill et al., 1980). Select some items for each skill and place them in order of increasing difficulty. Once the general area of difficulty is determined, a more extensive diagnostic test of that area can be given. A sample informal arithmetic test appears in Figure 14.1.

FIGURE 14.1
Informal Inventory of Arithmetic Skills

Addition

3	8	25	20	15	77	5
+5	+0	+71	+49	+ 7	+29	2
						+7

$5 + 7 = \square$ $3 + \square = 12$ $\square + 7 = 15$

	233		879		648
	+ 45		+ 48		745
					+286

Subtraction

7	25	78	72	546	6762
−5	− 9	− 23	− 49	− 222	−4859

$5 - 2 = \square$ $7 - \square = 4$ $\square - 3 = 5$

Multiplication

5	6	24	86	59	25
×3	×7	× 2	× 7	×34	×79

$6 \times 3 = \square$ $7 \times \square = 56$ $\square \times 5 = 20$

Division

$2\overline{)10}$ $4\overline{)16}$ $8\overline{)125}$ $11\overline{)121}$ $12\overline{)108}$

$12 \div 4 = \square$ $24 \div \square = 6$ $\square \div 9 = 6$

Analyzing Mathematics Errors

When working with a student with an arithmetic disability, teachers should be able to detect the type of errors the student is making so that instruction can be directed toward correcting that error. Teachers should examine the student's work or ask the student to explain how he or she went about solving a problem. A teacher needs to observe the methods used by the student and then determine the thought processes involved in those methods (Bachor, 1979; Reisman, 1981; Ashlock, 1982). The four types of mistakes listed below are among the most common errors of calculation.

Place Value. Pupils who make this error do not understand the concepts of place value, regrouping, carrying, or borrowing. For example:

$$\begin{array}{r} 75 \\ -\,27 \\ \hline 58 \end{array} \qquad \begin{array}{r} 63 \\ +\,18 \\ \hline 71 \end{array}$$

These students need concrete practice in the place value of 1s, 10s, 100s, and 1000s. Effective tools for such concrete practice are an abacus and a place value box or chart with compartments. Students can sort objects (sticks, straws, or chips) into compartments to show place value.

Computation Facts. Students who make errors in basic adding, subtracting, multiplying, and dividing need more practice and drill. A handy multiplication chart, like the one in Figure 14.2, might be useful in checking their work. For example:

$$\begin{array}{r} 6 \\ \times\,8 \\ \hline 46 \end{array} \qquad \begin{array}{r} 9 \\ \times\,7 \\ \hline 62 \end{array}$$

Using the Wrong Process. Some students use the wrong mathematical process, and this accounts for their errors. For example:

$$\begin{array}{r} 6 \\ \times\,2 \\ \hline 8 \end{array} \qquad \begin{array}{r} 15 \\ -\,3 \\ \hline 18 \end{array}$$

These students need work in recognizing symbols and signs.

Working from Right to Left. Some students reverse the direction of calculations and work from right to left. For example:

$$\begin{array}{r} 35 \\ +\,81 \\ \hline 17 \end{array} \qquad \begin{array}{r} 56 \\ +\,49 \\ \hline 49 \end{array}$$

These students need work in place value.

In addition, *poor writing skills* cause many math errors. When students cannot read their own writing or fail to align their numbers in columns, they may not understand what to do.

Standardized Survey Tests

Survey tests provide information on the general level of the student's mathematics performance. They are designed for groups, although they can be given to an individual as well. Usually, information is available on the test's reliability, validity, and standardization procedures. Often, there are accompanying manuals with tables for various kinds of score interpretation: grade scores, age scores, standard scores, percentiles Most of the survey tests in mathematics are part of a general achievement test battery. Among the widely used are the *California Achievement Test,* the *Metropolitan Achievement Test,* and the *SRA Achievement Test.*

Individual Clinical Tests

These tests are designed to be given to an individual rather than a group. Many of them yield more diagnostic information than the survey tests, providing information on specific areas of mathematics difficulty and more clues for planning instruction. Among the widely used clinical tests are the *Wide Range Achievement Test, Key Math Diagnostic Arithmetic Test, Peabody Individual Achievement Test,* the *Stanford Diagnostic Arithmetic Test,* the *Woodcock Johnson Achievement Test,* the *Brigance Diagnostic Inventory of Basic Skills,* and the *Brigance Diagnostic Mathematics Inventory.* Teachers should be aware that many of the diagnostic tests used in learning disabilities programs have been judged statistically inadequate by measurement experts (Salvia & Ysseldyke, 1981). Therefore, it is important to check the validity, reliability, and standardization procedures of tests before using them. These tests are described in Appendix C.

According to a survey of learning disabilities assessment programs, the *Key Math Diagnostic Arithmetic Test* is the most widely used instrument for arithmetic assessment (Ysseldyke, 1983). This test has fourteen subtests covering the following areas: content (numeration, fractions, geometry, and symbols); operations (addition, subtraction, multiplication, division, mental computation, and numerical reasoning); and applications (word problems, missing elements, money, measurement, and time).

Breen, Lehman, and Carlson (1984) note many common characteristics between the Key Math and the Woodcock-Johnson math subtest, and found a high correlation between these two tests. They suggest standard scores be utilized to a greater degree for comparing performance on different tests.

■ Teaching Strategies

The rest of this chapter presents teaching strategies for mathematics education. It includes a discussion of the mathematics curriculum in our schools, some principles of teaching mathematics, and activities for teaching mathematics concepts, skills, and problem solving.

The Mathematics Curriculum

Mainstream teachers, as well as resource room and special classroom teachers, need to have a general picture of the overall mathematics curriculum. It is important to know (1) what the student has learned before the present developmental stage and (2) what mathematics learnings lie ahead.

The Sequence of Mathematics Through the Grades

Mathematics is a subject that is naturally cumulative, and it is typically taught in a sequence that introduces certain skills at each grade level. For example, learning multiplication depends on knowing addition. Although the sequence may vary somewhat in different programs, the general timetables of instruction are as follows:

> *Kindergarten.* Basic number meanings, counting, classification, seriation or order, recognition of numerals, writing of numbers.
>
> *Grade 1.* Addition through 20, subtraction through 20, place value of 1s and 10s, time to the half-hour, money, simple measurement.
>
> *Grade 2.* Addition through 100, subtraction through 100, ordering of 0 to 100, skip counting (by twos), place value of 100, regrouping for adding and subtracting.
>
> *Grade 3.* Multiplication through 9s, odd or even skip counting, place value of 1000s, two and three-place numbers for addition and subtraction.
>
> *Grade 4.* Division facts, extended use of multiplication facts and related division facts through 9s, two-place multipliers.
>
> *Grade 5.* Fractions, addition and subtraction of fractions, mixed numbers, long division, two-place division, decimals.
>
> *Grade 6.* Percents, three-place multipliers, two-place division, addition and subtraction of decimals and mixed decimals, multiplication and division of decimals and mixed decimals by whole numbers.
>
> *Grade 7.* Geometry, rounding, ratios, simple probability.
>
> *Grade 8.* Scientific notion, using graphs, complex fractions, more complex applications, and word problems.

The major topics that are covered in the mathematics curriculum, grade 1 through 8, include numbers and numeration; whole numbers—addition and subtraction; whole numbers—multiplication and division; decimals; fractions; measurement; geometry; and computer education, a subject that is beginning to show up in many math programs (Thornton, Tucker, Dossey & Edna, 1983).

Mathematics Learning Disabilities at the Secondary Level

The mathematics difficulties for students in junior and senior high school are different from those at the elementary level. A survey of teachers working with learning-disabled students in mathematics at junior and senior high school levels showed that the most common mathematics difficulties were division of whole numbers, basic operations including fractions, decimals, and percentages, fraction terminology, multiplication of whole numbers, place value, measurement skills, and the language of mathematics (McLeod & Armstrong, 1982). For remedial instruction, the teachers in this survey reported that they used (1) mainstream texts, (2) other commercial materials, and (3) teacher-made instructional materials. All the teachers acknowledged a need for more specific math materials for learning-disabled adolescents.

Principles of Remedial Instruction in Mathematics

Certain principles are applicable to all types of mathematics learning and essential for effective teaching and remediation. The remediation principles discussed here include developing prenumber concepts—a readiness for mathematics learning; teaching from the concrete to the abstract; providing opportunities and time for practice; generalizing the concepts and skills that have been learned; working with the student's strengths and weaknesses; building a solid foundation of mathematics concepts and skills; and providing a balanced mathematics program.

Establish Readiness for Mathematics Learning

It is important to check back far enough into the previously acquired number learnings to insure that the student is ready for what needs to be learned now. Time and effort invested in building a firm foundation can prevent many later difficulties as students try to move on to more advanced and more abstract mathematics processes. The following basic prenumber learnings are essential (Bley & Thornton, 1981) and must be taught, if they are lacking:

1. Matching (concept of the "same" and grouping of objects)
2. Recognizing groups of objects (recognizing a group of three without counting)
3. Counting (matching numerals to objects)
4. Naming a number that comes after a given number (for example, what comes after 7?)
5. Writing numerals 0 to 10 (getting the sequence correct, overcoming reversals and distortions)
6. Measuring and paring (estimating, fitting objects, one-to-one correspondence)
7. Sequential values (arranging like objects in order by quantitative differences)
8. Relationships of parts to whole and parts to each other (experimentation with self-correcting materials to discover numerical relationships)
9. Operations (manipulation of number facts without reference to concrete objects—number facts to 10)
10. The decimal system (learning the system of numeration and notation beyond 10 and base 10)

Progress from the Concrete to the Abstract

Pupils can best understand a math concept when the teaching progresses from the concrete to the abstract. A teacher should plan three instructional stages: (1) *concrete,* (2) *representational,* and (3) *abstract.* In the concrete stage, the student manipulates real objects in learning the skill. For example, in the *concrete* stage, the student could see, hold, and move two blocks and three blocks to learn that they equal five blocks.

In the *representational* stage, a graphic representation is substituted for actual objects. For example, circles represent objects in the illustration from a worksheet below:

$$\circ\circ + \circ\circ\circ = 5$$

At the *abstract* level, numerals finally replace the graphic symbols.

$$2 + 3 = 5$$

Provide Opportunity for Practice and Review

Students need much review, drill, and practice to overlearn the math concepts, since they must be able to use the concepts almost automatically. There are many ways to provide this practice, and teachers should vary the method as often as possible. Different techniques for providing practice can include worksheets, flash cards, games, behavior modification techniques (rewards for work completed), and computer practice (special software programs that give immediate feedback).

Teach Student to Generalize to New Situations

Students must learn to generalize a skill to many situations. For example, they can practice computation facts with many story problems that the teacher or students create and then exchange. The point is to gain skill in recognizing and applying computational operations to various new situations.

Consider the Student's Strengths and Weaknesses

Before deciding on techniques for teaching mathematics, the teacher must understand the student's abilities and disabilities in relation to mathematics. Besides knowing the attainment levels and the mathematics operations that the student can perform, the teacher should try to understand what attributes and deficiencies the student brings to mathematics learning. How do the student's areas of disability affect the math learning? What other tasks does the student approach in this manner? How far back is it necessary to go to insure a firm foundation in number concepts? Considering these abilities and disabilities, what techniques, approaches, and materials appear to be most promising? Thus, it is useful to investigate characteristics related to math learning (Chalfant & Scheffelin, 1969; Bley & Thornton, 1981).

1. Determine if the student has comprehension of number structure and arithmetic operations. Is the student able to understand the meaning of spoken numbers? Can the student read and write numbers? Can the student perform basic arithmetic operations. Can the student tell which is larger and which is smaller?
2. Determine the student's skills in spatial orientation. Has the student

established a left-right directionality or shown evidence of spatial dis-
orientation?

3. To what extent does language ability contribute to problems in mathematics? Does the student's ability to understand language (receptive language) and use language (expressive language) affect mathematics learning?

4. Does poor reading ability interfere with mathematics learning? Can the
student read numbers? Can the student read the words in the directions
and in the story problems? Does the student understand the sentences in
the story problems?

5. Are there memory or attention problems that interfere with mathematics
learning? Does the student have difficulty remembering math facts?

Build a Solid Foundation of Mathematics Concepts and Skills

Poor teaching can actually make a student's mathematics problem even
worse. Mathematics should be taught in a way that solidifies the mathematics
concepts, so they are stable and remain available to the student. Bereiter
(1968) suggests that the following principles will help students develop a
solid foundation of mathematics thinking.

1. The emphasis in mathematics instruction should be on finding out answers to questions rather than on merely doing something.

2. Whatever is learned should be generalized to many different kinds of
applications and experiences with different ways of handling the problem.

3. Beginning mathematics should be made coherent instead of being taught
as a collection of unrelated topics and tricks.

4. Instruction must be thorough so that pupils have the needed practice. In
some math programs, insufficient time is devoted to practice.

5. The mathematics program should be taught so that the student gains
confidence in mathematics ability. Adults often become alarmed and
defensive when faced with a mathematical problem because they lost
confidence during their early arithmetic instruction.

Provide a Balanced Mathematics Program

A balanced program is needed for good mathematics instruction and should
include an appropriate combination of three elements: *concepts, skills,* and
problem solving. All three are essential for mathematics learning (Thornton,
Tucker, Dossey, & Edna, 1983).

Concepts

Concepts refer to basic understandings. Students develop a concept when
they are able to classify or group objects, or when they can associate a label

with a class. An example is recognizing that *round* objects form a group and that that class is called *circle*. Another example of a concept is the formulation of rules or regularities. To illustrate, a concept is developed when the student learns that when a number is multiplied by 10 the product is that number followed by a 0.

Skills

While concepts refer to basic understandings, skills refer to something one does. For example, the process of doing the number facts—the basic operations in addition, subtraction, multiplication, and division—are mathematics skills. A skill can be performed well or not so well, quickly or slowly, easily or with great difficulty. Skills tend to develop by degrees and can be improved through instructional activities.

Applications for Problem Solving

Application refers to using a skill or concept to accomplish some task or solve some problem. Usually, applications involve the selection and use of some combination of concepts or skills in a new or different setting. An example of application is the problem of measuring a board of lumber. The concepts involved in a rectangle and parallel sides come into play, as well as the skills of measuring, multiplying and adding. According to Thornton, Tucker, Dossey, & Edna (1983), to teach mathematics applications, the teacher must help a student identify analogous situations—that is, think of situations that are similar to the presented problem and then use these similarities by applying the same concepts and skills in both situations.

Activities for Teaching Mathematics

The remediation activities in this section are grouped into the three categories just discussed: *concepts, skills,* and *applications for problem solving.*

Teaching Mathematics Concepts

Classification and Grouping

1. ***Sorting games.***   Give students objects that differ in only one attribute, for example, color or texture, and ask them to sort the objects into two different boxes. For example, if the objects differ by color, have students put red items in one box and blue items in another box. At a more advanced level, increase the complexity of the classification of the attributes, for example, movable objects and stationary objects. Another variation is to use objects that have several attributes: for example, shape, color, and size. Present children with geometric cutouts of triangles, circles, and squares in three different colors (blue, yellow, and red) and two sizes (small and large). The three attributes of the objects overlap.

Ask the students to sort them according to shape and then according to color. Then ask them to discover a third way of sorting.

2. ***Matching and sorting.***   A first step in the development of number concepts is the ability to focus on and recognize a single object or shape. Have the pupil search through a collection of assorted objects to find a particular type of object. For example, the pupil might look in a box of colored beads or blocks for a red one, search through a collection of various kinds of nuts for all the almonds, choose the forks from a box of silverware, look in a box of buttons for the oval ones, sort a bagful of cardboard shapes to pick out the circles, or look in a container of nuts and bolts for the square pieces.

3. ***Recognition of groups of objects.***   Cards with colored discs, domino games, playing cards, concrete objects, felt boards, magnetic boards, mathematics workbooks—all provide excellent materials for developing concepts of groups.

4. ***Number stamp.***   Using a stamp pad and a stamp (the eraser on the end of a pencil will serve very well), the student can make a set of numerals with matching dots. Two students can play the classic card game "War" with one standard deck of cards and one deck made with stamped dots; the first player to recognize and claim matching cards can take them.

Ordering

1. ***Serial order and relationships.***   When teaching the concept of ordering, ask the student to tell the number that comes after 6 or before 5 or between 2 and 4. Also, ask the student to indicate the first, last, or third of a series of objects. Other measured quantities can be arranged by other dimensions, such as size, weight, intensity, color, volume, pitch of sound, and so forth.

2. ***Number lines.***   Number lines and number blocks to walk on are helpful in understanding the symbols and their relationships to each other.

```
     .     .     .     .     .     .     .
   ───────────────────────────────────────
     0     1     2     3     4     5     6
```

3. ***Pattern games.***   Ask the student to discover patterns by selecting the next object in a series that you have begun. For example, a pattern of red–white–red–white– will be followed by a red. Increase the complexity of patterns as the exercise progresses.

4. ***Relationship between concepts of size and length.***   Have the student compare and contrast objects of different size, formulating concepts of smaller, bigger, taller, shorter. Make cardboard objects such as circles, trees, houses, and so forth, or collect objects such as washers, paper clips, and screws. Have the student arrange them by size. Have the

student estimate the size of objects by guessing whether certain objects would fit into certain spaces.

One-to-One Correspondence

Pairing.   Pairing provides a foundation for counting. Activities designed to match or align one object with another are useful. Have the student arrange a row of pegs to match a prearranged row in a pegboard, set a table and place one cookie on each dish, and plan the allocation of materials to the group so that each person receives one object.

Counting

1. ***Motor activities for counting.*** Some students learn to count verbally, but without attaining the concept that each number corresponds to one object. Such students are helped by making a strong motor and tactile response along with the counting. Visual stimuli or pointing to the object may not be enough because such students will count erratically, skipping objects or saying two numbers for one object. Motor activities to help the student establish the counting principle include placing a peg in a hole, clipping clothespins on a line, and stringing beads onto a pipe cleaner. The auditory modality can be used to reinforce visual counting by having the student listen to the counts of a drumbeat with eyes closed. The student may make a mark for each sound and then count the marks. Have the student establish the counting principle through motor activities, for example, clap three times, jump four times, tap on the table two times.
2. ***Counting cups.***   Take a set of containers, such as cups, with a numeral to designate each container. Have the student fill each container with the correct number of objects, using items such as bottle caps, chips, buttons, screws, or washers.

Recognition of Numbers

1. ***Visual recognition of numbers.***   Students must learn to recognize the printed numbers (e.g., *7, 8, 3*) and the words expressing these numbers (*seven, eight, three*); and they must learn to integrate the written forms with the spoken symbol. For the student who confuses one number with another, color cues may be used to aid in recognition of the symbol: make the top of the 3 green and the bottom red. Have the student match the correct number with the correct set of objects; felt, cardboard, sandpaper symbols, and sets of objects can be used.
2. ***Parking lot poster.***   Draw a parking lot on a poster, numbering parking spaces with dots instead of numerals. Paint numerals on small cars and have the student park the car in the correct space.

Motor Activities

1. **Work space.**   A large table with equipment that can help in performing number tasks is helpful. Counting materials such as an abacus, beans, sticks, play money and rulers and other measuring instruments are among the items the student might use.
2. **Puzzles, peg boards, form boards.**   These are useful to help the student focus on shapes and spatial relations. For the student who has difficulty finding and fitting the missing piece, auditory cues and verbalization may be helpful. Discuss the shape being sought and ask the student to feel the edges for tactile cues.
3. **Measurement.**   Pouring sand, water, or beans from a container of one shape or size to a different container helps the student develop concepts of measurement. Estimating quantities, the use of measuring cups, and the introduction of fractions can be emphasized in such activities. Use actual containers and measuring devices to introduce the idea of measurement. Containers for pints, quarts, half-gallons, gallons, pounds, and half-pounds provide the opportunity to teach measurement and to demonstrate relationships of measurement.

Teaching Mathematics Skills

1. **Basic computational skills.**   Learning disabilities teachers report that many problems in arithmetic are due to deficiencies in basic computational skills. Each pupil's problem should be evaluated with reference to underlying deficits in learning processes—verbal, spatial, perceptual, or memory factors. In addition, however, one must consider teaching the basic computational skills that the student lacks, including addition, subtraction, multiplication, division, fractions, decimals, and percentages. Excellent suggestions for teaching computational skills are given by May (1974), Thornton (1984), and Thornton, Jones, & Toohey (1983).
2. **Addition.**   Knowledge of addition facts provides the foundation for all other computational skills in arithmetic. Addition is a short method of counting, and pupils should know that they can resort to counting when all else fails. Addition can be thought of as *part plus part equals whole.* Important symbols to learn are: + (plus or "put together") and = (equals or "the same as"). As with the other areas, first use concrete objects; then use cards with sets that represent numbers; and, finally, use the number sentence with the numbers alone: $3 + 2 = \square$. From this the pupil can also learn that: $3 + 2 = \square$; $\square + 2 = 5$; and $3 + \square = 5$.

   Addition using sums between 10 and 20 is more difficult. May (1974) suggests several approaches. It is easier to start with doubles, such as $8 + 8 = 16$. Then ask how much is $9 + 8$. One more than 16.

   Another way is to "make a 10." For example, in $7 + 5$, the pupil takes 3 of the 5, and adds the 3 to the 7 to make 10. Now the pupil can see that 10 + the remaining 2 = 12. Use movable disks so that the student can actually experience the process.

$$0 \ 0 \ 0 \ 0 \ 0 \ 0 \ 0 \ \bullet \ \bullet \ \bullet \qquad\qquad 10 + 2 = 12$$
$$0 \ 0 \ \bullet \ \bullet \ \bullet \qquad\qquad\qquad\qquad\qquad 7 + 5 = 12$$

The number line provides another way to teach addition.

3. **Subtraction.** After a good start on addition, introduce subtraction. An important new symbol is − (minus or "take away"). The pupil places a set of objects on the desk and then takes away a certain object. How many are left? 6 − 2 = □. Then use cards with sets on them. Find 6 by using a card with a set of 2 and a card with a set of 4. Tell the student you have a set of 6 when the cards are joined. Take away the set of 2 and ask the student what is left.

Another way of illustrating subtraction is using rods, such as Cuisenaire Rods. Start with the rod that represents a total sum. Place on top a type of rod that represents part of the sum. Ask the pupil to find the rod that fills the empty space.

The number line is useful in subtraction, too.

4. **Multiplication.** Very frequently the student with an arithmetic disability does not know multiplication facts (shown in Figure 14.2). In that case, division will also be impossible to learn.

Multiplication is a short method of adding. Instead of adding 2 + 2 + 2 + 2, the pupil can learn 2 × 4 = 8. May (1974) points out that subtraction is *not* a prerequisite of multiplication, and a student having difficulty with subtraction may do better with multiplication. The symbol to learn is × (times).

May suggests that there are a number of ways of explaining multiplication. One way is the *multiplication sentence.* How much are 3 sets of 2? Using sets of objects, the student can find the total either by counting objects or by adding equal addends.

The concept of reversals (turn-around) can be introduced. The sentence 3 × 5 = □ does not change in the form 5 × 3 = □.

In the *equal addend approach,* ask the student to show that

$$3 \times 5 = 5 + 5 + 5, \text{ or } 15$$

In the *number line* approach, pupils who can use number lines for addition will probably do well in using them for multiplication. The pupil adds a unit of 5 three times on the line, to end up at the 15 on the number line.

The *rectangular array approach* contains an equal number of objects in each row: 3 × 5 is shown as:

$$0 \quad 0 \quad 0 \quad 0 \quad 0$$
$$0 \quad 0 \quad 0 \quad 0 \quad 0$$
$$0 \quad 0 \quad 0 \quad 0 \quad 0$$

FIGURE 14.2
Multiplication Chart

1	2	3	4	5	6	7	8	9	10	11	12
2	4	6	8	10	12	14	16	18	20	22	24
3	6	9	12	15	18	21	24	27	30	33	36
4	8	12	16	20	24	28	32	36	40	44	48
5	10	15	20	25	30	35	40	45	50	55	60
6	12	18	24	30	36	42	48	54	60	66	72
7	14	21	28	35	42	49	56	63	70	77	84
8	16	24	32	40	48	56	64	72	80	88	96
9	18	27	36	45	54	63	72	81	90	99	108
10	20	30	40	50	60	70	80	90	100	110	120
11	22	33	44	55	66	77	88	99	110	121	132
12	24	36	48	60	72	84	96	108	120	132	144

5. ***Division.***   This computational skill is considered the most difficult to
learn and teach. Basic division facts come from knowledge of multiplication facts. Long division requires many operations, and students must be
able to do all the steps before they put them together. The new symbol is
÷ (divide).
   May (1974) suggests a number of ways to approach division. Sets can
be used: 6 ÷ 3 = □. Draw a set of 6 and enclose 3 equal sets. The
missing factor is seen as 2:

How many subsets are there? How many objects are there in each set?
   The *number line* can also be used. By jumping back a unit of 3, how
many jumps are needed?

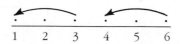

   The *missing factors* approach uses known multiplication facts and
reverses the process: 3 × □ = 12. Then change to a division sentence:
12 ÷ 3 = □.
6. ***Fractions.***   Geometric shapes are commonly used to introduce fractional numbers. The new symbol is shown below:

$\underline{1}$ → number of special parts
2 → total number of equal parts

FIGURE 14.3
Fractions

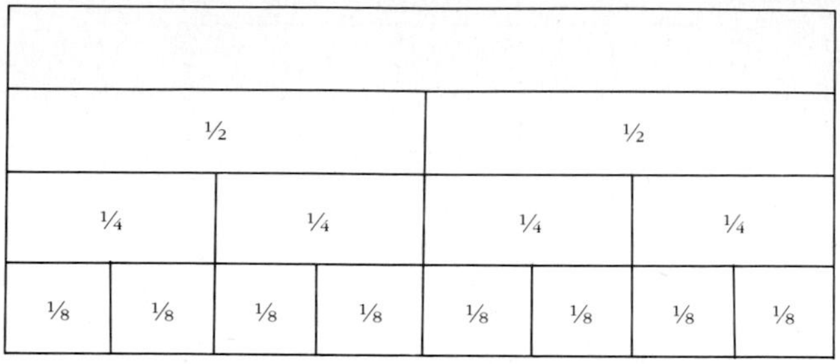

½	½
¼	¼	¼	¼
⅛	⅛	⅛	⅛	⅛	⅛	⅛	⅛

Start with halves, followed by quarters and then eighths. Cut shapes out of flannel board or paper plates. Figure 14.3 illustrates the fractions.

7. ***Learning the computational facts.***   Once the concepts behind the facts are known, the pupil must memorize the facts themselves. To do this it is necessary to write them, say them, play games with facts, take speed tests, and so forth. Also helpful are flash cards, rolling dice, playing cards, or even learning a fact a day. A wide variety of methods should be used (May, 1974).

To learn fractions, as well as other computational skills, the student with an arithmetic disability requires much experience with concrete and manipulative materials before moving to the abstract and symbolic level of numbers. Objects and materials that can be physically taken apart and put back together help the student to observe visually the relationship of the fractional parts of the whole.

There are fifty-six basic number facts to be mastered in each mode of arithmetic computation (addition, subtraction, multiplication, and division), if the facts involving the 1s ($3 + 1 = 4$) and doubles ($3 \times 3 = 9$) are not included (Otto, McMenemy, & Smith, 1973). Examples of number facts are $3 + 4 = 7$; $9 - 5 = 4$; $3 \times 7 = 21$; $18 \div 6 = 3$. In the computational skill of addition, for example, there are eighty-one separate facts involved in the span from $1 + 1 = 2$ to $9 + 9 = 18$. Few pupils have trouble with the 1s ($5 + 1 = 6$) or with the doubles ($2 + 2 = 4$). Therefore, if these facts are omitted, there are fifty-six basic addition facts to be mastered. Similarly, without the 1s and doubles, there are fifty-six facts to be mastered in each of the other computation areas—subtraction, multiplication, and division.

8. ***The two-weeks facts:*** **7 + 7.**   Students circle two full calendar weeks and count the number of days in each week to learn that $7 + 7 = 14$ (Thornton, 1984). See Figure 14.4.

9. ***Tapping out combinations.***   Tap out combinations of numbers on a table or have the student tap out the combinations. This reinforces the number learning with the kinesthetic and auditory modality.

FIGURE 14.4
Calendar for Learning Facts

Sun	Mon	Tue	Wed	Thur	Fri	Sat
1	2	3	4	5	6	7
8	9	10	11	12	13	14
15	16	17	18	19	20	21
22	23	24	25	26	27	28

10. ***Reinforcement of auditory expression.*** Some students find it help-ful to relate the number sequences and facts aloud.

11. ***Arrangements.*** Give students the numbers 1, 2, 3. Ask them in how many ways they can be arranged. 1–2–3; 1–3–2; 2–1–3; 2–3–1; 3–1–2; 3–2–1 (or 3 × 2 × 1 = 6). Another arrangement puzzle is this one: if four children sit around a square table, in how many ways can they arrange themselves? (4 × 3 × 2 × 1 = 24).

12. ***Puzzle cards of combinations.*** Make cardboard cards on which problems of additions, subtraction, multiplication, and division are worked. Cut each card in two so that the problem is on one part and the answer is on the other. Each card must be cut uniquely, so that when the student tries to assemble the puzzle, only the correct answer will fit.

13. ***Rate of perception of number facts.*** The use of a tachistoscope or flash cards is a way to increase the rate of recognition of sets of objects, number symbols, and answers to number facts. A tachistoscope can be improvised by putting information on transparencies, then cutting the transparencies into strips and inserting them in a filmstrip projector. By covering the lens with a sheet of cardboard and exposing the material for a short period of time, the teacher uses the projector as a tachistoscope (Lerner & Vaver, 1970).

14. ***Playing cards.*** A deck of ordinary cards becomes a versatile tool for teaching number concepts. Arranging suits in sequential order by num-ber, matching sets, adding and subtracting the individual cards, and quick recognition of the number in a set are some of the activities that can be accomplished with a deck of cards.

Teaching Applications for Problem Solving

The eventual goal of mathematics instruction is to apply the concepts and skills in problem solving. The goals set by the National Council for Teachers of Mathematics (1980) call for more emphasis on problem solving at all levels. Bley and Thornton (1981) suggest several effective strategies for teach-ing problem solving and applications to learning-disabled students.

1. ***Word story problems.*** Use word story problem situations that are of interest to the students and within their experience.

2. ***Posing problems orally.*** This is especially important for students with reading problems.

3. ***Visual reinforcements.*** Use concrete objects, drawings, graphs, or

other visual reinforcements to clarify the problem, demonstrate solutions, and verify the answers. Have students act out the problem.
4. **Simplifying.**   Have students substitute smaller and easier numbers for
problems with larger or more complex numbers so that they can understand the problem and verify the solution more readily.
5. **Restating.**   Have students restate the problems in their own words.
The verbalization helps the students structure the problem for themselves and also shows whether they understand the problem.
6. **Assessing given information.**   Select problems with too little or too
much information and have students determine what is still needed or
what is superfluous.
7. **Supplementary problems.**   Supplement textbook problems with
your own. These can deal with classroom experiences. Including the
students' names in the problem makes it more realistic
8. **Time for thinking.**   Allow students enough time to think. Ask for
alternative methods for solving the problem. Try to understand how the
student thought about the problem and went about solving it.
9. **Steps in solving word problems.**   Many learning-disabled students
have difficulty with word problems. Although difficulty in reading may
be a factor, often the difficulty is in thinking through the math problem.
Learning-disabled students tend to begin doing computations as soon as
they see the numbers in the word problem. Dunlap and McKnight (1980)
suggest that the following steps are helpful in teaching word problem
applications.

a. Seeing the situation. Have the student first read the word problem and
then relate the setting of the problem. Students do not need paper
and pencil for this task. They simply describe the setting or situation.
b. Determining the question. Have the student decide what is to be
found out—what is the problem to be solved?
c. Gathering data. The word problem often gives much data—some
relevant, some not relevant to the solution. Ask the student to read the
problem orally or silently and then list relevant and irrelevant data.
d. Analyzing relationships. Help the student analyze the relationships
among the data. For example, if the problem states that the down pay-
ment on an automobile costing $250 is 25 percent, the student must
see the relationship between these two facts. Seeing relationships is
a reasoning skill, which learning-disabled students often find difficult.
e. Deciding on a process. Students must decide what computational
process should be used to solve the problem. Here students should
be alert to key words such as "total" or "in all," suggesting adding, "is
left" or "remains," suggesting subtracting. They should next put the
problem into mathematical sentences.
f. Estimating answers. Have the students practice estimating what a reasonable answer might be. If students understand the reasoning behind the word problem, they should be able to estimate answers.

g. Practice and generalizations. After students have thought through and worked out one type of problem, the teacher can give similar problems with different numbers.

10. **Time.** Time is a difficult dimension for many students with learning disabilities to grasp, and they may require planned remediation to learn to tell time. Real clocks or teacher-made clocks are needed to teach this skill. A teacher-made clock can be created by using a paper plate and cardboard hands attached with a paper fastener. A sequence for teaching time might be (1) the hour (1:00); (2) the half-hour (4:30); (3) the quarter hour (7:15); (4) five-minute intervals (2:25); (5) before and after the hour; (6) minute intervals; and (7) seconds. Use television schedules of programs or classroom activities and relate them to clock time.

11. **Money.** The use of real money and lifelike situations is an effective way to teach number facts to some students. Have them play store, make change, order a meal from a restaurant menu, and then add up the cost and pay for it. All these situations provide concrete and meaningful practice for learning arithmetic.

Summary

• Some students with learning disabilities have severe difficulty in learning mathematics, even though for many learning-disabled students mathematics seems to be an area of strength.

• Students with a mathematics learning disability may display a number of characteristics. They may show a disturbance in spatial relationships, have motor and visual perception problems, and have a poor sense of direction and time. Oral language problems and reading difficulties can also interfere with mathematics learning. Poor memory is another characteristic of a mathematics disability.

• Ideas about teaching mathematics have been changing over the years in response to national concerns. We have witnessed a "modern math" movement and a back-to-basics movement. Now we are entering a period of consolidation, marked by concern with the cognitive skills of problem solving and by the use of computer technology.

• Three learning theories provide the basis of mathematics instruction: (1) developmental learning hierarchies, (2) mastery learning, and (3) problem solving and cognitive strategies.

• Developmental learning hierarchies theory emphasizes the normal developmental stages that the student goes through in intellectual learning. In teaching mathematics to the learning disabled, we must take these developmental stages into account.

• Mastery learning emphasizes the objectives to be taught and the sequential steps needed to reach those objectives.

• Cognitive learning strategies and information processing approaches emphasize the thinking strategies the student develops to solve mathematics problems.

• Technology available to help the mathematics student includes the calculator and the microcomputer. The calculator can be used to compute basic facts, as well as for drill and self-checking. The microcomputer can also be used to provide drill and practice programs in mathematics. In addition, learning-disabled students can be taught programming skills. The language called LOGO is particularly useful for students in the elementary and secondary schools.

• A student's mathematics abilities can be assessed through (1) informal inventories, (2) an analysis of the errors in the student's work, (3) standardized survey tests, and (4) individual clinical tests. Each method provides a different kind of information about the student's mathematics performance.

• The content of the mathematics curriculum is sequential. Different elements of mathematics are taught at different grade levels.

• Principles of remediation in mathematics include the following: the student should have prenumber concepts and possess the readiness for further mathematics learning; instruction should progress from the concrete to the abstract; ample opportunity for practice and review should be provided; students must learn to generalize concepts that have been learned; teachers should work with the student's strengths and weaknesses; teaching should build a solid foundation of mathematics skills and concepts; and a balanced mathematics program should be planned and should include teaching for concepts, skills, and problem solving.

• Teachers need a variety of teaching strategies for teaching mathematics concepts, skills, and problem solving. For a balanced mathematics program, learning-disabled students should receive adequate instruction with a variety of strategies for each of these three components of mathematics.

Key Terms

dyscalculia	time concepts	computer literacy
one-to-one correspondence	basic skills movement	mathematics computation
number line	place value	mastery learning
concrete instruction	mathematics problem solving	
spatial relationships	modern math	

Social Behavior and Emotional Status

Chapter 15

Introduction

This chapter discusses the social and emotional facets of learning disabilities. It is increasingly evident that learning disabilities encompasses more than academic difficulties and that a student's academic problems cannot be treated in isolation. As noted in Chapter 4, ecological systems of the student's social and emotional environments impinge on academic learning, either enhancing or diminishing it. Although the interactions between academic learning and the social-emotional realm are complex, they are essential considerations in trying to understand the puzzle of learning disabilities. The Theories section of this chapter considers concepts relating to social competence, emotion adjustments of learning-disabled students, and behavior management. The Teaching Strategies portion of the chapter discusses various therapies and methods to help students develop social competence, build self-esteem, and manage behavior.

■ Theories

The affective domain, the social and emotional side of learning disabilities, is as important to a student's success as academic learning. In discussing the social and emotional dimensions, this chapter considers (1) the concept of social skills disabilities, (2) the emotional effects of learning disabilities, (3) behavior analysis and management, and (4) methods of assessing social and emotional behaviors.

Social Skills Disabilities

The acquisition of social skills is a vital area of learning. Accumulating evidence shows that many learning-disabled students do poorly in social situations. Although these students may be average or even above average in areas such as verbal intelligence, they have difficulty in meeting the basic social demands of everyday life. Moreover, these social deficits are often related to other kinds of failure in school learning (Bryan, T., Pearl, Donahue, Bryan, J., & Pflaum, 1983; Bryan, T., 1983; Pearl, Bryan T., & Donahue, 1983; Deshler and Schumaker, 1983; Kronick, 1981).

Not all learning-disabled youngsters display incompetencies within the social realm. Some students have both social disabilities and academic disabilities; others have a social disability but do well in academic learning; and students in a third group have school-related academic problems but are competent in the social sphere. The discussion in this section pertains to those learning-disabled students who exhibit social perception problems.

Since a deficit in social skills implies a lack of sensitivity to people and a poor perception of social situations, the deficit affects almost every aspect of the student's life and is probably one of the most crippling disabilities the student can have. One school of thought views the social disability as a primary and discrete disability, separate from academic and learning problems. But of course, the failure to learn can create secondary emotional and social problems. In terms of total life functioning, the social problem may be far more disabling than academic dysfunction.

CASE EXAMPLES

Social Perception Disabilities

The following case examples illustrate social perception disabilities. Such problems may go unrecognized as a learning disability because the deficits may not prevent the students from using verbal language with fluency or from learning to read or write.

Impulsive Behavior

Nall (1971) described a twelve-year-old girl with a social disability, who, she predicted, would not be able to get along in a secondary school because of her poor skills in social perception. The girl read well, performed well in math, and wrote well; she just could not get along with others. She was too impulsive. What she thought, she said. She scratched where it itched. She went where she happened to look. When she finally was academically ready to enter high school, she could not be sent. She would not have lasted there a day.

Samuel: Disruptive Social Behavior

Six-year-old Samuel was judged by the psychologist to have an IQ in the high superior range. He was able to read simple stories by the time he entered first grade. However, Samuel's mother was frequently called for parent-teacher conferences because of her son's highly disruptive social behavior. The kindergarten teacher reported that Samuel was bossy, turned other children away from him, and had been a "social problem" all year. The first-grade teacher said that Samuel found it difficult to accept a "no" answer, stamped his feet, cried frequently, pushed others to be first in line himself, and alienated the other children by kissing and hugging them to gain affection.

Samuel's mother also described her son's social behavior at home as intolerable; sitting still for even a few minutes seemed to be impossible, and he ate so rapidly that he stuffed half of a sandwich into his mouth all at once. Samuel would invite a classmate to his house to play and would be so excited that he couldn't do much but run around. The friend would soon tearfully beg Samuel's mother to go home, and Samuel would also be in tears because of the frustration of trying so hard and not knowing what went wrong. Several other incidents typical of such children were reported by the mother. Once, for example, when a neighbor girl arrived to play with Samuel, he exclaimed to her, "You sure are a fat one," the would-be friend left in tears while Samuel could not understand what he had done wrong. On another occasion, when Samuel was invited to a birthday party, his behavior was so antisocial that the mother of the birthday child phoned to request that Samuel be taken home.

Becky: Inept Social Behavior

Becky, a thirteen-year old with high average intelligence, was constantly saying the wrong thing at the wrong time. She seemed to be unaware of the consequences of her inappropriate remarks. Her parents found they could not have any personal conversations at dinner because she would always tell someone about the personal situation. For example, she had told her Uncle Al that her parents said he was lazy and irresponsible. She desperately wanted to have friends and to have people like her, but her remarks often offended others and turned them away. For instance, Becky wanted very much to go to a summer camp, but she was rejected by the camp program because she failed the intake interview. When asked by the camp counselor why she would be attending camp, Becky replied that her parents wanted to go to Europe and that was the only way to get rid of her. With such a response, the interviewer decided that Becky was not a good candidate for the camp. Becky did not perceive the inappropriateness of this response nor the reaction of the interviewer.

Becky's social imperception problems continued in high school. Her classmates and teachers found her behavior and remarks annoying and disruptive. She did not know how to accept constructive criticism without an unsuitable rejoinder; and she did not know and use socially acceptable techniques for contradicting others. During class she was constantly raising her hand to demand recognition, making challenging remarks, and commenting critically in an undertone while the teacher was talking to the class. In her freshman year, her mother was informed by her science teacher that Becky would receive a grade of B. The science teacher explained that although her average numerical score in the course entitled her to a grade of A, he was lowering Becky's grade because of her behavior. Her poor perception of appropriate social behavior in the science class caused her to be an extremely disturbing and disruptive element in the class.

Characterisics of a Social Disability

What are the observable characteristics related to a deficit in social perception? Students with such deficits have been described in general as performing poorly in the kinds of independent activities expected of students of the same chronological age, inept in judging moods and attitudes of people, insensitive to the atmosphere of a social situation, displaying inappropriate behaviors, and making inappropriate remarks.

Lack of Judgment

The development of social perception is similar to the development of academic skills such as reading or mathematics. The individual learns to anticipate processes and then checks whether or not the confirmation is congruent

In school it is very important for students to have well-developed social and interactive skills with peers and adults; those who have social perception problems are often at a great disadvantage. *(Andrew Brilliant/The Picture Cube)*

with the expected result. Based on this feedback, the individual then adjusts his or her behavior. Students with social perception problems, however, may have difficulty in several of these steps. They may not be able to anticipate the process; they may be unable to confirm whether the action matches what is anticipated; and they may be unable to adjust their behavior in the light of the results. For these reasons, they appear to lack tact and sensitivity. They may inappropriately share very personal information with casual acquaintances. At the same time, they may not know how to make the appropriate investment in establishing a close relationship with those with whom they wish to be friends. (Kronick, 1981)

Difficulties in Perceiving How Others Feel

People with social disabilities appear to be less attuned than their peers to the feelings of others. They may use inappropriate behavior or language because they do not know if the person to whom they are reacting is sad or happy,

approving or disapproving, accepting or rejecting. In addition, they are insensitive to the general atmosphere of a social situation.

Research studies show that students with social disabilities are poor in
detecting or perceiving the subtle social cues given by others. This insensitiv-
ity may be a source of difficulty with peers and parents (Bryan et al., 1983).

Problems in Socializing and Making Friends

Parents often report that their learning-disabled children with social problems have much difficulty making friends. When there is no planned activity,
as during after school hours and weekends, and holidays, the problems
become especially acute. Research supports the observations of parents: the
social life of these youngsters is different from that of other students. They are
more often ignored when attempting to initiate a social interaction. Their
socially different behavior is even noted by strangers, who are able to detect
reliably differences between learning-disabled and non-learning-disabled
youngsters after viewing interactions for only a few minutes (Bryan et al.,
1983).

Problems in Establishing Family Relationships

The family is the core of the young child's life, and he or she desperately
needs the satisfaction and assurance of relations in the primary family. However, because of a learning-disabled youngster's numerous problems in social behavior, language, and temperament, even these relationships are hard
to establish. The youngster may not receive satisfaction from the family
sphere and is likely to be rejected by parents, as well as peers and teachers
(Bryan et al., 1983).

Social Disabilities in the School Setting

A lack of social competence also creates difficulties in school. Such students
are often ignored when attempting to initiate a social interaction with
teachers. Moreover, teachers tend to ignore them for reasons that are not
essentially academic. They also receive more negative and less positive reinforcement from teachers than their non-learning-disabled counterparts
(Bryan et al., 1983).

Poor Self-Concept

All these problems in the social realm can lead to disappointment, frustration, lowered self-esteem, and poor self-concept. Students need successful
social experiences to build confidence and feelings of self-worth, and these
experiences may be lacking in the life of the student with a social disability.
The emotional aspects of the problem are discussed later in this chapter.

CASE EXAMPLE

A Social Disability

Jimmy, nine and a half years old, is an example of a student with a disability in social perception. On the *Stanford-Binet Intelligence Test,* Jimmy received an IQ score of 127, putting him in a high intelligence classification. He did particularly well on the sections that required verbal and language responses. Yet on the *Goodenough-Harris Drawing Test,* his drawing of a man ranked at the sixth percentile for his age.

Jimmy had many problems in the area of social perception. Although he performed satisfactorily in many academic subjects, his teachers consistently reported that his social behavior in school was both strange and disturbing. The speech teacher dismissed him because of his abnormal delight and hilarity when others in the class made mistakes. Another teacher reported that he seemed unconscious of wrongdoing, that he made odd statements totally out of context, and that he was not well accepted by other children. Another report commented that Jimmy had not developed skills in social situations. Although he wanted to be accepted by others and have friends, he did not seem to know the appropriate manner of gaining friends and instead tended to antagonize other students. As seems to be

true of some other students with a disability in social perception, Jimmy also
did poorly in perceptual-motor tasks and
seemed to have a poor understanding of

space relationships. The psychologist reported poor performance in perceptual-
motor and coordination activities on the
Bender Visual-Motor Gestalt Test.

Research on the Social Behavior of Learning-Disabled Students

Many parents and teachers have observed that their learning-disabled youngsters have difficulties in social situations and are generally awkward in areas
of human interaction, often behaving in a socially inappropriate manner. To
verify these observations, the social competence of learning-disabled children was the focus of a series of research studies at the Chicago Institute for
the Study of Learning Disabilities (Bryan et al., 1983; Bryan, 1983; Pearl, Bryan,
& Donahue, 1983). The social behaviors of learning-disabled adolescents
were part of the research at the University of Kansas Institute for Research on
Learning Disabilities (Deshler & Schumaker, 1983; Schumaker, Deshler, Alley, & Warner, 1983).

The researchers at the Chicago Institute reached the following conclusions in their five-year study of the social behavior of learning-disabled children. Learning-disabled children do not do well in dealing with people.
Further, academic performance is affected by feelings of incompetence and
the student's perception of the expectations of others. Learning-disabled students are not well accepted by classmates. They are more negatively viewed
by their parents and teachers than non-learning-disabled children. In the
classroom setting, they behave differently in that they are more off-task, more
distractable, initiate more interactions with the teacher, and engage in more
nonproductive activity. In conversation situations, learning-disabled students
make more nasty statements and more competitive statements and receive
more rejections than non-learning-disabled youngsters. When working with a
partner, they tended to resist the initiatives of the partner for cooperative
work. Learning-disabled youngsters were described as both deferential and
hostile. Thus, this research found that learning-disabled students act in a
socially inappropriate manner and are at risk for social neglect and rejection.

The studies of the social skills of learning-disabled adolescents at the
University of Kansas (Deshler & Schumaker, 1983) found that although many
learning-disabled adolescents do not have social disabilities and are not social isolates, they tend to engage in fewer activities related to extracurricular
events and go out with friends less frequently than non-learning-disabled
adolescents. In addition to analyzing the social status of learning-disabled
adolescents, the Kansas Research Institute studied methods for teaching them
social skills. Deshler and Schumaker (1983) reported that direct instruction
of social skills improved the social behaviors of learning-disabled adoles-

cents. The effective methods included individual teaching, group teaching, and programmed written instruction.

In interpreting these research findings, it should be reiterated that learning-disabled students are very different from each other so that these characteristics do not describe all learning-disabled students. For some academically disabled students, at least, the social sphere is an area of strength and they do well in social relationships.

Emotional Status and its Effect on Learning

The emotional scars of repeated failure and the inability to achieve and develop a sense of competence and self-worth are often indelible. It is not surprising that learning-disabled students sometimes develop secondary emotional disturbances. Two constructs for analyzing the emotional reaction of learning failure are presented in this section: the psychodynamic perspective and the psychosocial perspective.

Psychodynamic Perspective

The psychodynamic analysis of the emotions involved in learning failure is based on theories of psychoanalysis. Psychodynamic development, personality structure, and ego functioning have important implications for understanding the emotional consequences of learning disabilities (Van Evra, 1983; Migden, 1983; Burka, 1983; Silver, 1983; Eisenberg, 1975; Rappaport, 1966). Viewing the student from a psychodynamic perspective, the critical question is how does the student with learning disabilities *feel*?

The ego development of the achieving student contrasts with that of the student with learning disabilities. The achieving student has the opportunity to develop important basic ego functions and hundreds of opportunities for self-satisfaction, as well as the satisfaction of pleasing others. The parent-child relationship can be mutually satisfying because normal accomplishments stimulate parental responses of approval and encouragement (Eisenberg, 1975; Rappaport, 1966).

Achieving children, as a result of both their own feelings about their accomplishments and their awareness of the approval of those around them, have the opportunity to develop a sense of self-worth and prideful identity. They feel positively about their experiences in the world, for they establish healthy identifications with their mothers, fathers, and other key figures in their lives. Ego functions, such as frustration tolerance and consideration for others, are developed in a normal manner. They learn to interact successfully with other people in their environment.

In contrast, the personality development of students with learning disabilities does not follow such a pattern. Ego functions are adversely affected if the central nervous system is not intact and is not maturing in a normal and even manner. A disturbance in such functions as motility and perception

Mastery of a skill or task; perceived respect from peers; and one's own feelings of competence are all sources of vital feelings of self-esteem. *(Evan Johnson/Jeroboam)*

leads to an inadequate development of ego functions. Attempts at mastery of tasks lead to feelings of frustration rather than feelings of accomplishment. Instead of building up self-esteem, the student's activities produce an attitude of self-derision and do not stimulate the parent's normal responses of pride. They cause the parents to experience feelings of anxiety and frustration, which finally result in rejection or overprotection.

For the learning-disabled, then, the feelings within themselves and the response from outside mold a concept of an insecure and threatening world and a view of themselves as inept persons without identity. Such an individual does not receive the normal satisfactions of recognition, achievement, or affection.

The battering of the developing personality continues and increases in school. Donald, a nine-year-old who was failing in school and had virtually no opportunities for success, was losing his self-concept and the belief that he was indeed a person with an individual identity. In response to a class assignment to write a biographical sketch, he poignantly revealed, "My name is Donald Turner. I am average."

Pupils who manifest learning problems when beginning academic work in school probably have been handicapped by learning disabilities in preschool life. The school may be a place where they face a situation that makes no allowances for their shortcomings and where those directing the learning are unable to comprehend the difficulties.

Ironically, the characteristic inconsistency and unpredictability of students with learning disabilities may account for an occasional academic breakthrough when they perform well, and such random moments of achievement may serve to make matters worse. Now the school may be convinced that "he could do it if he just tried harder." Failure now may be viewed purely in terms of behavior and poor attitude. Increased impatience and an attitude of blame on the part of the teacher intensifies the student's anxiety, frustration, and confusion, which brings disastrous consequences to the ego.

Thus, learning-disabled students often suffer from emotional problems. If the problems are so severe that they interfere with further learning, the student may be referred for psychological or psychiatric counseling. Harris and Sipay (1980) note the following forms of emotional reactions to learning problems: (1) conscious refusal to learn, (2) overt hostility, (3) negative conditioning to learning, (4) displacement of hostility, (5) resistance to pressure, (6) clinging to dependency, (7) quick discouragement, (8) the attitude that success is dangerous, (9) extreme distractability or restlessness, and (10) absorption in a private world.

Trying to determine if the learning failure or the emotional problem is the primary precipitating factor may be of little value. A more constructive approach is to help the student accomplish an educational task so that feelings of self-worth are oriented in a positive direction, reinforcing ego function and so increasing the capability to learn. The beginning of this mutual reinforcement cycle is also the beginning of effective treatment.

In summary, the student's feelings must be taken into consideration in an analysis of learning disabilities, for the psychodynamics and emotional status have an impact on the learning process. The important questions from this point of view are how does the student feel? are the student's needs being satisfied? what is the emotional status? Emotional well-being and a favorable attitude are essential prerequisites for effective learning.

Teaching strategies to build self-concept and to enhance a healthy mental attitude are presented in the Teaching Strategies section of this chapter and in Chapter 4, in the section Establishing a Therapeutic Relationship.

Psychosocial Perspective

The psychodynamic analysis shows how continual failure and frustration can affect the personality and lead to emotional disturbances. Yet many learning-disabled students do not develop emotional difficulties or low self-esteem as a result of their learning problems (Meyer, 1983; Sanders, 1983; Silverman & Zigmond, 1983). Why is it that some students do and some do not develop emotional disturbances in conjunction with their learning disabilities? Meyer (1983) discusses the origin and prevention of emotional disturbance in learning-disabled students from the perspective of psychosocial theory. She suggests that two major factors influence the development or prevention of emotional disorders: (1) whether or not one's self-esteem is preserved, and (2) whether one's motivation to achieve is preserved.

Self-Esteem

One's self-esteem, of course, is threatened by continual failure. Self-esteem is gained through mastery of a skill or task, through perceived respect from peers, and through one's feelings of competence. It is easy to follow the course of how the learning-disabled student can lose self-esteem, which in turn has emotional consequences.

It appears that those learning-disabled students who perceive that they have competencies in areas other than academic work are less likely to be devastated by school failure. Thus, in order to maintain their self-esteem, students need a support system from sources such as teachers, parents, and peers to acknowledge that they possess other competencies. Meyer (1983) suggests that the support system serves to help preserve self-esteem by: (1) keeping failure to a minimum, (2) increasing the visibility of non-academic talents, skills, and competencies (Baum & Kirschenbaum, 1984), and (3) emphasizing *learning goals* over *performance goals*. For example, the student is given credit for going about the task in the correct manner (learning goals) even though the final answer may not be accurate (performance goals).

Achievement Motivation

The *motivation* to learn and achieve is also threatened by continuous failure. When their attempts to learn are perceived as futile, the students' reaction is that they have lost control of the situation. For example, if they have tried their hardest, yet people tell them to try harder, they do not know what to do. They develop a "helpless" orientation toward the learning situation, withdraw effort, and appear to be without motivation.

Those learning-disabled students who do not develop such emotional responses to failure and continue to be motivated to learn, tend to perceive that they have maintained control. Therefore, the support system must strive to promote the students' feelings of control and power over their destiny. Meyer (1983) suggests the support group can promote perceptions of control by: (1) helping students develop skills in decision making and providing opportunities to make decisions, (2) helping students recognize the causes of success and failure so that instead of always blaming themselves they come to feel that their efforts will influence the outcome, and (3) developing coping mechanisms and strategies for responding constructively to failure.

The cognitive behavior modification approaches discussed in the Teaching Strategies section of this chapter suggest how to help students gain control.

Behavioral Analysis and Management

The study of a student's behavior, in contrast to the study of the student's emotional status, reflects a field of psychology known as behavior analysis (Lovitt, 1978; Gardner, 1978; O'Leary & O'Leary, 1977). A key interest of behavioral psychologists is modifying human activity, including academic and social learning. *Behavior modification* can be described as a systematic ar rangement of environmental events to produce a specific change in observable behavior.

The behavioral approach to studying human action is an outgrowth of concepts of operant conditioning developed by learning theorists such as Skinner (1963). The early experiments, conducted with animals, demonstrated that pigeons and rats would persist in behaviors (such as pressing a bar) if a positive reinforcement (such as a food pellet) was given immediately following the activity. The use of reinforcements conditioned the desired behavior. The concepts and procedures of operant conditioning and reinforcement theory are applied to human beings in behavioral analysis. These methods are used to modify and shape the student's behavior and learning— to improve unacceptable social behavior, as well as increase academic learning. The theory and techniques of behavior analysis have important implications for teaching students with learning disabilities.

Behavior Modification

Behavior modification procedures require the investigator to (1) carefully and systematically observe and tabulate the occurrence of specific events that precede the behavior of interest and the specific events that follow the behavior of interest and (2) manipulate those events to effect a desired change in the subject's behavior. The event preceding the behavior of interest is called the *antecedent event* or *stimulus,* and the event immediately following the behavior in question is called the *subsequent event* or *reinforcement.* For example, when John is asked to read, he begins to disturb others in the classroom by hitting them. The stimulus or antecedent event that precedes John's hitting behavior is the request that John read. When Betty reads five pages, she receives two tokens that are exchangeable for toys. The subsequent event of reinforcement following reading behavior is the receipt of the tokens.

The investigator working in this tradition observes the effects of various reinforcements or rewards on the individual behavior of a particular student and then analyzes the observations to determine patterns of response to rewards. Finally, the investigator attempts to construct a reward system that will promote the desired behavior.

Research suggests that reinforcements that are positive and immediate are most effective in promoting the desired behavior. Examples of positive reinforcers include candy, tokens, points earned, praise, flashing lights, or simply the satisfaction of knowing that the answer is correct. For example, in teaching reading, the desired behavior could be having the pupil say the sound equivalent of the letter *a* every time a stimulus card with the letter *a* is shown. For each correct response, the pupil may immediately receive a positive reinforcement, such as a piece of candy, cereal, stars, points, or money.

The behavior modification approach requires that the teacher determine a behavioral goal to be accomplished by the pupil. This goal must be specific rather than broad; moreover, evidence of learning should be observable instead of only being inferred. For example, the goal of teaching a pupil to be sociable is too broad and too difficult to observe; however, the behavior of saying "thank you" when the pupil is offered food is specific and observable.

Unlike some other theories of learning disabilities, the teacher using behavior modification techniques does not seek to discover the underlying causes of inappropriate behavior but tries to change the behavior by manipulating the environment of the learner. For example, the hyperactive student might be encouraged to modify hyperactive behavior if there is a positive reinforcement for a behavior of sitting quietly for a period of five minutes. The highly distractable student could be encouraged to modify behavior by receiving a positive reinforcement for reading a certain number of words, or pages or reading for a certain period of time.

Within this approach, the behaviors that interfere with learning a task are first identified; then plans are made to manipulate the environment to shape a desired behavior. For instance, Marion's hyperactivity and constant movement in the room during the reading lesson interfered with her learning to read. A desired behavior was to have Marion remain in her seat during the lesson. This behavior was shaped through a system of positive reinforcements. Each time Marion remained in her seat for a period of five minutes during the reading lesson, she was reinforced with a small piece of candy. As her attentive behavior was shaped by the candy reinforcer, she stayed in her seat for longer periods of time and her ability to attend improved.

Key Concepts in Behavior Management

Techniques of behavior management have become important tools in learning disabilities. A number of concepts essential for comprehending the work in this area are discussed below.

Reinforcement   A reinforcer is an event occurring after a person makes a response; it has the effect of controlling or modifying the response behavior. There are two types of reinforcers: positive and negative.

A *positive reinforcer* is a pleasurable event that follows the response and increases the likelihood that the person will make a similar response in similar situations in the future. For example, if Jim, who usually shouts out answers, is recognized by the teacher as soon as he raises his hand, he will tend to raise his hand in the future. If four-year-old Trudy, who has delayed speech, is given a piece of candy after she says a word, she is likely to try saying a word again.

A *negative reinforcer* is an unpleasant event following an unwanted response. In this case the person tries to escape the negative reinforcer or unpleasant situation by selecting an alternative mode of behavior—the desired behavior. For example, Joe's mother nags him to do his homework; Joe does his homework to avoid the negative reinforcer—his mother's nagging.

Extinction   This is the removing of sources of reinforcement that have been following a behavior so that the particular behavior will decrease in strength and eventually cease. Inappropriate classroom behavior is often unknowingly being reinforced by the teacher who gives the student attention in the form of reprimands or reminders. For example, every time Sam talks out in class, he becomes the center of attention as the teacher tells him how disturbing his actions are. The extinction concept implies that if Sam's behavior of making noises in the classroom is ignored instead of being reinforced by verbal comments, it will lessen and eventually cease.

Schedules of Reinforcement   The schedule of reinforcement is the plan of conditions under which reinforcement will occur. The plan of reinforcement is also called *contingencies,* that is, the arrangement of the relationship between the desired behavior and the occurrence of the reinforcement. The schedule of reinforcement may be either continuous or intermittent. *Continuous reinforcement* is the arrangement of reinforcing the desired behavior every time it occurs. For example, every time Joan completes an arithmetic problem, she receives a star.

Intermittent reinforcement means that reinforcement will be given every *nth* time rather than each time. For example, Joan is not given a star for each problem but for each page, then for two pages, five pages, and so forth. There are two kinds of intermittent reinforcement schedules: *interval* (based on reinforcements given at certain times) and *ratio* (based upon reinforcements given after so many responses). The interval schedule can be either a *fixed schedule* (reinforcement given after a predetermined time period, such as five minutes) or a *variable schedule* (reinforcement given somewhat randomly but with the time period varying around a certain average). The ratio schedule can be either a *fixed ratio* (reinforcement given after a fixed number of behaviors, such as after every fifth word read correctly) or a *variable ratio* (reinforcement given somewhat randomly but varying around a certain average).

Shaping Behavior   This term refers to the concept of breaking the desired goal into a sequence of ordered steps or tasks, then reinforcing a behavior that the student already shows and gradually increasing the requirement for reinforcement. This approach is sometimes referred to as *successive approximations*. For example, the eventual behavioral goal is to have Patty sit at her desk for a twenty-minute period. Patty's behavior may be shaped by reinforcing the following steps or successive approximations: first, she is reinforced for standing near her desk for a few seconds, then for touching her desk, then for kneeling on her desk, then for sitting at her desk for a few seconds, then for sitting two minutes, and so on.

Contingency Management   The concept that something desirable can be used to reinforce something the student does not wish to do is the essence of contingency management. What is known as the *Premack Principle* states that preferred activities can be used to reinforce less preferred activities (Premack, 1959). This contingency relationship is also referred to as "grandma's rule" because grandmothers are alleged to promise "If you finish your plate, then you can have dessert." For example, if Willie prefers constructing models to reading, the opportunity to work on a model would be contingent upon completing a certain reading assignment. Or Dave can play ball after he finishes his spelling work.

Contingency contracting is a technique used to make more formal arrangements. In such cases a written agreement is negotiated so that the student agrees to do something the teacher desires and the teacher agrees to provide something the student wants in return. For example, Karen writes an agreement that after she completes twenty arithmetic problems, she will be given an extra free period. The contract must be signed by both parties.

Token Reinforcements   In this method, the reinforcers are accumulated to be exchanged at a later time for a more meaningful "back-up" reinforcer. For example, the token reinforcer could be poker chips or plastic objects, which are saved to be exchanged for a more valuable object of the student's selection, such as toys, gum, comic books, candy, and so forth. Time must be scheduled for exchanges, and information about exchange rates must be made available. In some programs, a total *token economy* is built into the project.

In summary, behavioral analysis places great emphasis on the precise definition of the behavior of interest, on the careful observation, measurement, and recording of that behavior, and on an analysis of the environmental events surrounding that behavior. Specific methods and techniques for behavior modification are presented in the section Teaching Strategies.

Assessing Social and Emotional Behaviors

Assessing a student's social skills and emotional status is difficult. Observational techniques are probably the most direct way of judging a student's social and emotional behaviors. In fact, teachers who have daily contact with students in the classroom have proved to be excellent judges of the students' social and emotional reactions. There are also inventories, check lists, and rating scales that are used to assess a student's behavior. Several are briefly mentioned here but are described more fully in Appendix C.

Interview instruments are actually questionnaires that help a teacher interview the parent, the student, a teacher, or someone else who has contact with the student. They include the *AAMD Adaptive Behavior Scales,* the *Behavioral Rating Profile,* and the *Vineland Adaptive Behavior Scales.*

Rating scales are check lists completed by the teacher or parent. Some of the more widely used rating scales are the *Pupil Rating Scale, Devereaux Elementary School Behavior Rating Scale, Devereaux Adolescent School Behavior Rating Scale, Burk's Behavior Rating Scale,* and *Scales of Independent Behavior* (part of the Woodcock-Johnson Psychoeducational Battery) (See Chapter 3).

Inventories and *tests* are given to the student to complete and usually focus on measuring self-concept or personality variables. They include the *California Test of Personality, Self-Esteem Inventory,* and the *Piers-Harris Children's Self-Concept Scale.* All these measures are more completely described in Appendix C.

■ Teaching Strategies

This section presents teaching strategies for (1) developing social competencies, (2) building self-concept and establishing healthy emotional attitudes, (3) cognitive behavior modification, and (4) using behavior management techniques.

Developing Social Competencies

The normal student is able to learn social skills through daily living and observation, but the student with a deficit in social skills needs conscious effort and specific teaching to learn about the social world, its nuances, and its silent language. Just as we teach children to do schoolwork—to read, write, spell, do arithmetic, pass tests—we can teach them to learn to live with and around other people in a normal manner. Just as we must use different methods to teach school subjects, so we have to use different methods to teach students how to get along with others.

The activities given in this section represent ways that have been used to help students develop social skills. The activities are divided into the following categories: (1) body image and self-perception, (2) sensitivity to other people, (3) social situations, and (4) social maturity.

Body Image and Self-Perception

1. **Motor activities.**   See Chapter 10, the section on body image, for suggested motor activities for the development of concepts of body image.
2. **Body parts.**   Have students locate parts of the body on a doll, on a classmate, and finally on themselves. Discuss the function of each part of the body.
3. **Cardboard figures.**   Make a cardboard person with movable limbs. Put the person in various positions and have the student duplicate the positions. For example, put the left leg and right arm out.
4. **Puzzles.**   Make a puzzle from a picture of a person, and have the student assemble the pieces. Cut the puzzle so that each major part is easily identifiable.
5. **Completing pictures.**   Have the student complete a partially drawn figure or tell what is missing in an incomplete picture.
6. **Scrapbooks.**   Help students put together scrapbooks about themselves. Include pictures of them at different stages of growth, pictures of their families and pets, a list of their likes and dislikes, anecdotes of their past, accounts of trips, awards they have won, and so on.

Sensitivity to Other People

The spoken language is but one means of communication, but there is also a "silent language" in which people communicate with each other without the use of words, relying instead on gesture, stance, facial expression, or tone of voice. The students with social deficits, however, need help in learning how to decode the communication messages involved in this "silent language." For example, such students often fail to understand the meaning implied in facial expression and gesture.

1. **Pictures of faces.**   Draw pictures of faces or collect pictures of faces and have the student ascertain if the face conveys the emotion of happiness or sadness. Other emotions to be shown include anger, surprise, pain, and love.
2. **Gestures.**   Discuss the meanings of various gestures, such as waving good-by, shaking a finger for "no," shrugging a shoulder, turning away, tapping of a finger or foot in impatience, outstretched arms in gestures of welcome.
3. **Films, story situations.**   Find pictures, short filmed sequences, or story situations where the social implications of gesture, space, and time are presented.
4. **What the voice tells.**   Help the student learn to recognize implications in human voice beyond the words themselves. Have the student listen to

a voice on a tape recorder to determine the mood of the speaker and to decipher the communication beyond the words.

Social Situations

Students with social disabilities may be recognized as such by professionals, while members of their peer group may label them "weirdos," "queers," or "out of it." Such students appear unable to make the appropriate response in social situations without direct teaching.

1. *Judging behavior through stories and films.* Read or tell an incomplete story that involves social judgment. Have the student anticipate the ending or complete the story. A short film of a social situation provides an opportunity to discuss critically the activities of the people in the film. For example, discuss the consequences of a student's rudeness when an acquaintance tries to begin a conversation, or of a student's making a face when asked by her mother's friend if she likes her new dress, or of hitting someone at a party, and so on.

2. *Grasping social situations through pictures.* A series of pictures can be arranged to tell a story involving a social situation. Have the student arrange the pictures and explain the story. Comics, readiness books, beginning readers, and magazine advertising all provide good source materials for such activities. These series can also be pictures on transparencies.

3. *Social situations on film.* Use transparency overlays on an overhead projector to create a fairly complex social situation. Discuss the social situation as it develops. Start with a basic simple form and add additional concepts with each transparency overlay. The complete picture might show activities on a school playground, for example.

4. *Work with maps.* Space and directional concepts are often imprecise. Specific activities to help a student read maps, to practice following directions to reach specific places, and to estimate distances are helpful.

5. *Telling time.* Time concepts are often faulty. Learning to tell time, discussing appropriate activities for morning, afternoon, and evening, and estimating time needed to accomplish various activities may all be helpful.

6. *Distinguishing reality from make-believe.* Help the student learn to differentiate between real and make-believe situations. Do animals talk, sing, and dance in real life or only in the world of make-believe?

Social Maturity

Social development involves growing from immaturity to maturity. At the time of birth the human infant, among all species of animal life, is perhaps the most dependent on others for sheer survival. The road from complete dependence to relative independence is the long and gradual growth toward social maturity.

Behavior can be observed and recorded to indicate a level of social growth. Areas of social maturity include the recognition of rights and responsibilities of self and others, making friends, cooperating with a group, following procedures agreed upon by others, making moral and ethical judgments, gaining independence in going places, and so on.

1. ***Anticipating consequences of social acts.*** Role playing, creative play, stories, and discussions can help the child to see what happens if rules of the game or rules of manners are broken.
2. ***Establishing independence.*** Encourage the student to go places alone. Make simple maps with directions to follow, talk about the various steps to take in getting to the desired location. Use a walking map, if necessary. Plan activities so that the student makes simple purchases alone. Plan activities that provide opportunities to talk to other people, ask directions, interview others, and so on.
3. ***Ethical judgments.*** Help the student learn cultural mores and learn to make value judgments.
4. ***Planning and implementing.*** Have the student make plans for a trip, activity, party, picnic, or meeting. Then help the student successfully implement the plans to gain a feeling of independence and maturity.
5. ***The "weekend problem."*** As a consequence of a disability in social perception, some students have difficulty in making friends. Parents frequently complain of a "weekend problem" when their child appears to have nothing to do. Without companions and friends, summers and vacations often prove to be difficult periods for such youngsters. The initiative and cooperation of parent groups and community organizations will be needed to help develop solutions to such problems.

Building Self-Esteem and Emotional Well-Being

The student whose failure to learn is accompanied by emotional problems may be the victim of a continuous cycle of failure to learn and emotional reaction to the failure. In this cycle, the failure to learn leads to adverse emotional responses—feelings of self-derision, poor ego perception, and anxiety, which augment the failure-to-learn syndrome. Remediation must find a way to reverse this cycle—to build feelings of self-worth, to increase confidence and self-concept, and to provide an experience of success. Teaching strategies, thus, are designed to redirect this cycle of failure.

1. ***Psychiatric and psychological services.*** The most severely affected student may need psychiatric or psychological treatment before or during educational treatment. If so, appropriate referrals should be made.

2. **Building a psychotherapeutic relationship.** For most students, the learning disabilities teacher can provide a type of psychotherapy through skilled and sensitive clinical teaching. Specific techniques for building such a relationship are discussed in Chapter 4 in the section Establishing a Therapeutic Relationship.

3. **Bibliotherapy.** This is an approach to helping students understand themselves and their problems through books in which the characters learn to cope with problems similar to those faced by the students. By identifying with a character and working out the problem with the character, students are helped with their own problems (Lenkowsky & Lenkowsky, 1978). Books designed to explain the learning problem to the student are also useful (Hayes, 1974).

4. **Magic circle.** This is a human development approach in which students learn to communicate with other members of their group and learn to understand each other and themselves. Bessell and Palomares (1971) have a manual describing this approach. The students and their teacher, who serves as a catalyst, verbally explore themselves and each other through group interaction in activities related to specific goals. A daily twenty-minute session is held with participants seated in a circle. Students are encouraged to share their feelings, to learn to listen, and to observe others. The program seeks to promote active listening, to focus on feelings, to give recognition to each individual, and to promote greater understanding. Sample circle topics are such statements or questions as these:

> It made me feel good when I. . . .
> I made someone feel bad when I. . . .
> Something I do very well is. . . .
> What can I do for you. . . .

Current programs are available for prekindergarten to grade 6.

5. **Transactional analysis.** This technique is an adaptation of TA (transactional analysis) techniques (Harris, 1969) for use with children (Freed, 1971).

6. **Use of creative media.** Teachers can use art, dance, and music as therapy techniques for promoting the emotional involvement of children with learning disabilities (Long, Morse, & Newman, 1971; List, 1982).

7. **Materials.** The DUSO (Developing Understanding of Self and Others) program presents activities with accompanying kits of materials designed to stimulate social and emotional development (American Guidance Services, Inc.). The kits are designed for grades K through 4, and they focus on lessons such as learning to talk about feelings, accepting oneself, making responsible choices, and making friends. The TAD (Toward Affective Development) program consists of group activities, lessons, and materials designed to stimulate psychological and affective development for students in grades 3 to 6 (American Guidance Services, Inc.).

8. *Counseling.*   Reaction to failure and to success depends in part on attitude, emotional status, and beliefs and expectations. Healthier emotional attitudes can be developed through counseling, both individually and in groups.

Cognitive Behavior Modification

The method known as *cognitive behavior modification* focuses on training in cognitive strategies for learning. This approach seeks to change the student's regular pattern of response to a problem or learning situation by training the student to take control of the situation. Students are taught to develop new cognitive responses to problem situations, responses that are self-directed. In short, the students are trained to direct their own thinking behavior.

The techniques include teaching students to stop and think before responding, to verbalize and rehearse what they have seen, to visualize and imagine what they must remember, to preplan task approaches, and to organize their time. Among useful techniques are self-verbalization and self-monitoring. Cognitive behavior modification techniques are used to change both academic and social/behavioral responses (Meichenbaum, 1977; Meichenbaum, 1979; Brown & Alford, 1984; Hallahan & Sapona, 1983).

For example, the regular response of many learning-disabled students is impulsive—without consideration of what is required, without thinking through possible solutions or the consequences of various courses of action. In the cognitive behavior modification approach students are trained in self-control, to keep from an immediate nonreflective response. Often the learning-disabled students' pattern of response is described as "passive" or "learned helplessness." Instead of reacting in a passive manner, the students are trained to verbalize and ask themselves questions such as "What am I supposed to be doing?" In other words, they are taught to stop and think before responding. The teacher can model the cognitive strategy by talking out thoughts such as "Does this problem have similarities to other problems I have encountered?" or "What are three possible solutions?" The student then practices these skills of self-verbalization or thinking out loud. The self-monitoring method has been found to reduce attentional deficits in learning-disabled students (Hallahan & Sapona, 1983; Brown & Alford, 1984). The students become more actively involved and learn to attend to specific requirements of the task. The key techniques include these:

1. *Modeling.*   The teacher models the desired cognitive social behavior while solving a problem by thinking out loud as he or she goes about the steps of seeking solutions to the problem.
2. *Self-verbalization.*   The students follow the model of the teacher by talking out loud when solving the problem.
3. *Self-monitoring.*   The students question themselves as to how they are doing: does the answer make sense? is there another way of looking at the problem?

Behavioral Management Strategies

Behavior management techniques can be used with students with learning disabilities both for managing behavior and for teaching academic skills. The techniques focus on the student's actual behavior rather than its underlying cause.

Although many teachers recognize that behavior modification is similar to procedures they have intuitively used in the past, precise application of the theory of behavior modification requires that procedures be systematic, that the behaviors in question be observable, and that the techniques be very specific. Haphazard applications, including those that take into account unobservable changes, are not considered to be within the realm of behavior modification. Certain concepts of behavior modification, such as positive reinforcement, negative reinforcement, extinction, schedules of reinforcement, shaping, contingency management, and token reinforcement, were discussed in the theory section of this chapter. Specific procedures are presented below.

Basic Decisions in Behavior Management

The following basic decisions must be made if a behavior modification framework is to be effective (Lovitt, 1978).

1. Determine a consequence or reinforcement event that will accelerate a student's rate of performance on a specific task
2. Change the program of instructional materials so that the correct performance is facilitated.
3. When the student's performance is accurate, increase the reinforcer, and when the student makes an error, decrease the reinforcer.
4. Eventually, have the student make independent instructional decisions, such as corrections and establishment of reinforcement values.

Precise and accurate data describing the student's performance must be collected to form the basis for making decisions and planning the methods for modifying behavior.

Monitoring Behavior

Behavior modification stresses the importance of an objective record of the student's behavior as the basis for judging whether or not the desired change has occurred. A graph or chart is used to record daily observations. On a typical graph (Figure 15.1), the vertical axis shows countable behaviors, such as the number of times the behavior occurred, the percentage of correct responses, the rate or speed of behavior, the duration of behavior, or problems completed. The horizontal axis represents the successive days on which the behavior was recorded. Typically, the graph is also divided into periods.

FIGURE 15.1
Sample Behavior Modification Chart

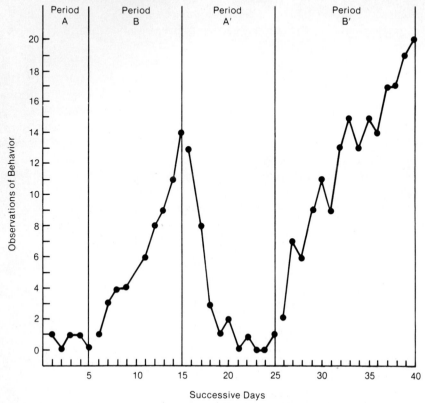

Period A = baseline; B = reinforcement; A′ = removal of reinforcement;
B′ = re-establishment of reinforcement

The graph in Figure 15.1 shows four time periods in which the student's behavior was observed: A, B, A′, B′. The first period, A, provides a *base line,* observations of the student's behavior before reinforcement; the second period, B, shows behavior with reinforcement; the third period, A′, shows behavior when reinforcement is removed; and the fourth period, B′, indicates behavior when reinforcement is reestablished. Figure 15.1 suggests that the reinforcement in this case was effective in increasing the desired behavior. Many other kinds of schedules are used in behavior modification procedures.

Finding Reinforcers

It is important to find the appropriate reinforcer. What is seen as desirable by one student may have little interest for another. Poteet (1973) suggests that there are several ways to find the appropriate reinforcer: observe the students to see what they choose for free time, ask them, and ask their parents. Reinforcers can be extrinsic—something external, such as candy or toys—or they can be intrinsic—something internal, such as the joy of mastering a task. The reinforcement can be social, such as praise or approval from teacher or parent. It can be a token to be exchanged for a later reinforcement, or it can take the form of a privilege. A good reinforcement for each individual is simply the one that works.

Several suggested reinforcements are noted below.

Foods: nuts, edible seeds, cereal, peanuts, popcorn, raisins, and fruit.

Play materials: toy animals and cars, marbles, jump ropes, gliders, crayons, coloring books, clay, dolls, kits, balls, puzzles, comic books, balloons, games, yoyos.

Tokens: marks on the blackboard, marks on the student's paper, gold or silver stars, marbles in a jar, plastic chips on a ring, poker chips, tickets, washers on a string.

Activities or privileges: presenting at "show and tell," going first, running errands, free time, helping with cleanup, taking the class pet home for the weekend, leading the songs, seeing a film strip, listening to music, doing artwork, having a longer recess period.

Modeling

Modeling, or demonstration of appropriate behavior, can be used for both academic and nonacademic behavior. Since students constantly observe the behavior of their peers and their teacher, this behavior can serve as an example that the student will tend to follow. When exemplary behavior in others is reinforced, it provides a model for the student, who receives vicarious reinforcement. For example, a model is provided for Kathy when the teacher says, "I like the way Roger is studying." Ignoring the poorly behaved student while focusing attention on the well-behaved one has proven to be an effective management technique. Teachers should be aware that they also provide a model for students, who observe teachers engaged in behaviors such as reading for pleasure, searching for information, or trying to discover solutions to problems.

Contracting

Contingency contracting is a behavioral management strategy that entails a written agreement between the student and the teacher. It is an agreement that the student will get to do something the student wants if the student first completes a task the teacher wants to be done. For example, the student may be given a free period upon completing a specific academic assignment. The contract may be oral or written but should specify the task to be completed, a time limit for the task, a reward for completing the task, and the individuals who have entered into the agreement. Examples of contracts are shown in Figures 15.2 and 15.3.

FIGURE 15.2
Sample Contract Between Student and Teacher for the Decrease of Noise in Classroom, with Specified Rewards

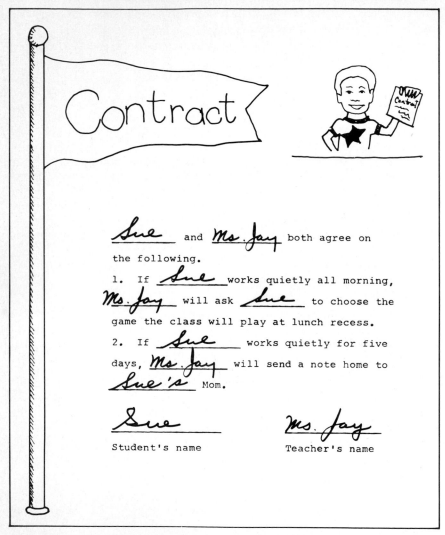

Source: S. Deno and P. Mirkin. *Data-based program modification: A manual.* Leadership Training Institute/ Special Education, Minneapolis: University of Minnesota, 1977, p. 138.

FIGURE 15.3
Contingency Contract

CONTRACT

This contract is an agreement between _____ and
                                              (student)

_____.
        (teacher)

_____ will _____
        (student)

_____

_____

by _____.
        (date of completion)

If the work described above is completed on time,

_____ will _____
        (teacher)

_____

by _____.
        (date of reward)

_____   _____
     Signature of student   date

_____   _____
     Signature of teacher   date

Precision Teaching

This is a variation of behavior modification. It offers a standardized system of monitoring behavior and charting daily improvement and change (Lindsley, 1974; Bates & Bates, 1971). In precision teaching, improvement is viewed as acceleration of the desired behavior; performance is measured, therefore, as frequency of occurrence (or rate). If a student begins to do something more frequently, then performance is improving. Performance is measured on a standardized six-cycle daily behavior chart. (See Figure 15.4) The chart has a six-cycle design to provide an adequate range of behaviors. Behaviors that occur once a day as well as those that occur as frequently as 1,000 times per minute can be charted. The standard Behavior Chart is also designed to help teachers measure many different types of behaviors. It also has the advantage of helping teachers who are familiar with the procedures of precision teaching to communicate about behaviors recorded without preliminary explanations of the graph used.

FIGURE 15.4
Standard Behavior Chart

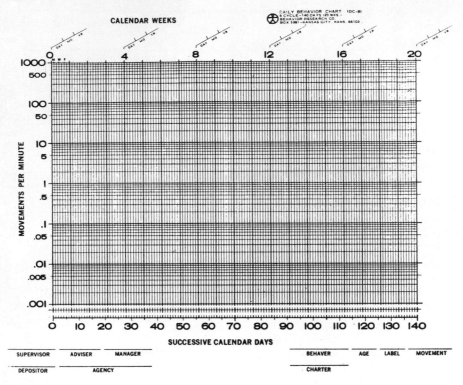

The numbers across the bottom of the chart indicate time by days and weeks. Thus, day lines go up and down the chart. The numbers up the left side of the chart indicate movements per minute or how many times a child does something. The lines going across the chart are thus frequency lines.

Since equal percent gains get equal distance on the Standard Behavior Chart, one can project the future course of behavior by drawing a straight line through the middle of the day frequencies previously charted. The direction of this line shows whether the frequency of performance is increasing, decreasing, or remaining the same. The developers of precision teaching claim that charting is very simple and that teachers are easily trained in the mechanics of it.

Finally, precision teaching is not viewed by its developers as a different approach but as a tool designed to improve and refine current teaching methods and materials. It is proposed simply as a way to present methods and a way to provide a more precise measurement instrument of present teaching.

Summary

- Many learning-disabled students have problems in social skills and social perception.

- The characteristics of the social difficulties include a lack of judgment, difficulty in perceiving the feelings of others, problems in socializing and making friends, problems in family relationships, and poor self-concept.

- A substantial quantity of research studies with learning-disabled children and adolescents has shown earlier observations of parents and teachers about their children's social problems to be true. Many learning-disabled students are not well accepted by classmates, behave differently from others in the classroom, do not do well in conversation with peers or in cooperative work, and are often described as hostile.

- The psychodynamic perspective of learning disabilities looks at the emotional consequences of failure. Learning-disabled students may grow up with little self-confidence, poor ego development, and few opportunities to develop feelings of self-worth. The emotional status of learning-disabled students may also further affect their ability to learn.

- Another perspective of the emotional consequences of learning disabilities is provided by psychosocial theory. Two factors are particularly important in determining if the student will develop emotional problems: preservation of self-esteem and achievement motivation.

- Behavior modification is a systematic arrangement of environmental events to produce a specific change in observable behavior. It can be used to change both social and academic behaviors.

- Key concepts in behavior modification include reinforcement (both positive and negative), extinction, schedules of reinforcement (intermittent, ratio, and variable reinforcement), shaping behavior, contingency management, contingency contracting, and token reinforcements.

- Assessment instruments for social-emotional factors include interviews, rating scales, check lists, inventories, and tests.

- Teaching strategies include developing social perception skills, building self-concept, cognitive behavior modification, and behavioral management techniques.

- Normal children usually learn social perception skills without direct instruction. However, learning-disabled students often need direct instruction in how to act and respond in social situations.

- Learning-disabled students often need help in building self-concept, self-esteem, and confidence so that they can learn.

• Cognitive behavior modification is a method that trains students to develop new cognitive strategies for learning. Students are taught to stop and think before responding, and to use self-verbalization and self-monitoring techniques.

• Behavioral approaches are effective in changing the behavior of learning-disabled students. It is important to determine what reinforcements will change the target behavior, to find workable reinforcers, and to monitor the behavior. Behavioral techniques include modeling, contracting, and precision teaching.

Key Terms

social skills	positive reinforcer	social perception
continuous reinforcement	Premack principle	achievement motivation
precision teaching	cognitive behavior	emotional well-being
psychodynamics of	modification	token reinforcers
emotional problems	self-esteem	behavior modification
contingency contract	modeling	successive approximation

Retrospective:

Learning Disabilities at the Crossroads

Many dimensions of learning disabilities are described in this book, reflecting the numerous and rapid changes that have taken place in the field over the past few years. These modifications occurred for a number of reasons: research in learning disabilities and related fields has opened new directions, experience that teachers have accrued over the past twenty years of teaching learning-disabled students has tested traditional approaches, current conditions in regular education and special education have added new dimensions, and pressures from outside sources, such as parents, legislators, and other political entities have been influential.

The changes are reflected in the contents of each section of the text.

Part 1: Overview of Learning Disabilities. The field of learning disabilities is now established and recognized. While the problem of definition remains one of controversy and debate, there is now a more stable concept of prevalence because of Child Count data. The past twenty years of experience in the field of learning disabilities provided the needed time to develop a clearer perspective of the historical development of the field.

Part 2: The Assessment-Teaching Process. The individualized education program (IEP) has become a familiar and accepted process for special educators. It has proved to be a workable tool for guiding assessment, clinical teaching, and delivery of educational services. The management of this process is becoming more efficient, and the technology of the microcomputer is being harnessed to improve it further.

Part 3: Theoretical Perspectives and Expanding Directions. This is one of the most exciting and promising areas of change in learning disabilities. The theoretical basis is extremely important because it is the foundation for all that occurs in the assessment and teaching process. Developments in the theory of cognitive learning strategies are opening new ways for understanding and helping students with learning disabilities and for conducting research. The preschool years are now generally recognized as the most productive years for successful intervention, and special teaching for the early childhood years has grown into a field of its own. Similarly, in the teaching of the learning-disabled adolescent, the need for programs, services, and research is clearly accepted. The topic of the learning-disabled adolescent is an area of new and productive research and practice.

Part 4: From Theories to Teaching Strategies. Teaching strategies is the practical side of teaching students with learning disabilities, and we have seen many changes in this area as well, with certain aspects receiving more emphasis and others less. For example, there is less interest in teaching motor skills and more stress on language skills. The concepts of cognitive learning strategies have crept into all areas of academic teaching. The use of the microcomputer is also finding its place in many parts of the curriculum.

Learning disabilities is now at a crossroads, as it seems to have been throughout its twenty-year history. The exact direction it will follow is hard to predict. Many of the innovative ideas are only in their beginning stages and will develop more fully in the years to come. We will see an expansion of the applications of cognitive learning strategies. There will be greater use of the microcomputer for management purposes and for teaching. Programs are likely to expand at the secondary level. There will be more integration of special education and regular education, and more learning-disabled students will receive services in the mainstream. As a result of all these shifts, the role of the learning-disabilities teacher will also have to change to meet the new demands.

We can predict with certainty that learning disabilities will continue to be highly controversial and a field of divergent opinions. We can also predict that it will *not* be a stable and static field of endeavor.

Since its inception in the 1960s at the instigation of parents whose children were unserved or poorly served in the schools, the field of learning disabilities has proved itself to be a dynamic discipline. Despite controversy, it has taken root and developed; it has also shown itself capable of adapting good ideas from related disciplines and establishing innovative and experimental programs. Most important, the establishment of the field of learning disabilities has made possible happier and more productive lives for thousands of children and adolescents.

Appendix A: **Case Study**

Introduction

Case studies are a useful pedagogical tool. They offer the opportunity to apply theoretical knowledge, combining the science and art elements of the assessment/teaching process in an actual situation. The case of Adam Z., a freshman high school student, follows the format outlined in Chapter 3. As noted earlier, any case presentation is necessarily influenced by the theoretical orientation of the case investigators, and professionals often differ about matters such as selection of assessment instruments, the way that assessment information is analyzed, and the recommended intervention procedures. The case of Adam Z. is followed through six stages of the assessment/teaching process.

Stage 1. Prereferral
Stage 2. Referral and initial planning
Stage 3. Multidisciplinary evaluation
Stage 4. Case conference; writing the IEP
Stage 5. Implementing the IEP
Stage 6. Reviewing student progress

Identifying Information: **Adam Z.**

Name of Student: Adam Z.
Age: 14 years 6 months
Current Placement: High School Freshman, Grade 9.4

Stage 1. Prereferral Information and Activities

Shortly after the semester started in September, Adam Z.'s high school departmental English teacher, Ms. Sloan, requested a prereferral staffing to discuss Adam Z., who was doing poorly in her English class. The informal prereferral staffing for Adam included Adam's departmental teachers: his English teacher (Ms. Sloan), his general science teacher, his American history teacher, and his Spanish teacher. Ms. Sloan reported that Adam's problem in English appeared to be that he was unable to read his literature assignments and therefore had no knowledge of material. After discussing Adam's problem, the members of the prereferral team recommended that a classmate in the English class tape-record the assigned literature readings for Adam so that he could listen to the material. Specifically, they recommended that Peter, a classmate of Adam's, be given this assignment; he was particularly interested in speech and drama and read well orally.

Ms. Sloan discussed this venture with Adam and Peter, and they agreed to give the plan a trial. Peter recorded two of the literature assignments to help Adam study his English homework. However, after a week into this plan, Peter won the lead role in the school play, and frequent rehearsals for the play kept him from making further recordings for Adam. As Peter's interest in the plan waned, so did Adam's, and he began to fall even further behind in English. At the next report period at the end of October, Adam received a failing grade in English. At this point, Ms. Sloan decided to refer Adam for a special education evaluation.

Stage 2. Referral and Initial Planning

Ms. Sloan met with Adam's mother, Mrs. Z., to discuss Adam's failing work in English class. Mrs. Z. related that Adam had difficulty in school all along, beginning with the primary grades. During the elementary years, grades 1 through 8, Adam had attended several schools, but he had not received any special education services. As Mrs. Z. signed the consent form to have the evaluation, she remarked that she was hoping that Adam would receive some help now that he was in high school.

Ms. Sloan subsequently submitted the referral to the special education coordinator in the high school. The initial planning for Adam's multidisciplinary evaluation included the following kinds of assessment information: (A) classroom observation, (B) review of health information and testing of auditory and visual acuity, (C) conference with Adam, (D) a relevant developmental and educational history, (E) a psychological report including measures of intellectual aptitude, (F) measures of present levels of academic achievement.

Stage 3. The Multidisciplinary Evaluation

The multidisciplinary evaluation team consisted of the school psychologist, the learning disabilities teacher, the high school guidance counselor, and the school nurse. Each member of the team was responsible for obtaining certain kinds of evaluation information. A summary of this information follows:

A. A Classroom Observation

The learning disabilities teacher observed Adam during a reading lesson in an American history class. The students in the class were assigned to read a passage concerning the U.S. Constitution and to answer 10 multiple-choice questions on the text. Adam exhibited behavior suggesting that he was completing the assignment: he appeared to be reading the selection, then he appeared to be answering the questions, exhibiting behaviors such as scratching his head and looking up at the ceiling, as if thinking, before marking each answer. Upon examination of his test paper and discussion with him, however, it became evident that the assignment was completely beyond his current achievement level. He had learned to feign the appropriate behavior to look as though he were doing the same work as the other students.

B. Review of Health and Auditory and Visual Acuity Information

The school nurse reviewed the health records, which showed that Adam had been absent often during the primary and elementary years because of frequent colds. Also, his mother had reported that during his early school years he had suffered from otitis media, an inflammatory condition of the middle ear resulting in fluctuating and temporary hearing loss. The school nurse tested his hearing with an audiometer, and his auditory acuity fell within normal limits.

The school nurse gave Adam a visual screening test, and no problems were noted. The other health history indicated no unusual health problems.

C. Conference with Adam

The guidance counselor met with Adam to discuss the evaluation. Adam clearly recognized that he had a learning problem, and he said he could not understand why he was so different from the other kids and had always so much difficulty learning to read. He thought he got along at his previous school because the teachers let him alone and never called on him. Adam also mentioned that he was worried that his parents did not like him because he caused them so much more trouble than his sister. He confided that he had once convinced a friend to rush into his house shouting, "Help, help! Adam's been run over!" so he could watch his mother's reaction through the window. He quite expected her to say, "Thank goodness for that." When she stood up in a panic, Adam rushed in telling her it was only a joke. His mother was very angry about his joke, but it was worth it to find out that she really cared.

D. Developmental and Educational History

The guidance counselor interviewed Mr. and Mrs. Z. and also reviewed Adam's educational history through his cumulative records.

Adam is the younger of two children. His sister is two years older and is an excellent student. Adam was born two months prematurely and weighed four pounds eight ounces at birth. He was a colicky baby and was put on a supplemental formula because his weight gain was slow. He was allergic to the formula and several changes had to be made. Motor developmental milestones were accomplished within the normal range: he crawled at eight months and walked at twelve months. Language development, however, was slow. He did not engage in activities such as cooing, verbalizing, or babbling during his infancy as his sister had. By age two he had not learned to say any words to express himself but only pointed and gestured. His pediatrician referred him to the University Language Disorders Clinic, where he received language therapy for one hour per week until age three. At that time the family moved to the Orient, where Mr. Z. was assigned for three years as part of his military service. During this period, Adam did not attend school or receive any language help. The family had a child-care helper who did not speak English. Mrs. Z. said that it wasn't until Adam was four years old that she was able to decipher and understand his verbalizations.

She said that Adam was an extremely active child, getting into everything, and that when he was young the family could not take him to restaurants or to the home of friends because of his extremely hyperactive behavior. He seemed to be driven, in constant motion, and touching everything. His poor communication skills and hyperactivity interfered with his making friends as a young child. He no longer is hyperactive, but he still is not very talkative. He does fairly well in sports activities and is a member of a football team.

Mrs. Z. said that Adam was placed in first grade when they returned to the States from their overseas assignment. At the end of the school year, the school suggested that Adam repeat first grade. However, his father would not hear of it, and he was enrolled in the second grade of a nonpublic school. They moved three times during his elementary years because of the military assignments. He never did repeat a grade during the elementary school years.

Although Adam does not enjoy school, he does not complain and tries hard to succeed. Just before the conference ended, Adam's father commented that as a child he had also had difficulty learning to read in school but has done well as an officer in the military service. Mr. and Mrs. Z. said they hoped that Adam could be helped through the special services of the school.

E. Psychological Report and Measures of Learning Aptitude

The school psychologist administered the Wechsler Intelligence Scale for Children-Revised (WISC-R) to assess intellectual potential and the Wide Range Achievement Test (WRAT) to screen academic achievement. The psychologist found that Adam was in the above-average range of intelligence, but his abilities in performance areas were substantially above his abilities in language areas. Adam did especially poorly in tasks requiring auditory memory abilities. The WRAT indicated severe problems in reading and spelling with less severe problems in mathematics. Adam was cooperative during the testing, was aware of his problem, and appeared to be anxious to succeed in school. He was well adjusted, considering the many years of failure he had encountered. He scored on these tests as follows:

WISC-R Full scale IQ 104; Performance IQ 120, Verbal IQ 91.

Verbal subtests	Scaled score	Performance subtests	Scaled score
Information	7	Picture arrangement	13
Comprehension	6	Picture completion	14
Arithmetic	9	Block design	15

Verbal subtests	Scaled score	Performance subtests	Scaled score
Vocabulary	7	Object assembly	14
Similarities	8	Coding	8
Digit span	6		

Wide Range Achievement Test (WRAT)

Reading (word recognition)	3.3
Arithmetic	6.0
Spelling	3.0

F. Measures of Present Levels of Academic Achievement

The following academic tests were administered by the learning disabilities teacher in their entirety or as a partial test: Brigance Inventory of Essential Skills, Woodcock-Johnson Psychoeducational Test Battery, Key Math Diagnostic Test, Clinical Evaluation of Language Function (CELF), Standard Reading Inventory, Test of Language Development (TOLD), and Test of Written Language (TOWL). A brief summary of test results in several academic areas follows.

Oral Language Abilities: Receptive   Adam scored at or above average on tests of comprehension of oral language sentences and words. When visual input was included, he seemed to do better in receiving and remembering the language.

Oral Language Abilities: Expressive   Problems were evident in his use of oral language, in word finding (retrieval of a precise word), and in syntax. He had difficulty repeating sentences with complex syntactical structures and words with difficult articulation patterns, and his word fluency was poor in terms of quantity, quality, and speed.

Reading   According to the oral reading inventory, Adam's instructional reading level was at the middle third-grade level. Although he knew basic word recognition skills, vowels, consonants, and simple word prefixes and suffixes, his efforts to apply this information were slow and laborious. His sight vocabulary was at the third-grade level, but recognition was somewhat slow. Adam's comprehension of the oral reading passages was surprisingly strong. Considering his difficulty with word recognition skills, he seemed to make good use of context clues to help understand the story.

Silent reading scores ranged from grade 3.5 to 5.0, generally below the fifth percentile for his age and grade. Observation of Adam during silent reading showed that he spent more time studying the questions than reading the text. He seemed to be looking for words he knew.

Mathematics   Mathematics was an area of significant strength for Adam. He did particularly well in computation and in mental mathematics.

When he had to read a mathematics word story problem, however, the task became more difficult.

Written Language   This was an area of great difficulty for Adam. He did poorly in usage, mechanics, and spelling. The quantity, as well as the quality, of output, was very meager. His handwriting, however, was legible.

Stage 4. The Case Conference

The case conference team met and included the following participants: the English teacher, the learning disabilities teacher, the school psychologist, the special education coordinator, Mr. and Mrs. Z., and Adam.

The case conference team agreed that Adam is learning disabled and requires special education services. He exhibits a severe discrepancy between his potential and achievement in reading, oral language, and written language.

Adam possesses a number of strengths: intellectual aptitude in the above-average range, with strong abilities in performance areas, mathematics concepts and computational skills, receptive oral language, and physical and motor performance. He does not exhibit behavior problems in school and appears to have a high desire to learn.

Areas of weakness that should be considered include poor reading skills (although he has a knowledge of basic word attack skills), inadequate skills in oral expressive language, poor written language skills and spelling, and inefficient strategies for coping with the demands of the high school curriculum.

The case conference team felt that Adam's academic problem was severe. Since he had not received any help in the past, he needs a rather intensive special education program at this time. The team recommended that Adam be placed in a self-contained learning disabilities class. They recommended that he be mainstreamed for several subjects—mathematics, physical education, and a career education class, to begin planning for his work life. Mr. and Mrs. Z. agreed to the plan and an IEP was written and signed by all members of the case conference team.

Stage 5. Implementing the Teaching Plan

The teacher in the learning disabilities self-contained classroom at the high school developed more specific plans to meet the objectives written into Adam's IEP. The plans included methods for solidifying and practicing reading word recognition skills, building reading comprehension skills through reading of content area books, placing Adam into a career education class, teaching metacognitive skills to improve his ability to help himself learn, and providing direct instruction in oral expression and in writing.

Stage 6. Monitoring Progress and Review

Adam's progress will be reviewed informally on a weekly basis by the learning disabilities teacher. Progress will be monitored in the learning disabilities class and a conference will be held with each of the departmental teachers (mathematics, career education). The school has special classes for learning-disabled students in the area of English, social studies, and science. Adam will be placed in these classes and in the learning disabilities resource room as his progress permits. A review of Adam's progress and a re-evaluation of his program will be held in six months.

Appendix B: **Phonics**

This appendix has two sections. The first part is a short phonics quiz to assess the teacher's knowledge of this subject area. The second part is a brief review of some phonic generalizations.

ə Fŏn'ĭks Kwĭz (a Phonics Quiz)

The purpose of the phonics quiz is to give teachers the opportunity to evaluate their knowledge of phonics, structural or morphemic analysis, and phonic generalizations. Even among advocates of conflicting approaches to the teaching of reading, there is agreement that skills in word recognition and phonics are essential for effective reading. And all reading authorities agree that teachers of reading and language arts have the responsibility to help students acquire the skills that will enable them to unlock unknown words. Without phonics, most students cannot become self-reliant, discriminating, efficient readers.

In spite of this strong and united stand taken by the reading experts, many teachers and prospective teachers, as well as prospective learning disabilities specialists, are not knowledgeable in this content area (Lerner and List, 1970; Horne, 1978). The *Torch Lighters* (Austin, 1961), an intensive and broad study of tomorrow's teachers of reading, supported by the Carnegie Corporation, revealed that many prospective teachers do not know techniques or generalizations of phonics. A major recommendation resulting from the study was that college instructors take responsibility for making certain that their students who will be teaching reading master the principles of phonics. Phonics and structural or morphemic analysis, then, should be part of the content area for the teacher of reading, language arts, and English.

It should be noted that the research on the utility of phonic generalizations reveals that these rules have many exceptions. In fact, some are applicable less than half the time. Therefore, certain generalizations may have a limited utility value (Clymer, 1963; Emans, 1967; Bailey, 1967; Burmeister, 1968; Lerner, 1969; Winkley, 1966). Nevertheless, these generalizations do provide a helpful start in analyzing unknown words.

Although knowledge of rules and facts concerning phonics is part of the content area for the teacher, this is not presented as a recommended way to teach phonics to a child. The strategies selected to teach a child the skill of unlocking words will depend on many factors.

To check your knowledge of phonics, select the correct answer for each of the following fifty questions. Compare your choices with the correct answers printed at the end of the phonics quiz. Score two points for each correct answer. Check the table that follows the answers for your rating and classification.

CHOOSE THE CORRECT ANSWER

Consonants

1. Which of the following words ends with a consonant sound?
   a) piano b) baby c) relay d) pencil e) below
2. A combination of two or three consonants pronounced so that each letter keeps its own identity is called a
   a) silent consonant b) consonant digraph c) diphthong d) schwa
   e) consonant blend
3. A word with a consonant digraph is
   a) stop b) blue c) bend d) stripe e) none of the above
4. A word with a consonant blend is
   a) chair b) ties c) thing d) strict e) where
5. A soft *c* is in the word
   a) city b) cat c) chair d) Chicago e) none of the above
6. A soft *g* is in the word
   a) great b) go c) ghost d) rig e) none of the above
7. A hard *c* is sounded in pronouncing which of the following nonsense words?
   a) cadur b) ceiter c) cymling d) ciblent e) chodly
8. A hard *g* would be likely to be found in which of the following nonsense words?
   a) gyfing b) gesturn c) gailing d) gimber e) geit
9. A *voiced* consonant digraph is in the word
   a) think b) ship c) whip d) the e) photo
10. An *unvoiced* consonant digraph is in the word
    a) those b) thirteen c) that d) bridge e) these

Vowels

11. Which of the following words contains a long vowel sound?
    a) paste b) stem c) urge d) ball e) off
12. Which of the following words contains a short vowel sound?
    a) treat b) start c) slip d) paw e) father
13. If *tife* were a word, the letter *i* would probably sound like the *i* in
    a) if b) beautiful c) find d) ceiling e) sing
    Why?
14. If *aik* were a word, the letter *a* would probably sound like the *a* in
    a) pack b) ball c) about d) boat e) cake
    Why?
15. If *ne* were a word, the letter *e* would probably sound like the *e* in
    a) fed b) seat c) batter d) friend e) weight
    Why?
16. A vowel sound represented by the alphabet letter name of that vowel is a
    a) short vowel b) long vowel c) diphthong d) digraph e) schwa

17. An example of the schwa sound is found in
    a) cotton b) phoneme c) stopping d) preview e) grouping
18. A diphthong is in the word
    a) coat b) boy c) battle d) retarded e) slow
19. Which of the following words contains a vowel digraph?
    a) toil b) amazing c) happy d) cape e) coat

Syllables

Indicate the correct way to divide the following nonsense words into syllables:

20. l i d b e r
    a) li—dber b) lidb—er c) lid—ber d) none of these
    Why?
21. s e f u m
    a) se—fum b) sef—um c) s—efum d) sefu—m e) none of these
    Why?
22. s k e b l e
    a) skeb—le b) ske—ble c) sk—eble d) none of these
    Why?
23. g o p h u l
    a) gop—hul b) go—phul c) goph—ul d) none of these
    Why?
24. r e p a i n l y
    a) rep—ain—ly b) re—pai—nly c) re—pain—ly d) none of these
    Why?
25. How many syllables are in the word *barked*?
    a) one b) two c) three d) four e) five
26. How many syllables are in the word *generalizations*?
    a) four b) five c) six d) seven e) eight
27. A word with an open syllable is
    a) pike b) go c) bend d) butter e) if
28. A word with a closed syllable is
    a) throw b) see c) why d) cow e) win

Accent

29. If *trigler* were a word, which syllable would probably be accented?
    a) trig b) ler c) neither d) both
    Why?
30. If *tronition* were a word, which syllable would probably be accented?
    a) tro b) ni c) tion d) none of these
    Why?
31. If *pretaineringly* were a word, which syllable would probably be accented?
    a) pre b) tain c) er d) ing e) ly
    Why?

Sound of Letter *y*

32. If *gly* were a word, the letter *y* would probably sound like
    a) the *e* in *eel* b) the *e* in *pet* c) the *i* in *isle* d) the *i* in *if* e) the *y* in *happy*
    Why?
33. If *agby* were a word, the letter *y* would probably sound like
    a) the *e* in *eel* b) the *e* in egg c) the *i* in *ice* d) the *i* in *if* e) the *y* in *cry*
    Why?

Silent Letters

34. *No* silent letters are found in which of the following nonsense words?
    a) knip b) gine c) camb d) wron e) shan
35. *No* silent letters are in
    a) nade b) fruting c) kettin d) foat e) pnam

Terminology

36. A printed symbol made up of two letters representing one single phoneme or speech sound is a
    a) schwa b) consonant blend c) phonetic d) digraph e) diphthong
37. The smallest sound-bearing unit or a basic sound of speech is a
    a) phoneme b) morpheme c) grapheme d) silent consonant e) schwa
38. A study of all the speech sounds in language and how these sounds are produced is
    a) phonics b) semantics c) orthography d) etymology e) phonetics
39. The application of speech sounds to the teaching of reading letters or groups of letters is called
    a) phonics b) phonemics c) orthography d) etymology e) phonetics
40. The study of the nature and function of human language utilizing the methodology and objectivity of the scientist is
    a) phonetics b) phonology c) linguistics d) morphology e) semantics
41. The approach to beginning reading that selects words that have a consistent sound-symbol relationship (CVC) is the
    a) basal reader approach b) phonics approach c) linguistics approach
    d) language-experience approach e) initial teaching alphabet approach
42. The approach to beginning reading that uses a simpler, more reliable alphabet to make the decoding of English phonemes less complex is the
    a) basal reader approach b) phonetic approach c) linguistic approach
    d) language-experience approach e) initial teaching alphabet approach
43. A *phonic element* is similar to which word in linguistic terminology?
    a) syntax b) phoneme c) morpheme d) grapheme e) intonation
44. The study of structural analysis is similar to what element of linguistics?
    a) syntax b) phonology c) morphology d) graphology e) intonation

The Utility of Phonic Generalizations

In examining both words that are exceptions to the rules and words that conform to the rules, researchers have found a varying percent of utility in the generalizations in items 45–48. How frequently does each hold true?

45. When there are two vowels side by side, the long sound of the first one is heard and the second is usually silent.
    a) 25% b) 45% c) 75% d) 90% e) 100% of the time
46. When there are two vowels, one of which is final *e*, the first vowel is long and the *e* is silent.
    a) 30% b) 60% c) 75% d) 90% e) 100%
47. When a vowel is in the middle of a one-syllable word, the vowel is short.
    a) 30% b) 50% c) 75% d) 90% e) 100%
48. When a word begins with *kn,* the *k* is silent.
    a) 30% b) 50% c) 70% d) 90% e) 100%
49. The first American educator to advocate the teaching of phonics as an aid to word recognition and pronunciation was
    a) Noah Webster in *The American Blueback Spelling Book,* 1790.
    b) William McGuffey in *McGuffey's Readers,* 1879.
    c) Leonard Bloomfield, *Language,* 1933.
    d) Rudolph Flesch in *Why Johnny Can't Read,* 1955.
    e) Charles Fries, *Linguistics and Reading,* 1963.
50. Most reading authorities agree that
    a) the sight word method is the best way to teach reading.
    b) the phonics method is the best way to teach reading.
    c) structural or morphemic analysis is the best way to teach reading.
    d) there is no *one* best way to teach reading.

Read the following nonsense words applying phonic generalizations to determine their appropriate pronunciations.

bongtrike	gingabution
plignel	recentively
abcealter	fudder
conborvement	gentropher
crangle	craipthrusher
magsletting	wonaprint
phister	knidderflicing
flabinstate	

Answers to Phonics Quiz

1.	d	14.	e: with two vowels, first is long, second is silent
2.	e		
3.	e	15.	b: one-syllable ending in vowel is long
4.	d		
5.	a	16.	b
6.	e	17.	a
7.	a	18.	b
8.	c	19.	e
9.	d	20.	c: divide between two consonants
10.	b		
11.	a	21.	a: vowel, consonant, vowel
12.	c	22.	b: words ending in *le*—consonant precedes the *le*
13.	c: long vowel with silent *e*		

23. b: consonant digraphs are not divided
24. c: prefix and suffix are separate syllables
25. a
26. c
27. b
28. e
29. a: accent first of two syllables
30. b: accent syllables before *tion* ending
31. b: accent syllable with two adjacent vowels
32. c: *y* at end of one syllable word has a long *i* sound
33. a: *y* at end of multisyllable word has long *e* sound
34. e
35. b
36. d
37. a
38. e
39. a
40. c
41. c
42. e
43. b
44. c
45. b
46. b
47. c
48. e
49. a
50. d

Rating Scale

Score	Rating
92–100	EXCELLENT Congratulations! You do know your phonics.
84–92	GOOD A brief refresher will help, though.
76–84	FAIR Study with your favorite third grader.
68–76	POOR You could be a case of "the blind leading the blind."

A Review of Common Phonic Generalizations

Consonants

Consonants are the letters in the alphabet that are not vowels. Consonant speech sounds are formed by modifying or altering or obstructing the stream of vocal sound with the organs of speech. These obstructions may be stops, fricatives, or resonants. Consonant sounds are relatively consistent and have a regular grapheme-phoneme relationship. They include: b, d, f, h, j, k, l, m, n, p, r, s, t, v, w, y (initial position).

Consonants *c* and *g*

Hard *c* pronounced like *k* when followed by a, o, u (cup, cat).
Soft *c* pronounced like *s* when followed by i, e, y (city, cent).
Hard *g* when followed by *a, o, u* (go, gay).
Soft *g* when followed by *i, e, y,* sounds like "j" (gentle, gyp).

Consonant Blends

A combination of two or three consonant letters blended in such a way that each letter in the blend keeps its own identity: bl, sl, cl, fl, gl, pl, br, cr, dr, fr, gr, pr, tr, sc, sk, sl, sw, sn, sp, sm, spl, spr, str, scr, ng, nk, tw, dw.

Consonant Digraphs

A combination of two consonant letters representing one phoneme or speech sound that is not a blend of the two letters: sh, ch, wh, ck, ph, gh, th.

Silent Consonants

Silent consonants are the consonants that, when combined with specific other letters, are not pronounced. In the examples below, the silent consonants are the ones enclosed in parentheses, and the letters shown with them are the specific letters that cause them to be silent in combination. (There are exceptions, however.)

i(gh)	sight, bright
m(b)	comb, lamb
(w)r	wren, wrong
(l)k	talk, walk
(k)n	knew, knife
s(t)	listen, hasten
f(t)	often, soften

Vowels

The vowels of the alphabet are the letters *a, e, i, o, u,* and sometimes *y.* The vowel speech sounds are produced in the resonance chamber formed by the stream of air passing through in the oral cavity.

Short vowels: a, e, i, o, u, (sometimes y). A single vowel in a medial position usually has the short vowel sound: consonant, vowel, consonant (CVC). A diacritical mark called a *breve* ˘ may indicate the short vowel: păt, săd, lĕd, sĭt, pŏt, cŭp, gў̆p.

Long vowels: a, e, i, o, u, (sometimes y). The long vowel sounds the same as the alphabet letter name of the vowel. It is indicated with the diacritical mark ē, called a macron: gō, cāke, ēel, īce, nō, ūniform, crȳ.

Double Vowels: Vowel Digraph

Frequently, when two vowels are adjacent, the first vowel has the long sound while the second is silent. Recent research has shown this generalization to hold true about 45 percent of the time: tie, coat, rain, eat, pay.

Final *e*

In words with a vowel-consonant-e pattern (VCe), the vowel frequently has the long sound while the *e* is silent. Research has shown this generalization to hold true about 60 percent of the time: make, Pete, slide, hope, cube.

Vowels Modified by *r*

Vowels followed by the letter *r* are neither long nor short, but the sound is modified by the letter *r*. This holds true about 85 percent of the time: star, her, stir, horn, fur.

Diphthong

This consists of two adjacent printed symbols representing two vowels, each of which contributes to a blended speech sound: joy, toil, cow, house, few.

Schwa Sound

This is the vowel sound in an unaccented syllable and is indicated with the symbol ə· balloon, eaten, beautify, button, circus

Syllabication

Number of Syllables

There are as many syllables in a word as there are vowel sounds heard: bruise (1 syllable), beautiful (3 syllables).

Two Consonants *(VC-CV)*

If the initial vowel is followed by two consonants, divide the word between the two consonants. This rule holds true about 80 percent of the time: con-tact, let-ter, mar-ket.

Single Consonant *(V-CV)*

If the initial vowel is followed by one consonant, the consonant usually begins the second syllable. There are many exceptions to this rule. The generalization holds true about 50 percent of the time: mo-tor, na-tion, student.

Consonant-*le (C-le)* Endings

If a word ends in *le,* the consonant preceding the *le* begins the last syllable. This generalization holds true about 95 percent of the time: ta-ble, pur-ple, han-dle.

Consonant Blends and Consonant Digraphs

Consonant blends and digraphs are not divided in separating a word into syllables. This holds true 100 percent of the time: teach-er, graph-ic, describe.

Prefixes and Suffixes

Prefixes and suffixes usually form a separate syllable: re-plac-ing, dis-appoint-ment.

Suffix *ed*

If the suffix *ed* is preceded by *d* or *t,* it does form a separate syllable and is pronounced *ed.* If the suffix *ed* is not preceded by a *d* or *t,* it does not form a separate syllable. It is pronounced like *t* when it follows an unvoiced consonant, and it is pronounced like *d* when it follows a voiced consonant: sanded (ed), patted (ed), asked (t), pushed (t), tamed (d), crazed (d).

Open and Closed Syllables

Syllables that end with a consonant are closed syllables and the vowel is short: *can*-vass. Syllables that end with a vowel are open syllables and the vowel is long: *ba*-by.

The *y* Sound in One-Syllable Words and Multisyllable Words

When the *y* is the final sound in a one-syllable word, it usually has the sound of a long *i*: cry, my, ply.

When the *y* is the final sound of a multisyllable word, it usually has the long *e* sound: funny, lady.

Accent

When there is no other clue in a two-syllable word, the accent frequently falls on the first syllable. This generalization is true about 80 percent of the time: pen'cil, sau'cer.

In inflected or derived forms of words, the primary accent usually falls on or within the root word: fix'es, un touched'.

Two vowels together in the last syllable of a word give a clue to an accented final syllable: re main', re peal'.

If two identical consonants are in a word, the syllable before the double consonant is usually accented: big'ger, win'ner.

The primary accent usually falls on the syllable preceding these suffixes: ion, ity, ic, ical, ian, ial, ious: at ten' tion, hys ter' ical, bar bar' ian, bil' ious.

References

Austin, M. C. (1961). *The Torch Lighters: Tomorrow's Teachers of Reading.* Cambridge, Mass.: Harvard University Press.

Bailey, M. H. (1967). The Utility of Phonic Generalizations in Grades One Through Six. *Reading Teacher, 20,* 413–418.

Burmeister, L. E. (1968). Usefulness of Phonic Generalizations. *Reading Teacher, 21,* 349–356.

Clymer, T. L. (1963). The Utility of Phonic Generalizations in the Primary Grades. *Reading Teacher, 16,* 252–258.

Emans, R. (1967). When Two Vowels Go Walking and Other Such Things. *Reading Teacher, 21,* 262–269.

Horne, M. (1978, November). Do Learning Disabilities Specialists Know Their Phonics? *Journal of Learning Disabilities, 11,* 580–585.

Lerner, J. W. (1969, March). The Utility of Phonic Generalizations—A Modification. *The Journal of the Reading Specialist, 8,* 117–118.

Lerner, J. W., & L. List. (1970, fall). The Phonics Knowledge of Prospective Teachers, Experienced Teachers, and Elementary Pupils. *Illinois School Research, 7,* 39–42.

Winkley, C. K. (1966). Which Accent Generalizations Are Worth Teaching? *Reading Teacher, 20,* 219–224.

Appendix C: **Tests**

This appendix provides an alphabetical listing of some tests that are useful in assessing students with learning disabilities. The list includes tests that have been referred to in this text, as well as tests that were not discussed. The descriptive material about each test is brief and not designed to be evaluative. Since tests are frequently revised and new forms of manuals are issued, it is desirable to obtain a current catalogue from the publisher before placing an order. The test publisher appears after the test name; publishers' addresses are provided in Appendix D.

In selecting tests, the user should consider the technical qualities of the test; its purpose, reliability, validity, standardization procedures, the types of scores that are provided, ease of administration and scoring, and time and training needed to administer the test. The *Standards for Educational and Psychologists Tests,* published by the American Psychological Association in 1974, is a comprehensive guide for test users and test developers; it sets the standard for the kinds of information that should be in test manuals, for the kinds of information that should be provided on the technical adequacy of tests, and for test use.

An Informal Reading Inventory (in Appendix D in M. Richek, L. List, and J. Lerner, *Reading Problems; Diagnosis and Remediation,* 1983). Prentice-Hall. An informal reading inventory of oral and silent reading, including word recognition and reading comprehension passages and questions (grades pp–8).

AAMD Adaptive Behavior Scale (Public School Version). American Association of Mental Deficiency. Assesses the total life-functioning abilities of students through an interview with an informant (grades 2–6).

Ammons Full-Range Picture Vocabulary Test. Psychological Test Specialists. Forms A and B. An individually administered test of receptive language vocabulary (preschool to adult).

Analytic Reading Inventory. Charles E. Merrill. Informal Reading Inventory. Comprehension passages yield independent, instructional, and frustration levels of reading (grades 1–9).

Basic Achieving Skills Individual Screener (BASIC). The Psychological Corp. Individual test of reading, mathematics, spelling, and writing (grades 1–12).

Basic Schools Skills Inventory. PRO-ED. Identifies areas of difficulty in school performance (ages 4–7).

Bender-Gestalt Test. Western Psychological Services. An individually administered test of a person's performance in copying designs. The Koppitz Scoring (The Bender Gestalt Test for Young Children: E. Koppitz. N.Y.: Grune & Stratton, 1963) provides a developmental scoring system for young children to age 10.

Brigance Diagnostic Inventory of Basic Skills. Curriculum Associates. Criterion-referenced tests of readiness, reading, language arts, and mathematics (grades K–6).

Brigance Diagnostic Inventory of Early Development. Curriculum Associates. Assesses functional skills of preschool children (ages 1–7).

Brigance Diagnostic Inventory of Essential Skills. Curriculum Associates. Measures minimal academic and vocational competencies. Designed for secondary students (grades 9–12).

Boehm Test of Basic Concepts. The Psychological Corp. Diagnostic group test of understanding of concepts (ages 5–6).

Brown-Carlsen Listening Comprehension Test. The Psychological Corp. A receptive language test designed for group use to determine ability to understand spoken English (grades 9–13).

California Achievement Tests. California Test Bureau. A battery of group tests to assess several areas of academic achievement. Also California Reading Tests (levels 1–college).

Carrow Elicited Language Inventory. DLM Teaching Resources. Assessment of language proficiency in spoken language (ages 3–8).

Carrow Screening Test for Auditory Comprehension of Language. DLM Teaching Resources. Assesses the child's understanding of language structure, using forms in Spanish and English (ages 3–10 and 6–11).

Classroom Reading Inventory. William C. Brown. A reading inventory that can be administered to individuals or groups (levels pp–8).

Clinical Evaluation of Language Functions (CELF). Charles E. Merrill. Individual screening test and diagnostic battery to measure oral language abilities (grades K–12).

Detroit Tests of Learning Aptitude (DTLA-2). PRO-ED. An individual test of mental functions. There are eleven subtests measuring various areas of mental processing. In addition to an overall general score, the test also gives nine composite scores (ages 6–17).

Developmental Test of Visual-Motor Integration. Follett. A visual-motor test of the subject's abilities in copying designs (ages 5–15).

Devereau Adolescent School Behavior Rating Scale. Devereau Foundation. A teacher rating scale for rating behavior of adolescents (ages 13–18).

Devereau Elementary School Behavior Rating Scale. Devereau Foundation. A rating scale for school-related behavior of elementary students (ages 5–12).

Diagnostic Tests and Self-Help in Arithmetic. California Test Bureau. Test designed to diagnose arithmetic difficulties (elementary).

DIAL-R (Developmental Indicators for the Assessment of Learning—Revised). Childcraft. A prekindergarten screening test for identifying children with learning problems (preschool age).

Doren Diagnostic Reading Test of Word Recognition Skills. American Guidance Services. Group or individually administered word skills test (grades 1–6).

Durrell Analysis of Reading Difficulty. The Psychological Corp. A battery of diagnostic tests designed to help in the analysis and evaluation of specific reading difficulties (grades 1–6).

Durrell Reading-Listening Series. The Psychological Corp. Group tests of listening and reading ability that permit a comparison of these two language skills. Primary (grades 1–3.5); intermediate (grades 3.5–6); advanced (grades 7–9).

Ekwall Reading Inventory. Allyn & Bacon. Informal reading inventory of oral and silent reading (grades pp–9).

Frostig Developmental Test of Visual Perception. Consulting Psychologists Press. This test measures abilities in five separate areas of visual perception (ages 4–8).

Gates-MacGinitie Reading Tests. Teachers College Press. A general test of silent reading designed for group administration. Five forms (grades 1–9).

Gates-McKillop-Horowitz Reading Diagnostic Tests. Teachers College Press. Battery of tests for individual administration, designed to give diagnostic information about a student's reading skills (grades 1–6).

Gilmore Oral Reading Test. Psychological Corp. An oral reading test, individually administered; gives information about word accuracy, rate, and comprehension (grades 1–8).

Goldman-Fristoe-Woodcock Auditory Skills Test Battery. American Guidance Services. Twelve tests of auditory skills (ages 3–adult).

Goldman-Fristoe Test of Articulation. American Guidance Services. Thirty-minute test for children over two years of age. Articulation of words and sentences.

Goldman-Fristoe-Woodcock Test of Auditory Discrimination. American Guidance Services. Tests auditory discrimination of phonemes against a quiet background and against a noisy background (ages 4–adult).

Goodenough-Harris Drawing Test. Psychological Corp. Provides a score of nonverbal intelligence obtained through an objective scoring of a student's drawings of a human figure (ages 3–15).

Gray Oral Reading Tests. PRO-ED. An individually administered oral reading test that combines rate and accuracy to obtain grade level scores. Comprehension questions available but not scored (grades pp–12).

Harris Tests of Lateral Dominance. Psychological Corp. Test to show right or left preference with hand, eye, foot (ages 7–adult).

Hiskey-Nebraska Test of Learning Aptitude. Marshall A. Hiskey. An individual test of intellectual potential, used widely with the deaf or hard of hearing (ages 3–17).

Illinois Test of Psycholinguistic Abilities. University of Illinois Press. Individually administered test containing twelve subtests of dimensions of mental processes. Scores obtained on subtests can be used for diagnostic purposes (ages 2–4 to 10–3).

Iowa Every-Pupil Test of Basic Skills. Houghton Mifflin. Group test of several academic areas: reading, arithmetic, language workstudy skills (ages 3–9).

Kaufman Assessment Battery for Children (K-ABC). American Guidance Services. Individual test of intelligence and achievement. Yields four major scores: Sequential Processing, Simultaneous Processing, Mental Processing Composite, and Achievement (ages 2½–12½).

Key Math Diagnostic Arithmetic Test. American Guidance Services. Measures fourteen arithmetic subskills. Individually administered. Four levels of evaluation (preschool–grade 6).

Keystone Visual Survey Service for Schools. Keystone View Co. Individually administered visual screening device to determine the need for further referral for a visual examination.

Leiter International Performance Scale. Stoelting. Nonverbal test of mental abilities (ages 2–18).

Lincoln-Oseretsky Motor Development Scale. Stoelting. Individual tests of a variety of motor skills (ages 6–14).

McCarthy Scales of Children's Abilities. The Psychological Corp. General intellectual levels and strengths and weaknesses in several ability areas (ages 2½–8½).

McCullough Word Analysis Tests. Ginn. Group test of word analysis skills (grades 4–8).

The Meeting Street School Screening Test. Meeting Street School. Early identification of children with learning disabilities: individually administered screening and diagnostic instrument, 30 minutes (ages 4½–6).

Metropolitan Achievement Tests. The Psychological Corp. Battery of tests. Group administration. Measures several areas of academic achievement: reading, spelling, arithmetic (grades 5–8).

Monroe Diagnostic Reading Tests. Stoelting. Individually administered diagnostic reading test of oral reading and word recognition.

Monroe Reading Aptitude Tests. Riverside. Group-administered test to measure readiness for reading. Nonreading test that assesses several areas of mental functioning (ages 6–9).

Motor-free Test of Visual Perception. Academic Therapy. Test of visual perception that does not require a motor component (ages 4–8).

Nelson-Denny Reading Test. Riverside. Group or individual general reading assessment (grade 9–adult level).

Nelson Reading Skills Test. Riverside. Diagnostic Reading Battery (grades 3–9).

Northwestern Syntax Screening Test. Northwestern University Press. Individually administered test of receptive and expressive language (ages 3–7).

Oseretsky Test of Motor Proficiency. American Guidance Services. Individual test of motor development (ages 4–16).

Ortho-rater. Bausch & Lomb. Individual visual screening test.

Otis-Lennon School Ability Test. Psychological Corp. Group test of general mental ability and scholastic aptitude (grades K–12).

Peabody Individual Achievement Test (PIAT). American Guidance Services. Individually administered test including five subjects: mathematics, reading recognition, reading comprehension, spelling, and general information. (K–adult).

Peabody Picture Vocabulary Test—Revised. American Guidance Services. An individually administered test of receptive language vocabulary (ages 2–8).

Picture Story Language Test—Revised. Grune & Stratton. An individually administered test of written language skills (ages 7–17).

Pupil Rating Scale. Grune & Stratton. A rating scale for elementary level students to be completed by the teacher (grades K–6).

Purdue Perceptual-Motor Survey. Charles E. Merrill. A series of tests for assessing motor development and motor skills (ages 4–10).

Reading Diagnosis. Jamestown Press. Diagnostic Reading Battery (grades 1–6).

Reading Miscue Inventory. Macmillan. Provides information on strategies used for oral reading (grades elementary–high school).

Roswell-Chall Auditory Blending Test. Essay Press. Individually administered short tests to assess ability to hear and blend sounds for word recognition (grades 1–4).

Roswell-Chall Diagnostic Reading Test. Essay Press. Individually administered short test to assess phonics abilities (grades 2–6).

Sequential Tests of Educational Progress (STEP). Addison-Wesley. A battery of achievement tests, including tests of reading vocabulary and comprehension (grades 3–12).

Slingerland Screening Tests for Identifying Children with Specific Language Disability. Educator's Publishing Services. Three sets of screening tests for early grades. Group administered. Informal scoring (grades 1–4).

Slosson Intelligence Test. Slosson Educational Publications. A short individual screening test of intelligence, for use by teachers and other professional persons for a quick estimate of mental ability (ages birth–adult).

Southern California Test Battery for Assessment of Dysfunction. Western Psychological Services. A battery containing the following separate tests: Southern California Kinesthesia and Tactile Perception Tests; Southern California Figure-Ground Visual Perception Test; Southern California Motor Accuracy Test; Southern California Perceptual-Motor Tests; and the Ayres Space Test (ages 3–10).

Spache Diagnostic Reading Scales. California Test Bureau. Individually administered battery of tests to diagnose reading difficulties (grades 1 and up).

SRA Achievement Scales. Science Research Associates. Group tests of several areas of academic achievement, including reading (grades 1–9).

SRA Primary Mental Abilities Tests. Science Research Associates. Group intelligence test designed to measure several subabilities of mental functioning. MA and IQ scores for verbal meaning, number facility, reasoning, perceptual speed, and spatial relations (grades K–adult).

Stanford Achievement Test. The Psychological Corp. Group test of academic achievement, including reading.

Stanford-Binet Intelligence Scale, Revised. Form LM Norms edition. Houghton Mifflin. Individual test of general intelligence, yielding MA and IQ scores; to be administered by trained examiners (ages 2–adult).

Stanford Diagnostic Arithmetic Test. Psychological Corp. Group test to diagnose nature of arithmetic difficulties.

Standard Reading Inventory. Klamath Printing Co. Informal reading inventory (pp–7).

Stanford Diagnostic Reading Test. Psychological Corp. Group test to diagnose nature of reading difficulties; measures performance in comprehension, vocabulary, syllabication, auditory skills, phonetic analysis, and reading rate (grades 2–9).

System of Multicultural Pluralistic Assessment (SOMPA). The Psychological Corp. Determines intellectual level and function based on a wide variety of measures. Separate norms available for black, Hispanic, and Caucasian American students (ages 5–11).

Templin-Darley Tests of Articulation. University of Iowa Bureau of Research and Service. Individual test of the articulation of speech sounds (grades 3–8).

Test of Adolescent Language (TOAL). PRO-ED. Assesses language ability of adolescent students (grades 6–12).

Test of Language Development (TOLD). PRO-ED. Individually administered diagnostic test of spoken language; articulation, word discrimination, oral vocabulary, picture vocabulary, sentence initiation, and grammar (grades 4–11).

Test of Reading Comprehension (TORC). PRO-ED. Assessment of reading comprehension abilities (grades 2–12).

Test of Written Language (TOWL). PRO-ED. A test of written expression.

Valett Developmental Survey of Basic Learning Abilities. Fearon Publishers. A survey of skill development in several areas of growth (ages 2–7).

Verbal Language Development Scale. American Guidance Service. An evaluation of language development obtained through an interview with an informant, usually a parent (ages one month–16).

Vineland Adaptive Behavior Scales. American Guidance Service. Individual measure of social maturity and independence. Information derived by interview with an informant, usually a parent (birth–adult).

Visual Retention Test—Revised. The Psychological Corp. Individually administered test of visual perception and memory of designs (ages 8–adult).

Wechsler Adult Intelligence Scale—Revised (WAIS-R). The Psychological Corp. An individual intelligence test of subjects over age 15; yields verbal, performance, and full-scale scores. To be administered by trained examiners (ages 15–adult).

Wechsler Intelligence Scale for Children—Revised (WISC-R). The Psychological Corp. Individual intelligence test that yields verbal and performance scores and a full-scale IQ score. To be administered by trained examiners (ages 6–16).

Wechsler Preschool and Primary Scale of Intelligence (WPPSI). The Psychological Corp. Individual intelligence test similar to the WISC-R for preschool children. Yields verbal, performance, and full-scale scores. To be administered by trained examiners (ages 4–6½).

Wepman Test of Auditory Discrimination. Language Research Associates. Individual test of auditory discrimination of phoneme sounds (ages 5–9).

Wide Range Achievement—Revised. Jastak Associates. A brief individual test of word recognition, spelling, and arithmetic computation (ages 5–adult).

Woodcock Reading Mastery Tests. American Guidance Services. Individual tests for identification of words, word attack, word comprehension, and passage comprehension. CRT and NRT interpretation (grades K–12).

Woodcock-Johnson Psychoeducational Battery. DLM Teaching Resources. Individual battery of twenty-seven tests in four parts: tests of cognitive ability, tests of achievement, tests of interest level, and scales of independent behavior (preschool through adult levels).

Appendix D: **Addresses of Publishers**

The following directory contains, in alphabetical order, the names and addresses of the publishers of tests and materials mentioned in this book, as well as other addresses that may be useful. The rapidity of changes in publishers and their addresses makes it inevitable that some entries will be changed during the life of this textbook.

Academic Therapy Publications, 20 Commercial Blvd., Novato, CA 94947.
ACLD, Association for Children and Adults with Learning Disabilities, 4156 Library Rd., Pittsburgh, PA 15234.
Addison-Wesley Publishing Co., Jacob Way, Reading, MA 01867.
Allied Education Council, PO Box 78, Galien, MI 49113.
Allyn & Bacon, 7 Wells Ave., Newton, MA 02159.
American Association of Mental Deficiency, 5201 Connecticut Avenue NW, Washington, DC 20015.
American Book Co., 135 W. 50th St., New York, NY 10020.
American Guidance Service, Inc., Publishers' Building, Circle Pines, MN 55014.
American Speech and Hearing Association, 9030 Old Georgetown Rd., Washington, DC 20014.
Ann Arbor Publishers, PO Box 338, Worthington, OH 43085.
Appleton-Century-Crofts, 440 Park Ave. South, NY 10016.
Arrow Book Club (Scholastic Book Services), 50 W. 44th St., NY 10036.
Barnell-Loft, 958 Church St., Baldwin, NY 11510.
Basic Books, Inc., 10 E. 53rd St., NY 10022.
Bausch & Lomb Optical Co., Rochester, NY 14602.
Beckley-Cardy, 1900 N. Narragansett, Chicago, IL 60639.
Bell and Howell, 7100 McCormick Rd., Chicago, IL 60645.
Benefic Press, 10300 W. Roosevelt Rd., Westchester, IL 60153.
Book-Lab, Inc., 1449 37 St., Brooklyn, NY 11218.
Borg-Warner Educational Systems, 7450 N. Natchez Ave., Niles, IL 60648.
William C. Brown Co., 2460 Kerper Blvd., Dubuque, IA 52001.
California Test Bureau, A Division of McGraw-Hill, Del Monte Research Park, Monterey, CA 93940.
Childcraft Education Corp., 20 Kilmer Rd., Edison, NJ 08817.
Consulting Psychologist Press, 577 College Ave., Palo Alto, CA 94306.
Continental Press, Inc., Elizabethtown, PA 17022.
Council for Exceptional Children, 1920 Association Dr., Reston, VA 22091.
Creative Playthings, Inc., Edinburgh Rd., Cranbury, NJ 08540.
Crestwood Company, PO Box 04513, Milwaukee, WI 53204.
Cuisenaire Company of America, Inc., 12 Church St., New Rochelle, NY 10805.
Curriculum Associates, Inc., 5 Esquire Rd., North Billerica, MA 08162.
Devereau Foundation, Devon, PA 19333.
DLM Teaching Resources, PO Box 4000, One DLM Park, Allen, TX 75002.
Easier to Learn Materials, PO Box 329, Garden City, NY 11530.

The Economy Company, 1901 N. Walnut Ave., Oklahoma City, OK 73125.

Edmark Associates, 655 S. Orcas St., Seattle, WA 98108.

Educational Performance Associates, 563 Westview Ave., Ridgefield, NJ 07657.

Educational Service, Inc., PO Box 219, Stevensville, MI 49127.

Educational Testing Service, Princeton, NJ 08540.

Essay Press, PO Box 2323, La Jolla, CA 92037.

Fearon Pitman Publishers, 6 Davis Dr., Belmont, CA 94002.

Garrard Publishing Co., 107 Cherry St., New Canaan, CT 06840.

Ginn & Co., 191 Spring St., Lexington, MA 02173.

Grune & Stratton, 111 Fifth Ave., New York, NY 10003.

Harper & Row Publishers, Inc., 10 E. 53rd St., New York, NY 10022.

Hiskey Publications, 5640 Baldwin, Lincoln, NE 68508.

Holt, Rinehart & Winston, Inc., 383 Madison Ave., New York, NY 10017.

Houghton Mifflin Co., One Beacon St., Boston, MA 02108.

Houston Press, University of Houston, Houston, TX 77000.

Incentives for Learning, 800 Van Buren St., Chicago, IL 60607.

Instructo Corp., 200 Cedar Hollow Rd., Paoli, PA 19301.

International Reading Association, 800 Barksdale Rd., Newark, DE 19711.

Jamestown Publishers, Box 5643, Providence, RI 02904.

Jastek Associates, 1526 Gilpin Ave., Wilmington, DE 19800.

Journal of Learning Disabilities, 101 E. Ontario St., Chicago, IL 60611.

Kendall/Hunt Publishing Co., 2460 Kerper Blvd., Dubuque, IA 52001.

Keystone View Co., 2212 E. 12th St., Davenport, IA 52803.

Klamath Printing Co., 320 Lowell St., Klamath Falls, OR 97601.

Language Research Associates, PO Box 2085, Palm Springs, CA 92262.

Lippincott Co., 521 Fifth Ave., New York, NY 10017.

Love Publishing Co., 6635 E. Villanova Pl., Denver, CO 80222.

The Macmillan Co., 866 Third Ave., New York, NY 10022.

Mafex Associates, Inc., 11 Barron Ave., Johnstown, PA 16906.

McCormick-Mathers Publishing Co., 450 W. 33rd St., New York, NY 10001.

McGraw-Hill Book Co., 1221 Avenue of the Americas, New York, NY 10020.

David McKay Co., 2 Park Ave., New York, NY 10016.

Meeting Street School, 667 Waterman Ave., East Providence, RI 02914.

Charles E. Merrill, 1300 Alum Creek Dr., Columbus, OH 43216.

Milton Bradley Co., 74 Park St., Springfield, MA 01101.

National Council of Teachers of English, 1111 Kenyon Rd., Urbana, IL 61801.

National Education Association Publications, 1201 16th St. NW, Washington, DC 20036.

Northwestern University Press, 1735 Benson Ave., Evanston, IL 60201.

Orton Dyslexia Society, 8415 Bellona Lane, Towson, MD 21204.

Prentice-Hall, Inc., Englewood Cliffs, NJ 07632.

PRO-ED, 5341 Industrial Oaks Blvd., Austin, TX 78735.

The Psychological Corp., 757 Third Ave., New York, NY 10017.

Reader's Digest Services, Educational Division, Pleasantville, NY 10570.

Recordings for the Blind, 214 E. 58th St., New York, NY 10022.

The Riverside Publishing Co., 3 O'Hare Towers, 8420 Bryn Mawr Road, Chicago, IL 60631.

Scholastic Magazine and Book Services, 50 W. 44th St., New York, NY 10036.

Science Research Associates, 155 N. Wacker Ave., Chicago, IL 60606.

Scott, Foresman and Co., 1900 E. Lake Ave., Glenview, IL 60025.

Slosson Educational Publications, 140 Pine St., East Aurora, NY 14052.

Steck-Vaughn Co., Box 2028, Austin, TX 78768.

Stoelting Co., 1350 S. Kostner, Chicago, IL 60623.

Teachers College Press, Teachers College, Columbia University, 1234 Amsterdam Ave., New York, NY 10027.

Teaching Resources (See DLM Teaching Resources).

United States Government Printing Office, Superintendent of Documents, Washington, DC 20025.

University of Illinois Press, 54 E. Gregory Dr., PO Box 5081, Station A, Champaign, IL 61820.

Walker Educational Book Corp., 720 Fifth Ave., New York, NY 10019.

Webster Division, McGraw-Hill, Manchester Rd., Manchester, MO 63011.

Western Psychological Services, 12031 Wilshire Blvd., Los Angeles, CA 90025.

Zaner-Bloser Co., 612 North Park St., Columbus, OH 43215.

Richard L. Zweig Associates, 20800 Beach Blvd., Huntington Beach, CA 92648.

Appendix E: **Glossary**

Agnosia The inability to obtain information through one of the input channels or senses, despite the fact that the receiving organ itself is not impaired. The medical term is associated with a neurological abnormality of the central nervous system.

Alexia The loss of ability to read because of some brain damage, such as a cerebral stroke. The term also refers to the complete failure to *acquire* reading skills as well as to a partial or complete loss of these skills through brain damage.

Annual goals Plans written in the individualized education program to be accomplished in the period of one year.

Aphasia Impairment of the ability to use or understand oral language. It is usually associated with an injury or abnormality of the speech centers of the brain. Several classifications are used, including expressive and receptive, congenital, and acquired aphasia.

Apraxia Difficulty in motor output or in performing purposeful motor movements. This medical term reflects an abnormality of the central nervous system.

Auding A level of auditory reception that involves comprehension as well as hearing and listening.

Auditory blending The ability to synthesize the phonemes of a word when they are pronounced with separations between phonemes so that the word can be recognized as a whole.

Auditory perception The ability to interpret or organize the sensory data received through the ear.

Basal reader approach A method of teaching reading in which instruction is given through the use of a series of basal readers. The sequence of skills, content, vocabulary, and activities is determined by the authors of the series. Teacher's manuals and children's activity books accompany the basal reading series.

Behavior modification A technique of changing human behavior based on the theory of operant behavior and conditioning. Careful observation of events preceding and following the behavior in question is required. The environment is manipulated to reinforce the desired responses, thereby bringing about the desired change in behavior.

Bibliotherapy The use of reading, particularly the use of characters in books with whom the child identifies, for therapeutic purposes.

Binocular difficulties A visual impairment due to the inability of two eyes to function together.

Body image   An awareness of one's own body and the relationship of the body parts to each other and to the outside environment.

Bonding   The process of building a close relationship between an infant and the mother.

Brain-injured child   A child who before, during, or after birth has received an injury to or suffered an infection of the brain. As a result of such organic impairment, there are disturbances that prevent or impede the normal learning process.

Cerebral dominance   The control of activities by the brain, with one hemisphere usually considered consistently dominant over the other. In most individuals, the left side of the brain controls language function, and the left side is considered the dominant hemisphere.

Clinical teaching   An approach to teaching that attempts to tailor learning experiences to the unique needs of a particular child. Consideration is given to the child's individual ways of learning and processing information.

Closure   The ability to recognize a whole or gestalt, especially when one or more parts of the whole are missing or when the continuity is interrupted by gaps.

Cloze procedure   A technique used in testing, teaching reading comprehension, and determining readability. It involves deletion of words from the text and leaving blank spaces. Measurement is made by rating the number of blanks that can be correctly filled.

Cognition   The act or process of knowing; the various thinking skills and processes are considered cognitive skills.

Concept   An abstract idea generalized from particular instances.

Conceptual disorders   A disturbance in the thinking process and in cognitive activities, or a disturbance in the ability to formulate concepts.

Content words (class words or lexical words)   Words in a language that have referential meaning, as opposed to words or morphemes with relational value (function or structure words). Content words are roughly similar to verbs, nouns, adjectives, and adverbs.

Continuum of alternative placements   An array of different placements available in a school to meet the varied needs of handicapped students.

Criterion-referenced tests   Tests that measure abilities in specific tasks (rather than tests that compare a student to others in a norm group).

Cross-categorical   Refers to a system of grouping handicapped students together without reference to a particular label or category of exceptionality.

Cross-modality perception   The neurological process of converting information received through one input modality to another system within the brain. The process is also referred to as "intersensory transfer," "intermodal transfer," and "transducing."

Developmental imbalance   A disparity in the developmental patterns of intellectual skills.

Developmental reading   The pattern and sequence of normal reading growth and development in a child in the learning-to-read process.

Diagnostic teaching   Teaching designed for the purpose of further assessing a student.

Dyscalculia   Lack of ability to perform mathematical functions, usually associated with neurological dysfunction or brain damage.

Dysgraphia   Extremely poor handwriting or the inability to perform the motor movements required for handwriting. The condition is often associated with neurological dysfunction.

Dyslexia   A disorder of children who, despite conventional classroom experience, fail to attain the skills of reading. The term is frequently used when neurological dysfunction is suspected as the cause of the reading disability.

Dysnomia   Difficulty in recalling or remembering words.

Echolalia   The parrot-like repetition of words, phrases, or sentences spoken by another person without understanding the meaning of the language.

Electroencephalograph   An instrument for graphically recording and measuring electrical energy generated by the cerebral cortex during brain functioning. It is often abbreviated as EEG.

Eligibility criteria   Standards for determining if a student will be admitted to the school's learning disabilities program.

Expressive language skills   Skills required to produce language for communication with other individuals. Speaking and writing are expressive language skills.

Figure-ground perception   The ability to attend to one aspect of the visual field while perceiving it in relation to the rest of the field.

Function words   See *Structure words.*

Grapheme   A written language symbol that represents an oral language code.

Heterogenous   Describing students with many different types of characteristics. The population of students with learning disabilities is heterogenous.

Holistic   A view of reading. Perceiving the whole process of reading, rather than a set of separate, discrete skills.

Hyperkinesis   Constant and excessive movement and motor activity.

Impulsivity   The behavioral characteristic of acting upon impulse without consideration of the consequences of an action.

Individualized education program (IEP)   The written plan for an individual handicapped student's education.

Individualized reading   The method of teaching reading that utilizes the student's interest; learning is structured through the student's own reading selections, using a variety of books. The teacher acts as a consultant, aid, and counselor.

Innate response system   The unlearned motor responses that the child has within him or her at birth.

Inner language   The process of internalizing and organizing experiences without the use of linguistic symbols.

Intrinsic   Within. Refers to factors within the individual causing the learning problem.

Language arts   School curricular activities that utilize language, namely, listening, speaking, reading, writing, handwriting, and spelling.

Language-experience approach to reading   A method of teaching reading and other language skills, based on the experiences of students. The method frequently involves the generation of experienced-based materials that are dictated by the student, written down by the teacher, then used in class as the material for teaching reading.

Language pathology   The study of the causes and treatment of disorders of symbolic behavior.

Laterality   Involves the awareness of the two sides of one's body and the ability to identify them as left or right correctly.

Least restrictive environment   Consideration of a handicapped student's school placement with reference to being with nonhandicapped students.

Lexical words   See *Structure words.*

Linguistics   The scientific study of the nature and function of human language.

Mainstreaming   Placing of children with handicaps within the regular education system of the school, particularly in the regular classroom.

Maturational lag   A slowness in certain specialized aspects of neurological development.

Metacognition   Knowing about knowing. Knowing how to go about the process of learning.

Minimal brain dysfunction   A mild or minimal neurological abnormality that causes learning difficulties in the student with near-average intelligence.

Mixed laterality   Tendency to perform some acts with a right-side preference and others with a left, or the shifting from right to left for certain activities.

Modality   The pathways through which an individual receives information and thereby learns. The "modality concept" postulates that some individuals learn better through one modality than through another. For example, a student may receive data better through the visual modality than the auditory modality.

Morpheme   The smallest meaning-bearing unit in a language.

Morphology   The linguistic system of meaning units in any particular language.

Multidisciplinary evaluation   Using several disciplines and instruments to evaluate a student.

Perception   The process of organizing or interpreting stimuli obtained through the senses.

Perceptual disorder   A disturbance in the awareness of objects, relations, or qualities, involving the interpretation of sensory stimulation.

Perceptual-motor   A term describing the interaction of the various channels of perception with motor activity. The channels of perception include the visual, auditory, tactual, and kinesthetic.

Perseveration   The tendency to continue an activity once it has been started and to be unable to modify or stop the activity even though it is acknowledged to have become inappropriate.

Phoneme   The smallest unit of sound in any particular language.

Phonetics   A study of all the speech sounds in language and how these sounds are produced.

Phonics   The application of portions of phonetics to the teaching of reading, particularly the teaching of reading in English. The establishment of the sound (or phoneme) of the language with the equivalent written symbol (or grapheme).

Phonology   The linguistic system of speech sounds in a particular language.

Prevalence   Refers to the frequency of the occurrence of learning disabilities in the general school population.

Psycholinguistics   The field of study that blends aspects of two disciplines—psychology and linguistics—to examine the total picture of the language process.

Receptive language   Language that is spoken or written by others and received by the individual. The receptive language skills are listening and reading.

Remediation   The special teaching of students who have learning problems.

Resource teacher   A specialist who works with children with learning disabilities and acts as a consultant to other teachers, providing materials and methods to help students who are having difficulty within the regular classroom. The resource teacher works from a centralized resource room within a school where appropriate materials are housed.

Semantics   A linguistic term referring to the meaning system in language.

Sensory-motor   A term applied to the combination of the input of sensations and the output of motor activity. The motor activity reflects what is happening to the sensory organs such as the visual, auditory, tactual, and kinesthetic sensations.

Short-term instructional objectives   Plans to be accomplished in a short period to meet the annual goal written in the individualized education plan.

Social perception   The ability to interpret stimuli in the social environment and appropriately relate such interpretations to the social situation.

Soft neurological signs   Neurological abnormalities that are mild or slight and difficult to detect, as contrasted with the gross or obvious neurological abnormalities.

Strauss Syndrome   A collection of behavioral characteristics describing the child who has difficulty in learning.

Strephosymbolia   Perception of visual stimuli, especially words, in reversed or twisted order. The condition may be explained as "twisted symbols."

Structure words (function words, lexical words)   Linguistic referents for words of a sentence that show the relationship between parts of the sentence, as opposed to content words. Structure words include these elements of traditional grammar: prepositions, conjunctions, modal and auxiliary verbs, and articles.

Syntax   The grammar system of a language. The linguistic rules of word order and the function of words in a sentence.

Tactile perception   The ability to interpret and give meaning to sensory stimuli that are experienced through the sense of touch.

Task analysis   The technique of carefully examining a particular task to discover the elements it comprises and the processes required to perform it.

Visual-motor coordination   The ability to coordinate vision with the movements of the body or parts of the body.

Visual perception   The identification, organization, and interpretation of sensory data received by the individual through the eye.

References

Abrams, J. (1970). Learning disabilities. A complex phenomenon. *The Reading Teacher, 23,* 299–303.

Adler, M. (1956). *How to read a book.* New York: Simon & Schuster.

Alder, S. (1979). Megavitamin treatment for behaviorally disturbed and learning disabled children. *Journal of Learning Disabilities, 12,* 678–681.

Alexander, N. (1983). A primer for developing a writing curriculum. *Topics in Learning and Learning Disabilities, 3*(3), 55–62.

Allen, R.V. (1976). *Language experiences in communication.* Boston: Houghton Mifflin.

Alley, G., & Deshler, D. (1979). *Teaching the learning disabled adolescent: Strategies and methods.* Denver, CO: Love.

Allington, R. (1978, March). *Are good and poor readers taught differently? Is that why poor readers are poor readers?* Paper presented at the meeting of the American Educational Research Association, Toronto.

Aloia, G. (1983). Special educators' perspectives of their roles as consultants. *Teacher Education and Special Education, 6,* 83–87.

Aman, M. (1980). Psychotropic drugs and learning problems—A selective review. *Journal of Learning Disabilities, 13,* 87–97.

American Academy of Pediatrics. (1982). Policy statement. The Doman-Delacato treatment of neurologically handicapped children. *Journal of Pediatrics, 70,* 810–812.

American Academy of Pediatrics. (1980). In-service training for physicians serving handicapped children (Bureau for Education of the Handicapped In-service Personnel Training Project). Evanston, IL: Author.

American Psychiatric Association. (1980). *Diagnostic and statistical manual of mental disorders* (3rd ed.). Washington, DC: American Psychiatric Association.

Anastasi, A. (1976). *Psychological testing.* New York: Macmillan.

Anderson, R., & Freebody, P. (1981). Vocabulary Knowledge. In J. Guthrie (Ed.), *Comprehension and teaching: Research views.* Newark, DE: International Reading Association.

Anderson, D., & Glowinski, D. (1982). Effective use of a computer managed instruction program. *Journal of Learning Disabilities, 15*(9), 555–557.

Anderson, R., Reynolds, R., Schallert, D., & Goetz, E. (1977). Frameworks for comprehension discourse. *American Educational Research Journal, 14,* 361–381.

Arbitman-Smith, R., & Haywood, H. (1980). Cognitive education for learning disabled adolescents. *Journal of Abnormal Child Psychology, 8,* 51–64.

Ashlock, R. (1982). *Error patterns in computation: A semi programmed approach.* Columbus, OH: Charles E. Merrill.

Assael, D., & Harrison, G. (1981). *1980–81 HCEEP overview and director.* Seattle, WA; TADS & WESTAR, University of Washington.

Atkinson, R., & Fletcher, J. (1972). Teaching children to read with a computer. *The Reading Teacher, 25,* 319–327.

Aulls, M. (1982). *Developing readers in today's elementary school.* Boston: Allyn & Bacon.

Ayres, A. (1981). *Sensory integration and the child.* Los Angeles: Western Psychological Services.

Ayres, A. (1978, January). Learning disabilities and the vestibular system. *Journal of Learning Disabilities, 11,* 18–29.

Bachor, D. (1979). Using work samples as diagnostic information. *Learning Disability Quarterly, 2,* 45–53.

Badian, N., & Ghublikian, M. (1983). The personal-social characteristics of children with poor mathematical computation skills. *Journal of Learning Disabilities, 16,* 154–157.

Bannatyne, A. (1974). Diagnosis: A note on recategorization of the WISC Scaled Scores. *Journal of Learning Disabilities, 7,* 272–274.

Barbe, W., Milone, M., & Wasylyk, T. (1983). Manuscript is the "write" start. *Academic Therapy, 18,* 397–406.

Barrett, T. (1965, January). Visual discrimination tasks as predictors of first-grade reading achievement. *Reading Teacher, 18,* 276–282.

Barsch, R. (1965). Six factors in learning. In J. Helmuth (Ed.), *Learning Disorders* (Vol. 1). Seattle: Special Child Publications.

Barsch, R. (1966). Teacher needs–motor training. In W. Cruickshank (Ed.), *The teacher of brain-injured children.* Syracuse, NY: Syracuse University Press.

Bateman, B. (1974). Educational implications of minimal brain dysfunction. *Reading Teacher, 27,* 662–688.

Bateman, B. (1979). Teaching reading to learning disabled and other hard-to-teach children. In L. Resnick & P. Weaver (Eds.), *Theory and practice of early reading, I.* Hillsdale, NJ: Erlbaum Associates.

Bates, S., & Bates, D. (1971). . . . and a child shall lead them: Stephanie's chart story. *Teaching Exceptional Children, 3,* 111–113.

Baum, S., & Kirschenbaum, R. (1984). Recognizing special talents in learning disabled students. *Teaching Exceptional Children, 16,* 92–98.

Beaver, J. (1968). Transformational grammar and the teaching of reading. *Research in the Teaching of English, 2,* 161–171.

Beckert, N., & Carnine, D. (1980). Direct instruction: An effective approach to educational intervention with disadvantaged and low performers. In B. Lahey & A. Kazdin (Eds.), *Advances in Clinical Psychology, 3.* New York: Plenum.

Beech, M., Blaski, K., Crump, D., & Smith, L. (1983). Generic teacher certification. *Council for Learning Disabilities Newsletter, 9*(2), 3–4.

Bender, L. (1957). Specific reading disability as maturational lag. *Bulletin of the Orton Society, 7,* 9–18.

Bennett, R. (1984). Myths and realities in automating special education information management. *Journal of Learning Disabilities, 17*(1), 52–54.

Bereiter, C. (1968). *Arithmetic and mathematics.* San Rafael, CA: Dimensions.

Bereiter, C., & Englemann, S. (1966). *Teaching disadvantaged children in the preschool.* Englewood Cliffs, NJ: Prentice-Hall.

Berger, N. (1978). Why can't John read? Perhaps he's not a good listener. *Journal of Learning Disabilities, 11,* 633–638.

Berko, J. (1958). The child's learning of English morphology. *Word, 14,* 15–177.

Berman, A. (1981). Research associating learning disabilities with juvenile delinquency In J. Gottlieb & S. Strichart (Eds.), *Developmental theory and research in learning disabilities.* Baltimore, MD: University Park Press.

Bernal, E. (1983). Trends in bilingual education. *Learning Disability Quarterly, 6,* 424–431.

Bernstein, B. (1964). Elaborated and restricted codes: Their social origins and some consequences. *American Anthropologist, 66,* 55–69.

Bessell, H., & Palomares, U. (1971). *Methods in human development: Theory manual.* San Diego, CA: Human Development Training Institute.

Bijou, S. (1970). What psychology has to offer education—now. *Journal of Applied Behavior Analysis, 3,* 65–71.

Blackhurst, A. (1982). Noncategorical special education teacher education. In M. Reynolds (Ed.), *The future of mainstreaming.* Reston, VA: Council for Exceptional Children.

Blalock, J. (1981). Persistent problems and concerns of young adults with learning disabilities. In W. Cruickshank & A. Silver (Eds.), *Bridges to tomorrow: Vol. 2. The best of ACLD.* Syracuse, NY: Syracuse University Press.

Blalock, J. (1982). Persistent language deficits in adults with learning disabilities. *Journal of Learning Disabilities, 15,* 604–609.

Blanton, G. (1984). Social and emotional development of learning disabled children. In W. Cruickshank & J. Kliebhan (Eds.), *Early adolescence to early adulthood: Vol. 5. The best of ACLD.* Syracuse, NY: Syracuse University Press.

Bley, N., & Thornton, C. (1981). *Teaching mathematics to the learning disabled.* Rockland, MD: Aspen.

Bloom, B. (Ed.) (1956). *Taxonomy of educational objectives: Handbook I,* Cognitive Domain. New York: David McKay.

Bloom, B. (1964). *Stability and change in human characteristics.* New York: John Wiley & Sons.

Bloom, B. (1976). *Human characteristics and school learning.* New York: McGraw-Hill.

Bloom, B. (1978). New views of the learner: Implications for instruction and curriculum. *Educational Leadership, 35,* 563–575.

Bloom, L. (1983). *Readings in language development.* New York: Wiley.

Bloom, L., & Lahey, M. (1978). *Language development and language disorders.* New York: Wiley.

Bloomfield, L., & Barnhart, C. (1963). *Let's read, Part I.* Bronxville, NY: C.L. Barnhart.

Boder, E. (1973). Developmental dyslexia: A diagnostic approach used on three atypical reading-spelling patterns. *Developmental Medicine and Child Neurology, 15*(5), 663–687.

Boder, E. (1976). School failure—Evaluation and treatment. *Journal of Pediatrics, 58*(3), 394–402.

Boder, E. (1982). *Screening test for developmental dyslexia.* New York: Grune & Stratton.

Boersma, F., Chapman, J., & Battle, J. (1979). Academic self-concept change in special education students: Some suggestions for interpreting self-concept scores. *Journal of Special Education, 13,* 433–442.

Bond, G., Tinker, M., Wasson, B., & Wasson, J. (1984). *Reading difficulties: Their diagnosis and correction.* Englewood Cliffs, NJ: Prentice-Hall.

Bond, G., & Dykstra, R. (1967, Summer). The cooperative research program in first-grade reading instruction. *Reading Research Quarterly, 2,* 5–142.

Bormuth, J. (1968). The Cloze readability procedure. *Elementary English, 45,* 429–436.

Bos, C., & Filip, D. (1984). Comprehension monitoring in learning disabled and average students. *Journal of Learning Disabilities, 17,* 229–233.

Bowlby, J. (1969). Attachment. New York: Basic Books.

Brady, M., Conroy, M., & Langford, C. (1984). Current issues and practices affecting the development of noncategorical programs for students and teachers. *Teacher Education and Special Education, 7,* 20–26.

Bransford, J., & Johnson, M. (1972). Contextual prerequisites for understanding: Some investigations of comprehension and recall. *Journal of Verbal Learning and Verbal Behavior, 11,* 726–727.

Breen, M., Lehman, J., & Carlson, M. (1984). Achievement correlates of the Woodcock-Johnson Reading and Math Subtests, Key Math, and Woodcock Reading in elementary aged school population. *Journal of Learning Disabilities, 17,* 258–261.

Brenner, A. (1982). The effects of megadoses of selected B complex vitamins on children with hyperkinesis: Controlled studies with long term follow-up. *Journal of Learning Disabilities, 15,* 258–264.

Broca, P. (1878). Anatomie comparée circonvolutions cérébrales. *Rev. Anthropology, 1,* 384–498.

Brothers, A., & Holsclaw, C. (1969, January). Fusing behaviors into spelling. *Elementary English, 46,* 297–342.

Brown, A. (1978). Knowing where, what, and how to remember: A problem of metacognition. In R. Glasser (Ed.), *Advances in instructional psychology.* Hillsdale, NJ: Lawrence Erlbaum.

Brown, R., & Alford, N. (1984). Ameliorating attentional deficits and concomitant academic deficiencies in learning disabled children through cognitive training. *Journal of Learning Disabilities, 17,* 20–26.

Brown, R., Cazden, C., & Bellugi-Klima, U. (1971). The child's grammar from I and III. In A. Bar-Ardon & W. Leopold (Eds.), *Child language: A book of readings.* Englewood Cliffs, NJ: Prentice-Hall.

Brueckner, L. (1955). *Diagnostic tests and self-helps in arithmetic.* Monterey, CA: CTB/McGraw-Hill.

Brueckner, L., & Bond, G. (1955). *The diagnosis and treatment of learning difficulties.* New York: Appleton-Century-Crofts.

Bruinniks, V. (1978). Actual and perceived peer status of learning disabled students in mainstream programs. *Journal of Special Education, 12,* 51–58.

Brutten, M., Richardson, S., & Mangel, C. (1973). *Something's wrong with my child.* New York: Harcourt, Brace, Jovanovich.

Bryan, T. (1983). Executive summary: The Chicago Institute for the Study of Learning Disabilities. In C. Collin (Ed.), *Keys to success* (Monograph of the Michigan ACLD Conference). Garden City, MI: Quality Printers.

Bryan, T., Donahue, M., & Pearl, R. (1981). Learning disabled children's peer interactions during a small group problem solving task. *Learning Disability Quarterly, 4,* 13–22.

Bryan, T., & McGrady, H. (1972). Use of a teacher rating scale. *Journal of Learning Disabilities, 5,* 199–208.

Bryan, T., Pearl, R., Donahue, M., Bryan, J., & Pflaum, S. (1983). The Chicago Institute for the Study of Learning Disabilities. *Exceptional Education Quarterly, 4*(1), 1–23.

Burka, A. (1983). The emotional reality of a learning disability. *Annals of Dyslexia: An Interdisciplinary Journal of the Orton Dyslexia Society, 33,* 289–302.

Buscaglia, L. (1975). Parents need to know: Parents and teachers working together. In S. Kirk & J. McCarthy (Eds.), *Learning Disabilities: selected ACLD papers.* Boston: Houghton Mifflin.

Bush, W., & Giles, M. (1977). *Aids to psycholinguistic teaching.* Columbus, OH: Merrill.

Buswell, G., & John, L. (1925). *Diagnostic chart for fundamental process in arithmetic.* Indianapolis, IN: Bobbs-Merrill.

Camp, B., & Bash, M. (1981). *Think aloud*. Champaign, IL: Illinois Research Press.

Camp, B., & Dolcourt, J. (1977, May). Reading and spelling in good and poor readers. *Journal of Learning Disabilities, 10,* 300–307.

Cantwell, D. (1980). Drugs and medial intervention. In H. Rie & E. Rie (Eds.), *Handbook of minimal brain dysfunction: A critical view*. New York: Wiley.

Carlberg, C., & Kavale, K. (1980). The efficacy of special versus regular class placement of exceptional children: A meta-analysis. *Journal of Special Education, 14,* 295–309.

Carpenter, T., & Moser, J. (1982). The development of addition and subtraction problem solving skills. In T. Carpenter, J. Moser, & T. Romberg (Eds.), *Addition and subtraction: A cognitive perspective*. Hillsdale, NJ: Lawrence Erlbaum.

Carpenter, T., Moser, J., & Romberg, T. (1982). *Addition and subtraction: A cognitive perspective*. Hillsdale, NJ: Lawrence Erlbaum.

Carroll, J. (1966). Some neglected relationships in reading and language learning. *Elementary English, 43,* 576–579.

Carroll, J. (1967). Psycholinguistics in the study of mental retardation. In R. Scheifelbusch, R. Copeland, & J. Smith (Eds.), *Language and mental retardation*. New York: Holt, Rinehart & Winston.

Cawley, J., Fitzmaurice, A., Shaw, R., Kahn, H., & Bates, H. (1979). Math word problems: Suggestions for learning disabled students. *Learning Disability Quarterly, 2,* 25–41.

Cegelka, P. (1981). Career education. In A. Blackhurst & W. Berdine (Eds.), *An introduction to special education*. Boston: Little, Brown.

Center for the Social Organization of Schools. (1983). *School uses of microcomputers: Report from a national survey*. Baltimore, MD: The Johns Hopkins University.

Chalfant, J., & Pysh, J. (1983). Teacher assistance teams. In C. Collin (Ed.). Keys to success. *Monograph of the Michigan ACLD Conference*. Garden City, MI: Quality Printers.

Chalfant, J., Pysh, M., & Moultrie, R. (1979). Teacher assistance teams: A model for within-building problem solving. *Learning Disability Quarterly, 2,* 85–96.

Chalfant, J., & Scheffelin, M. (1969). *Central processing dysfunction in children* (NINDS Monograph No. 9). Bethesda, MD: U.S. Department of Health, Education, and Welfare.

Chall, J. (1967). *Learning to read: The great debate*. New York: McGraw-Hill.

Chall, J., & Mirsky, A. (Eds.). (1978). *Education and the brain* (Seventy-seventh Yearbook of the National Society for the Study of Education). Chicago: University of Chicago Press.

Chall, J., & Stahl, S. (1982). *Reading*. In H.E. Mitzel (Ed.), *Encyclopedia of Educational Research* (5th ed.). New York: Free Press.

Chance, P. (1981, October). The remedial thinker. *Psychology Today,* pp. 63–73.

Chandler, H. (1982). A question of competence. *Journal of Learning Disabilities, 15,* 436–438.

Charcot, I. (1886/1953). New Lectures 1886. In S. Freud (Ed.), *On aphasia*. New York: International Universities Press.

Chicago Tribune, May 15, 1967.

Clements, J., Schweinhart, S., Barnett, S., Epstein, A. & Weikert, D. (1984). *Changed Lives* Ypsilanti. MI: High Scope Educational Foundations.

Clements, S. (1966). *Minimal brain dysfunction in children* (NINDS Monograph No. 3, Public Health Service Bulletin No. 1415). Washington, DC: U.S. Department of Health, Education, and Welfare.

Chomsky, N. (1965). *Aspects of the theory of syntax.* Cambridge, MA. MIT Press.

Cohen, S. (1971). Dyspedagogia as a cause of reading retardation in learning disorders. In B. Bateman (Ed.), *Learning Disorders—Reading* (Vol. 4). Seattle, WA: Special Child Publications.

Collins, K. (1982). The structure of learned outcomes; A refocusing for mathematics learning. In T. Carpenter, J. Moser, & T. Romberg (Eds.), *Addition and subtraction: A cognitive perspective.* Hillsdale, NJ: Lawrence Erlbaum.

Committee on Learning Disability. (1984). Learning disability: dyslexia and vision. *Journal of Pediatrics, 74,* 150–151.

Comptroller General of the United States. (1981). *Disparity still exists in who gets special education.* (Report to Chairman, Subcommittee on Select Education, Committee on Education and Labor, House of Representatives). Gaithersburg, MD: U.S. General Accounting Office.

Comptroller General of the United States. (1981). *Report to the Chairman, Subcommittee on Select Education* (Committee on Education and Labor, House of Representatives). Gaithersburg, MD: U.S. General Accounting Office.

Computers, Reading, and the Language Arts. (1983). *1*(1).

Cone, T., & Wilson, L. (1981). Quantifying a severe discrepancy: A critical analysis. *Learning Disability Quarterly, 4,* 359–372.

Conners, C. (1969). A teacher rating scale for use in drug studies with children. *American Journal of Psychiatry, 26.* 884–888.

Conners, C. (1973). What parents need to know about stimulant drugs and special education. *Journal of Learning Disabilities, 6,* 349–351.

Cook, R., & Armbruster, V. (1983). *Adapting early childhood curricula.* St. Louis, MO: Mosby.

Cordoni, Barbara. (1982). A directory of college learning disabilities services. *Journal of Learning Disabilities, 15,* 529–534.

Cott, A. (1972). Megavitamins: The orthomolecular approach to behavioral disorders and learning disabilities. *Academic Therapy, 7,* 245–259.

Cratty, B. (1971). *Active learning: Games to enhance academic abilities.* Englewood Cliffs, NJ: Prentice-Hall.

Cratty, B. (1973). *Intelligence in action.* Englewood Cliffs, NJ: Prentice-Hall.

Crawford, D. (1984). ACLD—R & D Project summary: A study investigating the link between learning disabilities and juvenile delinquency. In W. Cruickshank & J. Kliebhan (Eds.), *Early adolescence to early adulthood: Vol. 5. The best of ACLD.* Syracuse, NY: Syracuse University Press.

Crook, W. (1977). *Can your child read? Is he hyperactive?* Jackson, TN: Professional Books.

Crook, W. (1983). Let's look at what they eat. *Academic Therapy, 18,* 629–631.

Cruickshank, W. (1977). Myths and realities in learning disabilities. *Journal of Learning Disabilities, 10,* 57–64.

Cruickshank, W., Bentzen, F., Ratzeburg, F., & Tannhauser, M. (1961). *A teaching method for brain-injured and hyperactive children.* Syracuse, NY: Syracuse University Press.

Cummins, J. (1983). Bilingualism and special education: Program and pedagogical issues. *Learning Disability Quarterly, 6,* 373–386.

Davis, F. (1968). Psychometric research on comprehension in reading. *Reading Research Quarterly, 3,* 339–345.

Davis, H., & Silverman, S. (Eds.). (1970). *Hearing and deafness.* New York: Holt, Rinehart & Winston.

De Hirsch, I., Jansky, J., & Langford, W. (1966). *Predicting reading failure.* New York: Harper & Row.

Delacato, C. (1966). *Neurological organization and reading.* Springfield, IL: Charles C. Thomas.

Deno, E. (1970). Special education as developmental capital. *Exceptional Children, 37,* 229–237.

Deno, S., & Mirkin, P. (1977). *Data-based program modification.* Reston, VA: Council for Exceptional Children.

DeQuiros, J. (1976, January). Diagnosis of vestibular disorders in the learning disabled. *Journal of Learning Disabilities, 9,* 39–46.

Deshler, D., Alley, G., Warner, M., & Schumaker, J. (1981). Instructional practices for promoting skill acquisition and generalization in severely learning disabled adolescents. *Learning Disability Quarterly, 4,* 415–421.

Deshler, D., Lowrey, D., & Alley, G. (1979). Programming alternatives for learning disabled adolescents: A nationwide survey. *Academic Therapy, 14,* 389–398.

Deshler, D., & Schumaker, J. (1983). Social skills of learning disabled adolescents: A review of characteristics and intervention. *Topics in Learning and Learning Disabilities, 3,* 15–23.

Deshler, D., Schumaker, J., & Lenz, B. (1984). Academic and cognitive intervention for learning disabled adolescents, Part I. *Journal of Learning Disabilities, 17,* 108–119.

Deshler, D., Schumaker, J., Lenz, B., & Ellis, E. (1984). Academic and cognitive intervention for learning disabled adolescents, Part II. *Journal of Learning Disabilities, 17,* 170–187.

DeWeerd, J. (1981). Early education services for children with handicaps—where have we been, where are we now, and where are we going? *Journal of the Division for Early Childhood, 1,* 15–24.

Dewey, J. (1946). *The public and its problems.* Chicago: Gateway.

Diamond, G. (1983). The birthdate effect—A maturational effect? *Journal of Learning Disabilities, 16,* 161–164.

Di Pasquale, G., Moule, A., & Flewelling, R. (1980). The birthdate effect. *Journal of Learning Disabilities, 13,* 234–238.

DLD Times. (1983). *1*(1).

Doll, E. (1951). Neurophrenia. *American Journal of Psychiatry, 108,* 50–83.

Doman, R., Spitz, E., Zuckman, E., Delacato, C., & Doman, G. (1967). Children with severe brain injuries: Neurological organization in terms of mobility. In Frierson & Barbe (Eds.), *Educating children with learning disabilities.* New York: Appleton-Century-Crofts.

Donahue, M., Pearl, R., & Bryan, T. (1983). Communication competence in LD children. In I. Bialer & K. Gadow (Eds.), *Advances in learning and behavior disabilities, Vol. 2.* Greenwich, CT: JAI Press.

Downing, J. (1982). Reading—skill or skills? *The Reading Teacher, 35,* 534–537.

Duane, D. (1983). Neurobiological correlates of reading disorders. *Journal of Educational Research, 77,* 5–15.

Dunlap, W., & McKnight, M. (1980). Teaching strategies for solving word problems in mathematics. *Academic Therapy, 15,* 431–442.

Dunn, L. (1968). Special education for the mildly retarded—Is much of it justifiable? *Exceptional Children, 35,* 5–22.

Dunn, P. (1973, June). Neurological disorders and learning disabilities called a major problem. *Pediatric Herald.*

Dunn, R., Dunn, K., & Price, G. (1982). *Learning styles inventory.* Lawrence, KS: The Price Systems, P.O. Box 3271.

Durkin, D. (1974). Some questions about questionable instructional material. *The Reading Teacher, 28,* 13–17.

Durrell, D. (1956). *Improving reading instruction.* New York: Harcourt Brace & World.

Dykman, R., Ackerman, P., Holcomb, P., & Boudreau, A. (1983). Physiological manifestations of learning disability. In G. Senf & J. Torgesen (Eds.), *Annual Review of Learning Disabilities: Vol. 1. A Journal of Learning Disabilities Reader.* Chicago, IL: Professional Press.

Dykstra, R. (1966, Spring). Auditory discrimination abilities and beginning reading achievement. *Reading Research Quarterly, 1,* 5–34.

Egan, R. (1979). Research variables in CNS stimulant studies. (Doctoral dissertation, University of Michigan, 1978). *Dissertation Abstracts, 39.*

Eisenberg, L. (1975). Psychiatric aspects of language disability. In D. Duane & M. Rawson (Eds.), *Reading, perception and language:* Papers from the World Congress on Dyslexia. Baltimore, MD: York Press.

Eisenson, J. (1968). Developmental aphasia: A speculative view with therapeutic implications. *Journal of Speech and Hearing Disorders, 33,* 3–13.

Elkind, D. (1983). Viewpoint: The curriculum disabled child. *Topics in Learning and Learning Disabilities, 3,* 71–78.

Elliott, M. (1981). Quantitative evaluation procedures for learning disabilities. *Journal of Learning Disabilities, 14,* 84–87.

Emig, J. (1982). Writing, composition, and rhetoric. *Encyclopedia of Education Research* (5th ed.). New York: The Free Press.

Engelmann, S., Becker, W., Hanner, S., & Johnson, G. (1978). *Corrective reading program.* Chicago: Science Research Associates.

Engelmann, S., & Bruner, E. (1984). *Distar reading.* Chicago: Science Research Associates.

Epstein, M., Hallahan, D., & Kauffman, J. (1975). Implications of the reflexivity-impulsivity dimension for special education. *Journal of Special Education, 9,* 11–25.

Erickson, M. (1975). The z-score discrepancy method for identifying reading-disabled children. *Journal of Learning Disabilities, 8,* 308–312.

Evra, J. (1983). *Psychological disorders of children and adolescents.* Boston: Little, Brown.

Ewing, N., & Smith, J. (1981). Minimum competency testing and the handicapped. *Exceptional Children, 47,* 523–524.

Fader, D., & Schaevitz, M. (1966). *Hooked on books.* New York: Berkley.

Farr, R. (1969). *Reading: What can be measured?* Newark, DE: International Reading Association.

Feagans, L. (1983). A current view of learning disabilities. *Journal of Pediatrics, 102,* 487–493.

Feingold, B. (1975). *Why your child is hyperactive.* New York: Random House.

Feirer, J. (1982, September). Life skills for the '80's. *Industrial Education,* pp. 4–5.

Fernald, G. (1943). *Remedial techniques in basic school subjects.* New York: McGraw-Hill.

Festinger, L. (1964). *Conflict, decision, and dissonance.* Stanford, CA: Stanford University Press.

Feuerstein, R. (1978). *Just a minute . . . Let me think.* Baltimore, MD: University Park Press.

Feuerstein, R. (1979). *The dynamic assessment of retarded performers: The learning potential assessment device.* Baltimore, MD: University Park Press.

Feuerstein, R. (1980). *Instrumental enrichment: An intervention program for cognitive modifiability.* Baltimore, MD: University Park Press.

Fields, C., & Jacobson, R. (1980, January 21). Nader accuses ETS of "fraud," plans drive for testing reform. *The Chronicle of Higher Education, 19,* 5–6.

Fitzgerald, J. (1951). *A basic life spelling vocabulary.* Milwaukee, WI: Bruce.

Fitzgerald, J. (1955). Children's experiences in spelling. In V. Herrick & L. Jacobs (Eds.), *Children and the language arts.* Englewood Cliffs, NJ: Prentice-Hall.

Flavell, J. (1977). *Cognitive development.* Englewood Cliffs, NJ: Prentice-Hall.

Flax, N. (1973). The eye and learning disabilities. *Journal of Learning Disabilities, 6,* 328–333.

Ford, A., & Ford, J. (1979). Using cognitive discrimination exercise to foster social interaction with a withdrawn preschooler. *Directive Teacher, 2,* 24–25.

Forness, S., Sinclair, E., & Guthrie, D. (1983). Learning disability discrepancy formulas: Their use in actual practice. *Learning Disability Quarterly, 6,* 107–114.

Fox-Reid, G. (1982). Newly certified LD teachers' opinions of basic LD role competencies. *Teacher Education and Special Education, 6,* 61–68.

Freed, A. (1971). *TA for kids.* Sacramento, CA: A. Freed.

Freeman, M., & Becker, R. (1979). Competencies for professionals in LD: An analysis of teacher perceptions. *Learning Disability Quarterly, 2,* 70–79.

Freeman, R. (1967). Controversy over "patterning" as a treatment for brain damage in children. *Journal of the American Medical Association, 202,* 385–388.

Frostig, M. (1968). Education for children with learning disabilities. In H. Myklebust (Ed.), *Progress in learning disabilities.* New York: Grune & Stratton.

Furth, H. (1970). *Piaget for teachers.* Englewood Cliffs, NJ: Prentice-Hall.

Gaddes, W. (1980). *Learning disabilities and brain function: A neuropsychological approach.* New York: Springer.

Gaddes, W. (1983). Applied educational neuropsychology: Theories and problems. *Journal of Learning Disabilities, 16*(9), 511–514.

Gagné, R. (1984). *The conditions of learning.* New York: Holt, Rinehart & Winston.

Gagné, R. (1974). Task-analysis—and its relation to content analysis. *Educational Psychologist, 11,* 11–18.

Galaburda, A. (1983). Developmental dyslexia: Current anatomical research. *Annals of Dyslexia: An Interdisciplinary Journal of the Orton Dyslexia Society, 33,* 41–54.

Galaburda, A., & Kemper, T. (1979). Cytoarchitectonic abnormalities in developmental dyslexia: A case study. *Annals of Neurology.*

Gallagher, J. (1964). *Presidential address.* Annual Convention of the Council for Exceptional Children. Dallas, TX.

Gallagher, J. (1966). Children with developmental imbalances: A psychoeducational view. In W. Cruickshank (Ed.), *The teacher of brain-injured children.* Syracuse, NY: Syracuse University Press.

Gallagher, J. (1979). Rights of the next generation of children. *Exceptional Children, 46,* 98–105.

Gardner, W. (1978). *Children with learning and behavior problems: A behavioral management approach.* Boston: Allyn & Bacon.

Geraldi, R., & Coolidge, P. (1983). Steps before the referral. *Journal of Learning Disabilities, 16,* 534–536.

Gerber, H. (1983). Learning disabilities and cognitive strategies: A case for training or constraining problem solvency? *Journal of Learning Disabilities, 16,* 155–260.

Gerber, P. (1981). Learning disabilities and eligibility for vocational rehabilitation services: A chronology of events. *Learning Disability Quarterly, 4,* 422–434.

Geshwind, N. (1979). Specializations of the human brain. *Scientific American, 241,* 180–201.

Geshwind, N. (1982). Why Orton was right. *Annals of Dyslexia: An Interdisciplinary Journal of the Orton Dyslexia Society, 32,* 13–30.

Geshwind, N. (1984). Biological associations of left-handedness. *Annals of Dyslexia: An Interdisciplinary Journal of the Orton Dyslexia Society, 44,* 29–40.

Getman, G. (1965). The visuomotor complex of the acquisition of motor skills. In J. Hellmuth (Ed.), *Learning disorders* (Vol. 1). Seattle, WA: Special Child Publications, 49–76.

Getman, G., Kane, E., & McKee, G. (1968). *Developing learning readiness: A visual-motor tactile skills program.* Manchester, MO: Webster, McGraw-Hill.

Gilhool, T. (1982). The 1980's teacher preparation programs, handicapped children, and the courts. In M. Reynolds (Ed.), *The future of mainstreaming.* Reston, VA: Council for Exceptional Children.

Gillingham, A., & Stillman, B. (1966). *Remedial training for children with specific difficulty in reading, spelling, and penmanship* (7th ed.) Cambridge, MA: Educators Publishing Services.

Glass, G. (1973). *Teaching decoding as separate from reading.* Garden City, NY: Adelphi University Press.

Glass, G., & Burton, E. (1973). How do they decode: Verbalization and observed behaviors of successful decoders. *Education, 94,* 58–63.

Glass, G., & Robbins, M. (1967, Fall). A critique of experiments on the roles of neurological organization in reading performance. *Reading Research Quarterly, 3,* 5–52.

Gleason, J. (1969). Language development in early childhood. In J. Walden (Ed.), *Oral language and reading.* Champaign, IL: National Council of Teachers of English.

Goins, J. (1958). *Visual perceptual abilities and early reading problems* (Supplementary Educational Monographs No. 87). Chicago: University of Chicago Press.

Goldstein, K. (1939). *The Organism.* New York: American Book Co.

Good, T., & Bropby, J. (1978). *Looking in classrooms.* New York: Harper & Row.

Goodman, K. (1967). Reading: A psycholinguistic guessing game. *Journal of the Reading Specialist, 6,* 126–133.

Goodman, K. (1969). Analysis of oral reading miscues. *Reading Research Quarterly, 5,* 9–30.

Goodman, K. (1972). Reading: The key is in children's language. *The Reading Teacher, 25,* 505–508.

Goodman, K. (1974). Effective teachers of reading know language and children. *Elementary English, 5,* 823–828.

Goodman, K., & Gollasch, F. (1980–1981). Word omissions: Deliberate and non-deliberate. *Reading Research Quarterly, 14,* 6–31.

Goodman, L., & Hammill, D. (1973, February). The effectiveness of Kephart-Getman activities in developing perceptual-motor and cognitive skills. *Focus on Exceptional Children, 4,* 1–9.

Goodman, Y. (1976). Miscues, errors and reading comprehension. In J. Meritt (Ed.), *New horizons in reading.* Newark, DE: International Reading Association.

Goodman, Y., & Burke, C. (1972). *Reading miscue inventory.* New York: Macmillan.

Goodman, Y., & Burke, C. (1980). *Reading strategies: Focus on comprehension.* New York: Holt, Rinehart, & Winston.

Gordon, H. (1983). The learning disabled are cognitively right. *Topics in Learning and Learning Disabilities, 3*(1), 29–39.

Gordon, N. & McKinlay, I. (1980). *Helping clumsy children.* Edinburgh, Scotland: Churchill Livingstone.

Gouldner, H. (1978). *Teacher's pets, troublemakers, and nobodies.* Westport, CT: Greenwood Press.

Gray, L. (1984). LOGO helps remove children's handicaps. *Educational Computer, 4*(1), 33–37.

Gross, M. (1976). Growth of hyperkinetic children taking methylphenidate, dextroamphetamine, or imipramine/desipramine. *Pediatrics, 58,* 423.

Guerin, G., & Maier, A. (1983). *Informal assessment in education.* Palo Alto, CA: Mayfield.

Gunnison, J., Kaufman, N., & Kaufman, A. (1981). Reading remediation based on sequential and simultaneous processing. *Academic Therapy, 17,* 297–307.

Guthrie, J. (1973). Models of reading and reading disability. *Journal of Educational Psychology, 65,* 9–18.

Haddad, H., Isaacs, N., Onghena, K., Major, A. (1984). The use of orthoptics in dyslexia. *Journal of Learning Disabilities, 217,* 142–144.

Hagin, R. (1983). Write right—or left. *Journal of Learning Disabilities, 16,* 266–271.

Haight, S. (1984). Special education teacher consultant: Idealism versus realism. *Exceptional Children, 50,* 507–515.

Hallahan, D. (Ed.). (1983). *Exceptional Education Quarterly, 1*(1).

Hallahan, D. (Ed.). (1980). Teaching exceptional children to use cognitive strategies. *Exceptional Education Quarterly, 1*(1).

Hallahan, D., & Kauffman, J. (1982). *Exceptional Children.* Englewood Cliffs, NJ: Prentice-Hall.

Hallahan, D., & Reeve, R. (1980). Selective attention and distractibility. In B. Keogh (Ed.), *Advances in Special Education* (Vol. 1, pp. 141–181). Greenwich, CT: JAI Press.

Hallahan, D., & Sapona, R. (1983). Self-monitoring of attention and learning disabled children: Past research and current issues. *Journal of Learning Disabilities, 16,* 616–620.

Hamilton, S. (1984). Socialization for learning: Insights from ecological research in classrooms. *The Reading Teacher, 37,* 150–156.

Hammill, D., Goodman, L., & Wiederholt, L. (1974). Visual-motor processes—can we train them? *The Reading Teacher, 27,* 469–480.

Hammill, D., & Larsen, S. (1974a). The effectiveness of psycholinguistic training. *Exceptional Children, 41,* 5–15.

Hammill, D., & Larsen, S. (1974b). The relationship of selected auditory perceptual skills and reading ability. *Journal of Learning Disabilities, 7,* 429–435.

Hammill, D., & Larsen, S. (1978). The effectiveness of psycholinguistic training: A reaffirmation of position. *Exceptional Children, 44,* 402–414.

Hammill, D., Leigh, J., McNutt, G., & Larsen, S. (1981). A new definition of learning disabilities. *Learning Disability Quarterly, 4*(4), 336–342.

Hammill, D., & Wiederholt, L. (1972). Review of the Frostig Visual Perceptual Test and its related training program. In L. Mann & D. Sabatino (Eds.), *The First Review of Special Education.* Philadelphia: Journal of Special Education Press.

Hanna, G., Dyck, N., & Holen, M. (1979). Objective analysis of achievement-aptitude discrepancies in LD classification. *Learning Disability Quarterly, 2,* 32–38.

Hanna, P., Hodges, R., & Hanna, J. (1971). *Spelling structure and strategies.* Boston: Houghton Mifflin.

Hargrove, L., & Poteet, J. (1984). *Assessment in special education.* Englewood Cliffs, NJ: Prentice-Hall.

Haring, N., & Bateman, B. (1977). *Teaching the learning disabled child.* Englewood Cliffs, NJ: Prentice-Hall.

Harris, A. (1958). *Harris Test of Lateral Dominance.* New York: Psychological Corp.

Harris, A. (1961, 1970). *How to improve reading ability.* New York: David McKay.

Harris, A., & Sipay, E. (1980). *How to increase reading ability.* New York: Longman.

Harris, T. (1969). *I'm OK—You're OK.* New York: Avon Books.

Harth, R. (1982). The Feuerstein perspective on the modification of cognitive performance. *Focus on Exceptional Children, 15,* 1–12.

Hartlage, L. (1982). Neuropsychological assessment techniques. In C. Reynolds & T. Gutkin (Eds.), *Handbook of School Psychology.* New York: Wiley.

Hartlage, L., & Telzrow, C. (1983). The neuropsychological basis of educational intervention. *Journal of Learning Disabilities, 16*(9), 521–528.

Hasselbring, T., & Owens, S. (1983). Microcomputer-based analysis of spelling errors. *Computers, Reading, and Language Arts, 1*(1), 26–32.

Hawisher, M., & Calhoun, J. (1978). *The resource room.* Columbus, OH: Charles E. Merrill.

Hayden, D., Pommer, T., & Mark, D. (1983). Personal computer applications for the learning disabled: Managing instruction materials, Part I. *Learning Disabilities, 2*(7). New York: Grune & Stratton.

Hayden, D., Vance, B., & Irvin, M. (1982a). A special education management system. *Journal of Learning Disabilities, 15,* 374–375.

Hayden, D., Vance, B., & Irvin, M. (1982b). Establishing a special education management system SEMS *Journal of Learning Disabilities, 15,* 428–429.

Hayes, M. (1974). *The tuned-in, turned-on book about learning problems.* San Rafael, CA: Academic Therapy Publications.

Head, H. (1926). *Aphasia and kindred disorders of speech.* London: Cambridge University Press.

Hebb, D. (1949). *The organization of behavior.* New York: Wiley.

Heber, R., & Garber, H. (1975). The Milwaukee Project: A study of the use of family intervention to prevent cultural-familial mental retardation. In B. Friedlander, G. Sterritt, & G. Kirk (Eds.), *Exceptional Infant: Vol. 3, Assessment and Intervention.* New York: Bruner Mazel.

Heckelmann, R. (1969). A neurological impress method of remedial instruction. *Academic Therapy, 4,* 277–282.

Hegge, R., Kirk, S., & Kirk, W. (1965). *Remedial reading drills.* Ann Arbor, MI: George Wahr.

Heron, T., & Skinner, M. (1981). Criteria for defining the regular classroom as the least restrictive environment for LD students. *Exceptional Children, 4*(2), 115–121.

Heward, W., & Orlansky, M. (1984). *Exceptional children: An introductory survey to special education.* Columbus, OH: Charles E. Merrill.

Hildreth, G. (1947). Chapters 19–21 in *Learning the three R's.* Minneapolis, MN: Education Test Bureau.

Hinshelwood, J. (1917). *Congenital word blindness.* London: H.K. Lewis.

Hiscock, M. (1983). Do learning disabled children lack functional hemispheric lateralization: *Topics in Learning and Learning Disabilities, 3*(1), 14–28.

Hiscock, M., & Kinsbourne, M. (1980). Individual differences in cerebral lateralization: Are they relevant to learning disabilities? In W. Cruickshank (Ed.), *Approaches to Learning: Vol. 1. The best of ACLD.* Syracuse, NY: Syracuse University Press.

Hobbs, N. (1975). *Issues in the classification of children.* 1–2. San Francisco: Jossey-Bass.

Hoffer, K. (1983). Assessment and instruction of reading skills: Results with Mexican-American students. *Learning Disability Quarterly, 6,* 458–467.

Honey, J. (1983). *The language trap: Race, class, and the "standard English" issue in British schools.* National Council for Educational Standards, Kay-Shuttleworth Papers on Education: No. 3.

Horne, M. (1978). Do learning disabilities specialists know their phonics? *Journal of Learning Disabilities, 11,* 580–582.

Houck, C., & Sherman, A. (1979). Mainstreaming current flows two ways. *Academic Therapy, 15,* 133–140.

Howe, M. (1970). *Introduction to human memory.* New York: Harper & Row.

Hutton, J. (1984). Incidence of learning problems among children with middle ear pathology. *Journal of Learning Disabilities, 17,* 41–42.

Indiana Department of Public Instruction. (1984). *Microcomputers in the resource room: A handbook for teachers.* Indianapolis: Department of Special Education.

Ingersoll, G., Smith, C., & Elliott, P. (1983). Microcomputers in American public schools: A national survey. *Educational Computer, 3*(6), 28–33.

Itard, J. (1962). *The wild boy of Aveyron.* (Trans.). New York: Appleton-Century-Crofts. (Original work published 1801).

Jackson, J. (1874). On the nature of duality of the brain. In J. Taylor (Ed.). (1958). *Selected Writings of John Hughlings Jackson.* New York: Basic Books.

Jenkins, J., Deno, S., & Mirkin, P. (1979). Measuring pupil progress toward the least restrictive alternative. *Learning Disability Quarterly, 2,* 82–92.

Jenkins, J., & Pany, D. (1981). Instructional variables in reading comprehension. In J. Guthrie (Ed.), *Reading comprehension and teaching: Research views.* Newark, DE: International Reading Association.

Jenkins, J., Stein, M., & Osborn, J. (1981). What next after decoding? Instruction & research in reading comprehension. *Exceptional Education Quarterly, 2,* 27–39.

Jensen, R. (1969). How much can we boost IQ and scholastic achievement? *Harvard Educational Review, 39,* 1–123.

Jensen, R. (1978). *Bias in mental testing.* New York: Macmillan.

Johnson, D. (1967). Educational principles for children with learning disabilities. *Rehabilitation Literature, 28,* 317–322.

Johnson, D., & Myklebust, H. (1967). *Learning disabilities: Educational principles and practices.* New York: Grune & Stratton.

Johnson, D., & Myklebust, H. (1976). *Learning disabilities.* New York: Grune & Stratton.

Johnson, M., & Kress, R. (1965). *Informal reading inventories.* Newark, DE: International Reading Association.

Jones, J. (1972). *Intersensory transfer, perceptual shifting, model reference and reading.* Newark, DE: International Reading Association.

Kagan, J. (1976, March–April). Emergent themes in human development. *American Scientist,* pp. 186–196.

Karnes, M. (1972). *Goal program language development game.* Springfield, MA: Milton Bradley.

Karnes, M., Kokotovic, A., & Schwedel, A. (1982). Transporting a model program for young handicapped children: Issues, problems, and efficacy. *Journal of the Division for Early Childhood, 6,* 42–51.

Karnes, M., Linnemeyer, S., & Schwedel, A. (1981). A survey of federally funded model programs for handicapped infants: Implications for research and practice. *Journal of the Division for Early Childhood, 5,* 25–39.

Kaufman, A., & Kaufman, N. (1983). *Kaufman Assessment Battery for Children.* Circle Pines, MN: American Guidance Services.

Kauffman, J., Hallahan, D., Haas, K., Brame, T., & Born, R. (1978). Imitating children's errors to improve their spelling performance. *Journal of Learning Disabilities, 11,* 217–222.

Kavale, K. (1982). The efficacy of stimulant drug treatment for hyperactivity: A meta-analysis. *Journal of Learning Disabilities, 15,* 280–289.

Kavale, K. (1982). Meta-analysis of the relationship between visual perceptual skills and reading achievement. *Journal of Learning Disabilities, 15,* 42–51.

Kavale, K., & Forness, S. (1983). Hyperactivity and diet treatment: A meta-analysis of the Feingold hypothesis. In G. Senf & J. Torgesen (Eds.), *Annual Review of Learning Disabilities: Vol. 1. A Journal of Learning Disabilities Reader.* Chicago, IL: Professional Press.

Kavale, K., & Mattson, D. (1983). One jumped off the balance beam: Meta analysis of perceptual motor training. In G. Senf & J. Torgesen (Eds.), *Annual Review of Learning Disabilities: Vol. 1. A Journal of Learning Disabilities Reader.* Chicago, IL: Professional Press.

Keilitz, I., Zaremba, B., & Broder, P. (1979). The link between learning disabilities and juvenile delinquency: Some issues and answers. *Learning Disability Quarterly, 2,* 2–11.

Keller, H. (1961). *The story of my life.* New York: Dell.

Keogh, B. (1974). Optometric vision training programs for children with learning disabilities: Review of issues and research. *Journal of Learning Disabilities, 7,* 219–231.

Keogh, B. (1977). Research on cognitive styles. In R. Kneedler & S. Tarver (Eds.), *Changing perspectives in special education.* Columbus, OH: Charles E. Merrill.

Keogh, B., & Becker, L. (1973). Early detection of learning problems: Questions, cautions, and guidelines. *Exceptional Children, 40,* 5–13.

Keogh, B., Major-Kingsly, S., Omori-Gordon, H., & Reed, H. (1982). *A system of marker variables for the field of learning disabilities.* Syracuse, NY: Syracuse University Press.

Keogh, B., & Margolis, T. (1976). Learn to labor and wait: Attentional problems of children with learning disorders. *Journal of Learning Disabilities, 9,* 276–286.

Kephart, N. (1963). *The brain-injured child in the classroom.* Chicago: National Society for Crippled Children and Adults.

Kephart, N. (1967). Perceptual-motor aspects of learning disabilities. In E. Frierson & W. Barbe (Eds.), *Educating children with learning disabilities* (pp. 405–413). New York: Appleton-Century-Crofts.

Kephart, N. (1971). *The slow learner in the classroom.* Columbus, OH: Charles E. Merrill.

Kephart, N. (1972). Introduction to D. Woodward & N. Biondo, *Living around the now child.* Columbus, OH: Charles E. Merrill.

Kinsbourne, M. (1983). Models of learning disability. *Topics in Learning Disabilities, 3*(1), 1–13.

Kinsbourne, M., & Caplan, P. (1979). *Children's learning and attention problems.* Boston: Little, Brown.

Kirk, S. (1958). *Early education of the mentally retarded.* Urbana, IL: University of Illinois Press.

Kirk, S. (1963). Behavioral diagnosis and remediation of learning disabilities. In *Conference on the exploration into the problems of the perceptually handicapped child.* Evanston, IL: Fund for the Perceptually Handicapped Child.

Kirk, S. (1965). Diagnostic, cultural, and remedial factors in mental retardation. In S. Osler & R. Cook (Eds.), *Biosocial basis of mental retardation.* Baltimore, MD: Johns Hopkins University Press.

Kirk, S. (1967). Amelioration of mental abilities through psychodiagnostic and remedial procedures. In G. Jervis (Ed.), *Mental retardation.* Springfield, IL: Charles C. Thomas.

Kirk, S. (1974). Introduction. *State of the art: Where are we going?* Los Angeles: Association for Children with Learning Disabilities and California Association for Neurologically Handicapped Children.

Kirk, S., & Chalfant, J. (1984). *Academic and developmental learning disabilities.* Denver: Love Publishing.

Kirk, S., & Chalfant, J. (1984). *Developmental and academic learning disabilities.* Denver: Love Publishing.

Kirk, S., & Gallagher, J. (1983). *Educating exceptional children.* Boston: Houghton Mifflin.

Kirk, S., & Elkins, J. (1975). Characteristics of children enrolled in the Child Service Demonstration Centers. *Journal of Learning Disabilities, 8,* 630–637.

Kirk, S. & Kirk, W. (1971). *Psycholinguistic disabilities.* Urbana, IL: University of Illinois Press.

Kirk, S., Kliebhan, J., & Lerner, J. (1978). *Teaching reading to slow and disabled learners.* Boston: Houghton Mifflin.

Klein, R., Altman, S., Dreizen, K., Friedman, R., & Powers, L. (1981). Restructuring dysfunctional parental attitudes toward children's learning and behavior in school: Family-oriented psychotherapy. *Journal of Learning Disabilities, 14,* 15–19.

Koppitz, E. (1964). *Bender-Gestalt test for young children.* New York: Grune & Stratton.

Koppitz, E. (1972–1973). Special class pupils with learning disabilities: a five-year follow-up study. *Academic Therapy, 8,* 133–139.

Krevisky, J., & Linfield, J. (1963). *The bad speller's dictionary.* New York: Random House.

Kronick, D. (1978). An examination of psychosocial aspects of learning disabled adolescents. *Learning Disability Quarterly, 1,* 74–86.

Kronick, D. (1981). *Social development of learning disabled persons.* San Francisco, CA: Jossey-Bass.

Kuchinskas, G. (1983). Ways to use a microcomputer in reading and language arts classes. *Computers, Reading and Language Arts, 1*(1), 11–16.

Labov, W. (1973). The logic of nonstandard English. In J. DeStefano (Ed.), *Language, society, and education. A profile in black English.* Worthington, OH: Charles A. Jones.

Langsford, K., Slade, K., & Barnett, A. (1974). An explanation of impress techniques in remedial reading. *Academic Therapy, 9,* 309–319.

Larsen, S., & Hammill, D. (1975). Relationship of selected visual perceptual abilities to school learning. *Journal of Special Education, 9,* 282–291.

Larson, C. (1968, Fall). Teaching beginning writing. *Academic Therapy Quarterly, 4,* 61–66.

Laycock, M., & Watson, G. (1975). *The fabric of mathematics.* Hayward, CA: Activity Resources.

Lazar, I. (1979, Fall). Does prevention pay off? *The Communicator.* The Council for Exceptional Children, Division for Early Childhood, pp. 1–7.

Lazar, I., & Darlington, R. (1979, September). *Summary Report, Lasting Effects After Preschool.* (DHEW Publication No. OHDS 79–30, 179). Washington, DC: U.S. Government Printing Office.

Learning Disabilities Criteria Committee. (1983, March). *Learning disabilities criteria: Eligibility, severity, exit.* Palatine, IL: Northwest Suburban Special Education Organization.

Lee, L. (1974). *Developmental sentence analysis.* Evanston, IL: Northwestern University Press.

Lee, L., Koenigsnect, R., & Mulhern, S. (1975). *Interactive language development teaching: The clinical presentation of grammatical structure.* Evanston, IL: Northwestern University Press.

Lenkowsky, B., & Lenkowsky, R. (1978). Bibliotherapy of the LD adolescent. *Academic Therapy, 14,* 179–185.

Lenneberg, E. (1967). *Biological foundations of language.* New York: Wiley.

Lerner, J. (1975). Remedial reading and learning disabilities: Are they the same or different? *Journal of Special Education, 9,* 119–132.

Lerner, J. (1973). Systems analysis and special education. *Journal of Special Education, 9,* 16–26

Lerner, J., Bernstein, D., Stevenson, L., & Rubin, A. (1971, Summer). Bridging the gap in teacher education: A camping-academic program for children with school learning disorders. *Academic Therapy Quarterly, 5,* 367–374.

Lerner, J., & Cohn, S. (1981). Learning disabilities and the child-care physician. In W. Cruickshank & A. Silver (Eds.), *Bridges to tomorrow: Vol. 2. The best of ACLD.* Syracuse, NY: Syracuse University Press.

Lerner, J., Dawson, D., & Horvath, L. (1980). *Cases in learning and behavior problems: A guide to individualized education programs.* Boston: Houghton Mifflin.

Lerner, J., & Egan, R. (1979). Clinical teaching: update. *Journal of Clinical Psychology, 8,* 219–222.

Lerner, J., Evans, M., & Meyers, G. (1977). Learning disabilities programs at the secondary level. *Academic Therapy, 13,* 7–22.

Lerner, J., & List, L. (1970). The phonics knowledge of prospective teachers, experienced teachers, and elementary pupils. *Illinois School Research, 7,* 39–42.

Lerner, J., Mardell-Czudnowski, C., & Goldenberg, D. (1981). *Special education for the early childhood years.* Englewood Cliffs, NJ: Prentice-Hall.

Lerner, J., & Schuyler, J. (1974). Computer simulation: A method for training educational diagnosticians. *Journal of Learning Disabilities, 7,* 471–478.

Lerner, J., & Schuyler, J. (1975, February). *Computer applications in learning disabilities.* (ERIC Document Reproduction Service No. ED 096974).

Lerner, J., & Vaver, G. (1970, Summer). Filmstrips in learning. *Academic Therapy Quarterly, 4,* 320–325.

Levine, M., Brooks, R., & Shonkoff, J. (1980). *A pediatric approach to learning disorders.* New York: Wiley.

Levy, H. (1983). Developmental dyslexia: A pediatrician's perspective. *Schumpert Medical Quarterly, 1,* 200–207.

Lewis, R. (1983). Learning disabilities and reading: Instructional recommendations from current research. *Exceptional Children, 50,* 230–240.

Lewis, R., Strauss, A., & Lehtinen, L. (1960). *The Other Child.* New York: Grune & Stratton.

Liberman, I. (1973). Segmentation of the spoken word and reading acquisition. *Annals of Dyslexia: An Interdisciplinary Journal of the Orton Dyslexia Society, 23* (Reprint no. 54).

Liberman, I. (1982). Language-oriented view of reading and its disability. In H. Myklebust (Ed.), *Progress in learning disabilities, Vol. 5.* New York: Grune & Stratton.

Lieberman, L. (1982). Special educator's safety net. *Journal of Learning Disabilities, 15,* 439–440.

Lilly, M., & Givens-Olge, L. (1981). Teacher consultation: Past, present and future. *Behavior Disorders, 6,* 73–77.

Lilly, S. (1982). The education of mildly handicapped children and implications for teacher education. In M. Reynolds (Ed.), *The future of mainstreaming.* Reston, VA: Council for Exceptional Children.

Lindsey, J. (1983). Paraprofessionals in learning disabilities. *Journal of Learning Disabilities, 16,* 467–472.

Linsley, O. (1974). Precision teaching in perspective. In S. Kirk & F. Lord (Eds.), *Exceptional children: Educational resources and perspectives.* Boston: Houghton Mifflin.

List, L. (1982). *Music, art, and drama experiences in the elementary curriculum.* New York: Columbia Teachers College Press.

Loftus-Brighton, S. (1983). *Dyslexia need not be a disaster.* London: London Dyslexia Association.

Long, N., Morse, W., & Newman, R. (1971). *Conflict in the classroom: Education of children with problems.* Belmont, CA: Wadsworth.

Loper, A. (1980). Metacognitive development: Implications for cognitive training. *Exceptional Education Quarterly, 1,* 1–8.

Lovitt, T. (1975). Applied behavior analysis and learning disabilities—Part I. *Journal of Learning Disabilities, 8,* 432–443.

Lovitt, T. (1975). Applied behavior analysis and learning disabilities—Part II: Specific research recommendations and suggestions for practitioners. *Journal of Learning Disabilities, 8,* 504–518.

Lovitt, T. (1977). *In spite of my resistance, I've learned from children.* Columbus, OH: Charles E. Merrill.

Lovitt, T. (1978). The learning disabled. In N. Haring (Ed.), *Behavior of Exceptional Children.* Columbus, OH: Charles E. Merrill.

Lovitt, T. (1984). *Tactics for teaching.* Columbus, OH: Charles E. Merrill.

Lowenthal, B. (1984). Classroom classics: Natural language stimulation for language delayed children. *Illinois Council for Exceptional Children Quarterly, 33,* 13–15.

Lund, K., Foster, G., & McCall-Perez, F. (1978). The effectiveness of psycholinguistic training: A reevaluation. *Exceptional Children, 44,* 310–321.

Luria, A. (1961). *Speech and the regulation of behavior.* New York: Liveright.

Luria, A. (1966). *Human brain and psychological processes.* New York: Harper & Row.

Luria, A. (1968). *The mind of mnemonist.* New York: Basic Books.

Maddux, C. (1984). Using microcomputers with the learning disabled: Will the potential be realized? *Educational Computer, 4*(1), 31–32.

Mann, L. (1979). *On the trail of process.* New York: Grune & Stratton.

Mann, L., Cartwright, P., Kenowitz, L., Boyer, C., Metz, C., & Wolford, B. (1984). The child service demonstration centers: A summary report. *Exceptional Children, 50*(6), 532–541.

Mann, P., & Suiter, P. (1975). *Handbook in diagnostic teaching.* Boston: Allyn & Bacon.

Mardell-Czudnowski, C., & Goldenberg, D. (1983). *DIAL-R* (Developmental Indicators for the Assessment of Learning—Revised). Edison, NJ: Childcraft.

Marsh, G., & Price, B. (1980). *Methods of teaching the mildly handicapped adolescent.* St. Louis, MO: Mosby.

Martin, H. (1980). Nutrition, injury, illness, and minimal brain dysfunction. In H. Rie & E. Rie (Eds.), *Handbook of minimal brain dysfunction: A critical view.* New York: Wiley.

Martin, N. (1983). Genuine communications. *Topics in Learning and Learning Disabilities, 3*(3), 1–11.

Mattes, J. (1983). The Feingold diet: A current reappraisal. In G. Senf & J. Torgesen (Eds.), *Annual Review of Learning Disabilities: Vol. 1. A Journal of Learning Disabilities Reader*. Chicago, IL: Professional Press.

May, L. (1974). *Teaching mathematics in elementary school*. New York: Free Press.

McCarthy, D. (1954). Language development in children. In L. Carmichael (Ed.), *A manual of child psychology*. New York: Wiley.

McCarthy, J. (1968, April). Speech delivered to the Council on Understanding Learning Disabilities. Deerfield, IL.

McDonald, A., Carlson, K., Palmer, D., & Slay, T. (1983). Special education and medicine: A survey of physicians. *Journal of Learning Disabilities, 16,* 93–94.

McGinnis, M. (1963). *Aphasic children: Identification and education by the associa tion method*. Washington, DC: Volta Bureau.

McKinney, J. (1984). The search for subtypes of specific learning disability. *Journal of Learning Disabilities, 17,* 43–50.

McLeod, J. (1979). Educational underachievement: Toward a defensible psychometric definition. *Journal of Learning Disabilities, 12,* 322–330.

McLeod, T., & Armstrong, S. (1982). Learning disabilities in mathematics—skill deficits and remedial approaches at the intermediate and secondary level. *Learning Disability Quarterly, 5,* 305–311.

McLeod, T., & Crump, D. (1978). The relationship of visuospatial skills and verbal activity to learning disabilities in mathematics. *Journal of Learning Disabilities, 11,* 237–241.

Mehan, H. (1979). *Learning lessons: Social organizations in the classroom*. Cambridge, MA: Harvard University Press.

Meichenbaum, D. (1977). *Cognitive behavior modification*. New York: Plenum.

Meichenbaum, D. (1979). Teaching children self-control. In B. Lackey & A. Kazden (Eds.), *Advances in clinical child psychology* (Vol. 2). New York: Plenum

Meier, J. (1970). Prevalence and characteristics of learning disabilities in second-grade children. *Journal of Learning Disabilities, 4,* 6–21.

Menyuk, P. (1969). *Sentences children use*. Cambridge, MA: MIT Press.

Messerer, J., Hunt, E., Meyers, G., & Lerner, J. (1984). Feuerstein's instrumental enrichment: A new approach for activating intellectual potential in learning disabled youth. *Journal of Learning Disabilities, 17,* 322–325.

Meyer, A. (1983). Origins and prevention of emotional disorders among learning disabled children. *Topics in Learning and Learning Disabilities, 3,* 59–70.

Meyers, C., Macmillan, D., & Yoshida, R. (1980). Regular class education of EMR students, from efficacy to mainstreaming. In J. Gottlieb (Ed.), *Educating mentally retarded persons in the mainstream*. Baltimore, MD: University Park Press.

Meyers, P., & Hammill, D. (1982). *Learning disabilities*. Austin, TX: PRO-ED.

Miami Herald, October 9, 1979.

Miami Herald, October 11, 1980.

Migden, S. (1983). Issues in concurrent psychopathology—Remediation. *Annals of Dyslexia: An Interdisciplinary Journal of the Orton Dyslexia Society, 33,* 275–288.

Millichap, J. (1973). Drugs in management of minimal brain dysfunction. In F. DeLaCruz, B. Fox, & R. Roberts (Eds.), *Minimal brain dysfunction: Annals of the New York Academy of Sciences, 205,* 321–335.

Mills, R. (1956). *Learning methods test*. Fort Lauderdale, FL: Mills, 1612 E. Broward Blvd.

Minick, B., & School, B. (1982). The IEP process: Can computers help? *Academic Therapy, 18,* 141–148.

Minskoff, E. (1975). Research on psycholinguistic training: Critique and guidelines. *Exceptional Children, 42,* 136–144.

Minskoff, E., Wiseman, D., & Minskoff, J. (1973). *The MWM program of developing language abilities.* Ridgefield, NJ: Educational Performance Associates.

Moats, L. (1983). A comparison of the spelling errors of older dyslexics and second-grade normal children. *Annals of Dyslexia: An Interdisciplinary Journal of the Orton Dyslexia Association, 32,* 203–220.

Money, J. (1966). The laws of constancy and learning to read. In *International Approach to Learning Disabilities of Children and Youth: ACLD Conference* (pp. 80–97). Tulsa, OK: Association of Children with Learning Disabilities.

Montessori, M. (1912). *The Montessori method.* (A. E. George, Trans.). New York: Frederick Stokes.

Moran, M. (1978). *Assessment of the exceptional learner in the regular classroom.* Denver, CO: Love.

Moran, M. (1981). Performance of learning disabled and low achieving secondary students on formal features of a paragraph writing task. *Learning Disability Quarterly, 4,* 271–280.

Morgan, W. (1896, November). A case of congenital word blindness. *British Medical Journal,* pp. 1375–1379.

Moss, J., & Fielding, P. (Eds.). (1981). *National Directory of Four Year Colleges, Two Year Colleges and Post High School Training Programs for Young People with Learning Disabilities* (4th ed.). Tulsa, OK: Partners in Publishing, Box 50347.

Moyer, S. (1983). Repeated reading. In G. Senf & J. Torgesen (Eds.), *Annual Review of Learning Disabilities, 1,* 113–117.

Myklebust, H. (1964). *The psychology of deafness.* New York: Grune & Stratton.

Myklebust, H. (1965). *Picture story language test: The development and disorders of written language, Vol. 1.* New York: Grune & Stratton.

Myklebust, H. (1968). Learning disabilities: Definitions and overview. In H. Myklebust (Ed.), *Progress in learning disabilities* (Vol. 1). New York: Grune & Stratton.

Myklebust, H., & Boshes, B. (1969, June). *Minimal brain damage in children* (Final Report, U.S. Public Health Service Contract 108–65–142). Evanston, IL: Northwestern University Publication.

Nall, A. (1971). Prescriptive living. In J. Arena (Ed.), *The child with learning disabilities: His right to learn.* San Rafael, CA: Academic Therapy Publications.

National Advisory Committee on Handicapped Children. (1968, May). *Subcommittee on education of the committee on labor and public welfare* (First Annual Report). Washington, DC: U.S. Government Printing Office.

National Assessment of Educational Progress. (1981). *Reading, writing, and thinking.* (1979–80 Report). Washington, DC: U.S. Government Printing Office.

National Association of State Directors of Special Education (NASDE). (1983). Unpublished report of State Directors of Special Education.

National Commission on Excellence in Education. (1983). *A nation at risk: The imperative for educational reform.* Washington, DC: U.S. Department of Education.

National Council for Teachers of Mathematics. (1980). *An agenda for action: Recommendations for school mathematics for the 1980's.* Reston, VA: Council of Teachers of Mathematics.

Neisser, U. (1967). *Cognitive psychology.* New York: Appleton-Century-Crofts.

Nesher, P. (1982). Levels of description in the analysis of addition and subtraction of word problems. In T. Carpenter, J. Moser, & T. Romberg (Eds.), *Addition and subtraction: A cognitive perspective.* Hillsdale, NJ: Lawrence Erlbaum.

Newcomer, P. (1978). Competencies for professionals in learning disabilities. *Learning Disability Quarterly, 1,* 69–77.

Newcomer, P. (1982). Competencies for professionals in learning disabilities. *Learning Disability Quarterly, 6,* 241–252.

Newcomer, P., & Goodman, L. (1975). Effect of modality instruction on the learning of meaningful and nonmeaningful material by auditory and visual learners. *Journal of Special Education, 9,* 251–268.

Newcomer, P., & Hammill, D. (1975). ITPA and academic achievement: A survey. *Reading Teacher, 28,* 731–741.

Newcomer, P., & Hammill, D. (1976). *Psycholinguistics in the schools.* Columbus, OH: Charles E. Merrill.

Newcomer, P., Hare, B., Hammill, D., & McGettigan, J. (1974). Construct validity of the ITPA. *Exceptional Children, 40,* 509–510.

Nimmer, D., & Kinnison, L. (1980, July). Recommendations and practices for prescribed medicine in the schools. *Peabody Journal of Education, 57*(2).

Nodine, B. (1983). Forward: Process not product. *Topics in Learning and Learning Disabilities, 3*(3), ix–xii.

Obrzut, J., & Hynd, G. (1983). The neurobiological and neuropsychological foundations of learning disabilities. *Journal of Learning Disabilities, 1*(9), 515–520.

Ochoa, A., Pacheco, R., & Omark, D. (1984). Addressing the learning disabled needs of limited-English proficient students: Beyond language and race issues. *Learning Disability Quarterly, 6,* 416–423.

Ohio guidelines for interpretation of children with specific learning disabilities. (1983). Columbus, OH: State of Ohio.

O'Leary, K., & O'Leary, S. (1977). *Classroom management: The successful use of behavior modification.* New York: Pergamon.

Olsen, J., Wong, B., & Marx, R. (1983). Linguistic and metacognitive aspects of normally achieving and learning disabled children's communication process. *Learning Disability Quarterly, 6*(3), 289–304.

Orton, S. (1937). *Reading, writing and speech problems in children.* New York: Norton.

O'Shea, J., & Porter, S. (1981). Double-blind study of children with hyperactive syndrome treated with multi-allergic extract sublingually. *Journal of Learning Disabilities, 14,* 189–191.

Osman, B. (1979). *Learning disabilities: A family affair.* New York: Random House.

Osman, B. (with H. Binder). (1982). *No one to play with: The social side of learning disabilities.* New York: Random House.

Otto, W., & Askov, E. (1972). *Rationale and guidelines: The Wisconsin design for reading skills development.* Minneapolis: National Computer Systems.

Otto, W., McMenemy, L. & Smith, R. (1973). *Corrective and remedial teaching: Principles and practices.* Boston: Houghton Mifflin.

Papert, S. (1980). *Mindstorms.* New York: Basic Books.

Pateet, E. (1980). The diagnostic evaluation of written language skills (DEWS): Application of DEWS criteria to writing samples. *Learning Disability Quarterly, 3,* 88–98.

Patten, B. (1973). Visually mediating thinking: A report of the case of Albert Einstein, *Journal of Learning Disabilities, 6,* 415–420.

Patton, P. (1981). A model for developing vocational objectives in IEP. *Exceptional Children, 47,* 618–622.

Pearl, R., Bryan, T., & Donahue, M. (1983). Social behaviors of learning disabled children: A review. *Topics in Learning and Learning Disabilities, 2,* 1–14.

Peason, P., & Spiro, R. (1980). Toward a theory of reading comprehension. *Topics in Language Disorders, 1*(1), 71–88.

Pearson, R., & Johnson, D. (1978). *Teaching reading comprehension*. New York: Holt, Rinehart & Winston.

Personke, C., & Yee, A. (1966, March). A model for the analysis of spelling behavior. *Elementary English, 43,* 278–284.

Pfeiffer, S., & Naglieri, J. (1983). An integration of multidisciplinary team decision-making. *Journal of Learning Disabilities, 16,* 568–590.

Piaget, J. (1952). *The origins of intelligence in children.* (M. Cook, Trans.). New York: International University Press. (Original work published 1936).

Piaget, J. (1970). *The science of education of the psychology of the child.* New York: Grossman.

Poggio, J., & Salkind, N. (1979). A review and appraisal of instruments assessing hyperactivity in children. *Learning Disability Quarterly, 2,* 9–22.

Poplin, M. (1983). Assessing and developing writing abilities. *Topics in Learning and Learning Disabilities, 3*(3), 63–75.

Poplin, M., & Wright, P. (1983). The concept of cultural pluralism: Issues in special education. *Learning Disability Quarterly, 6,* 367–372.

Poteet, J. (1973). *Behavior modification: A practical guide for teachers.* Minneapolis, MN: Burgess.

Premack, D. (1959). Toward empirical behavior law I, positive reinforcement. *Psychological Review, 66,* 219–233.

Public Law 98–199, Education of the Handicapped Act Amendments, December, 1983.

Pyecha, J. (1981). A national survey of individual education programs for handicapped children. In U.S. General Accounting Office (Ed.), *Disparities still exist in who gets special education, 38.*

Ramey, C., & Bryant, D. (1982). Evidence for prevention of developmental retardation during infancy. *Journal of the Division for Early Childhood, 5,* 73–78.

Rapp, D. (1979). Food allergy treatment for hyperkinesis. *Journal of Learning Disabilities, 12,* 608–616.

Rappaport, S. (1966). Personality factors teachers need for relationship structure. In W. Cruickshank (Ed.), *The teacher of brain-injured children.* Syracuse, NY: Syracuse University Press.

Reger, R. (1979). Futile attempts at a simplistic definition. *Journal of Learning Disabilities, 12,* 529–532.

Rehabilitation Services Administration. (1982, July 27). *Acceptance of specific learning disabilities as a medically recognizable disability program instruction. Information Memorandum* (RSA-pi-81-22), pp. 1–7.

Reichman, J., & Healey, W. (1983). Learning disabilities in conductive hearing loss involving otitis media. In G. Senf and J. Torgesen (Eds.), *Annual Review of Learning Disabilities: Vol. 1. A Journal of Learning Disabilities Reader.* Chicago, IL: Professional Press.

Reid, D., Knight-Arest, I., & Hresko, W. (1981). Cognitive development in learning disabled children. In J. Gottlieb & S. Strichart (Eds.), *Developmental theory and research in learning disabilities.* Baltimore, MD: University Park Press.

Reid, G. (1982). Physical education for the learning disabled student: An update. *Learning Disability Quarterly, 5*(2), 190–193.

Reisman, F. (1981). *Teaching mathematics: Methods and content.* Boston: Houghton Mifflin.

Resnick, L. (1982). Syntax and semantics in learning to subtract. In T. Carpenter, J. Moser, & T. Romberg (Eds.), *Addition and subtraction: A cognitive perspective.* Hillsdale, NJ: Lawrence Erlbaum.

Resnick, L., & Ford, W. (1981). *The psychology of mathematics instruction.* Hillsdale, NJ: Erlbaum Associates.

Reynolds, M. (Ed.). (1982). *The future of mainstreaming.* Reston, VA: Council for Exceptional Children.

Reynolds, L., Egan, R., & Lerner, J. (1983). The efficacy of early intervention on preacademic deficits: Review of the literature. *Topics in Early Childhood Special Education, 3,* 47–76.

Ribner, S. (1978). The effects of special class placement on the self-concept of exceptional children. *Journal of Learning Disabilities, 11,* 319–323.

Richek, M., List, L., & Lerner, J. (1983). *Reading problems: Diagnosis and remediation.* Englewood Cliffs, NJ: Prentice-Hall.

Rimland, B. (1983). The Feingold diet: An assessment of the reviews by Mattes, by Kavale and Forness and others. In G. Senf and J. Torgesen (Eds.), *Annual Review of Learning Disabilities: Vol. 1. A Journal of Learning Disabilities Reader.* Chicago, IL: Professional Press.

Rinsland, H. (1945). *A basic vocabulary of elementary school children.* New York: Macmillan.

Roach, C., & Kephart, N. (1966). *The Purdue Perceptual-Motor Survey Test.* Columbus, OH: Charles E. Merrill.

Robbins, M. (1966). A study of the validity of Delacato's theory of neurological organization. *Experimental Children, 32,* 517–523.

Robertson, M. (1981). Motor development in learning disabled children. In J. Gottlieb & S. Strickhart (Eds.), *Developmental theory and research in learning disabilities* (pp. 80–109). Baltimore, MD: University Park Press.

Robinson, H. (1972). Visual and auditory modalities related to methods for beginning reading. *Reading Research Quarterly, 8,* 7–41.

Rockefeller, N. (1976, October 16). *TV Guide.*

Rosenthal, R., & Jacobson, L. (1968). *Pygmalion in the classroom: Teacher expectations and pupils' intelligence development.* New York: Holt, Rinehart & Winston.

Rosner, J. (1979). *Helping children overcome learning disabilities.* New York: Walker.

Ross, A. (1976). *Psychological aspects of learning disabilities and reading disorders.* New York: McGraw-Hill.

Roswell, F., & Natchez, G. (1971). *Reading disability: Diagnosis and treatment.* New York: Basic Books.

Rubin, H., & Liberman, I. (1983). Exploring the oral and written language errors made by language disabled children. *Annals of Dyslexia: An Interdisciplinary Journal of the Orton Dyslexia Society, 33,* 111–120.

Rumelhart, D. (1981). Schemata: The building blocks of cognition. In J. Guthrie (Ed.), *Comprehension and teaching: Research views.* Newark, DE: International Reading Association.

Runion, H. (1980). Hypoglycemia—fact or fiction. In W. Cruickshank (Ed.), *Approaches to learning: Vol. 1. The best of ACLD.* Syracuse, NY: Syracuse University Press.

Ryan, D. (1984). Mainstreaming isn't just for students anymore. *Journal of Learning Disabilities, 17,* 167–169.

Sabatino, D., & Dorfman, N. (1974). Matching learning aptitude to two commercial reading programs. *Exceptional Children, 44,* 85–90.

Safer, D., & Allen, R. (1973). Factors influencing the suppressant effects of two stimulant drugs on the growth of hyperactive children. *Pediatrics, 51,* 660.

Safer, D., Allen, R., & Barre, E. (1975). Growth rebound after termination of stimulant drugs. *Journal of Pediatrics, 86,* 113.

Salend, S. (1984). Factors contributing to the development of successful mainstreaming programs. *Exceptional Children, 50,* 409–416.

Salend, S., & Lutz, G. (1984). Mainstreaming or mainlining: A competency based approach to mainstreaming. *Journal of Learning Disabilities, 17,* 27–29.

Salvia, J., & Ysseldyke, J. (1981). *Assessment in special and remedial education.* Boston: Houghton Mifflin.

Samuels, S. (1981). Characteristics of exemplary programs. In J. Guthrie (Ed.), *Comprehension and teaching: Research views.* Newark, DE: International Reading Association.

Sanders, M. (1983). Assessing the interaction of learning disabilities and social emotional development. *Topics in Learning and Learning Disabilities, 3,* 37–47.

Schulz, J., & Turnbull, A. (1983). *Mainstreaming handicapped students: A guide for classroom teachers.* Boston: Allyn & Bacon.

Schumaker, J., Deshler, D., Alley, G., & Warner, M. (1983). Toward the development of an intervention model for learning disabled adolescents. The University of Kansas Institute for Research on Learning Disabilities. *Exceptional Education Quarterly, 4,* 44–47.

Schumaker, J., Deshler, D., & Denton, P. (1984). An integrated system for providing content to learning disabled adolescents using an audio-tape format. In J. Cruickshank & J. Kleibhan (Eds.), *Early adolescence to early childhood: Vol. 5. The best of ACLD.* Syracuse, NY: Syracuse University Press.

Schwartz, L. (1984). *Exceptional students in the mainstream.* Belmont, CA: Wadsworth.

Schweinhart, L., & Weikart, D. (1980). Young children grow up: The effects of the Perry Preschool Program on youths through age 15. *Monographs of the High/Scope Educational Research Foundation, 7.*

Schweinhart, L., & Weikart, D. (1981). Effects of the Perry Program on youths through age 15. *Journal of the Division for Early Childhood, 4,* 29–39.

Sequin, E. (1970). *Idiocy and its treatment by the physiological method.* New York: Columbia University Press. (Original work published in 1866).

Shearer, M., & Shearer, D. (1972). The Portage Project: A model for early childhood education. *Exceptional Children, 39,* 210–217.

Shepard, L. (1980). An evaluation of the regression discrepancy method for identifying children with learning disabilities. *Journal of Special Education, 14*(1), 79–80.

Sherrill, C. (1976). *Adapted physical education and recreation.* Dubuque, IA: W.C. Brown.

Shonkoff, J., Dworkin, P., Leviton, A., & Levine, M. (1979). Primary care approaches to developmental disabilities. *Pediatrics, 506,* 64.

Shuy, R. (1972). Speech differences in teaching strategies. How different is enough? In R. Hodges & E. Rudorf (Eds.), *Language and learning to read.* Boston: Houghton Mifflin.

Siegel, E., & Gold, R. (1982). *Educating the learning disabled.* New York: Macmillan.

Siegel, E., & Siegel, R. (1977). *Creating instructional sequences.* San Rafael, CA: Academic Therapy Publications.

Silver, A., & Hagin, R. (1966). Maturation of perceptual functions in children with specific reading disabilities. *The Reading Teacher, 19,* 253–259.

Silver, A., Hagin, R., & Kreeger, H. (1976). *SEARCH & TEACH.* New York: Walker Educational Book Corporation.

Silver, L. (1975). Acceptable and controversial approaches to treating learning disabilities. *Pediatrics, 55,* 406.

Silver, L. (1983). Introduction. In C. Brown (Ed.), *Childhood learning disabilities and prenatal risk.* Skillman, NJ: Johnson & Johnson Baby Products.

Silver, L. (1983). Therapeutic interventions with learning disabled students and their families. *Topics in Learning and Learning Disabilities, 3,* 48–58.

Silverman, R., & Zigmond, N. (1983). Self-concept in learning disabled adolescents. *Journal of Learning Disabilities, 16,* 478–490.

Simms, R., & Crump, W. (1983). Syntactic development in the oral language of learning disabled and normal students at the intermediate and secondary level. *Learning Disability Quarterly, 6*(2), 155–165.

Simopoulos, A. (1983). Nutrition. In C. Brown (Ed.), *Childhood learning disabilities and prenatal risk.* Skillman, NJ: Johnson & Johnson Baby Products.

Simpson, E. (1979). *Reversals: A personal account of victory over dyslexia.* Boston: Houghton Mifflin.

Skeels, H. (1942). A study of the effects of differential stimulation on mentally retarded children: A follow-up study. *American Journal of Mental Deficiency, 46,* 340–350.

Skeels, H. (1966). Adult status of children with contrasting early life experiences. *Monographs of the Society for Research in Child Development, 31.* Chicago: University of Chicago Press.

Skeels, H., & Dye, H. (1939). *A study of the effects of differential stimulation on mentally retarded children.* Proceedings and Addresses of the Sixty-third Annual Session of the American Association on Mental Deficiency, *44,* 114–130.

Skinner, B. (1957). *Verbal behavior.* New York: Appleton-Century-Crofts.

Skinner, B. (1963). Operant behavior. *American Psychologist, 18,* 503–515.

Slingerland, B. (1976). *A multisensory approach to language arts for specific language disability children: A guide for primary teachers.* Cambridge, MA: Educators Publishing Service.

Smith, C. (1983). *Learning disabilities: The interaction of learner, task, and setting.* Boston: Little, Brown.

Smith, F. (1972). The learner and his language. In R. Hodges & E. Rudorf (Eds.), *Language and learning to read.* Boston: Houghton Mifflin.

Smith, F. (1977). Making sense of reading and reading instruction. *Harvard Educational Review, 47,* 386–395.

Smith, F. (1982). *Understanding reading: Psycholinguistic analysis of reading.* New York: Holt, Rinehart & Winston.

Smith, F. (1982). *Writing and the writer.* New York: Holt, Rinehart & Winston.

Smith, S. (1980). *No easy answers: The learning disabled child at home and at school.* New York: Bantam Books.

Smith, S., Kimberling, W., Pennington, B., & Lubs, H. (1984, March). Specific reading disability: Identification of an inherited form through linkage analysis. *Science, 219,* 1345–1347.

Sperry, R. (1968). Hemisphere deconnection and unity in conscious awareness. *American Psychologist, 23,* 723–733.

Spradlin, J. (1967). Procedures for evaluating processes associated with receptive and expressive language. In R. Schiefelbush, R. Copeland, & J. Smith (Eds.), *Language and mental retardation.* New York: Holt, Rinehart & Winston.

Stauffer, R. (1975). *Directing the reading-thinking process.* New York: Harper & Row.

Stevens, G., & Birch, J. (1957). A proposed clarification of the terminology used to describe brain-injured children. *Exceptional Children, 23,* 346–349.

Strauss, A. (1951). The education of the brain injured child. *American Journal of Mental Deficiency, 56,* 712–718.

Strauss, A., & Lehtinen, L. (1947). *Psychopathology and education of the brain-injured child.* New York: Grune & Stratton.

Swan, W. (1980). Handicapped children's early education program. *Exceptional Children, 47,* 12–14.

Swan, W. (1981). Efficacy studies in early childhood special education. *Journal of the Division for Early Childhood, 4,* 1–4.

Tanyzer, H., & Mazurkiewicz, A. (1967). *Early to read i.t.a. program, Book 2.* New York: i/t/a/ Publications.

Tarver, S., & Dawson, M. (1978). Modality preference and the teaching of reading: A review. *Journal of Learning Disabilities, 11,* 5–17.

Thompson, L. (1971). Language disabilities in men of eminence. *Journal of Learning Disabilities, 4,* 34–45.

Thompson, R., & Dziuban, C. (1973). Criterion-referenced reading tests in perspective. *Reading Teacher, 27,* 292–294.

Thorndike, R. (1965). *The concepts of over- and under-achievement.* New York: Bureau of Publications, Teachers College, Columbia University.

Thornton, C. (1984). *Matter of facts.* Palo Alto, CA: Creative Publications.

Thornton, C., Jones, G., & Toohey, M. (1983). A multisensory approach to thinking strategies for remedial instruction in basic addition factors. *Journal for Research in Mathematics Education, 14,* 198–203.

Thornton, C., Tucker, B., Dossey, J., & Edna, F. (1983). *Teaching mathematics to children with special needs.* Menlo Park, CA: Addison-Wesley.

Thurber, D. (1983). Write on! With continuous stroke point. *Academic Therapy, 18,* 389–396.

Thurlow, M., & Ysseldyke, J. (1979). Current assessment and decision-making practices in model LD programs. *Learning Disability Quarterly, 2,* 15–24.

Time. (1974, September 2). 14–23.

Torgesen, J. (1979a). Factors related to poor performance on memory tasks in reading disabled children. *Learning Disability Quarterly, 2,* 17–23.

Torgesen, J. (1979b). What shall we do with psychological processes? *Journal of Learning Disabilities, 12,* 514–521.

Torgesen, J. (1980). Conceptual and educational implications of the use of efficient task strategies by learning disabled children. *Journal of Learning Disabilities, 13,* 364–371.

Torgesen, J. (1980). Memory processes in exceptional children. In B. Keogh (Ed.), *Basic constructs and theoretical orientation: A research annual.* Greenwich, CT: JAI Press.

Torgesen, J. (1982). The learning disabled child as an inactive learner: Educational implications. *Topics in Learning and Learning Disabilities, 2,* 45–52.

Traub, N., & Bloom, F. (1970). *Recipe for reading.* Cambridge, MA: Educators Publishing Service.

Treiber, F., & Lahey, B. (1983). Toward a behavioral model of academic remediation with learning disabled children. In G. Senf & J. Torgesen (Eds.), *Annual Review of Learning Disabilities, Vol. 1. A Journal of Learning Disabilities Reader.* Chicago, IL: Professional Press.

Turnbull, A., Strickland, B., & Brantley, J. (1982). *Developing and implementing individualized education programs.* Columbus, OH: Charles E. Merrill.

Underhill, R., Uprichard, A., & Heddens, J. (1980). *Diagnosing mathematics difficulties.* Columbus, OH: Charles E. Merrill.

U.S. Department of Education. (1979–1983). *To assure the free appropriate public education of all handicapped children.* Washington, DC: U.S. Department of Education.

U.S. Department of Education (1983). *A nation at risk: The imperative for educational reform.* Washington, DC: U.S. Government Printing Office.

U.S. General Accounting Office. (1981). *Disparities still exist in who gets special education.* Washington, DC: Comptroller General of the United States.

U.S. Office of Education. (1977, August 23). *Education of handicapped children.* Implementation of Part B of the Education for Handicapped Act. Federal Register, Part II. Washington, DC: U.S. Department of Health, Education, and Welfare.

U.S. Office of Education. (1977, December 19). Federal Register, Part III. *Education of handicapped children.* Assistance to the States: Procedures for Evaluating Specific Learning Disabilities. Washington, DC: U.S. Department of Health, Education, and Welfare.

Valett, R. (1983). Developing linguistic auditory memory patterns. *Journal of Learning Disabilities, 16,* 462–466.

Vance, B., & Hayden, D. (1982). Use of microcomputer and management assessment data. *Journal of Learning Disabilities, 15,* 496–498.

Van Evra, J. (1983). *Psychological disorders of children and adolescents.* Boston: Little, Brown.

Vellutino, F. (1977). Alternative conceptualizations of dyslexia: evidence in support of a verbal-deficit hypothesis. *Harvard Education Review, 47,* 334–354.

Vellutino, F., Steger, B., Moyer, S., Harding, C., & Niles, J. (1977). Has the perceptual deficit hypothesis led us astray? *Journal of Learning Disabilities, 10,* 375–385.

Vogel, S. (1975). *Syntactic abilities in normal and dyslexic children.* Baltimore, MD: University Park Press.

Vogel, S. (1977). Morphological ability in normal and dyslexic children. *Journal of Learning Disabilities, 10,* 41–49.

Vogel, S. (1982). On developing LD college programs. *Journal of Learning Disabilities, 15,* 518–528.

Vuckovich, D. (1968). Pediatric neurology and learning disabilities. In H. Myklebust (Ed.), *Progress in learning disabilities: Vol. 1.* New York: Grune & Stratton.

Vygotsky, L. (1962). *Thought and language.* Cambridge, MA: MIT Press.

Walker, D. (1983). Reflection on the educational potential and limitations of the microcomputer. *Phi Delta Kappan, 65,* 103–107.

Wallach, G., & Goldsmith, S. (1977). Language-based learning disabilities: Reading is language too. *Journal of Learning Disabilities, 3,* 57–62.

Wang, M., & Birch, J. (1984). Effective special education in regular class. *Exceptional Children, 50,* 391–398.

Weiner, E. (1980). The diagnostic evaluation of written language skills (DEWS): Application of DEWS criteria to writing samples. *Learning Disability Quarterly, 3,* 54–59.

Weisman, D. (1980). The nonreading parallel curriculum. *Academic Therapy, 20*(2), 14–20.

Wells, D., Schmid, R., Algozzine, B., & Maher, M. (1983). Teaching learning disabled adolescents. *Teacher Education and Special Education, 6,* 227–234.

Wepman, J. (1968). The modality concept. In H. Smith (Ed.), *Perception and reading.* Newark, DE: International Reading Association.

Wernicke, C. (1908). The symptom-complex of aphasia. In A. Church (Ed.), *Diseases of the Nervous System.* New York: Appleton.

Wiederholt, J. (1974). Historical perspectives in the education of the learning disabilities. In L. Mann & D. Sabatino (Eds.), *The second review of special education.* Philadelphia: Journal of Special Education Press.

Wiederholt, J., Hammill, D., & Brown, V. (1983). *The Resource Teacher.* Austin, TX: Pro-Ed.

Wiens, J. (1983). Metacognition and the adolescent passive learner. *Journal of Learning Disabilities, 16,* 144–149.

Wiig, E., & Semel, E. (1984). *Language disabilities in children and adolescents.* Columbus, OH: Charles E. Merrill.

Wong, B., & Jones, W. (1982). Increasing metacomprehension in learning disabled and normally achieving students through self-questioning training. *Learning Disability Quarterly, 5*(3), 228–240.

Wong, B., & Roadhouse, A. (1978). The test of language development (TOLD): A validation study. *Learning Disability Quarterly, 1,* 48–62.

Wood, M. (1980). Modern math and the LD child. *Academic Therapy, 15,* 279–290.

Yauman, B. (1980). Special education placement and the self-concepts of elementary-school age children. *Learning Disability Quarterly, 3*(3), 30–35.

Ysseldyke, J. (1977). *Assessing the learning disabled youngster: State of the art* (Research Report No. 1). Minneapolis, MN: Institute for Research on Learning Disabilities. University of Minnesota.

Ysseldyke, J. (1978). Remediation of ability deficits: Some major questions. In L. Mann, L. Goodman, & J. Wiederholt (Eds.), *Teaching the learning disabled adolescents.* Boston: Houghton Mifflin.

Ysseldyke, J. (1983). Current practices in making psychological decisions about learning disabled students. In G. Senf & J. Torgesen (Eds.), *Annual Review of Learning Disabilities, Vol. 1. A Journal of Learning Disabilities Reader.* Chicago, IL: Professional Press.

Ysseldyke, J., & Algozzine, B. (1979). Perspectives and assessment of learning disabled students. *Learning Disability Quarterly, 2,* 3–14.

Ysseldyke, J., & Algozzine, B. (1982). *Critical issues in special and remedial education.* Boston: Houghton Mifflin.

Ysseldyke, J., & Salvia, J. (1974). Diagnostic-prescriptive teaching: two models. *Exceptional Children, 40,* 181–186.

Zigmond, N., Vallecorsa, A., & Silverman, R. (1983). *Assessment for instructional planning in special education.* Englewood Cliffs, NJ: Prentice-Hall.

Author/Source Index

Subject Index

An Invitation to Respond

We would like to find out a little about your background and about your reactions to the Fourth Edition of *Learning Disabilities: Theories, Diagnosis, and Teaching Strategies*. Your evaluation of the book will help us to meet the interests and needs of students in future editions. We invite you to share your reactions by completing the questionnaire below and returning it to: *College Marketing; Houghton Mifflin Company; One Beacon Street; Boston, MA 02108*

1. How do you rate this textbook in the following areas?

		Excellent	*Good*	*Adequate*	*Poor*
a.	Understandable style of writing	____	____	____	____
b.	Physical appearance/ readability	____	____	____	____
c.	Fair coverage of topics	____	____	____	____
d	Comprehensiveness (covered major issues and topics)	____	____	____	____
e.	Practical activities and strategies	____	____	____	____
f.	Case Examples and Case Studies	____	____	____	____
g.	Appendixes	____	____	____	____
h.	Organization of chapters	____	____	____	____

2. Can you comment on or illustrate your above ratings? _____

_____

_____

_____

3. What chapters or features did you particularly like? _____

_____

_____

_____

4. What chapters or features did you dislike or think should be changed?

    _____

    _____

    _____

5. What material would you suggest adding or deleting? _____

    _____

    _____

    _____

6. What was the title of the course in which you used this book? _____

    _____

7. Are you an undergraduate student? _____ If so, what year? _____

8. Are you a graduate student? _____ If so, have you taught before?

    _____

9. What other courses in special education have you taken? _____

    _____

10. Will you be teaching in a regular classroom or in a special classroom?

    _____

11. Do you intend to keep this book for use during your teaching career?

    _____

12. Did you use the *Study Guide* that accompanies this textbook?

    _____ Yes   _____ No

13. We would appreciate any other comments or reactions you are willing
    to share. _____

    _____

    _____

    _____